Lecture Notes in Computer Science 10012

Commenced Publication in 1973
Founding and Former Series Editors:
Gerhard Goos, Juris Hartmanis, and Jan van Leeuwen

Editorial Board

More information about this series at http://www.springer.com/series/7408

Yliès Falcone · César Sánchez (Eds.)

Runtime Verification

16th International Conference, RV 2016
Madrid, Spain, September 23–30, 2016
Proceedings

 Springer

Editors
Yliès Falcone
Université Grenoble Alpes, Inria
Grenoble
France

César Sánchez
IMDEA Software Institute
Madrid
Spain

ISSN 0302-9743   ISSN 1611-3349   (electronic)
Lecture Notes in Computer Science
ISBN 978-3-319-46981-2   ISBN 978-3-319-46982-9   (eBook)
DOI 10.1007/978-3-319-46982-9

Library of Congress Control Number: 2016952525

LNCS Sublibrary: SL2 – Programming and Software Engineering

Printed on acid-free paper

This Springer imprint is published by Springer Nature
The registered company is Springer International Publishing AG
The registered company address is: Gewerbestrasse 11, 6330 Cham, Switzerland

Preface

This volume contains the proceedings of the 16th International Conference on Runtime Verification (RV 2016), which was held September 23–30, 2016, at La Residencia de Estudiantes of the Spanish Council for Scientific Research (CSIC) in Madrid, Spain.

During the first half of the twentieth century, La Residencia was a prestigious cultural institution that helped foster and create the intellectual environment for young thinkers, writers, and artists. It was one of the most vibrant and successful experiences of scientific and artistic creation and exchange of interwar Europe. Some of the brightest minds of the time, like Albert Einsten, Marie Curie, and Salvador Dali, visited La Residencia in this early epoch. In the last few years there has been a very intense attempt to recover the memory of La Residencia and its founding principles, and to promote new cultural and scientific activities based on the spirit of cooperation and sharing of knowledge. We hope that the attendees of RV 2016 enjoyed this unique venue.

The RV conference is concerned with all aspects of monitoring and analysis of hardware, sotfware, and more general system executions. Runtime verification techniques are lightweight techniques to asses correctness, reliability, and robustness; these techniques are significantly more powerful and versatile than conventional testing, and more practical than exhaustive formal verification.

RV started in 2001 as an annual workshop and turned into an annual conference in 2010. The proceedings from 2001 to 2005 were published in the *Electronic Notes in Theoretical Computer Science*. Since 2006, the RV proceedings have been published in Springer's *Lecture Notes in Computer Science*. The previous five editions of the RV conference took place in San Francisco, USA (2011), Istanbul, Turkey (2012), Rennes, France (2013), Toronto, Canada (2014), and Vienna, Austria (2015).

RV 2016 received 72 submissions, 49 of which were regular papers, ten short papers, six regular tool papers, two tool demonstration papers, and five tutorial proposals. Most papers were reviewed by four reviewers. The Program Committee accepted 18 regular papers, four short papers, three regular tool papers, two tool demonstration papers, and the five submitted tutorials.

The evaluation and selection process involved thorough discussions among the members of the Program Committee and external reviewers through the EasyChair conference manager, before reaching a consensus on the final decisions.

This year, the RV conference also included the organization of The First International Summer School on Runtime Verification, co-organized and sponsored by EU COST Action IC1402 "ArVi: Runtime Verification Beyond Monitoring." Additionally, the Third International Competition on Runtime Verification, also sponsored by EU COST Action IC1402, was colocated with RV 2016.

The conference program included the presentation of the peer-reviewed papers and tool demonstrations, tutorials, and invited keynote speeches. The conference program spanned over four rich days (see http://rv2016.imag.fr).

We are pleased to have hosted three top invited speakers:

- Gul Agha, Professor of Computer Science at the University of Illinois at Urbana-Champaign, talked about how to build dependable concurrent systems through probabilistic inference, predictive monitoring, and self-adaptation.
- Oded Maler, Research Director of CNRS at Verimag, talked about how to monitor qualitative and quantitative properties, in real and virtual executions of systems, in the online and offline approaches of runtime verification.
- Fred B. Schneider, Professor of Computer Science and Chair of Cornell's CS Department, talked about tag specification languages for policy enforcement.

The conference included the following five tutorials:

- Doron Peled presented a tutorial on "Using Genetic Programming for Software Reliability"
- Nikolaï Kosmatov and Julien Signoles presented a tutorial on "Frama-C, a Collaborative Framework for C Code Verification"
- Philip Daian, Dwight Guth, Chris Hathhorn, Yilong Li, Edgar Pek, Manasvi Saxena, Traian Florin Serbanuta, and Grigore Rosu presented a tutorial on "Runtime Verification at Work"
- Sylvain Hallé presented a tutorial on "When RV Meets CEP"
- Borzoo Bonakdarpour and Bernd Finkbeiner presented a tutorial on "Runtime Verification for HyperLTL"

We would like to thank the authors of all submitted papers, the members of the Program Committee, and the external reviewers for their exhaustive task of reviewing and evaluating all submitted papers. We would like to thank Christian Colombo for co-organizing the Summer School and Sylvain Hallé and Giles Reger for co-organizing the third edition of the competition on Runtime Verification (CRV 2016).

We would also like to thank Universidad Carlos III and the IMDEA Software Institute for their administrative support and their generous monetary contribution to the conference, the Laboratoire d'Informatique de Grenoble for its IT support, and La Residencia for sharing their facilities to hold the conference at reduced prices. We highly appreciate EasyChair for its system to manage submissions. Finally, we would like to extend our special thanks to the chair of the Steering Committee, Klaus Havelund, for his support during the organization of RV 2016.

August 2016   Yliès Falcone
                                                                     César Sánchez

Organization

Program Chairs

Yliès Falcone	Université Grenoble Alpes, Inria, Grenoble, France
César Sánchez	IMDEA Software Institute, Madrid, Spain

Tool Track Chair

Klaus Havelund	Nasa Jet Propulsion Laboratory, USA

Tool Committee

Steven Arzt	EC Spride, Germany
Howard Barringer	The University of Manchester, UK
Ezio Bartocci	TU Wien, Austria
Martin Leucker	University of Lübeck, Germany
Gordon Pace	University of Malta, Malta
Giles Reger	The University of Manchester, UK
Julien Signoles	CEA, France
Oleg Sokolsky	University of Pennsylvania, USA
Bernhard Steffen	University of Dortmund, Germany
Nikolai Tillmann	Microsoft Research, USA
Eugen Zalinescu	ETH Zurich, Switzerland

CRV'16 Chairs

Yliès Falcone	Université Grenoble Alpes, Inria, France
Sylvain Hallé	Université du Québec à Chicoutimi, Canada
Giles Reger	University of Manchester, Manchester, UK

Local Organization Chair

Juan Tapiador	Universidad Carlos III de Madrid, Madrid, Spain

Program Committee

Erika Abraham	RWTH Aachen University, Germany
Steven Artz	EC SPRIDE
Howard Barringer	The University of Manchester, UK
Ezio Bartocci	TU Wien, Austria
Andreas Bauer	NICTA and Australian National University, Australia

Bernhard Steffen   University of Dortmund, Germany
Scott Stoller   Stony Brook University, USA
Volker Stolz   University of Oslo, Norway
Jun Sun   Singapore University of Technology and Design,
                               Singapore
Juan Tapiador   Universidad Carlos III de Madrid, Spain
Serdar Tasiran   Koc University, Turkey
Nikolai Tillman   Microsoft Research
Michael Whalen   University of Minnesota, USA
Eugen Zalinescu   Technical University of Munich, Germany
Lenore Zuck   University of Illinois in Chicago, USA

Additional Reviewers

Assaf, Mounir   Kuester, Jan-Christoph   Schmitz, Malte
Azzopardi, Shaun   Le, Ton-Chanh   Selyunin, Konstantin
Bertrand, Nathalie   Lee, Benedict   Serwe, Wendelin
Dabaghchian, Maryam   Li, Yilong   Siddique, Umair
Daian, Philip   Matar, Hassan Salehe   Sirjani, Marjan
Decker, Normann   Maubert, Bastien   Srivastav, Abhinav
Della Monica, Dario   Mens, Irini-Eleftheria   Tan, Tian Huat
Duan, Lian   Mikučionis, Marius   Tekle, Tuncay
Duc Hiep, Chu   Mohammad Hasani,   Torfah, Hazem
Evrard, Hugues   Ramin   Traonouez, Louis-Marie
Faymonville, Peter   Mutlu, Erdal   Ulus, Dogan
Gossen, Frederik   Neubauer, Johannes   Vorobyov, Kostyantyn
Hedin, Daniel   Quilbeuf, Jean   Walulya, Ivan
Jaksic, Stefan   Ratasich, Denise   Yong, Chang
Khoury, Raphael   Rodionova, Alena   Zadok, Erez
Komp, John   Ruething, Oliver   Zhang, Yi
Kopetzki, Dawid   Scheffel, Torben

Invited Papers

Building Dependable Concurrent Systems Through Probabilistic Inference, Predictive Monitoring and Self-adaptation (Abstract)

Gul Agha

University of Illinois at Urbana-Champaign, Champaign, USA
http://osl.cs.illinois.edu

Abstract. The infeasibility of statically verifying complex software is well established; in concurrent systems, the difficulty is compounded by nondeterminism and the possibility of 'Heisenbugs'. Using runtime verification, one can not only monitor a concurrent system to check if it has violated a specification, but potentially predict future violations. However, a key challenge for runtime verification is that specifications are often incomplete. I will argue that the safety of concurrent systems could be improved by observing patterns of interaction and using probabilistic inference to capture intended coordination behavior. Actors reflecting on their choreography this way would enable deployed systems to continually improve their specifications. Mechanisms to dynamically add monitors and enforce coordination constraints during execution would then facilitate self-adaptation in concurrent systems. I will conclude by suggesting a program of research to extend runtime verification so systems an evolve robustness through such self-adaptation.

Acknowledgements. The work on this paper has been supported in part by Air Force Research Laboratory and the Air Force Office of Scientific Research under agreement number FA8750-11-2-0084, and by National Science Foundation under grant number CCF-1438982 and NSF CCF 16-17401.

References

1. Astley, M., Sturman, D.C., Agha,G.: Customizable middleware for modular distributed software. Communun. ACM, **44**(5), 99–107 (2001)
2. Donkervoet, B., Agha, G.: Reflecting on aspect-oriented programming, metaprogramming, and adaptive distributed monitoring. In: de Boer, F.S., Bonsangue, M.M., Graf, S., de Roever, W.P. (eds.) FMCO 2006. LNCS, vol. 4709, pp. 246–265. Springer, Heidelberg (2007)
3. Frolund, S., Agha, G.: A language framework for multi-object coordination. In: Nierstrasz, O. (ed.) ECOOP 1993. LNCS, vol. 707, pp. 346–360. Springer, Heidelberg (1993)
4. Sen, K., Rosu, G., Agha, G.: Online efficient predictive safety analysis of multi-threaded programs. In: Jensen, K., Podelski, A. (eds.) TACAS 2004. LNCS, vol. 2988, pp. 123–138. Springer, Heidelberg (2004)

5. Sen, K., Vardhan, A., Agha, G., Rosu, G.: Efficient decentralized monitoring of safety in distributed systems. In: Finkelstein, A., Estublier, J., Rosenblum, D.S. (eds.) ICSE 2004, Edinburgh, United Kingdom, 23–28 May 2004, pp. 418–427. IEEE Computer Society (2004)
6. Sturman, D.C., Agha, G.: A protocol description language for customizing semantics. In: 13th Symposium on Reliable Distributed Systems (SRDS 1994), Dana Point, California, 25–27 October 1994, pp. 148–157. ACM (1994)

Why Tags Could be It?
Keynote Lecture
Extended Abstract

Fred B. Schneider

Department of Computer Science, Cornell University, Ithaca,
New York, 14853, USA
fbs@cs.cornell.edu

Abstract. Reference monitors embody specifications about permitted and prohibited operation invocations. That limits what policies they can enforce. Those limitations have prompted us to explore alternative approaches to policy enforcement—specifically, expressive classes of labels that give permitted and prohibited uses for a piece of information. These *reactive information flow* (RIF) labels will be described, along with means for static and run-time verification of programs that process such labelled data. Use of RIF labels for specifying use-based privacy also will be discussed.

1 Introduction

Security policies can be enforced by defining guards on operations or by associating labels with values, as follows.

- A *guard* on an operation Op is checked each time Op is invoked; the guard blocks any invocation that would not comply with the policy.
- A *security label* on a value or variable V is checked before V is read or written; the access is blocked when it is inconsistent with what the security label allows.

Today's systems tend to be built in terms of guards on operations rather than in terms of security labels on values. This is unfortunate, because security labels specify and provide end-to-end guarantees about information use, whereas guards on operations do not.

For example, consider a system that creates and maintains a replica F' of some file F. A guard that prevented principal *Alice* from invoking a read operation naming F is not obliged to prevent *Alice* from invoking a read operation naming F'. But an end-to-end guarantee that stipulates *Alice* not read the contents in F would have to

Joint work with Cornell Ph.D. students Elisavet Kozyri and Eleanor Birrell.

F.B. Schneider—Supported in part by AFOSR grant F9550-16-0250 and grants from Microsoft. The views and conclusions contained herein are those of the author and should not be interpreted as necessarily representing the official policies or endorsements, either expressed or implied, of these organizations or the U.S. Government.

prevent attempts by *Alice* to learn the contents of F' or other values derived directly or indirectly from the contents in F. In addition, security tags can afford providers of information with flexibility to choose security policies after a system has been developed, deployed, or put into operation. Policy now accompanies a system's inputs instead of being fixed in the code.

2   Reactive Information Flow Specifications

The prevalence today of guards over security labels is not surprising, given limitations in the expressive power of currently available classes of security labels. To help overcome those limitations, we have been developing a new class of security labels: *reactive information flow* (RIF) specifications. Informally, a RIF specification for a value V gives

(i)   allowed uses for V, and
(ii)   the RIF specification for any value that might be directly or indirectly derived from V.

RIF specifications thus give allowed uses for the value produced by evaluating a function, where those restrictions may differ from the allowed uses for inputs to that evaluation. For instance, using RIF specifications as labels, the output of an encryption function can be public even though is inputs (plaintext and a key) are secret. In general, RIF specifications support *reclassifiers* that increase restrictions, decrease restrictions, or associate incomparable restrictions.

Various *carriers* can be instantiated to embody RIF specifications. A carrier must accept a language of reclassifiers, and it must associate a set of restrictions with each word in that language. Carriers for which language-inclusion is decidable are a good choice when we wish to treat RIF specifications as types, since the resulting type system will be statically checkable. To date, we have experience with two classes of (decidable) carriers.

–   Finite state automata suffice for many common security needs. Here, each automaton state gives a set of use restrictions; reclassifiers label transitions between automaton states, with the successor automaton state giving the new set of use restrictions for a derived value.
–   A simple form of push-down automata suffice for handling confidentiality when encryption and decryption are used to transform values (typically from secret to public and back). Encryption pushes a key onto the stack; decryption causes pop if the key being provided matches the key contained in top entry on the stack (and otherwise the decryption causes a push).

Type systems have been formulated for both kinds of carriers, where type correctness ensures that certain non-interference properties are satisfied. The conservative nature of type checking, however, is now leading us to contemplate run-time monitors for programs having RIF specifications as labels for values and variables. We also have been exploring practical aspects of using RIF specifications. For this, the information-flow type system in the JIF programming language has been replaced by a RIF type system based on finite-state automata. Prototype applications that we programmed in this JRIF language have given us experience with defining RIF specifications.

3   What RIF Tags May Restrict

Security labels traditionally have been interpreted as characterizing sets of principals. For confidentiality, a label specifies principals that are allowed to read a value (or any value derived); for integrity, a label describes principals that must be trusted for the labeled value to be trusted (which implies that the label defines a set of principals that may update the labeled value).

In practice, other forms of use restrictions are important too. In *use-based security*, pieces of information are labeled—actually or notionally—with tags that specify *use restrictions*, and principals who hold or process such pieces of information are obliged to comply with those restrictions. Use restrictions may come from those who submit or control the information, systems that process the information, and/or regulations imposed by the jurisdiction in which a system is located, the data originates, or its owners reside.

Use-based security can be quite general if we are given an expressive enough language for specifying the use restrictions. By choosing a suitable language, for example, we can support the various definitions of privacy that are being discussed, now that the failings of classical "notice and consent" have become apparent. We can also support regimes where data collection and use are limited by legislative authorities that specify when and how data may used, combined, how long it must be saved, etc.

RIF specifications seem well suited for defining restrictions for use-based security. Here, restrictions are not limited to being sets of principals; the restrictions instead can be permissions, prohibitions, and/or obligations for invoking arbitrary classes of operations. Reclassifiers, as before, allow derived values to be subject to different use restrictions. This capability, for example, would enable a RIF specification to assert that an individual's value must be kept confidential, but any derived value produced by statistical aggregation is public.

4   Enforcement

Formal verification, automated analysis, and run-time monitoring all are time-honored methods to ensure that a program will satisfy some property of interest. The trade-offs between expressiveness, conservatism, and automation are likely to be the same for RIF specifications as has been found for other classes of program properties. In connection with privacy, however, audit, with deterrence through accountability is sensible. So instead of preventing violations, a system detects violations and recovers. Prevention is not necessary, here.

Contents

Invited Paper

Some Thoughts on Runtime Verification

Oded Maler[(✉)]

VERIMAG, CNRS and the University of Grenoble Alpes (UGA),
Bat. IMAG, 700 av. Centrale, 38041 St Martin d'heres, France
oded.maler@imag.fr

Abstract. Some reflections on verification and runtime verification in general and of cyber-physical systems in particular.

1 Introduction

I was probably invited to present in this forum because of my work on checking simulation traces of cyber-physical (hybrid, mixed-signal) systems against specifications expressed using formalisms such as signal temporal logic [25] and timed regular expressions [2]. I will use the opportunity to discuss, in addition, some other issues that come to my mind in the context of runtime verification. I start in Sect. 2 with a reflection on the nature of words and then discuss some potential meanings of *runtime* verification as distinct from just *verification*. Section 3 describes one interpretation, the activity of monitoring simulation traces against formally defined properties. Section 4 discusses runtime verification interpreted as verification of something closer to the implementation. Section 5 is devoted to monitoring real working systems during their execution, an activity that differs in many aspects from monitoring during design and development time. Finally, Sect. 6 speaks briefly about robust satisfaction and the relation between properties and other quantitative performance measures traditionally applied to signals. The topics of Sects. 4 and 5 are outside my domain of expertise so what I write there is based on common sense and speculation. I am sure many of these issues have been studied by researchers in this community and I apologize in advance for not having the time and resources to make a comprehensive study of relevant work before writing this document.

2 Words Speak Louder Than They Should

Robert Anton Wilson, an overly-illuminated writer [32] and thinker [39], objected rather strongly to the usage of the word *is* based on some very reasonable grounds. Words are just tools, they do not have intrinsic absolute meaning and it is silly (but common) to argue about the *true* meaning of a word. The meaning depends on context and background and can differ from one occasion to the other, from one speaker or community to another and in general it shifts with time. One important aspect in studying word meanings is to consider the background against which they came to being, the specific additional distinctions and refinements of existing concepts they came to express.

© Springer International Publishing AG 2016
Y. Falcone and C. Sanchez (Eds.): RV 2016, LNCS 10012, pp. 3–14, 2016.
DOI: 10.1007/978-3-319-46982-9_1

As a concrete example consider the term *reactive systems* coined by Harel and Pnueli in a classical paper [14], published in 1985 some time before the emergence of CAV-style academic verification. Reactive systems are defined there as systems that maintain an *ongoing interaction* with their *external environment*. This should be understood against the background of classical computability (and complexity) theory, dealing with non-reactive (transformational) programs that map static inputs to static outputs without being in time, without interacting with the external world during computation (see some old ramblings of mine in [18]). The concept was useful in separating protocol verification (at least for some time) from other approaches to program verification.

In contrast, the term "reactive" does not have much meaning in control theory because all control systems are supposed to be reactive by definition.[1] The same holds, of course, for living systems, and those who preach reactive systems to biologists are, in fact, preaching for the introduction of discrete states and transitions into a modeling domain often dominated by continuous applied mathematics. In other contexts such as cognitive psychology, the word reactive might indicate a simple behavioral stimulus/response model, mathematically much narrower than the transducer model underlying the reactive systems of [14].

Coming to think of the possible meanings of *runtime verification* one has to think about what is particularly added by the *runtime* qualifier to the general background of the meaning of *verification*, which by itself is rather pluralistic. Verification can mean one thing to a practitioner (and this may depend on the type of software, hardware or physware development being practiced) and another thing to theoreticians of various degrees of practical inspiration, aspiration and pretention. I once received a book called *The verification Cookbook* from an EDA company and I did not find there anything remotely similar to concepts studied in most of CAV papers. Thus said, let me try to lay down the implicit semantics of verification I have been carrying in my head over the years. Needless to say after all this introduction, no claim is made for this semantics to be more truthful than any other.

So my version of verification, the algorithmic genre following [3,29], goes like this [19]. You have a system which is open (reactive), and each of its dynamic inputs may induce a different behavior. Behaviors are viewed as trajectories (runs, paths) in the state-space, which used traditionally to be that of a large state-exploded automaton. You want somehow to ensure correctness of the trajectories induced by all admissible inputs. Correctness of a run typically means the occurrence or non-occurrence of certain temporal patterns, expressible in a declarative language (temporal logic, regular expressions) or hacked manually into property observers composed with the system.

---

[1] Speaking about control, "reachability" (and to some extent "controllability") used not long ago to denote some very precise technical term in the Kalmanistic theory of linear systems before some barbarians came and kidnapped its meaning. As a punishment we have sometime to hear colleagues from others disciplines abuse theoretical computer science sacred terms such as *decidability* or *models of computation*.

Rather than enumerating all inputs up to a certain length and simulating in a black box fashion, formal verification does two things. First, by having access to the automaton model of the system, the verification algorithm can follow paths in the transition graph rather than trying to cover them by a blind selection of inputs. This yields an important complexity improvement [19]. Then, some systems are sufficiently small so that modern computers can explore all their paths within a reasonable time. Otherwise, an attempt is made to reason about all the behaviors in a more holistic manner. One direction is to try to prove something about all behaviors in a deductive/analytical way, a topic I will not touch here. Alternatively, one can do a kind of set-based breadth-first simulation, which came to be known as *symbolic model checking* [26], where symbolic means that logical formulae are used to describe the set of reachable states at successive time points.

Remark: In fact, the term *model-checking* is another example of a word shared by different meanings. Today, people from outside verification to whom the concept is presented, biologists for instance, probably take it to mean checking whether your model of some physical phenomenon makes sense, for example, whether it admits some counter-intuitive behaviors not supported by experiments, whether it is robust under parameter variations and so forth. So *model* is understood as the common concept of a *mathematical* model of something in the *real world*. This is *not* the original meaning of *model* as used in model checking, which is a purely technical logical concept stating that a given mathematical structure is a model of a system of logical axioms - there is a whole branch of logic called *model theory*, which studies the relation between these two classes of mathematical objects. Model checking was initially used in verification to contrast it with deductive (proof theoretic) methods of reasoning [13]. The story for LTL (linear-time temporal logic) goes like this: a given sequence w is a model of a temporal logic formula φ if w satisfies φ. Thus verification by model checking means to check whether all possible runs are models of φ. For branching-time logics like CTL, what is checked is whether the whole transition system (Kripke structure in modal logic parlance), viewed as a generator of a branching structure, is a model of the formula.

Other implicit assumptions in my story are the following.

1. The verification process takes place mostly during the *design* and *development* phase before we unleash the system to go wild in the streets and do what it is supposed to do;
2. In many cases, verification is done on a *model* of the system which is a kind of an automaton which abstracts away from data (rather than control) variables as well as some particular implementation details, including the programming language and execution platform. The more abstract this mathematical model is, that is, closer to an automaton/graph, the easier it is to reason about its behaviors in a global manner. Nevertheless, some syntactics is required to express the automaton for the purpose of verification and some connection with the program that realizes it should be eventually made;

3. The properties against which behaviors are evaluated have been traditionally *qualitative*, providing a yes/no answer concerning property satisfaction.

In the following I will contemplate on various interpretations of runtime verification by perturbing some of the abovementioned implicit assumptions. I will also discuss the adaptation of runtime verification techniques (and verification in general) to cyber-physical systems. In particular, I will touch upon the following topics:

1. Runtime verification viewed as good old simulation/testing without coverage guarantees but augmented with formal specifications;
2. Runtime verification viewed as getting closer to the real implemented artifact, further away from the abstract model;
3. Runtime indicating that we leave design/reflection time and get involved in the detection of patterns in *real* time while the system is up and running;
4. The quantitative semantics of temporal properties and the fusion of properties and assertions with other performance measures used by engineers to evaluate signals and systems.

3   Runtime Verification as Simulation Plus Formal Specification

This used to be my favorite interpretation that we exported successfully to the continuous and hybrid domain [22]. Verification is a glorious activity but it does not scale beyond certain system complexity and people will always resort to simulation, with or without renaming it as statistical model checking. We also separate concerns and say that coverage and exhaustiveness is someone else's responsibility. So what remains is plain simulation with the additional twist that the simulation trace is checked against formal properties specified in some rigorous and unambiguous formalism. It can still be debated whether some engineers' reluctance to use such clean declarative languages is a bug or a feature of their way of thinking. It is related, I think, to the issue of whether you want to use the same language for implementation and specification, or rather have two distinct languages. Maybe it is easier for a developer to build a property checker as a Simulink block or a piece of C code than to learn yet another language.

According to the automata-theoretic approach to verification [38], exhaustive verification corresponds to an *inclusion* problem between two formal languages:[2] the set of behaviors produced by the system and the set of behaviors defined by the property. For checking a single behavior, the problem simplifies into a *membership* problem: does a given behavior belong to the language defined by the property? Unlike verification, this activity, that we call *monitoring* from now on, does not require a respectable mathematical model and can work with *any*

---

[2] The term *formal language* provides yet another opportunity for terminological confusion. In theoretical computer science a formal language is nothing but a set of sequences, something very semantic in our context.

black box that generates simulation traces. In fact, monitoring is agnostic about the origin of those traces, which could be as well recordings of a real system. The complexity of the system, which is a critical limiting factor in exhaustive verification, influences only the simulation time and the number of simulations needed to properly cover its behaviors, but this is, as we said, not our problem.

In the context of digital hardware, monitoring is called *dynamic* verification against *assertions* while the term *static* or *formal* verification is used for model checking. Motivated initially by analog and mixed-signal circuits, we extended this idea[3] to continuous and hybrid systems [22, 25, 27] by introducing *signal temporal logic* (STL), which adds numerical predicates over real-valued variables on top of the dense time[4] *metric temporal logic* (MTL) [17]. We provided a simple efficient algorithm for checking satisfaction/membership for the future fragment of STL by backward interval marking. This procedure can, in principle, liberate users from the tedious task of classifying simulation traces manually by visual inspection or by writing programs for that purpose.

4   Runtime as More Real

Another interpretation of runtime is literally, *while a program is running*. This means that in contrast with the abstract automaton model, we deal here with something closer to the implementation: either we have generated real code from the abstract model or there was no such an abstract model to begin with. Software is a peculiar engineering artifact, closer in its very nature to its abstract model more than any physical system can be: compare the gap between an engine model and a real *physical* engine with the tiny gap between a model of a controller and its software implementation. For this reason, software developers may tend to skip what they perceive as a redundant modeling stage.

Cyber-physical systems admit heterogeneous components including the external environment which is modeled but not implemented, and the designed artifact itself which includes physical components, a hardware platform and software. In the development of such systems there is a multi-dimensional spectrum between abstract models and real systems, both in the implemented and unimplemented parts. This is attested by the existence of several kinds of testing, each using a different manifestations of the controller, the external environment and their interconnection. For example, hardware-in-the-loop simulation indicates that the real implemented controller, running on its execution platform is being tested. Model-in-the-loop testing, to take another example, means that

---

[3] I am indebted to a discussion with Yaron Wolfsthal before starting this project, in which he explained to me the workings of the FOCS property checker developed at IBM for discrete/digital systems.

[4] The advantage of dense time as used in MTL or in timed automata is in not committing to a fixed time step such as the clock tick in digital circuits. Otherwise, the major advantage of timed logics and automata is *not* in density but in the ability to reason about time arithmetically rather than by counting ticks. More opinions on timed systems can be found in [21].

the input to the implemented controller comes from a simulator, in contrast with more realistic settings where these inputs come from sensors or, at least, through real physical wires.

To perform verification while the program is running, the program should be properly instrumented to export the evolving values of the variables appearing in the property, thus producing traces that can be checked by your favorite property checker. Since we are talking about a real imperative program, not an interpreter of an automaton structure, only single runs (rather than set-based runs) can be naturally produced. This activity can still take place during the development phase (design, integration tests) but as will be discussed next, it can be applied to a working system.

5   Monitoring During the System's Lifetime

The most radical departure from classical verification is obtained by interpreting runtime as meaning that we monitor real systems during their normal (and abnormal) execution. Many such systems come to mind at different scales of space and time: nuclear reactors, highway and network traffic, air conditioning systems, industrial plants, medical devices, corporate information systems and anything that generates signals and time series.

A monitoring process that is simultaneous with the ongoing behavior of the system suggests new opportunities such as detecting important events and patterns, almost as soon as they happen, and reacting to them, either by alerting a human operator or by triggering some automatic action. Well, calling these opportunities "new" is appropriate only in the verification context: such monitors exist in low-tech ever since the industrial, or at least the electrical revolution. Just consider indicators in your car control panel for speed, temperature or fuel level and more modern features like alarming the driver while getting too close to other cars or activating the airbag upon detecting a collision.

This type of application deviates, as I attempt to show, from the standard story of verification and requires rethinking of what it is the thing that we want to specify (and monitor) using our favorite formalism. To understand what I probably mean let me introduce a naive straw man, a true believer in the verification myth. According to him, if φ is the (precise) system's specifications, characterizing exactly the acceptable behaviors, the most natural thing is to tell the monitor to watch for $\neg\varphi$ and cry out loud when it occurs. But on a second thought, our straw man will add, this will not happen anyway if we verified the system and showed that all its behaviors satisfy φ. Or if you want a control version of the myth, this will not happen if the controller has been designed correctly.

To understand what is wrong here, let us first see why verification of cyber-physical systems is different, hard and, in some sense, almost an oxymoron (some related observations and discussions concerning the rigorous design of *systems*, as opposed to programs, appear in [33,34]). The verification story is based on the following three premises:

1. You have a (very) faithful model of the system under verification;
2. You have formal requirements that indeed trace the boundary between acceptable and unacceptable behaviors;
3. The system is sufficiently small so that formal verification is computationally
   feasible.

The range of systems for which (1) and (2) above hold is very narrow in the cyber-
physical world. It is fair to say that it is restricted to some hardware and software
components, analyzed for their so called *functional* properties, those that care
only about their purely computational properties, not involving physical aspects
and interactions such as power consumption or timing.[5] Software is very peculiar
in admitting a chain of faithful semantics-preserving models, going all the way
from programs in a high-level language down to gates and transistors. Nothing
like this exists in the physical world where models are understood to be just
useful approximations.[6]

   The same holds for specifications: you can certainly write down a complete
set of properties that will characterize the valid behaviors of, say, a chip realizing
some hardware protocol, verify it on an exact model and expect that the real
chip will indeed work continuously without problems as long as the underlying
physical assumptions hold. For systems with physical functionalities, there is
typically never a comprehensive list of requirements that holds globally over the
whole state-space. In fact, such a global state-space (the one-world semantics of
[37]) by itself is not part of the conceptual map of most engineers. For physical
systems there are domain-specific intuitions about the shape of certain response
curves, the values of some quantitative measures, and so on, but you never have
an explicit formalized partition of all behaviors in the huge cyber-physical state-
space into good and bad behaviors. Airplanes fly, nevertheless, most of the time.[7]

   So we want to use some specification formalism to express observable conditions and temporal patterns that will trigger some responses:

$$\textbf{if } \textit{some pattern is observed } \textbf{then } \textit{do the right thing.} \tag{1}$$

The entity that does the right thing can be a human operator and in that case
the role of monitoring is just to create an alarm and bring the situation to her
attention. If the reaction is automatic, this is yet another instance of a feedback

---

[5] No program, no matter how thoroughly verified, will produce the correct result if
you hit the computer with a hammer or just unplug it from power.

[6] This fact renders our early heroic CS efforts to prove decidability results on hybrid
systems somewhat misguided, at least from an applicative point of view. In one of
the early hybrid systems meetings I organized in Grenoble in the 90s, Paul Caspi
presented a cartoon of a dialog between a control engineer, saying: *it is trivial* and a
theoretical computer scientist responding: *it is undecidable!*. But the noble activity
of doing math for its own sake is common in all academic engineering domains,
control included.

[7] Kurt Vonnegut's quote *Tiger got to hunt, bird got to fly; Man got to sit and wonder
'why, why, why?'* can be rephrased as *Governors govern and airplanes fly; It takes
a computer scientist to wonder why.*

control loop with actions based on observations, more appropriate for high-level supervisory control where discrete decisions are to be taken. Without giving a precise definition of hierarchical control, think of lower-levels controlling, say, torques and velocities in car engines or robots, essentially continuous processes and quantities, while higher levels decide whether to go right or left upon detecting an obstacle or whether to cancel the trip after observing traffic jams or fuel shortage.

Remark: Is there a particular advantage in using the format of (1) compared to standard controllers? Controllers with state variables and memory can encode in their state some abstraction of the input history that will influence their reaction. This is clearly visible for discrete-event systems where automaton states represent equivalence classes of input histories. This holds true, in principle, also for continuous controllers where you can integrate over the input signal but this is a very weak form of pattern detection. In fact, property monitors for logics such as STL are equivalent to some kind of timed automata over continuous signals that can be transformed into controllers by adding actions.   ⌐

If we want to react, the patterns that we specify need not be the negations of complete properties but, sometimes, prefixes of those. For example, if the specification is that $x(t)$ should always remain below c, we should raise a flag when x gets alarmingly close to c and try to steer the system in the opposite direction in order to *enforce* the property (see [11] for a discussion of enforcing specifications in the discrete context). Likewise, if the specification says that every request is granted within some time-bound d, a useful monitoring systems will detect customers that already wait for some $d' < d$ time while there is a chance to serve them before the deadline.[8]

Monitoring simulation traces can be done by offline procedures that wait for the end of the simulation and then may go through the trace back and forth in both directions. For monitoring real systems we should focus on online procedures that do not wait until the *end* of the trace (which is anyway a shaky concept for real reactive systems) to start the analysis. This is technically unfortunate for the future fragment of temporal logic which is by definition acausal, with satisfaction at time t typically defined based on values at time $t' > t$. This point of view is captured nicely by temporal testers [16,28] which are acausal transducers that provide for a compositional translation of temporal logic to automata (and timed temporal logic to timed automata [23]). Past LTL, which can express only safety properties, is causal and can report violation of a property by a prefix of the behavior as soon as it happens.

The traditional use of future temporal logic in verification is based on infinite behaviors whose time domain is $[0, \infty)$. A lot of effort, for example [9], was

---

[8] Are all the things that we want to monitor restricted to prefixes of behaviors that lead to a violation of the specifications? I do not have an answer at this moment and it probably depends also on whether we are in the hard (safety critical) or soft (quality of service) domain. It is also related to whether numerical quantities are involved: the car fuel indicator shows continuously the value of a real-valued variable and, in addition, emits a warning when it crosses a threshold.

invested in order to define a finitary semantics, appropriate for the very nature of monitoring. One may argue that unbounded liveness is not a useful notion for monitoring and we can do with bounded-response properties whose degree of acausality and non-determinism is bounded [24]. Traditionally, properties used in verification are supposed to hold from time zero and be satisfied or violated (accepted or rejected) by the whole behavior or its prefix. For runtime monitoring it might be more appropriate to use the more general *pattern matching* concept that speaks of segments of the behavior, starting and ending at arbitrary points in time. Regular expressions seem to be more appropriate for this purpose and we have recently developed offline [35] and online [36] pattern matching algorithms for timed regular expressions [2] over Boolean signals.

6   From Quality to Quantity

Properties and assertions are functions that map behaviors (sequences, signals) into $\{0, 1\}$ according to satisfaction or violation. In many contexts, especially in the cyber-physical world, we would like to have a more refined quantitative answer: not only whether the property has been satisfied or violated by the behavior, but also how robust the answer was [6,7,10,30]. For example, if we have a behavior which satisfies the requirement that $x(t)$ is always smaller than c, the distance between the maximal value of x and c will tell us the robustness of the satisfaction, how close far we were from violation. Likewise, in a behavior w where some response has missed a deadline d, the distance between d and the maximal response time occurring in w will tell us the severity of the violation and whether it can be fixed by relaxing the specification using some $d' > d$ which is still acceptable. For a given property φ and signal w, the quantitative (robustness) semantics returns a value $\rho = \rho(\varphi, w)$ having the following two important properties:

1. The robustness ρ is positive iff w satisifies φ;
2. The φ-satisfaction of any signal w', whose pointwise distance from w is smaller than ρ, is equal to that of w.

This semantics gives more information and moreover it opens new possibilities in the search for bad behaviors, also known as bug hunting or *falsification*, which is a very active domain in the verification of cyber-physical system. The idea is that the robustness value can be used by an optimization/search procedure that explores the space of system trajectories (and the input signals that induce them) trying the minimize the robustness value until a violating behavior is found, see for example [1,5,8,15,31].

Despite these advantages, the robustness semantics still suffers from the expressive limitations of traditional logic and its orientation toward extreme-case reasoning. The quantitative semantics of STL, as defined in [6,7], is obtained from the standard qualitative semantics by replacing Boolean values such as $x < c$ by numbers like $c - x$ and then replacing $\vee$, $\wedge$ and $\neg$ by min, max and $-$. Thus the robustness value is still determined by the worst value in the signal, regardless of whether the signal spent a lot of time near that value or just had a short spike, while being at much lower values most of the time.

Many other types of quantitative measures have been traditionally applied to signals. They are based on summation/averaging, noise filtering, applying frequency-domain transforms and many other functions that extract from the signal the performance measures appropriate for the application in question. In this context, one can view STL and similar formalisms as yet another family of performance measures which excels in extracting certain features of the signal such as the sequencing of threshold crossings and other events over time, including the temporal distances between them, while being weak in terms of other features. An early attempt to combine properties and quantitative measures into a single framework is reported in [4] for discrete time. A more recent one is described in [12] where pattern matching techniques are used to define segments of the signal where standard measurements (average, extremum) are to be applied. Combining properties and measures into a unified declarative language might help in further proliferation of verification ideas [20] into the real cyber-physical world.

Acknowledgment. This text benefitted from feedback given by Eugene Asarin, Jyo Deshmukh, Jim Kapinski, Dejan Nickovic, Joseph Sifakis and Dogan Ulus.

References

1. Annapureddy, Y., Liu, C., Fainekos, G.E., Sankaranarayanan, S., S-TaLiRo: a tool for temporal logic falsification for hybrid systems. In: TACAS, pp. 254–257 (2011)
2. Asarin, E., Caspi, P., Maler, O.: Timed regular expressions. J. ACM **49**(2), 172–206 (2002)
3. Clarke, E.M., Emerson, E.A.: Design and synthesis of synchronization skeletons using branching time temporal logic. In: Kozen, D. (ed.) Logic of Programs 1981. LNCS, vol. 131, pp. 52–71. Springer, Heidelberg (1982). doi:10.1007/BFb0025774
4. d'Angelo, B., Sankaranarayanan, S., Sanchez, C., Robinson, W., Finkbeiner, B., Sipma, H.B., Mehrotra, S., Manna, Z., Lola: Runtime monitoring of synchronous systems. In: TIME, pp. 166–174 (2005)
5. Deshmukh, J., Jin, X., Kapinski, J., Maler, O.: Stochastic local search for falsification of hybrid systems. In: Finkbeiner, B., Pu, G., Zhang, L. (eds.) ATVA 2015. LNCS, vol. 9364, pp. 500–517. Springer, Heidelberg (2015). doi:10.1007/978-3-319-24953-7_35
6. Donzé, A., Ferrère, T., Maler, O.: Efficient robust monitoring for STL. In: Sharygina, N., Veith, H. (eds.) CAV 2013. LNCS, vol. 8044, pp. 264–279. Springer, Heidelberg (2013). doi:10.1007/978-3-642-39799-8_19
7. Donzé, A., Maler, O.: Robust satisfaction of temporal logic over real-valued signals. In: Chatterjee, K., Henzinger, T.A. (eds.) FORMATS 2010. LNCS, vol. 6246, pp. 92–106. Springer, Heidelberg (2010). doi:10.1007/978-3-642-15297-9_9
8. Donzé, A.: Breach, a toolbox for verification and parameter synthesis of hybrid systems. In: Touili, T., Cook, B., Jackson, P. (eds.) CAV 2010. LNCS, vol. 6174, pp. 167–170. Springer, Heidelberg (2010). doi:10.1007/978-3-642-14295-6_17

9. Eisner, C., Fisman, D., Havlicek, J., Lustig, Y., McIsaac, A., Campenhout, D.: Reasoning with temporal logic on truncated paths. In: Hunt, W.A., Somenzi, F. (eds.) CAV 2003. LNCS, vol. 2725, pp. 27–39. Springer, Heidelberg (2003). doi:10. 1007/978-3-540-45069-6_3

10. Fainekos, G.E., Pappas, G.J.: Robustness of temporal logic specifications for continuous-time signals. Theoret. Comput. Sci. **410**(42), 4262–4291 (2009)

11. Falcone, Y.: You should better enforce than verify. In: Barringer, H., Falcone, Y., Finkbeiner, B., Havelund, K., Lee, I., Pace, G., Roşu, G., Sokolsky, O., Tillmann, N. (eds.) RV 2010. LNCS, vol. 6418, pp. 89–105. Springer, Heidelberg (2010). doi:10. 1007/978-3-642-16612-9_9

12. Ferrère, T., Maler, O., Ničković, D., Ulus, D.: Measuring with timed patterns. In: Kroening, D., Păsăreanu, C.S. (eds.) CAV 2015. LNCS, vol. 9207, pp. 322–337. Springer, Heidelberg (2015). doi:10.1007/978-3-319-21668-3_19

13. Halpern, J.Y., Vardi, M.Y.: Model checking vs. theorem proving: a manifesto. Artif. Intell. Math. Theory Comput. **212**, 151–176 (1991)

14. Harel, D., Pnueli, A.: On the development of reactive systems. In: Apt, K.R. (ed.) Logics and Models of Concurrent Systems, pp. 477–498. Springer, Heidelberg (1985)

15. Jin, X., Donzé, A., Deshmukh, J.V., Seshia, S.A.: Mining requirements from closed-loop control models. In: HSCC (2013)

16. Kesten, Y., Pnueli, A.: A compositional approach to CTL* verification. Theoretical Computer Science **331**(2–3), 397–428 (2005)

17. Koymans, R.: Specifying real-time properties with metric temporal logic. Real-Time Syst. **2**(4), 255–299 (1990)

18. Maler, O.: Hybrid systems and real-world computations (1992)

19. Maler, O.: Control from computer science. Ann. Rev. Control **26**(2), 175–187 (2002)

20. Maler, O.: Amir Pnueli and the dawn of hybrid systems. In: HSCC, pp. 293–295. ACM (2010)

21. Maler, O.: The unmet challenge of timed systems. In: From Programs to Systems (2014)

22. Maler, O., Nickovic, D.: Monitoring temporal properties of continuous signals. In: Lakhnech, Y., Yovine, S. (eds.) FORMATS/FTRTFT -2004. LNCS, vol. 3253, pp. 152–166. Springer, Heidelberg (2004). doi:10.1007/978-3-540-30206-3_12

23. Maler, O., Nickovic, D., Pnueli, A.: From MITL to timed automata. In: Asarin, E., Bouyer, P. (eds.) FORMATS 2006. LNCS, vol. 4202, pp. 274–289. Springer, Heidelberg (2006). doi:10.1007/11867340_20

24. Maler, O., Nickovic, D., Pnueli, A.: On synthesizing controllers from bounded-response properties. In: Damm, W., Hermanns, H. (eds.) CAV 2007. LNCS, vol. 4590, pp. 95–107. Springer, Heidelberg (2007). doi:10.1007/978-3-540-73368-3_12

25. Maler, O., Nickovic, D., Pnueli, A.: Checking temporal properties of discrete, timed and continuous behaviors. In: Avron, A., Dershowitz, N., Rabinovich, A. (eds.) Pillars of Computer Science. LNCS, pp. 475–505. Springer, Heidelberg (2008)

26. McMillan, K.L.: Symbolic Model Checking. Kluwer, Berlin (1993)

27. Nickovic, D.: Checking timed, hybrid properties: theory and applications. Ph.D. thesis, Université Joseph Fourier, Grenoble, France (2008)

28. Pnueli, A., Zaks, A.: On the merits of temporal testers. In: Grumberg, O., Veith, H. (eds.) 25 Years of Model Checking. LNCS, vol. 5000, pp. 172–195. Springer, Heidelberg (2008). doi:10.1007/978-3-540-69850-0_11

29. Queille, J.P., Sifakis, J.: Specification and verification of concurrent systems in CESAR. In: Dezani-Ciancaglini, M., Montanari, U. (eds.) Programming 1982. LNCS, vol. 137, pp. 337–351. Springer, Heidelberg (1982). doi:10.1007/3-540-11494-7_22

30. Rizk, A., Batt, G., Fages, F., Soliman, S.: A general computational method for robustness analysis with applications to synthetic gene networks. Bioinformatics **25**(12), 169–78 (2009)

31. Sankaranarayanan, S., Fainekos, G.E.: Falsification of temporal properties of hybrid systems using the cross-entropy method. In: HSCC (2012)

32. Shea, R., Wilson, R.A.: The Illuminatus! Trilogy. Dell Publishing, New York (1984)

33. Sifakis, J.: Rigorous system design. Found. Trends Electron. Des. Autom. **6**(4), 293–362 (2012)

34. Sifakis, J.: System design automation: challenges and limitations. Proc. IEEE **103**(11), 2093–2103 (2015)

35. Ulus, D., Ferrère, T., Asarin, E., Maler, O.: Timed pattern matching. In: Legay, A., Bozga, M. (eds.) FORMATS 2014. LNCS, vol. 8711, pp. 222–236. Springer, Heidelberg (2014). doi:10.1007/978-3-319-10512-3_16

36. Ulus, D., Ferrère, T., Asarin, E., Maler, O.: Online timed pattern matching using derivatives. In: Chechik, M., Raskin, J.-F. (eds.) TACAS 2016. LNCS, vol. 9636, pp. 736–751. Springer, Heidelberg (2016). doi:10.1007/978-3-662-49674-9_47

37. Varaiya, P.: A question about hierarchical systems. In: Djaferis, T.E., Schick, I.C. (eds.) System Theory, pp. 313–324. Springer, Heidelberg (2000)

38. Moshe, Y.: Vardi and Pierre Wolper. an automata-theoretic approach to automatic program verification. In: LICS (1986)

39. Wilson, R.A.: Quantum Psychology: How Brain Software Programs You & Your World. New Falcon Publication, New York (1990)

Satellite Events Papers

First International Summer School on Runtime Verification
As Part of the ArVi COST Action 1402

Christian Colombo[1] and Yliès Falcone[2(✉)]

[1] University of Malta, Msida, Malta
christian.colombo@um.edu.mt
[2] Univ. Grenoble-Alpes, Inria, LIG, 38000 Grenoble, France
ylies.falcone@imag.fr

Abstract. This paper briefly reports on the first international summer school on Runtime Verification: Branches of practical topics rooted in theory, co-organized and sponsored by COST Action IC1402 ArVi which was held September 23–25, Madrid, Spain as part of the 16th international conference on Runtime Verification (RV 2016).

Runtime Verification [1–5] is an umbrella term usually denoting the languages, techniques, and tools related to the verification of system executions against formally-specified behavioral properties. This field of research has been mainly represented by the Runtime Verification (RV) conference[1] which was held yearly for the last 16 years. As the field is growing and the techniques are becoming more and more mature, there is a pressing need in the community for documentation and lecture material to help students and practitioners entering the field, in spite of the existing (incomplete) tutorials and short overviews of the field. We foresee the organization of this summer school as one of the steps towards achieving this goal. By organizing the summer school, we wanted to build a short theoretical and practical program allowing to give in 3 days the necessary introductory knowledge to a practitioner or student entering the field.

Objectives. As the name of the summer school suggests, the summer school aimed to provide a balance of theory and practice: In the theoretical aspect, while all the core concepts were covered, participants were also exposed to cutting edge advances in the field. At the same time, the summer school was very hands-on and students followed up with practical work in the evenings so that by the end of the summer school, participants had created their own basic runtime verification tool.

For PhD students and researchers entering the field of RV, the school was a great opportunity to get to know other people working in the area, to meet distinguished scholars, and to establish contacts that may lead to research collaborations in the future. For people coming from industry, the school provided

---

[1] See http://runtime-verification.org.

© Springer International Publishing AG 2016
Y. Falcone and C. Sanchez (Eds.): RV 2016, LNCS 10012, pp. 17–20, 2016.
DOI: 10.1007/978-3-319-46982-9_2

an exposition of the major challenges as well as possible solutions to the application of RV in industry, an exposition to the major tools, as well as the basics of RV tool-building.

Lecturers. The following researchers lectured at the summer school:

- Prof. Wolfgang Ahrendt, Chalmers University of Technology and University of Gothenburg (Sweden).
- Prof. Ezio Bartocci, TU Wien (Austria).
- Prof. Borzoo Bonakdarpour, University of MacMaster (Canada).
- Dr. Marius Bozga, CNRS, Vérimag (France).
- Dr. Christian Colombo, University of Malta (Malta).
- Dr. Yliès Falcone, University of Grenoble (France).
- Dr. Adrian Francalanza, University of Malta (Malta).
- Dr. Klaus Havelund, NASA Jet Propulsion Laboratory (USA).
- Prof. Martin Leucker, University of Lübeck (Germany).
- Prof. Joao Lourenço, Universidade Nova de Lisboa (Portugal).
- Dr. Dejan Nickovic, Austrian Institute of Technology (Austria).
- Prof. Gordon Pace, University of Malta (Malta).
- Dr. Giles Reger, University of Manchester (UK).

Program Overview. The Summer School was organised over three days with a series of lectures from international experts during the day and a follow up practical session in the evening to enable the participants to incorporate the covered knowledge into their tool (see Tables 1, 2 and 3). The first day covered the fundamentals of runtime verification: starting with the basic concept of what is runtime verification, moving on to instrumentation techniques, and property specification languages. The second day covered the major practical aspects of runtime verification: handling data through monitor parametrisation, monitoring concurrency errors, and performance issues of monitors. The second day ended with a session on RV tools, giving the participants time to try tools and

Table 1. Programme overview - Day 1 - 23rd September

Time	Topic	Lecturer
09:00 09:45	RV overview, RV vs other verification techniques	Y. Falcone
09:45 10:30	Summer school Overview and manual monitoring	
11:00 11:45	Monitoring with AOP	G. Pace
11:45 12:30	Towards monitoring specification languages	
14:00 14:45	Monitoring LTL specifications	M. Leucker
14:45 15:30	Monitorability	
16:00 16:45	Hands on	C. Colombo
16:45 17:30		
18:00	Optional further assistance with hands on	

Table 2. Programme overview - Day 2 - 24th September

Time	Topic	Lecturer
09:00 09:45	Handling data in user-provided specifications	K. Havelund
09:45 10:30		
11:00 11:45	Monitoring concurrency errors: deadlocks, atomicity violations, and data races	J. Lourenco
11:45 12:30		
14:00 14:45	Performance issues and optimizations	G. Reger
14:45 15:30		
16:00 16:45	Hands on	C. Colombo
16:45 17:30		
18:00	Optional further assistance with hands on	

Table 3. Programme overview - Day 3 - 25th September

Time	Topic	Lecturer
09:00 09:45	Design and Monitoring of Component-Based Systems	M. Bozga
09:45 10:30	Distributed monitoring & monitoring distributed systems	B. Bonakdarpour
11:00 11:45	Time-Triggered monitoring	
11:45 12:30	From Monitoring quantitative properties to testing	D. Nickovic
14:00 14:45	Combined Static and Runtime Verification	W. Ahrendt
14:45 15:30	Bytecode manipulation for Runtime Verification	W. Binder
16:00 16:45	Runtime enforcement	Y. Falcone
16:45 17:30	A Theory of Monitors	A. Francalenza

interact with their creators. Finally, the third day covered advanced and cutting-edge research in the field with topics ranging from runtime enforcement to the combination of static and dynamic analysis, and from monitoring of distributed and transaction-based systems to low-level hardware monitoring.

Acknowledgment. We would like to warmly thank all the researchers for their lectures and all the participants to the summer school. We hope that the summer school will be continued in the future by becoming a regular event.

This summer school is based upon work from COST Action ARVI IC1402, supported by COST (European Cooperation in Science and Technology). The organizers are grateful to the COST association for sponsoring the summer school.

References

1. Colin, S., Mariani, L.: Run-time verification. In: Broy, M., Jonsson, B., Katoen, J.-P., Leucker, M., Pretschner, A. (eds.) Model-Based Testing of Reactive Systems. LNCS, vol. 3472, pp. 525–555. Springer, Heidelberg (2005). doi:10.1007/11498490_24
2. Falcone, Y., Havelund, K., Reger, G.: A tutorial on runtime verification. In: Broy, M., Peled, D.A., Kalus, G. (eds.) Engineering Dependable Software Systems, NATO Science for Peace and Security Series, D: Information and Communication Security, vol. 34, pp. 141–175. IOS Press (2013)

3. Havelund, K., Goldberg, A.: Verify your runs. In: Meyer, B., Woodcock, J. (eds.) VSTTE 2005. LNCS, vol. 4171, pp. 374–383. Springer, Heidelberg (2008). doi:10. 1007/978-3-540-69149-5_40
4. Leucker, M., Schallhart, C.: A brief account of runtime verification. J. Logic Algebraic Programm. **78**(5), 293–303 (2008)
5. Sokolsky, O., Havelund, K., Lee, I.: Introduction to the special section on runtime verification. STTT **14**(3), 243–247 (2012)

Third International Competition
on Runtime Verification
CRV 2016

Giles Reger[1]($\boxtimes$), Sylvain Hallé[2], and Yliès Falcone[3]

[1] University of Manchester, Manchester, UK
`giles.reger@manchester.ac.uk`
[2] Université du Québec à Chicoutimi, Saguenay, Canada
`shalle@acm.org`
[3] Univ. Grenoble Alpes, Inria, LIG, 38000 Grenoble, France
`ylies.falcone@imag.fr`

Abstract. We report on the Third International Competition on Runtime Verification (CRV-2016). The competition was held as a satellite event of the 16th International Conference on Runtime Verification (RV'16). The competition consisted of two tracks: offline monitoring of traces and online monitoring of Java programs. The intention was to also include a track on online monitoring of C programs but there were too few participants to proceed with this track. This report describes the format of the competition, the participating teams, the submitted benchmarks and the results. We also describe our experiences with transforming trace formats from other tools into the standard format required by the competition and report on feedback gathered from current and past participants and use this to make suggestions for the future of the competition.

1 Introduction

Runtime Verification (RV) [8,13] is a lightweight yet powerful formal specification-based technique for offline analysis (e.g., for testing) as well as runtime monitoring of system. RV is based on extracting information from a running system and checking if the observed behavior satisfies or violates the properties of interest. During the last decade, many important tools and techniques have been developed and successfully employed. However, it has been observed that there is a general lack of standard benchmark suites and evaluation methods for comparing different aspects of existing tools and techniques. For this reason, and inspired by the success of similar events in other areas of computer-aided verification (e.g., SV-COMP, SAT, SMT, CASC), the First International Competition on Software for Runtime Verification (CSRV-2014) was established [2]. See [3] for a more in-depth discussion of this first iteration where all submitted properties are presented and the results discussed. Additionally, [11] presents a study discussing how the properties from the competition could be written in two different specification languages. The first iteration of the competition was

© Springer International Publishing AG 2016
Y. Falcone and C. Sanchez (Eds.): RV 2016, LNCS 10012, pp. 21–37, 2016.
DOI: 10.1007/978-3-319-46982-9_3

followed by the second competition the following year which kept the same format but made some minor adjustments based on lessons learnt in the previous year (see [9]).

This is the third edition of the competition and the general aims remain the same:

- To stimulate the development of new efficient and practical runtime verification tools and the maintenance of the already developed ones.
- To produce benchmark suites for runtime verification tools, by sharing case studies and programs that researchers and developers can use in the future to test and to validate their prototypes.
- To discuss the metrics employed for comparing the tools.
- To compare different aspects of the tools running with different benchmarks and evaluating them using different criteria.
- To enhance the visibility of presented tools among different communities (verification, software engineering, distributed computing and cyber security) involved in monitoring.

CRV-2016 was held between May and August 2016 with the results presented in September 2016 in Madrid, Spain, as a satellite event of the 16th International Conference on Runtime Verification (RV'16).

Changes. The competition is broadly similar to the previous iteration [9]. The biggest change is that there were not enough participants to run the C track (see Sect. 7). The other changes were designed to make the competition run more smoothly: the number of benchmarks was reduced and an additional stage was introduced to ensure that benchmarks were clarified fully.

Report Structure. We begin by discussing the format of the competition (Sect. 2). We then present and briefly describe the participants to each track (Sect. 3), followed by an overview of the benchmarks submitted in each track (Sect. 4). The results of the competition are then presented (Sect. 5). This is followed by some reflections on the trace format used in the offline track (Sect. 6). Finally, we reflect on the challenges faced and give recommendations to future editions of the competition (Sect. 7) before making some concluding remarks (Sect. 8).

2   Format of the Competition

The format of the competition was broadly similar to that of the previous year (see [9]). The competition website contains a document outlining the full rules of the competition[1], which was distributed to participants before the start of the competition. This section summarises the key points from this document.

---

[1] http://crv.liflab.ca/CRV2016.pdf.

2.1 Tracks

As in previous years, the competition was originally meant to consist of three tracks with each track being treated slightly different in each phase. Here we give a brief overview of the general scope of what is covered by the competition and then the idea behind each track.

General Scope. There are many activities that could fall under the umbrella term of runtime verification. Here we describe and defend the *current* scope of the competition. Note that we (the general competition community) are open to suggestions for future iterations.

The general activity we consider is that of taking a trace τ and a specification ψ and answering the question whether τ satisfies/is a model for/is accepted by ψ. In some cases the trace τ is taken as a stand-alone artefact and in other cases it is being generated as a program is running. We restrict our attention to *linear* traces (i.e. we do not consider concurrency) and require programs that generate such traces to be (broadly) deterministic.

Note that our formulation precludes the other, related, activity of finding multiple *matches* between the trace and specification describing failure. In all cases it is sufficient to report failure as soon as it is detected. On a similar note, we do not restrict ourselves to safety properties, but (for obvious reasons) require all specification languages to have an interpretation on finite traces (i.e. one could have bounded liveness).

The Offline Track. This covers the scenario where the trace is collected, stored in a log file, and then processed *offline*. We define three acceptable formats for traces (log files) to be used in benchmarks. In previous years benchmarks in this track have focussed on parametric, or data-carrying, events. Note that this track does not (currently) support notions of time other than as data.

The Online Java Track. This covers a scenario where a Java program is instrumented to produce events that should be handled by a monitor. In the past the majority of instrumentation was carried out via AspectJ. We would like to standardise this where possible. Therefore, benchmark submissions will be required to include AspectJ instrumentation (again, where possible). Entrants may use alternative instrumentation techniques in their submissions but we ask that they justify this.

The Online C Track. This covers a scenario where a C program is run and it is asked whether a specification of that run holds. Starting this year, the C track will consist of two sub-tracks, although this is mainly for organisational reasons and we encourage entrants to participate in both sub-tracks. These are:

1. **Generic Specification.** The C version of the Java track where some instrumentation should abstract the program as a sequence of events to be passed to a monitor. Instrumentation can be automatic or manual.

2. **Implicit Specification.** This covers implicit properties (such as memory-safety and out of bounds array access). Such properties might typically be taken from a standardisation of C rather than formulated in a separate specification language. In this case the trace may also be implicit (although we note that it theoretically exists).

We note that this track did not run due to lack of participants.

2.2   Phases

The competition was divided into five phases as follows:

1. **Registration** collected information about entrants.
2. **Benchmark Phase** In this phase, entrants submitted benchmarks to be considered for inclusion in the competition.
3. **Clarification Phase** The benchmarks resulting from the previous phase were made available to entrants. This phase gave entrants an opportunity to seek clarifications from the authors of each benchmark. Only benchmarks that had all clarifications dealt with by the end of this phase were eligible for the next phase.
4. **Monitor Phase** In this phase entrants were asked to produce monitors for the eligible benchmarks. As described later, these had to be runnable via a script on a Linux system (therefore the tool had to be installable on such a system).
5. **Evaluation Phase** Submissions from the previous phase were collected and executed, with relevant data collected to compute scores as described later. Entrants were given an opportunity to test their submissions on the evaluation system. The output produced during evaluation will be made available after the competition.

Note that it was not necessary to participate in the Benchmark Phase, although not doing so would likely be disadvantageous. However, all entrants were required to take part in the remaining three phases, including the Clarification Phase.

2.3   Timeline

The competition was announced in relevant mailing lists in May 2016. This was much later than in previous years. This could have had an impact on the number of participants. Previous participants and tool developers known to the organisers were contacted directly. Potential participants were requested to declare their intent to participate in the competition using an online form collecting basic information about the participating tools.

The planned timeline was as follows:

Event	Starts	Ends (Deadline)
Registration	May 1st	June 5th
Benchmark submission	May 1st	May 29th
Clarifications	June 5th	June 12th
Monitor submission	June 19th	July 10th
Results		August 1st

Extensions were given for each deadline with the final submission deadline being the 22nd July.

2.4   Benchmark Submission Format

Benchmark submissions consisted of three parts:

1. **The Metadata.** Every benchmark requires a name, a description and a domain category.
2. **The Property.** This is a description of the property being monitored and should take the same form for all tracks (with the exception of the **Implicit Specification C subtrack** as described in the full rules document).
3. **The Trace Part.** This describes what the events to be monitored are and is necessarily track-specific. More details are given below.

We now review the last two parts below. The textual information about properties was uploaded to the competition wiki[2] and supporting files were uploaded to the competition server. Each team could submit up to three benchmarks. This is a reduction on previous years to reduce the workload for participants; we discuss the impact of this later.

Describing Properties. The information about a submitted property was formatted as follows:

1. An *informal* description. This should include the context of the property, the relevant events (their names and parameters, if any), and the ordering constraints between events that form the property. Moreover, any assumptions being made should have been reported.
2. Demonstration traces. At least 6 examples traces (3 that should be accepted, 3 rejected) should be provided. Traces can be given in an abstract form e.g. a(1).b(2) and should be explained in terms of the abstract property, not the formal description. The provided traces should ideally highlight edge cases.

---

[2] http://crv.liflab.ca/wiki.

3. A *formal* description. This should include resonable detail describing the specification written in a well-defined and documented specification language.

Optionally we encouraged participants to also describe the property in a standard form of first-order linear temporal logic but few participants did this (see later discussions).

Describing Traces. The trace formats fixed in the last iteration of the competition [9] have been kept. Traces could be in standardised CSV, XML or JSON formats. However, in XML and JSON no nesting of data values is supported. Along with the trace files, a benchmark should also include (i) an explanation of how concrete events in the trace relate to abstract events in the property, and (ii) additional statistics about the number of events in the trace.

Describing Programs. For programs, it was required that a benchmark includes the uninstrumented source files, two scripts `compile.sh` and `run.sh` to compile and run the program, and instrumentation information. For the Java track, we preferred instrumentation in the form of an AspectJ file. If it was not obvious, the relation between instrumentation and property should have been explained. Additionally, participants were encouraged to provide the facility to produce a trace file (in the above formats) from the program.

2.5   Monitor Submission Format

Once teams had written monitors for the benchmarks they wished to participate on they could upload these to the server and test that they worked in the competition environment (after installing their tool and all necessary libraries on the server).

Tools were required to give standardised outputs in the form of a status line. Monitors should output the verdict by printing a status line of the following form:

– **STATUS: Satisfied** if the property is satisfied,
– **STATUS: Violated** if the property is violated,
– **STATUS: TimeOut** if the status is not detected within the time limit,
– **STATUS: GaveUp** if the monitor fails to find the verdict for any reason.

If no status line is printed, it was assumed that the status is TimeOut.

For online tracks participants needed to provide a `setup.sh` script to prepare the benchmark, typically this performs automated instrumentation, and a `run.sh` script to run the benchmark, typically this will be the same as in the original submission (perhaps with additional inclusion of some libraries). For the offline track, a single script was required that took two inputs: (i) the name of the benchmark and (ii) the name of the trace file.

2.6 Scoring

The scoring remains the same as for the previous two iterations of the competition (see [2]). Each submission is awarded three scores for *correctness, running time* and *memory utilisation*. The correctness score is negative if there is an error e.g. an incorrect verdict. The scores for running time and memory utilisation are computed by distributing a fixed number of points per benchmark between the competing tools in proportion to their performance. For example, if tool A runs in 10 seconds and tool B runs in 40 seconds and there are 10 points to be awarded team A would get 8 points and team B would get 2 points for that benchmark.

3 Participating Teams

In this section, for each track, we report on the teams and tools that participated in CRV-2016. Tables 1 and 2 give a summary of the teams participating in the Java and Offline tracks respectively. In the following of this section, we provide a short overview of the tools involved in the competition. We note that the E-ACSL tool [7] from CEA LIST, France entered the C track but was the only tool to do so.

CRL. In the framework of Complex Event Processing, CRL [14] is a C++ library which allows for the analysis of complex event flows to recognise predetermined searched-for behaviours. These behaviours are defined as specific arrangements of events using a behaviour description language called the Chronicle Language. The recognition process has been completely formalised through a set semantics and the algorithms of CRL directly correspond to the mathematical definitions. CRL is available online[3].

Table 1. Tools participating in online monitoring of Java programs track.

Tool	Ref.	Contact person	Affiliation
Larva	[5]	Shaun Azzopardi	University of Malta, Malta
MarQ	[16]	Giles Reger	University of Manchester, UK
Mufin	[6]	Torben Scheffel	University of Lübeck, Germany

Table 2. Tools participating in the offline monitoring track.

Tool	Ref.	Contact person	Affiliation
BeepBeep 3	[10]	Sylvain Hallé	Université du Québec à Chicoutimi, Canada
CRL	[14]	Ariane Piel	ONERA, France
MarQ	[16]	Giles Reger	University of Manchester, UK

---

[3] http://chroniclerecognitionlibrary.github.io/crl/o.html.

BEEPBEEP 3 is a general purpose event stream processor that attempts to reconcile the capabilities of Runtime Verification and Complex Event Processing under a common framework [10]. In addition to Boolean properties used in monitoring, BEEPBEEP can compute queries that involve complex manipulations of event data and produce output traces of any type. BEEPBEEP 3 is under active development, and is available online[4].

LARVA is a Java tool [5] aimed specifically for monitoring Java systems with a specification language targeting business level logic rather than low level properties. The tool takes a specification in the form of a text file, generating the necessary code in Java and AspectJ which verifies that the properties in the script are being adhered to during the execution of the system. Its specification language (DATEs [4]) is a flavour of automata enriched with stopwatches. LARVA is available online[5].

MARQ (Monitoring at runtime with QEA) [16] monitors specifications written as Quantified Event Automata [1,15] (QEA). QEA is based on the notion of trace-slicing, extended with existential quantification and free variables. For online monitoring it relies on AspectJ. For offline monitoring of traces it provides a library of *translator* objects that allow the user to define the interface between the alphabets of the specification and trace. MARQ is available online[6].

MUFIN (Monitoring with Union-Find) [6] is a framework for monitoring Java programs. (Finite or infinite) monitors are defined using a simple API that allows to manage multiple instances of monitors. Internally MUFIN uses hash-tables and union-find-structures as well as additional fields injected into application classes to lookup these monitor instances efficiently. The main aim of MUFIN is to monitor properties involving large numbers of objects efficiently. MUFIN will hopefully be available online soon[7].

4 Benchmarks

We give a brief overview of the benchmarks submitted to each track.

4.1 Offline Track

There were 6 benchmarks submitted to the Offline track by 2 teams - MARQ and BEEPBEEP 3. An additional benchmark was submitted by CRL but this team withdrew. The three benchmarks from MARQ (taken from [1,15]) were

1. *AuctionBidding.* Items placed for auction should only be listed for the prescribed period, all bids should be strictly increasing and should be sold for no less than the reserve price.

---

[4] https://liflab.github.io/beepbeep-3.
[5] http://www.cs.um.edu.mt/svrg/Tools/LARVA/.
[6] https://github.com/selig/qea.
[7] http://www.isp.uni-luebeck.de/mufin.

2. *CandidateSelection.* For every voter there must exist a party that the voter is a member of, and the voter must rank all candidates for that party
3. *SQLInjection.* Every string derived from an input string must be sanitised before being used.

All three benchmarks appeared in last year's competition. The three benchmarks were designed to demonstrate the different ways data can be used within the specification language.

The three benchmarks from BEEPBEEP 3 where taken from a case study on applying runtime verfication to bug finding in video games [18]. The properties are therefore all about the interaction of *Pingu* characters within the game:

1. *PinguCreation.* From one event to the next, Pingus can only disappear from the game field; no Pingu can be created mid-game.
2. *EndlessBashing.* Every Basher must become a Walker when it stops bashing.
3. *TurnAround.* A Walker encountering a Blocker must turn around and keep on walking.

Traces for the benchmarks were generated by Pingu Generator[8]. These traces do not immediately conform to the competition format and we describe how they were translated in Sect. 6. As this was a new tool to the competition all benchmarks were new.

4.2　Java Track

There were 9 benchmarks submitted to the JAVA track by 3 teams - LARVA, MARQ, and MUFIN. All three teams used ASPECTJ as an instrumentation tool, allowing for easy reuse of instrumentation code.

The three benchmarks from LARVA were

1. *GreyListing.* Once greylisted, a user must perform at least three incoming transfers before being whitelisted.
2. *ReconcileAccounts.* The administrator must reconcile accounts after every 1000 attempted external money transfers or after an aggregate total of one million dollars in attempted external transfers.
3. *Logging.* Logging can only be made to an active session (i.e. between a login and a logout).

The first two benchmarks appeared in the first iteration of the competition (although the monitored programs have been extended to present a more challenging workload at the request of the competition organisers).

The three benchmarks from MARQ (taken from [1, 15]) were

1. *PublisherSubscriber.* For every publisher, there exists a subscriber that acknowledges every message sent by that publisher.

---

[8] https://bitbucket.org/sylvainhalle/pingu-generator.

2. *AnnonyingFriend.* Person A should not contact person B on at least three different social networking sites without any response from person B. There should not be 10 or more such messages across any number of sites.
3. *ResourceLifecycle.* Managed resources must obey their lifecycle e.g. not granted without first being requested nor released without first being granted.

The third benchmark appeared in last year's competition; the first two are new. The first two benchmarks were designed to demonstrate complex quantifier usage as they alternate universal and existential quantification.

The three benchmarks from MUFIN (also described in [6]) were

1. *Tree.* There is a tree of communicating nodes. The property is about communication between the nodes. For example, whenever a node receives a `sendCritical` message all descendent nodes must have received a `reset` message since the last `send` message.
2. *Multiplexer.* Clients attached to an inactive channel should not be used.
3. *Toggle.* A work piece may only be processed when it is not the same mode as its creating device.

All three benchmarks appeared in last year's competition. Each benchmark was designed to stress a certain element of the algorithm. *Tree* presents a scenario where the number of objects is not known in advance with complex relationships between objects. *Multiplexer* presents a scenario with many control states. *Toggle* includes global actions affecting all data values.

5   Results

For the first time the competition has been completed in time for the results to be included in the Runtime Verification conference proceedings rather than being announced for the first time at the conference (or in some cases shortly after). In this section, we report on the results and give some brief analysis.

5.1   Detailed Results

Tables 3 and 4 give the detailed results from the Offline and Java tracks respectively. The tables detail the running times and memory utilisation for each submission. The scores for each submission are then given. Negative correctness scores can be given for an incorrect result or error (which does not happen here) or for failing to give a result within the given resources (here we use TO to indicate time out, in this case 10 hours, and OM to indicate out of memory).

From Table 3 we see that MARQ failed to find a solution for its own *CandidateSelection* benchmark. On inspection it was found that MARQ required more than the 8GB of memory available on the competition machine. MARQ performed better than BEEPBEEP 3 in terms of running time in all cases. This is not very surprising given the low-level specification language used by MARQ. We note that the trace files being used for the two tools for the last three

Table 3. Detailed results for offline track

Benchmark	Tool	Time (seconds)	Memory (MB)	Scores		
				Correctness	Time	Memory
AuctionBidding	BEEPBEEP 3	36, 731.04	1,792	10	0.035	5.66
	MARQ	132.01	2,337	10	9.96	4.34
CandidateSelection	BEEPBEEP 3	6, 362.8	1,320	10	10	10
	MARQ	–	OM	-5	0	0
SQLInjection	BEEPBEEP 3	87.62	1,991	10	1.70	3.83
	MARQ	18.03	1,235	10	8.29	6.17
PinguCreation	BEEPBEEP 3	16.94	1,146	10	0.70	0.59
	MARQ	1.29	72	10	9.29	9.41
EndlessBashing	BEEPBEEP 3	116.95	1,473	10	0.26	1.03
	MARQ	3.08	168	10	9.74	8.97
TurnAround	BEEPBEEP 3	44.08	1,501	10	1.71	2.40
	MARQ	9.1	475	10	8.29	7.60

Table 4. Detailed results for Java track

Benchmark	Tool	Time (seconds)	Memory (MB)	Scores		
				Correctness	Time	Memory
GreyListing	LARVA	562.1	140	10	0.15	1.89
	MARQ	15.43	72	10	5.37	3.67
	MUFIN	18.48	59	10	4.48	4.45
ReoncileAccounts	LARVA	7.06	90	10	2.7	2.45
	MARQ	4.8	73	10	3.97	2.99
	MUFIN	5.73	48	10	3.32	4.56
Logging	LARVA	7691.68	181	10	0.07	2.49
	MARQ	104.62	129	10	5.68	3.49
	MUFIN	140.23	112	10	4.24	4.01
PublisherSubscriber	LARVA	0.44	46	10	6.22	4.62
	MARQ	4.86	335	10	0.56	0.63
	MUFIN	0.85	45	10	3.22	4.73
AnnoyingFriend	LARVA	51.63	836	10	1.73	2.04
	MARQ	26.35	718	10	3.40	2.37
	MUFIN	18.38	304	10	4.87	5.59
ResourceLifecycle	LARVA	TO	-	-5	0	0
	MARQ	282.87	752	10	0.85	2.69
	MUFIN	26.35	276	10	9.15	7.31
Tree	LARVA	TO	-	-5	0	0
	MARQ	-	-	0	0	0
	MUFIN	32.34	775	10	10	10
Multiplexer	LARVA	TO	-	-5	0	0
	MARQ	105.54	1703	10	0.38	1.06
	MUFIN	4.23	201	10	9.61	8.94
Toggle	LARVA	22,393.54	159	10	0.00	1.864
	MARQ	186.12	733	10	0.03	0.40
	MUFIN	0.52	38	10	9.97	7.73

Table 5. Total scores

Team	Submissions	Correctness	Time	Memory	Total	Average
Offline track						
BEEPBEEP 3	6	60	14.42	25.51	97.93	16.32
MARQ	6	45	45.58	36.49	127.07	21.18
Java Track						
LARVA	9	45	10.88	15.36	71.24	7.96
MARQ	8	80	20.25	17.30	117.65	14.71
MUFIN	9	90	58.87	57.34	206.21	22.91

benchmarks were not the same as MARQ first translated the trace files into the competition-compliant CSV format. This translation time is not included in the results.

The results of the Java track given in Table 4 are less obvious. We have four cases where LARVA failed to complete monitoring within the time limit. There was also one case where MARQ chose not to compete on a benchmark. According to the tool developer this was due to the complexity of the benchmark making it time-consuming to translate and debug. In general, MUFIN had significantly lower running times. Both LARVA and MARQ struggled due to garbage collection. LARVA is not optimised for memory leaks of this kind and MARQ switched off one of its optimisations prior to the competition due to a bug.

5.2   Scores and Winners

Table 5 gives the total scores for each tool in each track. This gives MARQ as the winner of the Offline track and MUFIN as the winner of the Java track. In previous years it has been the case that the ranking of average scores has not agreed with the ranking of total scores as some tools decided to only compete on a subset of the benchmarks they were suited to. This was not the case this year, with the average score and total score rankings being the same.

6   Discussion of Trace Formats

In this section we will briefly discuss some observations about the trace formats introduced for the Offline track. Throughout different iterations of the competition, tools have either been developed around the advertised competition trace formats or chosen to translate their existing format into one of the competition ones. There is a growing interest in the best way to capture traces [12] and we briefly discuss three cases where other traces have needed to be translated.

MONPOLY. In the first iteration of the competition the MONPOLY tool already had a native trace format that they translated into the CSV format of the competition. The main issue that needed to be overcome was that MONPOLY supports multiple events per time step i.e. an event is a set of labelled observations. The translation necessarily introduced an additional time step field and arbitrarily ordered events coming from the same time step.

BEEPBEEP 3. The trace files submitted by BEEPBEEP 3 this year did not conform to the XML requirements of the competition as they included nested data structures. A single event consisted of a variable number of character objects, each describing a different Pingu character. To translate this into the CSV format, the organisers introduced an event per character object, with the other metadata being copied between these new events. This led to additional orderings that did not occur in the original trace as a timestamp parameter was required to differentiate between characters occurring in different original events.

CRL. The benchmark submitted by CRL this year did not follow the required format. It consisted of separate files giving different parts of the overall behaviour. As the traces were related by timestamps it was relatively straightforward to merge the traces into a single trace file. However, the idea that different behaviour is recorded separately and then merged is reasonable. In this case, there was one trace file for inter-aircraft communication and one trace file per aircraft giving position information.

Discussion. These observations suggest that the trace format should be extended to allow either more complex structures as data values in events or the notion of multiple events occurring unordered at a single point in time. In both of the affected cases above, flattening the events led to more complex specifications that needed to deal with the arbitrary ordering of events that should be observed at the same point. Additionally, the last example suggests supporting traces in multiple files may be useful.

7   Feedback and Reflection

As part of preparing this report we contacted all participants in this and the two previous competitions and asked a number of questions about their experiences. More broadly we asked for general thoughts on the design and future of the competition. Here we summarise the result of this feedback, along with some thoughts of our own, organised around challenge areas.

7.1   Engagement and the Missing C Track

In the first year of the competition, 17 teams registered their interest and 10 teams submitted something. In the second year, 14 teams registered their interest and 7 teams submitted something. This year, 8 teams registered their interest and 5 submitted something.

Last year we identified the fact that entering the competition was a lot of work so this year we reduced the number of benchmarks. However, as one participant pointed out, this has drawbacks as there is more scope for over-fitting. The notion of a benchmark repository (discussed below) could sidestep this issue.

The main reason past participants gave for not re-entering was that they did not foresee any new insights coming from entering. One participant said *"We did not expect any new insights about the performance of our tool, since no major changes to our tool were made"*. Another made a suggestion *"I suggest to have such a competition every second year. I am not sure if there are many changes and improvements to too many tools within a year."*. This seems like a reasonable suggestion and we discuss this idea further below.

Whilst most participants were positive about the relevance of the competition the same participants expressed disappointment in the impact of the competition so far. One reason for this is the lack of engagement: *"even for the first competition, I was disappointed that only a few teams participated"*. Another pointed out that we have not taken full advantage of the process: *"I was hoping for a more sustainable report of the competition and its results."*. Lastly, due to logistic issues, the results from last years competition were only announced on a website some time after the announcement at the conference leading one participant to comment *"If winners are not announced, why participate?"*, a reasonable point.

Finally, it is disappointing that the C track is missing this year due to lack of participants. As mentioned earlier, we aimed to appeal to a wider range of tools by introducing the notion of implicit specifications and we received positive feedback on this from the one participant. However, it seems that the competition still lacks appeal to such tools.

7.2   A Benchmark Repository

The intention of the first competition organisers was for benchmarks to be reused from year to year. However, this has proved difficult for two main reasons. Firstly, a lack of common specification language means much of the effort in dealing with benchmarks involves translating properties from one specification language to another, we discuss this more later. Secondly, without a common format for capturing benchmarks it is not clear that we have captured enough information to fully describe the benchmark. This is an issue we have attempted to address by the addition of demonstration traces and clarification requests. But benchmarks still contain ambiguities and unwritten assumptions.

If these issues can be overcome then the development of an independent benchmark repository has clear benefits as resource for the community beyond the competition. Indeed, this is a continued aim of the COST Action associated with the competition.

This idea is supported by our feedback with one participant suggesting this approach, adding that benchmarks could be slightly mutated for use in the competition to avoid over-fitting. Another participant stated that *"creating benchmarks is the costly part of the competition"* suggesting that the perceived need to submit benchmarks is a barrier to entry. It was also pointed out that re-using benchmarks can be used to analyse a tools evolution. Finally, one participant expressed a wish for benchmarks to be released at the point the competition is announced to make the amount of work required clear from the beginning. This would require an independent benchmark repository.

7.3   A Common Specification Language

It is clear that without a common specification language the competition will continue to involve a lot of hard work. In the feedback, participants spoke of days spent translating specifications by hand and one spoke of this as a reason not to enter the competition again.

The main suggestion for a common specification language is first-order LTL. We encouraged benchmarks in such a language this year but this was seen as too much additional effort by participants. One issue is that there exist a number of variants of first-order LTL in the community and it is not clear if one of these should be used or a new language developed. Once a language has been selected then each tool developer needs to consider how the selected language relates to their specification language. Whilst there has been some work on relating different specification languages for runtime verification [17] we see this as a different hurdle for participants and it is not clear which is more significant.

7.4   Achieving Better Coverage

One criticism of the competition from two participants was the lack of coverage. Currently a single trace is used for evaluation. There is therefore no guarantee that the submitted monitor implements the property correctly beyond the single known trace. The suggestion here is to have multiple traces or workloads per benchmark with some being seen and others unseen. This allows the competition to check the completeness of the submitted monitor as well as the efficiency of the monitoring tool.

7.5   Beyond (or Ignoring) Performance

It has been suggested that holding the current version of the competition every year is not useful. The suggestion is to hold different styles of competition in years where the current style is not run. The question is then what such a competition should look like. One comment that came from the feedback is that a concentration on performance leads to a style of research that does not necessarily lead to usable tools. Below we list some suggestions for alternative focuses.

Different monitoring scenarios. One participant suggested a scenario where several properties are checked for a single trace. Another suggestion would be to detect multiple violations of a single safety property or explain violations.

Hardware. The previous point was about keeping the setting but changing the problem. Another approach would be to consider a different setting. Whilst most research on hardware monitoring is difficult to compare, setting a challenging problem to be solved in plenty of time may lead to new research on solving an interesting problem.

Concurrency. Currently the issue of monitoring distributed or concurrent systems has not played a large part in the competition. An iteration of the competition focussing on this issue could encourage more focussed research.

Usability. It is often mentioned that usability of tools and specification languages is a large barrier for uptake of formal methods tools. It is not immediately clear how usability could be measured objectively. One suggestion would be to have a showcase rather than a competition. One participant suggested the use of the summer school to carry out such a study. This is an interesting idea although complex logistically.

8   Concluding Remarks

This report described the Third Competition on Runtime Verification. The organisation of the competition was reviewed along with the competing teams. The results have been announced and some reflections on the structure and organisation of the competition have been given.

Acknowledgment. Thanks to Klaus Havelund, Julien Signoles, Torben Scheffel, Domenico Bianculli, Daniel Thoma and Felix Klaedtke for providing the feedback discussed in Sect. 7. The *Laboratoire d'informatique formelle* from Université du Québec à Chicoutimi lent the server for hosting the wiki and running the benchmarks. This article is based upon work from COST Action ARVI IC1402, supported by COST (European Cooperation in Science and Technology).

References

1. Barringer, H., Falcone, Y., Havelund, K., Reger, G., Rydeheard, D.: Quantified event automata: towards expressive and efficient runtime monitors. In: Giannakopoulou, D., Méry, D. (eds.) FM 2012. LNCS, vol. 7436, pp. 68–84. Springer, Heidelberg (2012). doi:10.1007/978-3-642-32759-9_9
2. Bartocci, E., Bonakdarpour, B., Falcone, Y.: First international competition on software for runtime verification. In: Bonakdarpour, B., Smolka, S.A. (eds.) RV 2014. LNCS, vol. 8734, pp. 1–9. Springer, Heidelberg (2014). doi:10.1007/978-3-319-11164-3_1
3. Bartocci, E., Bonakdarpour, B., Falcone, Y., Colombo, C., Decker, N., Klaedtke, F., Havelund, K., Joshi, Y., Milewicz, R., Reger, G., Rosu, G., Signoles, J., Thoma, D., Zalinescu, E., Zhang, Y.: First international competition on runtime verification. Int. J. Softw. Tools Technol. Trans. (STTT) (submitted)
4. Colombo, C., Pace, G.J., Schneider, G.: Dynamic event-based runtime monitoring of real-time and contextual properties. In: Cofer, D., Fantechi, A. (eds.) FMICS 2008. LNCS, vol. 5596, pp. 135–149. Springer, Heidelberg (2009). doi:10.1007/978-3-642-03240-0_13
5. Colombo, C., Pace, G.J., Schneider, G.: LARVA - safer monitoring of real-time Java programs (tool paper). In: Proceedings of the 2009 Seventh IEEE International Conference on Software Engineering and Formal Methods, SEFM 2009, pp. 33–37, 2009. IEEE Computer Society, Washington (2009)

6. Decker, N., Harder, J., Scheffel, T., Schmitz, M., Thoma, D.: Runtime monitoring with union-find structures. In: Chechik, M., Raskin, J.-F. (eds.) TACAS 2016. LNCS, vol. 9636, pp. 868–884. Springer, Heidelberg (2016). doi:10.1007/978-3-662-49674-9_54
7. Delahaye, M., Kosmatov, N., Signoles, J.: Common specification language for static, dynamic analysis of cprograms. In: Proceedings of SAC 2013: The 28th Annual ACM Symposium on Applied Computing, pp. 1230–1235. ACM (2013)
8. Falcone, Y., Havelund, K., Reger, G.: A tutorial on runtimeverification. In: Broy, M., Peled, D. (eds.) SummerSchool Marktoberdorf 2012 - Engineering Dependable Software Systems. IOS Press (2013) (to appear)
9. Falcone, Y., Ničković, D., Reger, G., Thoma, D.: Second international competition on runtime verification. In: Bartocci, E., Majumdar, R. (eds.) Runtime Verification. LNCS, vol. 9333, pp. 405–422. Springer, Cham (2015)
10. Hallé, S.: When RV meets CEP. In: Falcone, Y., Sanchez, C. (eds.) RV 2016. LNCS, vol. 10012, pp. 68–91. Springer, Heidelberg (2016)
11. Havelund, K., Reger, G.: Specification of parametric monitors. In: Drechsler, R., Kühne, U. (eds.) Formal Modeling, Verification of Cyber-Physical Systems, pp. 151–189. Springer, Heidelberg (2015)
12. Havelund, K., Reger, G.: What is a trace? a run time verification perspective. In: 7th International Symposium on Leveraging Applications of Formal Methods, Verification and Validation (ISoLA 2016) (accepted)
13. Leucker, M., Schallhart, C.: A brief account of run time verification. J. Logic Algebr. Programm. **78**(5), 293–303 (2008)
14. Piel, A.: Reconnaissance de comportements complexes partraitement en ligne de flux d'événements. (Online event flowprocessing for complex behaviour recognition). Ph.D. thesis, Paris 13 University, Villetaneuse, Saint-Denis, Bobigny, France (2014)
15. Reger, G.: Automata based monitoring and mining of execution traces. Ph.D. thesis, University of Manchester (2014)
16. Reger, G., Cruz, H.C., Rydeheard, D.: MarQ: monitoring at runtime with QEA. In: Baier, C., Tinelli, C. (eds.) TACAS 2015. LNCS, vol. 9035, pp. 596–610. Springer, Heidelberg (2015). doi:10.1007/978-3-662-46681-0_55
17. Reger, G., Rydeheard, D.: From first-order temporal logic to parametric trace slicing. In: Bartocci, E., Majumdar, R. (eds.) RV 2015. LNCS, vol. 9333, pp. 216–232. Springer, Heidelberg (2015). doi:10.1007/978-3-319-23820-3_14
18. Varvaressos, S., Lavoie, K., Massé, A.B., Gaboury, S.,Hallé, S.: Automated bug finding in video games: a case study for runtime monitoring. In: Proceedings of the 2014 IEEE International Conference on Software Testing, Verification, and Validation, ICST 2014, pp. 143–152. IEEE Computer Society, Washington (2014)

Tutorial Papers

Runtime Verification for HyperLTL

Borzoo Bonakdarpour[1]([✉]) and Bernd Finkbeiner[2]

[1] McMaster University, Hamilton, Canada
borzoo@mcmaster.ca
[2] Saarland University, Saarbrücken, Germany
finkbeiner@cs.uni-saarland.de

Abstract. Information flow security often involves reasoning about multiple execution traces. This subtlety stems from the fact that an intruder may gain knowledge about the system through observing and comparing several executions. The monitoring of such properties of sets of traces, also known as hyperproperties, is a challenge for runtime verification, because most monitoring techniques are limited to the analysis of a single trace. In this tutorial, we discuss this challenge with respect to HyperLTL, a temporal logic for the specification of hyperproperties.

1 Security Policies and Hyperproperties

Runtime verification (RV) is traditionally concerned with the monitoring of *trace properties* such as those expressed in linear-time temporal logic (LTL). Observing a growing prefix of a trace, we determine if the trace belongs to the set of traces that is characterized as correct by the specification.

Information flow security policies usually do not fit this pattern, because they express a relation between multiple traces. Noninterference, for example, requires that two traces that may differ in their high-security inputs, but have the same low-security inputs, must have the same low-security outputs. Such properties are therefore not properties of individual traces, but properties of sets of traces, also known as *hyperproperties*. This is not a matter of linear vs. branching time, as noninterference cannot even be expressed in branching-time temporal logics, such as CTL, CTL* or the modal μ-calculus [2,11]; the challenge, rather, is that information flow properties can be considered as properties on a system that results from the parallel composition of multiple copies of the original system [4,18].

Clarkson and Schneider proposed the notion of *hyperproperties* to account for properties that relate multiple executions of a system [7]. They showed that the class of hyperproperties comprises many of the properties proposed in the literature. A hyperproperty H is defined as a set of sets of executions traces, and a system is defined to satisfy H, if its set of execution traces is an *element* of H. Noninterference between an input h and an output o is, for example, the hyperproperty consisting of all sets of traces, in which all traces that only differ in h have the same output o at all times.

© Springer International Publishing AG 2016
Y. Falcone and C. Sanchez (Eds.): RV 2016, LNCS 10012, pp. 41–45, 2016.
DOI: 10.1007/978-3-319-46982-9_4

2   HyperLTL

Since hyperproperties cannot be expressed in the classic temporal logics like LTL
or CTL*, several extensions of the temporal logics have been proposed. Balliu
et al. encoded several standard information flow policies in epistemic temporal logics [3], which allows us to specify properties in terms of the knowledge
of agents. Another temporal logic that is sufficiently expressive to encode certain information flow policies is SecLTL, which specifies how information flow
requirements change over time and in response to events in the system [8]. We
focus here on the temporal logic HyperLTL [6,12], which adds explicit and simultaneous quantification over multiple traces to LTL. Compared to previous logical frameworks, HyperLTL significantly extends the range of security policies
under consideration, including complex information-flow properties like generalized noninterference, declassification, and quantitative noninterference.

Let AP be a set of *atomic propositions*, and let $\mathcal{V}$ be a set of trace variables.
The syntax of HyperLTL is given by the following grammar:

$$\psi ::= \exists \pi.\, \psi \mid \forall \pi.\, \psi \mid \varphi$$
$$\varphi ::= a_\pi \mid \neg \varphi \mid \varphi \vee \varphi \mid \bigcirc \varphi \mid \varphi \mathcal{U} \varphi$$

where $a \in AP$ is an atomic proposition and $\pi \in \mathcal{V}$ is a trace variable. Note that
atomic propositions are indexed by trace variables. The quantification over traces
makes it possible to express properties like "on all traces ψ must hold", which
is expressed by $\forall \pi.\, \psi$. Dually, one can express that "there exists a trace such
that ψ holds", which is denoted by $\exists \pi.\, \psi$. We use the usual derived Boolean
connectives. The derived temporal operators $\Diamond$, $\Box$, and $\mathcal{W}$ are defined as for
LTL: $\Diamond \varphi \equiv true\,\mathcal{U}\varphi$, $\Box \varphi \equiv \neg \Diamond \neg \varphi$, and $\varphi_1 \mathcal{W} \varphi_2 \equiv (\varphi_1 \mathcal{U} \varphi_2) \vee \Box \varphi_1$. We call
a HyperLTL formula ψ (quantifier) *alternation-free* iff the quantifier prefix only
consists of either only universal or only existential quantifiers.

It has been shown that many hyperproperties of interest can be expressed
in HyperLTL [6,12,16]. For many properties, it in fact suffices to use the
alternation-free fragment of HyperLTL. The following are two typical examples:

- *Observational determinism* [19] requires that every pair of traces with the
  same initial low observation remain indistinguishable for low users. That is,
  the program appears to be deterministic to low-security users. Observational
  determinism can be expressed in HyperLTL as follows:

$$\forall \pi.\forall \pi'.\, (lowIn_\pi \Leftrightarrow lowIn_{\pi'}) \;\Rightarrow\; \Box(lowOut_\pi \Leftrightarrow lowOut_{\pi'}),$$

  where *lowIn* and *LowOut* are atomic propositions representing the low-security
  inputs and outputs, respectively.
- *Shamir's secret sharing scheme* [17] is the following policy: A system stores a
  secret by splitting it into k shares. The requirement is that not all of the k
  shares are revealed:

$$\forall \pi_1 \; \ldots \; .\forall \pi_k.\, (\Box(\neg sr_{\pi_1}^1 \wedge \cdots \wedge \neg sr_{\pi_k}^1) \vee \; \ldots \; \vee \Box(\neg sr_{\pi_1}^k \wedge \cdots \wedge \neg sr_{\pi_k}^k)),$$

where the atomic proposition sr^i, $i \in [1, k]$, means that share i of the secret has been revealed.

The *satisfiability problem* of HyperLTL formulas is in general undecidable, but decidable for the fragment without quantifier alternations and for the $\exists^*\forall^*$-fragment. Since, in practice, many HyperLTL specifications only contain universal quantifiers, this means that the satisfiability, implication, and equivalence of such specifications can be checked automatically [10]. The *model checking problem* of HyperLTL formulas over finite-state Kripke structures is decidable for the full logic, and has, in fact, the same complexity (PSPACE-complete) as standard LTL model checking for the alternation-free fragment. MCHyper is an efficient tool implementation for hardware model checking against alternation-free HyperLTL formulas [12]. Beyond finite-state systems, it was recently shown that a first-order extension of HyperLTL can be checked automatically over workflows with arbitrarily many agents [13].

3   Runtime Verification for HyperLTL

For *runtime verification*, it is necessary to define finite-trace semantics for HyperLTL. Analogously to the three-valued semantics of LTL [5], such a finite-trace semantics for HyperLTL can be defined based on the truth values $\mathbb{B}_3 = \{\top, \bot, ?\}$. In this semantics, "?" means that for the given formula φ and the current set M of finite execution traces at run time, it is not possible to tell whether M satisfies or violates φ; i.e., both cases are possible in this or future extensions and/or executions.

Let M be a finite set of finite traces. The truth value of a closed HyperLTL formula φ with respect to M, denoted by $[M \models \varphi]$, is an element of the set $\mathbb{B}_3 = \{\top, \bot, ?\}$, and is defined as follows:

$$[M \models \varphi] = \begin{cases} \top & \text{if } \forall \text{ sets } T \text{ of infinite traces with } M \leq T, T \text{ satisfies } \varphi \\ \bot & \text{if } \forall \text{ sets } T \text{ of infinite traces with } M \leq T, T \text{ does not satisfy } \varphi \\ ? & \text{otherwise,} \end{cases}$$

where $\leq$ is a prefix relation on sets of traces defined as follows. Let u be a finite trace and v be a finite or infinite trace. We denote the concatenation of u and v by $\sigma = uv$. Also, $u \leq \sigma$ denotes the fact that u is a prefix of σ. If U is a set of finite traces and V is a finite or infinite set of traces, then $U \leq V$ is defined as $U \leq V \equiv \forall u \in U. (\exists v \in V. u \leq v)$. Note that V may contain traces that have no prefix in U.

Pnueli and Zaks [15] characterize an LTL formula φ as *monitorable* for a finite trace u, if u can be extended to one that can be evaluated with respect to φ at run time. For example, the LTL formula $\square\lozenge p$ is not monitorable, since there is no way to tell at run time whether or not p will be visited infinitely often in the future. By contrast, safety (e.g., $\square p$) and co-safety (e.g., $\lozenge p$) LTL formulas are monitorable. We can extend the concept of LTL-monitorability to HyperLTL by requiring that every finite set U of finite traces can be extended to a finite set V of finite traces such that every trace in U is the prefix of some trace in V and that V evaluates to $\top$ or $\bot$. It is easy to see that an alternation-free HyperLTL formula with monitorable inner LTL subformula is also monitorable. For example, observational determinism and Shamir's secret sharing scheme are both monitorable. Note, however, that only violations of such formulas can be detected at run time (detecting their satisfaction requires examining all traces of the system under inspection, which is a model checking problem).

A monitor for a HyperLTL formula must match the observed traces with the quantifiers of the HyperLTL formula and ensure that the inner LTL subformula is satisfied on the combined trace. For alternation-free HyperLTL formulas, this can be done by creating a monitor automaton for the LTL subformulas that are inter-trace independent, then *progressing* inter-trace dependent subformulas for each observed trace, and finally building a monitor automaton for each progressed formula [1]. This approach has proven successful on complex data sets, such as the GPS location data of 21 users taken over a period of eight weeks in the region of Seattle, USA. However, there is clear potential for further optimization, for example, by analyzing the observed execution trace in relation to an abstract model of the system at run time (cf. [9]). Another important line of work is the extension of the approach to a distributed monitoring framework (cf. [14]).

Acknowledgment. This work was partially supported by the German Research Foundation (DFG) in the Collaborative Research Center 1223 and by Canada NSERC Discovery Grant 418396-2012 and NSERC Strategic Grants 430575-2012 and 463324-2014.

References

1. Agrawal, S., Bonakdarpour, B.: Runtime verification of k-safety hyperproperties in hyperltl. In: Proceedings of the 29th IEEE Computer Security Foundations Symposium (CSF) (2016, to appear)
2. Alur, R., Černý, P., Zdancewic, S.: Preserving secrecy under refinement. In: Bugliesi, M., Preneel, B., Sassone, V., Wegener, I. (eds.) ICALP 2006. LNCS, vol. 4052, pp. 107–118. Springer, Heidelberg (2006). doi:10.1007/11787006_10
3. Balliu, M., Dam, M., Guernic, G.L.: Epistemic temporal logic for information flow security. In: Proceedings of the 2011 Workshop on Programming Languages and Analysis for Security, PLAS 2011, San Jose, CA, p. 6, June 2011
4. Barthe, G., D'Argenio, P.R., Rezk, T.: Secure information flow by self-composition. In: CSFW, pp. 100–114 (2004)
5. Bauer, A., Leucker, M., Schallhart, C.: Runtime verification for LTL and TLTL. ACM Trans. Softw. Eng. Methodol. **20**(4), 14 (2011)
6. Clarkson, M.R., Finkbeiner, B., Koleini, M., Micinski, K.K., Rabe, M.N., Sánchez, C.: Temporal logics for hyperproperties. In: Abadi, M., Kremer, S. (eds.) POST 2014. LNCS, vol. 8414, pp. 265–284. Springer, Heidelberg (2014). doi:10.1007/978-3-642-54792-8_15
7. Clarkson, M.R., Schneider, F.B.: Hyperproperties. J. Comput. Secur. **18**(6), 1157–1210 (2010)

8. Dimitrova, R., Finkbeiner, B., Kovács, M., Rabe, M.N., Seidl, H.: Model checking information flow in reactive systems. In: Kuncak, V., Rybalchenko, A. (eds.) VMCAI 2012. LNCS, vol. 7148, pp. 169–185. Springer, Heidelberg (2012). doi:10. 1007/978-3-642-27940-9_12

9. Dimitrova, R., Finkbeiner, B., Rabe, M.N.: Monitoring temporal information flow. In: Margaria, T., Steffen, B. (eds.) ISoLA 2012. LNCS, vol. 7609, pp. 342–357. Springer, Heidelberg (2012). doi:10.1007/978-3-642-34026-0_26

10. Finkbeiner, B., Hahn, C.: Deciding hyperproperties. In: Proceedings of the CONCUR 2016 (2016)

11. Finkbeiner, B., Rabe, M.N.: The linear-hyper-branching spectrum of temporal logics. IT Inform. Technol. **56**(6), 273–279 (2014)

12. Finkbeiner, B., Rabe, M.N., Sanchez, C.: Algorithms for model checking HyperLTL and HyperCTL*. In: Proceedings CAV 2015 (2015)

13. Finkbeiner, B., Seidl, H., Müller, C.: Specifying and verifying secrecy in workflows with arbitrarily many agents. In: Proceedings of the ATVA 2016 (2016)

14. Mostafa, M., Bonakdarpour, B.: Decentralized runtime verification of LTL specifications in distributed systems. In: IEEE International Parallel and Distributed Processing Symposium (IPDPS), pp. 494–503 (2015)

15. Pnueli, A., Zaks, A.: PSL model checking and run-time verification via testers. In: Misra, J., Nipkow, T., Sekerinski, E. (eds.) FM 2006. LNCS, vol. 4085, pp. 573–586. Springer, Heidelberg (2006). doi:10.1007/11813040_38

16. Rabe, M.N.: A Temporal Logic Approach to Information-flow Control. Ph.D. thesis, Saarland University (2016)

17. Shamir, A.: How to share a secret. Commun. ACM **22**(11), 612–613 (1979)

18. Terauchi, T., Aiken, A.: Secure information flow as a safety problem. In: Hankin, C., Siveroni, I. (eds.) SAS 2005. LNCS, vol. 3672, pp. 352–367. Springer, Heidelberg (2005). doi:10.1007/11547662_24

19. Zdancewic, S., Myers, A.C.: Observational determinism for concurrent program security. In: Proceedings IEEE Computer Security Foundations Workshop, pp. 29–43, June 2003

Runtime Verification at Work: A Tutorial

Philip Daian, Dwight Guth, Chris Hathhorn[✉], Yilong Li, Edgar Pek,
Manasvi Saxena, Traian Florin Şerbănuţă, and Grigore Roşu

Runtime Verification Inc., University of Illinois at Urbana-Champaign,
Champaign, USA
chris.hathhorn@runtimeverification.com

Abstract. We present a suite of runtime verification tools developed by
Runtime Verification Inc.: RV-MATCH, RV-PREDICT, and RV-MONITOR.
RV-MATCH is a tool for checking C programs for undefined behavior
and other common programmer mistakes. It is extracted from the most
complete formal semantics of the C11 language and beats many similar
tools in its ability to catch a broad range of undesirable behaviors. RV-
PREDICT is a dynamic data race detector for Java and C/C++ programs.
It is perhaps the only tool that is both sound and maximal: it only reports
real races and it can find all races that can be found by any other sound
data race detector analyzing the same execution trace. RV-MONITOR is
a runtime monitoring tool that checks and enforces safety and security
properties during program execution. Our tools focus on reporting no
false positives and are free for non-commercial use.

1 Introduction

Runtime verification is an analysis and execution approach based on extracting
information from a running system and using it to detect, and possibly react to,
observed behaviors satisfying or violating certain properties. In this session, we
present the practical applications of runtime verification technology that we are
currently exploring.

Runtime verification avoids the complexity of traditional formal verification
techniques (like model checking and theorem proving) by analyzing only one or a
few execution traces and working directly with the actual system. Thus, runtime
verification scales up relatively well and gives more confidence in the results
of the analysis because it avoids the tedious and error-prone step of formally
modeling the system (at the expense of reduced coverage). Moreover, through
its reflective capabilities, runtime verification can be made an integral part of
the target system, monitoring and guiding its execution during deployment.

We present three instantiations of the runtime verification approach: (1) RV-
MATCH, a dynamic analysis tool for finding a wide range of flaws in C programs,
(2) RV-PREDICT, a dynamic data race detector for Java and C, and (3) RV-
MONITOR, a runtime monitoring framework for checking and enforcing properties
of Java and C programs.[1]

---

[1] See https://runtimeverification.com/ for an overview of our tools and company.

© Springer International Publishing AG 2016
Y. Falcone and C. Sanchez (Eds.): RV 2016, LNCS 10012, pp. 46–67, 2016.
DOI: 10.1007/978-3-319-46982-9_5

2   RV-Match

RV-Match is a tool for checking C programs for undefined behavior and other common programmer mistakes. It is extracted from the most complete formal semantics of the C11 language. Previous versions of this tool were used primarily for testing the correctness of the semantics, but we have improved it into a tool for doing practical analysis of real C programs. It beats many similar tools in its ability to catch a broad range of undesirable behaviors. We demonstrate this below with comparisons based on a third-party benchmark.

2.1   Background: RV-Match

The $\mathbb{K}$ semantic framework[2] is a program analysis environment based on term rewriting [1]. Users define the formal semantics of a target programming language and the $\mathbb{K}$ framework provides a series of formal analysis tools specialized for that language, such as a symbolic execution engine, a semantic debugger, a systematic checker for undesired behaviors (model checker), and even a fully-fledged deductive program verifier. Our tool, RV-Match, is based on the $\mathbb{K}$ framework instantiated with the publicly-available C11 semantics[3] [8,9], a rigorous formalization of the current ISO C11 standard [15]. We have specially optimized RV-Match for the execution and detection of errors in C programs.

Unlike modern optimizing compilers, which have a goal to produce binaries that are as small and as fast as possible at the expense of compiling programs that may be semantically incorrect, RV-Match instead aims at mathematically rigorous dynamic checking of programs for strict conformance with the ISO C11 standard. A strictly-conforming program is one that does not rely on implementation-specific behaviors and is free of the most notorious feature of the C language, *undefined behavior*. Undefined behaviors are semantic holes left by the standard for implementations to fill in. They are the source of many subtle bugs and security issues [13].

2.2   Running RV-Match

Users interface with RV-Match through the `rv-match` executable, which behaves as a drop-in replacement for compilers like `gcc` and `clang`. Consider a file `undef.c` with contents:

```
int main(void) {
    int a;
    &a+2;
}
```

We compile the program with `rv-match` just as we would with `gcc` or `clang`. This produces an executable named `a.out` by default, which should behave just

---

[2] See http://kframework.org for details.
[3] Available at https://github.com/kframework/c-semantics.

as an executable produced by another compiler—for strictly-conforming, valid programs. For undefined or invalid programs, however, `rv-match` reports errors and exits if it cannot recover:

```
$ rv-match undef.c
$ ./a.out
Error: UB-CEA1
Description: A pointer (or array subscript) outside the
   bounds of an object.
Type: Undefined behavior.
See also: C11 sec. 6.5.6:8, J.2:1 item 46
   at main(undef.c:2)
```

In addition to location information and a stack trace, RV-MATCH also cites relevant sections of the standard [15].

2.3   Finding Undefined Behavior in C Using RV-MATCH

Below, we describe several examples demonstrating RV-MATCH's capabilities for detecting undefined behavior. Note that these examples cover only a small subset of the errors which RV-MATCH detects.

Unsequenced side effects. Consider a simple program:

```
int main(void) {
    int x = 0;
    return (x = 1) + (x = 2);
}
```

Compiled with `clang`, this program returns 3. With `gcc`, however, it returns 4, because `gcc` chooses to sequence both assignments before the addition expression. In general, compilers are allowed to introduce optimizations as long as they do not affect the behavior of well-defined programs. However, since this program is undefined, such optimizations can have unexpected consequences. When compiled with `rv-match`, we get the following output after running the program:

```
Error: UB-EI08
Description: Unsequenced side effect on scalar object
   with side effect of same object.
Type: Undefined behavior.
See also: C11 sec. 6.5:2, J.2:1 item 35
   at main(1-unsequenced-side-effect.c:3)
```

Buffer Overflows. Perhaps the most notorious errors in C programs are buffer overflows. RV-MATCH is capable of detecting all varieties of buffer overflows.[4]

---

[4] See `2-buffer-overflow.c` from the `examples/demo` directory of the `c-semantics` repository at https://github.com/kframework/c-semantics for examples of several varieties.

As a more subtle example, consider an overflow within the subobjects of an aggregate type (in this case, a `struct` of an array followed by an integer):

```
struct foo { char buffer[32]; int secret; };
int idx = 0;
void setIdx() { idx = 32; }
int main(void) {
    setIdx();
    struct foo x = {0};
    x.secret = 5;
    return x.buffer[idx];
}
```

We can safely assume the `struct` is laid out sequentially in memory, yet access to the 32nd index of this array is still undefined behavior. Tools like `valgrind` usually do not catch this sort of issue because the accesses will be to valid addresses for other pieces of the aggregate. But it is still undefined behavior. `gcc` compiles the program and execution leads to a leak of the secret integer. RV-MATCH, however, will detect the flaw:

```
Error: UB-CER4
Description: Dereferencing a pointer past the end of an
    array.
Type: Undefined behavior.
See also: C11 sec. 6.5.6:8, J.2:1 item 47
    at main(3-array-in-struct.c:16)
```

RV-MATCH reports more than 150 varieties of error, like UB-CER4 above, most of which concern undefined behavior.[5]

Implementation-Defined Behavior. RV-MATCH is also able to detect errors related to implementation-defined behavior, which the C standard defines as unspecified behavior where each implementation documents how the choice is made. `rv-match` can be instantiated with different profiles corresponding to different implementation choices (use `rv-match -v` for existing choices). An example of implementation-defined behavior is the conversion to a type that cannot store a specified value, thus triggering a loss of precision.

More examples of undefined behavior and the features of RV-MATCH are described in the "Running Examples" section of the RV-MATCH documentation [11].

2.4   Evaluation

Of course, there is no shortage of tools for analyzing C programs. To evaluate the strengths of our tool, we compare RV-MATCH against some popular C analyzers

---

[5] For a list of the errors and example programs demonstrating them, see https://github.com/kframework/c-semantics/blob/master/examples/error-codes.

on a benchmark from Toyota ITC. We also briefly mention our experience with running our tool on the SV-COMP benchmark. The other tools we consider are listed below:

- *GrammaTech CodeSonar* is a static analysis tool for identifying "bugs that can result in system crashes, unexpected behavior, and security breaches" [10].
- *MathWorks Polyspace Bug Finder* is a static analyzer for identifying "runtime errors, concurrency issues, security vulnerabilities, and other defects in C and C++ embedded software" [22].
- *MathWorks Polyspace Code Prover* is a tool based on abstract interpretation that "proves the absence of overflow, divide-by-zero, out-of-bounds array access, and certain other runtime errors in C and C++ source code" [23].
- *Clang UBSan, TSan, MSan, and ASan (version 3.7.1)* are all `clang` modules for instrumenting compiled binaries with various mechanisms for detecting undefined behavior, data races, uninitialized reads, and various memory issues, respectively [6].
- *Valgrind Memcheck and Helgrind (version 3.10.1, GCC version 4.8.4)* are tools for instrumenting binaries for the detection of several memory and thread-related issues (illegal reads/writes, use of uninitialized or unaddressable values, deadlocks, data races, etc.) [24].
- *The CompCert C interpreter (version 2.6)* uses an approach similar to our own. It executes programs according to the semantics used by the CompCert compiler [4] and reports undefined behavior.
- *Frama-C Value Analysis (version sodium-20150201)*, like Code Prover, is a tool based on static analysis and abstract interpretation for catching several forms of undefinedness [5].

The Toyota ITC Benchmark [25]. This publicly-available[6] benchmark consists of 1,276 tests, half with planted defects meant to evaluate the defect rate capability of analysis tools and the other half without defects meant to evaluate the false positive rate. The tests are grouped in nine categories: static memory, dynamic memory, stack-related, numerical, resource management, pointer-related, concurrency, inappropriate code, and miscellaneous.

We evaluated RV-MATCH along with the tools mentioned above on this benchmark. Our results appear in Fig. 1 and the tools we used for our evaluation are available online.[7] Following the method of Shiraishi, Mohan, and Marimuthu [25], we report the value of three metrics: DR is the detection rate, the percentage of tests containing errors where the error was detected; $\underline{FPR} = 100 - FPR$, where FPR is the false positive rate; and PM is a productivity metric, where $PM = \sqrt{DR \times \underline{FPR}}$, the geometric mean of DR and $\underline{FPR}$.

Interestingly, and similar to our experience with the SV-COMP benchmark mentioned below, the use of RV-MATCH on the Toyota ITC benchmark detected a number of flaws in the benchmark itself, both in the form of undefined behavior

---

[6] See https://github.com/Toyota-ITC-SSD/Software-Analysis-Benchmark.

[7] For tools and instructions on reproducing these results, see https://github.com/ runtimeverification/evaluation/tree/master/toyota-itc-benchmark.

that was not intended, and in the form of tests that were intended to contain a defect but were actually correct. Our fixes for these issues were accepted by the Toyota ITC authors and we used the fixed version of the benchmark in our experiments. Unfortunately, we do not have access to the MathWorks and GrammaTech static analysis tools, so in Fig. 1 we have reproduced the results reported in [25]. Thus, it is possible that the metrics scored for the other tools may be off by some amount.

The SV-COMP Benchmark Suite. This consist of a large number of C programs used as verification tasks during the International Competition on Software Verification (SV-COMP) [3]. We analyzed 1346 programs classified as correct with RV-MATCH and observed that 188 (14 %) of the programs exhibited undefined behavior. Issues ranged from using uninitialized values in expressions, potentially invalid conversions, incompatible declarations, to more subtle strict aliasing violations. Our detailed results are available online.[8]

3   RV-PREDICT

RV-PREDICT is a dynamic data race detector for Java and C/C++ programs. RV-PREDICT is perhaps the only tool that is both sound and maximal: it only reports real races and it can find all races that can be found by any other sound data race detector analyzing the same execution trace. We have evaluated our tool on a set of real Java programs and we have been able to find a large number of previously unknown data race violations. We report a case study on testing Tomcat, a widely used Java application server, using RV-PREDICT. Moreover, we have obtained encouraging results after evaluating RV-PREDICT on a smaller class of C programs. The more mature Java version can perform both online (i.e., data races detection as the program runs) and offline (i.e. data race detection after the program is run and traces are collected) analysis. The C/C++ version is a prototype and can only perform offline data race detection.

3.1   Background: RV-PREDICT

RV-PREDICT is based on an important theoretical result by Şerbănuţă, Chen, and Roşu [2]: given an execution trace, it is possible to build a *maximal and sound* causal model for concurrent computations. This model has the property that it consists of all traces that any program capable of generating the original trace can also generate.

Moreover, based on the results of Huang, Meredith, and Roşu [14], RV-PREDICT implements a technique that provides a provably higher detection capability than the state-of-the-art techniques. A crucial insight behind this technique is the inclusion of abstracted control flow information in the execution model, which expands the space of the causal model provided by classical

---

[8] Detailed SV-COMP benchmark results are available at https://github.com/runtimeverification/evaluation/tree/master/svcomp-benchmark.

Tool		Static memory	Dynamic memory	Stack-related	Numerical	Resource management	Pointer-related	Concurrency	Inappropriate code	Misc.	Avg. (unweighted)	Avg. (weighted)
RV-Match	DR	100	94	100	96	93	98	67	0	63	79	82
	FPR	100	100	100	100	100	100	100	–	100	100	100
	PM	100	97	100	98	96	99	82	0	79	89	91
GrammaTech CodeSonar	DR	100	89	0	48	61	52	70	46	69	59	68
	FPR	100	100	–	100	100	96	77	99	100	97	98
	PM	100	94	0	69	78	71	73	67	83	76	82
MathWorks Bug Finder	DR	97	90	15	41	55	69	0	28	69	52	62
	FPR	100	100	85	100	100	100	–	94	100	98	99
	PM	98	95	36	64	74	83	0	51	83	71	78
MathWorks Code Prover	DR	97	92	60	55	20	69	0	1	83	53	53
	FPR	100	95	70	99	90	93	–	97	100	94	95
	PM	98	93	65	74	42	80	0	10	91	71	71
UBSan + TSan + MSan + ASan (clang)	DR	79	16	95	59	47	58	67	0	37	51	47
	FPR	100	95	75	100	96	97	72	–	100	93	95
	PM	89	39	84	77	67	75	70	0	61	69	67
Valgrind + Helgrind (gcc)	DR	9	80	70	22	57	60	72	2	29	44	42
	FPR	100	95	80	100	100	100	79	100	100	95	97
	PM	30	87	75	47	76	77	76	13	53	65	65
CompCert interpreter	DR	97	29	35	48	32	87	58	17	63	52	51
	FPR	82	80	70	79	83	73	42	83	71	74	76
	PM	89	48	49	62	52	80	49	38	67	62	63
Frama-C Value Analysis	DR	82	79	45	79	63	81	7	33	83	61	66
	FPR	96	27	65	47	46	40	100	63	49	59	55
	PM	89	46	54	61	54	57	26	45	63	60	60

Fig. 1. Comparison of tools on the 1,276 tests of the ITC benchmark. The numbers for the GrammaTech and MathWorks tools come from Shiraishi, Mohan, and Marimuthu [25]. Blue indicates the best score in a category for a particular metric, while orange emphasizes the weighted average of the productivity metric for each tool. DR, FPR, and PM are, respectively, the detection rate, 100 − FPR (the complement of the false positive rate), and the productivity metric. The final average is weighted by the number of tests in each category. Italics and a dash indicate categories for which a tool has no support. (Color figure online)

happens-before or causally-precedes race detection techniques. We encode the control flow and a minimal set of feasibility constraints in first-order logic, thus reducing the race detection problem to a constraint satisfaction problem, which can be efficiently solved by SMT solvers.

3.2   Running RV-PREDICT

The Java Version. RV-PREDICT can be run both from the command line, as a drop-in replacement for the `java` command, and as an agent, to ease integration with IDEs and build management tools like Maven. For more details, please refer to the "Running RV-PREDICT" section of the documentation [19].

The C/C++ Version. Running RV-PREDICT for C/C++ involves two steps. In the first step, we create an instrumented version of the multithreaded C/C++ program. In the second step, RV-PREDICT's backend performs offline data race predictive analysis based on the principles described in the background section. Concretely, given a C program `file.c`, the two steps are shown below:

```
$ rv-predict-c-compile file.c
$ rv-predict-execute ./a.out
```

3.3   Detecting Common Data-Race Patterns Using RV-PREDICT

Data races are common concurrency bugs in multithreaded programs. A data race can be defined as two threads accessing a shared memory location concurrently and at least one of the accesses is a write. Data races are notoriously difficult to find and reproduce because they often happen under very specific circumstances. They usually manifest as intermittent or non-deterministic failures during testing. And when failures do occur, they typically produce mysterious error messages, far from the root cause of the data race.

Despite all of the work on solving this problem, it remains a challenge in practice to detect data races effectively and efficiently. In this section, we summarize common classes of data races and show how to detect them with RV-PREDICT. The examples described below can be found in the RV-PREDICT distribution.

A Simple Data Race. The simplest data race is also the most frequent in practice: two threads access a shared variable without synchronization. In Java, a shared variable is either a field (instance or static) or an array element. See JLS Sect. 17.4.1 for the precise definition. For example:

```java
public class SimpleRace {
    static int sharedVar;
    public static void main(String[] args) {
        new ThreadRunner() {
            @Override public void thread1() {sharedVar++;}
            @Override public void thread2() {sharedVar++;}
        };
    }
}
```

The access to sharedVar is not synchronized. Note that the ThreadRunner class (see the simple race description on our blog [18]) is a utility class containing boilerplate code that instantiates two threads with the defined tasks (it will be used throughout this section to simplify descriptions).

RV-PREDICT detects this race and the report it generates is below. For readability, the code above only shows the core of the problem, and so the lines in the report do not match line numbers in the code above.

```
Data race on field examples.SimpleRace.sharedVar: {{{
    Concurrent write in thread T10 (locks held: {})
 ---->   at examples.SimpleRace$1.thread1(SimpleRace.java:11)
         at examples.ThreadRunner$1.run(ThreadRunner.java:17)
    T10 is created by T1
         at examples.ThreadRunner.<init>(ThreadRunner.java:26)

    Concurrent read in thread T11 (locks held: {})
 ---->   at examples.SimpleRace$1.thread2(SimpleRace.java:16)
         at examples.ThreadRunner$2.run(ThreadRunner.java:23)
    T11 is created by T1
         at examples.ThreadRunner.<init>(ThreadRunner.java:27)
}}}
```

Although this particular data race might be easy to spot through code review, similar instances buried deep in thousands of lines of code can be very hard to discover. As shown above, RV-PREDICT can make detection of such bugs simple because it provides the precise location where conflicting memory accesses occur, the stack traces of the two threads involved in the race, the point of thread creation, and the locks held by each thread.

Even while developing RV-PREDICT, we were able to find a variation of this bug in our own RV-MATCH code base. Specifically, there was an intermittently occurring null pointer exception in the parser implementation. A (still) standard approach for debugging such issues relies on reproducing the bug and attempting to track the behavior backward to the root of the issue. Such an approach can be tedious and time consuming—RV-PREDICT, by contrast, finds these issues with minimal effort (for the story on our experience of using RV-PREDICT to debug RV-MATCH, see our blog [12]).

Using a Non-thread-Safe Class Without Synchronization. This class of bugs occurs if a developer assumes that the class being used is thread-safe. In fact many classes are not designed to be used in a multithreaded environment, e.g., java.util.ArrayList, java.util.HashMap, and many other classes in the Java Collections Framework, so unwarranted thread-safety assumptions can easily creep into the code. Consider this example:

```
import java.util.ArrayList;
import java.util.List;
public class RaceOnArrayList {
    static List<Integer> list = new ArrayList<>();
    public static void main(String[] args) {
        new ThreadRunner() {
LX:             @Override public void thread1() {list.add(0);}
LY:             @Override public void thread2() {list.add(1);}
        };
    }
}
```

Both threads are trying to add an element to the `ArrayList`. However, since the underlying data structure is not thread-safe, and the client code does not perform synchronization, there exists a data race.

Simply running this example will *occasionally* trigger an exception, indicating that something went wrong, but there is no guarantee this bug will appear during testing. Below is the shortened output from RV-PREDICT (exact values of line numbers are replaced with symbolic values LX and LY):

```
Data race on field java.util.ArrayList.$state: {{{
    Concurrent read in thread T10 (locks held: {})
 ---->   at examples.RaceOnArrayList$1.thread1(RaceOnArrayList.java:LX)
    ...

    Concurrent write in thread T11 (locks held: {})
 ---->   at examples.RaceOnArrayList$1.thread2(RaceOnArrayList.java:LY)
    ...
}}}
```

Notice that RV-PREDICT reports the race on the symbolic field `$state`, rather than the field inside the class `ArrayList` where the race actually occurs. This is by design: RV-PREDICT's error messages abstract away from the low-level implementation details of the Java class library to make identifying the root cause of a data race easier.

A more complex example violates rule LCK04-J from the CERT Oracle Coding Standard for Java: "Do not synchronize on a collection view if the backing collection is accessible." The CERT standard continues:

Any class that uses a collection view rather than the backing collection as the lock object may end up with two distinct locking strategies. When the backing collection is accessible to multiple threads, the class that locked on the collection view has violated the thread-safety properties and is unsafe. Consequently, programs that both require synchronization while iterating over collection views and have accessible backing collections must synchronize on the backing collection; synchronization on the view is a violation of this rule [20].

In the example below, `map` is an already synchronized map backed by a HashMap. When the first thread inserts a key-value pair into the map, the second thread acquires the monitor of `keySet` and iterates over the key set of the map. This is a direct violation of LCK04-J: thread 2 incorrectly synchronizes on `keySet` instead of `map`.

```
public class RaceOnSynchronizedMap {
    static Map<Integer, Integer> map =
        Collections.synchronizedMap(new HashMap<>());
    public static void main(String[] args) {
        new ThreadRunner() {
LX:         @Override public void thread1() {
                map.put(1, 1);
            }
            @Override public void thread2() {
                Set<Integer> keySet = map.keySet();
LY:             synchronized (keySet) {
LY':                for (int k : keySet)
                        System.out.println("key =" + k);
                }
            }
        };
    }
}
```

Thankfully, RV-PREDICT reports the race condition and reveals the underlying reason—two threads are holding different monitors:

```
Data race on field java.util.HashMap. $state: {{{
    Concurrent write in thread T10 (locks held: {Monitor@722c41f4})
  ----> at examples.RaceOnSynchronizedMap$1.thread1(
          RaceOnSynchronizedMap.java:LX)
        - locked Monitor@722c41f4 at
        examples.RaceOnSynchronizedMap$1.thread1
        (RaceOnSynchronizedMap.java:LX)
        ...

    Concurrent read in thread T11 (locks held: {Monitor@1f72ae1d})
  ----> at examples.RaceOnSynchronizedMap$1.thread2(
          RaceOnSynchronizedMap.java:LY')
        - locked Monitor@1f72ae1d at
        examples.RaceOnSynchronizedMap$1.thread2
        (RaceOnSynchronizedMap.java:LY)
        ...
}}}
```

Broken Spinning Loop. Often, we want to synchronize multiple threads based on some condition. We might achieve this by using a `while` loop to block until the condition becomes satisfied. For example:

```
public class BrokenSpinningLoop {
    static int sharedVar;
    static boolean condition = false;
    public static void main(String[] args) {
        new ThreadRunner() {
            @Override public void thread1() {
                sharedVar = 1;
                condition = true;
            }
            @Override public void thread2() {
                while (!condition) Thread.yield();
                if (sharedVar != 1)
                    throw new RuntimeException(
                        "How is this possible!?");
            }
        };
    }
}
```

How can this program ever throw the `RuntimeException`? The data race on `condition` might be obvious, but it appears to be innocuous. The exception should be impossible regardless of how accesses to `condition` are ordered.

Nonetheless, the exception can, in fact, be raised, because thread 2, after passing the `while` loop, might still read 0 instead of 1 from `sharedVar`. This can be due to several reasons, such as reordering and caching. In fact, the Java memory model allows such counter-intuitive behavior to happen when the program contains any data races at all. In one instance, this type of bug directly caused a loss of $12 million worth of lab equipment [26].

More examples of data race patterns that RV-PREDICT detects can be found on our website [18].

3.4   The RV-PREDICT Backend: Prediction Power vs. Efficiency

By default, RV-PREDICT attempts to strike a good balance between efficiency and prediction power. Nevertheless, while the default settings were engineered to work for most common cases, there might be cases where user input could improve the prediction process. We provide several options for advanced users to tune RV-PREDICT:

1. *Window size.* For efficiency reasons, RV-PREDICT splits the execution trace into segments (called windows) of a specified size. The default window size is 1000. Users can alter this size using the `--window` option, with the intuition that a larger size provides better coverage at the expense of increasing the analysis time.

2. *Excluding packages.* To allow better control over the efficiency, RV-PREDICT provides the option --exclude to remove certain packages from logging. This option takes a list of package pattern prefixes separated by commas and excludes from logging any class matched by one of the patterns. The patterns can use * to match any sequence of characters. Moreover, * is automatically assumed at the end of each pattern (to make sure inner classes are excluded together with their parent). Note that excluding packages might affect precision, as events from non-logged packages might prevent certain race conditions from occurring.
3. *Including packages.* For more flexibility in selecting which packages to include and exclude, RV-PREDICT also provides the --include option, which is similar to the --exclude option (it accepts a comma separated list of package patterns), but opposite in effect.

3.5 Running RV-PREDICT on Tomcat

When developers are dealing with a large project using multiple kinds of synchronization mechanisms, debugging becomes much more difficult and often requires a thorough understanding of the system. But RV-PREDICT can help with this task regardless of the code size of the project. As an example, we have run RV-PREDICT on Tomcat, one of the most widely used Java application servers.

Integrating RV-PREDICT into Tomcat's build cycle is straightforward. It essentially boils down to assuring that the RV-PREDICT agent is run with the unit tests. The only required change is in build.xml:

```
<jvmarg value="-javaagent:${rvPath}/rv-predict.jar=--base-log-dir log" />
```

Where ${rvPath} is RV-PREDICT's installation path and log is the location where RV-PREDICT will store its logs and results. RV-PREDICT runs along with unit-tests and its inclusion introduces a runtime overhead of roughly 5x (i.e., from 50 min to 260 min). We performed these experiments on Tomcat 8.0.26 and RV-PREDICT found almost 40 unique data races in only a few runs. All bugs were reported to developers and fixed in the next release.[9]

4   RV-MONITOR

RV-MONITOR is a software analysis and development framework that aims to reduce the gap between specification and implementation by allowing them together to form a system [21]. With RV-MONITOR, runtime monitoring is supported and encouraged as a fundamental principle for building reliable software: monitors are synthesized from specifications and integrated into the original system to check its behavior during execution.

---

[9] See https://goo.gl/L00hWt for a list of the bugs and http://tomcat.apache.org/tomcat-8.0-doc/changelog.html#Tomcat_8.0.27_(markt) for the Tomcat 8.0.27 changelog.

RV-MONITOR evolved from the popular JavaMOP runtime verification framework [16] and represents an effort to create a robust, extendable framework for monitoring library generation. In this section, we will show examples of RV-MONITOR compiling specifications into code, for both desktop applications and embedded systems.

4.1 Background: RV-MONITOR

Monitoring executions of a system against expected properties plays an important role in both the software development process (e.g., during debugging and testing) and as a mechanism for increasing the reliability and security of deployed systems. Monitoring a program execution generates a trace comprising events of interest. When an execution trace validates or violates a property, the monitor triggers actions appropriate to its purpose in the system [16]. RV-MONITOR is a parametric monitoring system, i.e., it allows the specifications of properties that relate objects in the program, as well as global properties. Our approach consists of two phases: in the first phase, the execution trace is sliced according to a parameter instance, while in the second phase each slice is checked by a monitor dedicated to the slice.

At its core, RV-MONITOR allows users to specify properties that the system should satisfy at runtime (safety or security properties, API protocols, etc.) and then generate efficient monitoring libraries for them. The generated libraries can then be used in two ways, either (1) manually, by calling the monitoring methods at the desired places, or (2) automatically, by inserting calls to the monitoring methods using instrumentation mechanisms.

When a specification is violated or validated during program execution, user-defined actions are triggered. The triggered actions can range from logging to runtime recovery. RV-MONITOR can be considered from at least three perspectives: (1) as a discipline allowing one to improve safety, reliability and dependability of a system by monitoring its requirements against its implementation at runtime; (2) as an extension of programming languages with logics (one can add logical statements anywhere in the program, referring to past or future states); and (3) as a lightweight formal method.

RV-MONITOR takes as input one or more specification files and generates Java classes that implement the monitoring functionality defined therein. Each RV-MONITOR specification defines a number of events, which represent abstractions of certain points in programs, e.g., a call to the hasNext() method in Java, or closing a file. With these event abstractions in mind, a user can define one or more properties over the events, taking the events as either atoms in logical formulae or as symbols in formal language descriptions. For example, the user may use these events as symbols in a regular expression or as atoms in a linear temporal logic formula. In the generated Java class, each event becomes a method that can be either called manually by a user or inserted automatically by using some means of instrumentation, such as AspectJ.

Each specification also has a number of handlers associated with each property that are run when the associated property matches some specific conditions. For instance, when a regular expression pattern matches, we run a handler designated by the keyword @match, and when a linear temporal logic property is violated, we run a handler designated by the keyword @violation. Additionally, RV-Monitor is able to generate monitors that enforce a given property by delaying threads in multithreaded programs.

4.2 Running RV-Monitor

As mentioned above, calls to the event methods generated by RV-Monitor can either be manually added to programs or programs can be automatically instrumented. Note that the examples in this section and the following sections are included as part of the RV-Monitor distribution and available online.[10]

The Manual Instrumentation Method. Manual calls may appear tedious at first, but they allow for fine grain use of RV-Monitor monitors as a programming paradigm. For example, consider the RV-Monitor HasNext.rvm property:

```
package rvm;
HasNext(Iterator i) {
    event hasnext(Iterator i) { }
    event next(Iterator i) { }
    ere : (hasnext hasnext* next)*
    @fail {
        System.out.println(
            "! hasNext() has not been called before"
            + "calling next() for an iterator");
            __RESET;
    }
}
```

Now the generated Java monitoring library (named HasNextRuntimeMonitor after the property) will contain two methods (one for each event), with the following signatures:

```
public static final void hasNextEvent(Iterator i)
public static final void nextEvent(Iterator i)
```

---

[10] See https://github.com/runtimeverification/javamop/tree/master/examples.

By calling these methods directly, we can control exactly what we wish to monitor. For instance, we can add a wrapper class for `Iterator` that has versions `hasNext` and `next` that call our monitoring code and only use them in places where correctness is crucial. The class could be defined as follows:

```
public class SafeIterator<E>
        implements java.util.Iterator<E> {
    private java.util.Iterator<E> it;
    public SafeIterator(java.util.Iterator it) {
        this.it = it;
    }
    public boolean hasNext() {
        rvm.HasNextRuntimeMonitor.hasnextEvent(it);
        return it.hasNext();
    }
    public E next() {
        rvm.HasNextRuntimeMonitor.nextEvent(it);
        return it.next();
    }
    public void remove() { it.remove(); }
}
```

Now programs of interest can distinguish between monitored and unmonitored iterators by simply creating `SafeIterators` from `Iterators`. For example, consider the program `Test.java`:

```
public class Test {
    public static void main(String[] args) {
        Vector<Integer> v = new Vector<Integer>();
        v.add(1); v.add(2); v.add(4); v.add(8);
        Iterator it = v.iterator();
        SafeIterator i = new SafeIterator(it);
        int sum = 0;
        if (i.hasNext()) {
            sum += (Integer)i.next();
            sum += (Integer)i.next();
            sum += (Integer)i.next();
            sum += (Integer)i.next();
        }
        System.out.println("sum:" + sum);
    }
}
```

Note that, to build this program, the javac and java commands require the RV-MONITOR runtime library (rv-monitor-rt.jar) and the monitor directory to be in the CLASSPATH. This allows the use of the RV-MONITOR runtime, required by the libraries generated by the rv-monitor command. With this in mind, and if the rvm directory contains the HasNext.rvm property and the corresponding generated library, HasNextRuntimeMonitor.java, the commands to compile and run the program above are as follows:

```
$ javac Test.java SafeIterator.java rvm/HasNextRuntimeMonitor.java
$ java Test
```

RV-MONITOR, then, outputs the following:

```
! hasNext() has not been called before calling next() for an iterator
  ! hasNext() has not been called before calling next() for an iterator
  ! hasNext() has not been called before calling next() for an iterator
  sum: 15
```

The Automated Instrumentation Method. In some use-cases, the manual insertion of calls to a monitoring library can be tedious and error-prone. In these cases, aspect-oriented programming [17] can be used to instrument large code bases automatically. We can create an AspectJ aspect that calls monitoring methods for all instances of next and hasNext in the program. This aspect can be weaved throughout any program to make all uses of Iterators safe. For example:

```
aspect HasNextAspect {
    after(Iterator i) : call(* Iterator.hasNext())
        && target(i) {
      rvm.HasNextRuntimeMonitor.hasnextEvent(i); }
    after(): before(Iterator i) : call(* Iterator.next())
        && target(i) {
      rvm.HasNextRuntimeMonitor.nextEvent(it); }
}
```

Additionally, the RV-MONITOR ecosystem includes a database of over 200 real, production-quality properties specifying the correct operation of the Java and Android APIs that may be automatically checked in Java programs using AspectJ and RV-MONITOR.[11] The RV-MONITOR distribution provides a pre-compiled suite of common Java API protocol properties together in an agent that is automatically invoked when java is replaced with rv-monitor-all in the command line.

---

[11] For more information, please see https://github.com/runtimeverification/property-db.

4.3   Specifying and Checking Properties with RV-MONITOR

In this section, we demonstrate monitors generated by RV-MONITOR from properties expressed in three different formalisms (as finite-state machines, regular expressions, and linear temporal logic) to check Java and C/C++ programs.

The Finite-State Machine (FSM) Formalism. First, we explore how we can leverage the FSM formalism to express the Java API property that the next method of an iterator must not be called without a previous call to the hasNext method. This property can be specified as shown below:

```
full-binding HasNext(Iterator i) {
    event hasnext(Iterator i) { } // after
    event next(Iterator i) { }     // before
    fsm :
        start [
            next -> unsafe
            hasnext -> safe ]
        safe [
            next -> start
            hasnext -> safe ]
        unsafe [
            next -> unsafe
            hasnext -> safe ]
    alias match = unsafe
    @match {
        System.out.println(
            "next called without hasNext!");
    }
}
```

After installing RV-MONITOR we can see what monitoring of this property looks like in action:

```
$ cd examples/FSM/HasNext
$ rv-monitor rvm/HasNext.rvm
$ javac rvm/HasNextRuntimeMonitor.java HasNext_1/HasNext_1.java
$ java HasNext_1.HasNext_1
```

RV-MONITOR reports that next has been called without hasNext four times in the corresponding Java code.

The FSM Formalism: An Example in C. In addition to Java, RV-MONITOR also supports C. Below is an example of a simple property about the state of a seat belt in a vehicle simulation:

```
SeatBelt {
    event seatBeltRemoved() {
        fprintf(stderr, "Seat belt removed.");
    }
    event seatBeltAttached() {
        fprintf(stderr, "Seat belt attached.");
    }
    fsm :
        unsafe [ seatBeltAttached -> safe ]
        safe [ seatBeltRemoved -> unsafe ]
    @safe {
        fprintf(stderr, "set max speed to user input.");
    }
    @unsafe {
        fprintf(stderr, "set max speed to 10 mph.");
    }
}
```

The Extended Regular Expression (ERE) Formalism. Consider the property expressed as a regular expression below. This property aims to ensure there are no writes to a file after the file is closed. As in the first example, this is a property of the Java API that is potentially a source of many program bugs. It can be defined as follows:

```
SafeFileWriter(FileWriter f) {
    static int counter = 0;
    int writes = 0;
    event open(FileWriter f) {     // after
        this.writes = 0;
    }
    event write(FileWriter f) {    // before
        this.writes ++;
    }
    event close(FileWriter f) { } // after
    ere : (open write write* close)*
    @fail  {
        System.out.println("write after close");
        __RESET;
    }
    @match {
        System.out.println(++counter + ":" + writes);
    }
}
```

In the previous examples of property checking, we defined properties of invalid program executions. This example, however, defines a property representing the correct execution of a `FileWriter` in Java. Specifically, this property formalizes the behavior of a file being opened, written to some number times, and then closed. Correct execution traces for a given `File` object contain this sequence of events occurring zero or more times. The above property can be exercised on the code from the RV-MONITOR distribution as shown below:

```
$ cd examples/ERE/SafeFileWriter
$ rv-monitor rvm/SafeFileWriter.rvm
$ javac rvm/SafeFileWriterRuntimeMonitor.java \
      SafeFileWriter_1/SafeFileWriter_1.java
$ java SafeFileWriter_1.SafeFileWriter_1
```

The Linear Temporal Logic (LTL) Formalism. The same specification about files mentioned above can be captured in another formalism, namely linear temporal logic. The only difference from the last specification is that we replace the ERE property with an LTL property:

```
ltl : [](write => (not close S open))
```

This property specifies that at a **write**, there should not have been in the past a call to **close**, and that **open** must have occurred after the start. This represents the same property as the extended regular expression property and demonstrates the ability of RV-MATCH to use multiple formalisms, depending on the knowledge and preferences of the property developer.

Analyzing Logs. In addition to monitoring software execution, RV-MONITOR is able to check logical properties over text-based log files. These properties can be anything that is Turing computable, and do not require storing the entire log files. This makes RV-MONITOR ideal for in-depth analysis of large log files which may be impractical to analyze with traditional techniques. For more details, please see the Running Examples section of RV-MONITOR documentation [7].

5   Conclusion

Whereas RV-MATCH is a tool for rigorously detecting all forms of undefinedness, RV-PREDICT targets the hard problem of efficiently detecting data races. RV-MATCH interprets programs according to a complete operational semantics, while RV-PREDICT is able to infer a maximal causal model of concurrent behavior from a single real execution trace. RV-MONITOR, on the other hand, confronts the problem of software correctness from a broader perspective by providing a framework for directly monitoring and enforcing adherence to a specification. Together, these tools represent a rigorous yet pragmatic and user-friendly approach to verification (eponymously) characterized by its focus on the analysis of programs at runtime.

References

1. Roşu, G., Şerbănuţă, T.F.: An overview of the K semantic framework. In: 79.6, pp. 397–434 (2010). doi:10.1016/j.jlap.03.012
2. Şerbănuţă, T.F., Chen, F., Roşu, G.: Maximal causal models for sequentially consistent systems. In: Qadeer, S., Tasiran, S. (eds.) RV 2012. LNCS, vol. 7687, pp. 136–150. Springer, Heidelberg (2013). doi:10.1007/978-3-642-35632-2_16
3. Beyer, D.: Reliable and reproducible competition results with BenchExec and witnesses (Report on SV-COMP 2016). In: Chechik, M., Raskin, J.-F. (eds.) TACAS 2016. LNCS, vol. 9636, pp. 887–904. Springer, Heidelberg (2016). doi:10.1007/978-3-662-49674-9_55
4. Campbell, B.: An executable semantics for CompCert C. In: Hawblitzel, C., Miller, D. (eds.) CPP 2012. LNCS, vol. 7679, pp. 60–75. Springer, Heidelberg (2012). doi:10.1007/978-3-642-35308-6_8
5. Canet, G., Cuoq, P., Monate, B.: A value analysis for C programs. In: Conference on Source Code Analysis and Manipulation (SCAM 2009), pp. 123–124. IEEE (2009). doi:10.1109/SCAM.2009.22
6. Clang: Clang 3.9 Documentation. http://clang.llvm.org/docs/index.html
7. Daian, P.: RV-Monitor Documentation (2015). https://runtimeverification.com/monitor/1.3/docs/
8. Ellison, C.: A formal semantics of C with applications. Ph.D. thesis. University of Illinois, July 2012. http://hdl.handle.net/2142/34297
9. Ellison, C., Roşu, G.: An executable formal semantics of C with applications. In: ACM SIGPLAN-SIGACT Symposium on Principles of Programming Languages (POPL 2012), pp. 533–544 (2012). doi:10.1145/2103656.2103719.
10. GrammaTech: CodeSonar. http://grammatech.com/products/codesonar
11. Guth, D.: RV-Match Documentation (2016). https://runtimeverification.com/match/1.0-SNAPSHOT/docs/
12. Guth, D.: Using RV-Predict to track down race conditions (2015). https://runtimeverification.com/blog/?p=47
13. Hathhorn, C., Ellison, C., Roşu, G.: Defining the undefinedness of C. In: 36th Conference on Programming Language Design and Implementation (PLDI 2015) (2015)
14. Huang, J., Meredith, Patrick O'Neil Roşu, G.: Maximal sound predictive race detection with control flow abstraction. In: PLDI 2015. doi:10.1145/2594291.2594315
15. ISO, IEC JTC 1, SC 22, WG 14. ISO, IEC 9899: 2011: Prog. Lang.–C. Tech. rep. International Organization for Standardization, 2012
16. Jin, D., et al.: JavaMOP: efficient parametric runtime monitoring framework. In: ICSE 2012, pp. 1427–1430. IEEE, June 2012. http://dx.doi.org/10.1109/ICSE.2012.6227231
17. Kiczales, G., Hilsdale, E., Hugunin, J., Kersten, M., Palm, J., Griswold, W.G.: An overview of AspectJ. In: Knudsen, J.L. (ed.) ECOOP 2001. LNCS, vol. 2072, pp. 327–354. Springer, Heidelberg (2001). doi:10.1007/3-540-45337-7_18
18. Li, Y.: Detecting popular data races in Java using RV-Predict (2015). https://runtimeverification.com/blog/?p=58
19. Li, Y.: RV-Predict Documentation (2015). https://runtimeverification.com/predict/1.8.2/docs/
20. Long, F., et al.: The CERT Oracle Secure Coding Standard for Java. The SEI Series in Software Engineering. Addison-Wesley, Upper Saddle River (2012). ISBN: 978-0-321-80395-5

21. Luo, Q., Zhang, Y., Lee, C., Jin, D., Meredith, P.O.N., Şerbănuţă, T.F., Roşu, G.:
    RV-Monitor: efficient parametric runtime verification with simultaneous properties.
    In: Bonakdarpour, B., Smolka, S.A. (eds.) RV 2014. LNCS, vol. 8734, pp. 285–300.
    Springer, Heidelberg (2014). doi:10.1007/978-3-319-11164-3_24
22. MathWorks. Polyspace Bug Finder. http://www.mathworks.com/products/
    polyspace-bug-finder
23. MathWorks. Polyspace Code Prover. http://www.mathworks.com/products/
    polyspace-code-prover
24. Nethercote, N., Seward, J.: Valgrind: a framework for heavyweight dynamic
    binary instrumentation. In: ACM SIGPLAN Conference on Programming Lan-
    guage Design and Implementation (PLDI 2007), pp. 89–100. ACM (2007). doi:10.
    1145/1250734.1250746
25. Shiraishi, S., Mohan, V., Marimuthu, H.: Test suites for benchmarks of static
    analysis tools. In: The 26th IEEE International Symposium on Software Reliability
    Engineering (ISSRE 2015), vol. Industrial Track (2015)
26. Why does this Java program terminate despite that apparently it
    shouldn't (and didn't)? (2013) http://stackoverflow.com/questions/16159203/
    whydoes-this-java-program-terminate-despite-that-apparently-itshouldnt-and-d

When RV Meets CEP

Sylvain Hallé[(✉)]

Laboratoire d'informatique formelle, Département d'informatique et de
mathématique, Université du Québec à Chicoutimi, Chicoutimi, Canada
shalle@acm.org

Abstract. This paper is an introduction to Complex Event Processing (CEP) intended for an practicioners of Runtime Verification. It first
describes typical CEP problems, popular tools and their query languages.
It then presents BeepBeep 3, an event stream processor that attempts
to bridge the gap between RV and CEP. Thanks to BeepBeep's generic
architecture and flexible input language, queries and properties from
both fields can be efficiently processed.

1 Introduction

Information systems generate a wealth of information in the form of event traces
or logs. The analysis of these logs, either offline or in real-time, can be put to
numerous uses: computation of various metrics, detection of anomalous patterns
or presence of bugs. A possible application of log analysis is Runtime Verification
(RV). In RV, a *monitor* is given a formal *specification* of some desirable property
that a trace should fulfill. The monitor is then fed events, either directly from
the execution of some instrumented system or by reading a pre-recorded file, and
is responsible for providing a *verdict*, as to whether the trace satisfies or violates
the property. Runtime monitors developed in the recent past include JavaMOP
[33], J-Lo [37], LARVA [18], MarQ [35], MonPoly [10], PoET [21], PQL [32],
PTQL [25], SpoX [20], and Tracematches [13].

Classical RV problems are centered around properties that deal with the way
events are ordered. For example, the canonical "HasNext" property stipulates
that, whenever an `Iterator` object is used in a program, any call to its `next()`
method must be preceded by a call to `hasNext()` that returns the value `true`.
Consequently, the languages used by monitors to specify properties all have a
strong temporal or sequential component: this includes finite-state automata,
temporal logic, μ-calculus, and multiple variations thereof.

Perhaps less known to RV practitioners is the existence of another field of
research, called Complex Event Processing (CEP). CEP frames the question of
processing an event trace as a *database* problem. A trace of events is seen as a
dynamic data source, on which *queries* are executed to extract a *result*. On the
surface, it seems that RV and CEP have a lot in common, since both seek to
evaluate a result on a trace made of events, and to update that result in real
time as the trace is being consumed. Yet, they also have notable differences,

Y. Falcone and C. Sanchez (Eds.): RV 2016, LNCS 10012, pp. 68–91, 2016.
DOI: 10.1007/978-3-319-46982-9_6

particularly in the nature of the properties (or queries) that are computed on event traces.

In this paper, we explore the ties between RV and CEP. In Sect. 2, we first define CEP, and study a few classical problems extracted from recent literature in that field; we also highlight the similarities and differences between RV and CEP. We then introduce BeepBeep 3, an event stream processing engine that attempts to reconcile the two fields under a common framework. Section 3 introduces the basic concepts of event streams, functions and processors. Section 4 then describes the basic processors included in BeepBeep's core engine, and Sect. 5 describes a few of its available extension packages. Finally, Sect. 6 puts it all together, and shows examples of complex BeepBeep queries subsuming both RV and CEP.

2   Complex Event Processing

Complex Event Processing (CEP) can be loosely defined as the task of analyzing and aggregating data produced by event-driven information systems [31]. A key feature of CEP is the possibility to correlate events from multiple sources, occurring at multiple moments in time. Information extracted from these events can be processed, and lead to the creation of new, "complex" events made of that computed data. This stream of complex events can itself be used as the source of another process, and be aggregated and correlated with other events.

2.1   Typical CEP Queries

In the same manner as RV, CEP literature has been crystallized around a set of more or less "canonical" use cases and problems. We present a few of them in this section. For more details and examples, the reader is referred to individual papers on CEP software that will be described in the next section.

Snapshot Query. A recurring scenario used in CEP to illustrate the performance of various tools is taken from the stock market [15]. One considers a stream of stock quotes, where each event is a tuple made of a stockSymbol attribute, the price of the stock at various moments (such as its minimumPrice and closingPrice), and a timestamp. A first, simple type of query one can compute over such a trace is called a *snapshot* query, such as the following:

Query 1. *Get the closing price of MSFT for the first five trading days.*

One can see how the result of that query is itself a trace of tuples, much in the same way the relational SELECT statement on a table returns another table. As a matter of fact, we shall see later on that in many CEP systems, queries are written using a syntax reminiscent of SQL.

Landmark Query. A refinement of the snapshot query is the *landmark* query, which returns only events that satisfy some criterion, such as:

> **Query 2.** *Select all the days after the hundredth trading day, on which the closing price of MSFT has been greater than $50.*

This simple query highlights two important elements of CEP. First, the result of a query must be computed monotonically: once a tuple is sent out, it cannot be "taken back" at a later time. Second, outputting a tuple may require waiting until more of the input trace is made available. In the worst case, MSFT may be the last stock symbol for which the price is known on a given day, and all events of that day must somehow be retained before knowing if they must be included in the result or discarded.

Sliding Query. In *window queries*, a computation is repeatedly made on a set of successive events. The size of that set is called the *width* of the window; the width is specified as a number of events or as a time interval. A *sliding query* is a particular case of window query where, after each computation, the window moves forward into the trace and a new set of successive events is considered. Often, the computation applied to the contents of the window is an aggregate function, such as a sum or an average. For example:

> **Query 3.** *On every fifth trading day starting today, calculate the average closing price of MSFT for the five most recent trading days.*

Join Query. A *join* query involves the comparison of multiple events together. For example:

> **Query 4.** *For the five most recent trading days starting today, select all stocks that closed higher than MSFT on a given day.*

When computing the result of such a query, a tuple is added to the output result depending on its relationship with respect to the price of MSFT for the same day. In most CEP systems, this is done by an operation similar to the JOIN operator in relational databases: the input trace is joined with itself, producing pairs of tuples (t_1, t_2) where t_1 belongs to the first "copy" of the trace, and t_2 belongs to the second. The join condition, in our example, is that timestamps of t_1 and t_2 must be equal. Since traces are potentially infinite, join operations generally require bounds of some kind to be usable in practice; for example, the join operation may only be done on events of the last minute, or on a window of n successive events.

Trend Query. We now move to a different field of application, that of medical record management. In this context, events are messages expressed in a structured format called HL7 [36]. An HL7 message is composed of one or more segments, each containing a number of fields. The analysis of HL7 event traces produced by health information systems can be used, among other things, to detect significant unexpected changes in data values that could compromise patient safety [12]. A general rule, which can apply to any numerical field, identifies whenever a data value starts to deviate from its current trend:

Query 5. *Notify the user when two out of three successive data points lie more than 2 standard deviations from the mean on the same side of the mean line.*

We call such a query a *trend* query, as it relates a field in the current event to an aggregation function applied on the past values of that field. Although our example query does not specify it, this aggregation can be computed over a window, such as the past 100 events, or events of the past hour.

Slice Query. The next example is taken from Microsoft's StreamInsight tutorial [30]. The scenario describes toll booths along a road sending out `TollReading` events whenever a car passes through the booth. Each event contains the `TollId` of that particular booth, the `LicensePlate`, `State`, `Make` and `Model` of the car, as well as the `Toll` paid by the driver. A *slice* query is the application of the same computation over multiple subsets (slices) of the input trace. An example of a slice query is the following (note that this query also incorporates the computation of a sum over a sliding window):

Query 6. *Compute the toll produced by each tool booth over three-minute intervals, with the window advancing in one minute hops.*

2.2   RV vs. CEP...

A variety of CEP software and theoretical frameworks have been developed over the years, which all differ in a number of dimensions. For example, TelegraphCQ [15] was built to fix the problem of continuous stream of data coming from networked environments; it shares similarities with the earlier STREAM system [7]. SASE [39] was brought as a solution to meet the needs of a range of RFID-enabled monitoring applications. On its side, Siddhi [34] focuses on the multi-threading aspect of evaluating CEP queries. Among other popular software, we shall also mention Borealis [6], Cayuga [14], Esper [1], StreamBase SQL [4], StreamInsight [30], and VoltDB [5].

Pointing out the differences in each of these tools is out of the scope of this paper. Some of them are research prototypes, while others are commercial products with a large user base. Nearly all of them provide their own distinct query language, whose expressiveness vastly varies from one tool to the next — as a rule, each of them can only handle a (different) subset of the examples we presented. Most, however, borrow syntactical elements from SQL to some extent. For example, the following code snippet shows how Query 4 can be written using TelegraphCQ:

```
Select c2.*
FROM ClosingStockPrices as c1, ClosingStockPrices as c2
WHERE c1.stockSymbol = 'MSFT' and c2.stockSymbol!= 'MSFT' and
    c2.closingPrice > c1.closingPrice and c2.timestamp = c1.timestamp
for (t = ST; t < ST + 20 ; t++){
    Windowls(c1, t − 4, t);
    Windowls(c2, t − 4, t);
}
```

We can identify a number of distinguishing elements between the problems and tools of Runtime Verification and Complex Event Processing.

Query Composition. As we have discussed, CEP aims at calculating the result of a *query* on a trace of events. The output of that query can itself be a sequence of events with data-rich contents, which can be reused as the input of another query. In contrast, a monitor evaluates a *property* over a trace. Intermediate results of its computation are seldom exposed or expected to be consumable, and its output (most often a single truth value) is not reusable as the input of another monitor for further processing.

We believe this is one area in particular where RV would benefit from integrating CEP concepts. Note that there do exist monitors whose specification language involves more advanced data computing capabilities (numerical aggregation functions, mostly), but they still compute the answer to what is fundamentally a yes/no question. Yet, if one sees a monitor, in the broader sense of the term, as a *diagnostics* tool for discovering and understanding bugs, then it should provide the possibility to compute results beyond a single Boolean value.

Data Transformation. As a consequence of the previous observation, it can be noted that CEP problems feature data-rich events, over which complex transformations and computations can made. For example, Query 3 computes the average of some numerical attribute over a sliding window of events, and Query 5 compares the value of a field to the mean and standard deviation of a set of past values for the same field. Such functionalities are considered standard for a CEP language. Indeed, the SELECT construct provided by most CEP engines makes it possible to produce output tuples made of attributes from multiple input tuples, coming from potentially different input traces, combine them and apply various built-in functions (mostly numerical).

In contrast, most monitors do support events with data fields, but only allow basic (again, Boolean) comparisons (=, ≤, etc.) between values of these fields. The handling of aggregation functions and other forms of computation over event data is not a common feature in RV, and only a handful of monitors so far support them [9,11,17,19,23].

Sequential Patterns and Quantification. Although they provide rich data manipulation facilities, CEP tools are far less advanced in terms of evaluating sequential patterns of events. In many of their input languages, the only way of correlating an event with past or future events is through a JOIN of the trace with itself —an expensive operation, which can only be done in restricted ways (such as by bounding the window of events that are joined). In a few cases, a language offers the possibility to describe primitive sequencing patterns (using a form of regular expression, or simple "A follows B" instructions). These patterns are very restricted in their use (for example, they do not allow negation) and, as empirical testing revealed, costly to evaluate.

This is in sharp contrast with RV, where the sequential aspect of event traces is central. Since the specification language of monitors is based on logic, it is also natural to find a form of first-order quantification in many of them. This quantification occurs in problems where some specific pattern must hold "for all elements". A few CEP systems allow a trace to be split into various slices, but as a rule, no true equivalent of universal and existential quantification is supported.

2.3   . . . and Beyond

The previous observations show that RV and CEP can borrow from each other's strengths. However, one may imagine a generic framework that not only encompasses both, but also goes beyond the current limitations of the two approaches.

Event Types. Both RV and CEP systems consider a single type of event. For example, many CEP tools, which have a strong background in databases, assume all events to be *tuples*. Every tuple of a trace must have the same fixed set of attributes, and events must differ only in the values they define for each attribute. Moreover, these values must be scalar. A query can transform an input trace into a different output, but the resulting trace will still be made of tuples, with possibly different attributes.[1] Monitors, on their side, handle various event types, depending on the system: tuples, predicates, or even richer events such as XML documents with an arbitrary nested structure. However, each monitor accepts a single of these types, and does not produce a new feed of events as its output.

A truly generic event processing system should not presuppose that any single type of events is appropriate for all problems. Rather, each type of event should come with its own set of *event manipulation functions* (EMF) to extract data, manipulate and create new events of that type. These functions should be distinct from *trace manipulation functions* (TMF), which, in contrast, should make very limited assumptions on the traces they manipulate. This clear separation of EMF and TMF should make it possible to easily mix events of different types into queries, and to write queries whose various intermediate traces may be of multiple types. It should also help avoid the "square peg in a round hole" problem, where one must write an overly complicated expression simply to work around the limitations of the single available event type.

---

[1] A few engines allow events to be user-defined objects, but these objects are accessed through methods that return scalar values, which is tantamount.

Query Language. A similar problem also arises with respect to the specification (or query) language of each tool. Again, the database foundations of CEP have led many solutions to compute everything through a tentacular SELECT statement, with optional constructs attempting to account for every possible use case. Monitors, again, have more varied specification languages, but since the output of a monitor cannot be used as the input of another one, every problem must be expressible in the language of a single tool to be solvable at all.

A modular event processing framework should alleviate this problem by proposing a set of basic processing units that can be freely composed. Therefore, rather than proposing a single, all-encompassing query language, it should accommodate multiple query languages, along with lightweight syntactical "glue" to allow their composition. This would allow every step of the computation to be expressed in the notation most appropriate for it.

3   The BeepBeep 3 Event Processing Engine

The observations made in the previous section motivated the design of Beep-Beep 3, a new event stream processing engine that aims to reconcile RV and CEP by supporting functionalities of both. As its name implies, it is the third incarnation of the BeepBeep line of monitoring software. Earlier versions of BeepBeep, which used a first-order extension of Linear Temporal Logic as their specification language, were successfully used in the detection of compliance violations in web services [29] and the runtime prevention of behavioural bugs in video games [38]. BeepBeep can be used either as a Java library embedded in another application's source code, or as a stand-alone query interpreter running from the command-line. Releases of BeepBeep 3 are publicly available for download through an open source license.[2]

3.1   Events, Functions and Processors

Let $\mathbb{T}$ be an arbitrary set of elements. An *event trace of type* $\mathbb{T}$ is a sequence $\bar{e} = e_0 e_1 \ldots$ where $e_i \in \mathbb{T}$ for all i. The set of all traces of type $\mathbb{T}$ is denoted $\mathbb{T}^*$. In line with the observations made previously, BeepBeep makes no assumption whatsoever as to what an event can be. Event types can be as simple as single characters or numbers, or as complex as matrices, XML documents, plots, logical predicates, polynomials or any other user-defined data structure. In terms of implementation, an event can potentially be any descendent of Java's Object class.

A *function* is an object that takes zero or more events as its input, and produces zero or more events as its output. The *arity* of a function is the number of input arguments and output values they have. For example, the addition function $+ : \mathbb{R}^2 \to \mathbb{R}$ is the 2:1 function that receives two real numbers as its input, and returns their sum as its output. In BeepBeep, functions are first-class

---

[2] https://liflab.github.io/beepbeep-3.

objects; they all descend from an abstract ancestor named `Function`, which declares a method called `evaluate()` so that outputs can be produced for a given array of inputs.

A *processor* is an object that takes zero or more event *traces*, and produces zero or more event *traces* as its output. The difference between a function and a processor is important. While a function is stateless, and operates on individual events, a processor is a stateful device: for a given input, its output may depend on events received in the past. Processors in BeepBeep all descend from the abstract class `Processor`, which provides a few common functionalities, such as obtaining a reference to the n-th input or output, getting the type of the n-th input or output, etc.

We shall use a notation that defines the output trace(s) of a processor in terms of its input trace(s). Let $\bar{e}_1, \ldots, \bar{e}_n$ be n input traces, and φ be a processor. The expression $[\![\bar{e}_1, \ldots, \bar{e}_n : \varphi]\!]$ will denote the output trace produced by φ, given these input traces. As a simple example, let us consider a processor, noted $\pitchfork_n$, that outputs every n-th event of its input and discards the others (this process is called *decimation*). This can be defined as:

$$[\![\bar{e} : \pitchfork_n]\!]_i \equiv e_{ni}$$

Each processor instance is also associated with a *context*. A context is a persistent and modifiable map that associates names to arbitrary objects. When a processor is duplicated, its context is duplicated as well. If a processor requires the evaluation of a function, the current context of the processor is passed to the function. Hence the function's arguments may contain references to names of context elements, which are replaced with their concrete values before evaluation. Basic processors, such as those described in Sect. 4, do not use context. However, some special processors defined in extensions to BeepBeep's core (the Moore machine and the first-order quantifiers, among others) manipulate their `Context` object.

3.2   Streaming, Piping and Buffering

A processor produces its output in a *streaming* fashion: it does not wait to read its entire input trace before starting to produce output events. However, a processor can require more than one input event to create an output event, and hence may not always output something. This can be seen in the case of the decimation processor described above. Given a trace $e_0 e_1, \ldots$, the processor outputs e_0 immediately after reading it. However, it does not produce any output after consuming e_1; it will only produce another output after reading n inputs.

Processors can be composed (or "piped") together, by letting the output of one processor be the input of another. Another important characteristic of BeepBeep is that this piping is possible as long as the type of the first processor's output matches the second processor's input type. The piping of processors can be represented graphically, as Fig. 1 illustrates. In this case, an input trace (of numbers) is duplicated into two copies; the first is sent as the first input of a

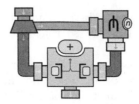

Fig. 1. A simple composition of processors, represented graphically

2:1 processor labelled "+"; the second is first sent to the decimation processor, whose output is connected to the second input of "+". The end result is that output event i will contain the value $e_i + e_{ni}$.

When a processor has an arity of 2 or more, the processing of its input is done *synchronously*. This means that a computation step will be performed if and only if an event can be consumed from each input trace. This is a strong assumption; many other CEP engines allow events to be processed asynchronously, meaning that the output of a query may depend on what input trace produced an event first. One can easily imagine situations where synchronous processing is not appropriate. However, in use cases where it is suitable, assuming synchronous processing greatly simplifies the definition and implementation of processors. The output result is no longer sensitive to the order in which events arrive at each input, or to the time it takes for an upstream processor to compute an output.[3]

This hypothesis entails that processors must implicitly manage *buffers* to store input events until a result can be computed. Consider the case of the processor chain illustrated in Fig. 1. When e_0 is made available in the input trace, both the top and bottom branches output it immediately, and processor "+" can compute their sum right away. When e_1 is made available, the first input of "+" receives it immediately. However, the decimation processor produces no output for this event. Hence "+" cannot produce an output, and must keep e_1 in a queue associated to its first input. Events e_2, e_3, ... will be accumulated into that queue, until event e_n is made available. This time, the decimation processor produces an output, and e_n arrives at the second output of "+". Now that one event can be consumed from each input trace, the processor can produce the result (in this case, $e_0 + e_n$) and remove an event from both input queues.

Note that while the queue for the second input becomes empty again, the queue for the first input still contains $e_2, \ldots e_n$. The process continues for the subsequent events, until e_{2n}, at which point "+" computes $e_2 + e_{2n}$, and so on. In this chain of processors, the size of the queue for the first input of "+" grows by one event except when i is a multiple of n.

This buffering is implicit: it is absent from both the formal definition of processors and any graphical representation of their piping. Nevertheless, the concrete implementation of a processor must take care of these buffers in order

---

[3] The order of arrival of events from the same input trace, obviously, is preserved.

to produce the correct output. In BeepBeep, this is done with the abstract class `SingleProcessor`; descendents of this class simply need to implement a method named `compute()`, which is called only when an event is ready to be consumed at each input.

3.3 "Pull" vs. "Push" Mode

The interaction with a `Processor` object is done through two interfaces: `Pullable` and `Pushable`. A `Pullable` object queries events on one of a processor's outputs. For a processor with an output arity of n, there exists n distinct pullables, namely one for each output trace. Every pullable works roughly like classical `Iterator`: it is possible to check whether new output events are available (`hasNext()`), and get one new output event (`next()`). However, contrarily to iterators, a `Pullable` has two versions of each method: a "soft" and a "hard" version.

"Soft" methods make a single attempt at producing an output event. Since processors are connected in a chain, this generally means pulling events from the input in order to produce the output. However, if pulling the input produces no event, no output event can be produced. In such a case, `hasNext()` will return a special value (`MAYBE`), and `pull()` will return `null`. Soft methods can be seen as doing "one turn of the crank" on the whole chain of processors —whether or not this outputs something.

"Hard" methods are actually calls to soft methods until an output event is produced: the "crank" is turned as long as necessary to produce something. This means that one call to, e.g. `pullHard()` may consume more than one event from a processor's input. Therefore, calls to `hasNextHard()` never return `MAYBE` (only `YES` or `NO`), and `pullHard()` returns `null` only if no event will ever be output in the future (this occurs, for example, when pulling events from a file, and the end of the file has been reached).

Interface `Pushable` is the opposite of `Pullable`: rather than querying events form a processor's output (i.e. "pulling"), it gives events to a processor's input. This has for effect of triggering the processor's computation and "pushing" results (if any) to the processor's output. It shall be noted that in BeepBeep, any processor can be used in both push and pull modes. In contrast, CEP systems and runtime monitors generally support a single of these modes.

The notion of push and pull is borrowed from event-based parsing of XML documents, where so-called "SAX" (push) parsers [3] are opposed to "StAX" (pull) parsers [24]. XQuery engines such as XQPull [22] implement these models to evaluate XQuery statements over XML documents. The use of such streaming XQuery engines to evaluate temporal logic properties on event traces had already been explored in an early form in [28].

3.4 Creating a Processor Pipe

BeepBeep provides multiple ways to create processor pipes and to fetch their results. The first way is programmatically, using BeepBeep as a library and Java as the glue code for creating the processors and connecting them. For example, the following code snippet creates the processor chain corresponding to Fig. 1.

```
Fork f = new Fork(2);
FunctionProcessor sum = new FunctionProcessor(Addition.instance);
CountDecimate decimate = new CountDecimate(n);
Connector.connect(fork, LEFT, sum, LEFT)
         .connect(fork, RIGHT, decimate, INPUT)
         .connect(decimate, OUTPUT, sum, RIGHT);
Pullable p = sum.getOutputPullable(OUTPUT);
while (p.hasNextHard() != NextStatus.NO) {
  Object o = p.nextHard();
  ...
}
```

A `Fork` is instructed to create two copies of its input. The first (or "left") output of the fork is connected to the "left" input of a processor performing an addition. The second (or "right") output of the fork is connected to the input of a decimation processor, which itself is connected to the "right" input of the sum processor. One then gets a reference to `sum`'s (only) `Pullable`, and start pulling events from that chain. The piping is done through the `connect()` method; when a processor has two inputs or outputs, the symbolic names LEFT/RIGHT and TOP/BOTTOM can be used instead of 0 and 1. The symbolic names INPUT and OUTPUT refer to the (only) input or output of a processor, and stand for the value 0.

Another powerful way of creating queries is by using BeepBeep's query language, the Event Stream Query Language (eSQL). A detailed presentation of eSQL would require a paper of its own; it will not be discussed here due to lack of space.

4   Built-In Processors

BeepBeep is organized along a modular architecture. The main part of BeepBeep is called the *engine*, which provides the basic classes for creating processors and functions, and contains a handful of general-purpose processors for manipulating traces. The rest of BeepBeep's functionalities is dispersed across a number of *palettes*. In the following, we describe the basic processors provided by Beep-Beep's engine. The next section will be devoted to processors and functions from a handful of domain-specific palettes that have already been developed.

4.1   Function Processors

A first way to create a processor is by lifting any $m : n$ function f into a $m : n$ processor. This is done by applying f successively to each tuple of input events, producing the output events. The processor responsible for this is called a `FunctionProcessor`. A first example of a function processor was shown in

Fig. 1. A function processor is created by applying the "+" (addition) function, represented by an oval, to the left and right inputs, producing the output. Recall that in BeepBeep, functions are first-class objects. Hence the `Addition` function can be passed as an argument when instantiating the `FunctionProcessor`. Since this function is 2:1, the resulting processor is also 2:1. Formally, the function processor can be noted as:

$$[\![\bar{e}_1, \ldots, \bar{e}_m : f]\!]_i \equiv f(\bar{e}_1[i], \ldots, \bar{e}_m[i])$$

Two special cases of function processors are worth mentioning. The `Mutator` is a $m : n$ processor where f returns the same output events, no matter its input. Hence, this processor "mutates" whatever its input is into the same output. The `Fork` is a $1 : n$ processor that simply copies its input to its n outputs. When $n - 1$, the fork is also called a *passthrough*.

A variant of the function processor is the `CumulativeProcessor`, noted Σ_f^t. Contrarily to the processors above, which are stateless, a cumulative processor is stateful. Given a binary function $f : \mathbb{T} \times \mathbb{U} \to \mathbb{T}$, a cumulative processor is defined as:

$$[\![\bar{e}_1, \bar{e}_2 : \Sigma_f^t]\!]_i \equiv f([\![\bar{e}_1, \bar{e}_2 : \Sigma_f^t]\!]_{i-1}, \bar{e}_2[i])$$

Intuitively, if x is the previous value returned by the processor, its output on the next event y will be $f(x, y)$. The processor requires an initial value $t \in \mathbb{T}$ to compute its first output.

Depending on the function f, cumulative processors can represent many things. If $f : \mathbb{R}^2 \to \mathbb{R}$ is the addition and $0 \in \mathbb{R}$ is the start value, the processor outputs the cumulative sum of all values received so far. If $f : \{\top, \bot, ?\}^2 \to \{\top, \bot, ?\}$ is the three-valued logical conjunction and ? is the start value, then the processor computes the three-valued conjunction of events received so far, and has the same semantics as the LTL$_3$ "Globally" operator.

4.2   Trace Manipulating Processors

A few processors can be used to alter the sequence of events received. We already mentioned the *decimator*, formally named `CountDecimate`, which returns every n-th input event and discards the others. The `Freeze` processor, noted $\downarrow$, repeats the first event received; it is formally defined as

$$[\![\bar{e} : \downarrow]\!] \equiv (\bar{e}_0)^*$$

Another operation that can be applied to a trace is trimming its output. Given a trace $\bar{e}$, the `Trim` processor, denoted as $\triangleright_n$, returns the trace starting at its n-th input event. This is formalized as follows:

$$[\![\bar{e} : \triangleright_n]\!] \equiv \bar{e}^n$$

Events can also be discarded from a trace based on a condition. The `Filter` processor F is a $n : n - 1$ processor defined as follows:

$$[\![\bar{e}_1, \ldots, \bar{e}_{n-1}, \bar{e}_n : \mathrm{F}]\!]_i \equiv \begin{cases} \bar{e}_1[i], \ldots, \bar{e}_{n-1}[i] & \text{if } \bar{e}_n[i] = \top \\ \epsilon & \text{otherwise} \end{cases}$$

The filter behaves like a passthrough on its first $n-1$ inputs, and uses its last input trace as a guard; the events are let through on its $n-1$ outputs, if the corresponding event of input trace n is $\top$; otherwise, no output is produced. A special case is a binary filter, where its first input trace contains the events to filter, and the second trace decides which ones to keep.

This filtering mechanism, although simple to define, turns out to be very generic. The processor does not impose any particular way to determine if the events should be kept or discarded. As long as it is connected to something that produces Boolean values, any input can be filtered, and according to any condition—including conditions that require knowledge of future events to be evaluated. Note also that the sequence of Booleans can come from a different trace than the events to filter. This should be contrasted with CEP systems, that allow filtering events only through the use of a WHERE clause inside a SELECT statement, and whose syntax is limited to a few simple functions.

4.3   Window Processor

Let $\varphi : \mathbb{T}^* \to \mathbb{U}^*$ be a 1:1 processor. The *window processor of φ of width n*, noted as $\Upsilon_n(\varphi)$, is defined as follows:

$$[\![\overline{e} : \Upsilon_n(\varphi)]\!]_i \equiv [\![\overline{e}^i : \varphi]\!]_n$$

One can see how this processor sends the first n events (i.e. events numbered 0 to $n-1$) to an instance of φ, which is then queried for its n-th output event. The processor also sends events 1 to n to a second instance of φ, which is then also queried for its n-th output event, and so on. The resulting trace is indeed the evaluation of φ on a sliding window of n successive events.

In existing CEP engines, window processors can be used in a restricted way, generally within a SELECT statement, and only a few simple functions (such as sum or average) can be applied to the window. In contrast, in BeepBeep, *any* processor can be encased in a sliding window, provided it outputs at least n events when given n inputs. This includes stateful processors: for example, a window of width n can contain a processor that increment a count whenever an event a is followed by a b. The output trace hence produces the number of times a is followed by b in a window of width n.

4.4   Slicer

The `Slicer` is a 1:1 processor that separates an input trace into different "slices". It takes as input a processor φ and a function $f : \mathbb{T} \to \mathbb{U}$, called the *slicing function*. There exists potentially one instance of φ for each value in the image of f. If $\mathbb{T}$ is the domain of the slicing function, and $\mathbb{V}$ is the output type of φ, the slicer is a processor whose input trace is of type $\mathbb{T}$ and whose output trace is of type $2^{\mathbb{V}}$.

When an event e is to be consumed, the slicer evaluates $c = f(e)$. This value determines to what instance of φ the event will be dispatched. If no instance of

φ is associated to c, a new copy of φ is initialized. Event e is then given to the appropriate instance of φ. Finally, the last event output by every instance of φ is collected into a set, and that set is the output event corresponding to input event e. The function f may return a special value $\#$, indicating that no new slice must be created, but that the incoming event must be dispatched to *all* slices.

A particular case of slicer is when φ is a processor returning Boolean values; the output of the slicer becomes a set of Boolean values. Applying the logical conjunction of all elements of the set results in checking that φ applies "for all slices", while applying the logical disjunction amounts to existential quantification over slices.

5   A Few Palettes

BeepBeep was designed from the start to be easily extensible. As was discussed earlier, it consists of only a small core of built-in processors and functions. The rest of its functionalities are implemented through custom processors and grammar extensions, grouped in packages called *palettes*. Concretely, a palette is implemented as a JAR file that is loaded with BeepBeep's main program to extend its functionalities in a particular way. Users can also create their own new processors, and extend the eSQL grammar so that these processors can be integrated in queries.

This modular organization has three advantages. First, they are a flexible and generic way to extend the engine to various application domains, in ways unforeseen by its original designers. Second, they make the engine's core (and each palette individually) relatively small and self-contained, easing the development and debugging process.[4] Finally, it is hoped that BeepBeep's palette architecture, combined with its simple extension mechanisms, will help third-party users contribute to the BeepBeep ecosystem by developing and distributing extensions suited to their own needs.

We describe a few of the palettes that have already been developed for Beep-Beep in the recent past. These processors are available alongside BeepBeep from the same software repository.

5.1   LTL-FO$^+$

This palette provides processors for evaluating all operators of Linear Temporal Logic (LTL), in addition to the first-order quantification defined in LTL-FO$^+$ (and present in previous versions of BeepBeep) [29]. Each of these operators comes in two flavours: Boolean and "Troolean".

Boolean processors are called Globally, Eventually, Until, Next, ForAll and Exists. If $a_0 a_1 a_2 \ldots$ is an input trace, the processor Globally produces an output trace $b_0 b_1 b_2 \ldots$ such that $b_i = \bot$ if and only there exists $j \geq i$ such

---

[4] The core of BeepBeep is made of less than 2,500 lines of code.

that $b_j = \perp$. In other words, the i-th output event is the two-valued verdict of evaluating $\mathbf{G}\,\varphi$ on the input trace, starting at the i-th event. A similar reasoning is applied to the other operators.

Troolean processors are called `Always`, `Sometime`, `UpTo`, `After`, `Every` and `Some`. Each is associated to the Boolean processor with a similar name. If $a_0 a_1 a_2 \ldots$ is an input trace, the processor `Always` produces an output trace $b_0 b_1 b_2 \ldots$ such that $b_i = \perp$ if there exists $j \leq i$ such that $b_j = \perp$, and "?" (the "inconclusive" value of LTL$_3$) otherwise. In other words, the i-th output event is the three-valued verdict of evaluating $\mathbf{G}\,\varphi$ on the input trace, after reading i events.

Note that these two semantics are distinct, and that both are necessary in the context of event stream processing. Consider the simple LTL property $a \to \mathbf{F}\,b$. In a monitoring context, one is interested in Troolean operators: the verdict of the monitor should be the partial result of evaluating an expression for the current prefix of the trace. Hence, in the case of the trace $accb$, the output trace should be ???$\top$: the monitor comes with a definite verdict after reading the fourth event.

However, one may also be interested in using an LTL expression φ as a filter: from the input trace, output only events such that φ holds. In such a case, Boolean operators are appropriate. Using the same property and the same trace as above, the expected behaviour is to retain the input events a, c, and c; when b arrives, all four events can be released at once, as the fate of a becomes defined (it has been followed by a b), and the expression is true right away on the remaining three events.

First-order quantifiers are of the form $\forall x \in f(e) : \varphi$ and $\exists x \in f(e) : \varphi$. Here, f is an arbitrary function that is evaluated over the current event; the only requirement is that it must return a collection (set, list or array) of values. An instance of the processor φ is created for each value c of that collection; for each instance, the processor's context is augmented with a new association $x \mapsto c$. Moreover, φ can be any processor; this entails it is possible to perform quantification over virtually anything.

5.2   FSM

This palette allows one to define a Moore machine, a special case of finite-state machine where each state is associated to an output symbol. This Moore machine allows its transitions to be guarded by arbitrary functions; hence it can operate on traces of events of any type.

Moreover, transitions can be associated to a list of `ContextAssignment` objects, meaning that the machine can also query and modify its `Context` object. Depending on the context object being manipulated, the machine can work as a pushdown automaton, an extended finite-state machine [16], and multiple variations thereof. Combined with the first-order quantifiers of the LTL-FO$^+$ package, a processing similar to Quantified Event Automata (QEA) [8] is also possible.

5.3 Other Palettes

Among other palettes, we mention:

Gnuplot. This palette allows the conversion of events into input files for the Gnuplot application. For example, an event that is a set of (x, y) coordinates can be transformed into a text file producing a 2D scatterplot of these points. An additional processor can receive these strings of text, call Gnuplot in the background and retrieve its output. The events of the output trace, in this case, are binary strings containing image files.[5]

Tuples. This palette provides the implementation of the named tuple event type. A named tuple is a map between names (i.e. Strings) and arbitrary objects. In addition, the palette includes a few utility functions for manipulating tuples. The `Select` processor allows a tuple to be created by naming and combining the contents of multiple input events. The `From` processor transforms input events from multiple traces into an array (which can be used by `Select`), and the `Where` processor internally duplicates an input trace and sends it into a `Filter` evaluating some function. Combined together, these processors provide the same kind of functionality as the SQL-like SELECT statement of other CEP engines.

XML, JSON and CSV. This palette provides a processor that converts text events into parsed XML documents. It also contains a `Function` object that can evaluate an XPath expression on an XML document. Another palette provides the same functionalities for events in the JSON and the CSV format.

6 Some Examples

In the spirit of BeepBeep's design, processors and functions from multiple palettes can be freely mixed. We end this tutorial by presenting a few examples of how BeepBeep can be used to compute various kinds of properties and queries.

6.1 Numerical Function Processors

As a first example, we will show how Query 5 can be computed using chains of function processors. First, let us calculate the *statistical moment of order* n of a set of values, noted $E^n(x)$. As Fig. 2a shows, the input trace is duplicated into two paths. Along the first path, the sequence of numerical values is sent to the `FunctionProcessor` computing the n-th power of each value; these values are then sent to a `CumulativeProcessor` that calculates the sum of these values. Along the second path, values are sent to a `Mutator` processor that transforms them into the constant 1; these values are then summed into another `CumulativeProcessor`. The corresponding values are divided by each

---

[5] An example of BeepBeep's plotting feature can be seen at: https://www.youtube.com/watch?v=XyPweHGVI9Q.

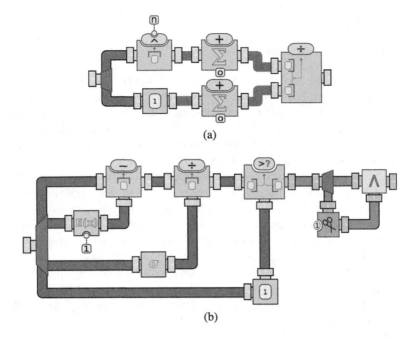

Fig. 2. (a) A chain of function processors for computing the statistical moment of order n on a trace of numerical events; (b) The chain of processors for Query 5

other, which corresponds to the statistical moment of order n of all numerical values received so far. A similar processor chain can be created to compute the standard deviation (i.e. $\sqrt{E^2(x)}$).

Equipped with such a processor chain, the desired property can be evaluated by the graph shown in Fig. 2b. The input trace is divided into four copies. The first copy is subtracted by the statistical moment of order 1 of the second copy, corresponding to the distance of a data point to the mean of all data points that have been read so far. This distance is then divided by the standard deviation (computed form the third copy of the trace). A `FunctionProcessor` then evaluates whether this value is greater than the constant trace with value 2.

The result is a trace of Boolean values. This trace is itself forked into two copies. One of these copies is sent into a `Trim` processor, that removes the first event of the input trace; both paths are sent to a processor computing their logical conjunction. Hence, an output event will have the value $\top$ whenever an input value and the next one are both more than two standard deviations from the mean.

Note how this chain of processors involves events of two different types: turquoise pipes carry events consisting of a single numerical value, while grey pipes contain Boolean events.

6.2   Quantifiers, Trim and XPath Processors

The next example is taken from our previous work on the monitoring of video games [38]. It focuses on the video game *Pingus*, a clone of the popular game *Lemmings*. In this game, individual characters called Pingus can be given skills (Walker, Blocker, Basher, etc.). An instrumented version of the game produces events in XML format at periodic intervals; each event is a snapshot of each character's state (ID, position, skills, velocity).

The property we wish to check is that every time a Walker encounters a Blocker, it must turn around and start walking in the opposite direction. An encounter occurs whenever the (x, y) coordinates of the Walker come within 6 pixels horizontally, and 10 pixels vertically, of some Blocker. When this happens, the Walker may continue walking towards the Blocker for a few more events, but eventually turns around and starts walking away.

Figure 3 shows the processor graph that verifies this. The XML trace is first sent into a universal quantifier. The domain function, represented by the oval at the top, is the evaluation of the XPath expression `//character[status=WALKER]/id/text()` on the current event; this fetches the value of attribute `id` of all characters whose status is `WALKER`. For every such value c, a new instance of the underlying processor will be created, and the context of this processor will be augmented with the association $p_1 \mapsto c$. The underlying processor, in this case, is yet another quantifier. This one fetches the

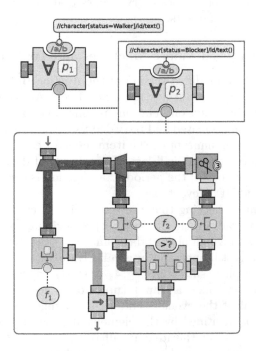

Fig. 3. Processor graph for property "Turn Around"

ID of every BLOCKER, and for each such value c', creates one instance of the underlying processor and adds to its context the association $p_2 \mapsto c'$.

The underlying processor is the graph enclosed in a large box at the bottom. It creates two copies of the input trace. The first goes to the input of a function processor evaluating function f_1 (not shown), on each event. This function evaluates $|x_1 - x_2| < 6 \wedge |y_1 - y_2| < 10$, where x_i and y_i are the coordinates of the Pingu with ID p_i. The resulting function returns a Boolean value, which is true whenever character p_1 collides with p_2.

The second copy of the input trace is duplicated one more time. The first is sent to a function processor evaluating f_2, which computes the horizontal distance between p_1 and p_2. The second is sent to the Trim processor, which is instructed to remove the first three events it receives and lets the others through. The resulting trace is also sent into a function processor evaluating f_2. Finally, the two traces are sent as the input of a function processor evaluating the condition >. Therefore, this processor checks whether the horizontal distance between p_1 and p_2 in the current event is smaller than the same distance three events later. If this is true, then p_1 moved away from p_2 during that interval.

The last step is to evaluate the overall expression. The "collides" Boolean trace is combined with the "moves away" Boolean trace in the Implies processor. For a given event e, the output of this processor will be ⊤ when, if p_1 and p_2 collide in e, then p_1 will have moved away from p_2 three events later.

Note how this property involves a mix of events of various kinds. Blue pipes carry XML events, turquoise pipes carry events that are scalar numbers, and grey pipes contain Boolean events.

6.3 Slicers, Generalized Moore Machines and Tuple Builders

The second example is a modified version of the Auction Bidding property presented in a recent paper introducing Quantified Event Automata (QEA) [8]. It describes a property about bids on items on an online auction site. When an item is being sold an auction is created and recorded using the create_auction(i, m, p) event where m is the minimum price the item named i can be sold for and p is the number of days the auction will last. The passing of days is recorded by a propositional endOfDay event; the period of an auction is over when there have been p number of endOfDay events.

Rather than simply checking that the sequencing of events for each item is followed, we will take advantage of BeepBeep's flexibility to compute a non-Boolean query: the average number of days since the start of the auction, for all items whose auction is still open and in a valid state.

The processor graph is shown in Fig. 4. It starts at the bottom left, with a Slicer processor that takes as input tuples of values. The slicing function is defined in the oval: if the event is endOfDay, it must be sent to all slices; otherwise, the slice is identified by the element at position 1 in the tuple (this corresponds to the name of the item in all other events). For each slice, an instance of a Moore machine will be created, as shown in the top part of the graph.

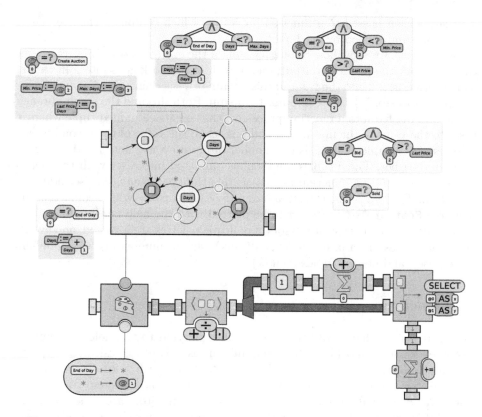

Fig. 4. Processor graph for the "Auction Bidding" query (Color figure online)

Each transition in this Moore machine contains two parts: the top part is a function to evaluate on the input event, to decide whether the transition should fire. The bottom part contains instructions on how to modify the `Context` object of the processor. For example, the top left transition fires if the first element of the event is the string "Create Auction". If so, the transition is taken, and the processor's context is updated with the associations *Last Price* $\mapsto$ 0, *Days* $\mapsto$ 0. The values of *Min. Price* and *Max. Days* are set with the content of the third and fourth element of the tuple, respectively. The remaining transitions take care of updating the minimum price and the number of days elapsed according to the events received.

Each state of the Moore machine is associated with an output value. For three of these states, the value to output is the empty event, meaning that no output should be produced. For the remaining two states, the value to output is the current content of *Days*, as defined in the processor's context.

According to the semantics of the `Slicer`, each output event will consist of a set, formed by the last output of every instance of the Moore machine. Thus, this set will contain the number of elapsed days of all items whose auction is currently open (the Moore machine for the other items outputs no number).

This set is then passed to a function processor, which computes the average of its values (sum divided by cardinality).

As a bonus, we show how to plot a graph of the evolution of this average over time. We fork the previous output; one branch of this fork goes into a `Mutator`, which turns the set into the value 1; this stream of 1 s is then sent to a cumulative function processor Σ_+^0 that computes their sum. Both this and the second branch of the fork are fed into a function processor, that creates a named tuple where x is set to the value of the first input, and y is set to the value of the second input. The result is a tuple where x is the number of input events, and y is the average computed earlier. These tuples are then accumulated into a set with the means of another cumulative function processor, this time performing the set addition operation. The end result is a stream of sets of (x, y) pairs, which could then be sent to a `Scatterplot` processor to be plotted with the help of Gnuplot.

One can see again that processors of multiple palettes are involved, and events of various types are mixed: predicates (pink), sets of numbers (grey), numbers (turquoise), and named tuples (yellow).

7   Conclusion

In this paper, we have presented a short introduction to the field of Complex Event Processing, and highlighted the differences between classical CEP problems and properties typically considered in Runtime Verification. In particular, we have seen how CEP problems involve intricate computations and transformations over data fields inside events, while runtime monitors are generally more powerful for evaluating properties that relate to the sequencing of events.

These observations motivated the development of BeepBeep, an event stream processing engine that attempts to reconcile these two fields. In BeepBeep's generic architecture, basic units of computation called *processors* can be freely composed to evaluate a wide range of expressions. Given an appropriate toolbox of processors, properties involving extended finite-state machines, temporal logic, aggregation and various other concepts can be evaluated. Moreover, through the modular mechanism of *palettes*, end users can easily create their own processors, thereby extending the expressiveness of the tool.

Still, several elements of BeepBeep have not been discussed due to lack of space. To start with, BeepBeep proposes its own declarative input language, eSQL, which provides an alternative to creating processor chains through "glue" code; the detailed exposition of this language, which is still under development, is left for a future publication. Performance is also a key aspect of both RV and CEP; benchmarks have been conducted to compare BeepBeep's throughput with a roster of CEP software on a set of queries; these results are, again, left for a future research paper devoted to the question.

Several research problems around BeepBeep's concepts of processors and event streams are also left unexplored. For example, BeepBeep currently does not support *lazy evaluation*; if the output of an n-ary processor can be determined by looking at fewer than n inputs, all inputs must still be computed and consumed.

Implementing lazy evaluation in a stream processing environment could provide some performance benefits, but is considered at the moment as a non-trivial task. In addition, since each processor represents an independent unit of computation communicating through message passing, chains of processors should be easily amenable to parallelization; whether this would bring tangible improvements in terms of throughput is currently unknown.

In time, it is hoped that BeepBeep will be adopted as a modular framework under which multiple event processing techniques can be developed and coexist, and that their potential for composition will make the sum greater than its parts.

References

1. Esper. http://espertech.com
2. LINQ (language-integrated query). http://msdn.microsoft.com/en-us/library/bb397926.aspx
3. Simple API for XML. http://docs.oracle.com/javaee/1.4/tutorial/doc/JAXPSAX.html. Accessed 13 Dec 2013
4. StreamBase SQL. http://streambase.com
5. VoltDB. http://voltdb.com
6. Abadi, D.J., Ahmad, Y., Balazinska, M., Çetintemel, U., Cherniack, M., Hwang, J.H., Lindner, W., Maskey, A., Rasin, A., Ryvkina, E., Tatbul, N., Xing, Y., Zdonik, S.B.: The design of the Borealis stream processing engine. In: CIDR, pp. 277–289 (2005)
7. Arasu, A., Babcock, B., Babu, S., Cieslewicz, J., Datar, M., Ito, K., Motwani,R., Srivastava, U., Widom, J.: Stream: the stanford data stream management system. Technical report 2004-20, Stanford InfoLab (2004). http://ilpubs.stanford.edu:8090/641/
8. Barringer, H., Falcone, Y., Havelund, K., Reger, G., Rydeheard, D.: Quantified event automata: towards expressive and efficient runtime monitors. In: Giannakopoulou, D., Méry, D. (eds.) FM 2012. LNCS, vol. 7436, pp. 68–84. Springer, Heidelberg (2012). doi:10.1007/978-3-642-32759-9_9
9. Barringer, H., Rydeheard, D.E., Havelund, K.: Rule systems for run-time monitoring: from Eagle to RuleR. J. Log. Comput. **20**(3), 675–706 (2010)
10. Basin, D., Harvan, M., Klaedtke, F., Zălinescu, E.: MONPOLY: monitoring usage-control policies. In: Khurshid, S., Sen, K. (eds.) RV 2011. LNCS, vol. 7186, pp. 360–364. Springer, Heidelberg (2012). doi:10.1007/978-3-642-29860-8_27
11. Basin, D.A., Klaedtke, F., Marinovic, S., Zalinescu, E.: Monitoring of temporal first-order properties with aggregations. Formal Methods Syst. Des. **46**(3), 262–285 (2015). http://dx.doi.org/10.1007/s10703-015-0222-7
12. Berry, A., Milosevic, Z.: Real-time analytics for legacy data streams in health: Monitoring health data quality. In: Gasevic, D., Hatala, M., Nezhad, H.R.M., Reichert, M. (eds.) EDOC, pp. 91–100. IEEE (2013)
13. Bodden, E., Hendren, L.J., Lam, P., Lhoták, O., Naeem, N.A.: Collaborative runtime verification with Tracematches. J. Log. Comput. **20**(3), 707–723 (2010)
14. Brenna, L., Gehrke, J., Hong, M., Johansen, D.: Distributed event stream processing with non-deterministic finite automata. In: Gokhale, A.S., Schmidt, D.C. (eds.) DEBS. ACM (2009)

15. Chandrasekaran, S., Cooper, O., Deshpande, A., Franklin, M.J., Hellerstein, J.M., Hong, W., Krishnamurthy, S., Madden, S., Raman, V., Reiss, F., Shah, M.A.: TelegraphCQ: continuous dataflow processing for an uncertain world. In: CIDR (2003)

16. Cheng, K., Krishnakumar, A.S.: Automatic functional test generation using the-extended finite state machine model. In: DAC, pp. 86–91 (1993). http://doi.acm.org/10.1145/157485.164585

17. Colombo, C., Gauci, A., Pace, G.J.: LarvaStat: monitoring of statistical properties. In: Barringer, H., Falcone, Y., Finkbeiner, B., Havelund, K., Lee, I., Pace, G., Roşu, G., Sokolsky, O., Tillmann, N. (eds.) RV 2010. LNCS, vol. 6418, pp. 480–484. Springer, Heidelberg (2010). doi:10.1007/978-3-642-16612-9_38

18. Colombo, C., Pace, G.J., Schneider, G.: LARVA - safer monitoring of real-time Java programs (tool paper). In: Seventh IEEE International Conference on Software Engineering and Formal Methods (SEFM), pp. 33–37. IEEE Computer Society, November 2009

19. D'Angelo, B., Sankaranarayanan, S., Sánchez, C., Robinson, W., Finkbeiner, B., Sipma, H.B., Mehrotra, S., Manna, Z.: LOLA: runtime monitoring of synchronous systems. In: 12th International Symposium on Temporal Representation and Reasoning (TIME 2005), 23–25 June 2005, Burlington, Vermont, USA, pp. 166–174. IEEE Computer Society (2005). http://dx.doi.org/10.1109/TIME.2005.26

20. Erlingsson, Ú., Pistoia, M. (eds.) Proceedings of the 2008 Workshop on Programming Languages and Analysis for Security, PLAS 2008, Tucson, AZ, USA, June 8, 2008. ACM (2008)

21. Erlingsson, Ú., Schneider, F.B.: IRM enforcement of Java stack inspection. In: IEEE Symposium on Security and Privacy, pp. 246–255 (2000)

22. Fegaras, L., Dash, R.K., Wang, Y.: A fully pipelined XQuery processor. In: XIME-P (2006)

23. Finkbeiner, B., Sankaranarayanan, S., Sipma, H.: Collecting statistics over runtime executions. Formal Methods Syst. Des. **27**(3), 253–274 (2005). http://dx.doi.org/10.1007/s10703-005-3399-3

24. Fry, C., Sagar, D.: Streaming API for XML, JSR 173 specification (2003). https://www.jcp.org/aboutJava/communityprocess/final/jsr173/

25. Goldsmith, S., O'Callahan, R., Aiken, A.: Relational queries over program traces. In: OOPSLA, pp. 385–402 (2005)

26. Hallé, S., Gaboury, S., Bouchard, B.: Towards user activity recognition through energy usage analysis and complex event processing. In: PETRA. ACM (2016)

27. Hallé, S., Varvaressos, S.: A formalization of complex event stream processing. In: Reichert, M., Rinderle-Ma, S., Grossmann, G. (eds.) 18th IEEE International Enterprise Distributed Object Computing Conference, EDOC 2014, Ulm, Germany, September 1–5, 2014, pp. 2–11. IEEE Computer Society (2014). http://dx.doi.org/10.1109/EDOC.2014.12

28. Hallé, S., Villemaire, R.: Runtime monitoring of web service choreographies using streaming XML. In: Shin, S.Y., Ossowski, S. (eds.) SAC, pp. 2118–2125. ACM (2009)

29. Hallé, S., Villemaire, R.: Runtime enforcement of web service message contracts with data. IEEE T. Serv. Comput. **5**(2), 192–206 (2012)

30. Krishnan, R., Goldstein, J., Raizman, A.: A hitchhiker's guide to StreamInsight queries, version 2.1 (2012). http://support.sas.com/documentation/onlinedoc/dfdmstudio/2.4/dfU_ELRG.pdf

31. Luckham, D.C.: The power of events - An introduction to complex event processing in distributed enterprise systems. ACM (2005)

32. Martin, M.C., Livshits, V.B., Lam, M.S.: Finding application errors and security flaws using PQL: a program query language. In: OOPSLA, pp. 365–383 (2005)

33. Meredith, P.O., Jin, D., Griffith, D., Chen, F., Rosu, G.: An overview of the MOP runtime verification framework. STTT **14**(3), 249–289 (2012). http://dx.doi.org/10.1007/s10009-011-0198-6

34. Perera, S., Suhothayan, S., Vivekanandalingam, M., Fremantle, P., Weerawarana, S.: Solving the grand challenge using an opensource CEP engine. In: Bellur,U., Kothari, R. (eds.) The 8th ACM International Conference on Distributed Event-Based Systems, DEBS 2014, Mumbai, India, May 26–29, 2014, pp.288–293. ACM (2014). http://doi.acm.org/10.1145/2611286.2611331

35. Reger, G., Cruz, H.C., Rydeheard, D.: MARQ: monitoring at runtime with QEA. In: Baier, C., Tinelli, C. (eds.) TACAS 2015. LNCS, vol. 9035, pp. 596–610. Springer, Heidelberg (2015). doi:10.1007/978-3-662-46681-0_55

36. Rodrigues, J.: Health Information Systems: Concepts, Methodologies, Tools, and Applications, vol. 1. IGI Global, Hershey (2010)

37. Stolz, V., Bodden, E.: Temporal assertions using AspectJ. Electr. Notes Theor. Comput. Sci. **144**(4), 109–124 (2006)

38. Varvaressos, S., Lavoie, K., Gaboury, S., Hallé, S.: Automated bug finding in video games: A case study for runtime monitoring. ACM Computers in Entertainment (2014, in press)

39. Wu, E., Diao, Y., Rizvi, S.: High-performance complex event processing over streams. In: Chaudhuri, S., Hristidis, V., Polyzotis, N. (eds.) SIGMOD Conference, pp. 407–418. ACM (2006)

Frama-C, A Collaborative Framework for C Code Verification: Tutorial Synopsis

Nikolai Kosmatov and Julien Signoles[(✉)]

CEA, LIST, Software Reliability and Security Laboratory, PC 174,
91191 Gif-sur-Yvette, France
{nikolai.kosmatov,julien.signoles}@cea.fr

Abstract. Frama-C is a source code analysis platform that aims at conducting verification of industrial-size C programs. It provides its users with a collection of plug-ins that perform static and dynamic analysis for safety- and security-critical software. Collaborative verification across cooperating plug-ins is enabled by their integration on top of a shared kernel, and their compliance to a common specification language, ACSL.

This paper presents a three-hour tutorial on Frama-C in which we provide a comprehensive overview of its most important plug-ins: the abstract-interpretation based plug-in Value, the deductive verification tool WP, the runtime verification tool E-ACSL and the test generation tool PathCrawler. We also emphasize different possible collaborations between these plug-ins and a few others. The presentation is illustrated on concrete examples of C programs.

Keywords: Frama-C · ACSL · Abstract interpretation · Deductive verification · Runtime verification · Test generation · Combinations of analyses

1 Introduction

The last few decades have seen much of the groundwork of formal software analysis being laid. Several angles and theoretical avenues have been explored, from deductive verification to abstract interpretation to program transformation to monitoring to concolic testing. While much remains to be done from an academic standpoint, these techniques have become mature enough to have been successfully implemented and used in industrial settings [1].

However, although verification of C programs is of paramount importance because the C programming language is still the language of choice for developing safety-critical systems and is also routinely used for security-based applications, verifying large C programs remains a time-consuming and challenging task. One of the reasons is related to the C programming language itself since it combines high level features like arrays and low level features like user-controlled memory allocations, bitfields and unions. Another reason comes from weaknesses

This work has received funding for the S3P project from French DGE and BPIFrance.

Y. Falcone and C. Sanchez (Eds.): RV 2016, LNCS 10012, pp. 92–115, 2016.
DOI: 10.1007/978-3-319-46982-9_7

of each verification technique: dynamic techniques are not bothered by C code complexity but are not exhaustive, abstract interpretation is exhaustive and almost automatic but may be imprecise and cannot verify complex functional properties, while deductive methods may tackle a broad varieties of properties but require formal specifications and may be less efficient in presence of low level code. One effective way to circumvent this problem is to combine several analyses in order to reduce weaknesses of each one thanks to the others. For instance, abstract interpretation can ensure the absence of most runtime errors, deductive verification can prove most functional properties, while monitoring can check at runtime the remaining properties. Such analysis combinations is the *raison d'être* of FRAMA-C.

The FRAMA-C software analysis platform [2] provides a collection of scalable, interoperable, and sound software analyses for the industrial analysis of ISO C99 source code. The platform is based on a kernel which hosts analyzers as collaborating plug-ins and uses the ACSL formal specification language [3] as a lingua franca. FRAMA-C includes plug-ins based on abstract interpretation, deductive verification, monitoring and test case generation, as well as a series of derived plug-ins which build elaborate analyses upon the basic ones. This large variety of analysis techniques and its unique collaboration capabilities make FRAMA-C most suitable for developing new code analyzers and applying code analysis techniques in many academic and industrial projects.

This article is a companion paper of a 3-h tutorial which brings participants to a journey into the FRAMA-C world along its main plug-ins. It aims at providing the essence of each technique and tool along with a few illustrating examples. While several tutorials about some parts of FRAMA-C have already been presented in previous conferences [4–8], none of them have already presented all these techniques altogether. Here, after a general overview of FRAMA-C (Sect. 2), we present deductive verification tool WP [2,9] (Sect. 3), abstract interpretation based plug-in VALUE [2,10] and its recent redesign EVA (Sect. 4), the runtime verification tool E-ACSL [11,12] (Sect. 5) and the test generation tool PathCrawler [13,14] (Sect. 6). A last section is dedicated to some of their possible collaborations (Sect. 7).

2 Overview of FRAMA-C

FRAMA-C is a platform which aims at analyzing source code written in ISO C99. This code may be annotated with formal specifications written in the ACSL formal specification language [3] (presented in Sect. 3). Recently FRAMA-CLANG has been released as a prototype FRAMA-C extension to handle C++ code. The platform is written in OCAML [15] and based on a plug-in architecture [16]: each analyzer is a plug-in which is linked against the FRAMA-C kernel.

The kernel provides a normalized representation of C programs and ACSL specifications. In addition, the kernel provides several general services for supporting plug-in development and providing convenient features to FRAMA-C's end-users. For instance, messages, source code and annotations are uniformly

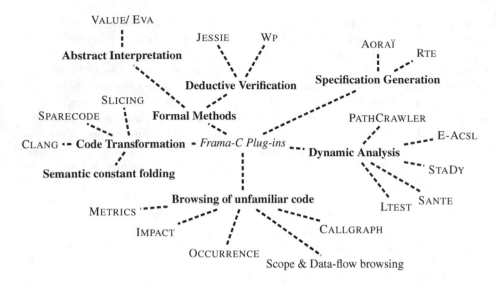

Fig. 1. FRAMA-C plug-in gallery

displayed, whereas parameters and command line options are homogeneously handled. The kernel also allows plug-ins to collaborate with each other either sequentially or in parallel. Sequential collaboration consists in a chain of analyses that perform operations one after another, while parallel collaboration combines partial analysis results from several analyzers to complete a full program verification. Examples of collaborations will be provided in Sect. 7. In particular, the kernel consolidates analysis results to provide the users with a synthesis of what is proven and ensure logical consistency when verifying dependent properties: the proof of a property P by analyzer A may depend on the validity of another property Q whose proof is done by analyzer B [17].

The FRAMA-C kernel is open source (under LGPL v2.1), as well as many of its plug-ins. Several plug-ins are presented in Fig. 1. Many important plug-ins are dedicated to program verification. First, FRAMA-C comes with a powerful abstract interpretation framework based on VALUE, which aims at computing over-approximations of possible values of program variables at each program point. VALUE is presented in Sect. 4. Next, FRAMA-C provides two alternative plug-ins for deductive verification: JESSIE (which is now deprecated) and WP. These plug-ins aim at verifying that a given C code satisfies its specification expressed as ACSL annotations. ACSL language and WP plug-in are presented in Sect. 3. Finally, FRAMA-C provides dynamic verification through the E-ACSL plug-in which aims at verifying annotations at runtime. This plug-in is presented in Sect. 5. Another dynamic tool, PATHCRAWLER [1] is dedicated to test

---

[1] unlike many other FRAMA-C analyzers, PATHCRAWLER is currently not open source but is available through the online test generation service http://pathcrawler-online. com.

case generation and is presented in Sect. 6. Plug-ins SANTE, STADY and LTEST implement different collaborations between static and dynamic analyses. They are introduced in Sect. 7.

Other plug-ins are not directly program verifiers. Some of them aim at helping the users to better understand a source code they are not familiar with: plug-in METRICS computes some useful metrics about the code, plug-in OCCURRENCES displays in the FRAMA-C GUI all occurrences of a particular left-value (taking into account aliasing), while a few other plug-ins compute scope and dataflow dependency information. Plug-in CALLGRAPH computes the callgraph, taking into consideration function pointers as soon as VALUE has been executed.

Some plug-ins perform program transformations. Plug-in SEMANTIC CONSTANT FOLDING replaces constant variables by their numerical values and propagates them along the dataflow by taking into account aliasing. Plug-in SLICING simplifies the code by removing code fragments that are irrelevant with respect to a given program property (e.g. preserve the effects of a particular statement). Plug-in SPARECODE can be seen as a particular case of SLICING which removes dead code. Plug-in IMPACT computes the values and statements impacted (directly or transitively) by the side effects of a given statement. It is the forward counterpart of the usual (backward) slicing, but it does not necessarily generate a new program: by default it just highlights the impacted statement.

FRAMA-C also allows analyzers to generate new ACSL annotations which encode specific properties. Plug-in AORAÏ takes as input a Büchi automaton or an LTL formula and generates ACSL annotations which encode the corresponding temporal property that can be verified by other means. In the same spirit, plug-in RTE generates an ACSL annotation for every possible undefined behavior of the source code. For instance, it generates a guard $y \neq 0$ before a division by y in the source code.

3   Specification and Deductive Verification with FRAMA-C/Wp

3.1   Specification of C Programs with ACSL

ACSL (ANSI/ISO C Specification Language) [3] is a formal behavioral specification language offered by FRAMA-C and shared by different FRAMA-C analyzers. It allows its users to specify functional properties of C programs similarly to Eiffel [18] and JML [19]. It is based on the notion of function contract. The *contract* of a function f specifies the preconditions that are supposed to be true before a call of f (i.e. ensured by the caller), and the postconditions that should be satisfied after the call of f (and should be thus established during the verification of f). The preconditions are specified in **requires** clauses, while the postconditions are stated in **ensures** clauses. An additional type of postconditions, specified in an **assigns** clause in ACSL and used for the so-called *frame rule*, states a list of locations of the global memory state that may have a different value before and after the call. When the contract of f contains such a clause, all locations that

```
1 /*@ requires n ≥ 0 && \valid(t+(0..n-1));
2       assigns \nothing;
3       ensures \result ≠ 0 ⟺
4           (\forall integer j; 0 ≤ j < n ⟹ t[j] == 0);
5 */
6 int all_zeros(int *t, int n) {
7    int k=0;
8    /*@ loop invariant 0 ≤ k ≤ n;
9        loop invariant \forall integer j; 0 ≤ j < k ⟹ t[j] == 0;
10       loop assigns k;
11       loop variant n-k;
12   */
13   while(k < n){
14     if (t[k] ≠ 0)
15       return 0;
16     k++;
17   }
18   return 1;
19 }
```

Fig. 2. Function `all_zeros` specified in ACSL (file `all_zeros.c`).

are not mentioned in it must have the same value before and after the call of f. Function contracts can be also represented in the form of different behaviors.

Predicates used in annotations are written in typed first-order logic. Variables have either a C type or a logical type (e.g. `integer` or `real` for mathematical integer or real numbers). The user can define custom functions and predicates and use them in annotations together with ACSL built-ins. Indeed, ACSL features its own functions and predicates to describe memory states. In particular, regarding memory-related properties, `\valid(p)` expresses validity of a pointer p (i.e. being a non-null pointer which can be safely accessed by the program); `\base_addr(p)`, `\block_length(p)`, and `\offset(p)` express respectively the base address, the size of the memory block containing p and the offset of p inside it (in bytes), while `\initialized(p)` is true whenever the pointed location *p has been initialized. We refer the reader to [3] for detailed documentation of all ACSL features.

Example of Specifications. Figure 2 illustrates a C function `all_zeros` specified in ACSL. This function receives as arguments an array t and its size n and checks whether all elements of the array are zeros. If yes, it returns a nonzero value, and 0 otherwise. The function contract contains a precondition (line 1) and postconditions (lines 2–4). The precondition states that the input array contains n valid memory locations at indices 0..(n-1) that can be safely read or written, and that the size n is non negative. This property must be ensured by the caller and should be thus specified in the precondition. The `assigns` clause at line 2 states that the function is not allowed to modify any non-local variable. Without this clause, an erroneous implementation writing zeros in all elements

```
1 /*@ requires len ≥ 0 && \valid(t+(0..len-1));
2     assigns \nothing;
3     behavior present:
4       assumes \exists integer i; 0 ≤ i < len && t[i] == elt;
5       ensures 0 ≤ \result < len && t[\result] == elt;
6     behavior absent:
7       assumes \forall integer i; 0 ≤ i < len ⟹ t[i] ≠ elt;
8       ensures \result == -1;
9     disjoint behaviors;
10    complete behaviors;
11  */
12 extern int find_value(int *t, int len, int elt);
```

Fig. 3. Function `find_value` specified in ACSL.

of the array and returning 1 would be considered correct with respect to the contract. Finally, the clause at lines 3–4 states that the result is nonzero if and only if all elements of the array are equal to zero. The loop contract at lines 8–12 will be discussed in the next section.

Figure 3 provides another example of a specified function. This function is only declared and takes as arguments an array `t` of size `n` and some element `elt`. It must return an index `i` such than `t[i]` = `elt`, or −1 if there is no such index. The precondition (line 1) and the `assigns` clause (line 2) are similar to the ones of the function `all_zeros`. The postcondition is expressed through two named behaviors. They correspond to the two different cases of the contract. First, the behavior **present** states that, if the searched element `elt` is present in the array (line 4), the function's result is an index with the expected property (line 5). The behavior **absent** corresponds to the opposite case (line 7). In that case, the function returns −1 (line 8). Additionally the `disjoint behaviors` clause states that these behaviors are mutually exclusive (line 9), while the `complete behaviors` clause indicates that their cover all the possible cases of the function (line 10). In other words, being both disjoint and complete guarantees that one and only one behavior applies at each function call.

3.2 Deductive Verification with FRAMA-C/Wp

Among other formal software verification techniques, deductive program verification consists in establishing a rigorous mathematical proof that a given program respects its specification. When no confusion is possible, one also says for short that deductive verification consists in "proving a program". The weakest precondition calculus proposed by Dijkstra [20] reduces any deductive verification problem to establishing the validity of first-order formulas called *verification conditions*. The WP plug-in [2,9] of FRAMA-C performs weakest precondition calculus for deductive verification of C programs. Various automatic SMT solvers, such as Alt-Ergo, CVC4 and Z3, can be used to prove the verification conditions generated by WP.

Example of Proof. Let us illustrate deductive verification with WP on the example of Fig. 2. The command `frama-c-gui -wp all_zeros.c` runs the proof with WP on this example and shows the results in the FRAMA-C GUI. Suppose first that the user has specified the contract at lines 1–4 without writing the loop contract at lines 8–12. In this case, the proof of the postcondition will not be successful. Indeed, in presence of loops, since the number of loop iterations is unknown, the deductive verification tool requires a *loop invariant*, i.e. an additional property on the program state that is true before the loop and after each complete loop iteration. It can be specified in a loop contract using `loop invariant` and `loop assigns` clauses. The clause at line 8 specifies the interval of values of the loop variable k. The clause at line 9 specifies that all elements at indices `0..(k-1)` are equal to 0 (that is indeed true after any complete loop iteration otherwise the loop execution was interrupted at line 15). Similarly to `assigns`, the `loop assigns` clause specifies the variables (but both global and local ones in this case) that may change their value during the loop. The loop contract can also contain a `loop variant`, which defines a decreasing natural measure corresponding to an upper bound of the number of remaining loop iterations and is used to prove that the loop terminates. In this example, `n-k` provides such a bound (cf. line 11).

On the complete program of Fig. 2 with the loop contract, WP successfully proves that this function respects its specification. In addition, it is possible to make WP check the absence of runtime errors using the option `-wp-rte`. In this case, thanks to the array validity assumed at line 1 and the interval of values specified at line 8, WP successfully proves that array access at line 14 is valid and the arithmetic operation at line 16 does not overflow (Fig. 4).

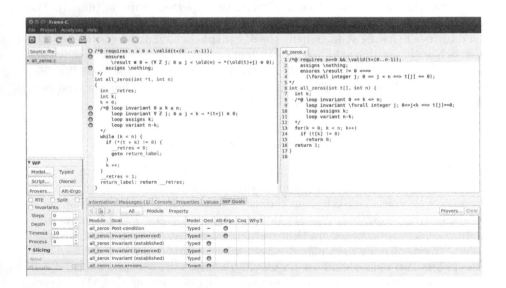

Fig. 4. Successful proof for the program of Fig. 2 with FRAMA-C/WP.

WP's *Models.* Deductive methods rely on *models.* For C programs, arithmetic models provide abstract representations of machine integers and/or floats, while memory models are abstractions of the program memory. These models are a trade-off between simplicity (making proof more automatic) and expressivity (being able to deal with more properties or programs at the price of making proof harder). WP's internal engine is generic, tries to simplify verification conditions and does not depend on a particular model [21]. WP actually comes with several different arithmetic and memory models. For arithmetics, the users can choose between mathematical integers or machine integers and between real numbers or floats. Machine integers make proofs easier, but the user must ensure the absence of integer overflows by other means (usually by using the -wp-rte option). Using reals converts float operations to real ones without rounding (that is unsafe with respect to norms, but tractable), while the float model introduces correct rounding but the proofs are rarely automatic and often require the use of a proof assistant (like Coq or PVS).

The WP's *Hoare* memory model, directly inspired by the historic definition of weakest precondition calculus, is very simple. However, it assumes a program with no pointer to be sound. A common programming C pattern is nevertheless to use pointers for function arguments passed by reference. In such cases, their adresses are never taken and so they are not aliased if they were not aliased when calling the function. Thus, it remains safe to use the a *Hoare*-like model: that is the purpose of the *Reference Parameters* model (shortly *Ref*). The last provided model is the *Typed* model which allows powerful reasoning on heap data. The special mode *Typed+Ref* uses the *Typed* model for expressiveness but is automatically able to detect when using the simpler *Ref* model is safe (making the proof more automatic).

For additional detail on specification with ACSL and deductive verification with WP, the reader may refer to articles [2, 21], dedicated tutorials [6, 22] and the WP manual [9].

4   Value Analysis with FRAMA-C/VALUE and EVA

The Value Analysis plug-in of FRAMA-C (VALUE for short) [10] automatically computes sets of possibles values for the variables of an analyzed program at each program point, by means of abstract interpretation [23]. It also warns about potential runtime errors. These objectives and means are shared with commercial tools like Polyspace [24] or Astrée [25]. However, VALUE has also distinct goals. First, it is *not* application directed: it aims at being directly usable on any C code in any applicative domain, from low level system libraries to safety-critical applications.[2] One consequence is that VALUE relies on an efficient generic domain which can nevertheless be less precise than specific domains designed for specific code like digital filters [26]. This drawback is circumvented by the FRAMA-C

---

[2] This goal is not yet reached but progress is regularly made in that direction and it is still an objective (which is not shared by other widely used tools, as far as we know).

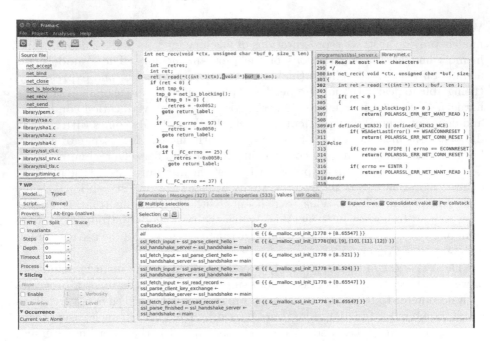

Fig. 5. FRAMA-C GUI with VALUE's results on PolarSSL's function `net_recv`. It displays the possible values of the function's parameter `buf` *per* callstack.

ecosystem: what cannot be proven by VALUE may still be proven by another plug-in, possibly a dedicated one.

Another originality of VALUE comes from its presence in the FRAMA-C ecosystem: one would like to reuse what it has computed in other plug-ins. Consequently, VALUE keeps the computed possible values of each variable of the program at each program point. This information is available in the FRAMA-C GUI and helps the user to better understand VALUE's results. An illustrative example for PolarSSL 1.1.7[3] is presented in Fig. 5. It also allows derived analyses like slicing to be sound. In particular it helps them to safely interpret function pointers and to find out potential aliasing. In this way, several plug-ins have been developed by academic and industrial users for specific goals in a safe way without spending too much time with pointer intricacies [27–30].

Abstract Domains. VALUE has hard-coded domains which can not be changed easily. They have been chosen for their good compromise between precision and efficiency and rely on heavily optimized datastructures and algorithms [31].

Integers are represented either by an exact set of possible values (when such a set remains small), or by intervals with congruence information (when the set of possible values becomes large). For example, an `int` variable could have values in the domain `[1..41],1,%2`, which means any positive odd integer smaller or

---

[3] See https://tls.mbed.org/.

equal to 41. Congruence is of particular interest to express offset properties like "the pointer p is a 32-bit aligned offset from &t[0]". Note that this domain is *not* relational: it does not keep any relation between program variables. For instance, if $x = y$, VALUE only knows that both variables have the same possible set of values (say, the interval $[a; b]$). It does not know that x and y have the same value in $[a; b]$.

Floating points are represented by IEEE 754 double-precision finite intervals. Rounding is performed when necessary (e.g. from simple-precision floats to double-precision). Infinities and NaN are considered as undesirable errors and reported as such.

Pointers are seen as a pair of a base address and an offset. This way, it is possible to verify the absence of buffer overflow by checking that the offset is positive and smaller than the size of the base. Consequently, VALUE's abstract representation of a pointer is a set of possible base addresses associated with possible offsets (in bytes). A base address can be either the address of a local or global variable, the address of a function formal parameter, the address of a literal string constant, or the special NULL base which is used to encode absolute addresses (denoted by their offsets). For instance, let P be a global pointer and t be a local array of 16-bit integers. Then a pointer Q could have values in the set { NULL; &P[0..24],0%8; &t[4..10],0%2 }. It means that pointer Q is either null, or equal to pointer P with an offset (in bytes) divisible by 8 between 0 and 24, or refers to one of the cells t[2],...,t[5].

In addition to one of the above-mentioned abstract values, VALUE associates to each memory location a flag which indicates if its contents may contain an indeterminate value like uninitialized local variables (ISO C99 standard [32], Sect. 6.2.4). Having a memory location containing such a value is not an error *per se* but accessing it is. The abstract memory representation maps each base address to a size and a chunk of memory cells. Each chunk itself maps a consecutive range of bits to abstract values. This representation is untyped and so can precisely interpret unions, bitfields and heterogeneous pointer conversions.

Parameterization. Abstract interpreters are automatic tools. However they rarely give useful results when running from scratch on a new large C program, because the analysis quickly diverges due to approximations. These tools always need parameterization to get more precise tractable results while consuming a decent amount of resources (computation time and computer memory). VALUE has a large variety of parameters [10], two of which are presented below.

The most important one is named slevel. It is an instance of trace partitioning [33] and, in particular, allows the user to unroll loops up to a certain limit. It may be set per loop, per function or for the whole program. Instead of having a single analysis state that approximates all the values of all possible executions, it allows the analysis to keep up to n separated states in parallel, which improves precision.

Another important way of parameterization is case splitting through ACSL trivial disjunctions (and slevel). Consider the following simple example.

```
1 /*@ ensures \result ≥ 0; */
2 int f(char x) {
3    if (x == 0) return 0;
4    else return x * x;
5 }
```

Without case splitting, VALUE is not able to prove the function's postcondition. Indeed, since VALUE is not relational and x may take any value from -128 to 127, it can only conclude that the returned value at line 4 belongs to the interval $[-16256..16384]$. However, the user may introduce the trivial assertion /*@ assert x <0 || x ==0 || x >0; */ before line 3 and set slevel to 3. This way, VALUE will split the 3 cases of the disjunctive predicate and keep them separated. In each case, it is able to verify the postcondition[4]. Of course, it is also able to prove the newly introduced trivial assertion. Interestingly, case splitting and aggressive trace partitioning often compensate for the absence of relational domains. It is true in this simple example, and it remains true in much larger applications.

Eva: Evolved Value Analysis. Since the very last open source release of FRAMA-C (namely, FRAMA-C Aluminium), an Evolved version of VALUE, named EVA, is available. It aims at reconciling the variety of target programs of VALUE with application-specific abstract domains, which allows to improve precision and/or efficiency in particular cases. Consequently, EVA transforms VALUE from a monolithic analyzer with hard-coded domains to a generic extendable analysis parameterized by cooperating abstract domains. In FRAMA-C Aluminium, the focus was made on supporting the very same domains as in VALUE for compatibility: case studies demonstrate that EVA gets comparable analysis time for better results. New domains will be introduced in the next releases of FRAMA-C, like support for Apron's domains [34] and Venet's Gauge [35].

5   Runtime Verification with FRAMA-C/E-ACSL

FRAMA-C was initially designed as a static analysis platform. Later on, it was extended to provide dynamic analysis tools as well. First, PATHCRAWLER, a preexisting test case generation tool (presented in Sect. 6), has been partially rewritten to become a FRAMA-C plug-in. Second, a runtime verification tool, namely E-ACSL, has been implemented as a FRAMA-C plug-in. The E-ACSL tool is the purpose of this section.

Since FRAMA-C was originally oriented towards static verification, ACSL has the same bias. In particular, it is based on mathematical logic that cannot be dynamically verified in its entirety. Consequently, an "executable" subset of this specification language has been designed, in which each annotation has an executable meaning. This specification language is also called E-ACSL ("E" stands

---

[4] Interval arithmetic guarantees that the product of two numbers of the same sign is positive here.

for "executable"). Given a C program p annotated in E-ACSL, the FRAMA-C plug-in E-ACSL generates another C program which observationally behaves like p if each annotation is satisfied, or reports the first failing annotation and exits otherwise. Section 5.1 introduces the annotation language, while Sect. 5.2 presents an overview of the tool.

5.1 E-ACSL Specification Language

The E-ACSL specification language [11,36] is a large strict subset of ACSL. It excludes ACSL constructs which have no significance at runtime. For instance, it includes neither mathematical lemmas nor axiomatics. There is no termination property as well, for example, to specify that a function does not terminate: it could not be verified in finite time at runtime. However, loop variants and `decreases` clauses—which are respectively used to prove termination of loops and recursive functions by specifying a measure which strictly decreases at each iteration/invocation—are still present because their verification only depends on (at most) two previous loop/function body runs.

Quantifications. The most important restriction of E-ACSL is certainly that every quantified variable must be syntactically bounded to a finite interval (whose bounds are not necessarily constant). For instance, if `arr` is an array of `len` cells, the predicate

$$\texttt{\\forall integer i; } 0{\leq}\texttt{i}{<}\texttt{len} \implies \texttt{arr[i]}{>}0 \tag{1}$$

means that every cell of `arr` is positive. However, because of an unbounded quantification over x, the ACSL predicate `\forall integer x, (2*x)%2 == 0` (stating that every even integer is dividable by 2) does not belong to the E-ACSL language. This restriction is not a strong limitation in practice because quantifications in program properties are usually constrained by the program context.

Integers. Example (1) of the previous paragraph illustrates that E-ACSL also supports mathematical integers in the same way as ACSL: E-ACSL remains compatible with tools supporting ACSL (in particular, other FRAMA-C plug-ins). It is still possible to use modular arithmetic in specifications through casts. For instance, the term `(int)(INT_MAX+1)` is interpreted as `INT_MIN`.[5] Although mathematical integers make the runtime verification harder, they can be safely implemented by using machine integers in almost all practical cases (see Sect. 5.2).

---

[5] Unlike the ISO C99 standard, ACSL and E-ACSL explicitly specify the semantics of cast overflows through modular interpretations (see ACSL reference manual [3, Sect. 2.2.4]).

Undefinedness. The most important change with respect to ACSL is the introduction of undefined terms and predicates *à la* Chalin [37] through tri-valued logic. Indeed, undefined terms like 1/0 would lead to an undefined C behavior if executed, while they introduce no issue in static tools: these tools just cannot prove any non-trivial property containing such terms except tautologies like 1/0==1/0 (by commutativity of equality). The E-ACSL semantics of such terms and predicates is undefined in order to overcome this issue.

Another important source of undefinedness is memory accesses like *p and t[i]. Tools supporting the E-ACSL language must ensure that undefined terms and predicates are never evaluated. Section 5.2 explains how our FRAMA-C plug-in handles them. In order to limit the impact of undefinedness, logical operators like &&, || and ⟹ are lazy in E-ACSL. For instance, the interpretation of n≠0 && 10/n==m is always well-defined. This semantics change remains nevertheless consistent with the original ACSL semantics: for any E-ACSL predicate p, if p is valid (resp. invalid) in ACSL then p is either valid (resp. invalid) or undefined in E-ACSL. Conversely, if p is valid (resp. invalid) in E-ACSL then p is also valid (resp. invalid) in ACSL. This fundamental property ensures tool compatibility between ACSL and E-ACSL.

5.2   E-ACSL Inline Monitoring Tool

The FRAMA-C plug-in E-ACSL is a program transformation tool: it takes as input a C program p annotated with E-ACSL specifications and generates another C program which observationally behaves like p if each annotation is satisfied, or stops on the first failing annotation otherwise. In other words, E-ACSL generates an *online* (more precisely, *inline*) monitor [38] for a C program based on its formal specification. This inline monitor is heavily optimized: E-ACSL got the second place of the first Competition of Runtime Verification tool (CRV) in 2014 [39], then won the second competition in 2015 (in the category of online monitoring of C programs in both cases).

Figure 6 shows how simple the E-ACSL transformation looks like in simple cases[6]: it mainly converts an ACSL assertion into an executable assertion through the use of a dedicated C function e_acsl_assert[7] which behaves by default in the same way as the standard C macro assert and can be customized by the end-user. However, a closer look at this simple example illustrates that the transformation is not as easy as it may sound. Indeed, E-ACSL generates long long integers 1LL and 0LL in order to perform the computation in this (bigger) type and ensure the absence of int overflows in y-1.[8] This section proposes a short overview of the transformation scheme which allows E-ACSL to generate efficient-but-sound code.

---

[6] The generated code shown in this paper is compliant with a 64-bit x86 architecture.

[7] It actually takes additional arguments in order to provide informative user feedback when a property is violated. They are omitted for clarity.

[8] The C99 semantics of subtraction ensures that, in the generated code, y is converted to long long through the usual arithmetic conversion before computing the subtraction (see ISO C99 standard [32, Sects. 6.3.1.8 and 6.5.6]).

```
int div(int x, int y) {           int div(int x, int y) {
  /*@ assert y-1 ≠ 0; */            /*@ assert y-1 ≠ 0; */
  return x/(y-1);                   e_acsl_assert(y-1LL ≠ 0LL);
}                                   return x/(y-1);
                                  }
```

Fig. 6. Naive E-ACSL translation. Original code (left) *vs.* translated code (right).

```
1  int div(int x, int y) {
2    /*@ assert y-1 ≠ 0; */
3    mpz_t e_acsl_y, e_acsl_1, e_acsl_sub, e_acsl__2;
4    int e_acsl_ne;
5    mpz_init_set_si(e_acsl_y,(long)y);         // e_acsl_y = y
6    mpz_init_set_si(e_acsl_1,1L);              // e_acsl_1 = 1
7    mpz_init(e_acsl_sub);
8    mpz_sub(e_acsl_sub, e_acsl_y, e_acsl_1);  // e_acsl_sub = y-1
9    mpz_init_set_si(e_acsl__2,0L);             // e_acsl_2 = 0
10   e_acsl_ne = mpz_cmp(e_acsl_sub, e_acsl__2); // y-1 == 0
11   e_acsl_assert(e_acsl_ne ≠ 0);                 // runtime check
12   mpz_clear(e_acsl_y); mpz_clear(e_acsl_1);    // deallocations
13   mpz_clear(e_acsl_sub); mpz_clear(e_acsl__2);
14   return x/(y-1);
15 }
```

Fig. 7. Translation of function div by using GMP.

Implementing Mathematical Integers. E-ACSL uses the GMP library[9] in order to implement mathematical integers. For instance, Fig. 7 presents the generated code for the previous example of function div when forcing E-ACSL to use GMP for integer operations. GMP integers are actually pointers that must be allocated and deallocated. In the example, lines 5–7 and 9 allocate (and initialize at the same time) four GMP integers, while lines 12–13 free them. Integer operations are performed through function calls. In our example, the subtraction is computed at line 8 and the comparison is done at line 10. The runtime check at line 11 consists in checking the result of this comparison.

Although safe, this translation scheme through GMP is quite heavy and inefficient: compare it with the direct translation scheme presented in Fig. 6 to see how more complex it is. Doing this GMP translation for every integer operation is not practical, but it allows us to translate any mathematical operations in a safe way. Consequently, E-ACSL implements a (sub-)type system based on interval inference which infers, for every integer term, the smallest C type that may contain all its possible values [11,40]. It is either a C integral type or a GMP. In our div example, it allows E-ACSL to safely use the type long long to perform the subtraction without overflow. Our experiments have demonstrated that almost no GMP code is generated by E-ACSL, except if the initial code does

---

[9] See http://gmplib.org/.

```
int foo(int u, int v) {            int foo(int u, int v) {
  /*@ assert u/v == 2; */   E-ACSL    /*@ assert u/v == 2; */
  return u/v;               ────────→  e_acsl_assert(u/v == 2);
}                                      return u/v;
                                     }
```

```
                                            │ RTE plug-in
                                            ↓
```

```
int foo(int u, int v) {            int foo(int u, int v) {
  /*@ assert v != 0; */              /*@ assert v != 0; */
  e_acsl_assert(v != 0);             /*@ assert u/v == 2; */
  /*@ assert u/v == 2; */ ←          e_acsl_assert(u/v == 2);
  e_acsl_assert(u/v == 2);  E-ACSL   return u/v;
  return u/v;                      }
}
```

Fig. 8. Preventing runtime errors in the code generated from specifications.

contain (signed or unsigned) long long integers. It is worth noting that AdaCore has adapted this solution to **SPARK 2014** in order to allow its users to specify mathematical properties without worrying about overflows while preserving efficiency at runtime.

Preventing Undefined Behaviors. In Sect. 5.1, we have said that every tool which aims at supporting the E-ACSL language must ensure that undefined terms and predicates are never executed. To reach this goal, the E-ACSL plug-in relies on the FRAMA-C plug-in RTE. As explained in Sect. 2, this plug-in generates an ACSL annotation with a guard to prevent every possible undefined behavior of the source code. All the annotations generated by RTE are actually E-ACSL-compliant and the RTE's API allows a developer to generate such annotations for a particular code fragment (for example, a C expression).

Consequently, when generating some code fragment C, E-ACSL asks RTE to generate annotations to prevent undefined behavior in C. Then it converts them into additional code fragment C' thanks to its own translator. No recursion is required because RTE's generated annotations never contain undefined terms or predicates: C' is always free of undefined behaviors. Figure 8 illustrates this translation scheme on a simple example: when translating the predicate u/v==2, E-ACSL generates an annotation v $\neq$ 0 thanks to the RTE plug-in. This extra annotation is then turned into C code by E-ACSL itself.

Supporting Memory-Related Constructs. An important feature of E-ACSL is memory-related constructs (introduced in Sect. 3.1), which allow the users to express complex properties about program memory. In particular, the RTE plug-in may use them to generate annotations preventing memory-related errors like dereferencing an invalid pointer: if the RTE plug-in has been executed on the original code in order to generate annotations for possible undefined behaviors, E-ACSL may be used to detect them at runtime.

```
 1  int main(void) {
 2    int x, y, z, *p;
 3    // local variable allocations
 4    __store_block(&p, 4U);
 5    __store_block(&z, 4U);                          // useless
 6    __store_block(&y, 4U);                          // useless
 7    __store_block(&x, 4U);
 8    __full_init(&p);  // initialization of p
 9    p = &x;
10    __full_init(&x);  // initialization of x  // useless
11    x = 0;
12    __full_init(&y);  // initialization of y  // useless
13    y = 1;
14    __full_init(&z);  // initialization de z  // useless
15    z = 2;
16  /*@ assert \valid(p); */
17    // runtime check
18    {
19      int __e_acsl_initialized;
20      int __e_acsl_and;
21      __e_acsl_initialized = __initialized((void *)(&
            p),sizeof(int *));
22      if (__e_acsl_initialized) {
23        int __e_acsl_valid;
24        __e_acsl_valid = __valid((void *)p, sizeof(int));
25        __e_acsl_and = __e_acsl_valid;
26      }
27      else __e_acsl_and = 0;
28      e_acsl_assert(__e_acsl_and);
29    }
30    *p = 3;
31    // memory deallocation
32    __delete_block(&p);
33    __delete_block(&z);                             // useless
34    __delete_block(&y);                             // useless
35    __delete_block(&x);
36    return 0;
37  }
```

Fig. 9. E-ACSL memory instrumentation.

In the general case, handling such constructs requires to query the program memory at runtime, for instance, to check whether some data has been fully initialized, to get the length of a memory block, or to get the offset of a pointer from its base address. For this purpose, E-ACSL comes with its own memory runtime library (mRTL) to be linked against the generated code [41]. This code records program memory modifications in a dedicated mRTL datastore, which can then be queried to evaluate memory-related E-ACSL constructs. Figure 9 shows such an instrumentation: memory allocations, deallocations and initializations are stored in the mRTL store, and checking an assertion requires to query the store.

However, this instrumentation is expensive: it is desirable to avoid it whenever possible. In our example, every line marked as *useless* is indeed not necessary since we are only interested in checking the validity of **p** at line 16 (that is, checking whether **p** is an initialized pointer that refers to a memory location which can be safely accessed by the program). It is worth noting that line 7 which stores the allocation of the local variable **x** must be kept because of the alias between **p** and **&x** is created at line 9: **p** is indeed valid because it is the address of this local variable.

In order to limit this instrumentation, E-ACSL implements a backward dataflow analysis that soundly over-approximates the memory locations to be monitored [40,42]: all other locations (all the lines marked as *useless* in our example) can safely be untracked by the monitor.

6   Test Case Generation with PATHCRAWLER

For structural unit testing of C code, FRAMA-C offers a test case generation tool, called PATHCRAWLER [13,14]. Given a C source code with a function under test f, it tries to generate test cases that *cover* (i.e. activate) all feasible execution paths in f, that is, to achieve the *all-paths* test coverage criterion. Its method combines symbolic execution, concrete execution and constraint solving similarly to Dynamic Symbolic Execution tools like DART/CUTE, PEX, SAGE, KLEE, etc. [43].

The main steps of the method are presented in Fig. 10. First, a chosen (partial) program path π is symbolically executed in order to construct its *path predicate* φ_π, that is, the constraints over the values of input variables that ensure the execution of π. Next, a constraint solver is used to solve the set of constraints φ_π. PATHCRAWLER relies on the COLIBRI constraint solver also developed at CEA List. If it succeeds, the resulting solution provides a test datum that covers the target path π. This test datum is then executed concretely on an instrumented version of the function in order to record the complete path and program outputs, and to double-check that it covers the target path π. If φ_π has no solution, path π is infeasible (i.e. impossible to activate). Finally, the next path to be covered is chosen. The tool continues similarly for all program paths that are explored in a depth-first search. When the number of paths is too large for an

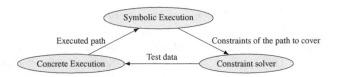

Fig. 10. Main steps of the PATHCRAWLER method.

Fig. 11. Example of test case generation results on pathcrawler-online.com where the user can find the test data, executed paths and branches, path predicates, concrete and symbolic outputs, pass or fail verdicts, etc.

exhaustive path coverage, the user can limit their exploration to paths with at most k consecutive iterations of loops (k-*paths* criterion).

PATHCRAWLER is sound, meaning that each test case activates the test objective for which it was generated. This is verified by concrete execution. PATHCRAWLER is also complete in the following sense: if the tool manages to explore all feasible paths of the program, then the absence of a test for some path means that this path is infeasible, since the tool does not approximate path constraints [14, Sect. 3.1].

PATHCRAWLER can accept user-provided test parameters that indicate the chosen strategy (*all-paths* or *k-paths*) and a precondition specifying the desired value intervals and relationships between input variables. They should be carefully specified in order to avoid generation of inadmissible test data. PATHCRAWLER can be used through the online test generation service http:// pathcrawler-online.com/. Figure 11 illustrates the results of a test generation session with this service. The reader can find more information on the tool and its usage in [4,5,13,14].

Recently, a new efficient variant of dynamic symbolic execution has been proposed for a rich set of test coverage criteria [44]. In this approach, test generation is highly optimized in order to avoid both unnecessary redundant attempts to cover a test objective and an exponential blow-up of the search space (in particular, by removing the constraints of a test objective from the constraint store while trying to cover other objectives). This technique has been implemented in the LTEST toolset [45] on top of PATHCRAWLER.

7   Combinations of Analyses

Various combinations of analyses have been designed and implemented within FRAMA-C. In this section, we present a few of them where different static and dynamic analyzers are advantageously combined together in FRAMA-C.

The SANTE method [46,47] aims at detecting runtime errors and combines three FRAMA-C analyzers. First it runs value analysis to detect potential errors, or *alarms*. Next, it runs slicing in order to simplify the program with respect to these alarms by preserving possible erroneous behavior. Finally, test generation with PATHCRAWLER tries to cover these alarms and trigger potential erroneous situations. PATHCRAWLER can confirm an alarm as a real bug, or sometimes, when it manages to cover all paths without triggerring the alarm, establish that it is safe (i.e. a false alarm). In this combination, the analyzers are complementary: error detection with abstract interpretation based value analysis is complete but imprecise, while testing is precise but incomplete since it is in general not exhaustive. Slicing removes irrelevant code, simplifies the search space and thus makes testing more efficient.

The SANTE method was recently extended to security flaw detection and successfully applied to the Heartbleed vulnerability in OpenSSL library [48]. Its methodology is shown in Fig. 12. In addition to value analysis that detects runtime errors, taint analysis is used to identify alarms that can be impacted by potentially malicious input values and are likely to be exploitable. After a program simplification step with slicing, a dynamic analysis step (with the fuzzing tool Flinder) is used to try to trigger the alarms. This work also demonstrates the possibilities of collaboration of FRAMA-C analyzers with external tools: indeed, taint analysis and fuzz testing tools used in this project were implemented by two industrial partners.

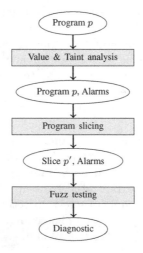

Fig. 12. Methodology of the Flinder-SCA tool.

Another interesting collaboration where dynamic analysis also improves a static verification technique is realized by the STADY tool [49]. During deductive verification, when some proof fails, STADY runs test generation to help the validation engineer to understand the reason of each proof failure and illustrate it by a counterexample.

Inversely, static analysis can be beneficial for dynamic analysis. In the context of the LTEST testing toolset [45], a combination of VALUE and WP is efficiently used to detect infeasible test objectives and therefore to avoid the waste of time of covering them during test generation [50]. Another combination, where static analysis helps to optimize runtime verification by removing irrelevant monitoring code, has been mentioned in Sect. 5.

8   Conclusion

Modern software has nowadays become increasingly critical and widely expanded in various domains of our life. Bugs and security flaws may have very expensive costs and sometimes lead to dramatic consequences. In this context, practical and efficient tools for software analysis and verification are necessary to ensure a high level of safety and security of software.

In this paper we have presented a synopsis of a tutorial on FRAMA-C, a rich and extensible platform for analysis of C code. FRAMA-C has been successfully applied in several industrial [28,51–54] and academic projects [27,29,55–59], and has become a reference for teaching software verification in several universities and engineering schools all around the world (including France, Germany, United Kingdom, Portugal, Russia, Brazil, China, United States). We have described its main analyzers based on abstract interpretation, deductive verification, runtime assertion checking and test case generation. These analyzers are publicly available in open-source or online versions. We have also emphasized a few combinations of analyses that appear to be practical and complementary to each other. FRAMA-C provides a convenient and powerful platform for combining different analyzers and development of new ones.

References

1. Boulanger, J.L. (ed.): Industrial Use of Formal Methods: Formal Verification. Wiley-ISTE, New York (2012)
2. Kirchner, F., Kosmatov, N., Prevosto, V., Signoles, J., Yakobowski, B.: Frama-C: a software analysis perspective. Formal Aspects Comput. **27**(3), 573–609 (2015)
3. Baudin, P., Filliâtre, J.C., Hubert, T., Marché, C., Monate, B., Moy, Y., Prevosto, V.: ACSL: ANSI/ISO C Specification Language. http://frama-c.com/acsl.html
4. Kosmatov, N., Williams, N., Botella, B., Roger, M., Chebaro, O.: A lesson on structural testing with PathCrawler-online.com. In: Brucker, A.D., Julliand, J. (eds.) TAP 2012. LNCS, vol. 7305, pp. 169–175. Springer, Heidelberg (2012). doi:10.1007/978-3-642-30473-6_15

5. Williams, N., Kosmatov, N.: Structural testing with PathCrawler: tutorial synopsis. In: International Conference on Quality Software (QSIC 2012), pp. 289–292. IEEE (2012)

6. Kosmatov, N., Prevosto, V., Signoles, J.: A lesson on proof of programs with frama-C. Invited Tutorial Paper. In: Veanes, M., Viganò, L. (eds.) TAP 2013. LNCS, vol. 7942, pp. 168–177. Springer, Heidelberg (2013). doi:10.1007/978-3-642-38916-0_10

7. Kosmatov, N., Signoles, J.: A lesson on runtime assertion checking with frama-C. In: Legay, A., Bensalem, S. (eds.) RV 2013. LNCS, vol. 8174, pp. 386–399. Springer, Heidelberg (2013). doi:10.1007/978-3-642-40787-1_29

8. Kosmatov, N., Signoles, J.: Runtime assertion checking and its combinations with static and dynamic analyses. In: Seidl, M., Tillmann, N. (eds.) TAP 2014. LNCS, vol. 8570, pp. 165–168. Springer, Heidelberg (2014). doi:10.1007/978-3-319-09099-3_13

9. Baudin, P., Bobot, F., Correnson, L., Dargaye, Z.: WP plug-in manual. http://frama-c.com/wp.html

10. Cuoq, P., Yakobowski, B., Prevosto, V.: Frama-C's value analysis plug-in. http://frama-c.com/download/value-analysis.pdf

11. Delahaye, M., Kosmatov, N., Signoles, J.: Common specification language for static and dynamic analysis of C programs. In: the 28th Annual ACM Symposium on Applied Computing (SAC 2013), pp. 1230–1235. ACM (2013)

12. Signoles, J.: E-ACSL user manual. http://frama-c.com/download/e-acsl/e-acsl-manual.pdf

13. Williams, N., Marre, B., Mouy, P., Roger, M.: PathCrawler: automatic generation of path tests by combining static and dynamic analysis. In: Cin, M., Kaâniche, M., Pataricza, A. (eds.) EDCC 2005. LNCS, vol. 3463, pp. 281–292. Springer, Heidelberg (2005). doi:10.1007/11408901_21

14. Botella, B., Delahaye, M., Hong-Tuan-Ha, S., Kosmatov, N., Mouy, P., Roger, M., Williams, N.: Automating structural testing of C programs: experience with PathCrawler. In: International Workshop on Automation of Software Test (AST 2009), pp. 70–78. IEEE (2009)

15. Cuoq, P., Signoles, J.: Experience report: Ocaml for an industrial-strength static analysis framework. In: International Confererence on Functional Programming (ICFP 2009), pp. 281–286 (2009)

16. Signoles, J.: Software architecture of code analysis frameworks matters: the Frama-C example. In: Workshop on Formal Integrated Development Environment (F-IDE 2015), pp. 86–96 (2015)

17. Correnson, L., Signoles, J.: Combining analyses for C program verification. In: Stoelinga, M., Pinger, R. (eds.) FMICS 2012. LNCS, vol. 7437, pp. 108–130. Springer, Heidelberg (2012). doi:10.1007/978-3-642-32469-7_8

18. Meyer, B.: Object-oriented Software Construction. Object-oriented Series, 2nd edn. Prentice Hall, New York (1997)

19. Leavens, G.T., Cheon, Y., Clifton, C., Ruby, C., Cok, D.R.: How the design of JML accommodates both runtime assertion checking and formal verification. In: Boer, F.S., Bonsangue, M.M., Graf, S., Roever, W.-P. (eds.) FMCO 2002. LNCS, vol. 2852, pp. 262–284. Springer, Heidelberg (2003). doi:10.1007/978-3-540-39656-7_11

20. Dijkstra, E.W.: Guarded commands, nondeterminacy and formal derivation of programs. Commun. ACM 18(8), 453–457 (1975)

21. Correnson, L.: Qed. Computing what remains to be proved. In: Badger, J.M., Rozier, K.Y. (eds.) NFM 2014. LNCS, vol. 8430, pp. 215–229. Springer, Heidelberg (2014). doi:10.1007/978-3-319-06200-6_17

22. Burghardt, J., Gerlach, J., Lapawczyk, T.: ACSL by example (2016). https://gitlab.fokus.fraunhofer.de/verification/open-acslbyexample/blob/master/ACSL-by-Example.pdf
23. Cousot, P., Cousot, R.: Abstract interpretation: a unified lattice model for static analysis of programs by construction or approximation of fixpoints. In: Principles of Programming Languages (POPL 1977), pp. 238–252. ACM Press (1977)
24. Deutsch, A.: Static verification of dynamic properties. PolySpace White Paper (2003)
25. Cousot, P., Cousot, R., Feret, J., Mauborgne, L., Min, A., Monniaux, D., Rival, X.: The ASTRE analyzer. In: Sagiv, M. (ed.) ESOP 2005. LNCS, vol. 3444, pp. 21–30. Springer, Heidelberg (2005)
26. Feret, J.: Static analysis of digital filters. In: Schmidt, D. (ed.) ESOP 2004. LNCS, vol. 2986, pp. 33–48. Springer, Heidelberg (2004). doi:10.1007/978-3-540-24725-8_4
27. Berthomé, P., Heydemann, K., Kauffmann-Tourkestansky, X., Lalande, J.F.: Attack model for verification of interval security properties for smart card C codes. In: Programming Languages and Analysis for Security (PLAS 2010), pp. 1–12. ACM (2010)
28. Cuoq, P., Delmas, D., Duprat, S., Moya Lamiel, V.: Fan-C, a Frama-C plug-in for data flow verification. In: Embedded Real-Time Software and Systems Congress (ERTS²2012) (2012)
29. Demay, J.C., Totel, E., Tronel, F.: SIDAN: a tool dedicated to software instrumentation for detecting attacks on non-control-data. In: International Conference on Risks and Security of Internet and Systems (CRiSIS 2009), pp. 51–58. IEEE (2009)
30. TrustInSoft: tis-ct blog post. http://trust-in-soft.com/tis-ct/
31. Bonichon, R., Cuoq, P.: A mergeable interval map. Studia Inform. Univ. **9**(1), 5–37 (2011)
32. ISO/IEC 9899:1999: Programming languages – C
33. Mauborgne, L., Rival, X.: Trace partitioning in abstract interpretation based static analyzers. In: Sagiv, M. (ed.) ESOP 2005. LNCS, vol. 3444, pp. 5–20. Springer, Heidelberg (2005). doi:10.1007/978-3-540-31987-0_2
34. Jeannet, B., Miné, A.: Apron: a library of numerical abstract domains for static analysis. In: Computer Aided Verification (CAV 2009), pp. 661–667 (2009)
35. Venet, A.J.: The gauge domain: scalable analysis of linear inequality invariants. In: Madhusudan, P., Seshia, S.A. (eds.) CAV 2012. LNCS, vol. 7358, pp. 139–154. Springer, Heidelberg (2012). doi:10.1007/978-3-642-31424-7_15
36. Signoles, J.: E-ACSL: Executable ANSI/ISO C Specification Language, May 2015. http://frama-c.com/download/e-acsl/e-acsl.pdf
37. Chalin, P.: Engineering a sound assertion semantics for the verifying compiler. IEEE Trans. Softw. Eng. **36**, 275–287 (2010)
38. Falcone, Y., Havelund, K., Reger, G.: A tutorial on runtime verification. In: Broy, M., Peled, D., Kalus, G. (eds.) Engineering Dependable Software Systems. NATO Science for Peace and Security Series - D: Information and Communication Security, vol. 34, pp. 141–175. IOS Press, Amsterdam (2013)
39. Bartocci, E., Bonakdarpour, B., Falcone, Y., Colombo, C., Decker, N., Klaedtke, F., Havelund, K., Joshi, Y., Milewicz, R., Reger, G., Rosu, G., Signoles, J., Thoma, D., Zalinescu, E., Zhang., Y.: First International Competition on Runtime Verification. Rules, Benchmarks, Tools and Final Results of CRV 2014 (Submitted)
40. Jakobsson, A., Kosmatov, N., Signoles, J.: Rester statique pour devenir plus rapide, plus précis et plus mince. In: Journes Francophones des Langages Applicatifs (JFLA 2015) (2015) (in French)

41. Kosmatov, N., Petiot, G., Signoles, J.: An optimized memory monitoring for run-time assertion checking of C programs. In: Legay, A., Bensalem, S. (eds.) RV 2013. LNCS, vol. 8174, pp. 167–182. Springer, Heidelberg (2013). doi:10.1007/978-3-642-40787-1_10

42. Jakobsson, A., Kosmatov, N., Signoles, J.: Expressive as a tree: optimized memory monitoring for C (Submitted)

43. Cadar, C., Godefroid, P., Khurshid, S., Pasareanu, C.S., Sen, K., Tillmann, N., Visser, W.: Symbolic execution for software testing in practice: preliminary assessment. In: International Conference on Software Engineering (ICSE 2011), pp. 1066–1071. ACM (2011)

44. Bardin, S., Kosmatov, N., Cheynier, F.: Efficient leveraging of symbolic execution to advanced coverage criteria. In: International Conference on Software Testing, Verification and Validation (ICST 2014), pp. 173–182. IEEE (2014)

45. Bardin, S., Chebaro, O., Delahaye, M., Kosmatov, N.: An all-in-one toolkit for automated white-box testing. In: Seidl, M., Tillmann, N. (eds.) TAP 2014. LNCS, vol. 8570, pp. 53–60. Springer, Heidelberg (2014). doi:10.1007/978-3-319-09099-3_4

46. Chebaro, O., Kosmatov, N., Giorgetti, A., Julliand, J.: Program slicing enhances a verification technique combining static and dynamic analysis. In: The ACM Symposium on Applied Computing (SAC 2012), pp. 1284–1291. ACM (2012)

47. Chebaro, O., Cuoq, P., Kosmatov, N., Marre, B., Pacalet, A., Williams, N., Yakobowski, B.: Behind the scenes in SANTE: a combination of static and dynamic analyses. Autom. Softw. Eng. 21(1), 107–143 (2014)

48. Kiss, B., Kosmatov, N., Pariente, D., Puccetti, A.: Combining static and dynamic analyses for vulnerability detection: illustration on heartbleed. In: Piterman, N. (ed.) HVC 2015. LNCS, vol. 9434, pp. 39–50. Springer, Heidelberg (2015). doi:10.1007/978-3-319-26287-1_3

49. Petiot, G., Kosmatov, N., Botella, B., Giorgetti, A., Julliand, J.: Your proof fails? Testing helps to find the reason. In: Aichernig, B.K.K., Furia, C.A.A. (eds.) TAP 2016. LNCS, vol. 9762, pp. 130–150. Springer, Heidelberg (2016). doi:10.1007/978-3-319-41135-4_8

50. Bardin, S., Delahaye, M., David, R., Kosmatov, N., Papadakis, M., Traon, Y.L., Marion, J.: Sound and quasi-complete detection of infeasible test requirements. In: International Conference on Software Testing, Verification and Validation (ICST 2015), pp. 1–10. IEEE (2015)

51. Bishop, P.G., Bloomfield, R.E., Cyra, L.: Combining testing and proof to gain high assurance in software: a case study. In: International Symposium on Software Reliability Engineering (ISSRE 2013), pp. 248–257. IEEE (2013)

52. Cuoq, P., Hilsenkopf, P., Kirchner, F., Labb, S., Thuy, N., Yakobowski, B.: Formal verification of software important to safety using the Frama-C tool suite. In: International Topical Meeting on Nuclear Plant Instrumentation, Control and Human Machine Interface Technologies (NPIC & HMIT) (2012)

53. Delmas, D., Duprat, S., Moya-Lamiel, V., Signoles, J.: Taster, a Frama-C plug-in to enforce coding standards. In: Embedded Real-Time Software and Systems Congress (ERTS^{2}2010)

54. Pariente, D., Ledinot, E.: Formal verification of industrial C code using Frama-C: a case study. In: International Conference on Formal Verification of Object-Oriented Software (FoVeOOS 2010) (2010)

55. Ceara, D., Mounier, L., Potet, M.L.: Taint dependency sequences: A characterization of insecure execution paths based on input-sensitive cause sequences. In: the 3rd International Conference on Software Testing, Verification and Validation Workshops (ICSTW 2010), pp. 371–380 (2010)

56. Ayache, N., Amadio, R., Régis-Gianas, Y.: Certifying and reasoning on cost anno-
    tations in C programs. In: Formal Methods for Industrial Critical Systems (FMICS
    2012) (2012)
57. Carvalho, N., Silva Sousa, C., Pinto, J.S., Tomb, A.: Formal verification of
    kLIBC with the WP frama-C plug-in. In: Badger, J.M., Rozier, K.Y. (eds.) NFM
    2014. LNCS, vol. 8430, pp. 343–358. Springer, Heidelberg (2014). doi:10.1007/
    978-3-319-06200-6_29
58. Gavran, I., Niksic, F., Kanade, A., Majumdar, R., Vafeiadis, V.: Rely/guarantee
    reasoning for asynchronous programs. In: International Conference on Concurrency
    Theory (CONCUR 2015), pp. 483–496 (2015)
59. Nguena-Timo, O., Langelier, G.: Test data generation for cyclic executives with
    CBMC and frama-C: a case study. Electr. Notes Theor. Comput. Sci. **320**, 35–51
    (2016)

Using Genetic Programming
for Software Reliability

Doron Peled[(✉)]

Department of Computer Science, Bar Ilan University, 52900 Ramat Gan, Israel
doron.peled@gmail.com

Abstract. Software reliability methods, such as testing and model checking, are well integrated into the software development process. They are complemented by safety enforcement mechanisms such as run time verification. However, even with a wealth of techniques and method-ologies for developing reliable systems, it is still quite challenging to eliminate all the bugs from software systems. One of the reasons is the magnitude of software systems, having to handle a very large number of use cases and possible interactions with an environment or between concurrent components. Genetic algorithms and programming provide a powerful heuristic search that involves randomization based on operators that simulate natural reproduction. We show various ways where genetic algorithms and programming can be integrated with formal methods to enhance software reliability.

1 Introduction

Computer applications surround our daily functions and well being, penetrating to a growing number of aspects of life and expanding in capabilities. Software development cannot exist nowadays without the intensive use of formal methods. Traditional methods of testing are still in extensive use, as well as more modern methods for the automatic testing of programs and systems, and algorithms that provide more comprehensive validation, such as model checking. There is also a growing interest in the automatic synthesis of (parts of) code directly from specification.

One of the problems in achieving software reliability is a combinatorial growth in complexity in the size of the system. A naive estimate for the complexity of the system is the number of possible states, representing the instantaneous values of all data stored. This is an enormous number, which is exponential in the number of bits that are used to hold all pieced of data, including internal representation of various items such as program counters and procedure call stacks. This number is larger than the actual number of states that the system may actually reach. Still, the actual number of involved states is not of a reasonable magnitude that can be enumerated as part of any formal method tool. Then, the number of possible executions, where the system moves between states, can be exponentially larger, in fact, it can even be unbounded. There seems to be a race between newly developed

© Springer International Publishing AG 2016
Y. Falcone and C. Sanchez (Eds.): RV 2016, LNCS 10012, pp. 116–131, 2016.
DOI: 10.1007/978-3-319-46982-9_8

testing and verification methods implemented within increasingly powerful tools, and the growing size and intricacy of new software projects.

There are several ways to combat the combinatorial explosion of system size. One principle is to check, test or verify a system *compositionally* instead of attacking the entire system or a large portion of it; the checks are designed in a way that would cover, when taken together, a large as possible part of the system. This approach still falls short of achieving comprehensiveness in many software projects, where sometimes even small parts of the system may witness a huge state space. The principle of *abstraction* allows one to map the state space of a system into a much smaller one. If we are interested only in the *sign* of a multiplication result, we may replace two 64 bits integers by the values -1, 0 and 1, having altogether 9 possible values to check. However, abstraction may also fall short of reducing the number of possibilities that we need to check. Other methods can help us to bound these possibilities. For example, partial order reduction (see e.g., [6]) can be used to partition the executions, based on inherent commutativity between actions in concurrent systems, into equivalence classes; the executions in each equivalence class are indifferent with respect to the checked properties, hence it is possible to check only representatives of the equivalence classes. A further technique with growing popularity is the use of randomization. In some cases where we cannot comprehensively check a system, we can at least sample it and provide some statistical results. We may use randomization to provide noncomprehensive model checking, as in [9].

Genetic algorithms provide a heuristic search strategy that uses randomization and is based on natural reproduction principles such as mutation and crossover. This is a beam search, progressing from one collection of points, called *generation*, to the next one, without backtracking. It promotes the propagation and evolution of individual points that show better potential through the calculation of a fitness function. There are a several places where the genetic principles can interface with formal methods, exploiting the combined power of these techniques. We will describe some of these combinations related to testing, verification and the automatic synthesis of correct-by-construction code.

2   Genetic Algorithms

During the 1970s, Holland [11] established the field known as *Genetic Algorithms* (GA). Individual candidate solutions are represented as fixed length strings of bits, corresponding to chromosomes in biological systems. Candidates are evaluated using a *fitness* function. This is a value that approximates the distance of the candidate from a desired solution. Genetic algorithms (and programming) differ from traditional search methods that progress from one point to another. Instead it is a kind of *beam search* in this sense that progress evolves a *set of candidates* (the beam) into a successor set. Each such set is a *generation*, and there is no backtracking. The different candidates in a single generation have a combined effect on the search, as progress tend to promote and improve the candidates that are better according to the fitness function and subsequently improve the fitness average.

Inspired by genetic selections, candidates progress from one generation to the next one according to one of the following cases:

- *Reproduction.* Part of the candidates are selected to propagate from one generation to the subsequent one. The reproduction is done at random, with probability relative to the fitness value or to the relation between the fitness of the selected individual and the average of fitness values in the current generation.
- *Crossover.* Some pairs of the candidates selected for reproduction are chosen, with some given probability p_c, to be combined using the crossover operation. This operation takes parts of bitstrings from two parent solutions and combines them into a two new solutions, which potentially inherit useful attributes from their parents. The lengths of the two parts needs to sum up to the fixed length of bitstrings representing candidates.
- *Mutation.* This operation randomly alters the content of small number of bits from candidates selected for reproduction (this can also be done after the crossover). To do that, one can decide on mutating each bit separately with some probability p_m.

A one-point crossover decides at random on the point k of splitting, where $1 \leq k < l$ for a bit-string of length l. One new candidate will consist of the first k prefix bits from the first selected candidate, and the $l - k$ suffix bits from the second, and the other new candidate will consist of the first k prefix bit from the second selected candidate and the $l - k$ suffix bit from the first. For example, the shuffle point between the following two strings

$$10110110 \ 11011010$$

is after 3 bits. The resulted strings are the following:

$$10111010 \ 11010110$$

The process of selecting candidates from the previous generation and deciding whether to apply crossover or mutate them continues until we complete a new generation. All generations are of some predefined size N. This can be, typically, a number between 50 and 500.

Genetic algorithms thus perform the following steps:

1. Randomly generate N initial candidates.
2. Evaluate the fitness of the candidates.
3. If a satisfactory solution is found, or the number of generations created exceeds a predefined limit (say hundreds or a few thousands), terminate.
4. Otherwise, select candidates for reproduction using randomization, proportional to the fitness values and apply crossover or mutation, again using randomization, until N candidates are obtained.
5. Go to step 2.

Holland [11] tried to explain the intuition behind the success of the genetic heuristic search with a *schema theorem*. We will present a simplified version that takes into account only mutations, but not crossover. The idea is that a good solution consists of good "building blocks" or "schemas" and that the search tends to quickly increase the density of candidate with better building blocks. A *schema*, (or template) represents a building block. In this analysis, it is a string of 1s, 0s and $*$s: the latter represents a "wildcard", i.e., can correspond to either 1 or 0. Thus, $1 * 0 * 1$ is a schema for candidates of length 5 that allows four possibilities, for all the cases of replacing the two $*$s with either 0 or 1. There are 3^l possible schemas (but 2^{2^l} sets of subsets of candidates).

Now, let $N(s,t)$ be the number of instances for the schema s at generation t and the average fitness of these instances $u(s,t)$. Statistically, the number of times a candidate x with fitness $f(x)$ is selected at a generation with average fitness $\bar{f}(t)$ is directly proportional to $f(x)/\bar{f}(t)$. Hence, the expected number of candidates to be selected for reproduction for schema s at generation t is:

$$\sum_{x \in s} \frac{f(x)}{\bar{f}(t)} = \frac{u(s,t)}{\bar{f}(t)} N(s,t)$$

Now we take into account mutation of candidates that are selected for reproduction. Suppose that for each bit of such a selected candidate we decide with small probability p_m whether to mutate the bit (from 1 to 0 or from 0 to 1). Let $o(s)$ be the *order* of the schema s, i.e., the number of its non $*$ characters (for $s = 1 * 0 * 1$, $o(s) = 3$). Then the probability that a selected candidate is *not* caused to leave the schema due to mutation is $(1 - p_m)^{o(s)}$. Overall (ignoring for simplicity the effect of mutation) this gives the expected number of schema s candidates in generation $t + 1$ to be:

$$E(N(s,t+1) \geq \frac{u(s,t)}{\bar{f}(t)} N(s,t)(1 - p_m)^{o(s)}$$

The reason we have $\geq$ rather than $=$ is that instances of a scheme s can also be randomly generated by mutation from instances of other schemes. Depending on how good the fitness of candidates of s with respect to other candidate, the population of candidates of s can grow exponentially with the number of generations.

An individual candidate can participate in an effort to increase the population of *multiple* good building blocks that it is comprised of. In that sense, each candidate can participate in a "parallel effort" to improve the quality of the population based on several schemas.

The operations of crossover and mutation can produce candidates with new helpful building blocks. Genetic algorithms were successfully applied to a large variety of domains, including strategies for games, optimization for economical systems, etc.

2.1 Testing Using Genetic Programming

Testing is the most common, and also oldest, software reliability method used. It is based on sampling the code while observing whether the inspected behaviors comply with the desired behavior. There are different principles to generate the test suite for code (see, e.g., the classical testing book by Myers [24]). The main challenge is to select a good test suite that will provide a high probability of detecting design programming errors but would have a reasonable size.

In [8] a genetic algorithm was used to select the execution paths that are tested. The idea is to use a crossover operator that is inspired by genetic programming. A finite execution path is represented as a bitstring of some length, a sort of a *chromosome*. A trivial description of a path would use k bits per each state to encode the next successor. This allows up to 2^k successors. However, the number of enabled successors per state is not fixed. Instead, the representation looks at the number of successors n from a state reached during testing using the current chromosome and reads the next $\lceil \log(n) \rceil$ bits. If this gives a value that is bigger than the number of currently enabled transitions, then these bits are corrected to a randomly chosen value between 0 and $n-1$, representing one possible successor. Then, the crossover just affixes together two parts from two parent chromosomes.

As the goal of testing, in this case, is finding deadlocks and checking violation of inline assertions, the following fitness calculation is used:

- The number of enabled transitions are summed up along the checked path. The fitness grows inversely proportional to this number, as paths with small number of enabled transitions are often more likely to lead to deadlocks.
- The fitness grows up with the number of states in which inline assertions are checked. One can also increase fitness for occurrences of tests (as in *if statement* conditions) that lead to the inline assertions.
- When checking programs with message passing, fitness grows up proportionally to the number of messages being sent.

3   Synthesis Using Genetic Programming

Software synthesis is a relatively new research direction. Manna and Wolper [23] suggested a transformation of temporal logic specification into automata. A similar idea appears also in the early model checking paper of Clarke and Emerson [5]. The translation into an automaton (on infinite sequences) provides an operational description of these sequences. Then, the operations that belong to different processes are projected out on these processes, while a centralized scheduler enforces globally the communication to occur in an order that is consistent with the specification. The main disadvantage of this approach is that due to the centralized scheduler, concurrency is lost.

Concurrent systems are complicated to synthesize: the specified task needs to be decomposed into different components, where each one has limited visibility and control over the behavior of the other components. Pnueli and Rosner [26] showed that automatic synthesis of concurrent systems with distributed components from Linear Temporal Logic specification is, in general, undecidable. Decidable cases are quite restrictive, see, e.g., [21].

Genetic programming [2,19] is a method for the automatic generation of computer programs by a process that mimics biological evolution and Darwinian natural selection. Turing [12] provided some initial insights about the connection between biological evolution, mutations and selection, and algorithmic iterative search in the space of candidate solutions or programs.

A number of researchers suggested methodologies of representing and evolving computer programs. One of the most influential works was by Koza [19], who gave the field its name. Genetic programming [19] is a direct successor of genetic algorithms. In GP, each individual organism represents a computer program. Instead of fixed length strings, programs are represented by variable length structures, such as trees or a sequences of instructions. Each individual solution is built from a set of functions and terminals, and corresponds to a program or an expression in a programming language that can be executed. The genetic operations were customized in order to match the flexible structure of individuals.

For instance, in tree-based genetic programming, crossover is performed by selecting subtrees on each of the parents, and then swapping between them. This forms two new programs, each having parts from both of its parents. Mutation can be carried out by choosing a subtree and replacing it by another randomly generated subtree. The fitness is calculated by directly running the generated programs on a large set of test cases and evaluating the results. In Koza's work, crossover is the main genetic operation, and mutations are negligible. On the other hand, there is an ongoing debate about the actual role and importance of crossover. The main question is whether it indeed combines building blocks into larger blocks of code, or just acts as a macro mutation. There were various suggestions of improving crossover, while other researches focused on the mutation operation [4].

GP has successfully generated complex solutions to problems in a broad range of domains, and it constantly yields human-competitive results [20]. Herman and Jones [10] subscribed genetic programming to a class of heuristic search methods that they termed *search-based software engineering*. These fitness guided search methods, which include also simulated annealing, are aimed at constructing, improving and correcting software artifacts.

Representation of code uses syntax trees, as shown in Fig. 1. It is quite easy to transfer between program and a syntax tree (this is the usual task of a compiler) and vice versa. One can use either of these representations for verification, however, the syntax tree representation can be easily utilized for applying the genetic operations of mutation and crossover. These trees are well-typed, which means that each node is classified as *code*, (Boolean) *condition* or *expression*. The genetic operations, need to respect these (and possibly further) types, e.g., expressions can be exchanged with expressions.

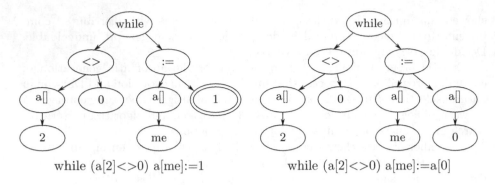

while (a[2]<>0) a[me]:=1   while (a[2]<>0) a[me]:=a[0]

Fig. 1. Mutation

There are several kinds of mutation operations. In *replacement* mutation, we pick at random a node in the tree, which roots a subtree. Then we throw away this subtree and replace it with a subtree of the same type, which we generate at random. Figure 1 demonstrate this kind of mutation. In this case, we chose the rightmost leaf node, which we marked with double ellipse. In this case, the subtree consists of this single node, representing the constant 1. Thus, it needs to be replaced with another expression, built at random. In this case we generated a new subtree consisting of two nodes, representing the expression $a[0]$.

In *insertion* mutation, we generate a new node of the same type as the selected subtree and insert it just above it (type permitting). This means that the new node needs to have the selected subtree as one of its descendants. Then we may need to complete other descendant of the newly inserted node, as required. For example, if we pick up an expression and insert above it a node that corresponds to addition +, we can make the expression one of the descendants to be added (left or right), but need to complete the tree with another expression to be added to make it syntactically correct. The *reduction* mutation has the opposite effect of *insertion*: the selected node is replaced with one of its offsprings (type permitting). The remaining of the offsprings are just deleted. In *deletion* mutation we remove the selected subtree, and recursively update the ancestors to make the program syntactically correct.

Crossover can be performed as followsL: we pick up two candidate trees, then select in them, at random, two nodes that are roots for subtrees of compatible types. Then we exchange the two subtrees to generate two new trees.

The syntax trees are not limited to a fixed size, as is the bit string representation of genetic algorithms. Therefore the candidates can shrink or grow after mutation and crossover. Because of this, there is actually a tendency of candidates to grow up with unnecessary code, for example, assignments such as $a[1] := a[1]$ or larger pieces of code that do not contribute anything. This is called *bloating*. the countermeasure for this, called *parsimony pressure*, is to provide a negative value to the fitness function corresponding to the length of the code. As a consequence, resulted solutions are not expected to have a perfect fitness value, but instead they need to pass all the tests/verifications performed.

3.1   Calculating Fitness

An important ingredient of genetic programming is providing a fitness function that helps promoting the good candidates for reproduction. In its simplest form, fitness is calculated by inspecting a collection of test cases, comparing their desired inputs against the observed inputs. This can be a test suite (also called here *training set*) that was prepared in advance, using some distribution of the input values with some fixed intervals or obtained using a random process.

It is important to be able to compare the observed outputs of the test cases against the correct ones. Given a test suite of n cases, with p_i the correct value for the ith case and o_i the observed value for this case, we can calculate the fitness, e.g., as $\sum_{i=1}^{n} |p_i - o_i|$. In other cases, it is argued, we may prefer to square the difference, as in $\sum_{i=1}^{n} |p_i - o_i|^2$. In both of these cases, the "best" fitness will be 0, and we may want to normalize it, e.g., to be between 0 and 1, or 0 and 100. We may also want to reverse it so that a higher fitness value will correspond to better fitness. All of that is done through simple arithmetic.

We can apply the following principle of mutation testing to check and improve a given test suite. The idea is that the test suite needs to be able to detect coding mistakes. Mutating the code would most likely generate an observable deviation of the behavior (e.g., in the obtained output values), hence one can check if at least one of the provided test cases would catch this behavior. In case that the current test suite cannot recognize the change in behavior introduced by mutation of some of the better fitted candidates, it is extended to include a test case that does so.

The principle of *coevolution* allows to reproduce and evolve test cases from one generation to another. The fitness of a test case can increase with the number of candidates for which it shows discrepancy between the expected and observed behavior. New test cases can be obtained from existing ones by using mutation or crossover.

The above description of calculating fitnes takes care of a simple case, where the sought after program is intended to obtain some initial input value, and calculate some output value. Things can get more complicated when we are interested in synthesizing an interactive program that repeatedly takes input and produces output. Even further, we may be interested in some temporal specification of a system, describing how it is behaves over time.

To illustrate this situation, we look at synthesizing a solution for the well known *mutual exclusion* problem. The problem has the following general form:

```
While W1 do          While W2 do
    NonCrit1             NonCrit2
    preCS1               preCS2
    CS1                  CS2
    postCS2              postCS2
end while            end while
```

The nonCSi represents the actions of the process i outside the critical section. It can actually be fixed as empty code. The CSi represents the critical section, which both processes want to enter a finite or unbounded number of times. It is not part of the synthesis task, and can be represented by trivial code, which serves only to allow checking that it is eventually entered upon request. The goal of the mutual exclusion problem is to allow eventual access to the critical section each time a process wants to enter it, but to disallow both processes to enter their critical section at the same time. Entering and exiting the critical section is controlled by the code in preCSi and postCSi. These are the two parts that consist of the mutual exclusion protocol and are the focus of the synthesis. The code for these two parts should be symmetric, although each one can index itself as i and the other as $2 - i$. The other code segments and the while loop are fixed.

We require the following Linear Temporal Logic properties:

Safety: $\Box \neg (p_0$ in CS1 $\wedge$ p_1 in CS2), i.e., there is no state where the program counters of both processes are in their corresponding critical sections simultaneously.

Liveness: $\Box (p_i$ in preCSi $\rightarrow \Diamond p_i$ in CSi), i.e., if a process wants to enter its critical section, then it will eventually do so. This has to apply for both processes, p_1 and p_2.

These two classical requirements from mutual exclusion are not sufficient as a requirement for the mutual exclusion problem, and there are further subtle considerations. The variables Wi are used to control whether processes want to keep entering their critical section. They serve an important purpose: we want to make sure that the liveness holds not only when the two processes want to enter the critical section indefinitely (W1 $\wedge$ W2), but also when only one process wants to do keep doing that (W1 $\wedge \neg$W2). This eliminates solutions where the processes are allowed to enter in alternation or any pattern of access that assume that *both* processes have an unbounded need to enter the critical section. Note that the candidates should be tested with both cases. This consideration puts us outside of the scope of Linear Temporal Logic, which postulates required properties of *all* the executions.

We also need to require that the duration of preCSi, postCSi and critical sections CSi are finite. E.g., by requiring $\neg \Diamond \Box p_i$ in CSi.

Another consideration is fairness [22]. Fairness requires that the computation will not prevent the execution of some process (or transition) that is enabled continuously (or frequently often). For many models of computation it is unreasonable to seek a solution that works without assuming *any* fairness. Even the classical solutions for mutual exclusion by Dekker [7], requires a (weak) fairness assumption in order to guarantee liveness. There, one process may perform actions that promote the other process into its critical section, but those can be constantly delayed (in the absence of fairness) by the other process, which just repeatedly checks for the moment it can progress.

Suppose that we want to provide a set of tests that would allow calculating a fitness value ranging between 0 and 100. We can run k tests in which only one process wants to enter its critical section (setting only W1 to *true*), and m runs in which both processes repeatedly want to enter their critical section.

Let k_1 be the number of runs in which process 1 managed to enter its critical section among the first k runs, m_1 the number of runs in which *only* process 1 or *only* process 2 manages to enter their critical section among the latter m runs, and m_2 the number of times both processes entered their critical section (thus, $m_1 + m_2 \leq m$). Let a, b and c be some numbers chosen such that $b < c$ and $a + c = 100$, the fitness can be calculated as

$$a \times \frac{k_1}{k} + b \times \frac{m_1}{m} + c \times \frac{m_2}{m}.$$

This gives small fitness value to candidates in which the critical section, is never managed, and checks that the critical section can be entered when there is (repeated) demand from only one process. It also gives preference to candidates that allow more executions in which processes enter both their critical section when there is demand from both processes. The analysis can (and should) be further refined, e.g., further separating k_1 and m_1 into cases where the critical sections are entered once or multiple times.

3.2   Genetic Programming Based on Verification

The direct translation from specification into a system that realizes it is undecidable for distributed systems and Linear Temporal Logic specification [26]. A simple idea is to bound the size of the system (in states, length of code, variables, values) and enumerate the possibilities and verify the resulting code. This was used successfully to synthesize mutual exclusion algorithms with three bits [3]. Systematic enumeration using powerful computing power will result in correct solutions if they exist within the limitations used. This is a generate-and-test approach that uses automatic verification (model checking) to sift the bad candidates. A related approach is Sketching [27], where some small parts of the code, e.g., constants or choices, are being left out and completed automatically through SAT solving.

Genetic programming can be used to harness the power of model checking to assist in searching for correct-by-design code, without being exhaustive. As a first approximation, we may assign fitness based on the number of properties that are satisfied [13]. As opposed to testing, with model checking, one checks *all* the executions, not only samples of them. For the mutual exclusion algorithm, instead of running two versions, one with only W1 set to *true* and one with both W1 and W2 set to *true*, we can change the code a little, making the two possibilities a nondeterministic choice. Model checking will automatically check all nondeterministic choices.

However, this approach is unlikely to work well in practice, unless we have a very large number of properties; in order for the fitness to separate among cases, it needs to be relatively smooth. In order to smooth out the fitness function, we can use additional verification levels between success and failure of the temporal properties. In particular, we can include the following levels per property:

- Not all the executions satisfy the property, but some of them do.
- The property is satisfied with probability 0.
- The property is satisfied with probability 1.
- The property holds under some fairness assumption that is stronger (ignores more executions) than the fairness provides by the actual hardware architecture used.
- Levels provided by statistical model checking, quantifying the portion of the executions satisfying the property.

We used a specially designed model checker and GP engine, which implement the methods [14–17] described earlier. This prototype tool was called MCGP and is described in [18]. It allows selecting the set of allowed commands and the number of variables and modes of communication (synchronous, asynchronous). Synthesis starts with a given program structure or architecture, where some parts are fixed. The architecture can also include the number of processes and the communication channels between them.

Experimental Results for Mutual Exclusion [14]. Program (a) shows one of the obtained candidates, which later evolved into program (b). The evolution first included the addition of the second line to the postCSi section. A replacement mutation then changed the inner while loop condition, leading to a perfect solution similar to Dekker's algorithm. Another interesting algorithm generated by one of the runs is program (c). This algorithm (also reported in [3]) is a perfect solution too, but it is shorter than Dekker's algorithm. On the other hand, it compares two variables, rather than a variable and a constant, in its while loop.

```
Non Critical Section          Non Critical Section          Non Critical Section
A[me] = 1                     A[me] = 1                     A[other] = other
While (A[other] == 1)         While (A[other] == 1)         if (A[2] == other)
   While (A[0] != other)         While (A[2] == me)            A[2] = me
      A[me] = 0                     A[me] = 0                While (A[me] == A[2])
   A[me] = 1                     A[me] = 1                 Critical Section
Critical Section              Critical Section             A[other] = me
A[me] = 0                     A[2] = me
                              A[me] = 0
```

       (a) [94.34]   (b) [96.70]   (c) [97.50]

4   Model Checking as Generalized Testing and Correcting Programs

Many interesting synthesis challenges are parametric. For example, sorting algorithms are developed for an arbitrary number of elements of arbitrary size, although are used with specific limits. Model checking is undecidable for parametric families of programs, e.g., with n processes, each with the same code, initialized with different parameters, even for a fixed property [1].

One possibility is to synthesize code that works with respect to a given finite constraint. Another possibility is to exploit model-checking as *generalized* testing: the automated verification is performed comprehensively multiple times, each time for specific values, parameters or architecture. These cases play the role of a test suite. They are selected in advance, or using randomization. We can also use coevolution to ameliorate this set, e.g., by elevating the fitness of those cases that managed to demote more candidates than others. For instance, we can make the fitness of such an individual case proportional to the number of properties not satisfied for a large enough portion of the candidates in the current generation.

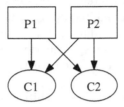

Fig. 2. An architecture of α-core that manifested an error

In [17] we approached the ambitious problem of correcting a known protocol for obtaining interprocess interaction called α-core [25]. The algorithm allows multiparty synchronization of several processes. Besides the processes that perform local and synchronized transitions there are *supervisory processes*, each responsible for a fixed interaction between multiple processes. It needs to function in a system that allows nondeterministic choices: processes that may *consider* one possible interaction may *decide* to be engaged in an alternative interaction. The algorithm uses asynchronous message passing between the processors and the synchronization supervisors in order to enforce a selection of the interactions by the involved processes without deadlock. In Fig. 2 we demonstrate two processes, P_1 and P_2, that are involved in two types of interactions with one another, through the supervision of managers C_1 and C_2. This nontrivial algorithm, which is used in practice in distributed systems, contains an error in its published version. The challenges in correcting this algorithm are the following:

Size. The protocol is quite big, involving sending different messages between the controlled processes and new processes, per each possible multiparty interaction. These messages include announcing the willingness to be engaged in an interaction, committing an interaction, canceling an interaction, requesting for commit from the interaction manager processes, as well as announcing that the interaction is now going on, or is canceled due to the departure of at least one participant. The state space of such a concurrent protocol is obviously high.

Varying architecture. The protocol can run on any number of processes, each process with arbitrary number of choices to be involves in interactions, and with each interaction involving any number of processes.

The parametric nature of the problem makes the model checking itself unde-cidable in general. In fact, we can used the genetic programming approach first to find the error, including finding the architecture instance that manifests the problem. We used two important ideas:

1. Employ the genetic engine not only to generate programs, but also to evolve different architectures on which programs can run.
2. Apply a co-evolution process, where evolution of candidate programs and of candidate architectures that fail these candidates is intermixed.

Specifically, the architecture for the candidate programs was also represented as code (or, equivalently, a syntactic tree) for spanning processes and their interactions, which can be subjected to genetic mutations. The fitness func-tion directed the search for an architecture that falsify the specification for the original α-core algorithm. After finding a "bad" architecture for a program, one that causes the program to fail its specification, our next goal was to reverse the genetic programming direction. Then we try to automatically correct the program.

For the α-core algorithm, the smallest architecture that manifested the failure included two processes, with two alternative communication between both of them. The architecture that was found to produce the error in the original α-core algorithm is the one appearing in Fig. 2. The message sequence chart in Fig. 3 demonstrates the bad scenario that was found. While we did not describe here the α-core algorithm, the scenario demonstrates the intricacy of the algorithm. The correction consisted of changing the following line of code

$$\text{if } n > 0 \text{ then } n := n - 1$$

into

$$\text{if } sender \in shared \text{ then } n := n - 1$$

In order to support the different capabilities of synthesizing and correcting code for fixed and varying architectures, the prototype tool MCGP [18], which we constructed for carrying out the experiments described here and in [14–17], can be used in different modes:

- Setting all parts as *static* will cause the tool to just run the model checking algorithm on the user-defined program, and provide detailed results.
- Setting an *init* process that defines the architecture of processes and the interaction between them as *static*, and all or some of the other processes as *dynamic*, will order the tool to synthesize code according to the specified architecture. This can be used for synthesizing programs from scratch, synthe-sizing only some missing parts of a given partial program, or trying to correct or improve a complete given program.
- Setting the *init* process as *dynamic*, and all other processes as static, is used when trying to falsify a given parametric program by searching for a configu-ration that violates its specification (see [17]).
- Setting both the *init* and the program processes as *dynamic*, is used for syn-thesizing parametric programs, where the tool alternatively evolves various programs, and configurations under which the programs have to be satisfied.

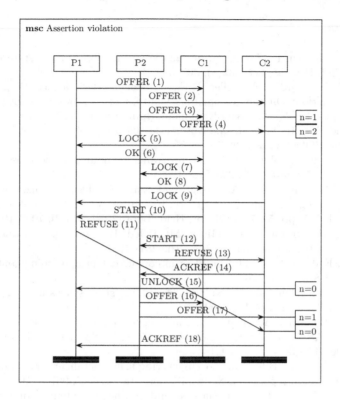

Fig. 3. A Message Sequence Chart showing the counterexample for the α-core protocol

5   Conclusions

We described here the combination of genetic algorithms and programming with formal methods. This was shown to help providing the following goals:

- Generating an effective test suite,
- synthesizing correct-by-design programs,
- finding errors in parametric programs,
- automatically correcting erroneous code with respect to a given specification.

We demonstrated the use of genetic programming for automatically synthesizing solutions for the classical mutual exclusion problem, and for detecting and correcting an error in a complicated multiparty synchronization algorithm called α-core.

The use of genetic programming with formal methods does not guarantee successful termination, neither for finding errors, nor for synthesizing programs from specification. Rather, it is a powerful heuristic that can be part of a human-assisted process for checking, correcting and synthesizing software.

References

1. Apt, K.R., Kozen, D.: Limits for automatic verification of finite-state concurrent systems. Inf. Process. Lett. **22**(6), 307–309 (1986)
2. Banzhaf, W., Nordin, P., Keller, R.E., Francone, F.D.: Genetic Programming - An Introduction; On the Automatic Evolution of Computer Programs and its Applications. 3rd edn. Morgan Kaufmann, dpunkt.verlag (2001)
3. Bar-David, Y., Taubenfeld, G.: Automatic discovery of mutual exclusion algorithms. In: PODC, p. 305 (2003)
4. Chellapilla, K.: Evolving computer programs without subtree crossover. IEEE Trans. Evol. Comput. **1**(3), 209–216 (1997)
5. Clarke, E.M., Emerson, E.A.: Design and synthesis of synchronization skeletons using branching time temporal logic. In: Kozen, D. (ed.) Logic of Programs 1981. LNCS, vol. 131, pp. 52–71. Springer, Heidelberg (1982). doi:10.1007/BFb0025774
6. Clarke, E.M., Grumberg, O., Minea, M., Peled, D.: State space reduction using partial order techniques. STTT **2**(3), 279–287 (1999)
7. Dijkstra, E.W.: Solution of a problem in concurrent programming control. Commun. ACM **8**(9), 569 (1965)
8. Godefroid, P., Khurshid, S.: Exploring very large state spaces using genetic algorithms. STTT **6**(2), 117–127 (2004)
9. Grosu, R., Smolka, S.A.: Monte carlo model checking. In: Halbwachs, N., Zuck, L.D. (eds.) TACAS 2005. LNCS, vol. 3440, pp. 271–286. Springer, Heidelberg (2005). doi:10.1007/978-3-540-31980-1_18
10. Harman, M., Jones, B.F.: Software engineering using metaheuristic innovative algorithms: workshop report. Inf. Softw. Technol. **43**(14), 905–907 (2001)
11. Holland, J.H.: Adaptation in Natural and Artificial Systems: An Introductory Analysis with Applications to Biology, Control and Artificial Intelligence. MIT Press, Cambridge (1992)
12. Ince, D.C. (ed.): Mechanical Intelligence (collected works of A.M. Turing). North-Holland Publishing Co., Amsterdam (1992)
13. Johnson, C.G.: Genetic programming with fitness based on model checking. In: Ebner, M., O'Neill, M., Ekárt, A., Vanneschi, L., Esparcia-Alcázar, A.I. (eds.) EuroGP 2007. LNCS, vol. 4445, pp. 114–124. Springer, Heidelberg (2007). doi:10.1007/978-3-540-71605-1_11
14. Katz, G., Peled, D.: Genetic programming and model checking: synthesizing new mutual exclusion algorithms. In: Cha, S.S., Choi, J.-Y., Kim, M., Lee, I., Viswanathan, M. (eds.) ATVA 2008. LNCS, vol. 5311, pp. 33–47. Springer, Heidelberg (2008). doi:10.1007/978-3-540-88387-6_5
15. Katz, G., Peled, D.: Model checking-based genetic programming with an application to mutual exclusion. In: Ramakrishnan, C.R., Rehof, J. (eds.) TACAS 2008. LNCS, vol. 4963, pp. 141–156. Springer, Heidelberg (2008). doi:10.1007/978-3-540-78800-3_11
16. Katz, G., Peled, D.: Synthesizing solutions to the leader election problem using model checking and genetic programming. In: Namjoshi, K., Zeller, A., Ziv, A. (eds.) HVC 2009. LNCS, vol. 6405, pp. 117–132. Springer, Heidelberg (2011). doi:10.1007/978-3-642-19237-1_13
17. Katz, G., Peled, D.: Code mutation in verification and automatic code correction. In: Esparza, J., Majumdar, R. (eds.) TACAS 2010. LNCS, vol. 6015, pp. 435–450. Springer, Heidelberg (2010). doi:10.1007/978-3-642-12002-2_36

18. Katz, G., Peled, D.: MCGP: a software synthesis tool based on model checking and genetic programming. In: Bouajjani, A., Chin, W.-N. (eds.) ATVA 2010. LNCS, vol. 6252, pp. 359–364. Springer, Heidelberg (2010). doi:10.1007/978-3-642-15643-4_28
19. Koza, J.R.: Genetic Programming: On the Programming of Computers by Means of Natural Selection. MIT Press, Cambridge (1992)
20. Koza, J.R.: Human-competitive results produced by genetic programming. Genet. Program. Evol. Mach. 11(3–4), 251–284 (2010)
21. Kupferman, O., Vardi, M.Y.: Synthesizing distributed systems. In: Proceedings of 16th Annual IEEE Symposium on Logic in Computer Science, Boston, 16–19 June 2001, pp. 389–398 (2001)
22. Manna, Z., Pnueli, A.: How to cook a temporal proof system for your pet language. In: Conference Record of the Tenth Annual ACM Symposium on Principles of Programming Languages, Austin, pp. 141–154, January 1983
23. Manna, Z., Wolper, P.: Synthesis of communicating processes from temporal logic specifications. ACM Trans. Program. Lang. Syst. 6(1), 68–93 (1984)
24. Myers, G.: The Art of Software Testing. Wiley, New York (1979)
25. Perez, J.A., Corchuelo, R., Toro, M.: An order-based algorithm for implementing multiparty synchronization. Concurr. Pract. Exp. 16(12), 1173–1206 (2004)
26. Pnueli, A., Rosner, R.: Distributed reactive systems are hard to synthesize. In: FOCS, pp. 746–757 (1990)
27. Solar-Lezama, A.: Program sketching. STTT 15(5–6), 475–495 (2013)

Regular Papers

Predicting Space Requirements for a Stream Monitor Specification Language

David M. Cerna[✉], Wolfgang Schreiner, and Temur Kutsia

Research Institute for Symbolic Computation (RISC),
Johannes Kepler University (JKU), Linz, Austria
David.Cerna@risc.jku.at

Abstract. The LogicGuard specification language for the runtime monitoring of message/event streams specifies monitors by predicate logic formulas of a certain kind. In this paper we present an algorithm that gives upper bounds for the space requirements of monitors specified in a formally elaborated core of this language. This algorithm has been implemented in the LogicGuard software and experiments have been carried out to demonstrate the accuracy of its predictions.

1 Introduction

We investigate the space complexity of the LogicGuard stream monitor specification language [14], which was developed in an industrial collaboration for the runtime monitoring of networks for security violations [11]. LogicGuard represents an alternative to the commonly used language of linear temporal logic (LTL) [12], from which efficient stream monitors can be generated but in which, due to its limited expressiveness, it can be difficult to formulate more complex properties of interest. The LogicGuard language is more expressive than LTL, because it encompasses a large fragment of predicate logic, in particular, it supports value computation and the construction of virtual streams by a form of set builder notation. However, the inclusion of such elements can make monitoring of specifications inefficient. We thus aim to identify such specifications expressing properties of interest for which monitoring is effectively possible.

First, since a LogicGuard monitor is able to "look into the past", it has in general to preserve the complete history of the stream in memory. Thus a static analysis was developed to determine whether a specification gives rise to a monitor that is able to operate with only a finite number of past messages in memory. This analysis was shown to be sound [10] and resulted in a "history pruning" optimization that enabled effective monitoring. For the soundness proof, a simplified core language with a formal operational semantics was devised.

Second, we investigated for the same core language a complementary analysis to determine the space requirements of monitors which "look into the future". In particular, we are interested in the number of formula instances which have

---

Supported by the Austrian Research Promotion Agency (FFG) in the frame of the BRIDGE program 846003 "LogicGuard II".

Y. Falcone and C. Sanchez (Eds.): RV 2016, LNCS 10012, pp. 135–151, 2016.
DOI: 10.1007/978-3-319-46982-9_9

to be preserved in memory, because their truth values cannot be determined from the observations made so far. Based on preliminary investigations we have in [3] provided upper bounds for the space complexity of monitors. The present paper improves this work by capturing these bounds more precisely, in some cases even optimally. Together with the history size, the result of this analysis bounds the memory requirements of the monitor and also the time required for processing every message/event. Also, these results seem to pinpoint a possible optimization by exchanging the order of logically independent nested quantifiers. This direction of research is based on the presented algorithm and the technical report [2].

The LogicGuard core language has much in common with Monadic First-Order Logic (MFO) [13]. LTL captures the class of star-free languages; its formulas can be translated into MFO formulas. The full language on the other hand is more closely related to Monadic Second-Order Logic (MSO) [1] which captures the class of omega-regular languages. Most space complexity results with respect to MFO and MSO use as a measure the size of the non-deterministic Büchi automaton that accepts the language of a formula. For MFO this size is in the worst case exponential in the formula size [15]; for MSO, it is in general even non-elementary [7]. These measures are relevant for model checkers which operate on non-deterministic automata; for runtime monitoring, the automata have to be determinized which results in another exponential blowup.

Because of this state space explosion, more restricted logics have been investigated. The hardware design language PSL [8] which is based on LTL defines a "simple subset" that restricts the use of disjunction to avoid exponential blow up. In [9], the class of "locally checkable" properties (a subclass of the "locally testable" properties introduced in [13]) is defined, where a word satisfies a property, if every k-length subword of the word does; such properties can be recognized by deterministic automata whose size is exponential in k but independent of the formula size. In [6] a procedure for synthesizing monitor circuits from LTL specifications is defined that restricts the exponential blow-up to those parts of a formula that involve unbounded-future operators.

LogicGuard shares some characteristics with two other systems, LOLA [5], for monitoring of synchronous systems, and LARVA [4] for real-time monitoring of Java programs. One of the main advantages of LOLA is independence of stream history, which is exactly the property shown in the history analysis of LogicGuard; however LogicGuard allows the users to run monitors without history bounds. Our work in this paper is tangent to this analysis, we focus on the memory usage of evaluation given independence of the monitor specification from stream history size. Concerning LARVA, which gives a more complete picture of resource requirements, our work in this paper plus the history analysis aims at providing a similar complete picture of monitor execution. Though, we do not provide time bounds, such bounds are closely related to the runtime representation size. More concerning this issue is discussed in the conclusion. LogicGuard can be thought of as similar to the above software, but more of an application specific monitoring specification language, that is a language for monitoring complex safety and security properties.

In our work we do not consider the translation of formulas to automata, nor use automata sizes as a space complexity measure. The operational form of a LogicGuard monitor is not an automaton but a structure that keeps in memory a (nested) set of formula instances that dynamically grows and shrinks during by the evaluation of the monitor on the stream. Thus we have investigated in [3] the number of instances kept in memory by abstracting the operational semantics into a rewriting system that is applied recursively to the formula structure. This allowed for complexity results not only in terms of asymptotic bounds but also in terms of concrete complexity functions. However, the method suffered from severe overestimation; in the present paper, we devise an analysis that provides much more accurate results. This analysis was also implemented in the LogicGuard software to estimate the space requirements of real monitors.

The rest of this paper is structured as follows: in Sect. 2, we present the core of the LogicGuard specification language and sketch its operational semantics. In Sect. 3, we define the space complexity of monitors and describe the algorithm that represents the core of the analysis. In Sects. 4 and 5, we present the formal details; in Sect. 6, we discuss experimental results. In Sect. 7, we conclude by outlining a few open problems which we would like to address in future work.

2   Core Language

The LogicGuard language [14] for monitoring event streams allows, for example, the derivation of a higher level stream (representing e.g. a sequence of messages transmitted by the datagrams) from a lower level input stream (representing e.g. a sequence of TCP/IP datagrams). Such a stream is processed by a monitor for a particular property (e.g. that every message is within a certain time bound followed by another message whose value is related in a particular way to the value of the first one). A specification of this kind has the following form:

```
type tcp; type message; ...
stream<tcp> IP;
stream<message> S = stream<IP> x satisfying start(@x) :
  value[seq,@x,combine]<IP> y
      with x < _ satisfying same(@x,@y) until end(@y) :
    @y ;
monitor<S> M = monitor<S> x satisfying trigger(@x) :
  exists<S> y with x < _ <=# x+T:
    match(@x,@y);
```

After the declaration of types tcp and message and external functions and predicates operating on objects of these types, a stream IP of TCP/IP datagrams is declared that is connected by the runtime system to the network interface. From this stream, a "virtual" stream S of "messages" is derived; each message is created by sequentially combining every datagram at position x on IP (whose value is denoted by @x) that satisfies a predicate start by application of a function combine with every subsequent datagram at position y that is related to the first one by a predicate same until a termination condition end is satisfied. The stream S is monitored by a monitor M that checks whether for every message on S that satisfies a trigger predicate within T time, a partner message appears that fits with the first message according to some match predicate.

To support a formal analysis, in [10] a core version of the LogicGuard language was defined and given a formal operational semantics. This core language has been subsequently used to analyze the complexity of monitoring and to derive the results presented in this paper. The analysis was also implemented in the LogicGuard system by translating specifications from the full language to the core language such that the analysis of the translated specification also predicts the complexity of monitoring the original specification (the translation is not semantics-preserving but generates a specification for which monitoring is at least as complex as the monitoring of the original one).

In the remainder of this section, we introduce this core language, partially relying on material from [3]. Its syntax is depicted to the left of Fig. 1 where the typed variables $M, F, \ldots$ denote elements of the syntactic domains $\mathbb{M}, \mathbb{F}, \ldots$ of monitors, formulas, etc. A monitor M has form $\forall_{0 \leq V} \colon F$ for some variable V and formula F; it processes an infinite stream of truth values $\top$ (true) or $\bot$ (false) by evaluating F for $V = 0, V = 1, \ldots$ The predicate @V denotes the value in the stream at position V, $\neg F$ denotes the negation of F, $F_1 \wedge F_2$ denotes parallel conjunction (both F_1 and F_2 are evaluated simultaneously), $F_1 \& F_2$ denotes sequential conjunction (evaluation of F_2 is delayed until the value of F_1 becomes available), $\forall_{V \in [B_1, B_2]} \colon F$ denotes quantification over the interval $[B_1, B_2]$.

$$
\begin{aligned}
M &::= \forall_{0 \leq V} \colon F. & m &::= \forall_{0 \leq V}^{\mathbb{P}(\mathbb{N} \times f \times c)} \colon f \\
F &::= @V \mid \neg F \mid F \wedge F \mid F \& F & f &::= \mathsf{d}(\top) \mid \mathsf{d}(\bot) \mid \mathsf{n}(g) \\
&\quad \mid \forall_{V \in [B,B]} \colon F. & g &::= @V \mid \neg f \mid f \wedge f \mid f \& f \\
B &::= 0 \mid \infty \mid V \mid \mid B \pm N. & &\quad \mid \forall_{V \in [b,b]} \colon f \mid \forall_{V \in [\mathsf{N}^\infty, \mathsf{N}^\infty]} \colon f \\
V &::= x \mid y \mid z \mid \ldots & &\quad \mid \forall_{V \leq \mathsf{N}^\infty}^{\mathbb{P}(\mathbb{N} \times f \times c)} \colon f \\
N &::= 0 \mid 1 \mid 2 \mid \ldots & b &::= c \to \mathsf{N}^\infty \\
& & c &::= (V \to^{\mathrm{part.}} \mathsf{N}) \times (V \to^{\mathrm{part.}} \{\top, \bot\})
\end{aligned}
$$

$$
\begin{aligned}
T(\forall_{0 \leq V} \colon F) &:= \forall_{0 \leq V}^{\emptyset} \colon T^{\mathrm{F}}(F) & T^{\mathrm{B}}(0) &:= \lambda c.\ 0 \\
T^{\mathrm{F}}(@V) &:= \mathsf{n}(@V) & T^{\mathrm{B}}(\infty) &:= \lambda c.\ \infty \\
T^{\mathrm{F}}(\neg F) &:= \mathsf{n}(\neg T^{\mathrm{F}}(F)) & T^{\mathrm{B}}(V) &:= \lambda c.\ c.1(V) \\
T^{\mathrm{F}}(F_1 \wedge F_2) &:= \mathsf{n}(T^{\mathrm{F}}(F_1) \wedge T^{\mathrm{F}}(F_2)) & T^{\mathrm{B}}(B \pm N) &:= \lambda c.\ T^{\mathrm{B}}(B)(c) \pm N \\
T^{\mathrm{F}}(F_1 \& F_2) &:= \mathsf{n}(T^{\mathrm{F}}(F_1) \& T^{\mathrm{F}}(F_2)) \\
T^{\mathrm{F}}(\forall_{V \in [B_1, B_2]} \colon F) &:= \forall_{V \in [T^{\mathrm{B}}(B_1), T^{\mathrm{B}}(B_2)]} \colon T^{\mathrm{F}}(F)
\end{aligned}
$$

Fig. 1. The core language: syntax, runtime representation, translation.

Monitor $M \in \mathbb{M}$ is translated by the function $T : \mathbb{M} \rightarrow \mathcal{M}$ defined at the bottom of Fig. 1 into its runtime representation $m = T(M) \in \mathcal{M}$ whose structure is depicted to the right; here the typed variables $m, f, \ldots$ denote elements of the runtime domains $\mathcal{M}, \mathcal{F}, \ldots$, i.e., the runtime representations of $M, F, \ldots$ Over the domain $\mathbb{N}^{\infty} = \mathbb{N} \cup \{\infty\}$ arithmetic operations are interpreted in the usual way, i.e., the operator $-$ is interpreted as truncated subtraction and for every $n \in \mathbb{N}$ we have $\infty \pm n = \infty$. The notions $\mathbb{P}(S)$, for some set S, and $A \rightarrow^{\text{part.}} B$ denote the powerset of S and the set of partial mappings from A to B, respectively. A context c consists of a pair of partial functions that assign to every variable its position and the truth value that the stream holds at that position, respectively.

During the execution of monitor M, its runtime representation $m = \forall_{0 \leq V}^{I} : f$ holds in set I those instances of its body F which could not yet be evaluated to $\top$ or $\bot$; each such instance is represented by a tuple $\langle p, f, c \rangle$ where p is the position assigned to V, f is the (current) runtime representation of F, and c represents the context to be used for the evaluation of f. A runtime representation f can be a tagged value $\mathsf{n}(g)$ where g represents the runtime representation of the formula to be evaluated in the next step; when the evaluation has completed, its value becomes $\mathsf{d}(t)$ where the truth value t represents the evaluation result.

The evaluation of a monitor's runtime representation is formally defined by a small-step operational semantics with a 6-ary transition relation $m \rightarrow_{p,s,v,R} m'$ where m is the runtime representation of the monitor prior to the transition, m' is its representation after the transition, p is the stream position of the next message value v to be processed, s denotes the sequence of p messages that have previously been processed, and R denotes the set of those positions which are reported by the transition to make the monitor body false. The monitor thus processes a stream $\langle v_0, v_1, \ldots \rangle$ by a sequence of transitions

$$\left(\forall_{0 \leq x}^{I_0} : f \right) \rightarrow_{0,s_0,v_0,R_0} \left(\forall_{0 \leq x}^{I_1} : f \right) \rightarrow_{1,s_1,v_1,R_1} \left(\forall_{0 \leq x}^{I_2} : f \right) \rightarrow \cdots$$

where $s_p = \langle v_0, \ldots, v_{p-1} \rangle$. Each set I_p contains those instances of the monitor which, by the p messages processed so far, could not be evaluated to a truth value yet and each set R_p contains the positions of those instances that were reported to become false by transition p. In particular, we have

$$I_{p+1} = \{(t, \mathsf{n}(g), c) \in \mathcal{I} \mid \exists f \in \mathcal{F} : (t, f, c) \in I' \wedge \vdash f \rightarrow_{p,s_p,v_p,c} \mathsf{n}(g)\}$$
$$R_{p+1} = \{t \in \mathbb{N} \mid \exists f \in \mathcal{F}, c \in \mathcal{C} : (t, f, c) \in I' \wedge \vdash f \rightarrow_{p,s_p,v_p,c} \mathsf{d}(\bot)\}$$

where $I' = I_p \cup \{(p, f, ((V, p), (V, v_p)))\}$. The transition relation on monitors depends on a corresponding transition relation $f \rightarrow_{p,s,v,c} f'$ on formulas where c represents the context for the evaluation of f. In each step p of the monitor transition, a new instance of the monitor body F is added to set I_p, and all instances in that set are evaluated according to the formula transition relation. Note that each formula instance in that set contains the runtime representation of a quantified formula (otherwise, it could have been immediately evaluated) which in turn contains its own instance set; thus instance sets are nested up to a depth that corresponds to the quantification depth of the monitor.

Atomic Formulas		
#	Transition	Constraints
A1	$n(@V) \to d(c.2(V)))$	$V \in dom(c.2)$

$$\cdots$$

Sequential conjunction		
C1	$n(f_1 \,\&\, f_2) \to n(n(f_1') \,\&\, f_2)$	$f_1 \to n(f_1')$
C2	$n(f_1 \,\&\, f_2) \to d(\bot)$	$f_1 \to d(\bot)$
C3	$n(f_1 \,\&\, f_2) \to n(f_2')$	$f_1 \to d(\top), f_2 \to n(f_2')$
Quantification		
Q1	$\forall_{V \in [b_1, b_2]}\colon f \to d(\top)$	$p_1 = b_1(c)\,,\ p_2 = b_2(c)\,,\ p_1 = \infty \vee p_1 > p_2$
Q2	$\forall_{V \in [b_1, b_2]}\colon f \to f'$	$p_1 = b_1(c)\,,\ p_2 = b_2(c), p_1 \neq \infty\,,\ p_1 \leq p_2,$ $n(\forall_{V \in [p_1, p_2]}\colon f) \to f'$
Q3	$n(\forall_{V \in [p_1, p_2]}\colon f) \to n(\forall_{V \in [p_1, p_2]}\colon f)$	$p < p_1$
Q4	$n(\forall_{V \in [p_1, p_2]}\colon f) \to f'$	$p_1 \leq p, n(\forall_{V \leq p_2}^{I_0}\colon f) \to f'$
Q5	$n(\forall_{V \leq p_2}^{I}\colon f) \to d(\bot)$	DF
Q6	$n(\forall_{V \leq p_2}^{I}\colon f) \to d(\top)$	$\neg DF, I'' = \emptyset, p_2 < p$
Q7	$n(\forall_{V \leq p_2}^{I}\colon f) \to n(\forall_{V \leq p_2}^{I''}\colon f)$	$\neg DF, (I'' \neq \emptyset \vee p \leq p_2)$

Fig. 2. The operational semantics of formula evaluation.

Figure 2 shows an excerpt of the operational semantics of formula evaluation (the full semantics is given in [10]) where the transition arrow $\to$ is to be read as $\to_{p,s,v,c}$ and rules Q4–Q7 are based on the following definitions.

$$I_0 = \{(i, f, (c.1[V \mapsto i], c.2[V \mapsto s(i + p - |s|)])) \mid p_1 \leq i \leq \min\{p_2 + 1, p\}\}$$

$$I' = \begin{cases} I & \text{if } p_2 < p \\ I \cup (p, f, (c.1[V \mapsto p], c.2[V \mapsto v])) & \text{otherwise} \end{cases}$$

$$I'' = \{(t, n(g), c) \in I' \mid (t, f, c) \in I' \wedge\, \vdash f \to n(g)\}$$

$$DF \equiv \exists t \in \mathbb{N}, f \in \mathcal{F}, c \in \mathcal{C} : (t, f, c) \in I' \wedge\, \vdash f \to d(\bot)$$

We provide an example adapted from [3] on the application of these rules.

Example 1. We take the monitor $M = \forall_{0 \leq x}\colon \forall_{y \in [x+1,\, x+2]}\colon @x \,\&\, @y$, which states that the current position of the stream is true as well as the next two future positions. We determine its runtime representation $m = T(M)$ as $m = \forall_{0 \leq x}^{\emptyset}\colon f$ with $f = \forall_{y \in [b_1, b_2]}\colon g$ for some b_1 and b_2 and $g = @x \,\&\, @y$. We evaluate m over the stream $\langle \top, \top, \bot, \ldots \rangle$. First consider the transition $(\forall_{0 \leq x}^{\emptyset}\colon f) \to_{0, \langle\rangle, \top, \emptyset} (\forall_{0 \leq x}^{I_0}\colon f)$. Which generates the instance set

$$I^0 = \{(0, n(\forall_{y \in [1, 2]}\colon g), (\{(x, 0)\}, \{(x, \top)\}))\}.$$

Performing another step $(\forall_{0 \leq x}^{I_0}\colon f) \to_{1, \langle\top\rangle, \top, \emptyset} (\forall_{0 \leq x}^{I_1}\colon f)$ we get

$$I^1 = \{(1, n(\forall_{y \in [2, 3]}\colon g), (\{(x, 1)\}, \{(x, \top)\})),$$
$$(0, n(\forall_{y \leq 2}^{\emptyset}\colon g), (\{(x, 0)\}, \{(x, \top)\}))\}.$$

The instance set $\emptyset$ in the runtime representation of the formula is empty, because the body of the quantified formula is propositional and evaluates instantly. Notice that the new instance is the same as the instance in I^0 but the positions are shifted by 1. The next step is $(\forall_{0 \leq x}^{I_1}\colon f) \rightarrow_{2,\langle \top, \top \rangle, \perp, \{0,1\}} (\forall_{0 \leq x}^{I_2}\colon f)$ where

$$I^2 = \left\{ (2, \mathsf{n}(\forall_{y \in [3,\,4]}\colon g), (\{(x,2)\}, \{(x, \perp)\})) \right\}.$$

The first two instances evaluate at this point and both violate the specification, thus yielding the set $\{0, 1\}$ of violating positions of the monitor. Again, the remaining instance is shifted by one position.

3   Space Complexity

Our goal is to determine the maximum size of the runtime representation of a monitor during its execution. For doing this we have to define the size of the runtime representation of monitors, formulas and formula instances.

Definition 1. *We define the functions $c_m : \mathcal{M} \to \mathbb{N}$, $c_f : \mathcal{F} \to^{part.} \mathbb{N}$, $c_g : \mathcal{G} \to \mathbb{N}$, and $c_i : \mathcal{I} \to \mathbb{N}$ which denote the size of the runtime representation of a monitor respectively unevaluated formula (with and without tag) respectively formula instance:*

$$
\begin{aligned}
c_m(\forall_{0 \leq V}^I\colon f) &= \textstyle\sum_{g \in I} c_i(g) & c_f(\mathsf{n}(g)) &= c_g(g) \\
c_g(@V) &= 0 & c_g(f_1 \wedge f_2) &= c_f(f_1) + c_f(f_2) \\
c_g(\neg f) &= c_f(f) & c_g(f_1 \,\&\, f_2) &= c_f(f_1) + c_f(f_2) \\
c_g(\forall_{V \in [b_1,\,b_2]}\colon f) &= 1 & c_g(\forall_{V \leq p}^I\colon f) &= 1 + \textstyle\sum_{g \in I} c_i(g) \\
c_g(\forall_{V \in [p_1,\,p_2]}\colon f) &= 1 & c_i((n, f, c)) &= c_f(f)
\end{aligned}
$$

Our notion of size thus only considers the quantifier structure of a monitor and its formulas that are being evaluated and ignores their propositional contents (because it is this structure that dominates the space complexity).

Now we can define a relation which determines the maximum size of the runtime representation of a monitor encountered during its execution.

Definition 2. *We define the relation $\multimap \subseteq \mathcal{M} \times \mathbb{N} \times \{\top, \perp\}^* \times \mathbb{N} \times \mathbb{N}$ inductively as follows:*

$$
\begin{aligned}
& M \multimap_{p,s,0} S' \leftrightarrow S' = c_m(M) \\
& M \multimap_{p,s,(n+1)} S' \leftrightarrow \\
& \qquad (\exists R.\ (M \rightarrow_{p,s,s(p),R} M') \wedge (M' \multimap_{p+1,s,n} S) \wedge S' = \max\{c_m(M), S\})
\end{aligned}
$$

Essentially, $M \multimap_{p,s,n} S$ states that S is the maximum size of the representation of monitor m during the execution of n transitions over the stream s starting at position p. Our goal is to compute/bound the value of S by a static analysis, i.e., without having to actually perform the transitions. We will later in Theorem 2 formalize the connection between our analysis and the relation given above. In a nutshell, this analysis proceeds as follows:

Algorithm 1. Space Requirements of an Annotated Quantifier Tree

1: **function** SR(aqt)   ▷ aqt is an annotated quantifier tree (A, a, b, qt')
2:     **if** $A = \infty$ **then**
3:         **return** ∞
4:     **else**
5:         **return** $\sum_{i=0}^{A-1} \text{SR}(aqt, i)$
6:     **end if**
7: **end function**
8:
9: **function** SR(aqt, i)   ▷ aqt is an annotated quantifier tree $(A, a, b, Q), i < A$
10:     $cil \leftarrow 1 + \min\{i, b\} - a$
11:     **if** $cil \leq 0$ & $b \geq a$ **then**
12:         **return** 1
13:     **else**
14:         **return** 0
15:     **end if**
16:     **if** $i \geq b$ **then**
17:         $inst \leftarrow 0$
18:     **else**
19:         $inst \leftarrow 1$
20:     **end if**
21:     **for all** $aqt' = (A', a', b', Q') \in Q$ **do**
22:         **if** $i < A'$ **then**
23:             $inst \leftarrow inst + cil \cdot \text{SR}(aqt', i)$
24:         **end if**
25:     **end for**
26:     **return** $inst$
27: **end function**

---

1. We compute from a monitor $M \in \mathbb{M}$ the *dominating monitor* $M' = D(M) \in \mathbb{M}$ whose space requirements on the one hand bound the requirements of M and on the other hand can be determined exactly by the subsequent analysis.
2. We translate $M' \in \mathbb{M}$ into a *quantifier tree* $qt = QT(M')$ which contains the essential information required for the analysis.
3. We translate qt into an *annotated quantifier tree* $aqt = AQT(qt)$ which labels every node with the maximum interval bound of the corresponding subtree.
4. Finally, we compute $SR(aqt) \in \mathbb{N}$ by application of Algorithm 1.

While the various steps will be explained in the following subsections, we will give a short account on the rationale behind this algorithm.

The core idea is that, if the monitor has a limit on the size of its runtime representation, it has also a limit on the number of instances stored in that representation. This limit will be reached in a finite number A of steps determined by the maximum distance that any subformula of the monitor will "look forward" in the stream in relation to the position of the message that is currently being processed. It then suffices, for every distance i in the interval $[0, A-1]$, to determine the number $N(i)$ of instances that are created by the monitor instance

$M(p)$ at position $p + i$; every monitor instance $M(p + A)$ then behaves identical to $M(p)$. In particular, if $p \geq A$ and the upper limit of the number of instances is reached, for every new instance added to some instance set another instance is removed. Thus it suffices to compute the sum of all $N(i)$ to determine the maximum space requirements of the monitor, which in essence explains the top-level function $SR(aqt)$ in the algorithm.

In the auxiliary function $SR(aqt, i)$ of the algorithm, we first determine the "current interval length" cil which essentially denotes the number of steps that have already been performed for the monitoring of the currently considered quantified formula. If $cil < 0$, the monitoring has not yet started, and the space requirements are 0. Otherwise, if i is less than the upper bound b of the quantifier interval, one more instance of the formula may be created at position i and stored for processing in future steps. Anyway, for every quantified subformula aqt', the number of instances $SR(aqt', i)$ has to be determined and multiplied with cil, since for every previous position that number of instances has been created.

After this short exposition, the following sections will elaborate the formal details of the analysis and also justify its soundness.

4   Dominating Monitor Transformation

A concept introduced in [3], *the Dominating Monitor formula*, allows us to restrict our analysis to quantified formulas whose variable intervals only depend on the outermost monitor variable, i.e. the size of every interval is the same for every value of the monitor variable.

Definition 3 (Dominating Monitor/Formula Transformation). *Let* $\mathbb{A} = \mathbb{V} \to^{part.} \mathbb{N}$ *be the domain of assignments that map variables to natural numbers. Then the* dominating monitor transformation $D : \mathbb{M} \to \mathbb{M}$ *respectively* formula transformation $D' : \mathbb{F} \times \mathbb{A} \times \mathbb{A} \to \mathbb{F}$ *are defined as follows:*

$$D(\forall_{0 \leq V}\colon F) = \forall_{0 \leq V}\colon D'(F, [V \mapsto 0], [V \mapsto 0])$$
$$D'(@V, a_l, a_h) = @V$$
$$D'(\neg F, a_l, a_h) = \neg D'(F, a_l, a_h)$$
$$D'(F_1 \,\&\, F_2, a_l, a_h) = D'(F_1, a_l, a_h) \,\&\, D'(F_2, a_l, a_h)$$
$$D'(F_1 \wedge F_2, a_l, a_h) = D'(F_1, a_l, a_h) \wedge D'(F_2, a_l, a_h)$$
$$D'(\forall_{V \in [B_1,\, B_2]}\colon F, a_l, a_h) = \forall_{V \in [h_L(B_1),\, h_H(B_2)]}\colon D'(F, a'_l, a'_h)$$

In the last equation we have $a'_l = a_l[V \mapsto h_L(B_1)]$, $a'_h = a_h[V \mapsto h_H(B_2)]$, $h_L(B_1) = \min\{[\![B_1]\!]^{a_l}, [\![B_1]\!]^{a_h}\}$, $h_H(B_2) = \max\{[\![B_2]\!]^{a_l}, [\![B_2]\!]^{a_h}\}$ *and* $[\![B]\!]^a$ *denotes the result* n *of the evaluation of bound expression* B *for assignment* a; *actually, if* B *contains the monitor variable* x, *the result shall be the expression* $x + n$ *(we omit the formal details, see the example below).*

The relationship, in terms of the maximum size of instance sets, between a monitor M and its dominating form $D(M)$ is summarized in the following theorem.

Theorem 1. *Let* $M \in \mathbb{M}$. *Then for all* $p, n, S, S' \in \mathbb{N}$ *and* $s \in \{\top, \bot\}^\omega$ *such that* $T(M) \multimap_{p,s,n} S$ *and* $T(D(M)) \multimap_{p,s,n} S'$, *we have* $S \leq S'$.

Proof. The correctness of this theorem follows from Definitions 2 and 3. Because the dominating formula considers the smallest lower bound and the largest upper bound only and creates a constant interval over which the quantifier is defined. The constant interval is the largest interval considered by the initial formula. The initial might have also considered smaller intervals which are a subset of this largest interval, thus we are checking extra instances. If $M = D(M)$, i.e., the monitor is already in its dominating form, then we have $S = S'$ because there are no extra instances being checked.

Example 2. Consider the following monitor M:

$$\forall_{0 \leq x}\colon \forall_{y \in [x+1, x+5]}\colon ((\forall_{z \in [y, x+3]}\colon \neg @z \,\&\, @z) \,\&\, G(x, y))$$
$$G(x, y) = \forall_{w \in [x+2, y+2]}\colon (\neg @y \,\&\, (\forall_{m \in [y, w]}\colon \neg @x \,\&\, @m))$$

The dominating form $D(M)$ of M is the following:

$$\forall_{0 \leq x}\colon \forall_{y \in [x+1, x+5]}\colon ((\forall_{z \in [x+1, x+3]}\colon \neg @z \,\&\, @z) \,\&\, G(x, y))$$
$$G(x, y) = \forall_{w \in [x+2, x+7]}\colon (\neg @y \,\&\, (\forall_{m \in [x+1, x+7]}\colon \neg @x \,\&\, @m))$$

Notice that additional instances are needed for the evaluation of $D(M)$.

Dominating monitors are used in the construction of *annotated quantifier trees* Which allow for a simpler space analysis of the core language. Theorem 1 makes it clear that space complexity results derived for dominating monitor provide upper bounds for the space complexity of general monitors.

5   Quantifier Trees

In this section we introduce the concept of *quantifier trees*. A quantifier tree represents the skeleton of a monitor that only describes its quantifier structure without the propositional connectives.

Definition 4 (Quantifier Trees). *A* quantifier tree *is inductively defined to be either* $\emptyset$ *or a tuple of the form* (y, b_1, b_2, Q) *where* $y \in V$, $b_1, b_2 \in B$ *and* Q *is a set of quantifier trees. Let* $\mathbb{QT}$ *be the set of all quantifier trees.*

Definition 5 (Quantifier Tree Transformation). *We define the* quantifier tree transformation $QT : \mathbb{M} \to \mathbb{QT}$, *respectively* $QT : \mathbb{F} \to \mathbb{QT}$, *recursively as follows:*

$$
\begin{array}{ll}
QT(\forall_{0 \leq V}\colon F) = (V, 0, 0, \{QT(F)\}) & QT(F \& G) = QT(F) \cup QT(G) \\
QT(F \wedge G) = QT(F) \cup QT(G) & QT(\neg F) = QT(F) \\
QT(\forall_{V \in [B_1, B_2]}\colon F) = (V, B_1, B_2, \{QT(F)\}) & QT(@V) = \emptyset
\end{array}
$$

By this transformation, every node of a quantifier tree consists of the variable bound by a quantifier, the interval bounds of the variable, and a set of nodes that represent the quantified subformulas. Thus a quantifier tree describes that internal structure of a monitor which essentially influences its space complexity.

In our analysis, we take a monitor $M \in \mathbb{M}$ and compute the quantifier tree $QT(D(M))$ of its dominating form $D(M)$. Every interval bound in a node of that tree can be only ∞, a constant c, or a term $x + c$ where x denotes the monitor variable. We may thus annotate each node of the tree with the maximum constant occurring in the bounds of the subtree rooted at that node (except in the cases of lower bound being infinity or lower bound constant and upper bound variable). The following definition formalizes this annotation.

Definition 6 (Size Annotation). *We define the size annotation* $A \,:\, \mathrm{QT}$ $\rightarrow^{part.} \mathbb{Z} \cup \{\infty\}$ *(whose domain is the set of quantifier trees resulting from the dominating form of a monitor) recursively as follows:*

$$A((V, \infty, B, qt)) \quad = 0$$
$$A((V, c_1, x + c_2, qt)) = \begin{cases} \max\{c_1, c_2\}, & \text{if } \forall q \in qt.\ A(q) \leq 0 \\ \infty, & \text{otherwise} \end{cases}$$
$$A((V, x + c_1, c_2, qt)) = A((V, x + c_1, x + c_2, qt)) = A((V, c_1, c_2, qt))$$
$$= \max\{c_1, c_2, \max_{q \in qt}\{A(q)\}\}$$
$$A((V, x + c_1, \infty, qt)) = A((V, c_1, \infty, qt)) = \infty$$

Notice that the annotation takes care of the cases when the evaluation of a formula requires an infinite amount of memory. There are three such cases, the most complex one being $(V, c_1, x + c_2, qt)$: here the amount of memory needed increases over time if qt requires a positive amount of memory, because every time we generate a new monitor instance the interval increases. This occurs while we are still evaluating the previous instances. These two factors together result in an unbounded number of instances.

The point of this annotation is to indicate at what position a monitor instance's runtime representation will have size zero. Assume we are dealing with monitor instance $x = m$, when this instance is evaluated at position $A + n$ for $m \leq n$, the runtime representation is of size zero. When $m \geq n$ the runtime representation will have a size greater than zero. When $m > A + n$, the monitor instance cannot be evaluated at all and we end up with a runtime representation with size one. Our Algorithm 1 considers monitor instance such that $n < m \leq A + n$.

Definition 7 (Annotated Quantifier Trees). *An annotated quantifier tree is inductively defined to be either $\emptyset$ or a tuple of the form (a, b_1, b_2, Q) where $a \in \mathbb{Z} \cup \{\infty\}$, $b_1, b_2 \in \mathbb{Z} \cup \{\infty\}$ and Q is a set of annotated quantifier trees. Let $\mathbb{AQT}$ be the set of all annotated quantifier trees.*

Definition 8 (Annotated Quantifier Tree Transformation). *We define* $AQT : \mathbf{QT} \to^{part.} \mathbf{AQT}$ *(whose domain is the set of quantifier trees where only the monitor variable x occurs in bounds) recursively as follows:*

$$
\begin{aligned}
AQT((V, x + c_1, x + c_2, qt)) &= (A((V, x + c_1, x + c_2, qt)), c_1, c_2, \cup_{q \in qt} AQT(q)) \\
AQT((V, c_1, c_2, qt)) &= (A((V, c_1, c_2, qt)), c_1, c_2, \cup_{q \in qt} AQT(q)) \\
AQT((V, x + c_1, c_2, qt)) &= (A((V, x + c_1, c_2, qt)), c_1, c_2, \cup_{q \in qt} AQT(q)) \\
AQT((V, x + c_1, \infty, qt)) &= (A((V, x + c_1, \infty, qt)), c_1, \infty, \cup_{q \in qt} AQT(q)) \\
AQT((V, c_1, \infty, qt)) &= (A((V, c_1, \infty, qt)), c_1, \infty, \cup_{q \in qt} AQT(q)) \\
AQT((V, \infty, x + c_1, qt)) &= (A((V, \infty, x + c_1, qt)), \infty, c_1, \cup_{q \in qt} AQT(q)) \\
AQT((V, \infty, c_1, qt)) &= (A((V, \infty, c_1, qt)), \infty, c_1, \cup_{q \in qt} AQT(q)) \\
AQT((V, c_1, x + c_2, qt)) &= (A((V, c_1, x + c_2, qt)), c_1, c_2, \cup_{q \in qt} AQT(q)) \\
AQT((V, c_1, c_2, qt)) &= (A((V, c_1, c_2, qt)), c_1, c_2, \cup_{q \in qt} AQT(q))
\end{aligned}
$$

Notice that if any subtree of an annotated quantifier tree requires infinite memory, then the uppermost node of the tree, i.e. the root, will have an annotation of ∞. Also, if the monitor represented by the annotated quantifier tree is completely backwards looking, then the annotation at the root will be 0. Thus, in these two cases no further computation is necessary to compute the space complexity of the monitor. This can be seen in function $SR(\cdot)$ of Algorithm 1. Also note that we drop the variable from the bounds. This means that the bounds c_1 and $x + c_1$ are treated the same. This is not problematic being that our algorithm only considers the case when x maps to zero. To deal with cases $x \geq 0$, we consider the monitor instance created at $x = 0$ at various future positions.

Example 3. Let us consider the monitor specification M from Example 2. Then $QT(M)$ and $AQT(QT(D(M)))$ are as depicted in Fig. 3.

We are now ready to formally state the soundness of our analysis.

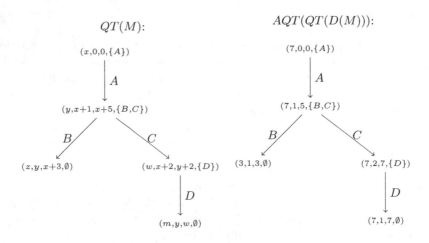

Fig. 3. (Annotated) Quantifier trees

Theorem 2. *Let $M \in \mathbb{M}$ and $aqt = AQT(QT(D(M)))$. Then for all $n, p, S \in \mathbb{N}$ and $s \in \{\top, \bot\}^{\omega}$ such that $T(M) \multimap_{p,s,n} S$, we have $S \leq SR(aqt)$.*

We informally sketch the argument for the correctness of this theorem.

Ignoring the special cases that the algorithm considers, i.e. the annotation of infinite memory, or subtrees which evaluate instantly, the heart of the algorithm is the observation that the quantifiers in dominating monitors can be treated the same independently of their position in the formula. This is not the case for non-dominating monitors because there is dependence between the intervals.

A second important observation is that the evaluation of the runtime monitors is independent of the position of the stream. Thus, we can take a single monitor instance and evaluate it as different positions to understand how all instances of the monitor will evaluate. See Sect. 3 for more detail.

Going back to the first observation and Definitions 1 and 2, we can consider the evaluation of a monitor M with a single quantifier whose interval is $[x + a, x + b]$, where $a \leq b$ and $a, b \in \mathbb{N}$. For $n \geq b$ it is easy to compute that $T(M) \multimap_{p,s,n} (b - a) + 1$. However, at positions $a \leq n < b$, $T(M) \multimap_{p,s,n} (n - a) + 1$. These results can already be found in [3]. Since the instance production of quantifiers is independent of their location in a formula, we can use these two basic results to compute the number of instances of the quantified formula produced. An elementary but tedious inductive argument leads to a soundness result and proof of Theorem 2. The argument would be, take a monitor with m quantifiers and construct a new monitor such that the monitor's formula has an additional quantifier added on top. The rest of the proof is just checking cases. We now give an asymptotic bound on the space complexity.

Theorem 3. *Let $aqt = (A, b_1, b_2, aqt') \in \mathbb{AQT}$. Then $SR(aqt) = O(A^n)$ where $n = d(aqt)$ is the quantifier depth of aqt inductively defined by $d(\emptyset) = 0$ and $d(a, b_1, b_2, Q) = 1 + \max_{aqt \in Q} d(aqt)$.*

Proof (sketch.). It is well known that $\sum_{i=0}^{A-1} i^n = O(A^n)$. If every quantifier in aqt has an interval $[0, A]$, then this summation accurately represents the computation of this algorithm: the outer $SR(\cdot)$ function represents the summation and the inner function $SR(\cdot, \cdot)$ computes the nth degree polynomial.

This result improves the $O(A^{2n})$ space complexity bound presented in [3].

6   Experimental Results

We have experimentally validated the predictions of our analysis for the following monitors where (1a) and (2a) represent the dominating forms of the monitors (1b) and (2b), respectively:

$$\forall_{0 \leq x}: \forall_{y \in [x, x+80]}: \forall_{z \in [x, x+80]}: @z \qquad (1a)$$

$$\forall_{0 \leq x}: \forall_{y \in [x, x+80]}: \forall_{z \in [x, y]}: @z \qquad (1b)$$

$$\forall_{0\leq x}\colon \forall_{y\in[x,\,x+40]}\colon \forall_{z\in[x,\,x+80]}\colon @z \tag{2a}$$

$$\forall_{0\leq x}\colon \forall_{y\in[x,\,x+40]}\colon \forall_{z\in[x,\,y+40]}\colon @z \tag{2b}$$

The diagram in Fig. 4 displays on the vertical axis the number of formula instances reported by the LogicGuard runtime system for corresponding monitors in the real specification language; the horizontal axis displays the number of messages observed so far on the stream. The monitors are defined such that the body of the innermost quantifier always evaluates to true and thus always the full quantifier range is monitored and the worst-case space complexity is exhibited. One should note that the runtime system reports the number of formula instances while our analysis determines a measure for the size of the monitor's runtime representation (which is difficult to determine in the real system); however, for monitors with less than three nested quantifiers, such as the ones given above, the results coincide (the z-quantifier does not store any instances, since its body is propositional; the y quantifier contains instances of size 1; the runtime system reports the number of these instances which is identical to the total size of these instances determined by our analysis).

As expected, we can observe that the number of instances eventually reaches, after the startup phase, an upper bound. For the dominating monitors 1a and 2a, the predictions 1 (3320) and 2 (2459) reported by the analysis accurately match the observations. As also expected, however, these predictions overestimate the number of instances observed for the non-dominating monitors 1b (160) and 2b (1659), from which the dominating monitors were derived. Interestingly, the overapproximation for monitor 2b (by a factor of 1.5) is much less than for monitor 1b (by a factor of 21). It seems that our analysis is better at predicting the number of instances for certain quantifier configurations. This would imply that quantifier configurations which we cannot predict well (i.e., where the difference between the actual space requirements and that of the dominating form is large) may have better performance in real-world scenarios. This is a topic that we are going to investigate further in future work.

We have also tested our algorithm with the following more realistic monitoring scenario which is based on the full language sketched in Sect. 2:

```
type int; type message; stream<int> IP;
stream<int> S = stream<IP> x satisfying @x>=0 :
      value[seq,@x,plus]<IP> y with x < _ <=# x+10000: @y;
monitor<S> M = monitor<S> x :
      forall<S> y with x < _ <=# x+15000:
        exists<S> z with y < _ <=# y+4000: IsEven(#z);
```

The predicate IsEven($\#z$) is true only when the message arrives at an even time. Notice that the internal quantifier of the monitor depends on the external quantifier, which as shown in Fig. 5 yields a less accurate prediction than for independent quantifiers.

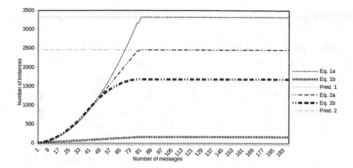

Fig. 4. Artificial experimental results versus predictions

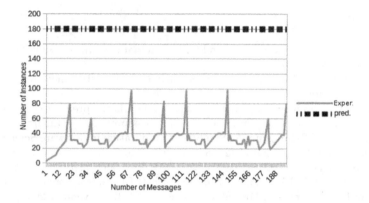

Fig. 5. Realistic experimental results versus predictions

7 Conclusions

In this paper we have studied the space complexity of runtime monitor execution. The monitors are written in the core version of the LogicGuard specification language. For this purpose, we have abstracted every monitor formula into a tree structure which contains only those aspects of the formula that influence the size of the runtime representation, which is determined by the number of instances. Using this structure, we developed an algorithm determining an upper bound for the number of formula instances that a monitor stores during execution. An essential part of this algorithm is the dominating monitor transformation, which over-approximates the actual number of instances stored. In our experimental results, it was shown that there are monitors whose instance number is accurately approximated by the algorithm's upper bound and monitors where the upper bound is far too conservative. The algorithm presented hints at a possible optimization when considered in conjunction with the technical report [2]. The ordering of quantifiers seems to greatly influence space complexity, that is larger quantifiers first implies lower space complexity. We plan to investigate optimizations based on quantifiers commutativity.

Another point we would like to address in future work is the variety of ways one can calculate the space complexity of a monitor specification. In Sect. 6, we brought up the subtle differences between our space calculation and the one used in the actual runtime system. The two measures diverge for quantifier depth three or greater. We plan to perform a similar analysis using this alternative approach to space complexity measures. On a similar note, both measures so far mentioned are closely related to possible time complexity measures. In the case of time complexity, we would like to count each individual step of the operational semantics. We want to develop a time complexity measure based on the space complexity measure devised here.

References

1. Büchi, J.R.: Weak SO arithmetic and finite automata. Z. Math. Logik Grundlagen Math. **6**, 66–92 (1960)
2. Cerna, D.: Space Complexity of LogicGuard Revisited. Technical report, RISC, JKU, Linz, October 2015
3. Cerna, D.M., Schreiner, W., Kutsia, T.: Space analysis of a predicate logic fragment for the specification of stream monitors. In: Davenport, J.H., Ghourabi, F. (eds.) 7th International Symposium on Symbolic Computation in Software Science. EPiC Computing, vol. 39, pp. 29–41 (2016)
4. Colombo, C., Pace, G.J., Schneider, G.: LARVA—safer monitoring of real-time Java programs (Tool Paper). In: 2009 Seventh IEEE International Conference on Software Engineering and Formal Methods, pp. 33–37, November 2009
5. D'Angelo, B., Sankaranarayanan, S., Sanchez, C., Robinson, W., Finkbeiner, B., Sipma, H.B., Mehrotra, S., Manna, Z.: LOLA: runtime monitoring of synchronous systems. In: 12th International Symposium on Temporal Representation and Reasoning (TIME 2005), pp. 166–174, June 2005
6. Finkbeiner, B., Kuhtz, L.: Monitor circuits for LTL with bounded and unbounded future. In: Bensalem, S., Peled, D.A. (eds.) RV 2009. LNCS, vol. 5779, pp. 60–75. Springer, Heidelberg (2009). doi:10.1007/978-3-642-04694-0_5
7. Frick, M., Grohe, M.: The complexity of FO and monadic SO logic revisited. Ann. Pure Appl. Logic **130**(1–3), 3–31 (2004)
8. IEEE Std 1850-2007: Standard for Property Specification Language (PSL) (2007)
9. Kupferman, O., Lustig, Y., Vardi, M.Y.: On locally checkable properties. In: Hermann, M., Voronkov, A. (eds.) LPAR 2006. LNCS (LNAI), vol. 4246, pp. 302–316. Springer, Heidelberg (2006). doi:10.1007/11916277_21
10. Kutsia, T., Schreiner, W.: Verifying the Soundness of Resource Analysis for LogicGuard Monitors. Technical Report 14–08, RISC, JKU, Linz (2014)
11. LogicGuard II, November 2015. http://www.risc.jku.at/projects/LogicGuard2/
12. Maler, O., Nickovic, D., Pnueli, A.: Real time temporal logic: past, present, future. In: Pettersson, P., Yi, W. (eds.) FORMATS 2005. LNCS, vol. 3829, pp. 2–16. Springer, Heidelberg (2005). doi:10.1007/11603009_2
13. McNaughton, R., Papert, S.: Counter-Free Automata. Research Monograph, vol. 65. MIT Press, Cambridge (1971)

14. Schreiner, W., Kutsia, T., Cerna, D., Krieger, M., Ahmad, B., Otto, H., Rummer-storfer, M., Gössl, T.: The LogicGuard Stream Monitor Specification Language (Version 1.01). Tutorial and Reference Manual, RISC, JKU, Linz (2015)
15. Vardi, M.Y., Wolper, P.: An automata-theoretic approach to automatic program verification. In: LICS 1986, 16–18 June, Cambridge, Massachusetts, USA, pp. 332–344. IEEE Computer Society (1986)

A Stream-Based Specification Language for Network Monitoring

Peter Faymonville, Bernd Finkbeiner$^{(\boxtimes)}$, Sebastian Schirmer, and Hazem Torfah

Saarland University, Saarbrücken, Germany
finkbeiner@react.uni-saarland.de

Abstract. We introduce Lola 2.0, a stream-based specification language for the precise description of complex security properties in network traffic. The language extends the specification language Lola with two new features: template stream expressions, which allow input data to be carried along the stream, and dynamic stream generation, where new monitors can be invoked during the monitoring process for the monitoring of new subtasks on their own time scale. Lola 2.0 is simple and expressive: it combines the ease-of-use of rule-based specification languages like Snort with the expressiveness of heavy-weight scripting languages or temporal logics previously needed for the description of complex stateful dependencies and statistical measures. Lola 2.0 specifications are monitored by incrementally constructing output streams from input streams, while maintaining a store of partially evaluated expressions. We demonstrate the flexibility and expressivity of Lola 2.0 using a prototype implementation on several practical examples.

Keywords: Runtime verification · Monitoring · Network intrusion detection

1 Introduction

Automatic support for the monitoring of network traffic has become essential in order to cope with the massive exchange of data over high-speed networks and the constantly rising number of attacks. With the help of *network intrusion detection systems* (NIDS), system administrators check the network against predefined malicious patterns and identify previously unknown attack patterns based on irregularities observed in the network traffic. For instance, to check whether a server is subject to a denial of service attack, one observes whether a large number of connections are established to the server in a short period of time from external IP addresses.

Traditionally, monitoring tasks in telecommunication networks have been specified in powerful scripting languages, such as the N-Code language in the Network Flight Recorder (NFR) [14]. Intrusion detection systems implemented

This work was partially supported by the German Research Foundation (DFG) in the Collaborative Research Center 1223 and by the Deutsche Telekom Foundation.

Y. Falcone and C. Sanchez (Eds.): RV 2016, LNCS 10012, pp. 152–168, 2016.
DOI: 10.1007/978-3-319-46982-9_10

in such languages extract from the network traffic a complex combination of temporal patterns and statistical measures that distinguish intrusions from normal network traffic. Such heavy-weight solutions are, however, expensive to develop and maintain, since specification and monitoring algorithm are typically not separated and dependencies on future behavior have to be explicitly encoded.

Descriptive specification languages allow us to naturally express future protocol behavior in concise and readable specifications. One such language is the stream-based specification language Lola [7], which describes complex temporal patterns with references into the past and the future in a simple way and can both monitor correctness properties and compute statistical measures. Lola specifications resemble programs in a synchronous programming language like Lustre [12], Esterel [5], or Signal [10], but may include formulas that refer to future values of streams. For network monitoring tasks, however, specifying properties for individual connections of a network stream is cumbersome, because every possible connection would need to be defined in a separate stream.

The contribution of the paper is to introduce new language features into the Lola language that allow us to run each stream on an *individual slice of the incoming data* and on an *individual time scale*. In this way, inexpensive patterns can be used as *filters* that produce streams that run at slower speeds with less data, and can therefore be analyzed against more expensive patterns.

To illustrate the need for the new language features of Lola, consider the classic Lola specification

input bool loginSuccess
output int attempts := ite(loginSuccess, 0, attempts[+1,0] + 1)

which computes, from a given position in the stream, the number of overall failed login attempts *until* that future point of time where either the login attempt succeeds or the stream ends. Now, to distinguish the login attempts of individual users, Lola 2.0 extends the streams of Lola to parameterized *stream templates*. The instantiation of a template, as well as the speed in which an instance runs, is determined dynamically by auxiliary *invocation* and *extension* streams. If, for example, we wish to count the number of failed login attempts *per user*, we might introduce a stream template

> **input bool** loginSuccess
> **input String** uid
> **output int** attempts<user> : **inv** :uid; **ext** :useraction :=
>   ite(loginSuccess,0,
>   attempts(user)[+1,0]+1)

where uid and useraction are auxiliary streams: the uid stream contains the id of the user who is currently logging in, and causes an invocation of the instance of the attempts stream corresponding to that user if that instance does not exist already, i.e., during the *first* login attempt of that user; the useraction stream extends the attempts stream whenever that user attempts *another* login:

> **output bool** useraction<u> := (uid=u)

As a result, the `attempts(u)` stream of a particular user u consists of those positions, and only those positions, where the user u tries to log on. The condition under which the monitor should raise an alarm is indicated in Lola with the keyword `trigger`. In Lola 2.0, the trigger condition might involve an aggregation over the instances of a stream template, as in the following example:

> **output bool** `bruteforce<user>` : **inv:** `uid`; **ext:** `useraction` :=
> `attempts(user)>3`
>
> **trigger** `any(bruteforce)`

The alarm is triggered if there exists a user who attempts more than three failed login attempts. Note that the only expensive part of the monitoring happens in the `attempts(user)` streams, which each run very slowly, at the pace of an individual user, and deal with very little data. While many instances of the `attempts` template might be active at the same time, this does not constitute a performance bottleneck as the instances could easily be distributed over several parallel machines.

Outline. In Sect. 2, we relate Lola 2.0 to other specification mechanisms for network monitoring. In Sect. 3 we discuss the syntax of Lola 2.0. In Sect. 4 we provide some illustrative examples of the application of Lola 2.0 to network intrusion detection. In Sect. 5 we turn to describing the semantics of Lola 2.0 in more detail. In Sect. 6, we present a monitoring algorithm for Lola 2.0 specifications. We report on experimental results in Sect. 7 and conclude in Sect. 8.

2   Related Work

Approaches to network intrusion detection are broadly classified into *signature-based* [1,11,16,17,19] and *anomaly-based* [8,15] approaches. Signature-based approaches monitor for known patterns of attacks, while anomaly-based approaches detect deviations from the usual behavior. Typically, signature-based approaches run the risk of missing attacks that do not follow a known pattern, anomaly-based approaches can recognize previously unseen attacks, but often produce false alarms. While our approach belongs to the category of signature-based approaches, it can, to some extent, emulate an anomaly-based approach by computing certain statistics and raising an alarm if the values fall out of the normal range.

Within the signature-based approaches, a wide range of specification languages has been proposed that differ significantly in expressiveness and ease-of-use. One of the most common NIDS is the Snort system [19]. Specifications for Snort are based on a simple rule-based model language that describes per packet tests and actions. Snort rules can define statistical anomaly patterns over packets and collect traffic based on data contained in the payload of the packets. Suricata[1], is a more recent implementation using the same rule-based

---

[1] https://suricata-ids.org.

input language as Snort. The focus on individual packets, rather than the relation between multiple packets, is the key weakness of light-weight specification approaches like Snort and Suricata rules. On the other end of the expressivity spectrum, systems like Bro [18], which use an event-based scripting language as a specification mechanism, fall into the category of heavy-weight specification mechanisms, which have the full power of a programming language.

As first pointed out by Roger and Goubault-Larrecq [20], the temporal patterns in the relations of multiple packets can naturally be expressed in a temporal logic. Approaches to intrusion detection based on temporal logic include the ORCHIDS [17], TeStID [2], and MONID [16] tools. ORCHIDS uses a specialized temporal logic tailored towards eventuality properties and employs an expressive underlying rule-based language as well as the capability to spawn monitors for individual instances of monitoring tasks. In comparison to Lola 2.0, non-determinism in the specification has to be handled explicitly. TeStID uses Many Sorted First Order Metric Temporal Logic (MSFOMTL). MONID uses the temporal logic EAGLE, which is based on parameterized recursive equations. A simpler, and often more efficient version of EAGLE is the rule-based specification language RuleR [4].

Our approach is based on the stream-based specification language Lola [7]. The definition of Lola output streams in terms of other streams resembles synchronous programming languages (notably Lustre [12], Esterel [5], and Signal [10]). Unlike these languages, Lola is not, however, an *executable* programming language, but a *descriptive* specification language. Lola subsumes many other specification languages, such as the temporal logics, and has been shown to provide natural encodings for both the temporal and the statistical measures needed to monitor industrial hardware designs. More theoretical work on Lola concerns the complexity, expressiveness, succinctness, and closure properties of Boolean streams [6]. The new version of Lola presented in this paper extends the original language with the concepts of *parameterization* and *multiple temporal time scales*.

Parameterization is a common concept in specification languages for runtime verification. In parametric temporal logic [9], parameters refer to quantitative measures, such as the number of steps until an eventuality is fulfilled. While this type of parametric specification can also be encoded in Lola, the purpose of the parameterization in Lola 2.0 is to run individual streams on small slices of the incoming data stream. This type of parameterization is similar to the parameterization in QEA (Quantified Event Automata) [3], an approach based on state machines, where a given trace is sliced into separate projections for different parameter values. Both types of parameterization appear in rule-based specification languages like LogFire [13], where a set of facts $F(v_1, \ldots, v_n)$ for some name F and parameter values $v_1, \ldots, v_n$ is maintained. A generic approach to add parameterization to an existing specification language was presented by Rosu and Chen [21]. The parameterization in Lola 2.0 extends these approaches with the dynamic creation and termination of streams and the aggregation of statistics over the instances of a stream template.

3   Stream-Based Specifications

We introduce the syntax of stream-based Lola specifications in two steps. We begin with "standard" Lola, as introduced in [7], where specifications are given by equations over stream variables. In the second step, we introduce Lola 2.0, by generalizing such stream equations to stream equation templates.

Lola 1.0. A *Lola specification* is a system of equations of stream expressions over typed *stream variables* of the following form:

$$\textbf{input } T_1 \ t_1$$
$$\vdots$$
$$\textbf{input } T_m \ t_m$$
$$\textbf{output } T_{m+1} \ s_1 := e_1(t_1, \ldots, t_m, s_1, \ldots s_n)$$
$$\vdots$$
$$\textbf{output } T_{m+n} \ s_n := e_n(t_1, \ldots, t_m, s_1, \ldots s_n)$$

Each stream expression $e_i(t_1, \ldots, t_m, s_1, \ldots s_n)$, for $1 \leq i \leq n$ is defined over a set of *independent* stream variables $t_1, \ldots, t_m$ and *dependent* stream variables $s_1, \ldots, s_n$. Independent stream variables refer to input stream values, and dependent stream variables refer to output stream values computed over the values of all streams. All stream variables are typed: the type of an independent stream variable t_i is T_i, the type of an dependent stream variable s_i is T_{m+i}.

A *stream expression* $e(t_1, \ldots, t_m, s_1, \ldots s_n)$ is defined recursively as follows:

- Let c be a constant of type T and let s_i for $1 \leq i \leq n$ be a stream variable of type T', then both $e = c$ and $e = s_i$ are atomic stream expressions of type T and T' respectively.
- Let $f : T_1 \times T_2 \times \ldots T_k \to T$ be a k-ary function, then for stream expressions $e_1, \ldots e_k$ of type $T_1, \ldots, T_k$, the expression $e = f(e_1, \ldots, e_k)$ is a stream expression of type T.
- Let b be a boolean stream expression and e_1, e_2 stream expressions of type T, then $e = \textbf{ite}(b, e_1, e_2)$ is a stream expression of type T. The expression evaluates to e_1 when b is *true* and to e_2 when b is *false*.
- Let e' be a stream expression of type T, d a constant of type T, and i an integer, then $e = e'[i, d]$ is a stream expression of type T. The stream expression $e'[i, d]$ refers to the value of expression e' offset i positions from the current position. If such a position is not defined, then the value of the stream is the default value d.

In addition to the stream equations, Lola specifications often contain a list of *triggers*

$$\textbf{trigger } \varphi_1, \varphi_2, \ldots, \varphi_k$$

where $\varphi_1, \varphi_2, \ldots, \varphi_k$ are expressions of type boolean over the stream variables. Triggers generate notifications when their value becomes *true*.

Lola 2.0. Lola 2.0 extends Lola with *stream equation templates* of the following form:

$$\textbf{output } T \; s\langle p_1 : T_1, \ldots, p_l : T_l \rangle : \textbf{inv} : s_{inv};$$
$$\textbf{ext} : s_{ext};$$
$$\textbf{ter} : s_{ter} :=$$
$$e(t_1, \ldots, t_m, s_1, \ldots s_n, p_1, \ldots, p_l)$$

Each such stream equation template introduces a *template variable s* of type T that depends on *parameters* $p_1, \ldots, p_l$ of types $T_{p_1}, \ldots T_{p_l}$, respectively. For given values $v_1, \ldots, v_l$ of matching types $T_{p_1}, \ldots T_{p_l}$ we call

$$s\langle v_1, \ldots, v_l \rangle = e(t_1, \ldots, t_m, s_1, \ldots s_n, p_1, \ldots, p_l)[p_1/v_1, \ldots p_l/v_l]$$

an *instance* of s. The template variables s_{inv}, s_{ext}, and s_{ter} indicate the following *auxiliary streams*:

- s_{inv} is the *invocation* template stream variable of s and has type $T_{p_1} \times \cdots \times T_{p_l}$. If some instance of s_{inv} has value $(v_1, \ldots v_l)$, then an instance $s\langle v_1, \ldots, v_l \rangle$ of s is invoked.
- s_{ext} is the *extension* template stream variable of s and has type *bool* and parameters of type $T_{p_1}, \ldots T_{p_l}$. If s is invoked with parameter values $\alpha = (v_1, \ldots, v_l)$, then an extension stream s_{ext}^{α} is invoked with the same parameter values. If s_{ext}^{α} is *true*, then the value of the output stream $s\langle v_1, \ldots, v_l \rangle$ is computed at the position.
- s_{ter} is the *termination* template stream variable of s and has type *bool* and parameters of type $T_{p_1}, \ldots T_{p_l}$. If s is invoked with parameter values $\alpha = (v_1, \ldots, v_l)$, then a terminate stream s_{ter}^{α} is invoked with the same parameter values. If s_{ter}^{α} is *true*, then the output stream $s\langle v_1, \ldots, v_l \rangle$ is terminated and not extended until it is invoked again.

A *template stream expression* $e(t_1, \ldots, t_m, s_1, \ldots s_n, p_1, \ldots, p_l)$ is defined like a stream expression in Lola 1.0, with the following additions:

- Let p_i for $i \in \{1, \ldots l\}$ be a parameter. Then p_i is a template stream expression of type T_i.
- Let s be a template variable, and Op be an *aggregation operator* of type T. For example, **any** is an aggregation operator of type **bool**, **count** is an aggregation operator of type **int**. Then $Op(s)$ is a template stream expression of type T.

If a stream equation template has no parameters, we omit the empty parameter tuple $\langle \rangle$. We also permit that any of the auxiliary streams may be omitted, in which case the invocation stream is set to the default stream σ_0, which is the constant stream that produces the empty tuple () in every position; the extension template stream is set to the constant stream that produces *true* in every position, and the termination template stream is set to the constant stream that produces *false* in every position. Note that in this way, Lola 1.0 stream equations are special cases of Lola 2.0 stream equation templates. The same also holds for independent stream variables. If omitted from the declaration, the invocation, extension and termination streams are set to the default values.

4   Example Specifications

In this section we show how we can employ Lola 2.0 to define properties over network traffic. Consider the Lola 2.0 specification given in Fig. 1. The specification defines a pattern for detecting a web application fingerprinting attack. In such an attack a hostile client sends arbitrary HTTP requests and awaits the responses from the server, which contain a HTTP response header with information about the server software vendor, its version, and more. Such information allows the client to determine known vulnerabilities according to the type of the server. The attacker mostly requests access to random URLs, which may lead in many cases to an HTTP response declaring either a bad HTTP request or a page not found message. One way to observe such an attack is to observe server responses containing either "Bad HTTP request" or "Page not found" messages and then check whether the IP address, which initiated the request, continues sending random requests to the server.

In the specification, the stream `webApplicationFingerprinting` is invoked for a pair of source and destination addresses every time the invocation stream `badHttpRequestInvoke` is extended with a new pair of addresses. Such a pair

```
input string Protocol, RequestMethod, ResponsePhrase, Source, Destination

output (string, string) badHttpRequestInvoke;
ext: Protocol="HTTP" & (ResponsePhrase="Bad Request" | "Not Found")
:= (Source, Destination)

output bool badHttpRequestExtend<src, dst>:
inv: badHttpRequestInvoke;
:= src=Source & dst=Destination &
ResponsePhrase = "Bad Request" | "Not Found"

output bool webApplicationFingerprintingTerminate<src,dst>:
inv: badHttpRequestInvoke;
:= src=Source & dst=Destination & ResponsePhrase = "OK"

output int webApplicationFingerprinting<src, dst>:
inv: badHttpRequestInvoke;
ext: badHttpRequestExtend;
ter: webApplicationFingerprintingTerminate
:= webApplicationFingerprinting(src, dst)[-1,0]+1

trigger any(webApplicationFingerprinting > threshold)
```

Fig. 1. A Lola 2.0 specification for a web application fingerprinting pattern

is recorded whenever a bad request or no page found response is sent out, as defined by the extension stream of `badHttpRequestInvoke`[2].

Once an instance of `webApplicationFingerprinting` is invoked it tracks the number of bad requests, using the extension stream `badHttpRequestExtend` which is invoked simultaneously with the same pair of addresses. If at some point the status code OK was returned then the instance is terminated via the termination stream `webApplicationFingerprintingTerminate`. This allows the monitoring process to discard many instances of the template that otherwise would cause many false positive alerts. If an instance is not terminated and its value exceeds a certain threshold, then the monitoring algorithm alerts about a potential web application fingerprinting threat. The latter is defined by the keywords `trigger` and `any`.

We consider another example involving denial of service attacks (DoS). One way of checking whether a server is subject to a DoS attack, is to observe whether a large number of connections are established to the server in a short period of time from external IP addresses. Consider a client that is trying to perform a DoS attack via a TCP-SYN scan. The hostile client sends a SYN request to the server to initiate a three-way handshake, upon which the server responds with a SYN/ACK packet including the port number it was sent from. The malicious client then sends no ACK packet to acknowledge the reception of the SYN/ACK package, or might even request a reset of the communication, which leaves the port and connection data structure open and thus leads to eventual resource exhaustion. One way to monitor such an attack is to check whether a large number of uncompleted handshakes are observed in the traffic.

Figure 2 shows a specification for checking whether the number of open TCP requests exceeds a given threshold using the stream template `tcpSynScan`. Whenever there is a TCP request from a client to the server, the monitor waits for an acknowledgment from the client. This is determined by the specification `waitForAck` which is invoked by the stream `incompleteHandshakeInvoke` for a pair of addresses. At the same time the stream `incompleteHandshakeInvoke` also invokes an instance of the template `tcpSynInvoke`. If a certain time passes without seeing an acknowledgement, then the instance is extended by the pair of source and destination addresses and an instance of `tcpSynScan` is invoked to monitor a potential TCP SYN scan attack for this pair of IP addresses. From this position on the monitor keeps track of how many TCP requests are received from an IP address or whether Syn requests keep being sent from one address without acknowledgements. When one of the thresholds `threshold2` and `threshold3` is exceeded, the monitor triggers an alert. This is achieved using the keywords `trigger`, `any` and `count`.

---

[2] In Fig. 1 the extension stream of `badHttpRequestInvoke` is defined explicitly in the output stream. This could also have been defined separately by a declaration of another boolean output stream with the same condition.

```
input string Protocol, Syn, Ack, Source, Destination

output (string,string) incompleteHandshakeInvoke:
ext: Protocol= "TCP" & Syn="Set" & Ack="Not Set";
:= (Source,Destination)

output bool incompleteHandshakeTerminate<src, dst>:
inv: incompleteHandshakeInvoke;
=Source=src & Destination=dst & Syn="Not Set" & Ack="Set"

output int waitForAck<src,dst>:
inv: incompleteHandshakeInvoke;
ter: incompleteHandshakeTerminate
= waitForAck(src, dst)[-1,0]+1

output (string,string) tcpSynInvoke<src, dst>:
inv: incompleteHandshakeInvoke;
ext: waitForAck(src,dst)[0,0] > threshold
ter: waitForAck(src,dst)[0,0] > threshold
= (src,dst)

output bool tcpSynExtend<src,dst>:
inv:tcpSynInvoke;
= src = Source & dst = Destination & Syn = "Set"

output bool tcpSynTerminate<src,dst>:
inv:tcpSynInvoke;
= src = Source & dst = Destination & Syn = "Not Set" & Ack="Set"

output int tcpSynScan<src,dst>:
inv:tcpSynInvoke;
ext:tcpSynExtend;
ter:tcpSynTerminate;
=tcpSynScan(src,dst)[-1,0] +1

trigger count(tcpSynScan) > threshold2
trigger any(tcpSynScan > threshold3)
```

Fig. 2. A specification of a TCP SYN scan pattern

5 Lola 2.0 Semantics

We now give a formal definition of the Lola 2.0 semantics. Let Φ be a specification with independent stream variables $t_1, \ldots, t_m$ of type $T_1, \ldots T_m$, respectively, and template stream variables $s_1, \ldots, s_n$ of types $T_{m+1}, \ldots T_{m+n}$, respectively.

We fix a natural number $N \geq 0$ as the length of the traces. An *evaluation model* of Φ is a set Γ of streams of length N, where each stream has type $T_{m+i} \cup \{\#\}$ for $1 \leq i \leq n$. The symbol $\#$ is added to the types to indicate that the stream does not exist yet at a particular position, for example if the stream has not been invoked yet. In the following, we use s_i^α to refer to the instance of a template variable s_i with parameter values α, and σ_i^α to refer to a corresponding stream in Γ.

We now pose several conditions that evaluation models must satisfy. Intuitively, the conditions concern the two mutually dependent requirements that (1) the evaluation model is populated with a sufficiently large set of streams, and that (2) each stream actually produces the right values. To guarantee requirement (1), we describe the elements of Γ inductively as follows:

- $\sigma_0 \in \Gamma$, where σ_0 is the constant stream that produces the empty tuple () in every position.
- For each template stream variable s_i, we consider the associated invocation stream variable s_{inv}. If Γ contains some stream σ_{inv}^α for some parameter values $\alpha \in T_1^{inv} \times \cdots \times T_{l_i}^{inv}$, then Γ must also contain a stream for every instance of s_i invoked by σ_{inv}^α at some position; i.e., for all $j < N$ where $\sigma_{inv}^\alpha(j) \neq \#$, there must exist some stream $\sigma_i^\beta \in \Gamma$ for the instance of s_i given by the parameter values $\beta = \sigma_{inv}^\alpha(j)$.

To guarantee condition (2), that each stream actually produces the right values, we first characterize the positions in which the stream exists.

Let $alive(s_i, (v_1, \ldots, v_{l_i}), j)$ be *true* for some stream position j if the stream was actually invoked, i.e., there is a stream $\sigma_{inv}^\beta \in \Gamma$ for some instance of the associated invocation stream variable s_{inv} (with arbitrary parameter values β) and an earlier stream position $j' < j$ such that $\sigma_{inv}^\beta(j') = (v_1, \ldots, v_l)$, and the stream was not terminated in the meantime, i.e., for $j' < j'' \leq j$ we have $\sigma_{ter}^{\beta'}(j'') = false$ for all instances of the termination stream variable with $\beta' = (v_1, \ldots, v_l)$.

If a stream exists in some position, we determine its value by evaluating the corresponding stream expression. For each stream $\sigma_i^\alpha \in \Gamma$ for the instance $\alpha = (v_1, \ldots, v_{l_i})$ of some stream template variable s_i,

$$\sigma_i^\alpha(j) = \begin{cases} val(e_i[p_1/v_1, \ldots, p_{l_i}/v_{l_i}], j) & \text{if } alive(s_i, (v_1, \ldots, v_{l_i}), j) \\ \# & \text{otherwise} \end{cases}$$

where the evaluation function $val(e_i[p_1/v_1, \ldots, p_{l_i}/v_{l_i}], j)$ is defined as follows:

- if $\sigma_{ext}^\alpha(j) = true$, where σ_{ext}^α is the extension stream of σ_i^α, then $val(e, j)$ is defined as follows:
  - $val(c)(j) = c$
  - $val(t_h)(j) = \tau_h(j)$ for $1 \leq h \leq m$
  - $val(f(e_1, \ldots, e_h))(j) = f(val(e_1)(j), \ldots, val(e_h)(j))$
  - $val(\textbf{ite}(b, e_1, e_2))(j) = \text{if } val(b)(j) \text{ then } val(e_1)(j) \text{ else } val(e_2)(j)$
  - $val(s_h^\beta[0, d])(j) = \begin{cases} \sigma_h^\beta(j) & alive(s_h, \beta, j) \\ d & \text{otherwise} \end{cases}$

$$\bullet \ val(s_h^\beta[k,d])(j) = \begin{cases} d & \text{if } j \geq N \text{ or } j < 0 \\ val(e[k-1,d])(j+1) & \text{if } k > 0, \sigma_{ext}^\beta(j) = true \\ val(e[k+1,d])(j-1) & \text{if } k < 0, \sigma_{ext}^\beta(j) = true \\ val(e[k,d])(j+1) & \text{if } k > 0 \\ val(e[k,d])(j-1) & \text{otherwise} \end{cases}$$

– otherwise $val(e_i[p_1/v_1, \ldots, p_{l_i}/v_{l_i}], j) = \#$

Intuitively, the extend stream defines a local clock for every template variable. Unlike in Lola, where all streams follow the same one clock, streams in Lola 2.0 follow several clocks depending on their invocation time and the extension pace. The invoke stream starts new instances of the template output stream whenever it evaluates to a fresh parameter instantiation. The extend stream is evaluated for all instances which are active on a current stream. Whenever it evaluates to *true*, the template output stream instance advances on its timeline. A template output stream instance is terminated whenever its terminate stream evaluates to true for its parameter instantiation. The clocks can be inductively defined on top of the clock of stream σ_0, which we call the base clock.

Well-defined specifications. We say a specification is *well-defined*, if for any set of appropriately typed input streams of length N for the independent stream variables, it has a unique evaluation model. In general, specifications need not be well-defined, for example through self-references without offsets in stream expressions or circular offsets via multiple stream variables, which lead to the non-existence of evaluation models or lead to infinitely many evaluation models for a given set of input streams.

Since well-definedness is a semantic condition and expensive to check, we give a syntactic criterion, called *well-formedness*, which implies well-definedness and can be checked by a simple check on the dependency graph. For a specification Φ, its associated *dependency graph* is a weighted and directed multi-graph $G = \langle V, E \rangle$ with $V = \{s_1, \ldots, s_n, t_1, \ldots, t_m\}$. We add an edge $e \in E$ where $e = \langle s_i, s_k, w \rangle$ from s_i to s_k with weight w iff the stream expression of s_i contains the subexpression $s_k[w,d]$ for some default value d. Edges leading to t_k are added analogously. Thus, the edges represent the fact that expression s_i depends on s_k at (positive or negative) offset w. Since each stream may be used more than once with different offsets in an expression, the graph may contain multiple edges between vertices. A *cycle* in the graph is a sequence $v_1 \xrightarrow{e_1, w_1} v_2 \ldots v_k \xrightarrow{e_k, w_k} v_{k+1}$ such that all $e_i = \langle v_i, v_{i+1}, w_i \rangle \in E$, and $v_1 = v_{k+1}$. The total weight of the cycle is the sum of all weights w_i along the cycle. A specification is *well-formed*, iff it does not contain a zero-weight cycle. Well-formed specifications are guaranteed to be well-defined.

6   The Monitoring Algorithm

We now describe a monitoring algorithm for the evaluation of a given Lola 2.0 specification on a set of input streams for the independent stream variables.

The streams become available *online*, i.e., one position at a time. The length of the streams is *a-priori* unknown and the full streams may be too large to store in memory.

The central data structure of the algorithm is the *equation store*, which consists of the following parts: A store S, in which we keep a set of the currently active instances of template stream variables; a store of *resolved* equations R, which are fully evaluated but may still be used by other streams, and a store of *unresolved* equations U, which are not yet fully evaluated.

For each position, we begin the evaluation by adding the input stream values at the current position to the store R. As we are adding resolved equations to R, we always check whether they start new invocations for any of the template stream expressions. Should this happen, we add these to the store S and add corresponding unresolved equations to the store U. We then continue by simplifying the equations in U by function applications, rewriting rules for conditionals and resolving stream access and offsets by the equations from store R. The invocation check and the simplification step are repeated until nothing new is added to R and no new streams are invoked. The number of repetitions depends on the structure and dependencies of the specification. Equations are removed from the store R whenever they are not needed anymore.

To simplify the presentation of the algorithm, we assume that all extension and termination streams are locally determined, i.e., their value at every position can be calculated just from the values of the input streams at the same or earlier positions. Let, for each independent stream variable t_i, the corresponding input stream be denoted by τ_i. Starting at position $j = 0$ with the empty equation stores, the algorithm performs the following steps for each position:

1. For each input stream t_i, add $\tau_i(j) = c$ to store R.
2. Add $\sigma_0(j) = ()$ to R.
3. Initialize the set of active stream valuations: For all template streams s_i, and valuations α such that $\alpha \in S(s_i, j - 1)$, if $\sigma_{\text{ext}}^\alpha = \text{true}$ and $\sigma_{\text{ter}}^\alpha = \text{false}$ then $\alpha \in S(s_i, j)$.

Then repeat the following steps until a fixpoint is reached:

1. Simplify all equations in U, if any expression is now constant, add to R.
2. Check for new invocations, extensions and terminations by the additions to R.
3. If for some stream template s_i, and any position k, $\sigma_{inv}^\alpha(k) = \beta$ is added to R, then $S(s_i, k) = S(s_i, k) \cup \beta$ and we add $\sigma_i^\beta(k) = e$ to U.
4. If for some stream template s_i, and any position k, $\sigma_{ext}^\alpha(k) = true$ is added to R, we add $\sigma_i^\alpha(k) = e$ to U.

The equations in U are simplified according to the following rules:

- Function application: e.g. $0 + x \rightarrow x$, ...
- Rewriting for conditionals: $\mathbf{ite}(true, e_1, e_2) \rightarrow e_1$, $\mathbf{ite}(false, e_1, e_2) \rightarrow e_2$.
- Resolve stream access: If $\sigma_{i,\alpha}(j) = c$ in R, replace every occurence of $\sigma_{i,\alpha}(j)$ by c in U.

- Resolve stream offsets: If some $\sigma_{i,\alpha}(j) = e_i$ in U contains a subexpression $\sigma_{i,\alpha}(j)[k,d]$, $\sigma_{ext}^{\alpha}(j) = c$ is in R for $c \in \{true, false\}$, and $\sigma_{ter}^{\alpha}(j) = false$ then

$$\sigma_{i,\alpha}(j)[k,d] \rightarrow \begin{cases} \sigma_{i,\alpha}(j) & \text{if } k = 0, \sigma_{ext}^{\alpha}(j) = true \\ \sigma_{i,\alpha}(j+1)[k-1,d] & \text{if } k > 0, \sigma_{ext}^{\alpha}(j) = true \\ \sigma_{i,\alpha}(j-1)[k+1,d] & \text{if } k < 0, \sigma_{ext}^{\alpha}(j) = true \\ \sigma_{i,\alpha}(j+1)[k,d] & \text{if } k > 0 \\ \sigma_{i,\alpha}(j-1)[k,d] & \text{if } k \geq 0, j > 0 \\ d & \text{otherwise} \end{cases}$$

- Resolve nonliving stream offsets: If some $\sigma_{i,\alpha}(j) = e_i$ in U contains a subexpression $\sigma_{i,\alpha}(j)[k,d]$, and $\alpha \notin S(s_i, j)$, then $\sigma_{i,\alpha}(j)[k,d] \rightarrow d$.

During the monitoring, we use a garbage collection process to remove entries from store R that are no longer needed. For each template stream expression s_i, we initially calculate the cutoff vector, which determines when a resolved stream expression can be cleared from store R. The vector records the usage of the stream expression within the definition of other streams and the maximal offset value. The vector contains one entry for every other stream, with default value 0. If there exits a reverse path in the dependency graph from stream s_k to stream s_i, we use the path with the smallest negative weight occuring on the edge originating in s_k on the path as the value. This yields the longest time we keep a value for s_i in memory for any dependency of s_k.

In an extra *garbage collection* store GC, we keep track of the current vectors of stream extensions which need to occur before a value can be eliminated. Whenever a new stream is invoked, we initialize $GC(s_i, \alpha, j) = (c_1, \ldots, c_n)$ with the cutoff vector $(c_1, \ldots, c_n)$. Whenever a stream s_k is extended, we increment the corresponding component c_k of all vectors in GC. If a vector in GC for any α and any s_i reaches strictly positive values in all elements at position j, we can safely remove $\sigma_{i,\alpha}(j)$ from R.

Once the stream has terminated, we replace all open offset expressions beyond the end of the stream with the specified default value and compute the fixpoint once again.

Efficiently monitorable specifications. A specification is called *efficiently monitorable* if its memory consumption is constant in the length of the input streams. In Lola 1.0, a specification is guaranteed to be efficiently monitorable, if the value of every stream depends, at every position, only on values of other streams up to a bounded number of steps into the future [7]. A corresponding result for Lola 2.0 does not hold, because we do not know how many streams are invoked during run-time. Thus, the memory needed for a Lola 2.0 specification therefore might grow with the length of generated traces. In practice, it is, however, often possible to bound the number of instances invoked during the monitoring process. This additional assumption in fact allows us to syntactically characterize a class of efficiently monitorable specifications. The restriction from Lola 1.0 that future dependencies are bounded is, however, not strong enough for Lola 2.0. The reason is that, even when a reference in a Lola 2.0 specification looks only a constant number of steps into the future, the actual occurrence of these future events might be delayed indefinitely by the extension stream. To obtain an efficiently monitorable fragment for Lola 2.0, we must therefore forbid all future references. Arbitrary references into the past remain allowed.

7   Experimental Results

We have implemented the monitoring algorithm for the efficiently monitorable fragment of Lola 2.0 as a command-line tool in C. As an input, it takes pre-processed network capture files (using the tool Wireshark[3]), which contain only the relevant input data defined by the input streams in the specification, and a Lola specification and produces output streams and statistics according to the specification.

Our experiments use network capture files from the Malware Capture Facility Project[4]. The network capture files range from 0.9 million up to 2.4 million packets and capture the traffic in a time frame of 24 h. All experiments were run on a single quad-core machine with an 3.6 GHz Intel Xeon processor with 32 GB RAM. The input stream files were stored on an internal SSD drive.

Table 1 shows the result of the monitoring tool on the specification in Fig. 2. We computed the number of **count** triggers, whose task was to observe the number of open handshake communications that have been waiting for more than 500 packets for an acknowledgment. We also observed the **any** trigger which checked whether any TCP request was not acknowledged after 600 packets. We compare the results of our specification with a Snort specification that checks whether the number of TCP Syn requests exceeds a threshold of 100 requests per 60 s. The results show that the specification in Fig. 2 never triggered, and therefore all Syn-requests were acknowledged eventually. In comparison, a large number of Snort alerts were issued on the trace files for the Snort specification. The reason for that is that Lola 2.0 allows an intermediate step using the templates **waitForAck** and **tcpSynScan**, where the monitor waits for the acknowledgment

Table 1. A comparison between our Lola 2.0 prototype and the rule-based language Snort for detecting a simple pattern of TCP SYN scans.

#Packets	Snort alerts	Invocation		Count trigger	Any trigger	Time (sec)
		Wait	Scan			
901710	613	53654	340	323	0	2550.31
1710372	472	95983	260	254	0	6279.87
1857752	1699	107721	280	274	0	6786.06
1954427	2428	115787	379	369	0	7160.27
2419006	2036	146748	869	835	0	10347.96

---

[3] http://www.wireshark.org.
[4] http://mcfp.weebly.com.

for a pair of IP-addresses before triggering. The high number of `waitForAck` invocations in comparison to the number of `tcpSynScan` invocations shows that Lola 2.0 allows to filter many TCP communications before starting the check for a possible TCP-Syn scan.

However, on the trace files used in the experiment of Table 1, Snort was able to return all the alerts in less than a minute. Since the following manual inspection of the Snort alerts is necessary to evaluate the potential TCP Syn Scan attack, this points to an interesting trade-off between the expressiveness of the specification mechanism and the time needed to analyze large trace files.

8   Conclusion

We have extended the stream-based specification language Lola with stream templates. Lola 2.0 is a descriptive language that subsumes many other specification languages and we showed how one can provide natural encodings for properties and attack patterns over network traffic. The extended language provides a bridge between more light-weight approaches and monitoring techniques based on expensive formalisms such as the temporal logics, combining both simplicity and expressiveness. During runtime, each template can be instantiated dynamically to obtain new streams. This allows each stream to run on an individual slice of the incoming data. In this way, Lola 2.0 can combine specifications that run on widely varying amount of data, and with widely varying speed. Inexpensive patterns can be used as filters that produce streams that run with less data, which can subsequently be analyzed against more expensive patterns.

Even though our prototype is an online monitoring tool, we have evaluated the tool on previously recorded pcap log data. In future work, we plan to deploy the monitor directly in the network. Since Lola specifications can easily be parallelized, such an implementation will likely consist of several connected nodes, placed at strategically chosen positions within the network. Further investigating the trade-off between the expressiveness and efficiency in descriptive, stream-based approaches for network monitoring remains an interesting topic for future work.

References

1. Ahmed, A., Lisitsa, A., Dixon, C.: A misuse-based network intrusion detection system using temporal logic and stream processing. In: 2011 5th International Conference on Network and System Security (NSS), pp. 1–8, September 2011
2. Ahmed, A., Lisitsa, A., Dixon, C.: TeStID: a high performance temporal intrusion detection system. In: Proceedings of the ICIMP, pp. 20–26 (2013)

3. Barringer, H., Falcone, Y., Havelund, K., Reger, G., Rydeheard, D.: Quantified event automata: towards expressive and efficient runtime monitors. In: Giannakopoulou, D., Méry, D. (eds.) FM 2012. LNCS, vol. 7436, pp. 68–84. Springer, Heidelberg (2012). doi:10.1007/978-3-642-32759-9_9

4. Barringer, H., Rydeheard, D.E., Havelund, K.: Rule systems for run-time monitoring: from eagle to ruler. J. Log. Comput. **20**(3), 675–706 (2010). http://dx.doi.org/10.1093/logcom/exn076

5. Berry, G.: Proof, Language, and Interaction: Essays in Honour of Robin Milner, Chap. The Foundations of Esterel, pp. 425–454. MIT Press, Cambridge (2000)

6. Bozzelli, L., Sánchez, C.: Foundations of boolean stream runtime verification. In: Bonakdarpour, B., Smolka, S.A. (eds.) RV 2014. LNCS, vol. 8734, pp. 64–79. Springer, Heidelberg (2014). doi:10.1007/978-3-319-11164-3_6

7. D'Angelo, B., Sankaranarayanan, S., Sánchez, C., Robinson, W., Finkbeiner, B., Sipma, H.B., Mehrotra, S., Manna, Z.: Lola: runtime monitoring of synchronous systems. In: 12th International Symposium on Temporal Representation and Reasoning (TIME 2005), pp. 166–174. IEEE Computer Society Press, June 2005

8. Debar, H., Becker, M., Siboni, D.: A neural network component for an intrusion detection system. In: Proceedings of 1992 IEEE Computer Society Symposium on Research in Security and Privacy, pp. 240–250, May 1992

9. Faymonville, P., Finkbeiner, B., Peled, D.: Monitoring parametric temporal logic. In: McMillan, K.L., Rival, X. (eds.) VMCAI 2014. LNCS, vol. 8318, pp. 357–375. Springer, Heidelberg (2014). doi:10.1007/978-3-642-54013-4_20

10. Gautier, T., Guernic, P., Besnard, L.: SIGNAL: a declarative language for synchronous programming of real-time systems. In: Kahn, G. (ed.) FPCA 1987. LNCS, vol. 274, pp. 257–277. Springer, Heidelberg (1987). doi:10.1007/3-540-18317-5_15

11. Goubault-Larrecq, J., Olivain, J.: A smell of ORCHIDS. In: Leucker, M. (ed.) RV 2008. LNCS, vol. 5289, pp. 1–20. Springer, Heidelberg (2008). doi:10.1007/978-3-540-89247-2_1

12. Halbwachs, N., Caspi, P., Raymond, P., Pilaud, D.: The synchronous dataflow programming language lustre. Proc. IEEE **79**(9), 1305–1320. citeseer.ist.psu.edu/halbwachs91synchronous.html

13. Havelund, K.: Rule-based runtime verification revisited. Int. J. Softw. Tools Technol. Transf. **17**(2), 143–170 (2015). http://dx.doi.org/10.1007/s10009-014-0309-2

14. Lee, W., Park, C.T., Stolfo, S.J.: Automated intrusion detection using NFR: methods and experiences. In: Proceedings of the Workshop on Intrusion Detection and Network Monitoring, Santa Clara, 9–12 April 1999, pp. 63–72. USENIX (1999). http://www.usenix.org/publications/library/proceedings/detection99/lee.html

15. Lee, W., Stolfo, S.J., Mok, K.W.: A data mining framework for building intrusion detection models. In: Proceedings of the 1999 IEEE Symposium on Security and Privacy, pp. 120–132 (1999)

16. Naldurg, P., Sen, K., Thati, P.: A temporal logic based framework for intrusion detection. In: Frutos-Escrig, D., Núñez, M. (eds.) FORTE 2004. LNCS, vol. 3235, pp. 359–376. Springer, Heidelberg (2004). doi:10.1007/978-3-540-30232-2_23

17. Olivain, J., Goubault-Larrecq, J.: The ORCHIDS intrusion detection tool. In: Etessami, K., Rajamani, S.K. (eds.) CAV 2005. LNCS, vol. 3576, pp. 286–290. Springer, Heidelberg (2005). doi:10.1007/11513988_28

18. Paxson, V.: Bro: a system for detecting network intruders in real-time. Comput. Netw. **31**(23–24), 2435–2463. http://dx.doi.org/10.1016/S1389-1286(99)00112-7

19. Roesch, M.: Snort - lightweight intrusion detection for networks. In: Proceedings of the 13th USENIX Conference on System Administration. LISA 1999, USENIX Association, Berkeley, pp. 229–238 (1999). http://dl.acm.org/citation.cfm?id=1039834.1039864
20. Roger, M., Goubault-Larrecq, J.: Log auditing through model-checking. In: Computer Security Foundations Workshop, p. 0220. IEEE (2001)
21. Rosu, G., Chen, F.: Semantics and algorithms for parametric monitoring. Log. Methods Comput. Sci. **8**(1) (2012). http://dx.doi.org/10.2168/LMCS-8(1:9)2012

On the Complexity of Monitoring Orchids Signatures

Jean Goubault-Larrecq[1]([✉]) and Jean-Philippe Lachance[1,2]

[1] LSV, ENS Cachan, CNRS, Université Paris-Saclay, 94235 Cachan, France
`goubault@lsv.ens-cachan.fr`
[2] Coveo Solutions, Inc., Québec City, QC G1W 2K7, Canada
`jplachance@coveo.com`

Abstract. Modern monitoring tools such as our intrusion detection tool Orchids work by firing new monitor instances dynamically. Given an Orchids signature (a.k.a. a rule, a specification), what is the complexity of checking that specification, that signature? In other words, let $f(n)$ be the maximum number of monitor instances that can be fired on a sequence of n events: we design an algorithm that decides whether $f(n)$ is asymptotically exponential or polynomial, and in the latter case returns an exponent d such that $f(n) = \Theta(n^d)$. Ultimately, the problem reduces to the following mathematical question, which may have other uses in other domains: given a system of recurrence equations described using the operators + and max, and defining integer sequences u_n, what is the asymptotic behavior of u_n as n tends to infinity? We show that, under simple assumptions, u_n is either exponential or polynomial, and that this can be decided, and the exponent computed, using a simple modification of Tarjan's strongly connected components algorithm, in linear time.

1 Introduction

Orchids [OG05, GO08] is an intrusion detection system. Given a trace σ of events, typically obtained in real-time, and a family of so-called signatures (variously otherwise called rules or specifications), Orchids tries to find a subsequence of σ that satisfies one of the signatures. Each signature is described as an automaton—not a finite-state automaton, though: each state comes with a piece of code, in a simple but expressive imperative language, that is executed whenever control flow enters that state. Orchids then waits for an event matching one of the transitions going out of the state.

See Fig. 1 for a slightly edited example of a signature that monitors legal user id (uid) and group id (gid) changes, and reports any system call done with an unexpected uid or gid (at state `alert`). Events are records with fields such as `.syscall` or `.euid` (we have slightly simplified the syntax), and variable names start with a dollar sign. Transitions are introduced by the `expect` keyword, so, e.g., the start state `init` has one outgoing transition, and `wait` has five. The last of the transitions of state `wait` is triggered whenever the currently monitored

© Springer International Publishing AG 2016
Y. Falcone and C. Sanchez (Eds.): RV 2016, LNCS 10012, pp. 169–184, 2016.
DOI: 10.1007/978-3-319-46982-9_11

```
rule pidtrack synchronized($pid) {        state wait! {
  state init {                              expect (.pid==$pid &&
    expect (.syscall==SYS_clone)                    .syscall==SYS_execve &&
      goto newpid;                                 (.uid!=.euid || .gid!=.egid))
  }                                           goto update_uid_gid;
  state newpid! {                           expect (.pid==$pid &&
    $pid = .exit;   $uid = .euid;                   .syscall==SYS_setresuid)
    $gid = .egid;   goto wait;              goto update_setuid;
  }                                         expect (.pid==$pid &&
  state update_uid_gid! {                          .syscall==SYS_setresgid)
    $uid = .euid; $gid = .egid;             goto update_setgid;
    goto wait;                              expect (.pid==$pid &&
  }                                                .syscall==SYS_exit)
  state update_setuid! {                    goto end;
    case (.egid!=$gid) goto alert;          expect (.pid==$pid &&
    else goto update_uid_gid;                      (.euid!=$uid || .egid!=$gid))
  }                                           goto alert;
  state update_setgid! {                  }
    case (.euid!=$uid) goto alert;        state alert! { report(); }
    else goto update_uid_gid;             state end! { }
  }                                     }
```

Fig. 1. The pid tracker signature

process (with pid $pid) executes an action with an effective user id .euid that is not the one we expected (in $uid), or with an unexpected effective group id.

Since Orchids cannot predict which of the five expect transitions will be matched by a subsequent event (and in fact, since, in principle, an event might match several of those transitions), Orchids must monitor all five. To implement that, the Orchids engine simulates so-called *threads*, and *forks* a new thread for each pending transition, each new thread waiting for a matching event. That is, on entering state wait, Orchids will create five threads.

This description of the working of Orchids is, of course, oversimplified, but is enough to explain the problem we attack in this paper: evaluating the *complexity* of detecting a subsequence that matches one of the signatures. A similar question occurs naturally in other modern monitors, such as JavaMOP or the more recent RV-Monitor [LZL+14], where signatures are called specifications, and threads are called monitor instances. As the authors argue, and as our own experience confirms, the main function that has to be estimated is the *number of threads* that the engine may create after reading n events.

In the worst case, for a signature S, the Orchids algorithm may create a number of threads $f_S(n)$ that is exponential in n, and that would be untenable. For an intrusion detection system, that would be dangerous, too, as that would open the door to an easy denial-of-service attack on the system itself.

Experience with practical signatures S shows that $f_S(n)$ is most often a polynomial of low degree. The exponential worst case behavior just means that one could instead craft specific signatures S such that $f_S(n)$ would be exponential.

Most signatures are not of this kind. But can we warn a signature writer of the complexity of his signatures? I.e., how does $f_S(n)$ vary as a function of S?

Our main contribution is the design, and proof, of a linear time algorithm that, given a signature S, computes the asymptotic behavior of $f_S(n)$ as n tends to $+\infty$. We shall see that $f_S(n)$ is either exponential or polynomial. In the second case, our algorithm computes the unique exponent d such that $f_S(n) = \Theta(n^d)$.

Outline. We review some recent related work in Sect. 2, and briefly describe how our task reduces to estimating the asymptotic growth of sequences defined by recurrence equations in Sect. 3. The core of our work lies in the subsequent sections: we define systems of recurrence equations and illustrate their possible asymptotic behaviors on several examples in Sect. 4; each such system Σ is better handled through its associated graph $G(\Sigma)$, which we introduce in Sect. 5; the building blocks of our complexity evaluation algorithm are then given in Sect. 6, relying on the decomposition of $G(\Sigma)$ in its strongly connected components (scc), and carefully distinguishing trivial and non-trivial sccs, cheap and expensive edges; the algorithm quickly follows in Sect. 7, as an easy adaptation of Tarjan's algorithm; we also report here on our implementation and the result it gives on the ten standard Orchids signatures. We conclude in Sect. 8.

2   Related Work

The question of evaluating the complexity of monitors at this level of detail does not seem to have been addressed already. Efficiency has always been an important subject in the field, and RV-Monitor [LZL+14] was recently advocated as a fast implementation of monitors, able to sustain a large number of monitor instances (a.k.a., our threads). This is backed by experimental evidence.

RV-Monitor's algorithm is data-driven. Given a specification with parameters $x_1, x_2, \ldots, x_k$, RV-Monitor organizes monitor instances inside an indexing tree, and if we agree to call N the maximal number of different values that parameters can take over an n event run, there can be at most N^k monitor instances at any given time. If we assume no fixed bound on N, it is however clear that $N = O(n)$, and that the RV-Monitor analogue of our function $f_S(n)$ above is polynomial in all cases (assuming the specification S fixed).

The Orchids algorithm is not data-driven, but trace-driven. That is, Orchids does not look merely for *values* of parameters that make a match, but for a *subsequence* of the input sequence. This is important for security. See Sect. 3.1 of [GO08] for a precise explanation: as we have argued there, Orchids needs to be able to sort matching subsequences (even with different sets of parameter values), so that only the smallest, lexicographically, is eventually reported: this is in most cases the most informative subsequence of events that characterizes a successful attack. Orchids signature matching is therefore necessarily more complex in general, and one can craft signatures that would make Orchids generate exponentially many threads. This is why the algorithm presented here is needed.

As a side matter, one can force the newest versions of Orchids to work in a data-driven way, using a specific "**synchronized**" construction. For example, the signature shown in Fig. 1 will only keep one Orchids thread per value of the $pid parameter, which keeps track of the pid of an actual Unix process monitored by Orchids. Such annotations will be ignored in this paper. They have little impact on the complexity analysis we shall do, in the worst case.

Efficiency is also one of the main concerns behind the MonPoly-Reg and MonPoly-Fin tools [BKMZ15]. The signature language there, MFOTL, is a real-time logic. Each variable varies in a domain of at most N elements, and it is assumed that there is an upper bound m on the number of successive events with the same timestamp. Time complexity is always polynomial. By carefully reading Sect. 5 of [BKMZ15], one sees that the polynomial degree is linear in the maximal number k of free variables in the monitored formula and in the number c of connectives of the formula. When $m = 1$ (i.e., event timestamps are strictly increasing) and there are no temporal future operators, the complexity is comparable with the $O(N^k)$ bound given for RV-Monitor: if $t(n)$ is the time to check one RV-Monitor instance, so that RV-Monitor takes time $O(N^k t(n))$, the MFOTL-based tools run in time $O(N^{O(k+c)})$.

We will not cite any other paper on the question of monitor complexity. Other (parametric) monitors such as QEA or LogFire are described in [HR15], with some features in common with Orchids and RV-Monitor respectively. Extra information can be gleaned by following references from the above papers.

Later, we will argue that our problem reduces to finding asymptotic estimates for sequences $(u_n)_{n \in \mathbb{N}}$ defined by so-called *recurrence equations*. Those are (systems of) equations of the form $u_{n+1} = f(u_n, v_n, w_n, \cdots)$, $v_{n+1} = g(u_n, v_n, w_n, \cdots)$, etc., where $f, g, \ldots$, are some explicitly given functions. There is a huge body of literature, specially in the mathematical literature, on those objects. One of the most relevant source is Flajolet and Sedgwick's book on analytic combinatorics [FS09]. Unfortunately, we shall need to deal with recurrence equations where u_{n+1} depend on u_n, v_n, w_n, etc., by using both the $+$ and max operations. The latter seems to be out of scope of what is known in analytic combinatorics.

3   Orchids, and Recurrence Equations

Let us have a quick look at how Orchids creates and handles threads (a.k.a., monitor instances). We shall ignore optimizations, both algorithmic and implementation-related, as they do not change the worst-case behavior of Orchids. Also, since 2008, Orchids has evolved a lot, and we warn the reader that the view we take of Orchids is rather remote, at least in form, from [GO08][1]. The algorithm is however the same from a conceptual standpoint.

---

[1] Historically, Orchids also evolved from previous attempts, starting from [RG01], which presents two approaches. The second approach was a forerunner of the 2008 approach [GO08], and corrected a few flaws from the first approach. That same first approach (not the second one) is covered by a patent [RGL99]. That patent does not cover Orchids. The main reason is that the main claims of that patent require a means of generating propositional Horn clauses from formulae in a temporal logic for each new event read. The Orchids algorithm is not based on any such mechanism.

An Orchids signature consists in finitely many *states*. One of them, init, is the initial state. Each state starts with an optional piece of code (e.g., $pid = .exit; $uid = .euid; $gid = .egid in state newpid), which gets executed on entering the state. That code can contain elementary computations, tests, but no loops: we consider it irrelevant as far as complexity is concerned.

The second part of the description of a state defines its outgoing transitions, and comes in two flavors. We may either see a block of expect clauses, labeled with conditions that must be satisfied to launch the transition, as in state wait; or a case-delimited multi-way conditional, as in state update_setuid for example (or as in the degenerate case of state update_uid_gid, where there is just one branch, hence no case keyword).

The latter kind of state has an obvious semantics. For example, a thread entering state update_setuid will compare the field .egid with the value of the variable $gid[2], and branch to state alert if they are different (a system call was made with a group id that is not what it was expected to be), or to update_uid_gid otherwise—such transitions were called *ε-transitions* in [GO08].

The former kind of state will *wait* for a subsequent event matching one of the expect clauses. A same event may match several expect clauses at once, and accordingly Orchids will fork as many threads as needed. We shall ignore the semantics of the tests performed by those clauses, and therefore a state with 5 expect clauses such as wait may fork 5 new threads.

The actual details are more complicated, and slightly different, but explaining it would involve examining the actual working of the Orchids algorithm in detail, and distract us from our goal.

We are now in a position to describe the basics of our complexity analysis. For each Orchids state q, let q_n denote the maximal number of threads that will descend from a single thread starting at state q, after reading n events. This is a *function* of $n \in \mathbb{N}$, and our goal is to evaluate its asymptotic behavior. The *definition* of q_n is derived from the semantics.

For a state q with 5 expect transitions leading to states s, t, u, v, w, for example, we must have the so-called *linear recurrence equation* $q_{n+1} = s_n + t_n + u_n + v_n + w_n$: if you consider a trace with $n + 1$ events, then on reading one event, only n remain, and forking a thread going to state s will contribute s_n new threads after those remaining n events, forking a thread to state t will contribute t_n, and so on.

For a state q with ϵ-transitions instead, such as update_setuid, the semantics is different: Orchids will not fork any new thread, rather it will make the current thread go to exactly one of the target states. Hence if q has, say, two ϵ-transitions going to states s and t, then we must have the following *non-linear* recurrence equation $q_{n+1} = \max(s_n, t_n)$.

Note that we can produce those recurrence equations in linear time from an Orchids signature given as input. As we have said already, the actual recurrence equations needed for Orchids are slightly more complex, but the way they are

---

[2] Variables are thread-local: if an Orchids thread modifies one of its variables, this does not affect any other thread.

built is entirely analogous. We now come to recurrence equations, the core of this paper.

4   Systems of Recurrence Equations

A *sequence* is an infinite family of natural numbers $(u_n)_{n\in\mathbb{N}}$ indexed by natural numbers. We say that a property P holds of u_n *for n large enough* if and only if there is an $n_0 \in \mathbb{N}$ such that P holds of u_n for every $n \geq n_0$. For a function $f \colon \mathbb{N} \to \mathbb{R}$, $u_n = \Theta(f(n))$ means that there are two real constants $m, M > 0$ such that, for n large enough, $mf(n) \leq u_n \leq Mf(n)$. If only the left-hand inequality is assumed, then we write $u_n = \Omega(f(n))$, and if only the right-hand inequality is assumed, then we write $u_n = O(f(n))$.

We shall say that $(u_n)_{n\in\mathbb{N}}$ has *exponential behavior* if and only if $u_n = \Omega(a^n)$ for some constant $a > 1$. It has *polynomial behavior* if and only if $u_n = \Theta(n^k)$ for some constant $k \in \mathbb{N}$.

Let $Q = \{u, v, \cdots\}$ be a finite non-empty set of symbols. Each symbol $u \in Q$ is meant to denote a sequence $(u_n)_{n\in\mathbb{N}}$ of natural numbers. A *system of recurrence equations* Σ for Q is, at least informally:

- an initial condition of the form $u_0 = a_u$, where $a_u \in \mathbb{N} \smallsetminus \{0\}$, one for each $u \in Q$;
- for each $u \in Q$, an equation that defines u_{n+1} in terms of the terms v_n, $v \in Q$, and natural number constants, using the operations max and $+$. Semantically, since max distributes over $+$, this means defining u_{n+1} as $\max_{i=1}^{m_u}(\sum_{v\in Q} a_{uiv} v_n + b_{ui})$, where a_{uiv} and b_{ui} are natural number constants. For reasons that will be explained below, we require $m_u \neq 0$, and for each u and i, either $b_{ui} \neq 0$ or $a_{uiv} \neq 0$ for some $v \in Q$.

We shall use a slightly different *formal* definition below.

Sticking to the above definition for now, Σ defines a unique family of sequences $(u_n)_{n\in\mathbb{N}}$, one for each $u \in Q$, in the obvious way. Our purpose is to show that one can decide, in linear time, which of these sequences have exponential behavior, and which have polynomial behavior; in the latter case, our algorithm will return a natural number d such that $u_n = \Theta(n^d)$. Note that this will imply that $(u_n)_{n\in\mathbb{N}}$ has either exponential or polynomial behavior, nothing else—e.g., not logarithmic, $\Theta(2^{\sqrt{n}})$ or $\Theta(n^{\log n})$ for example.

Example 1. Consider $Q = \{u\}$, the system $u_0 = 1$, $u_{n+1} = 2u_n$ is a system of recurrence equations; it defines a unique sequence $u_n = 2^n$, which has exponential behavior.

Example 2. Instead, consider $Q = \{u, v, w\}$ and the system $u_0 = 1$, $v_0 = 1$, $w_0 = 1$, $u_{n+1} = v_n + 1$, $v_{n+1} = u_n + w_n$, $w_{n+1} = w_n + 2$. Its unique solution is given by $w_n = 2n+1$, $v_n = \frac{1}{2}n^2 + n + 1$ if n is even, $v_n = \frac{1}{2}n^2 + n + \frac{1}{2}$ if n is odd, $u_n = \frac{1}{2}n^2 + 1$ if n is even, $u_n = \frac{1}{2}n^2 + \frac{3}{2}$ if n is odd. In that case, $w_n = \Theta(n)$, $u_n = \Theta(n^2)$, $v_n = \Theta(n^2)$ all have polynomial behavior.

Notice the slightly oscillating behavior of $(u_n)_{n \in \mathbb{N}}$ and $(v_n)_{n \in \mathbb{N}}$. Although those sequences have polynomial behavior, we cannot find an actual, unique polynomial $p(n)$ such that $u_n = p(n)$ for every $n \in \mathbb{N}$.

Our recurrence equations have a few constraints attached: a_u is non-zero, m_u is non-zero, and either $b_{ui} \neq 0$ or $a_{uiv} \neq 0$ for some $v \in Q$. This will be the case in all applications. Without this condition, the behaviors of the corresponding sequences might be much wilder, as exemplified below.

Example 3. Consider $Q = \{u, v, s, t\}$ with $u_0 = 0$, $v_0 = 1$, $s_0 = 1$, $t_0 = 1$, $u_{n+1} = 2v_n$, $v_{n+1} = u_n$, $s_{n+1} = s_n + 1$, $t_{n+1} = v_n + s_n$. This is not a system of recurrence equations in our sense, because the initial value a_u for u is equal to 0. Its unique solution is $u_n = 0$ if n is even, $2^{(n+1)/2}$ if n is odd; $v_n = 2^{n/2}$ if n is even, 0 if n is odd; $s_n = n+1$; $t_n = 1$ if $n = 0$, n if n is even, and $2^{(n-1)/2} + n$ if n is odd. Note that $(t_n)_{n \in \mathbb{N}}$ exhibits neither polynomial nor exponential behavior, as it oscillates between the two. Such a system is forbidden by our definition.

We claimed that, for every vertex $u \in Q$, $(u_n)_{n \in \mathbb{N}}$ would either have exponential or polynomial behavior, and that in the latter case, we would be able to find a degree $d \in \mathbb{N}$ such that $u_n = \Theta(n^d)$. One may wonder whether it would be possible to refine this, and to also find a coefficient a such that $u_n \sim a n^d$ (meaning that $u/(a n^d)$ would tend to 1 as n tends to $+\infty$). This is not possible, as the following example shows.

Example 4. Let $Q = \{u, v, s, t\}$ with $u_0 = 1$, $v_0 = 2$, $s_0 = 1$, $t_0 = 1$, $u_{n+1} = v_n$, $v_{n+1} = u_n$, $s_{n+1} = t_n$, $t_{n+1} = s_n + u_n$. Its unique solution is: $u_n = 1$ if n is even, 2 if n is odd; $v_n = 2$ if n is even, 1 if n is odd; $s_n = n/2 + 1$ if n is even, n if n is odd; $t_n = n + 1$ if n is even, $(n + 3)/2$ if n is odd. Note that both s and t exhibit polynomial behavior, as they are $\Theta(n)$, but we cannot find an a such that $s_n \sim an$ or $t_n \sim an$: for example, s_n oscillates between $n/2 + 1$ and n.

Let us give a formal definition of systems of recurrence equations. One might do this in the obvious way, by the data of Q and families of numbers a_{uiv} and b_{ui}. However, we would also like some equations such as

$$u_{n+1} = u_n + \max(v_n, \max(u_n, w_n + 2) + \max(2u_n, w_n)) \tag{1}$$

where the max and + operators are freely mixed. Distributing max over + would produce an equivalent system of the right shape, but this transformation takes exponential time and space in the worst case.

Instead, we use the following folklore transform, which works in linear time, at the expense of introducing new symbols to Q (clearly, only linearly many more). For each non-variable proper subexpression of the term on the right (here, $u_n + \max(v_n, \max(u_n, w_n + 2) + \max(2u_n, w_n)))$, we introduce a fresh symbol. By *non-variable* we mean any subexpression except the non-constant leaves (here, u_n, v_n, w_n); this includes all non-leaf expressions, such as $\max(u_n, w_n + 2)$, and all constant leaves, such as 2. Let us do so on (1). There are seven non-variable proper subexpressions there, and we create seven fresh symbols, call them a, b,

c, d, e, f and *two*. The sequence two_n is meant to be the constant sequence equal to 2, and is defined by $two_0 = 2$, $two_{n+1} = two_n$. The sequence a_n denotes $w_n + 2$, b_n denotes $\max(u_n, w_n + 2)$, c_n denotes $2u_n$, d_n denotes $\max(2u_n, w_n)$, e_n denotes $\max(u_n, w_n + 2) + \max(2u_n, w_n)$, and f_n denotes $\max(v_n, \max(u_n, w_n + 2) + \max(2u_n, w_n))$. Accordingly, we replace (1) by the following eight equations:

$$u_{n+1} = u_n + f_n \quad f_n = \max(v_n, e_n) \quad e_n = b_n + d_n$$
$$d_n = \max(c_n, w_n) \quad c_n = 2u_n \quad b_n = \max(u_n, a_n)$$
$$a_n = w_n + two_n \quad two_{n+1} = two_n$$

plus the initial condition $two_0 = 2$.

Doing so only requires us to be able to state three kinds of equations:

1. equations of the form $u_{n+k} = \max(v_n, w_n, \cdots)$, for some non-empty subset of symbols $v, w, \cdots \in Q$,
2. and equations of the form $u_{n+k} = \sum_{v \in Q} a_{uv} v_n$, where at least one a_{uv}, $v \in Q$, is non-zero,

where k is equal to 0 or 1, and if $k = 1$, then we also need an initial condition $u_0 = a_u$, for some constant $a_u \in \mathbb{N} \smallsetminus \{0\}$. Note that constants b_{ui} have disappeared in the process, being replaced by fresh symbols (such as *two* in the above example).

This leads us to the following, formal, definition. A *system of recurrence equations* Σ on the set of symbols Q is a Q-indexed family of *recurrence equations* E_u, each one being of one of the above two forms, plus initial conditions. We represent equations $u_{n+k} = \sum_{v \in Q} a_{uv} v_n$ in sparse form, that is, as a list of pairs (v, a_{uv}) for each $v \in Q$ such that $a_{uv} \neq 0$.

Our formal definition includes strictly more systems than our previous, informal definition. Systems defined per our previous definition always have exactly one solution; in other words, for each $u \in Q$, they define exactly one sequence $(u_n)_{n \in \mathbb{N}}$. A contrario, our new definition allows for systems of the form $u_n = u_n$, which have infinitely many solutions; or of the form $u_n = u_n + one_n$, $one_{n+1} = one_n$, $one_0 = 1$, which have no solution. We repair this shortly.

5   Graphs

Given a system Σ of recurrence equations on the set of symbols Q, let us define its *graph* $G(\Sigma)$ as follows. We write $s \to t$ to say there is an edge from s to t. $G(\Sigma)$ is a labelled directed graph, and both vertices and edges receive labels. Its vertices are the elements of Q, and are split in two kinds, corresponding to the two kinds of allowed equations:

1. the *max* vertices u are those whose associated equation E_u is of the form $u_{n+k} = \max(v_n, w_n, \cdots)$; there is one edge from u to v, one from u to w, and so on; u itself is labeled with k, and the edges receive label 1;
2. the *plus* vertices u are those whose associated equation E_u is of the form $u_{n+k} = \sum_{v \in Q} a_{uv} v_n$; there is one edge from u to each $v \in Q$ such that $a_{uv} \neq 0$, and it is labeled with a_{uv}; the vertex u itself is labeled with k;
3. there is no other edge.

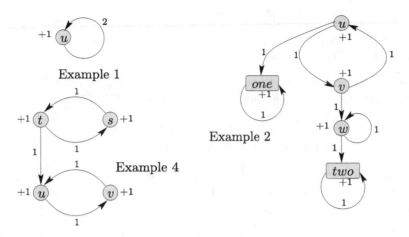

Fig. 2. Three examples of graphs $G(\Sigma)$

Introducing auxiliary symbols as necessary, Example 1 is really the system:

$$u_{n+1} = 2u_n \qquad u_0 = 1$$

Its graph is shown on the top left of Fig. 2. We distinguish the plus vertices by showing them on a light grey background. We also distinguish the vertex labels by writing them with a plus sign, viz., +1, not 1. The right-hand graph is that of the system of Example 2, put into the adequate form:

$$u_{n+1}=v_n + one_n \qquad u_0=1 \qquad v_{n+1}=u_n + w_n \qquad v_0=1 \qquad w_{n+1}=w_n + two_n$$
$$one_{n+1}=one_n \qquad one_0=1 \qquad two_{n+1}=two_n \qquad two_0=2 \qquad w_0=1$$

Similarly for the graph of Example 4, shown at the bottom left.

Using the graph $G(\Sigma)$, we evacuate the problem of those systems Σ that have non-unique solutions, or no solution: we say that Σ is *well-formed* if and only if there is no cycle in the graph that goes only through vertices labeled +0.

Proposition 1. *Every well-formed system Σ has a unique solution, consisting of uniquely-defined sequences $(u_n)_{n \in \mathbb{N}}$ for each $u \in Q$, which satisfy all the equations in Σ.*

Note that $G(\Sigma)$ has no provision for specifying initial conditions such as $u_0 = 1$. They are not needed for Proposition 1. They will be useless in our subsequent developments as well: the asymptotic behavior of u_n will be independent of u_0.

6   Sccs, and Asymptotics

We shall see that the key to understanding the asymptotic behavior of sequences defined by a well-formed system of recurrence equations Σ lies in the strongly connected components of $G(\Sigma)$.

We fix a well-formed system Σ of recurrence equations for the rest of the section, as well as its set of symbols Q, and the unique sequences $(u_n)_{n\in\mathbb{N}}$ that it defines. The following trivial lemma is crucial.

Lemma 1. *Assume two vertices u, v in Q such that v is reachable from u, namely, such that there is a path from u to v in $G(\Sigma)$. There is a constant $k \in \mathbb{N}$ such that, for every $n \in \mathbb{N}$, $u_{n+k} \geq v_n$.*

More precisely, k can be taken as the sum of vertex labels on any given path from u to v, including u but excluding v.

Proof. The key argument is that for every edge of the form $s \to t$, where s is labeled a, $s_{n+a} \geq t_n$ for every $n \in \mathbb{N}$. This holds whether s is a max or a plus vertex.   □

A subset A of vertices is *strongly connected* if and only if every vertex from A is reachable from any other vertex of A. The maximal strongly connected subsets are called the *strongly connected components* of the graph, and we abbreviate that as *scc*. They partition the graph, and in particular every vertex u belongs to a unique scc, which we write $scc(u)$.

Computing the sccs of a graph can be done, in linear time, by Tarjan's algorithm [Tar72].

On Fig. 2, the top left graph is its unique scc. The right-hand graph has four sccs, the top cycle $\{u, v\}$, the middle cycle $\{w\}$, and the two cycles $\{one\}$ and $\{two\}$. The bottom left graph has two sccs, the top cycle $\{s, t\}$, and the bottom cycle $\{u, v\}$.

In general, an scc can be more complex than a mere cycle, but if one wants to picture a non-trivial scc, a cycle is a good first approximation. Sccs can also be *trivial*, i.e., consist of no cycle at all, just a single vertex with no self-loop. Figure 3 displays a more complex graph, with sccs shown as darker gray rectangles. The topmost scc is an example of an scc that is not just a cycle. There are also trivial sccs: $\{c\}$ and $\{f\}$. We let the reader reconstruct a system of recurrence equations associated with this graph. Note that, contrarily to previous examples, this one involves the max operator in order to define $(u_n)_{n\in\mathbb{N}}$, $(v_n)_{n\in\mathbb{N}}$, $(s_n)_{n\in\mathbb{N}}$, $(t_n)_{n\in\mathbb{N}}$, $(w_n)_{n\in\mathbb{N}}$, $(r_n)_{n\in\mathbb{N}}$. Although this may seem like a complicated graph, it will follow from our algorithm that $u_n = \Theta(n)$ and $v_n = \Theta(n)$, and all other vertices have constant behavior.

Call a vertex $u \in Q$ *bad* if and only if it is a plus vertex, and given its associated equation $u_{n+k} = \sum_{v\in Q} a_{uv} v_n$, the sum of the coefficients a_{uv} where v ranges over $scc(u)$ is at least 2. Equivalently, u is bad if and only if it is a plus vertex, and at least one of the following possibilities occurs:

1. there is an edge (u, v) of label at least 2 to a vertex v in the same scc as u,
2. or there are at least two edges $u \to v$ and $u \to w$ to vertices v and w that are both in the same scc as u.

In Example 1, u is bad. There is no bad vertex in Example 2 or in Example 4. There is no bad vertex either in Fig. 3: although there are several edges with label

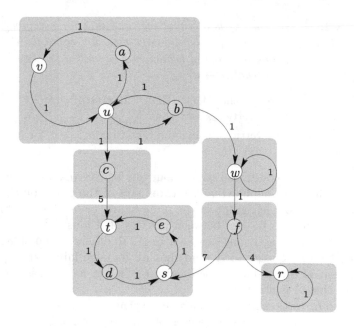

Fig. 3. Sccs in a graph $G(\Sigma)$

at least 2, they all go out of their start scc. (Vertex labels have been removed for clarity; they are all $+1$, although this is not important.)

Say that a vertex $u \in Q$ is bad^* if and only if some bad vertex is reachable from it, namely if and only if there is a path from u to some bad vertex v. We shall see that the bad* vertices u are exactly those such that $(u_n)_{n \in \mathbb{N}}$ has exponential behavior. In Example 1, u is bad*. There is no bad* vertex in Example 2 or in Example 4, or in Fig. 3.

Proposition 2. *For every bad* vertex u in Q, $(u_n)_{n \in \mathbb{N}}$ has exponential behavior.*

Proof (Sketch). There is a path from u to some bad vertex v. We show that $(v_n)_{n \in \mathbb{N}}$ will have exponential behavior, which implies the claim by Lemma 1. Since v is bad, for some $a \in \{0, 1\}$, v_{n+a} is defined as a sum of at least two values s_n, t_n (where it may be that $s = t$). Since v is again reachable from both s and t, s_n and t_n are larger than or equal to v_{n-k} for some constant k. Hence $v_{n+a} \geq 2v_{n-k}$, which entails the claim. ☐

If an scc contains a bad* vertex, then all its vertices are bad*. Let us consider the case of sccs A without any bad* vertex. We shall illustrate the various cases we need to consider on the graph shown in Fig. 3. The idea of our algorithm is that we shall iterate on all sccs A, from bottom to top, deducing a characteristic degree d_A such that $u_n = \Theta(n^{d_A})$ for every vertex u in A from the characteristic degrees of sccs below A.

We first deal with the case of *trivial* sccs, i.e., sccs with only one vertex and no self-loop. By abuse of language, say that u is a trivial scc iff $\{u\}$ is.

Proposition 3. *Assume $u \in Q$ is a trivial scc, and that for every edge $u \to v$, the sequence $(v_n)_{n \in \mathbb{N}}$ has polynomial behavior, viz., for some $d_v \in \mathbb{N}$, $v_n = \Theta(n^{d_v})$. Then $(u_n)_{n \in \mathbb{N}}$ has polynomial behavior, too, and $u_n = \Theta(n^{d_u})$, where $d_u = \max\{d_v \mid v \in Q \text{ such that } u \to v\}$.*

Proof. This follows from the fact that $\max(\Theta(n^{d_v}), \Theta(n^{d_w}), \cdots) = \Theta(n^{\max(d_v, d_w, \cdots)})$ for max vertices, and that $\sum_{v \in Q \text{ such that } u \to v} a_{uv} \Theta(n^{d_v}) = \Theta(n^{\max\{d_v | u \to v\}})$ for plus vertices, using the fact that $a_{uv} \geq 1$ for every $v \in Q$ such that $u \to v$. □

Now assume A is a non-trivial scc without any bad vertex. Such an scc must have a special shape, exemplified on the three sccs of the graph on the right of Fig. 2, or on the bottom left graph of the same figure, or on the non-trivial sccs of Fig. 3: the weights of all edges between vertices of A must be equal to 1, and every plus vertex has exactly one successor in A (all others are outside A). That it has at most one successor in A (and that all its edge labels are equal to 1) is a consequence of the absence of bad vertices. That it has at least one follows from the fact that A is non-trivial.

Note that plus vertices in A may have more than one successor; but only one can be in A. For example, v has two successors in the graph of Example 2 (Fig. 2, right), but only u is in the scc $A = \{u, v\}$ that v belongs to. Example 4 displays a similar situation. Figure 3 does, too: b has two successors, but only one in its own scc.

Definition 1 (Expensive, cheap edges). *Say that an edge $u \to v$ goes out of A if and only if $u \in A$ and $v \notin A$. If u is a plus vertex, then we say that it is an expensive edge out of A, otherwise it is a cheap edge out of A.*

In Fig. 3, there is only one expensive edge out of a non-trivial scc, namely the edge $b \to w$, with label 1. There are two other edges going out of non-trivial sccs, namely $u \to c$ and $w \to f$. They are both cheap.

Note that being cheap or expensive is entirely independent of the label it carries. Here the expensive edge has the lowest possible label of the whole graph.

The key argument in Proposition 4 consists in noting that $\sum_{j=0}^{n} j^N = \Theta(n^{N+1})$ when n tends to $+\infty$—a well-known identity. The way we use that is probably best explained on a small test case. Imagine one of the simplest possible non-trivial sccs: a one-vertex loop, as shown on the right, and assume that we know that $v_n = \Theta(n^N)$, and even, to make things simpler, that $v_n = n^N$.

The equation defining $(u_n)_{n \in \mathbb{N}}$ is $u_{n+1} = u_n + v_n = u_n + n^N$. It follows easily that $u_n = (n-1)^N + (n-2)^N + \cdots + 1^N + 0^N + u_0 = u_0 + \sum_{j=0}^{n-1} j^N$, and that is $\Theta(n^{N+1})$, as we have just seen. Note that the edge $u \to v$ is expensive. The name "expensive" was chosen so as to suggest that those are the edges that are responsible for the increase in the exponent, from N to $N+1$. Cheap edges will incur no such increase.

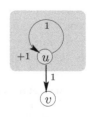

In general, the proof of the bounds in the following proposition uses a similar argument. The case of non-trivial sccs A

without any bad vertex, and with only + vertices (no max vertex) is easier to argue. There is a single elementary cycle from u back to u, and all its weights are equal to 1; all edges out of this path go out of A. Semantically u_{n+a} can be written as u_{n-k} (for some constant k) plus values v_n, for v outside of A. If v_n has polynomial growth, viz. if $v_n = \Theta(n^{d_v})$, then n^{d_v} will enter a summation defining u_{n+a}, and a similar argument as above shows that u_n will grow as a polynomial in n whose degree is the largest exponent d_v plus 1. The fact that + and max vertices can be used freely inside A makes the (omitted) proof of the following proposition slightly more involved.

Proposition 4. *Let A be a non-trivial scc of $G(\Sigma)$ without a bad vertex. For each edge $u \to v$ going out of A, assume that $(v_n)_{n \in \mathbb{N}}$ has polynomial behavior. Precisely, assume that $v_n = \Theta(n^{d_v})$.*

Then every vertex of A has polynomial behavior, with the same degree d_A, where d_A is the maximum of:

- *all the quantities d_v, where $u \to v$ ranges over the cheap edges out of A,*
- *and all the quantities $d_v + 1$, where $u \to v$ ranges over the expensive edges out of A.*

To be completely formal, we agree that the maximum of an empty set of numbers is 0; this is needed in case there is no edge going out of A at all.

Let us use all those results to determine the asymptotic behavior of all the sequences defined in the system associated with the graph of Fig. 3. Recall that there is no bad* vertex in that example. We start from the sccs at the bottom, and work our way up:

- The non-trivial sccs $\{r\}$ and $\{s, e, t, d\}$ have no outgoing edge at all, hence their associated sequences are $\Theta(n^0)$ (bounded from below and from above by constants).
- The scc $\{f\}$ is trivial, and its two successors behave as $\Theta(n^0)$, hence it itself behaves as $\Theta(n^0)$, by Proposition 3.
- Similarly for the trivial scc $\{c\}$.
- The scc $\{w\}$ is not trivial, but it does not have any expensive edge out of it; by Proposition 4, it also behaves as $\Theta(n^0)$.
- The topmost scc is non-trivial, it has one cheap outgoing edge, $u \to c$, and one expensive outgoing edge $b \to w$. By applying Proposition 4, all the sequences associated with vertices in that scc behave as $\Theta(n^{\max(0, 0+1)})$, that is, $\Theta(n)$.

7   The Algorithm

To conclude, we need a final, standard ingredient: the *condensation* of a directed graph G is the graph whose vertices are the sccs of G, and such that there is an edge from A to B if and only if there are vertices $q \in A$ and $r \in B$ and an edge $q \to r$ in G. The condensation is always acyclic, meaning that working our way up, that is, from the leaves to the roots of the condensation, must terminate (hence terminate in a linear number of steps). In the case of a graph G of the form $G(\Sigma)$, we shall say that an edge $A \to B$ as above in the condensation is *expensive* if and only if A is non-trivial, and we can find a $q \in A$ and an $r \in B$ such that the edge $q \to r$ is expensive in G; it is *cheap* otherwise, namely when A is trivial, or A is non-trivial and all the edges $q \to r$ in G with $q \in A$ and $r \in B$ are cheap.

Theorem 1. *Given any system Σ of recurrence equations with set Q of symbols, we can compute a table of numbers $d_u \in \mathbb{N} \cup \{+\infty\}$, $u \in Q$, in linear time, such that $d_u = +\infty$ iff $(u_n)_{n \in \mathbb{N}}$ has exponential behavior, and otherwise $u_n = \Theta(n^{d_u})$. The algorithm works as follows:*

1. *Compute $G(\Sigma)$ and its sccs, building its condensation G'.*
2. *Traverse G' in reverse topological order (i.e., from the bottom up). For each visited scc A, decide whether A contains a bad vertex. If so, let $d_A := +\infty$. Otherwise, for every successor B of A in G', d_B has already been computed, and let $d_A := \max(\max_{A \to B\ cheap}\ d_B, \max_{A \to B\ expensive}\ (d_B + 1))$, where by convention we agree that the maximum of the empty set is zero.*
3. *Finally, for each $u \in Q$, let $d_u := d_{scc(u)}$.*

The correctness of the algorithm is a direct consequence of Propositions 2, 3, and 4. That it works in linear time is easy. Notably, the second phase sweeps through all the sccs A once, and for each, takes time proportional to the number of vertices in A plus the number of edges that go out of A. The sum over all sccs A of those values is the size of $G(\Sigma)$.

In practice, this is implemented by simply modifying Tarjan's scc algorithm [Tar72]. In any description of that algorithm, there is a single line of code where it has just found an scc A, and it must emit it by repeatedly popping a stack. It is enough to compute d_A there, by the formula given in Theorem 1, item 2, knowing that at that point, all the values d_B will have been computed earlier.

We have implemented that algorithm inside Orchids, and its ten standard signatures. Execution time was negligible. We had the pleasant surprise of observing that all our signatures had polynomial thread complexity, confirming our intuition that human experts do not write signatures with exponential behavior.

The largest observed complexity is $\Theta(n^3)$ for the `lin24_ptrace.rule`, a signature that attempts to detect the `ptrace` attack [Pur03]. This is actually over-estimated: the actual complexity is $\Theta(n^2)$. There is a loop in that signature that our algorithm thinks may create a linear number of threads, but that loop can only be traversed 10 times, due to a counting mechanism implemented in the Orchids programming language.

The second largest is $\Theta(n^2)$ for the `apachessl.rule`, a signature that tries to correlate abnormal variations in message entropy [GO13] with specific failure events from the Apache server. Out of our ten signatures, seven others have linear behavior, including the pid tracker of Fig. 1. We have instrumented our algorithm so that it reports the main causes of complexity. For example, on the pid tracker, our algorithm reports:

```
rule pidtrack may have worst case linear behavior, i.e., O(#events).
each event may fork a new thread going to 'init'.
```

And indeed, each newly created Unix process (through the `clone` system call, a Linux abstraction behind the more well-known `fork` call) may cause the creation of a new Orchids thread for that signature, starting at state `init`.

The last of the ten signatures, `taint_auditd.rule`, a tainting mechanism for detecting illegal transitive information flows, is not even flagged by our algorithm: it is correctly classified as generating a *constant* number of threads.

8 Conclusion

We have described, and proved, a linear time algorithm that decides the asymptotic complexity of sequences defined by certain forms of systems of recurrence equations, using both the + and max operators. Our goal was to analyze, automatically, which Orchids signatures have polynomial detection complexity (in terms of numbers of created Orchids threads), and with which exponent.

This turns out to be an extremely reliable and useful tool to Orchids signature writers. Personal experience shows that a high degree in the polynomial, or worse, an estimation of exponential complexity, is indicative of a mistake in the writing of the signature.

Beyond Orchids, it seems obvious that our simple algorithm for estimating the asymptotic complexity of recurrence equations should find applications outside of security or of runtime verification. Mounir Assaf recently proposed a (yet unpublished) static analysis that detects whether leakage of sensitive data in security programs is negligible or not [Ass15]. This is based on estimating the rate of growth of a sequence u_n as the number of steps taken, n, tends to infinity, and we hope that our algorithm, or similar techniques, apply.

Acknowledgement. This research was partially funded by INRIA-DGA grant 12 81 0312 (2013–2016). This, in particular, funded the second author's internship at LSV, ENS Cachan, in the spring of 2013, who implemented two prototypes for a precursor of the algorithm described here. The second author also thanks Hydro-Québec and Les Offices jeunesse internationaux du Québec (LOJIQ) for their financial support.

The first author would like to thank Mounir Assaf for drawing his attention to analytic combinatorics, and the anonymous referees for their suggestions.

References

[Ass15] Assaf, M.: From qualitative to quantitative program analysis: permissive enforcement of secure information flow. PhD thesis, Université Rennes I (2015)

[BKMZ15] Basin, D., Klaedtke, F., Müller, S., Zălinescu, E.: Monitoring metric first-order temporal properties. J. ACM **62**(2), 15:1–15:45 (2015)

[FS09] Flajolet, P., Sedgwick, R.: Analytic Combinatorics. Cambridge University Press, New York (2009)

[GO08]   Goubault-Larrecq, J., Olivain, J.: A smell of ORCHIDS. In: Leucker, M. (ed.) RV 2008. LNCS, vol. 5289, pp. 1–20. Springer, Heidelberg (2008). doi:10. 1007/978-3-540-89247-2_1

[GO13]   Goubault-Larrecq, J., Olivain, J.: On the efficiency of mathematics in intrusion detection: the NetEntropy case. In: Danger, J.-L., Debbabi, M., Marion, J.-Y., Garcia-Alfaro, J., Zincir Heywood, N. (eds.) FPS - 2013. LNCS, vol. 8352, pp. 3–16. Springer, Heidelberg (2014). doi:10.1007/ 978-3-319-05302-8_1

[HR15]   Havelund, K., Reger, G.: Specification of parametric monitors - quantified event automata versus rule systems. In: Drechsler, R., Kuhne, U. (eds.) Formal Modeling and Verification of Cyber-Physical Systems, pp. 151–189. Springer, Wiesbaden (2015)

[LZL+14] Luo, Q., Zhang, Y., Lee, C., Jin, D., Meredith, P.O.N., Şerbănuţă, T.F., Roşu, G.: RV-Monitor: efficient parametric runtime verification with simultaneous properties. In: Bonakdarpour, B., Smolka, S.A. (eds.) RV 2014. LNCS, vol. 8734, pp. 285–300. Springer, Heidelberg (2014). doi:10.1007/ 978-3-319-11164-3_24

[OG05]   Olivain, J., Goubault-Larrecq, J.: The ORCHIDS intrusion detection tool. In: Etessami, K., Rajamani, S.K. (eds.) CAV 2005. LNCS, vol. 3576, pp. 286–290. Springer, Heidelberg (2005). doi:10.1007/11513988_28

[Pur03] Purczyński, W.: Linux kernel privileged process hijacking vulnerability. BugTraq Id 7112, March 2003. http://www.securityfocus.com/bid/7112

[RG01]   Roger, M., Goubault-Larrecq, J.: Log auditing through model checking. In: Proceedings of the 14th IEEE Computer Security Foundations Workshop (CSFW 2001), Cape Breton, pp. 220–236. IEEE Computer Society Press, June 2001

[RGL99] Roger, M., Goubault-Larrecq, J.: Procédé et dispositif de résolution de modèles, utilisation pour la détection des attaques contre les systèmes informatiques. Dépôt français du 13, correspondant Dyade, demandeurs: 1. INRIA 2. Bull S.A. Numéro de publication: 2 798 490. Numéro d'enregistrement national: 99 11716. Classification: G 06 F 19/00. Date de mise à la disposition du public de la demande: 16 mars 2001, bulletin 01/11, 1999, September 1999

[Tar72] Tarjan, R.E.: Depth-first search and linear graph algorithms. SIAM J. Comput. **1**(2), 146–160 (1972)

Input Attribution for Statistical Model Checking Using Logistic Regression

Jeffery P. Hansen$^{(\boxtimes)}$, Sagar Chaki, Scott Hissam, James Edmondson,
Gabriel A. Moreno, and David Kyle

Carnegie Mellon University, Pittsburgh, PA, USA
{jhansen,chaki,shissam,jredmondson,gmoreno,dskyle}@sei.cmu.edu

Abstract. We describe an approach to Statistical Model Checking (SMC) that produces not only an estimate of the probability that specified properties (a.k.a. predicates) are satisfied, but also an "input attribution" for those predicates. We use logistic regression to generate the input attribution as a set of linear and non-linear functions of the inputs that explain conditions under which a predicate is satisfied. These functions provide quantitative insight into factors that influence the predicate outcome. We have implemented our approach on a distributed SMC infrastructure, DEMETER, that uses Linux Docker containers to isolate simulations (a.k.a. trials) from each other. Currently, DEMETER is deployed on six 20-core blade servers, and can perform tens of thousands of trials in a few hours. We demonstrate our approach on examples involving robotic agents interacting in a simulated physical environment. Our approach synthesizes input attributions that are both meaningful to the investigator and have predictive value on the predicate outcomes.

1 Introduction

Statistical model checking (SMC) [4, 23] has emerged as a key technique for quantitative analysis of stochastic systems. Given a stochastic system $\mathcal{M}$ depending on random input x, and a predicate Φ, the primary goal of SMC is to estimate the probability $P[\mathcal{M} \models \Phi]$ that Φ is satisfied in $\mathcal{M}$ within some specified level of confidence (e.g., relative error). SMC, which is based on Monte-Carlo methods, has some major advantages over methods such as probabilistic model checking. It can be applied to larger and more complex systems, and to the actual system software rather than an abstract model of that software. Moreover, it can analyze a system as a "black box" observing only its inputs and outputs.

While estimating the probability that a predicate holds is important, it is also important to understand the factors that contribute to that estimate. We refer to this as *input attribution*. More specifically, an input attribution is a

This material is based upon work funded and supported by the Department of Defense under Contract No. FA8721-05-C-0003 with Carnegie Mellon University for the operation of the Software Engineering Institute, a federally funded research and development center, DM-0003895.

Y. Falcone and C. Sanchez (Eds.): RV 2016, LNCS 10012, pp. 185–200, 2016.
DOI: 10.1007/978-3-319-46982-9_12

human-understandable quantitative model explaining the relationship between the random inputs and the specified predicate Φ (e.g., a mathematical expression of the input variables that predicts whether Φ will be satisfied). A good input attribution must: (i) describe a relationship that actually exists in the system; (ii) be presented in a way that is quantitative, meaningful and understandable to the investigator; (iii) give the investigator new insights into the system; and (iv) be resilient to additional hidden or uncontrolled randomness (e.g., randomness due to the physics in the system not included in the input x).

In this paper, we address the input attribution problem for SMC, and make the following contributions. First, we present an approach to input attribution that builds a statistical model from the simulation data collected during SMC. Among several potential statistical modeling methods, we focus on logistic regression [14] (LR). Logistic regression is targeted at systems with a binary (or categorical) dependent variable, which is exactly the case in SMC. The result of an LR analysis is a function that predicts the probability that the dependent binary variable will be 1 as a function of the input variables. One advantage of LR over other techniques, such as linear discriminant analysis, is that it makes no assumptions on the distribution of the inputs. We show how to compute both linear and polynomial input attributions via LR.

Second, we implement our approach in a distributed SMC infrastructure, called DEMETER, that uses a dispatch and join pattern to run many simulations in parallel across a set of machines. DEMETER uses Docker [17] containers to isolate simulations from each other, and batching to avoid statistical bias in results [22]. Using six blade servers, DEMETER has to date run millions of simulations over many days, demonstrating its robustness. Finally, we validate our approach over a set of examples involving one or more agents that operate under uncertainty to achieve specific goals. Our results indicate that the LR-based approach is able to synthesize input attributions that are both meaningful to the investigator and have predictive value on the predicate outcomes.

The rest of this paper is organized as follows. In Sect. 2 we discuss related work; in Sect. 3 we discuss some basic concepts and theory of Statistical Model Checking; in Sect. 4 we discuss our approach to input attribution; in Sect. 5 we describe DEMETER; in Sect. 6 we present our results in applying our techniques to three different examples; and in Sect. 7 we conclude.

2   Related Work

SMC, developed by Younes [23], has been applied to a wide variety of system models including stochastic hybrid automata [7], real time systems [8], and Simulink models for cyber-physical systems [4]. In contrast, we apply SMC directly to the system executing in an operating environment that includes uncertainty from scheduling and communication. Our prior work [16] also presented a distributed SMC infrastructure for DMPL [3] programs, but used a manually managed set of virtual machines to isolate trials from each other logically. In contrast, DEMETER uses lighter weight Docker [17] containers for isolation, and

Rancher [1] for automated launching and failover. In addition, it is able to carry out trials involving a broader class of applications, not just those generated from DMPL programs.

The PRISMATIC [19] project investigated "counterexample generation and culprit identification" in the context of probabilistic verification. It used machine learning (specifically the Waffles tool) to construct decision trees from runs of the system. From the decision tree, one can infer the component that is most responsible for failure. Their approach has limited effectiveness when a combination of several components leads to failure. In contrast, we use LR to give numeric weights to input variables, as well as polynomial terms of such variables. This makes our approach more effective when a combination of multiple random inputs is the more likely cause of failure. In addition, the PRISMATIC tool is built on top of PRISM [15] and can analyze models, while we analyze system executables.

The problem of determining under which conditions a program will fail has also been explored in the context of non-stochastic software. For example, Cousot et al. [6] use abstract interpretation [5] to statically compute an expression over a function's parameters (i.e., a precondition) under which the function will always fail a target assertion. Similarly, the DAIKON system [11] dynamically constructs likely program invariants from collected execution traces using machine learning techniques. Our goals are similar, in that we want to produce artifacts that provide insight about a program's behavior, but our focus is on stochastic systems, and we use logistic regression.

3   Background

Consider a system $\mathcal{M}$ with a finite vector of random inputs x over domain D_x. The SMC problem is to estimate the probability $p = P[\mathcal{M} \models \Phi]$ that $\mathcal{M}$ satisfies a predicate Φ given a joint probability distribution f on x. Let us write $x \sim f$ to mean x has distribution f. SMC involves a series of Bernoulli trials, modeling each trial as a Bernoulli random variable having value 1 with probability p, and 0 with probability $1 - p$. For each trial i, a random vector $x_i \sim f$ is generated, and the system $\mathcal{M}$ is simulated with input x_i to generate a trace σ_i. The trial's outcome, y_i, is 1 if Φ holds on σ_i, and 0 otherwise.

Traditionally, we would assume that whether $\mathcal{M} \models \Phi$ is satisfied under a specific input x is deterministic. However, since we are considering physical simulations of agents, the physics engine itself may introduce additional randomness that is not under our control. For this reason, we weaken our deterministic output assumption and assume the outcome y_i of $\mathcal{M} \models \Phi$ for a specific input x_i is itself a Bernoulli random variable with an unknown probability $J_{\mathcal{M} \models \Phi}(x_i)$ that $\mathcal{M} \models \Phi$ is satisfied. An alternative and equivalent way to model this is to introduce a hidden random variable $u \sim \mathcal{U}(0, 1)$ to represent randomness inherent in the simulation.[1] We then have a system with input x, u for which $\mathcal{M} \models \Phi$ is satisfied when $J_{\mathcal{M} \models \Phi}(x) \geq u$.

Define an indicator function $I_{\mathcal{M} \models \Phi} : D_x \times [0, 1] \rightarrow \{0, 1\}$ that returns 1 if $\mathcal{M} \models \Phi$ under input x, u, and 0 otherwise. Then, when $x \sim f$, and $u \sim \mathcal{U}(0, 1)$, the probability $p = E[I_{\mathcal{M} \models \Phi}(x, u)]$ that $\mathcal{M} \models \Phi$ holds can be estimated as $\hat{p} = \frac{1}{N} \sum_{i=1}^{N} I_{\mathcal{M} \models \Phi}(x_i, u_i)$, where N is the number of trials. Note that, while we observe the values of x_i for each trial simulation, we can see only the resulting outcome $I_{\mathcal{M} \models \Phi}(x_i, u_i)$ and not the value of the hidden variable u_i itself.

The precision of $\hat{p}$ is quantified by its *relative error* $RE(\hat{p}) = \frac{\sqrt{Var(\hat{p})}}{\hat{p}}$ where $Var(\hat{p})$ is the variance of the estimator. It is known [4] that for Bernoulli trials, relative error is related to the number of trials N and the probability of the event p as $RE(\hat{p}) = \sqrt{\frac{1-p}{pN}} \approx \frac{1}{\sqrt{pN}}$. Thus, we have $N = \frac{1-p}{pRE^2(\hat{p})} \approx \frac{1}{pRE^2(\hat{p})}$.

4   Input Attribution

Statistical learning is a field of statistics that is concerned with finding a model that relates a stimulus to some response [12]. In the case of statistical model checking, the stimulus is the set of random input variables and the response is the outcome of a trial. There are two main uses for these learned models: prediction and inference. Prediction is using the model to predict the response given a stimulus, while inference is learning something about the relationship between the stimulus and the response. Input attribution is primarily concerned with inference, though we do evaluate the predictive power of the model to ensure validity of any input attribution generated by our approach.

One technique used in statistical learning is logistic regression. In logistic regression, a linear function of "predictors" is fit to the log of the odds (often called a "logit") ratio that a binary response variable holds. Here, odds are simply an alternative way of representing probability such that $p = \frac{\gamma}{1+\gamma}$ is the probability where γ is the odds. For example, if the odds of an event are 4 to 3, then $\gamma = \frac{4}{3}$ and the probability is $p \approx 0.57$.

In this paper, we take the predictors to be either the input variables, or a combination of the input variables and functions of the input variables. For simplicity we assume all random variables are continuous or countable, though it is possible to generalize these results to categorical random variables. The analysis is performed independently for each predicate defined by the investigator with a separate result for each. Let x_{ij} be the inputs over a set of trials $1 \leq i \leq N$ with predictors $1 \leq j \leq M$ for each input, and y_i be the result of each trial. Logistic regression will find a linear function of the form:

$$L : x \mapsto \beta_0 + \sum_{j=1}^{M} \beta_j x_j \tag{1}$$

---

[1] In this paper we use $\mathcal{U}(a, b)$ for the uniform distribution between two real numbers $a \leq b$, and $\mathcal{U}\{a, b\}$ for the uniform integer distribution between a and b, inclusive.

such that $\hat{p} = \frac{1}{1+e^{-L(x_i)}}$ is the predicted probability that we will get a response of $y_i = 1$ given input x_i. The β_j for a continuous random variable x_j represents the increase in the "logit" for each unit increase in of x_j. When interpreting the coefficients, it is sometimes useful to think of an "odds ratio", the factor by which the odds changes in response to some change. For an increase of Δ on variable x_j the odds ratio will be $e^{\beta_j \Delta}$. Note that β_j itself does not necessarily indicate the importantance of x_i as it is also dependentant on the units.

We use the R statistical analysis system [20] to perform the logistic regression. For each predictor x_j, R generates a maximum likelihood estimate $\hat{\beta}_j$ and a standard error $se(\hat{\beta}_j)$ of the coefficient β_j for that predictor. The standard error is used to perform a Wald test [14] on the significance of β_j against the null-hypothesis that β_j could be 0 (i.e., the hypothesis that predictor x_j is not important for determining the outcome). The Wald test involves calculating a z-value $z_j = \frac{\hat{\beta}_j - 0}{se(\hat{\beta}_j)}$ representing the number of standard deviations from zero of the $\hat{\beta}_j$ estimate, then looking up that value in the Normal distribution table to find the p-value representing the probability that the null-hypothesis could occur by chance. Typically a p-value <0.05 is considered statistically significant.

Since our goal is to discover relationships between the predictors and the predicate, the $\hat{\beta}_j$ and the associated p-values for each coefficient are the most useful for us. Low p-values tell us that a predictor is significant, and the $\hat{\beta}_j$ tells us the factor by which the log of the odds for the predicate being satisfied increases which each unit increase in predictor x_j.

4.1   Linear Input Attribution

The most straight-forward application of logistic regression is to use each input x_j as a predictor, and report those for which the p-value is below the selected threshold. Our approach includes this as one of its options, and is the easiest to use when relationships between input variables and predicates are linear.

Example. As an illustrative example consider a data set consisting of 500 samples of random vectors $x = (x_1, x_2, x_3)$ where $x_1 \sim \mathcal{U}\{1,6\}$, $x_2 \sim \mathcal{U}\{1,6\}$, $x_3 \sim \mathcal{U}\{1,12\}$. Also assume there is a hidden random variable $u \sim \mathcal{U}\{1,10\}$ that affects the outcome of the trial, but cannot be directly observed. Now assume the predicate y we are testing is 1 when $x_2 + x_3 + u > 10$ and 0 otherwise. When we apply logistic regression on this data set using R we get: $L : x \mapsto -2.8 - 0.03x_1 + 0.50x_2 + 0.64x_3$, with p-factors well below 0.01 for both x_2 and x_3, and a p-factor of 0.78 for x_1 indicating it is not statistically significant (which is expected since it was not involved in the predicate being tested). For this example, our approach generates the input attribution: $0.50x_2 + 0.64x_3$, excluding the x_1 term because it was not statistically significant. The positive coefficients for both x_2 and x_3 indicate the probability of y being 1 increases with an increase in either input, as expected.

Before accepting the result of the logistic regression analysis, we must verify that the overall logistic model fits the data. We do this using ROC (Receiver

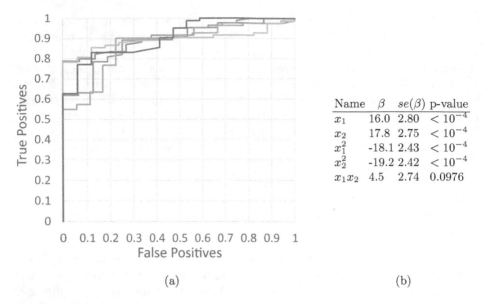

Name	β	$se(\beta)$	p-value
x_1	16.0	2.80	$< 10^{-4}$
x_2	17.8	2.75	$< 10^{-4}$
x_1^2	-18.1	2.43	$< 10^{-4}$
x_2^2	-19.2	2.42	$< 10^{-4}$
$x_1 x_2$	4.5	2.74	0.0976

(a)   (b)

Fig. 1. (a) ROC curves for linear example; (b) Logistic regression results for polynomial example.

Operating Characteristic) analysis [13]. In ROC analysis, we consider $L(x) > T$ for some threshold T to be the prediction that is compared to the actual result of the predicate y. We then plot the true positive rate $P[y = 1|L(x) > T]$ against the false positive rate $P[y = 0|L(x) > T]$ for $-\infty < T < \infty$.

The ROC curve for our example data using 5-fold cross validation is shown in Fig. 1(a). In 5-fold cross validation, the trials are randomly partitioned into 5 chunks then 4/5 of the data are used to build the logistic model while the remaining 1/5 is used to validate the model. This process is repeated 5 times with each chunk taking its turn as the test data resulting in curves for each of the 5 folds shown in the figure. In ROC analysis, curves that approach the upper left corner are considered "good" detectors while a detector near the diagonal from the lower left to upper right are no better than random guessing. Another more succinct way to present the results of an ROC analysis is the AUC (Area Under Curve). It is known [13] that the AUC is equivalent to the probability $P[L(x_{sat}) > L(x_{unsat})]$ where x_{sat} is a randomly selected input that satisfies the predicate and x_{unsat} is a randomly selected input that does not satisfy the predicate. An AUC of 1 corresponds to a perfect detector, while an AUC of 0.5 corresponds to a detector that is no better than guessing. Using our sample data, we computed AUC for each fold yielding values be 0.87 and 0.91 with a mean of 0.90 indicating good predictive value of the model, and thus indicating our input attribution is valid.

4.2   Non-linear Input Attribution

If there are non-linear dependencies between a predictor and the predicate, the linear analysis techniques described above will fail to find a statistically significant relationship. To solve this problem, we include non-linear functions of the inputs as predictors. In effect, the non-linear functions are "guesses" on potential relationships between the inputs and the predicate. Some guesses may result in statistically significant relationships, while others may not and be discarded.

In this paper, we restrict our guesses to 2nd order polynomials over the input variables. These are important because in sets of random variables describing points in space, distances between fixed points, or between pairs of random points can be described as 2nd order polynomials. Note that it is not necessary to actually include every possible polynomial of the inputs, we need only include the monomial building blocks of the possible polynomials. More specifically, in addition to the linear input terms $\{x_1, \ldots, x_M\}$, we include the additional predictors $\{x_j^2 \mid 1 \leq j \leq M\}$, and the predictors $\{x_j x_k \mid 1 \leq j < k \leq M\}$.

Factored Polynomials. In order to present relationships that are easy to interpret, our algorithm further attempts to find factored polynomials where possible. Two types of factors are considered: single variable and two variable. In each case, we look for subsets of the log odds expression (1) that can be factored. In the single variable case, we look for predictors $\beta_a x_j^2$ and $\beta_b x_j$ where both have a low p-value and factor by completing the squares as:

$$\beta_a (x_j + \frac{\beta_b}{2\beta_a})^2 + C = \beta_a x_j^2 + \beta_b x_j \tag{2}$$

where C is the constant needed to complete the square. But since our goal is to show relationships, our algorithm only outputs the $\beta_a(x_i + \frac{\beta_b}{2\beta_a})^2$ part.

Factored Two-Variable Polynomials. Similarly, in the two variable case, we look for predictors $\beta_a x_j^2$, $\beta_b x_j x_k$ and $\beta_c x_k^2$ with low p-values, and factor as:

$$\beta_a x_j^2 + \beta_b x_j x_k + \beta_c x_k^2 = \beta_a(x_j + (h+g)x_k)(x_j + (h-g)x_k) \tag{3}$$

where $h = \frac{\beta_b}{2\beta_a}$ and $g = \frac{\sqrt{\beta_b^2 - 4\beta_a \beta_c}}{2\beta_a}$ when g is real. Since all of the β_i are approximations, our algorithm suggests the simpler factoring:

$$\beta_a x_j^2 + \beta_b x_j x_k + \beta_c x_k^2 \approx \beta_a(x_j + hx_k)^2 \tag{4}$$

when $|\beta_c - \beta_a h^2| < K se(\beta_c)$ (i.e., when the polynomial coefficient of the x_k^2 term in $\beta_a(x_j + hx_k)^2$ is within K standard error of its original value). We use $K = 3$ in this paper.

Example. Now consider an example with 500 trials with inputs $x = (x_1, x_2)$ where $x_1 \sim \mathcal{U}(0, 1)$ and $x_2 \sim \mathcal{U}(0, 1)$ are uniformly distributed between 0 and 1 and represent coordinates in a 2D square. Define the predicate y as being true when the point x is within distance $u \sim \mathcal{U}(0, 0.5)$ of the center $(0.5, 0.5)$ of the square but with u being a hidden random variable.

When we first try a linear analysis, we find that the p-factors for both x_1 and x_2 are not significant. When we repeat the analysis using polynomial terms we get the results shown in Table 1(b). The 5-fold cross validation for this example results in an average AUC of 0.85 indicating reasonable predictive strength for the model. Since the p-value for the $x_1 x_2$ term is greater than 0.05, it is not statistically significant and so we only look for single variable polynomial expressions. Completing the squares for the x_1 and x_2 gives us the input attribution: $-18.1(x_1 - 0.44)^2 - 19.2(x_2 - 0.46)^2$. We see from the form of this expression that the analysis synthesizes an expression for distance between (x_1, x_2) and $(0.44, 0.46)$ which is close to the expected distance from the center point at $(0.5, 0.5)$. We also see this expression is negative meaning that the further (x_1, x_2) is from the center point, the lower the probability that y is satisfied.

5   SMC Infrastructure: DEMETER

We have implemented our approach in a distributed SMC infrastructure called DEMETER (Distributed Execution of Multiple Experiments and Transfer of Empirical Results). DEMETER uses a dispatch and join pattern for parallel processing across a set of machines. Dispatch is managed by an *SMC Master* (see Fig. 2) which queues SMC *jobs*. A job is described via a .smc file, which includes the system $\mathcal{M}$, the input variables x_i and their probability distribution f, target predicate(s) Φ, and the target relative error for each predicate $RE(\hat{p})_\Phi$.

A job is conducted by the Master as a series of Bernoulli trials. Each trial in the series is allocated to an *SMC Runner* which simulates the system $\mathcal{M}$ with the trial inputs, and reports the outcome. The system $\mathcal{M}$ can be any arbitrary piece of software that can be invoked from a shell script dispatched by the Runner, potentially with multiple communicating processes. The trial input to the Runner is an instance of a random input vector, $x_i \sim f$, generated by the Master for that trial. The outcome, produced by $\mathcal{M}$, is either 1 if Φ holds on σ_i, and 0 otherwise for each Φ described by the job. The Master records the input

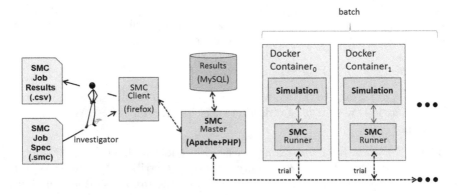

Fig. 2. The Master-Runner architecture of DEMETER.

and outcome for each trial in the *Results* database and the Master will continue to perform trials until the target relative error computed for each $\hat{p}_\Phi$ is reached.

A job may require thousands of trials to reach the target $RE(\hat{p}_\Phi)$. The Master dispatches trials in parallel as a sequence of *batches* allowing all trials in a batch to complete before starting the next batch to avoid bias [22]. The default batch size equals the number of available Runners, but this can be controlled via the "weight" specification for the job (discussed later in *Load Management*). Once a batch is dispatched, the Master waits for all trials in that batch to complete before dispatching the next batch. A batch is complete if every trial in it completes with either 0 or 1 for all predicates defined for the job. Any other result (e.g., an infrastructure error) is considered an error for the trial, and the entire batch is discarded to avoid bias. Trials from a complete batch are used to compute $RE(\hat{p}_\Phi)$ for each predicate.

For our experiments, we deployed DEMETER over six Dell PowerEdge blades with each blade having 128 Gb of RAM and 2 Intel Xeon E5-2687W 3.1 GHz processors with each processor having 10 processing cores and 2 cpu threads per core. A pool of 216 Runners (36 *Runners* ∗ 6 *blades*²) were used. We now discuss how DEMETER achieves isolation between trials.

Logical Isolation is achieved by running each trial within a separate Docker [17] instance. Docker has the following twofold advantage over other virtual machine approaches: (i) startup, shutdown and failover for each Runner can be managed by open source tools like Rancher [1] with low learning curve; and (ii) Docker's overhead is low compared to other full operating system virtualization technologies [21].

Network Isolation. Processes in Docker containers can communicate at the network level with each other. By default, multicast messages (used in our simulations) cross container boundaries. This can result in processes from one simulation receiving messages from another simulation. Using Docker's `icc=false` configuration directive disables such inter-container communication, but also disables Rancher's ability to manage the Runners. As such, `iptables` was used in conjunction with `icc=true` to drop all multicast traffic emanating from the `docker0` interface. This minimalistically isolates Runners from each other, avoiding network interference within the simulation, while allowing Rancher management.

Load Management. DEMETER allows a numeric "weight" to be specified for the job. Intuitively, the weight w is the number of CPU cores required to execute each trial. Note that w can be greater than 1 if, for example, the application is distributed and consists of several nodes executing in parallel. The Master executes at most $\lfloor \frac{216}{w} \rfloor$ trials in parallel at a time. Thus, CPU overload can be avoided by specifying a suitably large value of w.

---

² This leaves a few CPU threads for host processing independent of simulation activities.

6   Results

We validated our approach on three scenarios with increasing complexity. In each experiment, one or more agents are realized by a quadcopter model in the physics simulator V-REP [9]. An additional Linux process is used as a controller for each agent, communicating over a socket with V-REP. For each scenario we show that DEMETER.constructs effective input attributions.

6.1   Pursuer/Evader Scenario

Scenario Overview. The goal of this example was to validate the effectiveness of non-linear input attribution via logistic regression. It consists of two agents— a pursuer P and an evader E—moving on a 2-dimensional 20×20 grid of cells. Each cell is identified by its coordinate, with the cell at the lower-left corner of the grid being $(0,0)$ and the cell at the upper-right corner being $(19,19)$. Each trial runs as follows: (i) the pursuer starts in a random initial cell (x_p, y_p) and the evader starts in a random initial cell (x_e, y_e) such that x_p, y_p, x_e and y_e are all uniformly selected from $\mathcal{U}\{6, 13\}$; note that this means that initially P and E are located in the sub-grid whose lower-left cell is $(6,6)$ and upper-right cell is $(13,13)$; (ii) the evader moves toward the grid corner away from the pursuer with velocity v, and the pursuer moves toward the evader with velocity kv where $k > 1$ is the factor by which P is faster than E; (iii) if P is able to reach within distance d of E by time $t_{\max}$ then P wins and the trial results in 0; otherwise, E wins and the trial results in 1. The constants v and $t_{\max}$ are such that E can never reach a grid corner by time $t_{\max}$, and hence always has space to move. Intuitively, the result of a trial depends on the initial distance between E and P, i.e., on $(x_e - x_p)^2 + (y_e - y_p)^2$. Moreover, this is a polynomial and hence requires non-linear input attribution. Purely linear logistic regression will not be able to detect this dependency. Our results, discussed next, confirm these intuitions.

Analysis of Results. Using DEMETER, we estimated the probability $\hat{p}$ that the evader escapes the pursuer with a result of $\hat{p} = 0.214$. This was estimated to a target relative error of 0.01 and required 36,960 trials, of which 7,900 satisfied the predicate. Total run time was 5 h and 20 min with 120 trials per batch. When we perform the Logistic Regression for the linear analysis, we get the results shown in Table 1(a). Only x_e results in a p-value less than 0.05. However, an ROC analysis with 5-fold cross validation results in an average AUC of 0.51, indicating that the predictive value of the model is no better than chance. For this reason, we do not accept the results of the linear analysis.

When we include the polynomial terms, we get the results shown in Table 1(b) (only terms for which the p-value was below 0.05 are shown). The AUC for the 5-fold cross validation including the polynomial terms was 0.77, considerably better than that including only linear terms. When we apply the factoring heuristics from Sect. 4.2, we get the following polynomial input attribution expressions: $0.0602(x_e - 1.03x_p)^2$ and $0.0561(y_e - 1.09y_p)^2$. These expressions, generated automatically from just the simulation data, are very close to our

Table 1. Logistic analysis results of pursuer/evader experiment.

(a) Linear Analysis

Name	β	$se(\beta)$	p-value
x_e	-0.0178	0.0055	0.0013
y_e	0.0106	0.0055	0.0554
x_p	0.0026	0.0056	0.6458
y_y	-0.0009	0.0055	0.8689

(b) Polynomial Analysis

Name	β	$se(\beta)$	p-value
$x_e x_p$	-0.124	0.0027	$< 10^{-4}$
$y_e y_p$	-0.122	0.0027	$< 10^{-4}$
x_e^2	0.060	0.0031	$< 10^{-4}$
y_e^2	0.056	0.0031	$< 10^{-4}$
x_p^2	0.056	0.0031	$< 10^{-4}$
y_p^2	0.056	0.0031	$< 10^{-4}$

expectation that the probability of escape for the evader depends on the initial distance between the pursuer and evader. The positive leading coefficient on both of the expressions tell us that the probability of escape increases as the initial distance increases, which is also what we expect.

6.2   Target/Threat Scenario

Scenario Overview. This scenario involves self-adaptive behavior by an agent that must fly a pre-planned route over a 2D grid at constant forward speed, detecting as many targets on the ground as possible. Target detection is done using a downward-looking sensor whose performance is inversely proportional to the distance from the ground. There are also threats along the route, but the probability of being destroyed by a threat is inversely proportional to the height of the agent. Clearly, when deciding at what height the agent should fly there is a tradeoff between detecting targets and avoiding threats.

The number and location of targets and threats is random and unknown. However, the agent has a forward-looking sensor that observes the environment ahead with some finite horizon to detect threats and targets, albeit with false positive and false negative rates. The agent self-adapts proactively [18] to this uncertainty by changing its altitude as it flies. It aims to maximize the number of targets detected, taking into account that if it is destroyed, no more targets are detected and the mission fails. Specifically, using the forward-looking sensor information, the agent periodically constructs at run time a probabilistic model of the environment, which is then used to make the adaptation decision—either stay at the current altitude, or increase/decrease altitude by one level.

In this scenario, mission success is defined as detecting at least 50 % of the existing targets without being destroyed. We break this down into three predicates with the predicate Φ_t being "at least 50 % of the existing targets are detected", Φ_s being the "the agent survives to end of run", and $\Phi_m = \Phi_t \wedge \Phi_s$ being the predicate for mission success. The random variables upon which these results depend are shown in Table 2.

Analysis of Results. The estimated probabilities produced by DEMETER for the predicates tested are $\hat{P}[\Phi_t] = 0.361$, $\hat{P}[\Phi_s] = 0.618$ and $\hat{P}[\Phi_m] = 0.308$. Thus, while the agent survived most trials, the mission success rate is low because of

Table 2. Inputs for target/threat scenario.

Name	Dist.	Description
N_E	$\mathcal{U}\{10,40\}$	Total number of existing targets
N_T	$\mathcal{U}\{5,20\}$	Total number of existing threats
d_{LA}	$\mathcal{U}\{1,5\}$	Number of cells in front of the agent scanned by the forward-looking sensor, and decision horizon for proactive adaptation
p_{EFP}	$\mathcal{U}(0,0.5)$	False positive rate for target detection with the forward-looking sensor
p_{EFN}	$\mathcal{U}(0,0.5)$	False negative rate for target detection with the forward-looking sensor
p_{TFP}	$\mathcal{U}(0,0.5)$	False positive rate for threat detection with the forward-looking sensor
p_{TFN}	$\mathcal{U}(0,0.5)$	False negative rate for threat detection with the forward-looking sensor
r_E	$\mathcal{U}\{1,5\}$	Downward-looking sensor range (i.e., maximum height from which a target can possibly be detected)
r_T	$\mathcal{U}\{1,3\}$	Threat range (i.e., maximum height at which agent can be destroyed)

failure to detect the required number of targets. The target relative error was 0.01, and 22,560 trials were completed in 10 h and 6 min, with 120 trials per batch. The 5-fold cross validated mean AUCs for the linear and polynomial versions of the logistic regression analysis for each of the three predicates were approximately equal, ranging between 0.891 and 0.926. Since the polynomial model provides no additional predictive quality, we focus our analysis on the linear results shown in Table 3 (coefficients that were not statistically significant for a predicate are not shown). Notable conclusions from these results are:

(a) The most important variables affecting Φ_m are r_E, r_T, N_T, d_{LA} and p_{TFP}. Mission success $\hat{P}[\Phi_m]$ increases as r_E and d_{LA} increase, but decreases as the other input variables increase.

(b) As the target false-positive rate p_{TFP} increases, $P[\Phi_s]$ increases but $P[\Phi_t]$ decreases. The increase in $P[\Phi_s]$ is explained by the fact that falsely detecting a threat causes the agent to fly at a higher altitude on average. This results in it being at a higher than necessary altitude when it actually encounters a threat, thus increasing its probability of survival. On the other hand, being higher than necessary causes it to miss targets, thus lowering $P[\Phi_t]$.

(c) Increasing the number of targets N_T results in decreases to all three predicates. While it is not surprising that increasing the number of targets makes it more difficult to meet the 50 % requirement, the effect on the survival probability $P[\Phi_s]$ is less obvious. A possible explanation for this is that detections of a potential target cause the agent to take more risk flying at lower altitude and thus increasing its chances for being destroyed.

Table 3. Results for target/threat scenario

Name	Φ_s			Φ_t			Φ_m		
	β	$se(\beta)$	p-value	β	$se(\beta)$	p-value	β	$se(\beta)$	p-value
r_E				1.46	0.0195	$<10^{-4}$	1.33	0.0194	$<10^{-4}$
r_T	-2.37	0.0308	$<10^{-4}$	-1.189	0.0195	$<10^{-4}$	-1.57	0.0288	$<10^{-4}$
d_{LA}	0.377	0.0137	$<10^{-4}$	0.194	0.0137	$<10^{-4}$	0.233	0.0140	$<10^{-4}$
N_T	-0.0792	0.0041	$<10^{-4}$	-0.0943	0.0043	$<10^{-4}$	-0.0892	0.0043	$<10^{-4}$
N_E	-0.0296	0.0021	$<10^{-4}$						
p_{EFP}	-17.8130	1.3026	$<10^{-4}$						
p_{TFP}	32.7410	1.3363	$<10^{-4}$	-10.0390	1.3358	$<10^{-4}$	-3.2583	1.3569	0.0163

(d) Increasing d_{LA} increases all three predicates. This happens for two reasons. First, the agent accumulates observations done with the forward-looking sensor as it flies. Thus, the larger the look-ahead, the more time a target/threat will be within the sensor range and the more times it will be sensed. Second, using a longer horizon for the adaptation decision allows the agent to consider not only immediate, but also upcoming needs (e.g., to start increasing altitude to avoid a threat likely present three cells ahead).

(e) The target and threat sensor false-negative rates – p_{EFN} and p_{TFN} – have no predictive value on the outcome. This is surprising since the corresponding false-positive rates are predictive, and we expect the input-attribution to be symmetric. However, we validated these results by repeating our experiments with different combinations of (high and low) values of these rates. Our results showed that while changing p_{EFP} and p_{TFP} changed the $\hat{p}$ significantly, changing p_{EFN} and p_{TFN} had no effect. This demonstrates the effectiveness of our approach in producing counter-intuitive input-attributions, and its predictive value.

6.3   Paparazzi Scenario

Scenario Overview. This scenario involves multiple collaborating autonomous agents attempting to protect another agent from being clearly photographed. There is one paparazzi photographer (P) agent, one famous celebrity (C) agent, and one or more unmanned autonomous quadcopter guardian (G) agents. All agents start at random initial locations on a 3D map. Guardians must position themselves between P and C, while P moves around C to get a clear shot.

The guardians G execute an "onion-defense" formation between C and P. An onion-defense is a layered formation with the number of layers being a function of the number of guardians, and each layer forming an arc around C, resembling the layers of an onion as it is peeled. The goal is to provide redundant line-of-sight blocking for any direction P might move to attempt to get a picture of C.

The more guardians G in the formation, the more protected C is from a nimble P that tries to flank members of G. Once in stable formation, members of G try to maintain a spacing buffer $S_G = 1$ between each other.

Each guardian G has a block radius B_G which is the range around its center-of-mass that it blocks effectively. Each trial has a random number of guardians $N_G \sim \mathcal{U}\{1, 14\}$, each having a random $B_G \sim \mathcal{U}(1, 4)$ (note that $B_G \geq S_G$). P has a minimal distance D_P that he must be from C to take a useful photograph, and an initial distance I_P that he starts north from C. Once P reaches D_P from C, he moves counter-clockwise around C until he either has line of sight (success) or a 300 s timeout occurs (failure). We keep D_P a constant, but $I_P \sim \mathcal{U}(D_P, 1.5D_P)$. To prevent guardians from blocking all possible photograph angles on initialization, each member of G has an initial distance $I_G \sim \mathcal{U}(0.4D_P, 1.2D_P)$ from C in a random direction $\theta_G \sim \mathcal{U}(0, 360)$. The farther any G is from C and other G, the longer it takes to get into formation and the better chance P should have to get a good photograph of C once the actual distance A_P between P and C equals the useful photograph distance D_P.

Our experiments are built atop the Group Autonomy for Mobile Systems [2] toolkit (which provides the onion defense algorithm), the Multi-Agent Distributed Adaptive Resource Allocation [10] middleware, and V-REP.

Analysis of Results. DEMETER estimated the probability that P photographs C as $\hat{p} = 0.0023$, with a target relative error of 0.05, using 170,424 trials of which 400 satisfied the predicate (i.e., the photographer succeeded 0.23 % of the time). Total run time was 1 day 17 h and 37 min with 120 trials per batch. The Logistic Regression for linear and polynomial analysis is shown in Table 4. The ROC analysis for linear analysis had a good predictive value with an AUC of 0.73. However, the ROC for polynomial analysis was a more distinctive curve with average AUC of 0.87. Consequently, we will focus on the results of the polynomial analysis over the linear analysis.

Table 4(b) shows results for polynomial terms with p-values below 0.0002. Applying the factoring heuristics from Sect. 4.2 results in the input attribution expressions: $0.0208(N_G - 1.53\theta_1)(N_G + 2.96\theta_1)$ and $0.0939(\theta_1 - 7.82)^2$. This result illuminates the peculiarities of the onion-defense, which gets more protective with more defenders (N_G). The first defender (G_1) is especially important because it is located directly between P and C. G_2 is then placed to its left in an arc around C and G_3 to the immediate right of G_1. Each subsequent member builds

Table 4. Logistic analysis results for Paparazzi experiment.

(a) Linear Analysis

Name	β	$se(\beta)$	p-value
N_G	0.1166	0.0133	0.0000
θ_1	0.1792	0.0284	0.0000
θ_2	-0.1452	0.281	0.0000
I_P	-1.6228	0.3524	0.0000

(b) Polynomial Analysis

Name	β	$se(\beta)$	p-value
θ_2^2	0.0939	0.0170	0.0000
θ_1^2	0.0939	0.0173	0.0000
N_G^2	-0.0208	0.0044	0.0000

outward from G_1 and new layers are added behind it as N_G gets larger. θ_1 is important because P always starts due north of C, and if θ_1 is more northward, then G_1 gets to its assigned position quickly to block P. θ_2 is also important because G_2 is to the left of G_1, and if it can get into position quickly, it can block the counter-clockwise movement of P.

We were surprised by θ_1 being more important than I_1 (the initial distance from C). Through this analysis, we were able to give guidance to the onion-defense designer on potential fixes to deal with P being detected very close to C. For instance, instead of the current algorithm using fixed formations based on indices of agents, the algorithm could use intercept times to assign agent positions in formations to protect C from P. This highlights the usefulness of our approach to diagnose and fix issues in stochastic systems.

7   Conclusion

We have presented an approach for input-attribution in SMC and have implemented it in DEMETER, a distributed SMC infrastructure. We have shown that our approach synthesizes input attributions that satisfy the four conditions we stated are necessary for a good input attribution in Sect. 1 as follows: (i) by showing that the generated models have predictive power, we demonstrated that synthesized expressions correspond to actual relationships in the system; (ii) synthesized attributions are numeric in nature and backed up with confidence scores on individual coefficients and on the overall predictive power of the model; (iii) results from our experiments were able to validate our hypotheses and in some cases such as in the paparazzi scenario resulted in new and unexpected insights; and (iv) all of these results were obtained despite substantial noise from other hidden and explicit random variables in the system.

Note that while in this paper we focused on inputs, we believe that it is also possible to "watch" internal variables in the system and include them in the attribution. We also expect that other relationships, besides polynomial, could also be found by adding predictors to the logistic regression analysis, and believe this to be an important area for future work.

References

1. A platform for operating docker in production. http://github.com/rancher/rancher
2. Dukeman, A., Adams, J.A., Edmondson, J.: Extensible collaborative autonomy using GAMS. In: Proceedings of IRMAS (2016)
3. Chaki, S., Kyle, D.: DMPL: programming and verifying distributed mixed-synchrony and mixed-critical software. Technical report CMU/SEI-2016-TR-005, Software Engineering Institute, Carnegie Mellon University, Pittsburgh (2016). http://resources.sei.cmu.edu/library/asset-view.cfm?assetid=464254
4. Clarke, E.M., Zuliani, P.: Statistical model checking for cyber-physical systems. In: Bultan, T., Hsiung, P.-A. (eds.) ATVA 2011. LNCS, vol. 6996, pp. 1–12. Springer, Heidelberg (2011). doi:10.1007/978-3-642-24372-1_1

5. Cousot, P., Cousot, R.: Abstract interpretation: a unified lattice model for static analysis of programs by construction or approximation of fixpoints. In: Proceedings of POPL (1977)
6. Cousot, P., Cousot, R., Fähndrich, M., Logozzo, F.: Automatic inference of necessary preconditions. In: Giacobazzi, R., Berdine, J., Mastroeni, I. (eds.) VMCAI 2013. LNCS, vol. 7737, pp. 128–148. Springer, Heidelberg (2013). doi:10.1007/978-3-642-35873-9_10
7. David, A., Du, D., Guldstrand Larsen, K., Legay, A., Mikučionis, M.: Optimizing control strategy using statistical model checking. In: Brat, G., Rungta, N., Venet, A. (eds.) NFM 2013. LNCS, vol. 7871, pp. 352–367. Springer, Heidelberg (2013). doi:10.1007/978-3-642-38088-4_24
8. David, A., Larsen, K.G., Legay, A., Mikučionis, M., Wang, Z.: Time for statistical model checking of real-time systems. In: Gopalakrishnan, G., Qadeer, S. (eds.) CAV 2011. LNCS, vol. 6806, pp. 349–355. Springer, Heidelberg (2011). doi:10.1007/978-3-642-22110-1_27
9. Rohmer, E., Signgh, S.P.N., Freese, M.: V-REP: a versatile and scalable robot simulation framework. In: Proceedings of IROS (2013)
10. Edmondson, J., Gokhale, A.: Design of a scalable reasoning engine for distributed, real-time and embedded systems. In: Xiong, H., Lee, W.B. (eds.) KSEM 2011. LNCS (LNAI), vol. 7091, pp. 221–232. Springer, Heidelberg (2011). doi:10.1007/978-3-642-25975-3_20
11. Ernst, M.D., Cockrell, J., Griswold, W.G., Notkin, D.: Dynamically discovering likely program invariants to support program evolution. In: Proceedings of ICSE (1999)
12. James, G., Witten, D., Hastie, T., Tibshirani, R.: An Introduction to Statistical Learning, 6th edn. Springer, New York (2015)
13. Hanley, J., McNeil, B.: The meaning and use of the area under a receiver operating characteristic (ROC) curve. Radiology 143(1), 29–36 (1982)
14. Hosmer, D., Lemeshow, S.: Applied Logistic Regression, 3rd edn. Wiley, Hoboken (2013)
15. Kwiatkowska, M., Norman, G., Parker, D.: PRISM 4.0: verification of probabilistic real-time systems. In: Gopalakrishnan, G., Qadeer, S. (eds.) CAV 2011. LNCS, vol. 6806, pp. 585–591. Springer, Heidelberg (2011). doi:10.1007/978-3-642-22110-1_47
16. Kyle, D., Hansen, J., Chaki, S.: Statistical model checking of distributed adaptive real-time software. In: Bartocci, E., Majumdar, R. (eds.) RV 2015. LNCS, vol. 9333, pp. 269–274. Springer, Heidelberg (2015). doi:10.1007/978-3-319-23820-3_17
17. Merkel, D.: Docker: lightweight Linux containers for consistent development and deployment. Linux J. http://dl.acm.org/citation.cfm?id=2600239.2600241
18. Moreno, G.A., Cámara, J., Garlan, D., Schmerl, B.: Efficient decision-making under uncertainty for proactive self-adaptation. In: Proceedings of ICAC (2016, to appear)
19. Musliner, D.J., Engstrom, E.: PRISMATIC: unified hierarchical probabilistic verification tool. Technical report AFRL-RZ-WP-TR-2011-2097 (2011)
20. R Development Core Team: R: A Language and Environment for Statistical Computing (2008). http://www.R-project.org
21. Seshachala, S.: Docker vs VMs. http://devops.com/2014/11/24/docker-vs-vms
22. Younes, H.L.S.: Ymer: a statistical model checker. In: Etessami, K., Rajamani, S.K. (eds.) CAV 2005. LNCS, vol. 3576, pp. 429–433. Springer, Heidelberg (2005). doi:10.1007/11513988_43
23. Younes, H.L.S.: Verification and planning for stochastic processes with asynchronous events. Ph.D. thesis, CMU, Technical report no. CMU-CS-05-105 (2005)

Quantitative Monitoring of STL with Edit Distance

Stefan Jakšić[1,2]($\boxtimes$), Ezio Bartocci[2], Radu Grosu[2], and Dejan Ničković[1]

[1] AIT Austrian Institute of Technology, Seibersdorf, Austria
Stefan.Jaksic.fl@ait.ac.at
[2] Faculty of Informatics, Vienna University of Technology, Vienna, Austria

Abstract. In cyber-physical systems (CPS), physical behaviors are typically controlled by digital hardware. As a consequence, continuous behaviors are discretized by sampling and quantization prior to their processing. Quantifying the similarity between CPS behaviors and their specification is an important ingredient in evaluating correctness and quality of such systems. We propose a novel procedure for measuring robustness between digitized CPS signals and Signal Temporal Logic (STL) specifications. We first equip STL with quantitative semantics based on the *weighted edit distance* (WED), a metric that quantifies both space and time mismatches between digitized CPS behaviors. We then develop a dynamic programming algorithm for computing the robustness degree between digitized signals and STL specifications. We implemented our approach and evaluated it on an automotive case study.

1 Introduction

Cyber-physical systems (CPS) integrate heterogeneous collaborative components that are interconnected between themselves and their physical environment. They exhibit complex behaviors that often combine discrete and continuous dynamics. The sophistication, complexity and heterogeneity of CPS makes their verification a difficult task. Runtime monitoring addresses this problem by providing a formal, yet scalable, verification method. It achieves both rigor and efficiency by enabling evaluation of systems according to the properties of their individual behaviors.

In the recent past, property-based runtime monitoring of CPS centered around Signal Temporal Logic (STL) [18] and its variants have received considerable attention [1,5,6,10–12,20]. STL is a formal specification language for describing properties of continuous and hybrid behaviors. In its original form, STL allows to distinguish correct from incorrect behaviors. However, the binary true/false classification may not be sufficient for real-valued behaviors. In fact, systems with continuous dynamics are often sensitive to small perturbations in initial conditions, system parameters and the accuracy of sensors, which may influence the correctness of the verdict. In order to address this problem, the satisfaction relation can be replaced by the *robustness degree* [10–12] of a behavior with respect to a temporal specification. The robustness degree gives a finer measure of how far is the behavior from satisfying or violating of the specification.

© Springer International Publishing AG 2016
Y. Falcone and C. Sanchez (Eds.): RV 2016, LNCS 10012, pp. 201–218, 2016.
DOI: 10.1007/978-3-319-46982-9_13

In this paper, we propose a novel quantitative semantics for STL that measures the behavior mismatches in both *space* and *time*. We consider applications in which continuous CPS behaviors are observed by a digital device. In this scenario, continuous behaviors are typically discretized, both in time and space, by an analog-to-digital converter (ADC). As a consequence, we interpret STL over discrete-time digitized behaviors. We first define the *weighted* edit distance as an appropriate metric for measuring combined space-time similarity between discretized CPS behaviors. We then provide the quantitative semantics for STL based on this distance and discuss the effects of sampling and quantization on the distance value. We develop an efficient on-line algorithm for computing the robustness degree between a behavior and a STL formula. The algorithm can be directly implemented both in software and hardware. In the former case, the implemented procedure can be connected to the simulation engine of the CPS design and used to monitor its correctness and quality. In the latter case, the resulting implementation can be deployed on the Field Programmable Gate Array (FPGA) and used to monitor real systems or design emulations. We implement the above procedure in Verilog and evaluate it on an automotive benchmark.

Related Work. The Levenshtein (edit) distance [17] has been extensively used in information theory, computer science and bioinformatics for many applications, including approximate string matching, spell checking and fuzzy string searching. Levenshtein automata [24] were introduced to reason about the edit distance from a reference string. A Levenshtein automaton of degree n for a string w recognizes the set of all words whose edit distance from w is at most n. A dynamic programming procedure for computing the edit distance between a string and a regular language has been proposed in [26]. The problem of computing the smallest edit distance between any pair of distinct strings in a regular language has been studied in [15]. In contrast to our work, these classical approaches to edit distance consider only operations with simple weights on unordered alphabets and do not relate the distance to specification formalisms.

The edit distance for weighted automata was studied in [19], where the authors propose a procedure for computing the edit distance between weighted transducers. A space efficient algorithm for computing the edit distance between a string and a weighted automaton over a tropical semiring was developed in [2]. The resulting approach is generic and allows for instance to assign an arbitrary cost to each substitution pair. However, all substitution pairs must be enumerated by separate transitions. In contrast, we consider signals with naturally ordered alphabets as input strings and hence can efficiently handle substitution over large alphabets by treating allowed input values with symbolic constraints. In addition, we use the edit distance to define the semantics of a temporal specification formalism. Finally, we provide insights into the effect of sampling and quantization to the computation of the distance. The weighted Hamming and edit distances between behaviors are also proposed in [23], where the authors use it to develop procedures for reasoning about the introduce the Lipshitz-robustness of Mealy machines and string transducers. The notion of robustness is different from ours, and in contrast to our work it is not computed against a specification.

The quantitative semantics for temporal logics were first proposed in [12,22], with the focus on the *spatial* similarity of behaviors, given by their point-wise comparison. The spatial quantitative semantics is sensitive to phase shifts and temporal inaccuracies in behaviors – a small temporal shift in the behavior may result in a large robustness degree change. This problem was addressed in [11], in which STL with spatial quantitative semantics is extended with time robustness. In [1], the authors propose another approach of combining space and time robustness, by extending STL with *averaged* temporal operators. Another approach to determining robustness of hybrid systems using self-validated arithmetics is shown in [13]. Monitoring of different quantitative semantics is implemented in tools S-TaLiRo [3] and Breach [9]. These works differ from ours in that they all assume continuous behaviors, in contrast to our approach where behaviors are quantized and sampled.

The recent results on using Skorokhod metric to compute the distance between piecewise-linear or piecewise-constant continuous behaviors [8] partially inspired our work. Skorokhod metric quantifies both space and time mismatches between continuous behaviors by allowing application of time distortions in behaviors in order to minimize their pointwise distance. The distortion of the timeline is achieved by applying a retiming function - a continuous bijective strictly increasing function from time domain to time domain. Given a behavior $x(t)$, the resulting retimed behavior $r(x(t))$ preserves the values and their order but not the duration between two values. This information-preserving distance relies on continuous time and is not applicable to the discrete time domain – stretching and compressing the discrete time axis results inevitably in an information loss. Finally, computation of the Skorokhod distance was extended to the flow-pipes in [7], but we are not aware of any work that addrsses the problem of computing the Skorokhod distance between a behavior and a temporal specification.

2   Preliminaries

In this section, we provide the necessary definitions to develop the algorithm presented in subsequent sections of the paper. We first shortly recall the notion of metric spaces and distances. We then define signals and Signal Temporal Logic. Finally, we introduce a variant of symbolic and weighted symbolic automata.

Metric Spaces and Distances. A metric space is a set for which distances between all elements in the set are defined.

Definition 1 (Metric space and distance). *Suppose that $\mathcal{M}$ is a set and $d :$ $\mathcal{M} \times \mathcal{M} \rightarrow \mathbb{R}$ is a function that maps pairs of elements in $\mathcal{M}$ into the real numbers. Then $\mathcal{M}$ is a* metric space *with the* distance measure *d, if (1) $d(m_1, m_2) \geq 0$ for all m_1, m_2 in $\mathcal{M}$; (2) $d(m_1, m_2) = 0$ if and only if $m_1 = m_2$; (3) $d(m_1, m_2) =$*

$d(m_2, m_1)$ for all m_1, m_2 in $\mathcal{M}$; and (4) $d(m_1, m_2) \leq d(m_1, m) + d(m, m_2)$ for all m, m_1, m_2 in $\mathcal{M}$.

Given $m \in \mathcal{M}$ and $M \subseteq \mathcal{M}$, we can lift the above definition to reason about the distance between an element m of $\mathcal{M}$ and the subset M of $\mathcal{M}$ as follows

$$d(m, M) = \min_{m' \in M} d(m, m')$$

We define the *robustness degree* $\rho(m, M)$ of m with respect to the set M as follows

$$\rho(m, M) = \begin{cases} d(m, \mathcal{M} \backslash M) & \text{if } m \in M \\ -d(m, M) & \text{otherwise} \end{cases}$$

Signals. Let X be a finite set of variables defined over some domain $\mathbb{D}$. Then, a *signal* s is a function $s : \mathbb{T} \times X \to \mathbb{D}$, where $\mathbb{T}$ is the time domain[1]. We distinguish between *analog*, *discrete* and *digital* signals. Analog signals have continuous value and time domains. The time domain of discrete signals is the set of integers, while digital signals have in addition their value domain restricted to a finite set. Digital signals can be obtained by *sampling* and *quantization* of analog signals. The conversion of analog to digital signals is at the core of the signal processing field and is in practice done by an *analog-to-digital converter* (ADC).

Sampling is the process of reducing the continuous time in analog signals to the discrete time in the resulting discrete signal. The ideal theoretical sampling function periodically measures the value of the analog signal every T time units, where T denotes the *sampling interval*. Similarly, we denote by f the *sampling frequency*, that is the average number of measurements obtained by sampling in one second, where $f = 1/T$. Given an analog signal $s_a : \mathbb{R}_{\geq 0} \times X \to \mathbb{R}^n$ and a sampling interval T, applying the ideal sampling function to s_a results in a discrete signal $s_{disc} : \mathbb{N} \times X \to \mathbb{R}$ such that $s_{disc}(i, x) = s_a(iT, x)$ for all $i \geq 0$ and $x \in X$.

When sampling real-valued signals, it is impossible to maintain the arbitrary precision of its values, which consequently must be restricted to a finite set. Quantization consists of converting real values to their discrete numerical approximations, and thus allows to map discrete to digital signals. We consider the basic uniform quantization function with a *quantization step* Q which is defined as follows

$$Q(r) = Q \cdot \lfloor |r|/Q + 0.5 \rfloor,$$

where $r \in \mathbb{R}$. We note that the quantization can be decomposed into two stages, *classification* and *reconstruction*. The classification function c maps the real input value into an integer index k, and the reconstruction function y converts k into the actual discrete approximation of the input. Hence, we have that $Q(r) = y(c(r))$ where

---

[1] We use $s(t)$ to denote the valuation vector of the variables in X at time t.

$$c(r) = \lfloor |r|/Q + 0.5 \rfloor$$
$$y(k) = Q \cdot k$$

The decomposition of the quantization into two independent stages has a practical advantage – without loss of generality, we can from now directly work with digital signals obtained after the classification stage with their value domain being a finite subset of $\mathbb{N}$. We also restrict ourselves to signals that have *finite-length* and hence are of the form $s_{dig} : [0, l) \times X \rightarrow [v_{min}, v_{max}]$, where $[0, l)$ and $[v_{min}, v_{max}]$ are intervals in $\mathbb{N}$, and X is now the set of variables defined over the domain $[v_{min}, v_{max}]$. We extend the signal notation $s(i, X)$ to denote the vector $\mathbb{D}^{|X|}$ of all variable values in X at time i. From now on, we refer to digital signals of finite length simply as signals and denote them by s.

Signal Temporal Logic. In this paper, we study Signal Temporal Logic (STL) with both *past* and *future* operators interpreted over digital signals of final length[2].

Let X be a finite set of variables defined over a finite interval domain $\mathbb{D} = [v_{min}, v_{max}] \subseteq \mathbb{N}$. We assume that X is a metric space equiped with a distance d. The syntax of a STL formula φ over X is defined by the grammar

$$\varphi := x \sim u \mid \neg \varphi \mid \varphi_1 \vee \varphi_2 \mid \varphi_1 \, \mathcal{U}_I \, \varphi_2 \mid \varphi_1 \, \mathcal{S}_I \, \varphi_2$$

where $x \in X$, $\sim \in \{<, \leq\}$, $u \in \mathbb{D}$, I is of the form $[a, b]$ or $[a, \infty)$ such that $a, b \in \mathbb{N}$ and $0 \leq a \leq b$. The other standard operators are derived as follows: true $= p \vee \neg p$, false $= \neg$true, $\varphi_1 \wedge \varphi_2 = \neg(\neg \varphi_1 \vee \neg \varphi_2)$, $\Diamond_I \, \varphi = $ true$\mathcal{U}_I \, \varphi$, $\Box_I \, \varphi = \neg \, \Diamond_I \, \neg \varphi$, $\Diamond_I \, \varphi = $ true$\mathcal{S}_I \, \varphi$, $\boxminus_I \, \varphi = \neg \, \Diamond_I \neg \varphi$, $\bigcirc \, \varphi = $ false$\mathcal{U}_{[1,1]} \, \varphi$ and $\ominus \, \varphi = $ false$\mathcal{S}_{[1,1]} \, \varphi$.

The semantics of a STL formula with respect to a signal s of length l is described via the satisfiability relation $(s, i) \models \varphi$, indicating that the signal s satisfies φ at the time index i, according to the following definition where $\mathbb{T} = [0, l)$.

$$
\begin{aligned}
(s, i) &\models x \sim u & &\leftrightarrow s(i, x) \sim u \\
(s, i) &\models \neg \varphi & &\leftrightarrow (s, i) \not\models \varphi \\
(s, i) &\models \varphi_1 \vee \varphi_2 & &\leftrightarrow (s, i) \models \varphi_1 \text{ or } (s, i) \models \varphi_2 \\
(s, i) &\models \varphi_1 \, \mathcal{U}_I \, \varphi_2 & &\leftrightarrow \exists j \in (i + I) \cap \mathbb{T} : (s, j) \models \varphi_2 \text{ and } \forall i < k < j, (s, k) \models \varphi_1 \\
(s, i) &\models \varphi_1 \, \mathcal{S}_I \, \varphi_2 & &\leftrightarrow \exists j \in (i - I) \cap \mathbb{T} : (s, j) \models \varphi_2 \text{ and } \forall j < k < i, (s, k) \models \varphi_1
\end{aligned}
$$

We note that we use the semantics for $_I$ and $_I$ that is strict in both arguments and that we allow punctual modalities due to the discrete time semantics. Given an STL formula φ, we denote by $L(\varphi)$ the *language* of φ, which is the set of all signals s such that $(s, 0) \models \varphi$.

---

[2] Although this segment of STL is expressively equivalent to LTL, use the STL name to highlight the explicit notions of real-time and quantitative values in the language.

Automata and Weighted Automata. In this section, we define a variant of *symbolic automata* [25] and also introduce its *weighted* extension. Similarly to the definition of STL, we consider $\mathbb{D} = [v_{min}, v_{max}]$ to be the finite interval of integers equipped with the distance d and let X to be a finite set of variables defined over $\mathbb{D}$. The variable valuation $v(x)$ is a function $v : X \to \mathbb{D}$, which we naturally extend to the valuation $v(X)$ of the set X. A variable *constraint* γ over X is defined by the grammar in negation normal form $\gamma := x \le c \mid \neg(x \le c) \mid \gamma_1 \vee \gamma_2 \mid \gamma_1 \wedge \gamma_2$, where $x \in X$ and $c \in \mathbb{D}$. We denote by $\Gamma(X)$ the set of all constraints definable over X. Given the valuation $v(X)$ and a constraint γ over X, we write $v(X) \models \gamma$ when $v(X)$ satisfies γ.

Definition 2 (Symbolic Automata). *We define a symbolic automaton $\mathcal{A}$ as the tuple $\mathcal{A} = (\mathbb{D}, X, Q, I, F, \Delta)$, where $\mathbb{D}$ is the finite alphabet, X is a finite set of variables over $\mathbb{D}$, Q is a finite set of states, $I \subseteq Q$ is the set of initial states, $F \subseteq Q$ is the set of final states and $\Delta = \Delta_X \cup \Delta_\epsilon$ is the transition relation, where $\Delta_X \subseteq Q \times \Gamma(X) \times Q$ and $\Delta_\epsilon \subseteq Q \times \{\epsilon\} \times Q$ are sets of transitions that consume an input letter and silent transitions.*

Given a $q \in Q$, let $\mathcal{E}(q)$ denote the set of states reachable from q by following ϵ-transitions in Δ only. Formally, we say that $p \in \mathcal{E}(q)$ iff there exists a sequence of states $q_1, \ldots, q_k$ such that $q = q_1$, $(q_i, \epsilon, q_{i+1}) \in \Delta$ for all $0 \le i < k$, and $p = q_k$. Let $s : [0, l) \times X \to \mathbb{D}$ be a signal. We say that s is a *trace* of $\mathcal{A}$ if there exists a sequence of states $q_0, \ldots, q_l$ in Q such that $q_0 \in \mathcal{E}(q)$ for some $q \in I$, for all $0 \le i < l$, there exists $(q_i, \gamma, q) \in \Delta$ for some γ such that $s(i, X) \models \gamma$ and $q_{i+1} \in \mathcal{E}(q)$ and $q_l \in F$. We denote by $L(\mathcal{A})$ the set of all traces of $\mathcal{A}$. A *path* π in $\mathcal{A}$ is a sequence $\pi = q_0 \cdot \delta_0 \cdot q_1 \cdots \delta_{n-1} \cdot q_n$ such that $q_0 \in I$ and for all $0 \le i < n$, δ_i is either of the form (q_i, γ, q_{i+1}) or (q_i, ϵ, q_{i+1}). We say that π is *accepting* if $q_n \in F$. Given a trace $s : [0, l) \times X \to \mathbb{D}$ and a path $\pi = q_0 \cdot \delta_0 \cdot q_1 \cdot \delta_1 \cdots \delta_{n-1} \cdot q_n$, we say that s induces π in $\mathcal{A}$ if π is an accepting path in $\mathcal{A}$ and there exists a monotonic injective function $f : [0, l) \to [0, n]$ such that for all $0 \le i < l$, $\delta_i = (q_i, \gamma, q_{i+1})$ such that $s(i, X) \models \gamma$ and $\delta_j = (q_j, \epsilon, q_{j+1})$ for all $j \in \bigcup_{0 \le i < n} (f(i), f(i+1)) \cup [0, f(0)) \cup (f(l), n]$. We denote by $\Pi(\mathcal{A}, s) = \{\pi \mid s \text{ induces } \pi \text{ in } \mathcal{A}\}$ the set of all paths in $\mathcal{A}$ induced by s.

We now introduce *weighted* symbolic automata, by adding a weight function to the transitions of the symbolic automaton, relative to the consumed input letter.

Definition 3 (Weighted symbolic automata). *A weighted symbolic automaton $\mathcal{W}$ is the tuple $\mathcal{W} = (\mathbb{D}, X, Q, I, F, \Delta, \lambda)$, where $\mathcal{A} = (\mathbb{D}, X, Q, I, F, \Delta)$ is a symbolic automaton and $\lambda : \Delta \times (\mathbb{D}^{|X|} \cup \{\epsilon\}) \to \mathbb{Q}^+$ is the weight function.*

Let s be a signal of size l and $\pi = q_0 \cdot \delta_0 \cdots \delta_{n-1} \cdot q_n$ a path in $\mathcal{W}$ induced by s. The value of π in $\mathcal{W}$ subject to s, denoted by $v(s, \pi, \mathcal{W})$, is the sum of weights associated to the transitions in the path π and subject to the signal s. We define the *value* $v(s, \mathcal{W})$ of s as the minimum value from all the paths in $\mathcal{W}$ induced by s, i.e. $v(s, \mathcal{W}) = \min_{\pi \in \Pi(\mathcal{W}, s)} v(s, \pi, \mathcal{W})$.

3   Weighted Edit Distance

Measuring the similarity of sequences is important in many application areas, such as information theory, spell checking and bioinformatics. The *Hamming distance* d_H is the most basic and common string measure arising from the information theory. It measures the minimum number of *substitution* operations needed to match equal length sequences. The *edit distance* d_E extends the Hamming distance with two additional operations, *insertion* and *deletion* and is defined as the minimum accumulation of edit operation costs used to transform one sequence into the other.

Neither of these metrics provide satisfactory solution for comparing digitized signals. They are defined over unordered alphabets and associate fixed costs to different kinds of operations. In contrast, the value domain of digital signals admits a natural notion of a distance representing the difference between two signal valuations. In addition, the Hamming distance provides only pointwise comparisons between sequences and consequently does not account for potential timing discrepancies in the sampled signals. Two discrete signals that differ only in a constant time delay will typically have a large Hamming distance. The edit distance addresses this problem by allowing us to bridge the time shifts using insertion and deletion operations.

Inspired by [19,23], we propose the *weighted edit distance* as the measure for comparing the similarity of two discrete signals. It adopts the insertion and deletion operations from the edit distance and adapts the substitution operation to the ordered alphabets. Since we consider multi-dimensional signals, we extend the cost of the substitution operation to take into account different variable valuations.

Let X be a finite set of variables defined over some interval domain $\mathbb{D} = [v_{min}, v_{max}]$. Given two valuation vectors $a, b \in \mathbb{D}^{|X|}$ of X, we denote by $d_M(a, b)$ the *Manhattan distance* [16] between a and b, where $d_M(a, b) = \Sigma_{i=0}^{|X|-1} |a_i - b_i|$. Let $w_i, w_d \in \mathbb{Q}$ be weight constants for the insertion and deletion operations. We then define the *costs* of the substitution c_s, insertion c_i and deletion c_d operations as follows: (1) $c_s(a, b) = d_M(a, b)$; (2) $c_i = w_i$; (3) $c_d = w_d$. The definition of the WED adapts the classical edit distance recursive definition with the new costs.

Definition 4 (Weighted edit distance). *Let* $s_1 : [0, l) \times X \to \mathbb{D}$ *and* $s_2 : [0, l) \times X \to \mathbb{D}$ *be discrete-time signals. The* weighted edit distance $d_W(s_1, s_2)$ *equals to* $d_{l,l}(s_1, s_2)$:

$$d_{-1,-1}(s_1, s_2) = 0$$
$$d_{i,-1}(s_1, s_2) = d_{i-1,-1}(s_1, s_2) + c_i$$
$$d_{-1,j}(s_1, s_2) = d_{-1,j-1}(s_1, s_2) + c_d$$
$$d_{i,j}(s_1, s_2) = min \begin{cases} d_{i-1,j-1}(s_1, s_2) + c_s(s_1(i, X), s_2(j, X)) \\ d_{i-1,j}(s_1, s_2) + c_i \\ d_{i,j-1}(s_1, s_2) + c_d \end{cases}$$

Proposition 1. *The weighted edit distance is a distance.*

Remark. We chose the Manhattan distance for the substitution cost because it combines the absolute difference of several signal components.

We first note that the distance is additive in two dimensions - the Manhattan distance adds substitution costs for each variable in the signal, and the edit operation costs are accumulated over the signal length. In addition, the distance is sensitive to the sampling period used to discretize the signal. As a consequence, this distance can be *normalized*, in order to provide more uniform results. Given signals s_1, s_2 of length l defined over X and sampled with a period T, the value domain $\mathbb{D} = [v_{max}, v_{min}]$, we define the normalized weigted edit distance, which is always bounded by $[0, 1]$ as follows:

$$d_W^{\#}(s_1, s_2) = \frac{T \cdot d_W(s_1, s_2)}{l|X|(v_{max} - v_{min})}.$$

3.1   Sampling, Quantization and Weighted Edit Distance

We compute the WED between digital signals resulting from physical behavior observations after sampling and quantization. In this section, we discuss the effect of inaccuracies introduced by these operations on the WED.

Let s be an analog signal, T a sampling period and Q a quantization step. We assume that s has a band limit f_M and $T \leq 1/(2f_M)$. We denote by $s[T]$ the discrete signal obtained from s by sampling with the period T, and by $s[T][Q]$ the digital signal obtained from $s[T]$ by quantization with the step Q.

We cannot directly relate the WED to the analog signals, because it is not defined in continuous time. However, this distance allows tackling phase shifts in the sampled signals. Consider two analog signals $s_1(t)$ and $s_2(t - \tau)$ such that $\tau = iT$ for some $i \geq 0$ and their sampled variants $s_1[T](t)$ and $s_2[T](t)$. It is clear that with $2 \cdot i$ insertion and deletion operations, $s_2[T]$ can be transformed into $s_1[T]$ such that their remaining substitution cost equals to 0. This situation is illustrated in Fig. 1 (see signals s_1 and s_2). We see that the distance between the two signals initially grows due to the insertion and deletion operations, but that eventually it becomes perfectly stable.

Now consider another signal $s_3(t) = s_1(t - \tau)$ such that τ is not a multiple of T. In this case, the sampled signal $s_3[T](t)$ cannot be perfectly transformed into $s_1[T](t)$ by using insertion and deletion operations because of the mismatch between the sampling period and the phase shift. As a consequence, the distance between $s_1[T](t)$ and $s_3[T](t)$ will accumulate substitution costs due to this mismatch. This scenario is also depicted in Fig. 1 (see signals s_1 and s_3). The figure shows that after an initial steep increase of the distance due to the insertion and deletion operations, its value does not converge, but continues slowly increasing due to the accumulation of remaining substitution costs.

We define the *sampling error* as the maximum difference in value between two periods in a sampled signal. Intuitively, this value gives an impression about the error that can be accumulated when comparing sampled variants of two

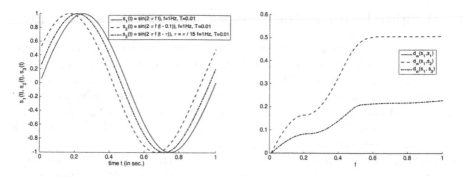

Fig. 1. Weighted edit distances $d_W(s_1, s_2)$ and $d_W(s_1, s_3)$, where $s_1(t) = \sin(2\pi f t)$, $s_2(t) = \sin(2\pi f(t - 0.1))$, $s_3(t) = \sin(2\pi f(t - \tau))$, $T = 0.01$, $f = 1\,Hz$ and $\tau = \pi/15$.

phase-shifted signals, when the phase shift is not a multiple of the sampling period.

Definition 5 (Sampling error). *Let s be an analog signal with band-limit f_M and sampling period T, such that $T \leq 1/(2f_M)$. The sampling error is defined as $err_T(s, i) = ||s[T](i) - s[T](i+1)| - \max_{0 \leq \tau \leq T} |s(iT) - s(iT + \tau)||$*

We show that this error converges to 0 when the sampling period goes to 0.

Proposition 2. $\lim_{T \to 0} err_T(s, i) = 0$

Intuitively, the quantization step abstracts the real value of $s[T]$ to the nearest multiple of the quantization step. This approximation inevitably introduces an accumulative error to the distance between quantized signals. We provide a bound on this error as a function of Q and the length of the signals, and show that the error bound decreases with smaller quantization steps. We now formalize this result. We first define the WED error due to quantization.

Definition 6 (Weighted Edit Distance Error). *Let $s_1[T]$ and $s_2[T]$ be two discrete signals of length l and Q a quantization step. The WED error, denoted by $err_Q(s_1[T], s_2[T])$, is defined as follows*

$$err_Q(s_1, s_2) = |d_W(s_1[T], s_2[T]) - d_W(s_1[T][Q], s_2[T][Q])|$$

The following theorem bounds the WED error due to quantization and states that the error bound improves as the quantization step approaches 0.

Theorem 1. *For arbitrary discrete signals $s_1[T]$ and $s_2[T]$ of length l defined over the same value domain and quantization step Q,*

1. *$err_Q(s_1[T], s_2[T]) \leq Q|X|l$*
2. *$\lim_{Q \to 0} err_Q(s_1[T], s_2[T]) = 0$*

4   Weighted Edit Robustness for Signal Temporal Logic

In this section, we propose a novel procedure for computing the *robustness degree* of a discrete signal with respect to a STL property. In our approach, we set c_i and c_d to be equal to $|X|(v_{max} - v_{min})$. In other words, the deletion and insertion costs are at most the largest substitution cost. Our procedure relies on computing the WED between a signal and a set of signals, defined by the specification. It consists of several steps, illustrated in Fig. 2. We first translate the STL formula φ into a symbolic automaton $\mathcal{A}_\varphi$ that accepts the same language as the specification. The automaton $\mathcal{A}_\varphi$ treats timing constraints from the formula enumeratively, but keeps symbolic guards on data variables[3]. We then transform $\mathcal{A}_\varphi$ into a *weighted edit automaton* $\mathcal{W}_\varphi$, a weighted symbolic automaton that accepts all the signals but with the value that corresponds to the WED between the signal and the specification (Fig. 2 (a)). We propose an algorithm for computing this distance. Computing the robustness degree between a signal and an STL specification follows from the calculation of their WED, as shown in Fig. 2 (b).

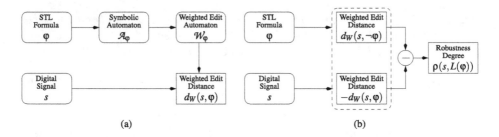

Fig. 2. Computation of (a) $d_W(s, \varphi)$ and $\rho(s, \varphi)$.

4.1   From STL to Weighted Edit Automata

Let X be a set of finite variables defined over the domain $\mathbb{D} = [v_{min}, v_{max}] \subseteq \mathbb{N}$. We consider an STL formula φ defined over X. Let $s : [0, l) \times X \to \mathbb{D}$ be a digital signal.

From φ to $\mathcal{A}_\varphi$. In the first step, we translate the STL specification φ into the automaton $\mathcal{A}_\varphi$ such that $L(\varphi) = L(\mathcal{A}_\varphi)$. The translation from STL interpreted over discrete time and finite valued domains to finite automata is standard, and can be achieved by using for instance on-the-fly tableau construction [14] or the temporal testers approach [21].

Example 1. Consider the past STL formula $\varphi = \Box\,(x = 4 \to \Diamond\,(x < 3))$, where x is defined over the domain $[0, 5]$. The resulting automaton $\mathcal{A}_\varphi$ is shown in Fig. 3(a).

---

[3] The time in $\mathcal{A}_\varphi$ cannot be treated symbolically with digital clocks since every pair of states and clock valuation may behave differently with respect to the WED.

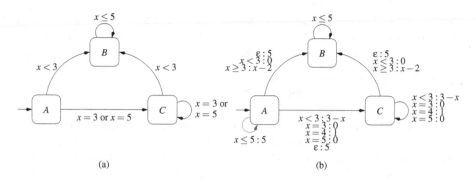

(a)   (b)

Fig. 3. (a) $\mathcal{A}_\varphi$ accepting $L(\varphi)$ - all states are accepting and (b) $\mathcal{W}_\varphi$. (Color figure online)

From $\mathcal{A}_\varphi$ to $\mathcal{W}_\varphi$. In this step, we translate the automaton $\mathcal{A}_\varphi$ to the weighted edit automaton $\mathcal{W}_\varphi$. The automaton $\mathcal{W}_\varphi$ reads an input signal and mimics the weighted edit operations. In essence, $\mathcal{W}_\varphi$ accepts every signal along multiple paths. Each accepting path induced by the signal corresponds to a sequence of weighted edit operations needed to transform the input signal into another one allowed by the specification. The value of the least expensive path corresponds to the weighted edit distance between the input signal and the specification. The weighted automaton $\mathcal{W}_\varphi$ explicitly treats substitution, insertion and deletion operations, by augmenting $\mathcal{A}_\varphi$ with additional transitions and associating to them the appropriate weight function. We now provide details of the translation and describe the handling of weighted edit operations. Let $\mathcal{A}_\varphi = (\mathbb{D}, X, Q, I, F, \Delta)$ be the symbolic automaton accepting the language of the specification φ.

Substitution. In order to address substitutions in the automaton, we define a new set of *substitution* transitions Δ_s and associate to them the weight function λ_s as follows. Given $q, q' \in Q$, let $\gamma(q, q') = \bigvee_{(q,\gamma,q')\in\Delta} \gamma$. Then, we have:

- $(q, \mathsf{true}, q') \in \Delta_s$ if there exists $(q, \gamma, q') \in \Delta$ for some γ; and
- $\lambda_s((q, \mathsf{true}, q'), v) = d_M(v, \gamma(q, q'))$, for all $v \in \mathbb{D}^{|X|}$.

Intuitively, we replace all the transitions in $\mathcal{A}_\varphi$ with new ones that have the same source and target states. We relax the guards in the new transitions and make them enabled for *any* input. On the other hand, we control the cost of making a transition with the weight function λ_s, which computes the substitution cost needed to take the transition with a specific input. This cost is the Manhattan distance between the input value and the guard associated to the original transition.

Deletion. Addressing deletion operations consists in adding self-loop transitions that consume all the input letters to all the states with the deletion cost $c_d = |X|(v_{max} - v_{min})$, thus mimicking deletion operations. We skip adding a self-loop transition to states that already have the same substitution self-loop transition – according to our definition $c_d \geq c_s(a, X)$ for all a, hence taking the deletion transition instead of the substitution one can never improve the value of a path and is therefore redundant. We define the set of deletion transitions Δ_d and the associated weight function λ_d as follows:

- $(q, \text{true}, q) \in \Delta_d$ if $(q, \text{true}, q) \notin \Delta_s$; and
- $\lambda_d(\delta, v) = c_d$ for all $\delta \in \Delta_d$ and $v \in \mathbb{D}^{|X|}$.

Insertion. In order to mimic the insertion operations, we augment the transitions relation of $\mathcal{W}_\varphi$ with silent transitions. For every original transition in Δ, we associate another transition with the same source and target states, but labeled with ϵ and having the insertion cost $c_i = |X|(v_{max} - v_{min})$. Formally, we define the set of insertion transitions Δ_i and the associated weight function λ_i as follows:

- $(q, \epsilon, q') \in \Delta_i$ if $(q, \gamma, q') \in \Delta$ for some γ; and
- $\lambda_i(\delta, \{\epsilon\}) = c_i$ for all $\delta \in \Delta_i$.

Given the symbolic automaton $\mathcal{A}_\psi = (\mathbb{D}, X, Q, I, F, \Delta)$ accepting the language of the specification φ, its associated symbolic weigthed edit automaton $\mathcal{W}_\psi$ is the tuple $(\mathbb{D}, X, Q, I, F, \Delta', \lambda')$, where $\Delta' = \Delta_s \cup \Delta_d \cup \Delta_i$ and $\lambda'(\delta, v) = \lambda_s(\delta, v)$ if $\delta \in \Delta_s$, $\lambda'(\delta, v) = \lambda_d(\delta, v)$ if $\delta \in \Delta_d$ and $\lambda'(\delta, \epsilon) = \lambda_i(\delta, \epsilon)$ if $\delta \in \Delta_i$.

Example 2. The weighted edit automaton $\mathcal{W}_\varphi$ obtained from $\mathcal{A}_\varphi$ is illustrated in Fig. 3(b). The blue transitions, such as $(A, 0, A)$ with weight 5, correspond to the deletion transitions. The red transitions, such as (A, ϵ, B), correspond to the insertion transitions.

The resulting weighted automaton $\mathcal{W}_\varphi$ allows determining the weighted edit distance between a signal w and the formula φ, by computing the value of s in $\mathcal{W}_\varphi$.

Theorem 2. $d_W(s, \varphi) = v(s, \mathcal{W}_\varphi)$.

4.2   Computing the Value of a Signal in a Weighted Edit Automaton

We now present an on-the-fly algorithm Val, shown in Algorithm 1, that computes the value of a signal s in a weighted automaton $\mathcal{W}$. In every step i, the algorithm computes the minimum cost of reaching the state q with the prefix of s consisting of its first i values. After reading a prefix of s, we may reach a state $q \in Q$ in different ways with different costs. Note that it is sufficient to keep the state with the minimum value in each iteration. It follows that the algorithm requires book keeping $|Q|$ state value fields in every iteration. We now explain the details of the algorithm. The procedure first initializes the costs of all the states in $\mathcal{W}$ (see Algorithm 2). The initial states are set to 0 and the non-initial ones to ∞. Then, we compute the effect of taking the ϵ transitions without reading any signal value. It is sufficient to iterate this step $|Q|$ times, since within $|Q|$ iterations, one is guaranteed to reach a state q that was already visited with a smaller value v. In every subsequent iteration i, we first update the state values by applying the cost of taking all transitions labeled by $s(i, X)$ and then update the effect of taking ϵ transitions $|Q|$ times. The weight function of a substitution cost is computed as follows: $\lambda(v, x \leq k)$ gives 0 if $v \leq k$, and $v - k$ otherwise; $\lambda(v, \neg(x \leq k))$ is symmetric; $\lambda(v, \varphi_1 \wedge \varphi_2) = \max(\lambda(v, \varphi_1), \lambda(v, \varphi_2))$ and $\lambda(v, \varphi_1 \vee \varphi_2) = \min(\lambda(v, \varphi_1), \lambda(v, \varphi_2))$.

Upon termination, the algorithm returns the minimum cost of reaching an accepting state in the automaton.

Theorem 3. $\mathsf{Val}(s, \mathcal{W}) = v(s, \mathcal{W})$.

Theorem 4. *Given a signal s of length l defined over X and a weighted automaton $\mathcal{W}$ with n states and m transitions, $\mathsf{Val}(s, \mathcal{W})$ takes in the order of $O(lnm))$ iterations to compute the value of s in $\mathcal{W}$, and requires in the order of $O(n(\lceil log(l(v_{\max} - v_{\min})) \rceil))$ memory.*

Algorithm 1. $\mathsf{Val}(s, \mathcal{W})$

Input: s and $\mathcal{W}_\psi$
Output: v
$\quad$ InitVal($\mathcal{W}$)
$\quad$ **for all** $i \in [0, l)$ **do**
$\quad\quad$ **for all** $\delta = (q, \gamma, q') \in \Delta$ **do**
$\quad\quad\quad$ $v'(q') \leftarrow \min(v'(q'), v(q) + \lambda(s(i, X), \delta))$
$\quad\quad$ **end for**
$\quad\quad$ **for** $i = 0; i < |Q|; i++$ **do**
$\quad\quad\quad$ **for all** $\delta = (q, \epsilon, q') \in \Delta$ **do**
$\quad\quad\quad\quad$ $v'(q') \leftarrow \min(v'(q'), v(q) + \lambda(\delta, \epsilon))$
$\quad\quad\quad$ **end for**
$\quad\quad\quad$ **for all** $q \in Q$ **do**
$\quad\quad\quad\quad$ $v(q) \leftarrow v'(q)$
$\quad\quad\quad\quad$ $v'(q) \leftarrow \infty$
$\quad\quad\quad$ **end for**
$\quad\quad$ **end for**
$\quad$ **end for**
$\quad$ $v \leftarrow \min_{q \in F} v(q)$
$\quad\quad\quad$ **return** v

Algorithm 2. InitVal($\mathcal{W}$)

$\quad$ **for all** $q \in Q$ **do**
$\quad\quad$ $v(q) \leftarrow (q \in I) ? 0 : \infty; v'(q) \leftarrow \infty$
$\quad$ **end for**
$\quad$ **for** $i = 0; i < |Q|; i++$ **do**
$\quad\quad$ **for all** $\delta = (q, \epsilon, q') \in \Delta$ **do**
$\quad\quad\quad$ $v'(q') \leftarrow \min(v'(q'), v(q) + \lambda(\delta, \epsilon))$
$\quad\quad$ **end for**
$\quad\quad$ **for all** $q \in Q$ **do**
$\quad\quad\quad$ $v(q) \leftarrow v'(q)$
$\quad\quad\quad$ $v'(q) \leftarrow \infty$
$\quad\quad$ **end for**
$\quad$ **end for**

Example 3. Consider the STL property φ from Example 1, the associated weighted edit automaton $\mathcal{W}_\varphi$ from Fig. 1 and the signal[4] $s : [0, 2] \rightarrow [0, 5]$ such that $s(0) = 5$, $s(1) = 5$ and $s(2) = 4$. It is clear that $(s, 0) \not\models \varphi$, since $s(2) = 4$, while there was not a single $0 \leq i < 2$ where $s(i) < 3$. We illustrate in Fig. 4 the computation of $v(s, \mathcal{W}_\varphi)$. We can see that with the signal s, we can reach one of the accepting states (B or C) with the value 1. This value corresponds to one substitution operation, replacing the value of 4 in $s(2)$ by 5, which allows vacuous satisfaction of the property φ.

---

[4] Since s has only one component, we skip the variable name.

$$s(0) = 5 \qquad s(1) = 5 \qquad s(2) = 4$$

A	0	0	5	5	10	10	15	15
B	∞	5	3	3	3	3	3	3
C	∞	5	0	0	0	0	1	1

init   update   update   update
ε-init   ε-update   ε-update   ε-update

Fig. 4. Example - computation of $v(s, \mathcal{W}_\varphi)$.

5   Implementation and Case Study

We now describe our implementation of quantitative monitors for STL. The parser for the STL formulas is developed using Java and ANTLR. We translate STL properties into temporal testers, and convert them to acceptor automata. We use JAutomata library to represent the testers and the acceptors. We then generate quantitative monitor code in Verilog HDL. The resulting monitor is a hardware implementation of the weighted automata and the underlying algorithm for computing the weighted edit distance.

Table 1. Automatic transmission properties [4].

ID	φ
φ_1	$\square\,(\omega < 4500)$
φ_2	$\square\,((\omega < 4500) \wedge (v < 120))$
φ_3	$\square\,((g_2 \wedge \bigcirc g_1) \rightarrow \square_{(0,2.5]} \neg g_2)$
φ_4	$\square\,((\neg g_1 \wedge \bigcirc g_1) \rightarrow \square_{(0,2.5]} g_1)$
φ_5	$\bigwedge_{i=1}^{4} \square\,((\neg g_i \wedge \bigcirc g_i) \rightarrow \square_{(0,2.5]} g_i)$
φ_6	$\neg(\Diamond_{[0,4]}\,(v > 120) \wedge \square\,(\omega < 4500))$
φ_7	$\Diamond_{[0,4]}\,((v > 120) \wedge \square\,(\omega < 4500))$
φ_8	$((g_1 \,\mathcal{U} g_2 \,\mathcal{U} g_3 \,\mathcal{U} g_4) \wedge \Diamond_{[0,10]}\,(g_4 \wedge \Diamond_{[0,2]}\,(\omega > 4500))) \rightarrow \Diamond_{[0,10]}\,(g_4 \rightarrow \bigcirc\,(g_4 \,\mathcal{U}_{[0,1]}(v \geq 120)))$

For the evaluation of our approach, we apply it to an automotive benchmark problem published in [4]. We consider the slightly modified Automatic Transmission deterministic Simulink demo provided by Mathworks as our system-under-test (SUT). It is a model of an automatic transmission controller that exhibits both continuous and discrete behavior. The system has two inputs – the throttle u_t and the break u_b. The break allows the user to model variable load on the engine. The system has two continuous-time state variables – the speed of the engine ω (RPM), the speed of the vehicle v (mph) and the active gear g_i. The system is initialized with zero vehicle and engine speed. It follows that the output trajectories depend only on the input signals u_t and u_b, which can take any value between 0 and 100 at any point in time. The Simulink model contains 69 blocks including 2 integrators, 3 look-up tables, 2 two-dimensional look-up tables and a Stateflow chart with 2 concurrently executing finite state machines with 4 and 3 states, respectively. The benchmark defines 8 STL formalized requirements that the system shall satisfy, shown in Table 1.

We now describe the evaluation setup. We simulated the Simulink model with fixed-step sampling and recorded the results. The obtained traces, as the one shown in Fig. 5, were then further discretized with the uniform quantization. We have obtained 751 samples from the Simulink model and normalized all variables' value domain to the interval $[0, 5000]$ which is the range of RPM variable, thus achieving fair reasoning about their substitution cost. We designed a test-bench in Verilog to stimulate the monitor with the generated values from the Simulink model. We used Xilinx Vivado to perform monitor simulation and synthesis.

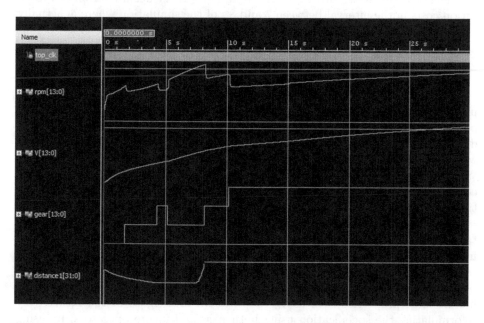

Fig. 5. A simulation trace s from the Automatic Transmission model and $d_W(s, \neg \varphi_6)$.

Figure 5 illustrates the monitoring results for φ_6 on a specific gear input. In the depicted scenario, the speed does not reach 120 mph in 4 s, a sufficient condition for the satisfaction of the formula. In order to violate the formula, we need to alter both v and ω signals such that (1) v reaches 120 mph at any moment within the first 4 s; and (2) ω remains continuously below 4500 rpm. These alterations result in (1) a single substitution happening within the first

Table 2. Evaluation results.

φ	ρ	φ				$\neg\,\varphi$			
		$|Q|$	$|\Delta|$	#FF	#LUT	$|Q|$	$|\Delta|$	#FF	#LUT
φ_1	-2528	2	2	62	260	4	8	94	657
φ_2	-11423	2	2	75	306	4	11	107	799
φ_3	1000	496	1374	4106	53033	992	2878	8127	106937
φ_4	1000	496	692	3061	22777	992	1445	6025	44968
φ_5	n/a	n/a	n/a	n/a	n/a	n/a	n/a	n/a	n/a
φ_6	5337	405	813	6540	66085	409	903	6504	73657
φ_7	-5336	403	903	6504	73766	405	813	6545	66116
φ_8	n/a	n/a	n/a	n/a	n/a	n/a	n/a	n/a	n/a

4 s which is necessary to bring v to 120 mph; and (2) the accumulation of substitution costs in the interval between 7 and 8 s of the simulation where ω actually exceeds 4500 rpm. Note that the robustness degree decreases in the first 4 s. This happens because the actual v increases and the substitution cost needed for v to reach 120 mph is continuously being improved.

The evaluation results are shown in Table 2. We tested the correctness of STL to automata translation by generating both acceptors for φ and $\neg\,\varphi$. The presented robustness degrees are not normalized, which can be statically computed using the formula from Sect. 3. It is clear from our table that either the distance from φ or from its negation is always 0. The dominant type of resources when implementing our monitors on FPGA hardware are LUTs. This is not surprising, due to the large combinatorial and arithmetic requirements of the computation. We can also note that the size of our monitors is sensitive to the timing bounds in the formulas and the sampling period of the input signals. Our monitor automata enumerate clock ticks instead of using a symbolic representation. The enumeration is necessary because state - clock valuation pairs can have different values associated and thus cannot be grouped. We were not able to generate monitors for φ_5 and φ_8 due to the state explosion. However, φ_5 can be decomposed into 4 independent sub-properties. We can see several ways to handle large properties such as φ_8 that we will investigate in the future – by reformulating the specification using both past and future operators, by using larger sampling periods (and thus smaller time bounds in the formula) and by using more powerful FPGA hardware.

6   Conclusions

In this paper, we proposed a new procedure for measuring robustness of STL properties based on the weighted edit distance. Weighted edit distance is an accumulative measure, and provides insight on how often the property is violated.

It is thus sensitive to the length of the signal, but also to the sampling rate and the number of components in the signal. Normalizing the distance enables obtaining a uniform measure of "goodness" of a behavior. While the focus is on the quantitative semantics of STL, our approach is applicable to other regular specification languages interpreted over finite signals.

In the future, we will study more closely the effect of sampling to the computed distance. We will apply our approach on more relevant examples, in order to get better insight on the interpretation of the values obtained by the robustness measurements. Finally, we will work on the optimization of our procedure in order to obtain smaller weighted automata that can be efficiently implemented on hardware, and will deploy our implementation on FPGA and evaluate it in the lab environment.

Acknowledgements. We would like to thank Oded Maler, Mario Klima and the anonymous reviewers for their comments on the earlier drafts of the paper.

We acknowledge the support of the IKT der Zukunft of Austrian FFG project HARMONIA (nr. 845631), the ICT COST Action IC1402 Runtime Verification beyond Monitoring (ARVI), the Austrian National Research Network S 11405-N23 and S 11412-N23 (RiSE/SHiNE) of the Austrian Science Fund (FWF) and the Doctoral Program Logical Methods in Computer Science of the Austrian Science Fund (FWF).

References

1. Akazaki, T., Hasuo, I.: Time robustness in MTL and expressivity in hybrid system falsification. In: Kroening, D., Păsăreanu, C.S. (eds.) CAV 2015. LNCS, vol. 9207, pp. 356–374. Springer, Heidelberg (2015). doi:10.1007/978-3-319-21668-3_21

2. Allauzen, C., Mohri, M.: Linear-space computation of the edit-distance between a string and a finite automaton. CoRR abs/0904.4686 (2009)

3. Annpureddy, Y., Liu, C., Fainekos, G., Sankaranarayanan, S.: S-TaLiRo: a tool for temporal logic falsification for hybrid systems. In: Abdulla, P.A., Leino, K.R.M. (eds.) TACAS 2011. LNCS, vol. 6605, pp. 254–257. Springer, Heidelberg (2011). doi:10.1007/978-3-642-19835-9_21

4. Abbas, H., Hoxha, B., Fainekos, G.: Benchmarks for temporal logic requirements for automotive systems. In: Proceedings of Applied Verification for Continuous and Hybrid Systems (2014)

5. Bartocci, E., Bortolussi, L., Sanguinetti, G.: Data-driven statistical learning of temporal logic properties. In: Legay, A., Bozga, M. (eds.) FORMATS 2014. LNCS, vol. 8711, pp. 23–37. Springer, Heidelberg (2014). doi:10.1007/978-3-319-10512-3_3

6. Brim, L., Dluhos, P., Safránek, D., Vejpustek, T.: STL*: extending signal temporal logic with signal-value freezing operator. Inf. Comput. **236**, 52–67 (2014)

7. Deshmukh, J.V., Majumdar, R., Prabhu, V.S.: Quantifying conformance using the Skorokhod metric. In: Kroening, D., Păsăreanu, C.S. (eds.) CAV 2015. LNCS, vol. 9207, pp. 234–250. Springer, Heidelberg (2015). doi:10.1007/978-3-319-21668-3_14

8. Deshmukh, J.V., Majumdar, R., Prabhu, V.S.: Quantifying conformance using the Skorokhod metric (full version). CoRR abs/1505.05832 (2015)

9. Donzé, A.: Breach, a toolbox for verification and parameter synthesis of hybrid systems. In: Touili, T., Cook, B., Jackson, P. (eds.) CAV 2010. LNCS, vol. 6174, pp. 167–170. Springer, Heidelberg (2010). doi:10.1007/978-3-642-14295-6_17

10. Donzé, A., Ferrère, T., Maler, O.: Efficient robust monitoring for STL. In: Sharygina, N., Veith, H. (eds.) CAV 2013. LNCS, vol. 8044, pp. 264–279. Springer, Heidelberg (2013). doi:10.1007/978-3-642-39799-8_19

11. Donzé, A., Maler, O.: Robust satisfaction of temporal logic over real-valued signals. In: Chatterjee, K., Henzinger, T.A. (eds.) FORMATS 2010. LNCS, vol. 6246, pp. 92–106. Springer, Heidelberg (2010). doi:10.1007/978-3-642-15297-9_9

12. Fainekos, G.E., Pappas, G.J.: Robustness of temporal logic specifications for continuous-time signals. Theor. Comput. Sci. **410**(42), 4262–4291 (2009)

13. Fainekos, G.E., Sankaranarayanan, S., Ivancic, F., Gupta, A.: Robustness of model-based simulations. In: Proceedings of the 30th IEEE Real-Time Systems Symposium, RTSS 2009, Washington, DC, USA, 1–4 December 2009, pp. 345–354 (2009)

14. Gerth, R., Peled, D., Vardi, M.Y., Wolper, P.: Simple on-the-fly automatic verification of linear temporal logic. In: Protocol Specification, Testing and Verification XV, Proceedings of the Fifteenth IFIP WG6.1 International Symposium on Protocol Specification, Testing and Verification, Warsaw, Poland, pp. 3–18 (1995)

15. Konstantinidis, S.: Computing the edit distance of a regular language. Inf. Comput. **205**(9), 1307–1316 (2007)

16. Krause, E.F.: Taxicab Geometry: An Adventure in Non-Euclidean Geometry. Courier Corporation, North Chelmsford (2012)

17. Levenshtein, V.I.: Binary codes capable of correcting deletions, insertions, reversals. Sov. Phys. Dokl. **10**, 707 (1966)

18. Maler, O., Nickovic, D.: Monitoring properties of analog and mixed-signal circuits. STTT **15**(3), 247–268 (2013)

19. Mohri, M.: Edit-distance of weighted automata: general definitions and algorithms. Int. J. Found. Comput. Sci. **14**(6), 957–982 (2003)

20. Nguyen, T., Ničković, D.: Assertion-based monitoring in practice–checking correctness of an automotive sensor interface. In: Lang, F., Flammini, F. (eds.) FMICS 2014. LNCS, vol. 8718, pp. 16–32. Springer, Heidelberg (2014). doi:10.1007/978-3-319-10702-8_2

21. Pnueli, A., Zaks, A.: On the merits of temporal testers. In: Grumberg, O., Veith, H. (eds.) 25 Years of Model Checking. LNCS, vol. 5000, pp. 172–195. Springer, Heidelberg (2008). doi:10.1007/978-3-540-69850-0_11

22. Rizk, A., Batt, G., Fages, F., Soliman, S.: On a continuous degree of satisfaction of temporal logic formulae with applications to systems biology. In: Heiner, M., Uhrmacher, A.M. (eds.) CMSB 2008. LNCS (LNBI), vol. 5307, pp. 251–268. Springer, Heidelberg (2008). doi:10.1007/978-3-540-88562-7_19

23. Samanta, R., Deshmukh, J.V., Chaudhuri, S.: Robustness analysis of string transducers. In: Van Hung, D., Ogawa, M. (eds.) ATVA 2013. LNCS, vol. 8172, pp. 427–441. Springer, Heidelberg (2013). doi:10.1007/978-3-319-02444-8_30

24. Schulz, K.U., Mihov, S.: Fast string correction with Levenshtein automata. Int. J. Doc. Anal. Recogn. **5**(1), 67–85 (2002)

25. Veanes, M., Bjørner, N., de Moura, L.: Symbolic automata constraint solving. In: Fermüller, C.G., Voronkov, A. (eds.) LPAR-17. LNCS, vol. 6397, pp. 640–654. Springer, Heidelberg (2010). doi:10.1007/978-3-642-16242-8_45

26. Wagner, R.A.: Order-n correction for regular languages. Commun. ACM **17**(5), 265–268 (1974)

Extended Code Coverage for AspectJ-Based Runtime Verification Tools

Omar Javed[✉], Yudi Zheng, Andrea Rosà, Haiyang Sun, and Walter Binder

Faculty of Informatics, Università della Svizzera Italiana (USI), Lugano, Switzerland
{omar.javed,yudi.zheng,andrea.rosa,haiyang.sun,walter.binder}@usi.ch

Abstract. Many runtime verification tools for the Java virtual machine rely on aspect-oriented programming, particularly on AspectJ, to weave the verification logic into the observed program. However, AspectJ imposes several limitations on the verification tools, such as a restricted join point model and the inability of weaving certain classes, particularly the Java and Android class libraries. In this paper, we show that our domain-specific aspect language DiSL can overcome these limitations. While offering a programming model akin to AspectJ, DiSL features an extensible join point model and ensures weaving with complete bytecode coverage for Java and Android. We present a new compiler that translates runtime-verification aspects written in AspectJ to DiSL. Hence, it is possible to use existing, unmodified runtime verification tools on top of the DiSL framework to bypass the limitations of AspectJ. As a case study, we show that the AspectJ-based runtime verification tool Java-MOP significantly benefits from the automated translation of AspectJ to DiSL code, gaining increased code coverage. Thanks to DiSL, JavaMOP analyses are able to unveil violations in the Java class library that cannot be detected when using AspectJ.

1 Introduction

Many state-of-the-art runtime verification tools, such as JavaMOP [1], LARVA [2], Tracematches [3], and MARQ [4], target the Java Virtual Machine (JVM). Often, such tools rely on Aspect-Oriented Programming (AOP), in particular on AspectJ [5], to weave the verification logic into the observed program at specified join points[1].

Unfortunately, while offering a convenient programming model, AspectJ suffers from severe shortcomings that may impair the development of effective runtime verification tools. First, AspectJ provides only a limited set of join points that can be instrumented. Second, AspectJ is unable to weave aspects in certain classes, in particular, those in the class libraries of Java and Android. While the first limitation has been addressed in the approach described in [6], the second

---

[1] In this paper, we use the following terms related to AOP: *join points* (i.e., any identifiable execution point in a system), *pointcuts* (i.e., a set of join points of interest), and *advice* (i.e., code to be executed when a join point of a pointcut is reached).

© Springer International Publishing AG 2016
Y. Falcone and C. Sanchez (Eds.): RV 2016, LNCS 10012, pp. 219–234, 2016.
DOI: 10.1007/978-3-319-46982-9_14

limitation results in monitoring tools with only limited code coverage[2], which may fail to fully verify program correctness.

In this paper, we argue that the aforementioned limitations of AspectJ can be overcome by DiSL [7], our instrumentation framework for runtime verification. In particular, our work targets runtime verification tools that generate aspects to express the verification logic and rely on AspectJ to weave that logic into the observed program. By translating verification aspects expressed in AspectJ into DiSL instrumentations, the code coverage of existing AspectJ-based tools [1–4] can be significantly extended, enabling runtime verification on classes (such as those in the Java class library) which otherwise cannot be processed with AspectJ, as well as on Android applications. Such feature enables library developers to easily apply out-of-the-box tools on the library code, which demands a better code quality than the application code. To this end, we present a novel AspectJ-to-DiSL compiler that can be readily integrated with unmodified AspectJ-based runtime verification tools.

This work makes the following contributions. We show that DiSL achieves better code coverage than AspectJ, which results in the discovery of violations in Java that cannot be found by AspectJ. Moreover, we present a novel compiler to translate a subset of AspectJ constructs into DiSL code (detail of supported subset is mentioned in Sect. 3.1). The constructs supported by the compiler are particularly important for runtime monitoring and verification.

Our evaluation results demonstrate that applying our compiler to the Java-MOP runtime verification tool [1] results in a more versatile, enhanced tool that presents a considerably increased code coverage and is able to detect violations in the Java class library. In particular, this enhanced tool has led to the discovery of previously unknown violations found by JavaMOP analyses in the Java Development Kit (JDK) 8.

In the rest of the paper, we present an overview of DiSL in Sect. 2, while we detail our novel AspectJ-to-DiSL compiler in Sect. 3. Section 4 shows the benefits of using DiSL over AspectJ for runtime verification, discussing our evaluation results on both the JVM and on Android. Finally, we discuss related work in Sect. 5 and conclude in Sect. 6.

2   DiSL Overview

In this section we give a brief overview of DiSL; see [7] for more information.

Language Constructs. With DiSL, any region of bytecodes can be used as a join point. Pointcuts are expressed with *markers* that select bytecode regions. DiSL provides an extensible library of such markers, including those for selecting method bodies, exception handlers, basic blocks, and single bytecodes. Join points selected by a marker can be further restricted by *guards*, i.e., side-effect-free predicate methods executed at weave-time. Advice in DiSL are expressed

---

[2] We use the term "code coverage" to refer to the degree to which the program is monitored by runtime verification tools.

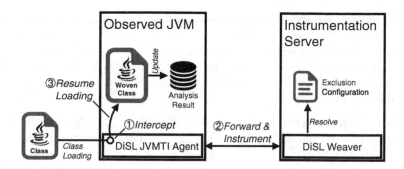

Fig. 1. DiSL architecture (configuration for JVM in-process analysis).

in the form of code *snippets*, which serve as code templates to be inserted at certain join points indicated by *annotations*. Snippets are instantiated by the weaver using contextual information.

Context Information. Snippets have access to complete context information provided via method arguments. Context information can be of two types: static (i.e., static reflective join point information limited to constants: primitive values, strings, or class literals) or dynamic (i.e., including local variables and the operand stack). DiSL provides an extensible library of both kinds of context information. Guards have access only to static context information.

Data Passing. DiSL supports *synthetic local variables* that enable efficient data passing between snippets woven into the same method body. To allow snippets to access the same variables, snippets are inlined by the DiSL weaver. Synthetic local variables are expressed as annotated static fields. DiSL also supports *thread-local variables* that are efficiently implemented by extra instance fields in `java.lang.Thread`. They are also expressed as annotated static fields.

Architecture. The architecture of DiSL (when instrumenting applications on the JVM) is shown in Fig. 1. DiSL uses a separate process for instrumentation to reduce perturbations and interferences in the observed JVM. All classes (including those from the Java class library) are intercepted at load-time by the DiSL JVMTI agent and forwarded to the instrumentation process, which executes the DiSL weaver. Instrumented classes are then returned to the observed JVM where they are linked.

Instrumentation. When a snippet is selected to be woven at a join point, it is first instantiated using the context of the join point. The DiSL weaver replaces invocations of static-context methods with the corresponding constants, i.e., static-context method invocations in a snippet are pseudo method calls that are substituted with concrete constants. Similarly, dynamic-context method invocations in a snippet are pseudo method calls that are replaced with bytecode sequences to access local variables or to copy operands from the stack. DiSL relies on polymorphic bytecode instrumentation [8] to achieve complete bytecode coverage.

Out-of-Process Analysis. DiSL also supports a deployment setting to enforce isolation between the analysis and the observed program [9]. In this setting analysis code in executed in a separate process, avoiding any shared state between the analysis and the observed program. This setting prevents interference problems often found in systems that execute the analysis code and the observed program within the same process [10].

Android Support. DiSL supports instrumentation on the Dalvik Virtual Machine (DVM) employed in Android [11]. The DiSL instrumentation server receives Dalvik bytecode from Android, converts it to Java bytecode, instruments it, and converts the result to Dalvik bytecode before sending it back. By intercepting class loading on Android, DiSL achieves load-time weaving and ensures full bytecode coverage [12], enabling also the instrumentation of the Android system library and of dynamically loaded classes. Moreover, DiSL integrates a bypass mechanism which dynamically activates or deactivates an instrumentation [13]. This approach is useful for shared libraries and allows applying multiple instrumentations in a single weaving pass, as each instrumentation can be selectively enabled or disabled.

3   AspectJ-to-DiSL Compiler

Here we present our compiler that translates AspectJ aspects to DiSL instrumentations. It allows unmodified AspectJ-based runtime verification tools to take advantage of the increased bytecode coverage of DiSL. We refer any interested reader to [13] for how DiSL achieves comprehensive code coverage. We start with an overview of the compiler in Sect. 3.1, followed by an explanation of the implementation in Sect. 3.2. Finally, we illustrate the compiler with a running example in Sect. 3.3.

3.1   Overview

Our AspectJ-to-DiSL compiler takes compiled AspectJ classes as input and generates a corresponding DiSL instrumentation. We employ ASM[3], a Java bytecode manipulation framework, to parse the AspectJ constructs. An alternative approach would be to modify the AspectJ compiler to directly emit a DiSL instrumentation. While the latter approach would require more development effort, it would result in a tighter integration of DiSL with AspectJ.

Our compiler transforms AspectJ *pointcuts* and *advice*. Because DiSL only supports instrumentations for monitoring tasks and prevents structural modifications of the woven code, our AspectJ-to-DiSL compiler supports neither *around advice* that alters the control flow[4], nor *inter-type declarations* that may modify the class structure or even the class hierarchy.

---

[3] http://asm.ow2.org/.

[4] We show a solution for around advice that does not alter the control flow in Sect. 3.2.

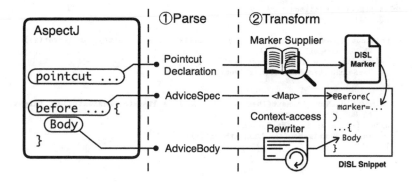

Fig. 2. Overview of the AspectJ-to-DiSL compiler.

An overview of the AspectJ-to-DiSL compiler is shown in Fig. 2. The compiler first parses the AspectJ pointcut declarations and advice specifications, instantiates custom DiSL markers, and assembles them into concrete DiSL snippet annotations. Then, it copies the body of the AspectJ advice and adapts code accessing context information.

3.2   Implementation

AspectJ advice is translated into DiSL snippets. Depending on the advice specification, the corresponding DiSL snippet is annotated with @Before, @AfterReturning, @AfterThrowing, or @After[5]. For around advice which does not alter the control flow in the observed program (i.e., proceed is guaranteed to be invoked exactly once, which is checked by a static analysis), our compiler transforms the advice into two DiSL snippets annotated with @Before and @After, respectively, and introduces synthetic local variables for sharing data between these two DiSL snippets if necessary.

Pointcut declarations in AspectJ aspects are translated to custom DiSL markers as follows. For each type of pointcut, we create a method template that selects the corresponding bytecode regions. This method template must be specialized with the parameter of the pointcut before being instantiated to a custom marker class. For instance, a call(* Iterator.hasNext()) pointcut will be mapped to our CallMarkerTemplate. During compilation, we instantiate a custom CallMarker class with a parameter to the call pointcut, i.e., "* Iterator.hasNext()". For a pointcut that composes multiple pointcuts using logical operators such as && or ||, the custom DiSL marker embeds such logic into its top level marking method, and composites the marker classes instantiated from the corresponding method templates.

---

[5] Such annotations denote a DiSL snippet to be inserted, respectively, before the marked code region, after a normal exit, after an exceptional exit, and after any exit from the marked code region.

```
1   public aspect HasNextMonitorAspect {
2      ...
3
4      pointcut HasNext_next(Iterator i) : (call(* Iterator.next()) && target(i))
5         && MOP_CommonPointCut();
6      before (Iterator i) : HasNext_next(i) {
7         HasNextRuntimeMonitor.nextEvent(i);
8      }
9
10     pointcut HasNext_hasnext(Iterator i) : (call(* Iterator.hasNext()) && target(i))
11        && MOP_CommonPointCut();
12     after (Iterator i) : HasNext_hasnext(i) {
13        HasNextRuntimeMonitor.hasnextEvent(i);
14     }
15  }
```

(a)

```
1   public class HasNextMonitorInstrumentation {
2      ...
3
4      @Before(marker = NextInvocationMarker.class)
5      static void before$HasNext_next$1 (ArgumentProcessorContext pc){
6         Iterator i = (Iterator) pc.getReceiver(ArgumentProcessorMode.CALLSITE_ARGS);
7         HasNextRuntimeMonitor.nextEvent(i);
8      }
9
10     @After(marker = HasNextInvocationMarker.class)
11     static void after$HasNext_hasnext$2 (ArgumentProcessorContext pc) {
12        Iterator i = (Iterator) pc.getReceiver(ArgumentProcessorMode.CALLSITE_ARGS);
13        HasNextRuntimeMonitor.hasnextEvent(i);
14     }
15  }
```

(b)

Fig. 3. (a) AspectJ code for the *HasNext* property in JavaMOP. The naming convention is derived from JavaMOP. (b) DiSL code generated for the AspectJ code in Fig. (a).

The body of the AspectJ advice is reused in the DiSL snippet, yet access to the context information is adapted. Our compiler maintains a mapping from each kind of join point context into specific methods for accessing the same context information in the DiSL library. When the compiler encounters an access to the join point context in the AspectJ advice, including those defined in the pointcut or advice declaration (e.g. target, arg or this), it will be replaced with an invocation to the corresponding method. For optimization purposes, the compiler distinguishes between static context information and dynamic context information. The compiler folds multiple identical accesses to the latter, and place them at the beginning of the DiSL snippet.

3.3   Example

To illustrate our AspectJ-to-DiSL compiler, we use the *HasNext* property in JavaMOP as an example. This property is used for specifying constraints on the invocation of Iterator.hasNext() and Iterator.next() for each Iterator instance. Figure 3(a) shows the AspectJ code related to the *HasNext* property, while Fig. 3(b) demonstrates the output of our AspectJ-to-DiSL compiler. The semantics of the pointcuts are encapsulated into two custom DiSL markers, i.e.,

Table 1. JavaMOP properties evaluated.

Property	Description
HasNext	Program should always call hasNext() before next() on an iterator.
UnsafeIterator	When the iterator associated with a collection is accessed, the collection should not be updated.
SafeSyncMap	When the iterator associated with a map is accessed, the map should not be updated.
SafeSyncCollection	A synchronized collection should always be accessed by a synchronized iterator, and the iterator should always be accessed in a synchronized manner

NextInvocationMarker and HasNextInvocationMarker. The two markers apply the library method corresponding to the call pointcut, marking bytecodes that invoke Iterator.next() or Iterator.hasNext(). In the body of the DiSL snippets, the compiler adapts the access to the receiver of the invocations by using ArgumentProcessorContext[6].

4   Evaluation

In this section, we demonstrate the prominence of DiSL over AspectJ in terms of code coverage and violation detection, and show how existing runtime verification tools can benefit from our AspectJ-to-DiSL compiler. In particular, we apply the proposed compiler to the JavaMOP [1] verification tool, and show how the compiler enhances JavaMOP analyses by converting AspectJ aspects generated by JavaMOP into DiSL instrumentation[7].

We start by describing the setting of our evaluation in Sect. 4.1; then, we compare AspectJ and DiSL instrumentation along different dimensions, i.e., the number of join points executed (Sect. 4.2), violations detected in the Java class library (Sect. 4.3) and bytecode coverage on the Android platform (Sect. 4.4.).

4.1   Evaluation Setup

We choose multiple well-known JavaMOP properties (shown in Table 1), and evaluate two versions of each property: (1) the AspectJ aspect as generated by JavaMOP, and (2) the translated DiSL instrumentation.

---

[6] The ArgumentProcessorContext interface allows one to access method arguments within snippets. Here, this features is used to get the receivers of method invocations.

[7] Note that some AspectJ constructs in such aspects are not supported by our compiler, as DiSL does not support them (see Sect. 3.1).

To guarantee a fair comparison between AspectJ and DiSL, we did not include any class or method in the exclusion list[8] of both frameworks. Because the generated JavaMOP aspects exclude the Java class library using the !within pointcut, we also manually modify the generated DiSL markers to enable the instrumentation of the Java class library. Concerning the experiments on the Android platform, since the AspectJ load-time weaver is not available on Android, we conduct the evaluation by comparing the DiSL instrumentation applied on application code only V_{DISL} (i.e., excluding the Android class library) and with full coverage V_{DISL+}.

We have confirmed the correctness of our compiler as follows. First, we defined an exclusion list for DiSL with all the classes that could not be woven by AspectJ[9]; then, for each JavaMOP property, we compared the number of joint points executed by both the original AspectJ code and the translated DiSL instrumentation. In all cases, the results showed no relevant differences (apart from minor fluctuations due to non-determinism between different runs of some benchmarks) between the two frameworks, confirming that the same join points were intercepted by both AspectJ and DiSL.

On the JVM, our base programs come from the DaCapo[10] and Scala benchmark suites[11]. The experiments are run on a 64-bit multicore platform with Oracle Hotspot Server VM[12]. We use JavaMOP 4.2, AspectJ 1.8.9, and DiSL 2.1. On Android, the base programs are applications in the Android Open Source Project (AOSP)[13]. We evaluate theses applications on Android 4.4.

4.2 Join Point Executions on the JVM

Figure 4 shows the number of join point executions for each JavaMOP property. The shaded region of each bar denotes the number of join points intercepted by AspectJ, while the unshaded region of the bar denotes the difference between the join points intercepted by DiSL and those intercepted by AspectJ. In all benchmarks DiSL intercepts more join points than AspectJ, because DiSL provides full bytecode coverage, allowing the same JavaMOP property to cover the Java class library as well as all AspectJ dependencies (i.e., classes that are implicitly excluded from load-time weaving in AspectJ). We expect the increase

---

[8] The exclusion list allows one to specify a list of classes and methods that must not be considered in the weaving process.

[9] Such classes are hard-coded in the AspectJ weaver, and cannot be woven even when specified in the weaver's inpath flag.

[10] Release 9.12-bach, http://www.dacapobench.org/. We excluded tradesoap, tradebeans and tomcat due to well-known issues. See bug #70 (hardcoded timeout in tradesoap and tradebeans) and bug #68 (StackOverflowError in tomcat) in the DaCapo bugtracker at https://sourceforge.net/p/dacapobench/bugs/.

[11] http://www.benchmarks.scalabench.org/.

[12] Intel Core i7, 2.5 GHz, Oracle JDK 1.8.0_60 Hotspot Server VM (64-bit) on Darwin Kernel Version 15.4.0.

[13] https://source.android.com/.

in the number of join points intercepted to expose more violation of JavaMOP properties, especially within the Java class library.

From the figure, we can see that there is a significant coverage difference between AspectJ and DiSL in most of the benchmarks. However, the difference is smaller for *avrora* and *h2*, because most intercepted join points stem from an application class. The two join points java.util.Iterator.hasNext() and java.util.Iterator.next() are the most frequent ones, and in the case of *h2* and *avrora*, they occur frequently in application classes. This behavior is different from other benchmarks, where the major contribution to the total number of join point executions is within the Java class library. When weaving with AspectJ, we observe that *h2* shows the same number of join points in three different properties: *HasNext*, *SafeSyncCollection*, and *SafeSyncMap*, caused by a common pointcut which intercepts calls to both java.util.Iterator.hasNext() and java.util.Iterator.next(). For instance, org.h2.command.dml.Select.is Everything()[14] contains join points which are intercepted by all three properties.

Amongst the four properties, *SafeSyncMap* yields the biggest difference between the number of join points executed by AspectJ and DiSL, with an exception in the *avrora* benchmark. In this benchmark, method calls to java.util.List.iterator() and java.util.Iterator.hasNext() are intercepted most of the time, and, among all properties, only *SafeSyncCollection* employs pointcuts to intercept the aforementioned two join points. For many benchmarks, the property *HasNext* shows the lowest number of joint point executions among all properties. The reason is that this property employs pointcuts which can be considered as a subset of the pointcuts employed by other properties. For example, pointcuts which intercept java.util.Iterator.hasNext() and java.util.Iterator.next(), apart from being defined in *HasNext*, are similarly defined in *SafeSyncCollection* and *SafeSyncMap*. An exception is *h2*, where java.util.Iterator.next() and java.util.Iterator.hasNext() account for the majority of join point executions. Since *UnsafeIterator* only intercepts java.util.Iterator.hasNext() (but not java.util.Iterator.next()), the total number of join points executed in this property is lower than for *HasNext*.

Overall, most of the benchmarks show a low number of join points intercepted by AspectJ, especially in Scala benchmarks (i.e., the last 12 benchmarks shown in Fig. 4). The reason is that AspectJ can only instrument application classes, in contrast to DiSL. In the case of Scala benchmarks, the number of join points executed by AspectJ are very low when compared to DiSL (in some cases, they are not even visible in the figure). With full bytecode coverage, most join point executions are in library code rather than in application code, with the exception of the *actor* benchmark.

---

[14] For brevity, we do not report parameters and return type for methods.

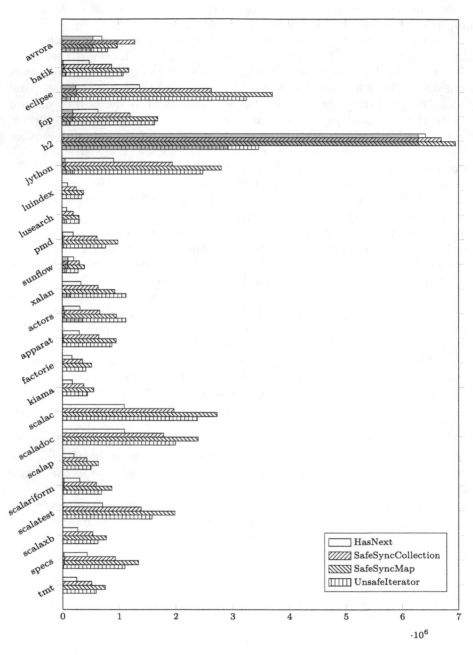

Fig. 4. Number of join points executed in different benchmarks for the four considered properties of JavaMOP. Pattern ▨ shows the number of join points in AspectJ. Pattern □ shows the difference of join points executed between AspectJ and DiSL (DiSL - AspectJ).

4.3 Violations in the Java Class Library

JavaMOP analyses, after being translated to DiSL instrumentations, reveal the existence of two property violations in the Java class library which cannot be detected by standard AspectJ code.

The first violation concerns **java.util.EnumSet.copyOf(Collection)** (source code at Fig. 5), which violates the *HasNext* property. Further investigation reveals that this library method invokes Iterator.next() at line 8 without calling Iterator.hasNext(). While the code is valid, as it asserts whether the input Collection is empty, the implicit dependency between the assertion and the invocation of Iterator.next() is error-prone during code evolution—a developer may support copying an empty collection and drop the assertion. For this reason, we consider the reported violation as a valid one, which cannot be detected by the AspectJ code generated by JavaMOP.

The second violation is related to **com.sun.org.apache.xerces.internal. jaxp.SAXParserImpl.setFeatures(Hashtable)** (source code at Fig. 6), which violates the *SafeSyncCollection* property. After investigating this matter further, we found that this library method iterates through an instance of Hashtable, which is a synchronized Collection, without explicit synchronization (i.e., without specifying the **synchronized** keyword).

If the invocation to this method is not synchronized by the user, line 6 may throw a ConcurrentModificationException if the content of the Hashtable instance is modified concurrently after calling java.util.Iterator.hasNext() at line 5. In the newer version of Oracle JDK (e.g., 1.8.0_91), the responsibility of synchronization is explicitly shifted to the user by having this method accepting a Map argument instead of a Hashtable. When passing an Hashtable instance, the user should guarantee that the invocation is properly synchronized.

Overall, the increased number of join point executions intercepted by DiSL has enabled the discovery of two previously unknown property violations in the Java class library. Thanks to our AspectJ-to-DiSL compiler and to the DiSL framework, runtime verification tools such as JavaMOP can also support the developers of the Java class library.

```
1    public static <E extends Enum<E>> EnumSet<E> copyOf(Collection<E> c) {
2        if (c instanceof EnumSet) {
3            return ((EnumSet<E>)c).clone();
4        } else {
5            if (c.isEmpty())
6                throw new IllegalArgumentException("Collection is empty");
7            Iterator<E> i = c.iterator();
8            E first = i.next(); // invoked without calling hasNext()
9            EnumSet<E> result = EnumSet.of(first);
10           while (i.hasNext())
11               result.add(i.next());
12           return result;
13       }
14   }
```

Fig. 5. Source code of java.util.EnumSet.copyOf(Collection).

```
1    private void setFeatures(Hashtable features)
2        throws SAXNotSupportedException, SAXNotRecognizedException {
3        if (features != null) {
4            Iterator entries = features.entrySet().iterator();
5            while (entries.hasNext()) {
6                Map.Entry entry = (Map.Entry) entries.next();
7                String feature = (String) entry.getKey();
8                boolean value = ((Boolean) entry.getValue()).booleanValue();
9                xmlReader.setFeature0(feature, value);
10           }
11       }
12   }
```

Fig. 6. Source code of com.sun.org.apache.xerces.internal.jaxp.SAXParserImpl.setFeatures. (Oracle JDK 1.8.0_60)

4.4 Join Point Executions on Android

Here, we show the number of join points intercepted by JavaMOP analyses in Android applications (after translation of the analyses to DiSL instrumentations), remarking that such an analysis is not possible with AspectJ's load-time weaver. We note that the evaluation on V_{DISL} is meant to simulate the code coverage that AspectJ would have had if it had been applicable to Android applications. That is, V_{DISL} does not weave any classes that cannot be woven by AspectJ. To illustrate the effectiveness of our work, we apply the translated JavaMOP analyses on built-in applications from the AOSP, which are standard and well-known applications for the Android system. We report our results in Fig. 7.

It can be seen from the figure that V_{DISL+} (i.e., DiSL instrumentation applied on all classes) shows a significant increase in the number of join point executions wrt. V_{DISL}. This behavior follows our expectation, since V_{DISL+} intercepts join points in the Android class library, which are not covered by V_{DISL}.

Amongst all applications, *inputmethod* shows the highest coverage at the application level, It is because two join points, Iterator.next() and Iterator.hasHext() are the most frequent ones, and in the case of *inputmethod*, they occur frequently in application classes. However, in all other applications, the coverage at the application level is rather low, showing the need for employing full bytecode coverage also to the Android system.

5 Related Work

There are many runtime monitoring and verification frameworks, most of them based on AspectJ. JavaMOP [1] supports parametric properties and uses decentralized indexing to reduce the runtime overhead. LARVA [2] provides runtime verification of real-time properties, while Tracematches [3] can process traces of events instead of single events by specifying regular expressions of symbols with free variables. Finally, MARQ [4] generates monitors based on the structural characteristics of the properties being monitored in order to optimize runtime monitoring. Since all these tools use AspectJ for generating events, they suffer

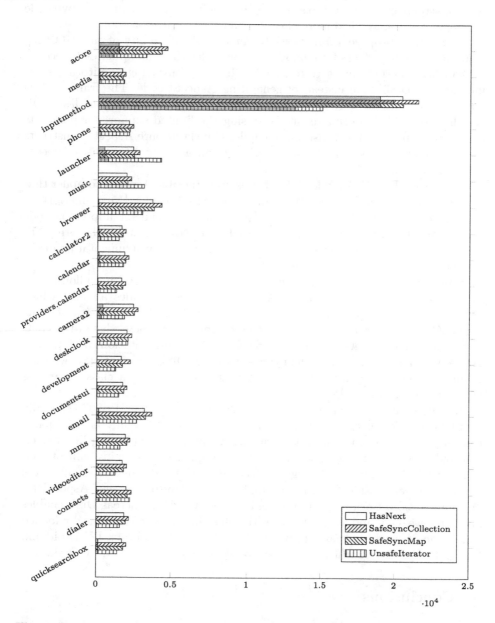

Fig. 7. Number of join points executed in different Android applications for the four considered properties of JavaMOP. Pattern ▨ shows number of join points in DiSL when excluding the Android class library. Pattern □ shows the difference of join points executed between V_{DISL+} and V_{DISL}.

from the shortcomings pinpointed in this paper. By integrating our AspectJ-to-DiSL compiler in these tools, they can benefit from an increased bytecode coverage, which may yield more effective runtime verification tools.

Xiang et al. propose a framework to enhance the flexibility of JavaMOP [6]. The framework consists of a deployment controller that manipulates bytecodes for capturing events, and a translator for directly converting monitoring specifications to DiSL code instead of generating AspectJ code. The framework is applicable only to JavaMOP, as it directly generates DiSL code from JavaMOP specifications. Their work aims at addressing the limited support for pointcuts offered by AspectJ. In contrast, our compiler translates pure AspectJ constructs to DiSL, providing benefits to any runtime verification tool that uses AspectJ for instrumentation.

The AspectBench Compiler (abc) [14] is an extensible AspectJ compiler that makes it possible to add new features. It uses the Polyglot [15] framework as its front-end and the Soot framework [16] as its back-end for improving code generation. The compiler can also be applied on the Android platform [17]. However, abc supports neither load-time weaving nor the instrumentation of the core class library, which are supported by DiSL.

InterAspect [18] is an instrumentation framework for GCC that allows writing instrumentation plugins using AOP. InterAspect provides an API which defines pointcuts to ease the instrumentation, hiding the intricacies of writing GCC instrumentation plugins, which requires expert knowledge of the GCC internals. While InterAspect manipulates GIMPLE representations of Java programs, weaving takes place at the bytecode level in DiSL. It is not clear whether an instrumentation generated by InterAspect covers the Java class library, as DiSL instrumentations do.

Instrumenting Android applications with AOP is popular [19,20], especially for monitoring security and privacy threats. RV-Droid [21] relies on third-party runtime verification tools such as JavaMOP to produce monitoring libraries on Android. The authors modified the AspectJ compiler to enable instrumentation on Android. RV-Android [22] targets safety properties and provides a unified tool for runtime verification for Android applications. It also leverages AspectJ for instrumentation. Both tools support only static weaving, whereas DiSL enables load-time weaving and is able to cover the class library and dynamically loaded code. Since AspectJ is unable to weave the Android class library, RV-Droid and RV-Android could benefit from the full bytecode coverage offered by DiSL.

6   Conclusions

Several state-of-the-art runtime verification tools for the JVM leverage AspectJ for instrumentation. Unfortunately, AspectJ suffers from severe drawbacks, such as a restricted join point model and limited weaving capabilities that reduce code coverage, especially in the Java class library. In this paper, we have demonstrated that such limitations can be overcome by DiSL, our instrumentation framework for runtime verification. Moreover, we have presented a compiler to translate a subset of AspectJ constructs to DiSL. Our evaluation results show that applying our compiler to unmodified AspectJ-based runtime verification tools results in significantly increased code coverage, which allows one to find violations in the Java class library. Thanks to DiSL, runtime verification tools can also gain complete bytecode coverage on the Android platform.

DiSL is open-source and available at http://disl.ow2.org/. A new release is currently under preparation. In our ongoing research, we are improving the AspectJ-to-DiSL compiler to produce highly optimized woven code, aiming at outperforming AspectJ for runtime verification tasks. We plan to add support for inter-type declarations to minimize the impact on the monitoring performance. Moreover, we are investigating how to support ART on Android.

Acknowledgement. The research presented in this paper was supported by Oracle (ERO project 1332), by the Swiss National Science Foundation (project 200021_141002), by the European Commission (contract ACP2-GA-2013-605442), and by the Swiss Government Excellence Scholarship (ESKAS-Nr: 2015.0989).

References

1. Jin, D., Meredith, P.O.N., Lee, C., Roşu, G.: JavaMOP: efficient parametric runtime monitoring framework. In: ICSE, pp. 1427–1430 (2012)
2. Colombo, C., Pace, G.J., Schneider, G.: LARVA–safer monitoring of real-time Java programs (tool paper). In: SEFM, pp. 33–37 (2009)
3. Bodden, E., Hendren, L., Lam, P., Lhoták, O., Naeem, N.A.: Collaborative runtime verification with tracematches. In: Sokolsky, O., Taşıran, S. (eds.) RV 2007. LNCS, vol. 4839, pp. 22–37. Springer, Heidelberg (2007). doi:10.1007/978-3-540-77395-5_3
4. Reger, G., Cruz, H.C., Rydeheard, D.: MARQ: monitoring at runtime with QEA. In: Baier, C., Tinelli, C. (eds.) TACAS 2015. LNCS, vol. 9035, pp. 596–610. Springer, Heidelberg (2015). doi:10.1007/978-3-662-46681-0_55
5. Kiczales, G., Hilsdale, E., Hugunin, J., Kersten, M., Palm, J., Griswold, W.G.: An overview of AspectJ. In: Knudsen, J.L. (ed.) ECOOP 2001. LNCS, vol. 2072, pp. 327–354. Springer, Heidelberg (2001). doi:10.1007/3-540-45337-7_18
6. Xiang, C., Qi, Z., Binder, W.: Flexible and extensible runtime verification for Java (Extended Version). Int. J. Softw. Eng. Knowl. Eng. **25**, 1595–1609 (2015)
7. Marek, L., Villazón, A., Zheng, Y., Ansaloni, D., Binder, W., Qi, Z.: DiSL: a domain-specific language for bytecode instrumentation. In: AOSD, pp. 239–250 (2012)
8. Binder, W., Moret, P., Tanter, É., Ansaloni, D.: Polymorphic bytecode instrumentation. Softw. Pract. Exp. (2015) doi:10.1002/spe.2385
9. Marek, L., Kell, S., Zheng, Y., Bulej, L., Binder, W., Tůma, P., Ansaloni, D., Sarimbekov, A., Sewe, A.: ShadowVM: robust and comprehensive dynamic program analysis for the Java platform. In: GPCE, pp. 105–114 (2013)
10. Kell, S., Ansaloni, D., Binder, W., Marek, L.: The JVM is not observable enough (and What to do about it). In: VMIL, pp. 33–38 (2012)
11. Sun, H., Zheng, Y., Bulej, L., Villazón, A., Qi, Z., Tůma, P., Binder, W.: A programming model and framework for comprehensive dynamic analysis on Android. In: MODULARITY, pp. 133–145 (2015)

12. Zheng, Y., Kell, S., Bulej, L., Sun, H., Binder, W.: Comprehensive multi-platform dynamic program analysis for Java and Android. IEEE Softw. **33**, 55–63 (2016)
13. Moret, P., Binder, W., Tanter, E.: Polymorphic bytecode instrumentation. In: AOSD, pp. 129–140 (2011)
14. Avgustinov, P., Christensen, A.S., Hendren, L., Kuzins, S., Lhoták, J., Lhoták, O., de Moor, O., Sereni, D., Sittampalam, G., Tibble, J.: Abc: an extensible AspectJ compiler. In: AOSD, pp. 87–98 (2005)
15. Nystrom, N., Clarkson, M.R., Myers, A.C.: Polyglot: an extensible compiler framework for Java. In: Hedin, G. (ed.) CC 2003. LNCS, vol. 2622, pp. 138–152. Springer, Heidelberg (2003). doi:10.1007/3-540-36579-6_11
16. Vallée-Rai, R., Gagnon, E., Hendren, L., Lam, P., Pominville, P., Sundaresan, V.: Optimizing Java bytecode using the Soot framework: is it feasible? In: Watt, D.A. (ed.) CC 2000. LNCS, vol. 1781, pp. 18–34. Springer, Heidelberg (2000). doi:10.1007/3-540-46423-9_2
17. Arzt, S., Rasthofer, S., Bodden, E.: Instrumenting Android and Java applications as easy as abc. In: Legay, A., Bensalem, S. (eds.) RV 2013. LNCS, vol. 8174, pp. 364–381. Springer, Heidelberg (2013). doi:10.1007/978-3-642-40787-1_26
18. Seyster, J., Dixit, K., Huang, X., Grosu, R., Havelund, K., Smolka, S.A., Stoller, S.D., Zadok, E.: InterAspect: aspect-oriented instrumentation with GCC. Formal Methods Syst. Des. **41**, 295–320 (2012)
19. Falcone, Y., Currea, S.: Weave droid: aspect-oriented programming on Android devices: fully embedded or in the cloud. In: ASE, pp. 350–353 (2012)
20. Bodden, E.: Easily instrumenting Android applications for security purposes. In: CCS, pp. 1499–1502 (2013)
21. Falcone, Y., Currea, S., Jaber, M.: Runtime verification and enforcement for Android applications with RV-Droid. In: Qadeer, S., Tasiran, S. (eds.) RV 2012. LNCS, vol. 7687, pp. 88–95. Springer, Heidelberg (2013). doi:10.1007/978-3-642-35632-2_11
22. Daian, P., Falcone, Y., Meredith, P., Şerbănuţă, T.F., Shiriashi, S., Iwai, A., Rosu, G.: RV-Android: efficient parametric Android runtime verification, a brief tutorial. In: Bartocci, E., Majumdar, R. (eds.) RV 2015. LNCS, vol. 9333, pp. 342–357. Springer, Heidelberg (2015). doi:10.1007/978-3-319-23820-3_24

nfer – A Notation and System for Inferring Event Stream Abstractions

Sean Kauffman[1], Klaus Havelund[2]([⊠]), and Rajeev Joshi[2]

[1] University of Waterloo, Waterloo, Canada
[2] Jet Propulsion Laboratory, California Institute of Technology, Pasadena, USA
klaus.havelund@jpl.nasa.gov

Abstract. We propose a notation for specifying event stream abstractions for use in spacecraft telemetry processing. Our work is motivated by the need to quickly process streams with millions of events generated by the Curiosity rover on Mars. The approach builds a hierarchy of event abstractions for telemetry visualization and querying to aid human comprehension. Such abstractions can also be used as input to other runtime verification tools. Our notation is inspired by Allen's Temporal Logic, and provides a rule-based declarative way to express event abstractions. The system is written in Scala, with the specification language implemented as an internal DSL. It is based on parallel executing actors communicating via a publish-subscribe model. We illustrate the solution with several examples, including a real telemetry analysis scenario.

1 Introduction

A key challenge in operating remote spacecraft is that human operators must rely on telemetry to assess the status of the spacecraft. Telemetry can be thought of as an execution trace, a stream consisting of millions of discrete events. These event streams are difficult to interpret and validate because of their size and complexity. The current approach to analyzing spacecraft telemetry relies on ad-hoc scripts that are difficult to write and maintain. We propose a notation for computing abstractions of event streams, resulting in a hierarchy of interval abstractions, which is useful for telemetry visualization and querying to aid human comprehension. Our notation is inspired by interval logics, specifically Allen's Temporal Logic [2], commonly used in the planning and artificial intelligence (AI) domains. We extend a variation of this logic with a rule-based declarative way to express event abstractions. We also present a system named nfer (**infer**ence), written in Scala, which implements the notation as an internal Scala (DSL). The nfer system is based on concurrently executing actors communicating via a publish-subscribe model. We show the application of nfer to telemetry received from the Curiosity Mars rover.

The research performed by the last two authors was carried out at Jet Propulsion Laboratory, California Institute of Technology, under a contract with the National Aeronautics and Space Administration.

© Springer International Publishing AG 2016
Y. Falcone and C. Sanchez (Eds.): RV 2016, LNCS 10012, pp. 235–250, 2016.
DOI: 10.1007/978-3-319-46982-9_15

Our system differs from traditional runtime verification (RV) systems, in which a program execution trace is checked against a user-provided specification. RV usually results in a binary decision (true/false) as to whether the execution trace satisfies the specification, although variations on this theme have been developed. These include 3-valued logics (true, false, don't know) [8] and 4-valued logics (true, false, true-so-far, false-so-far) [6].

The remaining content of the paper is as follows. Section 2 introduces preliminary notation. Section 3 provides the problem statement and motivation for this work. Section 4 defines the `nfer` notation. Section 5 describes the implementation of the system in Scala, including the DSL. Section 6 illustrates the application of `nfer` to a scenario from the Mars Science Laboratory. Section 7 discusses related work. Finally, Sect. 8 concludes the paper.

2   Preliminary Notation

By $\mathbb{B}$ we denote the set of Boolean values $\{true, false\}$. By $\mathbb{N}$ we denote the set of natural numbers $\{0, 1, 2, \ldots\}$ and by $\mathbb{R}$ we denote the set of real numbers. For readability, we use the type $\mathbb{C} = \mathbb{R}$ to represent clock time stamps. By $A \times B$ we denote the cross product of types A and B. By $A \rightarrow B$ we denote the set of total functions from A to B. Functions in $A \rightarrow B$ can be denoted by lambda terms: $\lambda x.e$. A function of type $A \rightarrow \mathbb{B}$ is referred to as a predicate. Predicates with the same domain type can be composed with Boolean operators. For example, given $f : A \rightarrow \mathbb{B}$ and $g : A \rightarrow \mathbb{B}$, then $(f \wedge g)(x) = f(x) \wedge g(x)$. Given a set S, 2^S denotes the power set of S containing as elements all subsets of S. S^* denotes the set of finite sequences over S where each sequence element is of type S. A sequence σ of length N is a function of type: $\{n \in \mathbb{N} | n < N\} \rightarrow S$. The i'th element of a sequence is denoted $\sigma(i)$. We say that a value v is in σ, denoted by $v \in \sigma$ iff $\exists i \in \mathbb{N}$ such that $\sigma(i) = v$. Given a set S, by S^n for a given $n \in \mathbb{N}$ $(n \geq 2)$ we denote the tuple type: $S \times S \times \ldots \times S$ (n times).

Let $\mathcal{I}$ be a set of identifiers, and let $\mathcal{V}$ be a set of values, including strings, integers, and floating point numbers[1]. A *map* is a partial function from identifiers to values with a finite domain, that is, a function of type $\mathcal{I} \xrightarrow{m} \mathcal{V}$. We use $\mathbb{M}$ to denote the type of all maps. The empty map is denoted by $[\,]$. We denote by $\mathbb{M}_\perp$ the extension of $\mathbb{M}$ with a bottom element: $\mathbb{M}_\perp = \mathbb{M} \cup \{\perp\}$. Here $\perp$ represents a "no map" value.

An event is a timestamped named tuple of the type $\mathbb{E} = \mathcal{I} \times \mathbb{C} \times \mathbb{M}$. An element (id, t, M) of type $\mathbb{E}$ is written as $id(t, M)$. A trace is a sequence of events. The type of traces is denoted by $\mathbb{T}$ and is defined by $\mathbb{T} = \mathbb{E}^*$. In our context a trace corresponds to a telemetry stream.

3   Problem Statement

In this section, we briefly outline the requirements to our specification language. We first illustrate a concrete problem with an example. Subsequently, we outline the specific needs.

---

[1] $\mathcal{V}$ can be any set of values that are part of monitored events.

3.1 Illustrating Example

Consider the trace shown on the left part of Fig. 1, that we assume has been generated by a spacecraft[2]. The trace consists of a sequence of events, or EVent Reports (EVRs) as they are named in space mission operations, each with a name, a time stamp, and a list of parameters. The events in this particular trace represent such activities as a boot process starting, a boot process ending, downlink of data to ground, and operating the antenna and radio.

NAME	TIME	PARAMS			
DOWNLINK	10	size -> 430			
BOOT_S	42	count -> 3			
TURN_ANTENNA	80				
START_RADIO	90		*BOOT*		
DOWNLINK	100	size -> 420			
BOOT_E	160			*DBOOT*	*RISK*
STOP_RADIO	205				
BOOT_S	255	count -> 4			
START_RADIO	286		*BOOT*		
BOOT_E	312				
TURN_ANTENNA	412				

Fig. 1. An event trace and its abstractions

Our concern, in this case, is whether there is a downlink operation during a 5-min time interval where the flight computer reboots twice. This scenario could cause a potential loss of downlink information. Notice the use of the term *interval*. We need a form of interval notation. We suggest imposing a structure on the trace, where these intervals are named and highlighted, as shown on the right part of Fig. 1. Specifically, we want to identify the following intervals: A BOOT represents an interval during which the spacecraft software is rebooting. A DBOOT (double boot) represents an interval during which the spacecraft reboots twice within a 5-min timeframe. A RISK represents an interval during which the spacecraft reboots twice and at the same time also attempts to downlink information.

Our objective now is to formalize the definition of such intervals in a specification language. Specifically, in this case, we need a rule-based formalism for formally defining the following three intervals:

1. A BOOT interval starts with a BOOT_S (boot start) event and ends with a BOOT_E (boot end) event.
2. A DBOOT (double boot) interval consists of two consecutive BOOT intervals, with no more than 5-min from the start of the first BOOT interval to the end of the second BOOT interval.
3. A RISK interval is a DBOOT interval during which a DOWNLINK occurs.

---

[2] The trace is artificially constructed to have no resemblance to real artifacts.

3.2 Desired Features

The specification language should allow a user to:

1. **define intervals** as a composition of other intervals/events. For example to define the label BOOT as an interval delimited by the events BOOT_S and BOOT_E, or to define a DBOOT to be composed sequentially of two BOOT intervals.
2. **refer to time stamps** associated with events, as well as generate and later read start and end times of generated intervals. It should be possible to define complex time constraints.
3. **refer to data** associated with events, as well as generate and later read data of generated intervals using a rich expression language. For example, a generated interval may have a datum value defined as the sum of two lower-level interval data.

We believe that Allen's Temporal Logic (ATL) [2], specifically its operators for expressing temporal constraints on time intervals, is a good starting point. In ATL, a time interval represents an action or a system state taking place over a period. A time interval has a name, a start time, and an end time. ATL offers 13 mutually exclusive binary relations. Examples are: $Before(i, j)$ which holds iff interval i ends before interval j starts, and $During(i, j)$ which holds iff i starts strictly after j starts and ends before or when j ends, or i starts when or after j starts and ends strictly before j ends. An ATL formula is a conjunction[3] of such relationships, for example, $Before(A, B) \land Contains(B, C)$. A model is a set of intervals satisfying such a conjunction of constraints. ATL is typically used in planning for generating a plan (effectively a model) from a formula, but ATL can also be used for checking a model against a formula, as described in [20].

Our objective is different from planning and verification. Given a trace, we want to generate a model (a set of intervals), guided by a specification that we provide, that represents a layered view of the trace, and is used for system comprehension.

4 The nfer Notation

4.1 Intervals

Before we more formally introduce the **nfer** notation, we shall introduce some further basic semantic concepts. As already mentioned in Sect. 2, a telemetry stream (for example received from a spacecraft) is a sequence of events, also referred to as a trace. In contrast to most runtime verification systems, however, the **nfer** notation does not directly operate on such traces. Instead, it operates on a set of *intervals* (defined below). We will provide the definition and intuition behind intervals, and how a trace is converted into an initial set of intervals, on which **nfer** operates.

---

[3] A limited form of disjunction is also allowed but not described here.

An interval represents a named section of a trace, spanning a certain time period. An interval can carry data as well, using a map. Concretely, an *interval* is a 4-tuple of the form (η, t_1, t_2, M), where $\eta \in \mathcal{I}$ is an interval name, $t_1, t_2 \in \mathbb{C}$ are time stamps[4] representing the start and end time of the interval, satisfying the condition $t_1 \leq t_2$, and M is a map in $\mathbb{M}$, the data that the interval carries. The type of all intervals is denoted by $\mathbb{I}$.

A *pool* is a set of intervals, that is, an element of type $\mathbb{P} = 2^{\mathbb{I}}$. A trace τ is converted into an initial pool by a function *init* of type $\mathbb{T} \rightarrow \mathbb{P}$:

$$init(\tau) = \{ \ (\eta, t, t, M) \mid \eta(t, M) \ \in \ \tau \ \}$$

nfer subsequently transforms this initial pool of intervals to a pool containing as well all abstractions defined by the specification. In the following, we shall illustrate how such specifications are written.

4.2   Syntax of the nfer Notation

An nfer specification consists of a list of *labeling* rules of the form:

$$\eta \leftarrow \eta_1 \ \oplus \ \eta_2 \ \textbf{map} \ \Phi \tag{1}$$

where, $\eta, \eta_1, \eta_2 \in \mathcal{I}$ are identifiers, $\oplus : \mathbb{C}^6 \rightarrow \mathbb{B}$ is a *clock predicate* on six time stamps, and $\Phi : \mathbb{M} \times \mathbb{M} \rightarrow \mathbb{M}_\perp$ is a *map function* taking two maps and returning a map or $\perp$. The syntax contains mathematical functions to simplify the presentation.

The informal interpretation of such a rule is as follows. Given a pool π, the rule generates a set of new intervals (a pool), each of the form (η, s, e, M), provided that in π there exist two intervals (η_1, s_1, e_1, M_1) and (η_2, s_2, e_2, M_2), such that the time constraint defined by $\oplus$ is satisfied: $\oplus(s_1, e_1, s_2, e_2, s, e)$, and such that the map function Φ produces a well-defined map as a function of the maps of the two input intervals: $M = \Phi(M_1, M_2) \neq \perp$. Note that the $\oplus$ time constraint constrains the start time s and end time e of the result interval as well. Hence, one can control the time values of the generated interval.

The time constraint can, for example, express that one interval ends before the other interval starts ($e_1 < s_2$), which is one of the Allen operators. Likewise, the map function can check whether the input maps M_1 and M_2 satisfy certain conditions: if not return $\perp$, but if so, return a new map to be part of the generated interval. The time constraint must evaluate to true and the resulting map not be $\perp$ for the rule to apply.

As an example, the following rule generates an abstraction interval named BOOT from a BOOT_S (boot start) event that occurs before a BOOT_E (boot end) event, and furthermore carries the boot count contained in the BOOT_S interval:

$$\text{BOOT} \leftarrow \text{BOOT\_S} \ \oplus \ \text{BOOT\_E} \ \textbf{map} \ \Phi$$

---

[4] Time stamps have no specified units.

where the two functions $\oplus$ and Φ are defined as follows:

$$\oplus(s_1, e_1, s_2, e_2, s, e) = e_1 < s_2 \land s = s_1 \land e = e_2$$
$$\Phi(m_1, m_2) = [count \mapsto m_1(count)]$$

Note how the resulting interval's start time s is constrained to be the start time of the BOOT_S event, and likewise the end time e is constrained to be the end time of the BOOT_E event. Below, we introduce a pre-defined set of candidate functions for $\oplus$ inspired by Allen logic to make specifications easier to write, allowing us instead to write this rule as follows (with the same Φ function and **before** denoting the $\oplus$ function above):

$$\text{BOOT} \leftarrow \text{BOOT\_S before BOOT\_E map } \Phi$$

4.3   Semantics of the nfer Notation

The semantics is provided in two steps. First the semantics for the core notation is provided, second a collection of derived symbols (called operators) are defined, which map to the core notation.

Semantics of Core Notation. The semantics of the core notation is defined in three steps: the semantics R of individual rules on pools, the semantics S of a specification (a list of rules) on pools, and finally the semantics T of a specification on traces.

Let Δ be the type of rules. We define the semantics of labeling rules with the *interpretation* function R, with the type and definition below, and using the brackets $[\![\_]\!]$ around syntax being given semantics:

$$
\begin{aligned}
&R[\![\_]\!] \; : \; \Delta \to \mathbb{P} \to \mathbb{P} \\
&R[\![\eta \leftarrow \eta_1 \oplus \eta_2 \textbf{ map } \Phi]\!] \; \pi \; = \\
&\quad \{ \; (\eta, s, e, M) \in \mathbb{I} \; | \\
&\qquad\qquad \exists \; s_1, e_1, s_2, e_2 \in \mathbb{C} \; \bullet \; \exists \; J, K \in M \; \bullet \\
&\qquad\qquad (\eta_1, s_1, e_1, J) \in \pi \; \land \\
&\qquad\qquad (\eta_2, s_2, e_2, K) \in \pi \; \land \\
&\qquad\qquad \oplus(s_1, e_1, s_2, e_2, s, e) \; \land \\
&\qquad\qquad M = \Phi(J, K) \neq \bot \\
&\quad \}
\end{aligned}
$$

That is, given a rule δ and a pool π, a new pool is returned by: $R[\![\delta]\!]\pi$, containing (only) the new intervals generated. The definition reads as follows. A pool is returned containing intervals (η, s, e, M), where there exist two intervals in π, with names η_1 and η_2, and where the time constraint is satisfied, and the map resulting from applying Φ to the respective sub-maps is not $\bot$.

Next, we define the semantics of a list of rules, also referred to as a specification. For this we define the following one-step interpretation function S, which, given a set of rules and a pool, returns a new pool extending the input pool with added abstraction intervals resulting from taking the union of the pools generated by each rule:

$$S \, [\![\_]\!] \; : \; \Delta^* \to \mathbb{P} \to \mathbb{P}$$
$$S \, [\![\, \delta_1 \ldots \delta_n \,]\!] \; \pi \; = \; \pi \; \cup \; R \, [\![\, \delta_1 \,]\!] \; \pi \; \cup \; \ldots \cup \; R \, [\![\, \delta_n \,]\!] \; \pi$$

That is, given a specification $\delta_1 \ldots \delta_n$ and a pool π, a new pool is returned by: $S[\![\delta_1, \ldots, \delta_n]\!] \, \pi$. Finally, we define the semantics of a specification applied to a trace (a sequence of events). For this we define the interpretation function T, which given a list of rules and a trace returns a pool containing abstraction intervals:

$$T \, [\![\_]\!] \; : \; \Delta^* \to \mathbb{T} \to \mathbb{P}$$
$$T \, [\![\, \delta_1 \ldots \delta_n \,]\!] \; \tau \; =$$
$$\textbf{least } \pi \in \mathbb{P} \textbf{ such that}$$
$$init(\tau) \subseteq \pi$$
$$\wedge$$
$$\pi \; = \; S \, [\![\, \delta_1 \ldots \delta_n \,]\!] \, (\pi)$$

That is, given a specification $\delta_1 \ldots \delta_n$ and a trace τ, a pool of abstractions is returned by: $T[\![\delta_1, \ldots, \delta_n]\!] \tau$. The resulting pool is defined as the least fixed-point of $S[\![\delta_1 \ldots \delta_N]\!] : \mathbb{P} \to \mathbb{P}$ that includes $init(\tau)$, corresponding to repeatedly applying $S[\![\delta_1 \ldots \delta_N]\!]$, starting with $init(\tau)$, and until no new intervals are generated. Note that the least fixed-point exists since the semantic functions are monotonic. However, our simple iterative algorithm may not reach the least fixed-point if it is an infinite set. In practice, the **nfer** tool processes rules in a slightly different, but equivalent, order to improve performance.

4.4   Derived Forms

As hinted at the end of Sect. 4.2, a collection of $\oplus$ functions have been pre-defined, along with symbols (operators) denoting them. These symbols are shown in Table 1 together with their function definitions. Note that s_1 and e_1 are the start and end times for the left-hand interval, s_2 and e_2 are the start and end times for the right-hand interval, and s and e are the start and end times for the resulting interval. For all operators, except the **slice** operator, the start and end times of the resulting interval is the respectively left-most and right-most time stamps of the involved intervals. For the **slice** operator, the resulting time span denotes the overlapping section of two intervals. Note that the definitions of these operators differ from those of the Allen logic operators in [2], which are defined to be mutually exclusive, whereas **nfer**'s operators are not. This is due to our different practical needs.

The informal explanation of the operators is as follows: A **before** B: A ends before B starts; A **meet** B: A ends where B starts; A **during** B: all of A occurs during B; A **coincide** B: A and B occur at the exact same time; A **start** B:

Table 1. nfer operators

Operator $\oplus$	$\oplus(s_1, e_1, s_2, e_2, s, e)$
before	$e_1 < s_2 \land s = s_1 \land e = e_2$
meet	$e_1 = s_2 \land s = s_1 \land e = e_2$
during	$s_1 \geqslant s_2 \land e_1 \leqslant e_2 \land s = s_2 \land e = e_2$
coincide	$s = s_1 = s_2 \land e = e_1 = e_2$
start	$s = s_1 = s_2 \land e = \max(e_1, e_2)$
finish	$s = \min(s_1, s_2) \land e = e_1 = e_2$
overlap	$s_1 < e_2 \land s_2 < e_1 \land s = \min(s_1, s_2) \land e = \max(e_1, e_2)$
slice	$s_1 < e_2 \land s_2 < e_1 \land s = \max(s_1, s_2) \land e = \min(e_1, e_2)$

A starts at the same time as B; A **finish** B: A finishes at the same time as B; A **overlap** B: A and B overlap in time; A **slice** B: A and B overlap in time, and only the overlapping time span is returned. For the **before** operator, the nfer tool returns the shortest matching intervals, whereas the semantics specifies that all matching intervals are returned.

The next abbreviation concerns further time constraints a user may want to impose. The core rule notation, see (1) on page 5, allows for any time constraints to be expressed. Possible constraints include the just introduced relational operators, but also time spans, such as stating that an event B should follow an event A within 10 time units. We present the following shorthand for allowing the specification of additional time constraints in addition to the just introduced operators. Let $\odot \in \{\textbf{before}, \textbf{meet}, \textbf{during}, \textbf{coincide}, \textbf{start}, \textbf{finish}, \textbf{overlap}, \textbf{slice}\}$, and let $\odot_p$ denote the corresponding clock predicate. The following abbreviation is introduced:

$$\eta \leftarrow \eta_1 \odot \eta_2 \textbf{ within } \Theta \textbf{ map } \Phi$$

where $\Theta : \mathbb{C}^6 \rightarrow \mathbb{B}$ is a predicate on six time stamps. This is synonymous with:

$$\eta \leftarrow \eta_1 (\odot_p \land \Theta) \eta_2 \textbf{ map } \Phi$$

The one operator (clock predicate) rule format (1) on page 5 presents a simple notation with a clean semantics. However, further convenient syntax allows rules containing more than one operator on the right-hand side, for example: $A \leftarrow (B \textbf{ before } C) \textbf{ overlap } D$. Such rules are mapped into the core form resulting in additional auxiliary rules. The internal Scala DSL described in Sect. 5 allows such enriched rules. Note that we shall allow time constraints (**within**) and map transformations (**map**) to be left out in rules, in which case they assume the default function values respectively $\lambda s_1, e_1, s_2, e_2, s, e. \; true$ and $\lambda m_1, m_2. [\,]$.

4.5   Example

As an example, we will formalize the three rules that were informally stated in Sect. 3.1. The specification similarly consists of three rules:

BOOT ← BOOT_S **before** BOOT_E **map** (λ m_1,m_2 . [$count \mapsto m_1(count)$])

DBOOT ← BOOT **before** BOOT **within** (λ s_1,e_1,s_2,e_2,s,e . $e-s \leqslant 300$)
map snd

RISK ← DOWNLINK **during** DBOOT **map** snd

The rules should be mostly self-explanatory (time is assumed measured in seconds). The first rule creates from the two sub-maps m_1 and m_2 a new map, mapping count to the same value as in m_1. The function snd selects m_2 from a binary tuple (m_1, m_2).

Let us illustrate how this specification is evaluated on the trace in Fig. 1. This trace is first converted into an initial pool. The semantic S function on (page 7) will go through three iterations when applied to this initial pool before a fixed-point is reached. The added intervals in each iteration are as follows:

1 : { (BOOT, 42, 160, [$count \mapsto 3$]), (BOOT, 255, 312, [$count \mapsto 4$]) }
2 : { (DBOOT, 42, 312, [$count \mapsto 4$]) }
3 : { (RISK, 42, 312, [$count \mapsto 4$]) }

5   Implementation

In this section, we outline the **nfer** infrastructure and internal DSL, implemented in the Scala programming language.

5.1   The Nfer Infrastructure

The **nfer** implementation is based on Scala actors communicating via asynchronous message passing through a publish/subscribe model built with Apache Kafka [16]. Figure 2 shows the **nfer** implementation's internal configuration corresponding to the double boot example from Sect. 4.5. The Kafka publish/subscribe framework is represented in the center by the Shared Telemetry Bus. Each actor is represented by a circle, with arrows showing the messages that are passed to the actor (those it subscribes to), as well as the messages the actor publishes back.

Specifically, each rule in an **nfer** specification results in an actor, which subscribes to events/intervals occurring on the right-hand side of the rule, and publishes the interval mentioned on the left-hand side of the rule to the shared bus. This means that rule actors are only passed events and intervals which are pertinent to their execution. For example, the RISK actor subscribes to both DBOOT intervals and DOWNLINK events, and publishes back RISK intervals. A special actor receives messages from the spacecraft and publishes them to the bus. When a rule actor publishes an interval, any subscribers will be notified

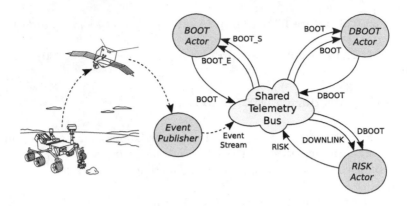

Fig. 2. Implementation of the example from Sect. 4.5

and can build on this interval to create yet new intervals. The `nfer` notation is declarative and the order in which rules are declared is unimportant. Likewise, the order in which actors execute is also unimportant, since the results of one actor cannot inhibit the behavior of any other actor. If the DSL offered a negation operator that would not be the case.

The implementation can process events *online*, as they come down to ground from the spacecraft, as well as events produced at an earlier point in time, and stored in a database. The full telemetry stream in principle includes all events from the start of the mission. Normally ground operators are only interested in recent events. However, there can be a need to analyze the telemetry stream from the start of the mission. It is not expedient to process all events in the full telemetry stream from the start of the mission whenever the `nfer` system is activated. Instead, `nfer` can be used to incrementally create intervals, which can then be stored for later use as an abstraction of the entire telemetry stream.

5.2 The Internal Scala DSL

This section introduces the internal Scala DSL for writing `nfer` specifications. Consider the double boot example written in the `nfer` notation in Sect. 4.5. This example can be written as follows in the internal DSL that we shall describe:

```
class DoubleBoot extends Nfer {
  "BOOT" :- ("BOOT_S" before "BOOT_E" map {
    case (m1,m2) => Map("count" -> m1("count"))
  })

  "DBOOT" :- ("BOOT" before "BOOT" within 300 map (_._2))

  "RISK" :- ("DOWNLINK" during "DBOOT" map (_._2))
}
```

The complete specification is a class, named DoubleBoot, that extends the Nfer class, which provides all the operators needed for writing rules. The specification in the DSL has largely the same format as the specification in our notation. Some differences include the use of the symbol :- instead of ←, and the map function defined using Scala's partial function **case**-notation. Also, note that the constant 300 is automatically lifted by an *implicit* function (defined in the Nfer class) into a predicate on six time stamps with the expected semantics. Each rule in turn is essentially a function call having the side-effect of creating an actor that subscribes and publishes on the shared telemetry bus. For example, the first rule corresponds to a function call (series of function calls really) that will create an actor, which consumes BOOT_S and BOOT_E events (represented as intervals) from the telemetry bus and returns BOOT intervals back to the bus. Although it does not look like a normal function call, it is equivalent to the following call:

```
liftRuleName("BOOT").:-(
  (liftOperand("BOOT_S").before(liftOperand("BOOT_E"))).map {
    case (m1,m2) ⇒ Map("count" → m1("count"))
  )
```

This equivalence holds due to Scala's features for defining domain-specific languages. First of all, Scala allows method names to be non-alphanumeric, as for example :−. Second, Scala allows the omission of dots and parentheses in calls of methods on objects. For example, "BOOT" :− (...) is just another way of writing "BOOT".:−(...). Finally, we notice that the method :− is called on the string object "BOOT". However, no such method is defined on strings. Scala's implicit function concept can again be used here to lift the "BOOT" string to an object which defines a :− method. The following function (defined in the Nfer class) is applied automatically by the Scala compiler to resolve the typing conflict, as shown above:

```
implicit def liftRuleName(s: String) = new {
  def :−(op: Op) = makeRules(s, op)
}
```

The right-hand side of the rule contains the expression: "BOOT_S" before "BOOT_E", which again is equivalent to: "BOOT_S".before("BOOT_E"), and again implicit lifting is needed. The following implicit function lifts "BOOT_S" to an object of type Op, on which methods like before are defined:

```
implicit def liftOperand(s: String) = new Op(s)
```

The Op class itself provides all the infix binary temporal operators, such as before, during, etc. as well as the functions within and map for defining time constraint and map functions (the latter two update variables holding these functions). Note how these functions return new instances of the Op class such that further infix binary methods can be applied in a chain-like manner.

```
case class Op(s : String, left : Op = null, right : Op = null, op: Fun = null)
{
  def before(e: Op) = Op(..., this, e, BEFORE)
```

```
def during(e: Op) = Op(..., this, e, DURING)
    ...
}
```

Each instantiation of the Op class takes two arguments and an operator defining how they should be related. For example, BEFORE is defined as follows:

```
def BEFORE(...) {
  makeRule(...,
    { case (i1: Interval, i2: Interval) ⇒ (i1.end < i2.start)},
    { case (i1: Interval, i2: Interval) ⇒ (i1.start, i2.end) })
}
```

The parameters to the makeRule function are (some dotted out): the name of the rule, two patterns (interval names essentially) that the generated actor subscribes to, the function evaluating the map, the function evaluating any added time constraints beyond the before, during, etc. constraints, and finally two functions (shown) defining respectively (1) the temporal operator, in this case an interval occurs before another if the end time of the first is less than the start time of the second, and (2) the boundary times of the generated interval as the start time of the first and the end time of the second.

6   Example Application to Warning Analysis

As noted earlier, we are currently applying the **nfer** tool to processing telemetry from the Curiosity rover. In this section, we briefly describe an application to a task, that is traditionally performed either manually or by ad-hoc scripts. We consider the problem of automatically labeling warning messages that are expected due to known idiosyncrasies of the system. EVRs produced by Curiosity are associated with a *severity* level, which is used to distinguish between expected and unexpected behavior. One of the severity levels is *WARNING*, which indicates potentially anomalous behavior. Unfortunately, due to various idiosyncrasies of hardware and software, there are several situations in which warning EVRs do not denote real anomalies. As a result, one of the roles of the ground operations team is to label those received warnings that are to be ignored; this work needs to be completed before the next plan can be uplinked to the spacecraft. To speed up analysis, we have implemented a set of rules that can label EVRs corresponding to known idiosyncrasies. As a result, ground operators can limit their attention to only unlabeled warning EVRs. We describe some of these rules below.

The first pair of rules capture a known (benign) race condition in the software caused by a thread reading from a shared buffer before another thread has finished its write. While race conditions can be serious, in this case, the effect is that the reading thread generates a warning, and ignores the data. Because the error was discovered late in the mission, and the impact is benign, no code fix was deemed necessary. The rule below looks for this known scenario by checking for an occurrence of TLM_TR_ERROR during execution of either a MOB_PRM or an

ARM_PRM command. A command execution interval itself is defined by a pair of
CMD_DISPATCH and CMD_COMPLETE events whose maps agree on the "cmd" key,
which denotes the command name.

```
"cmdExec" :− ("CMD_DISPATCH" before "CMD_COMPLETE" map {
    case (m1, m2) ⇒
        if (m1("cmd") == m2("cmd")) Some(Map("cmd" → m1("cmd"))) else None
})
```

```
"telecom0208" :− ("TLM_TR_ERROR" during "cmdExec" map {
    case (_ , m2) ⇒ if ((m2("cmd") == "MOB_PRM") || (m2("cmd") == "ARM_PRM"))
        Some(Map()) else None
})
```

The second rule involves a timing consideration. In this case, a power-on command fails and then recovers within 15 seconds. Since the behavior is predictable,
and benign, the two warnings about command failure and subsequent recovery
are labeled as expected. Note that for readability we have simplified the signature
of the delay15 function.

```
def delay15(s1,e1,s2,e2,s,e : Double): Boolean = e − s <= 15
```

```
"instCmdFail" :− ("INST_PWR_ON" before
    ("INST_CMD_FAIL" before "INST_RECOVER") within delay15)
```

As we illustrated in Sect. 5.2, this can be written more simply by just providing
15 as argument to the within function, which would have the same effect.

```
"instCmdFail" :− ("INST_PWR_ON" before
    ("INST_CMD_FAIL" before "INST_RECOVER") within 15)
```

The third set of rules labels a situation in which a warning about task starvation
is expected whenever the vdp activity overlaps with a communications activity
(labeled comm). In this case, we use the slice operator to identify the interval of
overlap between the vdp and comm intervals:

```
"comm" :− ("WIN_BEGIN" before "WIN_END" map {
    case (m1, _) ⇒ Map("wid" → m1("wid"))
})
```

```
"vdp" :− ("VDP_START" before "VDP_STOP")
```

```
"starvationOk" :− "TASK_STARVATION" during ("vdp" slice "comm")
```

7 Related Work

An earlier effort to develop a telemetry comprehension tool is described in [14],
which provided a Scala DSL for writing a subset of the specifications offered in
this paper. That work was inspired by yet earlier efforts using the rule-based
system LogFire [13] for analyzing telemetry streams, as described in [15]. Log-
Fire, however, offers a more traditional rule notation, which becomes verbose for

writing the desired specifications (similar to state machines being more verbose than regular expressions).

Interval logics are common in the planning domain. Allen formalized his algebra [2], which has come to be known as ATL, for modeling time intervals. He argued that it was necessary to model relative timing with significant imprecision, and proposed his algebra's use in planning systems [3]. Many other planning languages have been proposed which rely on these same concepts, including PDDL [18] and ANMLite [7].

The concepts introduced and formalized by these interval logics are useful for modeling telemetry data, but the languages themselves have been principally designed for planning, not verification. Some efforts have been made to adapt them to that role, however. An effort is described in [22], where the suitability of the ANMLite system for verification was evaluated, with some positive results, but it was ultimately concluded that the solver techniques were not yet mature enough to be useful. A translation from LTL to PDDL is described in [1] as a means to leverage PDDL's solver for verification.

Conversely, [20] defines a translation of a modified ATL to LTL for monitoring. It is concluded, however, that this approach is impractical since the generated monitoring automata become too large, even for small ATL formulas. Instead, they introduce a simple algorithm for that purpose using a state machine for each relationship. For example, a state machine is created for $Before(A, B)$, which is violated if a B is seen before an A. Our work differs in some respects: (i) Instead of monitoring ATL relationships for verification, we generate a relationship hierarchy for supporting system execution comprehension. (ii) We handle parameterized intervals. (iii) We allow any constraints on time and parameter values, not just the 13 ATL constraints. (iv) In their system, an interval is unique, while in nfer it can occur multiple times. Other interval logics have been designed specifically for verification purposes, such as Interval Temporal Logic (ITL) [19], the Duration Calculus (DC) [12], and Graphical Interval Logic (GIL) [9].

Our work has strong similarities to data-flow (data streaming) languages. A recent example is QRE [4], which is based on regular expressions, and offers a solution for computing numeric results from traces. QRE allows the use of regular programming to break up the stream for modular processing, but is limited in that the resulting sub-streams may only be used for computing a single quantitative result, and only using a limited set of numeric operations, such as sum, difference, minimum, maximum, and average, to achieve linear time (in the length of the trace) performance. Our approach is based on Allen logic, and instead of a numeric result produces a set of named intervals, useful for visualization (and thereby systems comprehension). Furthermore, data arguments to intervals can be computed using arbitrary functions.

RV systems have been developed which aggregate data as part of the verification [5,11]. Statistical model checking [17] is an approach collecting statistical information about the degree to which a specification is satisfied on multiple traces. Pushing statistical analysis further, in specification mining [10,21] the user provides no specification, and the system learns one by sampling nominal runs or by static analysis of the source code. This approach relieves the user of writing specifications and allows them to better understand the behavior of the software.

8   Conclusion

We have introduced the nfer rule-based notation and system for labeling event streams. The result of a labelling is a set of intervals: named sections of the event stream, each including a start time, and end time, and a map holding data selected from the events and sub-intervals making up the interval. Typically intervals are built on top of intervals, forming a hierarchy of abstractions. The result can for example be visualized, and can generally help engineers to better comprehend the structure of an event stream. The nfer system is implemented as an internal Scala DSL. Each interval-generating rule spawns an actor, that subscribes to events and/or sub-intervals, and publishes new intervals in the publish/subscribe architecture. Future work includes optimizing the implementation; handling missing telemetry; support for visual entering of rules and visualization of results; improving the internal Scala DSL; and allowing rules to be written in Python (commonly used by engineers) and encoded in JSON. The problem has been inspired by actual planetary space mission operations, specifically the Mars Curiosity rover, and the solution is being evaluated for use by the next Mars rover mission in 2020.

References

1. Albarghouthi, A., Baier, J.A., McIlraith, S.A.: On the use of planning technology for verification. In: Proceedings of the ICAPS Workshop on Verification and Validation of Planning and Scheduling Systems (VVPS). Citeseer (2009)
2. Allen, J.F.: Maintaining knowledge about temporal intervals. Commun. ACM **26**(11), 832–843 (1983)
3. Allen, J.F.: Towards a general theory of action and time. Artif. Intell. **23**(2), 123–154 (1984)
4. Alur, R., Fisman, D., Raghothaman, M.: Regular programming for quantitative properties of data streams. In: Thiemann, P. (ed.) ESOP 2016. LNCS, vol. 9632, pp. 15–40. Springer, Heidelberg (2016). doi:10.1007/978-3-662-49498-1_2
5. Basin, D., Harvan, M., Klaedtke, F., Zălinescu, E.: MONPOLY: monitoring usage-control policies. In: Khurshid, S., Sen, K. (eds.) RV 2011. LNCS, vol. 7186, pp. 360–364. Springer, Heidelberg (2012)
6. Bauer, A., Leucker, M., Schallhart, C.: The good, the bad, and the ugly, but how ugly is ugly? In: Sokolsky, O., Taşıran, S. (eds.) RV 2007. LNCS, vol. 4839, pp. 126–138. Springer, Heidelberg (2007)
7. Butler, R.W., Siminiceanu, R.I., Muno, C.: The ANMLite language and logic for specifying planning problems. Report No. 215088, 23681–2199 (2007)
8. Chen, F., Roşu, G.: MOP: an efficient and generic runtime verification framework. In: ACM SIGPLAN Notices, vol. 42, pp. 569–588. ACM (2007)

9. Dillon, L.K., Kutty, G., Moser, L.E., Melliar-Smith, P.M., Ramakrishna, Y.S.: A graphical interval logic for specifying concurrent systems. ACM Trans. Softw. Eng. Methodol. **3**, 131–165 (1994)
10. Ernst, M.D., Perkins, J.H., Guo, P.J., McCamant, S., Pacheco, C., Tschantz, M.S., Xiao, C.: The Daikon system for dynamic detection of likely invariants. Sci. Comput. Program. **69**(1), 35–45 (2007)
11. Finkbeiner, B., Sankaranarayanan, S., Sipma, H.: Collecting statistics over runtime executions. Formal Meth. Syst. Des. **27**(3), 253–274 (2005)
12. Hansen, M.R., Van Hung, D.: A theory of duration calculus with application. In: George, C.W., Liu, Z., Woodcock, J. (eds.) Domaine Modeling. LNCS, vol. 4710, pp. 119–176. Springer, Heidelberg (2007)
13. Havelund, K.: Rule-based runtime verification revisited. Softw. Tools Technol. Transf. (STTT) **17**, 143–170 (2015)
14. Havelund, K., Joshi, R.: Comprehension of spacecraft telemetry using hierarchical specifications of behavior. In: Merz, S., Pang, J. (eds.) ICFEM 2014. LNCS, vol. 8829, pp. 187–202. Springer, Heidelberg (2014)
15. Havelund, K., Joshi, R.: Experience with rule-based analysis of spacecraft logs. In: Artho, C., Ölveczky, P.C. (eds.) FTSCS 2014. CCIS, vol. 476, pp. 1–16. Springer, Heidelberg (2015)
16. Kreps, J., Narkhede, N., Rao, J.: Kafka: a distributed messaging system for log processing. In: Proceedings of the 6th International Workshop on Networking Meets Databases (NetDB 2011), pp. 1–7. ACM (2011)
17. Legay, A., Delahaye, B., Bensalem, S.: Statistical model checking: an overview. In: Barringer, H., Falcone, Y., Finkbeiner, B., Havelund, K., Lee, I., Pace, G., Roşu, G., Sokolsky, O., Tillmann, N. (eds.) RV 2010. LNCS, vol. 6418, pp. 122–135. Springer, Heidelberg (2010)
18. McDermott, D., Ghallab, M., Howe, A., Knoblock, C., Ram, A., Veloso, M., Weld, D., Wilkins, D.: PDDL-the planning domain definition language (1998)
19. Moszkowski, B.C.: A temporal logic for multilevel reasoning about hardware. IEEE Comput. **18**, 10–19 (1985)
20. Roşu, G., Bensalem, S.: Allen linear (interval) temporal logic–translation to LTL and monitor synthesis. In: Ball, T., Jones, R.B. (eds.) CAV 2006. LNCS, vol. 4144, pp. 263–277. Springer, Heidelberg (2006)
21. Shoham, S., Yahav, E., Fink, S.J., Pistoia, M.: Static specification mining using automata-based abstractions. IEEE Trans. Softw. Eng. **34**(5), 651–666 (2008)
22. Siminiceanu, R.I., Butler, R.W., Muñoz, C.A.: Experimental evaluation of a planning language suitable for formal verification. In: Peled, D.A., Wooldridge, M.J. (eds.) MoChArt 2008. LNCS, vol. 5348, pp. 132–146. Springer, Heidelberg (2009)

Accelerated Runtime Verification of LTL Specifications with Counting Semantics

Ramy Medhat[2]($\boxtimes$), Borzoo Bonakdarpour[1], Sebastian Fischmeister[2], and Yogi Joshi[2]

[1] McMaster University, Hamilton, Canada
[2] University of Waterloo, Waterloo, Canada
rmedhat@uwaterloo.ca

Abstract. This paper presents a novel and efficient parallel algorithm for runtime verification of an extension of LTL that allows for nested quantifiers subject to numerical constraints. Such constraints are useful in evaluating thresholds (e.g., expected uptime of a web server). Our algorithm uses the *MapReduce* programming model to split a program trace into variable-based clusters at run time. Each cluster is then mapped to its respective monitor instances, verified, and reduced collectively on a multi-core CPU or the GPU. Our experiments on real-world case studies show that the algorithm imposes negligible monitoring overhead.

1 Introduction

Runtime verification (RV) is an automated specification-based technique, where a *monitor* evaluates the correctness of a set of logical properties on a particular execution. RV complements exhaustive approaches such as model checking and theorem proving and under-approximated methods such as testing. RV can be particularly helpful in scenarios, where one needs to monitor parametric requirements on types of execution entities (e.g., processes and threads), user- and kernel-level events and objects (e.g., locks, files, sockets), web services (e.g., requests and responses), and network traffic. For example, the requirement 'every open file should eventually be closed' specifies a rule for causal and temporal order of opening and closing individual objects which generalizes to *all* files. Such properties can become even more complex by incorporating numerical constraints such as thresholds, floors, ceilings. However, to our knowledge existing RV frameworks fall short in expressing counting semantics.

In this paper, we extend the 4-valued semantics of LTL (denoted RV-LTL in this paper) [6] by adding counting semantics with numerical constraints and propose an efficient parallel algorithm for their verification at run time. Inspired by the work in [15], the syntax of our language (denoted LTL_4-C) extends LTL syntax by the addition of *counting quantifiers*. That is, we introduce two quantifiers: the *instance counting quantifier* ($\mathbb{E}$) which allows expressing properties that reason about the number of satisfied or violated instances, and the *percentage counting quantifier* ($\mathbb{A}$) which allows reasoning about the percentage of satisfied

© Springer International Publishing AG 2016
Y. Falcone and C. Sanchez (Eds.): RV 2016, LNCS 10012, pp. 251–267, 2016.
DOI: 10.1007/978-3-319-46982-9_16

or violated instances out of all instances in a trace. These quantifiers are sub-scripted with numerical constraints to express the conditions used to evaluate the count. For example, the following LTL_4-C formula:

$$\mathbb{A}_{\geq 0.95}\, s : \mathsf{socket}(s) \cdot (\mathbf{G}\,\mathsf{receive}\,(s) \Rightarrow \mathbf{F}\,\mathsf{respond}\,(s))$$

intends to express the property that 'at least 95 % of TCP/UDP sockets must eventually respond to a received request'. For a web admin, ideally the number of dropped requests is zero, however in reality requests will be dropped some-times [19]. Thus it is beneficial for a monitor to keep track of the percentage of dropped requests and fire an alert once a certain threshold is exceeded.

The first contribution of the paper is extending RV-LTL by redefining pre-sumably true/false within the context of counting semantics. Consider the exam-ple demonstrated above, where it is required that a web server drops less than 5 % of the requests. For such a property, counting semantics justify the need for presumably true/false in a similar fashion to incomplete executions in RV-LTL. For instance, if only 4 % of the requests have been dropped so far, that does not mean that the property is permanently satisfied. There could be more requests that arrive in the future and are dropped, increasing the percentage of dropped requests beyond 5 %. A verdict of true is incorrect, since the property can be violated in the future. In LTL_4-C, this property is presumably satisfied, with a potential to be violated by more requests. For a web admin, this verdict indicates that the system is currently healthy.

The second contribution of this paper is a divide-and-conquer-based online monitor generation technique for LTL_4-C specifications. Our technique first synthesizes an RV-LTL monitor for the inner LTL formula of the given LTL_4-C formula at pre-compile time using the technique in [6]. Then, based upon the values of variables observed at run time, submonitors are generated and merged to compute the current truth value of a property for the current program trace.

Our third contribution is a monitoring algorithm that implements the above approach for verification of LTL_4-C properties at run time. The monitoring algorithm evaluates properties in parallel, utilizing multicore CPUs or GPUs and maximizing the throughput of the monitor. The algorithm utilizes the popular *MapReduce* programming model to (1) spawn submonitors that aim at eval-uating subformulas using partial quantifier elimination, and (2) merge partial evaluations to compute the current truth value of properties.

Our parallel algorithm for verification of LTL_4-C properties is fully imple-mented on multi-core CPU and GPU technologies using our own simple imple-mentation of the MapReduce programming model. We report experimental results by conducting three real-world independent case studies. The first case study is a monitor for HTTP requests and responses on an Apache Web Server. The second case study is a monitor for upload chunk size based on a dataset for profiling DropBox traffic. The third case study monitors a network proxy cache to reduce the bandwidth usage of online video services, based on a YouTube request dataset. We present performance results comparing single-core CPU, multi-core CPU, and GPU implementations. Our results show that our GPU-based imple-mentation provides an average speed up of 6.3x when compared to single-core

CPU, and 1.75x when compared to multi-core CPU. The CPU utilization of the GPU-based implementation is negligible compared to multi-core CPU, freeing up the system to perform more computation. Thus, the GPU-based implementation manages to provide competitive speedup while maintaining a low CPU utilization, which are two goals that the CPU cannot achieve at the same time. Put it another way, the GPU-based implementation incurs minimal monitoring costs while maintaining a high throughput.

2   LTL with Counting Semantics

Let IP be a finite set of interpreted predicates, and let $\Sigma = 2^{IP}$ be the power set of IP. We call each element of Σ an *event*.

Definition 1 (Trace). *A trace $w = w_0 w_1 \cdots$ is a finite or infinite sequence of events where each event consists of interpreted predicates; i.e., $w_i \in \Sigma$, for all $i \geq 0$.* ∎

We denote the set of all infinite traces by Σ^ω and the set of all finite traces by Σ^*.

2.1   Syntax of LTL4-C

LTL$_4$−C extends RV-LTL [6] (also known as RV-LTL) with two counting quantifiers: the instance counting quantifier ($\mathbb{E}$) and the percentage counting quantifier ($\mathbb{A}$). The semantics of these quantifiers are introduced in Subsect. 2.4. The syntax of LTL$_4$−C is defined as follows:

Definition 2 (LTL$_4$–C Syntax). LTL$_4$−C *formulas are defined using the following grammar:*

$$\varphi ::= \mathbb{A}_{\sim k} \, x : p(x) \cdot \varphi \mid \mathbb{E}_{\sim l} \, x : p(x) \cdot \varphi \mid \psi$$
$$\psi ::= \top \mid a \mid p(x_1 \cdots x_n) \mid \neg\psi \mid \psi_1 \wedge \psi_2 \mid \mathbf{X}\,\psi \mid \psi_1 \, \mathbf{U} \, \psi_2$$

where $\mathbb{A}$ is the percentage counting quantifier, $\mathbb{E}$ is the instance counting quantifier, x, $x_1 \cdots x_n$ are variables with finite domains $\mathcal{D}, \mathcal{D}_1, \cdots \mathcal{D}_n$, $\sim \in \{<, \leq, >, \geq, =\}$, $k : \mathbb{R} \in [0,1]$, $l \in \mathbb{Z}^+$, a is an atomic proposition, $\mathbf{X}$ is the next, and $\mathbf{U}$ is the until temporal operators. ∎

If we omit the numerical constraint in $\mathbb{A}_{\sim k}$ (respectively, $\mathbb{E}_{\sim l}$), we mean $\mathbb{A}_{=1}$ (respectively, $\mathbb{E}_{\geq 1}$). The syntax of LTL$_4$−C forces constructing formulas, where a string of counting quantifiers is followed by a quantifier-free formula. We emphasize that $\mathbb{A}$ and $\mathbb{E}$ do not necessarily resemble standard first order quantifiers $\forall$ and $\exists$. In fact, $\neg\mathbb{A}$ and $\mathbb{E}$ are not equivalent.

Consider the LTL$_4$−C property $\varphi = \mathbb{A}x : p(x) \cdot \psi$, where the domain of x is $\mathcal{D}$. This property denotes that for any possible valuation of the variable x ($[x := v]$), if $p(v)$ holds, then ψ should hold. If $p(v)$ does not hold, then $p(v) \cdot \psi$

evaluates to true. This effectively means that the quantifier $\mathbb{A}x$ is in fact applied only over the sub-domain $\{v \in \mathcal{D} \mid p(v)\} \subseteq \mathcal{D}$.

To give an intuition, consider the scenarios where file management anomalies can cause serious problems at run time (e.g., in NASA's Spirit Rover on Mars in 2004). For example, the following $\text{LTL}_4{-}\text{C}$ property expresses "at least half of the files that a process has previously opened must be closed":

$$\varphi = \mathbb{A}_{\geq 50\%} f : \mathsf{inevent}(f) \cdot \mathbf{G}(\mathsf{opened}(f) \mathbf{U} \mathsf{close}(f)) \tag{1}$$

where inevent is the p predicate of the quantifier, denoting that the concrete file appeared in an event in the trace.

2.2   Truth Values of LTL4-C

The objective of $\text{LTL}_4{-}\text{C}$ is to verify the correctness of quantified properties at run time with respect to finite program traces. Such verification attempts to produce a sound verdict regardless of future continuations.

Similar to RV-LTL, we incorporate four truth values to define the semantics of $\text{LTL}_4{-}\text{C}$: $\mathbb{B}_4 = \{\top, \bot, \top_p, \bot_p\}$; *true, false, presumably true,* and *presumably false,* respectively. The values in $\mathbb{B}_4$ form a lattice ordered as follows: $\bot < \bot_p < \top_p < \top$. Given a finite trace u and an $\text{LTL}_4{-}\text{C}$ property φ, the informal description of evaluation of u with respect to φ is as follows:

- **True** ($\top$) denotes that any infinite extension of u satisfies φ. For example, $\varphi_1 = \mathbb{E}_{\geq 1}t : \mathsf{thread}(t) \cdot \mathsf{log}(t)$ is a property that checks a process has at least one log thread. If one log thread is found in the trace, the property is permanently satisfied.
- **False** ($\bot$) denotes that any infinite extension of u violates φ. For example, $\varphi_2 = \mathbb{E}_{=1}t : \mathsf{thread}(t) \cdot \mathsf{log}(t)$ is a property that checks a process has *exactly* one log thread. If more than one log thread is found in the trace, the property is permanently violated.
- **Presumably true** ($\top_p$) extends the definition of *presumably true* in RV-LTL [6], where $\top_p$ denotes that u satisfies the inner LTL property and the counting quantifier constraint in φ, if the program terminates after execution of u. An example is

$$\varphi_3 = \mathbb{E}_{\geq 1}t : \mathsf{thread}(t) \cdot \mathsf{log}(t) \wedge \mathbf{G}(\mathsf{event}(t) \Rightarrow \mathbf{F}\mathsf{write}(t))$$

which evaluates to $\top_p$ if there is only one log thread that has received an event and has written it, but can still potentially receive another event and never write it, thus violating the property.
- **Presumably false** ($\bot_p$) extends the definition of *presumably false* in RV-LTL [6], which denotes that u presumably violates the quantifier constraint in φ. For example, Property φ_3 evaluates to $\bot_p$ if there is one log thread that has received an event and not yet written it. A future extension of the trace can potentially contain a write event, thus transforming the valuation of the property to $\top_p$.

2.3   Valuation in LTL₄−C

An $\mathrm{LTL_4-C}$ property essentially defines a set of traces, where each trace is a sequence of events (i.e., sets of predicates). We define the semantics of $\mathrm{LTL_4-C}$ with respect to finite traces and present a method of utilizing these semantics for runtime verification. In the context of runtime verification, the objective is to ensure that a trace is in the set of traces that the property defines.

To introduce the semantics of $\mathrm{LTL_4-C}$, we examine counting quantifiers further. Since the syntax of $\mathrm{LTL_4-C}$ allows nesting of counting quantifiers, a canonical form of properties is $\varphi = \mathbb{Q}_\varphi \, \psi$ where ψ is an LTL property and $\mathbb{Q}_\varphi$ is a sequence of counting quantifiers $\mathbb{Q}_\varphi = \mathcal{Q}_0 \mathcal{Q}_1 \cdots \mathcal{Q}_{n-1}$ such that each $\mathcal{Q}_i = \langle q_i, \sim_i, c_i, x_i, p_i \rangle$, $0 \le i \le n-1$, is a tuple encapsulating the counting quantifier information. That is, $q_i \in \{\mathbb{A}, \mathbb{E}\}$, $\sim_i \in \{<, \le, >, \ge, =\}$, c_i is the constraint constant, x_i is the bound variable, and p_i is the predicate within the quantifier (see Definition 2).

Variable Valuation. We define a vector D_φ with respect to a property φ as $D_\varphi = \langle d_0, d_1, \cdots, d_{n-1} \rangle$ where $n = |\mathbb{Q}_\varphi|$ and d_i, $0 \le i \le n-1$, is a value for variable x_i. We denote the first m components of the vector D_φ (i.e., $\langle d_0, d_1, \cdots, d_{m-1} \rangle$) by $D_\varphi|^m$. We refer to D_φ as a *value vector* and to $D_\varphi|^m$ as a *partial value vector*.

A *property instance* $\hat{\varphi}(D_\varphi|^m)$ is obtained by replacing every occurrence of the variables $x_0 \cdots x_{m-1}$ in φ with the values $d_0 \cdots d_{m-1}$, respectively. Thus, $\hat{\varphi}(D_\varphi|^m)$ is free of quantifiers of index less than m, yet remains quantified over variables $x_m \cdots x_{n-1}$. $\hat{\varphi}(D_\varphi)$ denotes replacing all quantified variables with values in D_φ, resulting in an unquantified LTL property. For instance, for the following property $\varphi = \mathbb{A}_{>c_1} \, x : p_x(x) \cdot (\mathbb{A}_{<c_2} \, y : p_y(y) \cdot \mathbf{G} \, q(x, y))$ and value vector $D_\varphi = \langle 1, 2 \rangle$ (i.e., the vector of values for variables x and y, respectively), $\hat{\varphi}(D_\varphi)$ will be $\hat{\varphi}(\langle 1, 2 \rangle) = p_x(1) \cdot (p_y(2) \cdot \mathbf{G} \, q(1, 2)) = \mathbf{G} \, q(1, 2)$.

We now define the set $\mathbb{D}_{\varphi,u}$ as the set of all value vectors with respect to a property $\varphi = \mathbb{Q}_\varphi \, \psi$ and a trace $u = u_0 u_1 \cdots$:

$$\mathbb{D}_{\varphi,u} = \{ D_\varphi \mid \exists j \ge 0 : \forall i \in [0, |\mathbb{Q}_\varphi|) : p_i(d_i) \in u_j \} \qquad (2)$$

Valuation of Property Instances. As per the definition of $\mathbb{D}_{\varphi,u}$, every value vector $D_\varphi = \langle d_0 \cdots d_{n-1} \rangle$ in $\mathbb{D}_{\varphi,u}$ contains values for which the predicates $p_i(d_i)$ hold in some trace event u_j. For simplicity, we denote this as a value vector *in* a trace event u_j. These value vectors can possibly be in multiple and interleaved events in the trace. Thus, we define a trace $u^{D_\varphi} = u_0^{D_\varphi} u_1^{D_\varphi} \cdots$ as a subsequence of the trace u such that the value vector D_φ is in every event:

$$\forall j \ge 0 : \forall i \in [0, n-1] : p_i(d_i) \in u_j^{D_\varphi}$$

2.4   Semantics of LTL4-C

Definition 3 (LTL₄–C **Satisfaction Relation**). *Given an* $\mathrm{LTL_4-C}$ *property* $\varphi = \mathcal{Q} \, \psi$ *where* $\mathcal{Q}$ *is a quantifier (either* $\mathbb{A}$ *or* $\mathbb{E}$*), and* ψ *is an* $\mathrm{LTL_4-C}$ *formula.*

Also, given an infinite trace w, we define the satisfaction relation $w \models_4 \varphi$ as follows:

$$w \models_4 \psi \quad \textit{iff } w \models \psi \textit{ and } \psi \textit{ is an LTL property}$$

$$w \models_4 \mathbb{E}_{\sim c}x : p_x(x) \cdot \psi \quad \textit{iff } \exists \mathbb{D}'_{\varphi,w} \subset \mathbb{D}_{\varphi,w} \textit{ s.t. } \forall D_\varphi \in \mathbb{D}'_{\varphi,w} : w^{D_\varphi} \models \hat{\varphi}(D_\varphi) \wedge$$
$$\forall D_\varphi \notin \mathbb{D}'_{\varphi,w} : w^{D_\varphi} \not\models \hat{\varphi}(D_\varphi) \wedge |\mathbb{D}'_{\varphi,w}| \sim c$$

$$w \models_4 \mathbb{A}_{\sim c}x : p_x(x) \cdot \psi \quad \textit{iff } \exists \mathbb{D}'_{\varphi,w} \subset \mathbb{D}_{\varphi,w} \textit{ s.t. } \forall D_\varphi \in \mathbb{D}'_{\varphi,w} : w^{D_\varphi} \models \hat{\varphi}(D_\varphi) \wedge$$
$$\forall D_\varphi \notin \mathbb{D}'_{\varphi,w} : w^{D_\varphi} \not\models \hat{\varphi}(D_\varphi) \wedge |\mathbb{D}'_{\varphi,w}|/|\mathbb{D}_{\varphi,w}| \sim c$$

where $\mathbb{D}_{\varphi,w}$ is the finite set of all value vectors in the infinite trace w. $\hat{\varphi}(D_\varphi)$ is an LTL property and $\models$ is the satisfaction relation as defined in LTL semantics.

Definition 4 (LTL$_4$–C Semantics for finite prefixes). *Given an LTL$_4$–C property $\varphi = \mathcal{Q}_{\sim c} \psi$ where $\mathcal{Q}$ is a quantifier and ψ is an LTL$_4$–C formula. Also, given a finite prefix u of a trace, LTL$_4$–C semantics are defined as follows:*

$$[u \models_4 \varphi] = \begin{cases}
[u \models_{\text{RV-LTL}} \varphi] & \textit{iff } \varphi \textit{ is an LTL property} \\[4pt]
\top & \textit{iff } \exists \mathbb{D}'_{\varphi,u} \subset \mathbb{D}_{\varphi,u} \textit{ s.t.} \\
& \quad \forall D_\varphi \in \mathbb{D}'_{\varphi,u} : [u^{D_\varphi} \models_4 \hat{\varphi}(D_\varphi)] = \top \wedge \\
& \quad \forall D_\varphi \notin \mathbb{D}'_{\varphi,u} : [u^{D_\varphi} \models_4 \hat{\varphi}(D_\varphi)] \neq \top \wedge \\
& \quad |\mathbb{D}'_{\varphi,u}| \sim c \textit{ if } \mathcal{Q} = \mathbb{E} \textit{ else } |\mathbb{D}'_{\varphi,u}|/|\mathbb{D}_{\varphi,u}| \sim c \wedge \\
& \quad \forall v \in \Sigma^\omega : uv \models_4 \varphi \\[4pt]
\bot & \textit{iff } \exists \mathbb{D}'_{\varphi,u} \subset \mathbb{D}_{\varphi,u} \textit{ s.t.} \\
& \quad \forall D_\varphi \in \mathbb{D}'_{\varphi,u} : [u^{D_\varphi} \models_4 \hat{\varphi}(D_\varphi)] \neq \bot \wedge \\
& \quad \forall D_\varphi \notin \mathbb{D}'_{\varphi,u} : [u^{D_\varphi} \models_4 \hat{\varphi}(D_\varphi)] = \bot \wedge \\
& \quad |\mathbb{D}'_{\varphi,u}| \not\sim c \textit{ if } \mathcal{Q} = \mathbb{E} \textit{ else } |\mathbb{D}'_{\varphi,u}|/|\mathbb{D}_{\varphi,u}| \not\sim c \wedge \\
& \quad \forall v \in \Sigma^\omega : uv \not\models_4 \varphi \\[4pt]
\top_p & \textit{iff } \exists \mathbb{D}'_{\varphi,u} \subset \mathbb{D}_{\varphi,u} \textit{ s.t.} \\
& \quad \forall D_\varphi \in \mathbb{D}'_{\varphi,u} : [u^{D_\varphi} \models_4 \hat{\varphi}(D_\varphi)] \in \{\top, \top_p\} \wedge \\
& \quad \forall D_\varphi \notin \mathbb{D}'_{\varphi,u} : [u^{D_\varphi} \models_4 \hat{\varphi}(D_\varphi)] \notin \{\top, \top_p\} \wedge \\
& \quad |\mathbb{D}'_{\varphi,u}| \sim c \textit{ if } \mathcal{Q} = \mathbb{E} \textit{ else } |\mathbb{D}'_{\varphi,u}|/|\mathbb{D}_{\varphi,u}| \sim c \wedge \\
& \quad \exists v \in \Sigma^\omega : uv \not\models_4 \varphi \\[4pt]
\bot_p & \textit{iff } \exists \mathbb{D}'_{\varphi,u} \subset \mathbb{D}_{\varphi,u} \textit{ s.t.} \\
& \quad \forall D_\varphi \in \mathbb{D}'_{\varphi,u} : [u^{D_\varphi} \models_4 \hat{\varphi}(D_\varphi)] \in \{\top, \top_p\} \wedge \\
& \quad \forall D_\varphi \notin \mathbb{D}'_{\varphi,u} : [u^{D_\varphi} \models_4 \hat{\varphi}(D_\varphi)] \notin \{\top, \top_p\} \wedge \\
& \quad |\mathbb{D}'_{\varphi,u}| \not\sim c \textit{ if } \mathcal{Q} = \mathbb{E} \textit{ else } |\mathbb{D}'_{\varphi,u}|/|\mathbb{D}_{\varphi,u}| \not\sim c \wedge \\
& \quad \exists v \in \Sigma^\omega : uv \models_4 \varphi
\end{cases}$$

The semantics are defined for five cases:

- If φ is an LTL property, then we use the four-valued semantics in RV-LTL.
- Let $\mathbb{D}'_{\varphi,u}$ be a subset that contains all values of the quantified variable that satisfy the inner property. If the cardinality of this subset satisfies the numerical constraint on the quantifier, and no infinite extension of the trace can violate it, the valuation is $\top$.
- Now, let $\mathbb{D}'_{\varphi,u}$ contain all values for which the inner property is not $\bot$, i.e. it could be $\top$, $\top_p$, or $\bot_p$. If the cardinality of this subset violates the numerical constraint on the quantifier, and no infinite extension of the trace can satisfy it, the valuation is $\bot$.
- $\top_p$ is similar to $\top$, except that $\mathbb{D}'_{\varphi,u}$ can include values with which the inner property evaluates to $\top_p$, and there exists an extension to the trace prefix that can violate the quantifier constraint.
- $\bot_p$ is the opposite of $\top_p$, where $\mathbb{D}'_{\varphi,u}$ violates the quantifier constraint, and there exists an extension to the trace prefix that can satisfy the constraint.

Note that LTL_4-C semantics are defined recursively from the outermost quantifier. The recursion can be observed in $[u^{D_\varphi} \models_4 \hat{\varphi}(D_\varphi)]$ where D_φ is a value vector $\langle d \rangle$ for the quantified variable in $\mathcal{Q}$, and $\hat{\varphi}(D_\varphi)$ is property φ without quantifier $\mathcal{Q}$. Hence, the semantics recurse with one less quantifier at each step until there are no counting quantifiers and φ is an LTL property, at which case we use RV-LTL semantics. Also note that for a finite prefix of a trace, the semantics of LTL_4-C is decidable since the quantification is over a finite set of objects that exist in the trace.

3   Divide-and-Conquer-based Monitoring of LTL4-C

In this section, we describe our technique inspired by divide-and-conquer for evaluating LTL_4-C properties at run time. This approach forms the basis of our parallel verification algorithm in Sect. 4.

Unlike runtime verification of propositional RV-LTL properties, where the structure of a monitor is determined solely based on the property itself, a monitor for an LTL_4-C needs to evolve at run time, since the valuation of quantified variables change over time. More specifically, the monitor $\mathcal{M}_\varphi$ for an LTL_4-C property $\varphi = \mathcal{Q}_\varphi \psi$ relies on instantiating a *submonitor* for each property instance $\hat{\varphi}$ obtained at run time. We incorporate two type of submonitors: (1) RV-LTL *submonitors* evaluate the inner LTL property ψ. An RV-LTL submonitor instance is denoted as $\mathcal{M}^*_{D_\varphi}$, where D_φ is the unique value vector that binds all quantified variables in the property, leaving only a simple LTL property to be monitored. (2) The second time of submonitors is *quantifier submonitors*, described in Subsect. 3.1. In Subsect. 3.2, we explain the conditions under which a submonitor is instantiated at run time. Finally, in Subsect. 3.3, we elaborate on how submonitors evaluate an LTL_4-C property.

3.1   Quantifier Submonitors

Given a finite trace u and an $\textsc{Ltl}_4-\textsc{C}$ property $\varphi = \mathbb{Q}_\varphi \psi$, a *quantifier submonitor* $(\mathcal{M}^{\mathbb{Q}})$ is a monitor responsible for determining the valuation of a property instance $\hat\varphi(D_\varphi|^i)$ with respect to a trace subsequence $u^{D_\varphi|^i}$, if $i < |\mathbb{Q}_\varphi|$.

Definition 5 (Quantifier Submonitor). *Let* $\varphi = \mathbb{Q}_\varphi \psi$ *be an* $\textsc{Ltl}_4-\textsc{C}$ *property and* $\hat\varphi(D_\varphi|^i)$ *be a property instance, with* $i \in [0, |\mathbb{Q}_\varphi| - 1]$. *The quantifier submonitor for* $\hat\varphi(D_\varphi|^i)$ *is the tuple* $\mathcal{M}^{\mathbb{Q}}_{D_\varphi|^i} = \langle \mathcal{Q}_i, \mathbb{M}_{D_\varphi|^i}, \mathcal{F} \rangle$, *where*

- $\mathcal{Q}_i$ *encapsulates the quantifier information (see Subsect. 2.4)*
- $\mathbb{M}_{D_\varphi|^i}$ *is the set of child submonitors (submonitors of child property instances) defined as follows:*

$$\mathbb{M}_{D_\varphi|^i} = \begin{cases} \{\mathcal{M}^*_{D'_\varphi} \mid D'_\varphi|^i = D_\varphi|^i\} & \textit{if } i = |\mathbb{Q}_\varphi| - 1 \\ \{\mathcal{M}^{\mathbb{Q}}_{D'_\varphi|^{i+1}} \mid D'_\varphi|^i = D_\varphi|^i\} & \textit{if } i < |\mathbb{Q}_\varphi| - 1 \end{cases}$$

- $\mathcal{F}$ *is a function that applies the quantifier constraint* $\mathcal{Q}_i$ *on the truth values of all the child submonitors* $\mathbb{M}_{D_\varphi|^i}$.

Thus, if $i = |\mathbb{Q}_\varphi| - 1$, *all child submonitors are* RV-$\textsc{Ltl}$ *submonitors. Otherwise, they are quantifier submonitors of the respective child property instances.* ∎

3.2   Instantiating Submonitors

Let an $\textsc{Ltl}_4-\textsc{C}$ monitor $\mathcal{M}_\varphi$ for property φ evaluate the property with respect to a finite trace $u = u_0 u_1 \cdots$. Let $D_\varphi = \langle d_0, d_1, \cdots \rangle$ be a value vector and u_0 the first trace event such that $\forall d_i : p_i(d_i) \in u_0$. In this case, the $\textsc{Ltl}_4-\textsc{C}$ monitor instantiates submonitors for every property instance resulting from that value vector. A value vector of length $|\mathbb{Q}_\varphi|$ results in $|\mathbb{Q}_\varphi| + 1$ prop-

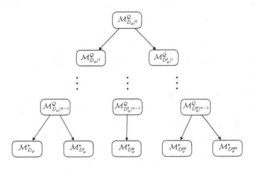

Fig. 1. Tree structure of an $\textsc{Ltl}_4-\textsc{C}$ monitor

erty instances: one for each quantifier in addition to an RV-$\textsc{Ltl}$ inner property. Figure 1 demonstrates the tree structure of submonitors graphically.

3.3   Evaluating LTL4-C Properties

Once the $\textsc{Ltl}_4-\textsc{C}$ monitor instantiates its submonitors, every submonitor is responsible for updating its truth value. The truth value of an RV-$\textsc{Ltl}$ submonitor $(\mathcal{M}^*)$ is determined by its automaton. Quantifier submonitors update their truth value by applying the quantifier constraint on their child submonitors and producing a valuation based on $\textsc{Ltl}_4-\textsc{C}$ semantics.

4   Parallel RV Algorithm

The main challenge in designing a runtime monitor is to ensure that its behavior does not intervene with functional and extra-functional (e.g., timing constraints) behavior of the program under scrutiny. This section presents a parallel algorithm for verification of LTL_4-C properties. Our idea is that such a parallel algorithm enables us to offload the monitoring tasks into a different computing unit (e.g., the GPU). The algorithm utilizes the *MapReduce* programming model to spawn and merge submonitors to determine the final verdict. It is important to note that the algorithm supports both online and offline monitoring. We generalize the input to the algorithm as a trace, which could be the entire program trace in the case of offline monitoring, or an event or a buffered sequence of events in the case of online monitoring.

This section is organized as follows: Subsect. 4.1 describes how valuations are extracted from a trace in run time, and Subsect. 4.2 describes the steps of the algorithm in detail.

4.1   Valuation Extraction

Valuation extraction refers to obtaining a valuation of quantified variables from the trace. As described in LTL_4-C semantics, the predicate $p_i(x_i)$ identifies the subset of the domain of x_i over which the quantifier is applied: namely the subset that exists in the trace. From a theoretical perspective, we check whether the predicate is a member of some trace event, which is a set of predicates. From an implementation perspective, the trace event is a key-value structure, where the key is for instance a string identifying the quantified variable, and the value is the concrete value of the quantified variable in that trace event.

4.2   Algorithm Steps

Algorithm 1 presents the pseudocode of the parallel monitoring algorithm. Given an LTL_4-C property $\varphi = \mathbb{Q}_\varphi \, \psi$, the input to the algorithm is the RV-LTL monitor $\mathcal{M}^*$ of RV-LTL property ψ, a finite trace u, the set of quantifiers $\mathbb{Q}_\varphi$, and the vector of keys K used to extract valuations. Note that the algorithm supports both online and offline runtime verification. Offline mode is straightforward since the algorithm receives a finite trace that it can evaluate.

In the case of online mode, the algorithm maintains data structures that represent the tree structure shown in Fig. 1, and repeated invocation of the monitor updates these data structures incrementally. Thus, an online monitor will receive batches of events in run time and process them, building the tree of monitors with every invocation of the monitor. These invocations can be periodic or event based, and the batches can be of any length.

The entry point to the algorithm is at Line 5 which is invoked when the monitor receives a trace to process. This can be the entire trace in offline monitoring, or a buffered segment of the trace in online monitoring. The algorithm returns a truth value of the property at Line 8. Subsect. 4.2 describe the functional calls between Lines 5–8.

The MapReduce operations are visible in functions *SortTrace* and *ApplyQuantifiers*, which perform a *map* ($\Rightarrow$) in Lines 10 and 40 respectively. *ApplyQuantifiers* also performs a reduction ($\rightarrowtail$) in Line 41.

Trace Sorting. As shown in Algorithm 1, the first step in the algorithm is to sort the input trace u (Line 5). The function *SortTrace* performs this functionality as follows:

1. The function performs a parallel map of every trace event to the value vector that it holds (Line 10).
2. The mapped trace is sorted in parallel using the quantifier variable as a key (Line 11).
3. The sorted trace is then compacted based on valuations, and the function returns a map μ where keys are value vectors and values are the ranges of where these value vectors exist in trace u (Line 12). A range contains the start and end index. This essentially defines the subsequences u^{D_φ} for each property instance $\hat\varphi(D_\varphi)$ (refer to Subsect. 2.4).

Monitor Spawning. Monitor spawning is the second step of the algorithm (Line 6).

Algorithm 1. LTL$_4$−C Monitor

1: INPUT: An RV-LTL monitor $\mathcal{M}^*$ of LTL property ψ, a finite trace u, a set of quantifiers $\mathbb{Q}_\varphi$, and a vector of keys K to extract valuations of quantified variables.
2: declare $T = \{\mathcal{M}^{\mathbb{Q}}_{D|0}\}$ ▷ Tree of quantifier submonitors
3: declare $\mathbb{D} = \{\}$,   ▷ Value vector set
4: declare $\mathbb{M}^* = \{\}$ ▷ RV-LTL submonitor set
5: $\mu \leftarrow$ SORTTRACE(u)   ▷ The entry point
6: SPAWNMONITORS(μ)
7: DISTRIBUTE(u,μ)
8: return APPLYQUANTIFIERS($|\mathbb{Q}_\varphi - 1|$)

9: **function** SORTTRACE(u)▷ Trace sorting and compaction
10:    $u_i \Rightarrow u'_i :=$VALUEVEC(u_i, K)   ▷ ‖ map to value vectors
11:    PARALLELSORT(u',K)
12:    $\mu\langle D, r\rangle \leftarrow$ PARALLELCOMPACT(u')
13:    return μ

14: **function** SPAWNMONITORS(μ)   ▷ Monitor spawning
15:    **for** $D \in \mu$ **do in parallel**
16:       **if** $D \notin \mathbb{D}$ **then**
17:          ADD($\mathbb{D}$,D)
18:          $t \leftarrow$ ADDTOTREE(D)
19:          t.addMonitor(CREATEMONITOR(D))

20: **function** ADDTOTREE(D)
21:    $t = T$.root
22:    **for** $i \in [1, |\mathbb{Q}_\varphi| - 1]$ **do**
23:       **if** $\mathcal{M}^{\mathbb{Q}}_{D|i} \notin t$.children **then**
24:          t.addchild($\mathcal{M}^{\mathbb{Q}}_{D|i}$)
25:          $t \leftarrow t$.children$\left[\mathcal{M}^{\mathbb{Q}}_{D|i}\right]$
26:    return t

27: **function** CREATEMONITOR(D)   ▷ Monitor creation
28:    $\mathcal{M}^*_D \leftarrow$ LAUNCHMONITORTHREAD(D)
29:    $\mathcal{M}^*_D.D \leftarrow D$
30:    ADD($\mathbb{M}^*$,$\mathcal{M}^*_D$)
31:    return $\mathcal{M}^*_D$

32: **function** DISTRIBUTE(u,μ)   ▷ Distribute trace to monitors
33:    **for** $\mathcal{M}^*_D \in \mathbb{M}^*$ **do in parallel**
34:       PROCESSBUFFER($\mathcal{M}^*_D$,u,$\mu[\mathcal{M}^*_D.D]$)

35: **function** PROCESSBUFFER($\mathcal{M}^*_D$,u,r)   ▷ Process trace
36:    filter include $u \Rightarrow u' := u[r.\text{start}, r.\text{end}]$ ▷ ‖ filter
37:    $\mathcal{M}^*_D.b \leftarrow$ UPDATEMONITOR($\mathcal{M}^*_D$, u')

38: **function** APPLYQUANTIFIERS(i)   ▷ Apply quantifiers
39:    **for** $t \in T$.nodesAtDepth(i) **do in parallel**
40:       t.children $\Rightarrow \{s := [v, v', \cdots]\}$ ▷ ‖ map
41:       $s \rightarrowtail t.v$ ▷ ‖ reduction to truth vector
42:       $t.b \leftarrow$ VALUATION(t)   ▷ LTL$_4$−C semantics
43:    **if** $i = 0$ **then**
44:       return $t.b$
45:    return APPLYQUANTIFIERS($i - 1$)

The function *SpawnMonitors* receives a map μ and searches the cached collection of previously encountered value vectors $\mathbb{D}$ for duplicates. If a value vector in μ is new, it creates submonitors and inserts them in the tree of submonitors

T (Line 18). The function *AddToTree* attempts to generate $|\mathbb{Q}_\varphi| - 1$ quantifier submonitors $\mathcal{M}^\mathcal{Q}$ (Line 22) ensuring there are no duplicate monitors in the tree (Line 23).

After all quantifier submonitors are created, *SpawnMonitors* creates an RV-LTL submonitor $\mathcal{M}^*$ and adds it as a child to the leaf quantifier submonitor in the tree representing the value vector (Line 19). This resembles the structure in Fig. 1.

Checking whether submonitors do not already exist and the creation of new submonitors is performed in parallel for all value vectors in trace u. This is because the trace has been sorted and grouped by unique value vectors in the previous step. Thus, each subtree of monitors that corresponds to a unique value vector is created in parallel, and connected to its parent via locks.

Distributing the Trace. The next step in the algorithm is to distribute the sorted trace to all RV-LTL submonitors (Line 7). The function *Distribute* instructs every RV-LTL submonitor to process its respective trace by passing the full trace and the range of its respective subsequence, which is provided by the map μ (Line 34). The RV-LTL monitor updates its state according to the trace subsequence and stores its truth value b.

Applying Quantifiers. Applying quantifiers is a recursive process, beginning with the leaf quantifier submonitors and proceeding upwards towards the root of the tree (Line 8). Function *ApplyQuantifiers* operates in the following steps:

1. The function retrieves all quantifier submonitors at the ith level in the tree T (Line 39).
2. In parallel, for each quantifier submonitor, all child submonitor truth values are reduced into a single truth value of that quantifier submonitor (Lines 40–42). This step *reduces* all child truth vectors into a single vector and then applies LTL_4-C semantics to determine the truth value of the current submonitor, essentially applying function $\mathcal{F}$ on the truth values of all child submonitors.
3. The function proceeds recursively calling itself on submonitors that are one level higher. It terminates when the root of the tree is reached, where the truth value is the final verdict of the property with respect to the trace.

5   Implementation and Experimental Results

We have implemented Algorithm 1 for two computing technologies: Multi-core CPUs and GPUs. We applied three optimizations in our GPU-based implementation: (1) we use *CUDA Thrust API* to implement parallel sort, (2) we use *Zero-Copy Memory* which parallelizes data transfer with kernel operation without caching, and (3) we enforced alignment, which enables coalesced read of trace events into monitor instances. In order to intercept systems calls, we have integrated our algorithm with the Linux `strace` application, which logs all system calls made by a process, including the parameters passed, the return value, the time the call was made, etc. Notice that using `strace` has the benefit of eliminating static analysis for instrumentation.

5.1   Case Studies

We have conducted three case studies, the first demonstrates using our implementation for online monitoring, while case study 2 and 3 are monitored offline. Following is a detailed description of the case studies:

1. **Ensuring every request on a socket is responded to.** This case study monitors the responsiveness of a web server. Web servers under heavy load may experience some timeouts, which results in requests that are not responded to. This is a factor contributing to the uptime of the server, along with other factors like power failure, or system failure. Thus, we monitor that at least 95 % of requests are indeed responded to:

$$\mathbb{A}_{\geq 0.95}\, s: \mathsf{socket}(s) \cdot (\mathbf{G}\, \mathsf{receive}\,(s) \Rightarrow \mathbf{F}\, \mathsf{respond}\,(s))$$

   We use the Apache Benchmarking tool to create varying loads on the Apache web server, and monitor the property *online*.
2. **Ensuring fairness in utilization of personal cloud storage services.** This case study is based on the work in [12], which discusses how profiling DropBox traffic can identify the bottlenecks and improve the performance. Among the issues detected during this analysis, is a user repeatedly uploading chunks of maximum size to DropBox servers. Thus, it is beneficial for a runtime verification system to ensure that the majority of chunks are not of maximum size, ensuring fairness of service use. The corresponding $\mathrm{LTL_4-C}$ property is as follows:

$$\mathbb{A}u: \mathsf{user}(u) \cdot \mathbb{A}_{<0.5}\, c: \mathsf{chunk}(c) \cdot \mathsf{ismaxchunksize}\,(u, c)$$

3. **Ensuring proxy cache is functioning correctly.** This experiment is based on a study that shows the effectiveness of utilizing proxy cache in decreasing YouTube videos requests in a large university campus [20]. Thus, we monitor that no video is requested externally more than once:

$$\mathbb{A}v: \mathsf{vid}(v) \cdot \mathbb{E}_{\leq 1}\, r: \mathsf{req}(r, v) \cdot \mathsf{external}(r, v)$$

Notice that the formulas in the above case studies utilize counting semantics to express properties that cannot be expressed in standard LTL. Moreover, evaluation of these properties can never result in permanent satisfaction nor permanent violation (Case Study 1 and 2 only). Thus, the use of four-valued logic allows the monitor to produce a meaningful verdict for these properties.

5.2   Experimental Setup

Experiment Platform. The experiments machine comprises of a 12-core Intel Xeon E5-1650 CPU, an Nvidia Tesla K20c GPU, and 32GB of RAM, running Ubuntu 12.04.

Experimental Factors. We experiment with three implementations: single CPU, parallel CPU, and a GPU based implementation. We also experiment with multiple trace sizes to demonstrate scalability.

Experimental Metrics. We measure the total execution time and the monitor's CPU utilization. This is to demonstrate the impact of monitoring on overall CPU utilization. We perform 20 replicates of each experiment and present error bars of a 95 % confidence interval.

5.3   Results

First of all, the case studies have been evaluated with real-world datasets, except in Case Study 1, where we use the Apache benchmark tool to generate traces. We have validated that the monitor works correctly by ensuring that verdicts of presumably true/false are produced appropriately for Case Studies 1 and 2, and verdicts of presumably true/permanently false are produced appropriately for Case Study 3.

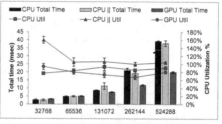

(a) Case Study 1

The performance results of Case Study 1 are shown in Fig. 2a. As seen in the figure, the GPU implementation scales efficiently with increasing trace size, resulting in the lowest monitoring time of all three implementations. The GPU versus single core CPU speedup ranges from 0.8 to 1.6, increasing with the increasing trace size. When compared to parallel CPU (CPU ||), the speedup ranges from 0.78 to 1.59. This indicates that parallel CPU outperforms GPU for smaller traces (32768), yet does not scale as well as GPU in this case study. This is attributed to the low number of individual objects in the trace, making parallelism less impactful.

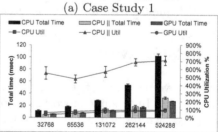

(b) Case Study 2

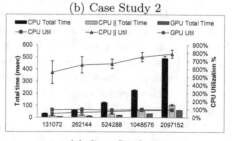

(c) Case Study 3

Fig. 2. Experimental results

CPU utilization results in Fig. 2a show a common trend with the increase of trace size. When the trace size is small, parallel implementations incur high CPU utilization as opposed to a single core implementation, which could be attributed to the overhead of parallelization relative to the small trace size. On the other hand, GPU shows a stable utilization percentage, with a 78 % average utilization. The single core CPU implementation shows a similar trend, yet slightly elevated average utilization (average 86 %). The parallel CPU implementation imposes a higher CPU utilization (average 115 %), since more cores are being used to process the trace. This result indicates that shipping the monitoring workload to GPU consistently provides more time for CPU to execute other processes including the monitored process. The results of Case Study 2 and Case Study 3 in Figs. 2b and c respectively demonstrate a more prominent advantage of using GPU in terms of speedup. The number of individual objects in these traces are large, making parallelism highly effective. For Case Study 2, the speedup of the GPU implementation over single core CPU ranges from 1.8 to 3.6, and 0.83 to 1.18 over parallel CPU. The average CPU utilization of GPU, single core CPU, and parallel CPU is 64 %, 82 %, and 598 % respectively. For Case Study 3, speedup is more significant, with 6.3 average speedup of GPU over single core CPU, and 1.75 over parallel CPU. The average CPU utilization of GPU, single core CPU, and parallel CPU is 73 %, 95 %, and 680 % respectively. Thus, the parallel CPU implementation is showing large speedup similar to the GPU implementation, yet also results in a commensurate CPU utilization percentage, since most cores of the system are fully utilized.

> *Although the parallel CPU implementation provides reasonable speedup and the single-core CPU implementation imposes low CPU overhead, the GPU implementation manages to achieve both simultaneously.*

6   Related Work

Runtime verification of parametric properties has been studied by Rosu et al. [13,16]. In this line of work, it is possible to build a runtime monitor parameterized by objects in a Java program. The work by Chen and Rosu [9] presents a method of monitoring parametric properties in which a trace is divided into slices, such that each monitor operates on its slice. This resembles our method of identifying trace subsequences and how they are processed by submonitors. However, parametric monitoring does not provide a formalization of applying existential and numerically constrained quantifiers over objects.

Bauer et al. [5] present a formalization of a variant of first order logic combined with LTL. The work by Leucker et al. presents a generic approach for monitoring modulo theories [11]. This work provides a more expressive specification language. Our work enforces a canonical syntax which is not required in [11], resulting in more expressiveness. However, the monitoring solution provided requires SMT solving at run time. LTL_4-C extends RV-LTL by redefining $\top_p$ and $\bot_p$ to support quantifiers and their numerical constraints. This four-valued semantics provides a more accurate assessment of the satisfaction of the property based on finite traces as opposed to the three-valued semantics in [11].

The work in [14] presents an extension to LTL that allows counting events associated with the *Until* operator. In this work, it is possible to apply a numerical constraint on the number of events satisfying subformulas. This differs from LTL_4-C, where numerical constraints are applied on quantified objects, allowing us to reason about the number or percentage of objects that satisfy a property. The work in [2] allows a limited form of quantification over values of a variable, yet does not support a higher level of quantification on the entire LTL property parameterized by the quantified variable, as is possible in LTL_4-C. The work in [18] presents a property specification language that allows quantification, and separates propositional evaluation from quantifier evaluation, similar to LTL_4-C. However, LTL_4-C supports LTL operators and quantification with numerical constraints.

The work in [1] presents a method of using MapReduce to evaluate LTL properties. The algorithm is capable of processing arbitrary fragments of the trace in parallel. The work in [3] presents a MapReduce method for offline verification of LTL properties with first-order quantifiers. Our approach supports both offline and online monitoring by extending RV-LTL's four valued semantics, which are capable of reasoning about the satisfaction of a partial trace. This is unclear in [3], since there is no evidence of supporting online monitoring.

The work in [10] presents a specification language for defining properties on input streams. The work in [4] presents an extension to metric first order temporal logic that allows aggregate operations.

Finally, the work in [7,8] presents two parallel algorithms for verification of propositional LTL specifications at run time. These algorithms are implemented in the tool RiTHM [17]. This paper enhances the framework in [7,8,17] by introducing a significantly more expressive formal specification language along with a parallel runtime verification system.

7   Conclusion

In this paper, we proposed a specification language (LTL_4-C) for runtime verification of properties of types of objects in software and networked systems. Our language is an extension of LTL that adds counting semantics with numerical constraints. The four truth values of the semantics of LTL_4-C allows system designers to obtain informative verdicts about the status of system properties at run time. We also introduced an efficient and effective parallel algorithm with two implementations on multi-core CPU and GPU technologies. The results of our experiments on real-world case studies show that runtime monitoring using GPU provides us with the best throughput and CPU utilization, resulting in minimal intervention in the normal operation of the system under inspection.

For future work, we are planning to design a framework for monitoring LTL_4-C properties in distributed systems and cloud services. Another direction is to extend LTL_4-C such that it allows non-canonical strings of quantifiers. Finally, we are currently integrating LTL_4-C in our tool RiTHM [17].

Acknowledgments. This work was partially sponsored by Canada NSERC Discovery Grant 418396-2012 and NSERC Strategic Grants 430575-2012 and 463324-2014.

References

1. Barre, B., Klein, M., Soucy-Boivin, M., Ollivier, P.-A., Hallé, S.: MapReduce for Parallel trace validation of LTL properties. In: Qadeer, S., Tasiran, S. (eds.) RV 2012. LNCS, vol. 7687, pp. 184–198. Springer, Heidelberg (2013). doi:10.1007/978-3-642-35632-2_20

2. Barringer, H., Goldberg, A., Havelund, K., Sen, K.: Program monitoring with LTL in eagle. In: 2004 Proceedings of the 18th International Parallel and Distributed Processing Symposium, p. 264. IEEE (2004)

3. Basin, D., Caronni, G., Ereth, S., Harvan, M., Klaedtke, F., Mantel, H.: Scalable offline monitoring. In: Bonakdarpour, B., Smolka, S.A. (eds.) RV 2014. LNCS, vol. 8734, pp. 31–47. Springer, Heidelberg (2014). doi:10.1007/978-3-319-11164-3_4

4. Basin, D., Klaedtke, F., Marinovic, S., Zălinescu, E.: Monitoring of temporal first-order properties with aggregations. Formal Methods Syst. Des. **46**(3), 262–285 (2015)

5. Bauer, A., Küster, J.-C., Vegliach, G.: From propositional to first-order monitoring. In: Legay, A., Bensalem, S. (eds.) RV 2013. LNCS, vol. 8174, pp. 59–75. Springer, Heidelberg (2013)

6. Bauer, A., Leucker, M., Schallhart, C.: Comparing LTL semantics for runtime verification. J. Logic Comput. **20**(3), 651–674 (2010)

7. Berkovich, S., Bonakdarpour, B., Fischmeister, S.: GPU-based runtime verification. In: IEEE International Parallel and Distributed Processing Symposium (IPDPS), pp. 1025–1036 (2013)

8. Berkovich, S., Bonakdarpour, B., Fischmeister, S.: Runtime verification with minimal intrusion through parallelism. Formal Methods Syst. Des. **46**(3), 317–348 (2015)

9. Chen, F., Roşu, G.: Parametric trace slicing and monitoring. In: Kowalewski, S., Philippou, A. (eds.) TACAS 2009. LNCS, vol. 5505, pp. 246–261. Springer, Heidelberg (2009)

10. d'Angelo, B., Sankaranarayanan, S., Sánchez, C., Robinson, W., Finkbeiner, B., Sipma, H.B., Mehrotra, S., Manna, Z.: LOLA: runtime monitoring of synchronous systems. In: 12th International Symposium on Temporal Representation and Reasoning (TIME 2005), pp. 166–174. IEEE (2005)

11. Decker, N., Leucker, M., Thoma, D.: Monitoring modulo theories. In: Ábrahám, E., Havelund, K. (eds.) TACAS 2014 (ETAPS). LNCS, vol. 8413, pp. 341–356. Springer, Heidelberg (2014)

12. Drago, I., Mellia, M., Munafo, M.M., Sperotto, A., Sadre, R., Pras, A.: Inside dropbox: understanding personal cloud storage services. In: Proceedings of the 2012 ACM Conference on Internet Measurement Conference, pp. 481–494. ACM (2012)

13. Jin, D., Meredith, P.O., Lee, C., Rosu, G.: JavaMOP: efficient parametric runtime monitoring framework. In: 2012 34th International Conference on Software Engineering (ICSE), pp. 1427–1430, June 2012

14. Laroussinie, F., Meyer, A., Petonnet, E.: Counting LTL. In; Proceedings of the 2010 17th International Symposium on Temporal Representation and Reasoning, TIME 2010, pp. 51–58. IEEE Computer Society, Washington, DC (2010)

15. Libkin, L.: Elements of Finite Model Theory. Springer, New York (2004)
16. Meredith, P., Rosu, G.: Efficient parametric runtime verification with deterministic string rewriting. In: 2013 IEEE/ACM 28th International Conference on Automated Software Engineering (ASE), pp. 70–80. IEEE (2013)
17. Navabpour, S., Joshi, Y., Wu, W., Berkovich, S., Medhat, R., Bonakdarpour, B., Fischmeister, S.: RiTHM: a tool for enabling time-triggered runtime verification for C programs. In: ACM Symposium on the Foundations of Software Engineering (FSE), pp. 603–606 (2013)
18. Sokolsky, O., Sammapun, U., Lee, I., Kim, J.: Run-time checking of dynamic properties. Electron. Notes Theoret. Comput. Sci. **144**(4), 91–108 (2006)
19. Williams, M.: Scaling Web Applications with NGINX, Part II: Caching and Monitoring (2015). https://www.nginx.com/blog/. Accessed 27 May 2016
20. Zink, M., Suh, K., Gu, Y., Kurose, J.: Watch global, cache local: Youtube network traffic at a campus network: measurements and implications. In: Electronic Imaging 2008, p. 681805. International Society for Optics and Photonics (2008)

Non-intrusive Runtime Monitoring Through Power Consumption: A Signals and System Analysis Approach to Reconstruct the Trace

Carlos Moreno[✉] and Sebastian Fischmeister

Electrical and Computer Engineering, University of Waterloo, Waterloo, Canada
{cmoreno,sfischme}@uwaterloo.ca

Abstract. The increasing complexity and connectivity of modern embedded systems highlight the importance of runtime monitoring to ensure correctness and security. This poses a significant challenge, since monitoring tools can break extra-functional requirements such as timing constraints. Non-intrusive program tracing through side-channel analysis techniques have recently appeared in the literature and constitute a promising approach. Existing techniques, however, exhibit important limitations.

In this paper, we present a novel technique for non-intrusive program tracing from power consumption, based on a signals and system analysis approach: we view the power consumption signal as the output of a system with the power consumption of training samples as input. Using spectral analysis, we compute the impulse response to identify the system; the intuition is that for the correct training sample, the system will appear close to a system that outputs a shifted copy of the input signal, for which the impulse response is an impulse at the position corresponding to the shift. We also use the Control Flow Graph (CFG) from the source code to constrain the classifier to valid sequences only, leading to substantial performance improvements over previous works.

Experimental results confirm the effectiveness of our technique and show its applicability to runtime monitoring. The experiments include tracing programs that execute randomly generated sequences of functions as well as tracing a real application developed with SCADE. The experimental evaluation also includes a case-study as evidence of the usability of our technique to detect anomalous execution through runtime monitoring.

Keywords: Program tracing · Runtime monitoring · Embedded software security · Side-channel analysis · Power-based program tracing · Signal processing · Signals and systems analysis

1 Introduction

Modern embedded devices are rapidly increasing in complexity and connectivity, making it ever more important to incorporate runtime monitoring systems for

© Springer International Publishing AG 2016
Y. Falcone and C. Sanchez (Eds.): RV 2016, LNCS 10012, pp. 268–284, 2016.
DOI: 10.1007/978-3-319-46982-9_17

the purpose of ensuring correctness and security. This introduces an important challenge, as instrumentation added to the system can break extra-functional requirements such as real-time constraints in the operation. Non-intrusive program tracing through side-channel analysis techniques have recently appeared in the literature and constitute a promising approach. These techniques use an external device to measure power consumption and reconstruct the program trace. From the perspective of runtime monitoring, there are several benefits: (i) we obtain the program trace without any instrumentation that could affect the device's functionality; (ii) once the program trace is obtained, additional monitoring (processing/analysis) tools can be introduced without the risk of interfering with the device's functionality or breaking any extra-functional requirements; and (iii) the runtime monitor is *tamper-proof* in the sense that it is not affected by system "crashes" or even deliberate cyber-attacks.

Moreno et al. presented a novel technique for non-intrusive program tracing and debugging through side-channel analysis [19]. In that work, they used power consumption measurements — *power traces* — to determine blocks of source code being executed. That work was an important step in showing the technical feasibility of these program tracing techniques. However, it exhibits important limitations with respect to both methodology and performance. In particular, it requires a user-assisted training phase where fragments of source code have to be isolated and individually executed. Moreover, the technique in [19] operated at the granularity level of whole functions, which may be too coarse to be practical. Indeed, [19] does not present any case-studies to support the idea of this non-intrusive tracing technique being useful in practice. The work in [20] proposes a technique that can be combined with the approach in [19], and indeed can be combined with our proposed technique, potentially increasing its performance through a compiler-assisted transformation of the generated binary code. Eisenbarth et al. [9] presented a different approach, introducing the idea of a side-channel disassembler. Without using information about source code, they attempted to obtain the sequence of CPU instructions from power consumption. However, their results showed a performance far too low to be applicable in practice. Clark et al. [5] used side-channel analysis to identify execution traces in medical devices for the purpose of tamper-detection. That work is limited in the sense that it only works at the granularity level of the entire execution trace, and relies on the assumption that the device's task is simple and highly repetitive.

Using online trace information, our approach can work within the conceptual scheme of traditional runtime monitoring and verification systems [22], but it exhibits important advantages with respect to their implementation. The main benefits derive from the fact that in our system, the external monitor is a physically isolated subsystem, yet suitable for low-cost microcontrollers that have little or no hardware support for debugging, tracing, or in general runtime monitoring. Both event-triggered [4,12–14,25] and time-triggered frameworks [21] typically rely on components or instrumentation that run together with the monitored system, making them vulnerable to security threats and failures involving memory corruption ("system crashes").

1.1   Our Contributions

In this work, we propose and implement a novel technique for non-intrusive program tracing through side-channel analysis, and show its application to online runtime monitoring through anomaly detection. We introduce conceptual changes that improve the effectiveness and efficiency of power-based program tracing, thus addressing most of the limitations in [5, 9, 19]. Our proposed technique has several aspects that account for these improvements over previous work:

- **Novel use of signal processing for classification in power-based program tracing.** Instead of standard statistical pattern recognition techniques, we propose a novel approach based on signal processing; specifically, a form of system identification. We use a computationally efficient procedure that determines the best match for a trace segment and also the position of the match (without requiring any extra, separate computation). This addresses one of the important limitations in [19]: the system is given a single power trace and has to split it into segments to be classified, maintaining alignment with the correct segments boundaries (of which the system is given no information as input). Our signals and system analysis approach proved to not only work well in terms of the performance of the system, but also contributed to a substantial improvement in processing speed, with a measured speedup of more than 4× attributable to this aspect.
- **Use of code analysis to improve performance.** Using the Control Flow Graph (CFG) obtained from the source code, we assist the classification system by constraining the blocks to those that are part of valid sequences. The intuition is that the probability of misclassification is lower if the classifier counts on additional information that reduces the set of candidates. This is illustrated by Fig. 1, where sub-figure (a) represents classification when considering all possible blocks, and sub-figure (b) represents classification where a reduced set of candidates is considered. Our technique builds upon this intuition: by expanding the CFG using a dynamic programming approach, we validate sequences of blocks; this can be seen as a mechanism where we obtain fine granularity, but with the equivalent of the classifier working at a coarser granularity so that it reduces the probability of misclassification by working with larger segments.
- **Improved methodology and nearly fully automated work flow.** We instrumented the source code using the CFG, allowing us to achieve nearly full automation of both the training phase and the performance evaluation phases of the system.

In addition to the experimental evaluation where we measure the performance of our system, we include a case-study presented as evidence of the usability of this technique. This case-study applies in the context of runtime monitoring as well as in the context of computer security, where our technique may be used as an Intrusion Detection System (IDS) [17] for embedded devices. The case-study involves introducing a buffer-overflow bug/vulnerability, exploited in two

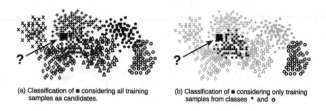

(a) Classification of ■ considering all training
samples as candidates.

(b) Classification of ■ considering only training
samples from classes * and o

Fig. 1. Reducing the set of candidates for classification

distinct ways: (i) overflowing the stack to make execution return to a random address (a "bug" in the conventional sense); and (ii) through a buffer-overflow attack [1,7], where the stack is overwritten in a controlled way to hijack the device's execution. Results from the case-study confirm our approach's potential and usability in these two contexts.

1.2 Organization of the Paper

The remaining of this paper proceeds as follows: Sect. 2 presents a brief review of signals and system analysis tools. Section 3 describes our proposed approach. Our experimental setup is described in Sect. 4, followed by the results in Sect. 5, including the case-study. Finally, a discussion and concluding remarks are presented (Sects. 6 and 7).

2 Background – Frequency Domain Analysis of Signals and Systems

A discrete-time linear time-invariant (LTI) system can be fully described by its impulse response, $h(n)$. This impulse response is the output of the system when the input is the impulse signal $\delta(n)$, where $\delta(0) \triangleq 1$ and $\delta(k) \triangleq 0 \ \forall \ k \neq 0$. For an arbitrary input signal $x(n)$, the system's output $y(n)$ is obtained through the *convolution* relationship [24]:

$$y(n) = \sum_{k=-\infty}^{\infty} h(k)\, x(n-k) \tag{1}$$

A frequency domain representation of a discrete-time signal $x(n)$ can be obtained through the (Discrete-Time) Fourier Transform $\mathcal{F}$, defined as [24]:

$$\mathcal{F}\{x\} = \mathcal{X}(\omega) = \sum_{k=-\infty}^{\infty} x(k)\, e^{-j\omega k} \tag{2}$$

where ω is the *angular frequency* $(-\pi < \omega < \pi)$, and j denotes the imaginary unit (i.e., $j^2 = -1$).[1]

---

[1] We adopt the electrical engineering convention of using j to denote the imaginary unit, to avoid ambiguity with the symbol for electrical current or intensity, i.

Given the Fourier Transform $\mathcal{X}(\omega)$, the signal $x(n)$ can be obtained through the inverse Fourier Transform $\mathcal{F}^{-1}$, defined as [24]:

$$\mathcal{F}^{-1}\{\mathcal{X}\} = x(n) = \int_{-\pi}^{\pi} \mathcal{X}(\omega)e^{j\omega n}d\omega \tag{3}$$

The properties of the Fourier Transform for discrete-time signals regarding convolution in the time domain are the same as those of the Fourier Transform for continuous-time signals. In particular, if $x(n)$, $y(n)$, and $h(n)$ follow the relationship described in Eq. (1), then it holds that:

$$\mathcal{Y}(\omega) = \mathcal{X}(\omega)\mathcal{H}(\omega) \tag{4}$$

where $\mathcal{X}(\omega)$, $\mathcal{Y}(\omega)$, $\mathcal{H}(\omega)$ are the Fourier Transforms of $x(n)$, $y(n)$, $h(n)$, respectively. Thus, given an input signal $x(n)$ and its corresponding output signal $y(n)$, the impulse response $h(n)$ of the system can be obtained as:

$$h(n) = \mathcal{F}^{-1}\left\{\frac{\mathcal{Y}(\omega)}{\mathcal{X}(\omega)}\right\} = \mathcal{F}^{-1}\left\{\frac{\mathcal{F}\{y\}}{\mathcal{F}\{x\}}\right\} \tag{5}$$

To apply frequency domain analysis to a segment or a window of a signal of length N (viewed as a signal $x(n)$ with $0 \leqslant n < N$), we use the discrete Fourier Transform (DFT), defined as [24]:

$$\mathcal{DFT}(x) = \mathcal{X}(k) = \sum_{n=0}^{N-1} x(n)e^{-j\frac{2\pi kn}{N}} \tag{6}$$

with $0 \leqslant k < N$. Its inverse operation is given by:

$$\mathcal{DFT}^{-1}(X) = x(n) = \frac{1}{N}\sum_{k=0}^{N-1} \mathcal{X}(k)e^{j\frac{2\pi kn}{N}} \tag{7}$$

The DFT can be efficiently computed through the Fast Fourier Transform (FFT) algorithm [24]. In our case, we used the FFTW library [10], which efficiently computes both FFT and inverse FFT. The DFT represents the Fourier Transform of a periodic signal with period N where $x(n)$ comprises one period of the signal. The properties shown above hold, with the system's output being given by the *circular convolution* of the input signal and the impulse response — convolution computed with time indexes treated in a modulo N fashion. This allows us to obtain the impulse response of a system when looking at N-samples windows of the related signals:

$$h(n) = \mathcal{DFT}^{-1}\left\{\mathcal{H} = \frac{\mathcal{Y}}{\mathcal{X}}\right\} \tag{8}$$

where the quotient $\mathcal{H}$ is computed through sample-wise division. That is, for each $k \in [0, N)$, $\mathcal{H}(k) = \frac{\mathcal{Y}(k)}{\mathcal{X}(k)}$.

3   Proposed Technique

This section describes the main aspects and novelty of our proposed technique.

3.1   Frequency Analysis: Classifying and Determining the Shift in the Power Trace Segments

The main idea and novel aspect behind our proposed approach for classification is to view the power trace segments as the output of a system whose input is the power trace of the training samples. For each of the training samples (corresponding to fragments of code) we perform a system identification; in particular, we obtain the impulse response as described in Sect. 2. The intuition is that for the correct fragment, the identified system will correspond to a system that outputs a copy of the input signal shifted by a certain amount of samples. For this time-shift system, we know that the impulse response is a single pulse at the position corresponding to the shift [24].

A key detail is that as the system advances through the trace, the exact positions where the trace segments begin (i.e., the position at which the corresponding fragment of code started execution) are not given. One advantage of this system identification approach is that once we determine the best match among the training samples, the shift in the impulse response reveals the position where the match occurs. In terms of execution speed, this represents an important advantage with respect to the technique in [19], where the system needs to attempt classification over a somewhat large range of possible starting positions around the nominal starting point given by the outcome of the previous classification (see [18] for details).

We have to be careful, however, with the "circular" nature of the DFT-based analysis: consider a system that shifts the signal by n_0 samples, with impulse response $h(n) = \delta(n - n_0)$. If we look at an N-samples window of a periodic signal, the shift occurs circularly within the window. However, for the case of a non-periodic signal (as it is our case), shifting the signal and comparing input and output in the same N-samples window corresponds to truncating the signal on one end and introducing an alien fragment on the other end. Thus, the impulse response obtained through DFT analysis within an N-samples window will not be a single pulse.

The key observation is that for small values of n_0 compared to N, the impulse response will be close to a single pulse, since the output corresponds to the linear superposition of a large fraction of the signal shifted and two signals that are nonzero only in a small fraction of the interval. Figure 2 illustrates this intuition, with sub-figure (a) showing the computed impulse response for a shift by a small amount (5 positions in a 128 samples window) and sub-figure (b) showing the response for a larger shift (40 positions). The impulse response for the small shift shows a very prominent pulse at index 5, whereas the response for the larger shift exhibits a higher "noise level" outside the main pulse near index 40, thus making the pulse less prominent. It should be obvious that the response

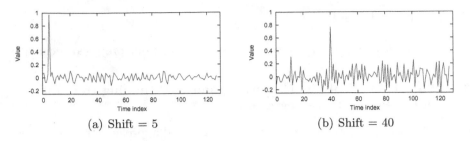

(a) Shift = 5   (b) Shift = 40

Fig. 2. Examples of impulse responses

for two unrelated signals should not have any prominent pulses, so we omit any examples.

3.2 Statistical Pattern Recognition

Though the use of pattern recognition as the main classification technique was largely replaced by the signal processing approach, some elements from this field are present. In particular, we use a distance metric to quantify how close the impulse response is from a single pulse, and this distance is evaluated for the elements of a database of training samples; we determine the k closest matches from the database and evaluate the average distance — a logic similar to that behind the k nearest neighbors (k-NN) rule [26].

For the distance metric, we used the following heuristics: we quantify how close a given impulse response is from a single pulse based on the following parameters (computed in the same order as listed):

- Highest value of the signal (the "height" of the main pulse; denoted H_p) and position where it occurs (denoted n_0).
- Median of the absolute values of the signal; denoted $\tilde{h}$.
- Width of the main pulse (obtained from the interval around n_0 for which the absolute value of the signal is above $\tilde{h}$; denoted W_p).
- Highest absolute value of the signal outside the interval corresponding to the main pulse (the "noise" level; denoted L_n).

With these parameters, the distance, d (a metric corresponding to the natural notion that the smaller the distance, the closer the match), is given by:

$$d \;=\; W_p \times \frac{L_n}{H_p} \tag{9}$$

The first term accounts for the effect that the narrower the main pulse, the closer it is to a single pulse. The second term accounts for the effect that the smaller the values outside the main pulse (relative to the height of the main pulse), the closer it is to being a single pulse.

3.3   Static Analysis: Using the Control Flow Graph

The second important aspect introduced in this work is the addition of static analysis tools to assist the classifier by restricting the classification choices to blocks that constitute allowed sequences. In particular, use of the CFG allows us to constrain the choice of best match to those that are part of valid sequences. To this end, we used a dynamic programming approach [6]: at each point in the classification, we expand the CFG to determine the set of possible paths up to a given depth (given as a configuration parameter). For each of the nodes in this expanded/unrolled CFG, we evaluate the distance (as described in Sect. 3.2). We choose the path $\mathcal{P}$ with lowest sum of distances, and the classifier's decision corresponds to the first node in $\mathcal{P}$.

This can be seen as a mechanism where we obtain fine granularity in the execution trace, but with the equivalent of using a coarse granularity for the classification, reducing the probability of misclassification by working with longer traces. The dynamic programming implementation improves computational efficiency: we advance through the tree, discarding the subtrees of the sibling nodes to the selected one, but keeping the subtree of the selected node so that we avoid redundant calculations when expanding the CFG at the new node. Algorithm 1 shows the details of this procedure. In the algorithm, the expression $\{\mathrm{Suc}(\cdot)\}$ denotes the set of successors of the argument $\cdot$, and G_n denotes the CFG G with a state indicating that it is currently at node n.

Algorithm 1. Classification Procedure.

Input: G (CFG), P_T (Power Trace), D (Depth)

Output: T (Program Trace) Expressed as sequence of blocks

begin
  $R \leftarrow RootNode$;
  repeat D times;
      for each leaf node $n \in R$ **do**
          $n.child\_nodes \leftarrow \{\mathrm{Suc}(G_n)\}$;
          Compute distance and start pos. (shift) for added nodes
  end
  while R *leaf nodes not at end of* P_T **do**
      $\mathcal{P} \leftarrow$ Path to leaf with lowest sum of distances;
      $T \leftarrow T \parallel \mathcal{P}(1)$;
      $R \leftarrow$ *Subtree with root* $\mathcal{P}(1)$;
      for each leaf node $n \in R$ **do**
          $n.child\_nodes \leftarrow \{\mathrm{Suc}(G_n)\}$;
          Compute distance and shift for added nodes
      end
  end
end

Notice that this "recursion forward" is possible because we have the complete trace for analysis; in an actual implementation where the system has to operate online (i.e., classify traces on-the-fly), this simply means that we have to allow for a small delay in the classification process, so that at block n of the trace, the classifier is making the decision for block $n - D$, where D is the depth of the expanded CFG.

We also highlight the aspect that this dynamic programming approach of expanding the CFG can be combined with other classification techniques, since it relies on a distance metric that quantifies how close given samples are from training samples. Though our signals and system analysis approach proved effective, other techniques may be suitable under different conditions, and could exhibit better results in terms of classifier's performance. Being able to combine any such techniques with the CFG expansion approach ensures that one can improve the classifier's performance while targeting a fine granularity regardless of the classification technique being used.

3.4 Segmentation of Traces and Fragments of Source Code

One important limitation in the approach proposed in [19] relates to the difficulty in training the system. For the training phase, fragments of code (whole functions, in that work) had to be run in isolation and surrounded by markers. In our proposed approach, during the training phase we run the fragments of code in the natural sequence as they occur in the source code. An instrumented version of the source code allows us to segment the trace into the sections that correspond to the fragments in the source code by flipping a port bit at the boundaries between fragments. This was done in a way such that the effect on the power traces is negligible (Sect. 4.1 describes this setup in more detail).

For the training phase, where we require a priori knowledge of the fragment of code being executed, an additional instrumented version is created with print statements at the boundaries between segments. This instrumented instance is run outside the target, in "offline" mode; both instrumented versions produce the same execution trace, since the source code is the same for both cases and the input data is the same (it is chosen at random, but once chosen it is "hard coded" into the programs — Sect. 4.1 includes a more detailed description). Thus, the system can automatically determine the fragment of code corresponding to each segment of the trace, as marked by the edges in the port bit signal.

3.5 Instrumenting the Source Code

We used LLVM [16] to extract a CFG from the source code. However, for our setup — with an AVR Atmega2560 [2] operating at 1 MHz — basic blocks produce trace segments that are too short for the classifier to operate successfully. We devised a procedure to merge CFG nodes into nodes representing larger

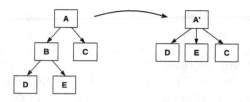

Fig. 3. Example of merging CFG nodes

blocks of source code, yet maintaining a valid CFG structure[2] where the beginning of execution of each block can be marked in the source code.

Since we require markers between segment boundaries, and segments correspond directly with blocks of code associated to CFG nodes, the important aspect to maintain is preserving the beginning of the block by merging nodes corresponding to short blocks into their predecessor nodes. As an example, consider the subgraph of a CFG shown at the left in Fig. 3, where block B is too short.

We merge node B into node A to create node A'. The result is consistent with the initial CFG: the meaning of this new CFG subgraph is that if we enter node A', then the possible successors are node C (if block B does not get executed) or nodes D or E (if B does execute). The beginning of block A' (the line in the source code) remains the same as the beginning of block A, and there is no ambiguity. Block B no longer needs its beginning marked, since block B is no longer being considered, and instead, it is part of block A'. When executing, marks are correctly applied at the beginning of each block. Blocks with multiple possible internal paths are not a problem; we enter block A' and its starting point is marked. The next mark will occur at the beginning of one of its successors, and execution of any instance of block A' will be enclosed between the mark at its beginning and the next mark that appears.

4   Experimental Evaluation

The experimental evaluation includes two parts:

- **Random sequence of functions.** We evaluate our system against a target executing randomly generated sequences of MiBench [11] functions, with a random choice of two functions to execute next at each step in the sequence. The experiment is run multiple times, and we randomly generate a different sequence for each execution. The rationale for this choice is twofold: (i) it allows us to compare the performance against previous works, especially against the results reported in [19]; and (ii), a sequence of code with a "random CFG" constitutes a highly demanding task for our classifier, and

---

[2] Technically, the resulting graph is not a CFG, since the blocks can contain conditionals; however, it maintains the aspect that is relevant to our application: edges indicate the possible sequences during execution.

this has two important consequences: the results obtained are not "helped" by any particular structure of specific software that one may choose for this purpose; and also, the results are more statistically meaningful.

- **Cruise Control application.** The target device executes a SCADE 6 [8] Cruise Control application. This application follows the periodic, real-time tick based scheme where execution alternates between an interval of computations and idle. The rationale for using a concrete, real-world application is also clear: as much as the execution of random sequences of functions has important advantages, we still want to demonstrate the effectiveness of our technique on real applications. Not surprisingly, the performance of our system was substantially better for this case, given the simpler structure of the software and the more systematic patterns in the execution.

Many aspects in the experimental setup are common for both parts. The following section describes the setup.

4.1   Workflow

Figure 4 shows the hardware setup, including the use of two workstations to automate the experimentation (Fig. 4(a)) and the interface subsystem to capture the power trace and markers through the sound card (Fig. 4(b)). The workflow itself does not require two workstations; but the connections for the signals capture forced us to electrically isolate the flashing from the capture.

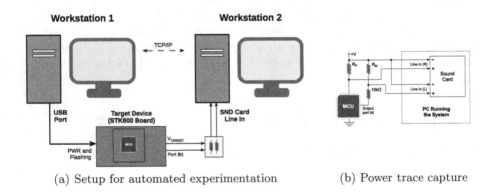

(a) Setup for automated experimentation   (b) Power trace capture

Fig. 4. Experimental setup

The workstations communicate via TCP/IP to synchronize the required actions: Workstation 2 is the "master" in that it instructs Workstation 1 to generate an instance of the software and flash the target device. The software running on Workstation 2 captures and processes the traces. It detects the bit flips (markers at the boundaries between trace segments) by looking for inflection points between neighboring minima and maxima. We used the standard

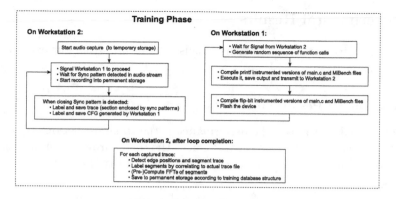

Fig. 5. Procedure for the training phase

numeric approximations for the derivatives [23], with interpolation to find the position of the inflection point with sub-sample resolution.

We used a *custom-made* pseudorandom number generator (PRNG) to randomize the input data and the choice of functions to execute. This ensures that execution on the target and on the print-instrumented version produce the same trace. This is not guaranteed if we use the Standard Library PRNG, since it can potentially vary between compilers. We used a linear congruential generator with 64-bit internal state, as described in [15]. The PRNG is seeded by the code generator software running on Workstation 1, using `/dev/urandom`.

We emphasize the aspect that the training phase and the operation phase in our experiments always use different input data, to ensure that the results are meaningful. This is the case since every execution of a function (for either training or operation purposes) operates on randomly selected input data.

Figures 5 and 6 show the experimental procedures for the training phase and the performance evaluation phase, respectively.

The implementations are in fact coded as infinite loops, simply relying on the user to interrupt the program when they estimate that a sufficient amount of data has been collected.

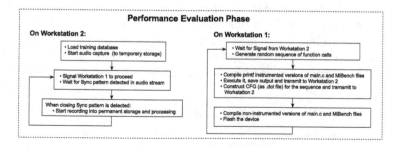

Fig. 6. Operation phase and performance evaluation

5   Experimental Results

In this section we present and briefly discuss the results from our experimental evaluation.

5.1   Classifier's Performance

The metric used to evaluate the performance is the standard notion of precision. In our case, this corresponds to the fraction of the time during which the classifier output corresponds to the correct segment or block (a true positive):

$$P \triangleq \frac{\sum |I_{T_P}|}{\sum |I_{T_P}| + \sum |I_{F_P}|} \tag{10}$$

where P denotes the precision, I_{T_P} are the intervals for which the output of the classifier is a true positive, I_{F_P} are the intervals where the output is a false positive (a misclassification), and $|\cdot|$ denotes the length of the argument $\cdot$ (the length of the interval). The notion of recall is not applicable, since at all times the classifier outputs something—either a true positive or a false positive.

Table 1 shows the measured precision for the various experiments, including 95 % confidence intervals. The "Raw" measurement is the precision obtained while the system is in sync with the CFG—roughly speaking, it corresponds to the probability of correct classification when the candidates are restricted to the actual possible options. It was measured by counting misclassifications but correcting them so that the next classification is done with the correct set of candidates. The purpose of this metric is to isolate the effect of using the CFG to narrow down the set of candidates for the classifier from the issue of having to maintain sync with the CFG. This allows for a more direct comparison against the results in [19], as they report the precision when classifying functions executed in isolation as well as the overall system precision including the task of maintaining sync after misclassifications. With the use of the dynamic programming/CFG expansion approach, the experiment with random sequence of functions used a depth of 8 for the tree, and with the cruise control application, a depth of 5.

The results show a reasonably good precision, given the granularity at which our system operates—800 functions correspond to approx. 3000 nodes, giving a granularity close to four times finer than that reported in [19]. Working at this substantially finer granularity, the precisions that we obtain are similar to those in [19]: 97.1 % precision for classification of individual blocks; close to the 98 %

Table 1. Classifier precision

	Random sequence	Cruise control application
Raw	97.1 % ± 0.3 %	--
With CFG Expansion	86.25 % ± 3.4 %	**95.68 % ± 0.01 %**

reported in [19] when classifying individual functions in isolation. And 86.25 % overall precision, with the classifier never going out of sync; in the same order as the 88 % reported in [19]. For the SCADE application, the performance was substantially higher, even when working with a lower recursion depth (which also improves execution speed), and the classifier never went out of sync.

Observation of the classifier's output additionally gave us several interesting insights that will be discussed in Sect. 6.

5.2   A Case-Study: Buffer Overflows

As a case-study to assess the usability of our runtime monitoring technique in practice, we repeated the experiments with a deliberately introduced defect that allows buffer overflows. We performed this modified experiment in two distinct ways: overwriting the return address with a random value (a "bug" in the conventional sense); and overwriting the return address with a crafted value to cause execution to return to a different address (a buffer-overflow/code reuse attack). As expected, for both scenarios the system irrecoverably went out of sync with the CFG and misclassified essentially every segment after the buffer overflow occurred.

The shifts in the trace segments (the deviation of the starting point with respect to the "nominal" position, given by the outcome of the previous classification) provide a good indicator of an out-of-sync condition. When the system is operating normally, we expect the shifts to be small, to compensate for minor deviations due to measurement noise. When operating on a trace that is not consistent with the CFG, the matches are found at somewhat random positions, resulting in large values of the shifts. Figure 7 shows the shift values for the case where the buffer overflow occurs at the seventh block; as expected, we observe a noticeable increase in the values after that position.

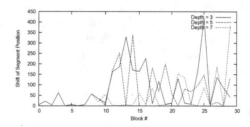

Fig. 7. Effect of a buffer overflow bug/attack on the classifier's shifts

Though we did not incorporate any formal anomaly detection techniques [3] to automate the reporting of these unrecognized segments, the results represent encouraging evidence to the usability of our technique in the context of either monitoring to detect faulty behavior or as an IDS.

6   Discussion and Future Work

One of the positive aspects to highlight relates to the potential for usability of our system as a runtime monitoring tool in real-world systems; the experimental results confirm this potential for cases where execution follows the CFG but deviating from specifications (e.g., an infinite loop due to lack of validation of input data) and also the cases where execution violates the CFG constraints (e.g., stack corruption, invalid pointer accesses, malware/tampering, etc.). Combining our approach with the technique in [20] is a promising avenue to further improve our system's performance, and is one of the aspects suggested as future work.

The following are some of the interesting insights that we obtained from this work, in particular from analysis of the classifier's output from the experiments:

- **Use of additional static analysis to improve the precision of the classifier.** We could observe that one of the main opportunities for misclassifications arises from segments that are short in length and where the CFG expansion allows a substitution without getting out of sync. Static analysis could reduce the set of paths that can execute (with respect to using the CFG alone). This would also improve speed, as it reduces the size of the expanded CFG in our dynamic programming algorithm in the classifier.
- **Using the shifts to avoid misclassifications.** We could observe several instances where the shifts (the deviation from the nominal starting point of a segment) could help correct misclassifications; indeed, several errors occurred for instances where the correct path was $A \to B \to C$ and the classifier output $A \to C$, with a large positive shift for A and a large negative shift for C, which suggests that the choice $A \to B \to C$ was likely the correct one (in any case, the system could confirm this if it verifies that the shifts for the former case are small).
- **Optimizing the choice of CFG blocks.** The choice of CFG blocks could be adjusted to improve the classifier's performance; for example, this could address the aspect mentioned above, where a short segment is incorrectly selected without getting out of sync. By looking at the training samples and estimating probabilities of correct classification, situations prone to errors could be identified and avoided through a different choice of CFG blocks, obtained by merging blocks in different combinations.

7   Conclusions

In this paper, we presented a non-intrusive program tracing technique and showed its applicability to runtime monitoring. We used a novel signals and system analysis approach, combined with static analysis to further improve both performance and methodology. The proposed technique exhibits substantially better performance compared to previous work on power-based program tracing, as it has comparable precision while working at a granularity level close to four times finer. A case-study confirmed the potential of our technique either as a runtime monitoring tool or as an IDS for embedded devices.

Acknowledgments. The authors would like to thank Pansy Arafa, Hany Kashif, and Samaneh Navabpour for their valuable assistance with the CFG and instrumentation infrastructure as well as related discussions.

This research was supported in part by the Natural Sciences and Engineering Research Council of Canada and the Ontario Research Fund.

References

1. One, A.: Smashing the stack for fun and profit. Phrack Magazine (1996)
2. Atmel Corporation: ATmega2560 (2016). http://www.atmel.com/devices/ATMEGA2560.aspx
3. Chandola, V., Banerjee, A., Kumar, V.: Anomaly detection: a survey. ACM Computing Surveys (CSUR) **41**(3), 15 (2009)
4. Chen, F., Roşu, G.: Java-MOP: a monitoring oriented programming environment for Java. In: Halbwachs, N., Zuck, L.D. (eds.) TACAS 2005. LNCS, vol. 3440, pp. 546–550. Springer, Heidelberg (2005). doi:10.1007/978-3-540-31980-1_36
5. Clark, S.S., Ransford, B., Rahmati, A., Guineau, S., Sorber, J., Fu, K., Xu, W.: WattsUpDoc: power side channels to nonintrusively discover untargeted malware on embedded medical devices. In: USENIX Workshop on Health Information Technologies. USENIX (2013)
6. Cormen, T.H., Leiserson, C.E., Rivest, R.L., Stein, C.: Introduction to Algorithms, 3rd edn. The MIT Press, Cambridge (2009)
7. Solar Designer: "return-to-libc" Attack, Bugtraq, August 1997
8. Dormoy, F.X.: SCADE 6: a model based solution for safety critical software development. In: Proceedings of the 4th European Congress on Embedded Real Time Software (ERTS 2008) (2008)
9. Eisenbarth, T., Paar, C., Weghenkel, B.: Building a side channel based disassembler. In: Gavrilova, M.L., Tan, C.J.K., Moreno, E.D. (eds.) Transactions on Computational Science X. LNCS, vol. 6340, pp. 78–99. Springer, Heidelberg (2010). doi:10.1007/978-3-642-17499-5_4
10. Frigo, M., Johnson, S.G.: The design and implementation of FFTW3. In: Proceedings of the IEEE special issue on "Program Generation, Optimization, and Platform Adaptation" (2005)
11. Guthaus, M.R., Ringenberg, J.S., Ernst, D., Austin, T.M., Mudge, T., Brown, R.B.: MiBench: a free, commercially representative embedded benchmark suite. In: Proceedings of the Workload Characterization. IEEE Computer Society (2001)
12. Havelund, K.: Runtime verification of C programs. In: International Conference on Testing of Software and Communicating Systems (2008)
13. Havelund, K., Roşu, G.: Monitoring Java programs with Java PathExplorer. Electron. Notes Theoret. Comput. Sci. **55**(2), 200–217 (2001). Runtime Verification (RV 2001)
14. Kim, M., Viswanathan, M., Kannan, S., Lee, I., Sokolsky, O.: Java-MaC: a runtime assurance approach for Java programs. Formal Methods Syst. Des. **24**(2), 129–155 (2004)
15. Knuth, D.E.: The Art of Computer Programming, Volume 2: Seminumerical Algorithms, 3rd edn. Addison-Wesley, Reading (1998)
16. Lattner, C., the LLVM Developer Group: The LLVM Compiler Infrastructure - online documentation. http://llvm.org
17. Bishop, M.: Computer Security: Art and Science. Addison-Wesley, Reading (2003)

18. Moreno, C.: Side-channel analysis: countermeasures and application to embedded systems debugging. Ph.D. Thesis (University of Waterloo) (2013)
19. Moreno, C., Fischmeister, S., Hasan, M.A.: Non-intrusive program tracing and debugging of deployed embedded systems through side-channel analysis. In: Conference on Languages, Compilers and Tools for Embedded Systems, pp. 77–88 (2013)
20. Moreno, C., Kauffman, S., Fischmeister, S.: Efficient program tracing and monitoring through power consumption - with a little help from the compiler. In: Design, Automation, and Test (DATE) (2016)
21. Navabpour, S., Joshi, Y., Wu, W., Berkovich, S., Medhat, R., Bonakdarpour, B., Fischmeister, S.: RiTHM: a tool for enabling time-triggered runtime verification for C programs. In: Foundations of Software Engineering, pp. 603–606. ACM (2013)
22. Pnueli, A., Zacks, A.: PSL model checking and run-time verification via testers. In: 14th International Symposium on Formal Methods (2006)
23. Press, W., Teukolsky, S., Vetterling, W., Flannery, B.: Numerical Recipes in C, 2nd edn. Cambridge University Press, Cambridge (1992)
24. Proakis, J.G., Manolakis, D.G.: Digital Signal Processing: Principles, Algorithms, and Applications, 4th edn. Prentice Hall, Upper Saddle River (2006)
25. Seyster, J., Dixit, K., Huang, X., Grosu, R., Havelund, K., Smolka, S.A., Stoller, S.D., Zadok, E.: Aspect-oriented instrumentation with GCC. In: Barringer, H., et al. (eds.) RV 2010. LNCS, vol. 6418, pp. 405–420. Springer, Heidelberg (2010). doi:10.1007/978-3-642-16612-9_31
26. Webb, A.R., Copsey, K.D.: Statistical Pattern Recognition, 3rd edn. Wiley, New York (2011)

An Automata-Based Approach to Evolving Privacy Policies for Social Networks

Raúl Pardo[1]($\boxtimes$), Christian Colombo[3], Gordon J. Pace[3], and Gerardo Schneider[2]

[1] Department of Computer Science and Engineering,
Chalmers University of Technology, Gothenburg, Sweden
{pardo,gersch}@chalmers.se
[2] Department of Computer Science and Engineering,
University of Gothenburg, Gothenburg, Sweden
[3] Department of Computer Science, University of Malta, Msida, Malta
{christian.colombo,gordon.pace}@um.edu.mt

Abstract. *Online Social Networks* (OSNs) are ubiquitous, with more than 70 % of Internet users being active users of such networking services. This widespread use of OSNs brings with it big threats and challenges, privacy being one of them. Most OSNs today offer a limited set of (static) privacy settings and do not allow for the definition, even less enforcement, of more dynamic privacy policies. In this paper we are concerned with the specification and enforcement of *dynamic* (and *recurrent*) privacy policies that are activated or deactivated by context (events). In particular, we present a novel formalism of *policy automata*, transition systems where privacy policies may be defined per state. We further propose an approach based on runtime verification techniques to define and enforce such policies. We provide a proof-of-concept implementation for the distributed social network Diaspora, using the runtime verification tool LARVA to synthesise enforcement monitors.

1 Introduction

As stated in [21] by Weitzner et al., "[p]rotecting privacy is more challenging than ever due to the proliferation of personal information on the Web and the increasing analytical power available to large institutions (and to everyone else) through Web search engines and other facilities". The problem being not only to determine *who* might be able to access *what* information and *when* but also *how* the information is going to be used (for which *purpose*). Addressing all these privacy-related questions is complex, and as today there is no ultimate solution.

The above is particularly true for *Online Social Networks* (OSNs) (also known as *Social Networking Sites* or *Social Networking Services* — SNSs), due to their explosion in popularity in the last years. Sites like Facebook, Twitter and LinkedIn are in the top 20 most visited Web sites in the world [1]. Nearly 70 % of the Internet users are active on OSNs as shown in a recent survey [12], and this number is increasing. A number of studies show that the number of privacy breaches is keeping pace with this growth [10,14–16]. The reasons for

© Springer International Publishing AG 2016
Y. Falcone and C. Sanchez (Eds.): RV 2016, LNCS 10012, pp. 285–301, 2016.
DOI: 10.1007/978-3-319-46982-9_18

this increase on privacy breaches are manifold; just to mention a few: (i) Many users are not aware of the implications of content sharing on OSNs, and do not foresee the consequences until it is too late; (ii) Most users do not take the time to check/change the default privacy settings, which are usually quite permissive; (iii) The privacy settings offered by existing OSNs are limited and are not fine-grained enough to capture desirable privacy policies; (iv) Side knowledge and indirect disclosure, e.g. through aggregation of information from different sources, it is difficult to foresee and detect; (v) There currently are no good warning mechanisms informing users of the potential breach of privacy, before a given action is taken; (vi) Privacy settings are static (they are not time- nor context-dependent), thus not being able to capture the possibility of defining repetitive or recurrent privacy policies.

Recently, the following privacy flaw was pointed out in the Facebook messenger app [3]. It was shown that it is possible to track users based on their previous conversations. It was enough to chat several times per day with users to accurately track their locations and even infer their daily routines. It was possible since the app adds by default the location of the sender to all the messages. This problem arises because of some of the reasons in the previous list such as (i), (ii) and (v). Facebook solution was to disable location sharing by default, which might be seen as a too radical solution. However, it is the best Facebook developers can do given the current state of privacy protection mechanisms. We believe that there is room for better solutions that offer protection to users while not restricting the sharing functionalities of the OSN. For instance, this privacy flaw could have been solved with a privacy policy that says *"My location can only be disclosed 3 times per day"*. This policy prevents tracking users while still allowing users to share their location in a controlled manner. We called this type of privacy policies *evolving* polices and they are the focus of this paper. Other examples of evolving policies are *"Co-workers cannot see my posts while I am not at work, and only family can see my location while I am at home"* or *"My supervisor cannot see my pictures during the weekend"*.

In this paper we address the above problem, through the following contributions: (i) The definition of *policy automata* (finite state automata enriched with privacy policies in their states), the definition of a subsumption and a conflict relation between policy automata, and the proofs of some properties about these relations (Sect. 2); (ii) A translation from policy automata into DATEs [4], the underlying data structure of the runtime verification tool LARVA [5] (Sect. 3); (iii) A proof-of-concept implementation of dynamic/recurrent privacy policies for the open source distributed OSN Diaspora* [6] using LARVA (Sects. 4 and 5).

2   Policy Automata

In order to describe evolving policies, we adopt the approach of taking a static policy language and use it to describe temporal snapshots of the policies in force. We then use a graph structure to describe how a policy is discarded and another enforced, depending on the events taking place e.g. user actions or system events.

2.1   Semantics of Policy Automata

Policy automata are defined as structures such that progressing through structure represents evolving policies, parametrised by a static policy language SPL. This approach allows us to define a whole family of evolving policy languages, depending on the underlying static language used.

Assumption 1. *We assume that SPL has the notion of conjunction of policies such that, for any two policies[1] $p_1, p_2 \in SPL$, $p_1 \,\&\, p_2 \in SPL$.*

Definition 1. *A policy automaton over a static privacy policy language SPL is a 4-tuple $\langle \Sigma, Q, q_0, \rightarrow, \pi \rangle$ where: Σ is the alphabet — effectively the set of observable actions of the underlying system; Q is the set of states in the automaton; $q_0 \in Q$ is the initial state of the automaton; $\rightarrow \subseteq Q \times \Sigma \times Q$ is the transition relation; and $\pi \in Q \rightarrow SPL$ is a function which maps each state to a privacy policy in SPL.*

We will write $q \xrightarrow{a} q'$ to indicate that there is a transition from state q to state q', labelled by a: $q \xrightarrow{a} q' \stackrel{df}{=} (q, a, q') \in \rightarrow$. We will take the transitive closure of the transition relation to enable us to write $q \stackrel{es}{\Rightarrow} q'$ to denote that the sequence of events es takes the automaton from state q to state q'.

Example 1. To illustrate policy automata let us consider the policy *'Co-workers cannot see my posts while I am not at work, and only family can see my location while I am at home'* (P1). If we use the static policy operator $\mathcal{F}_g(x)$ to denote that anyone in group g is forbidden from performing action x (where x can refer to posting, viewing a post, liking a post, etc.), we can express the first part of P1 to be $\mathcal{F}_{co\text{-}workers}(read\text{-}post)$, and the second part to be $\mathcal{F}_{\overline{family}}(see\text{-}location)$ (we use $\bar{g}$ to denote the complement of a group of users g). By synchronising with the actions of our social network application through events marking the arrival at and departure from a location (*enter(l)* and *leave(l)* respectively), we can express the evolving policy in the following manner[2]:

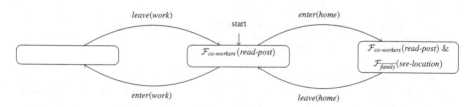

Non-deterministic and non-total transition relations in a policy automaton can lead to policy behaviour which is typically not required in real-life policy analysis. For instance, we do not want to consider automata that under the

---

[1] In the rest of the paper we take SPL to be the set of well-formed policy formulae of the static policy language.

[2] When we draw a policy automaton, transitions for events that are not explicitly drawn are assumed to be reflexive.

execution of an event, randomly choose between the activation of two different static policies. For this reason, we define the subset of sane policy automata which behave deterministically and never deadlock.

Definition 2. *We say that a policy automaton* $\mathcal{P} = \langle \Sigma, Q, q_0, \rightarrow, \pi \rangle$ *is* sane *if its transition relation is total and deterministic (functional). With sane policies, we write* $q \xrightarrow{e}$ *and* $q \xRightarrow{es}$ *(with* $e \in \Sigma$ *and* $es \in \Sigma^*$*) to denote the unique state reachable from state* q*, following action* e *and sequence* es *respectively. Finally, we will write* $policy_{\mathcal{P}}(es)$ *to denote the policy in force after following event sequence* es *from the initial state:* $policy_{\mathcal{P}}(es) \overset{df}{=} \pi(q_0 \xRightarrow{es})$.

In order to give a semantics to policy automata, we require the semantics of the underlying static policy language. Let $\sigma \in SN$ be the state of the social network where SN is the universe of all possible social network states. Given a static policy language SPL, we write $\sigma, e \vdash_{SPL} p$ to denote that in the social network state σ an event e respects privacy policy p. We assume that the social network (but not the policy) may evolve over time through events via the relation $\rightarrow_{SN} \subseteq SN \times \Sigma \times SN$ which is assumed to be a total function on the two first parameters.

Based on the semantics of the static policy language, we can now define the semantics of policy automata:

Definition 3. *The* configuration *of a policy automaton consists of the state of the automaton*[3]. *The initial configuration is taken to be* q_0. *Whether an event respects a policy automaton in a particular configuration* C *is defined as follows:*

$$\frac{\sigma, e \vdash_{SPL} \pi(C)}{\sigma, e \vdash_{PA} C}\text{SPL}$$

This is extended over traces in the following manner:

$$\frac{}{\sigma, \varepsilon \vdash_{PA} C}\text{BASETRACE}$$

$$\frac{\sigma, e \vdash_{PA} C \qquad \sigma \xrightarrow{e}_{SN} \sigma' \qquad C \xrightarrow{e} C' \qquad \sigma', es \vdash_{PA} C'}{\sigma, e : es \vdash_{PA} C}\text{INDTRACE}$$

Example 2. Consider the policy *'Only up to 3 posts disclosing my location are allowed per day in my timeline'* (P2), which can be encoded as the following automaton (we will assume that from left to right, the states are named q_0, q_1, q_2 and q_3):

---

[3] We present these semantics in terms of general configurations, rather than the automata states, since we envisage the extension of the automata to handle local symbolic state, requiring a richer configuration but still in line with the definitions given in this paper.

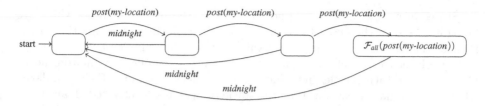

Since we expect that posting the location when a policy prohibiting it is in force is a violation, we would expect the static policy language semantics to show that for any social network state σ: σ, $post(my\text{-}location) \not\vdash_{SPL} \mathcal{F}_{all}(post(my\text{-}location))$.

From this, and given that $\pi(q_3) = \mathcal{F}_{all}(post(my\text{-}location))$ we can deduce that in state q_3, the policy clause is likewise violated whenever a post disclosing $my\text{-}location$ is performed, no matter the state of the social network: σ, $post(my\text{-}location) \not\vdash_{PA} q_3$.

Using the rule INDTRACE, provided there is σ' such that $\sigma \xrightarrow{post(my\text{-}location)^3} \sigma'$, we have:[4] σ, $post(my\text{-}location)^4 \not\vdash_{PA} q_0$.

Note that here we write $post(my\text{-}location)^4$ because we want to check that after disclosing 3 times the user's location, the forth one would be a violation of $\pi(q_3)$.

If the maximum number of posts were to be increased, the number of states in the automaton would grow quickly. For the sake of presentation, in the rest of the paper, we will also be enriching our notation in the examples to transition systems which have an implicit symbolic state. Transitions are labelled by a triple: $event/condition/state\text{-}update$ — triggering when the specified event happens and the condition holds, performing the state update before proceeding. The property allowing for 10 location posts can be expressed in this notation in the following manner:

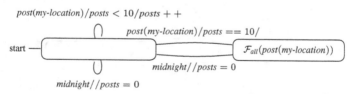

Such a symbolic automaton can be unfolded into a policy automaton possibly with an infinite number of states. For instance, in the above example, the set of states would be $\{(q, n) \mid q \in \{q_0, q_1\}, n \in \mathbb{N}\}$ where q holds the value of the (explicit) state, and n the value of $posts$. Since in this paper we are concerned with runtime verification — enforcing a dynamic policy along a single trace, the infinite number of states poses no challenge to the decidability question.

---

[4] The supra-index over events represent the number of occurrences of the event, so $my\text{-}location^3$ represent the sequence of events $my\text{-}location; my\text{-}location; my\text{-}location$.

States in policy automata do not contain all the privacy policies which are being enforced in the OSN. Internally the OSN could be enforcing other static policies that have been manually activated by the users. Policy automata are a separate layer to control some static policies. When a policy automaton moves to a state, the static policies in the new state are activated in the OSN. Similarly, when the automaton leaves a state, the static polices are deactivated. Transitions to and from an empty state just mean that there is no update of static policies.

One advantage of using policy automata is that one can combine them synchronously to get the equivalent of conjunction over evolving policies. In order to do so, we require the underlying SPL to have a notion of conjunction (cf. Assumption 1).

Policy automata can now be combined using standard synchronous composition over a particular alphabet:

Definition 4. *Given two policy automata* $\mathcal{P}_1$ *and* $\mathcal{P}_2$ *(such that* $\mathcal{P}_i = \langle \Sigma_i, Q_i, q_{0_i}, \rightarrow_i, \pi_i \rangle$*), the synchronous composition of the automata synchronising over actions* G*, is defined to be the policy automaton* $\mathcal{P}_1 \|_G \mathcal{P}_2 = \langle \Sigma_1 \cup \Sigma_2, Q_1 \times Q_2, (q_{01}, q_{02}), \rightarrow, \pi \rangle$ *where* $\pi(q_1, q_2) \overset{df}{=} \pi_1(q_1) \,\&\, \pi_2(q_2)$ *and the transition relation is defined as follows:*

$$\frac{q_1 \xrightarrow{a}_1 q_1' \qquad q_2 \xrightarrow{a}_2 q_2'}{(q_1, q_2) \xrightarrow{a} (q_1', q_2')} \; a \in G$$

$$\frac{q_1 \xrightarrow{a}_1 q_1'}{(q_1, q_2) \xrightarrow{a} (q_1', q_2)} \; a \notin G \qquad\qquad \frac{q_2 \xrightarrow{a}_2 q_2'}{(q_1, q_2) \xrightarrow{a} (q_1, q_2')} \; a \notin G$$

Example 3. The policy automaton of Example 1 effectively is a composition of two individual evolving policies. First *"Colleagues cannot see my posts when I am not at work"*, which can be represented in the following automaton

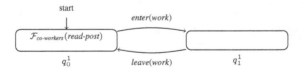

and secondly, *"Only my family can see my location while I am at home"*:

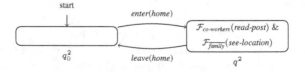

Let $\mathcal{P}_1$ and $\mathcal{P}_2$ denote the previous two automata, respectively. The following diagram shows $\mathcal{P}_{12}$, the parallel composition of the previous automata

$\mathcal{P}_1 \|_{\emptyset} \mathcal{P}_2$ (the synchronisation set is empty because $\mathcal{P}_1$ and $\mathcal{P}_2$ do not communicate over any event):

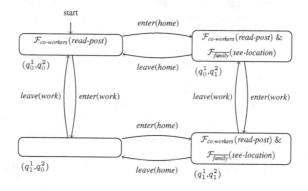

Note that this automaton is not equivalent to that of Example 1. In some transitions that Example 1's automaton do not update the static privacy policies (i.e., the automaton remains in the same state) this synchronous composition updates the policies accordingly. Imagine, for instance, that a user goes from work to home without leaving work (it is a possible scenario if the user lives at her workplace). After receiving *enter(work)*, *enter(home)*, the automaton resulting from the synchronous composition would active the policy $\mathcal{F}_{co\text{-}workers}(read\text{-}post)$ & $\mathcal{F}_{\overline{family}}(see\text{-}location)$ whereas Example 1's automaton would activate no policies. Formally, the state (q_0^1, q_1^2) should contain the static policy $\mathcal{F}_{co\text{-}workers}(read\text{-}post)$ & $\mathcal{F}_{co\text{-}workers}(read\text{-}post)$ & $\mathcal{F}_{\overline{family}}(see\text{-}location)$. However, we require the & operator of the static policy language to be idempotent (cf. Assumption 2, see below), thus being able to reduce the policy to $\mathcal{F}_{co\text{-}workers}(read\text{-}post)$ & $\mathcal{F}_{\overline{family}}(see\text{-}location)$.

Though formally the evolving policies can thus be combined into a single one, in practice one can keep them separate and enforce them independently, e.g. possibly on separate machines, thus avoiding information leaks (if all the policies) have to be communicated to a central server for enforcement. For instance, one can see a user's set of policies being combined together over his or her local alphabet, and then synchronising globally at a global level across users:

$$(p_{1,1} \|_{U_1} \cdots \|_{U_1} p_{1,n}) \;\|_{\text{Global}}\; (p_{m,1} \|_{U_m} \cdots \|_{U_m} p_{m,n'})$$

2.2   Subsumption of Dynamic Privacy Policies

Many notions can be carried over from the underlying static policy language to dynamic policies expressed using policy automata. Provided that the static policy language has a notion of semantic equivalence (which encompasses the usual properties of idempotency, commutativity and associativity of conjunction), we can derive equivalence and strictness ordering over policy automata.

Assumption 2. *We assume that the static policy language SPL has the notion of semantic equivalence $=_{SPL}$ which is assumed to be an equivalence relation.*

Furthermore, conjunction is assumed to be commutative, associative and idempotent under this equivalence: (i) $p_1 \& p_2 =_{SPL} p_2 \& p_1$; (ii) $p_1 \& (p_2 \& p_3) =_{SPL} (p_1 \& p_2) \& p_3$; and (iii) $p \& p =_{SPL} p$.

Based on this equivalence, we can extend this to policy automata equivalence by quantifying over traces:

Definition 5. *Two policy automata $\mathcal{P}_1$ and $\mathcal{P}_2$ (with $\mathcal{P}_i = \langle \Sigma_i, Q_i, q_{0i}, \to_i, \pi_i \rangle$) with a common alphabet Σ (which requires $\Sigma_1 = \Sigma_2$) are equivalent if after following any trace, they both end up in a state in which the policies are equivalent:*

$$\mathcal{P}_1 =_{PA} \mathcal{P}_2 \overset{df}{=} \forall es : \Sigma^* \cdot policy_{\mathcal{P}_1}(es) =_{SPL} policy_{\mathcal{P}_2}(es).$$

Using standard approach, we can now define policy strictness ordering — a policy is considered stricter than another if all behaviour allowed by the former is also allowed by the latter.

Definition 6. *Given policy automata $\mathcal{P}_1$ and $\mathcal{P}_2$ over alphabet Σ, we say that $\mathcal{P}_1$ is stricter than $\mathcal{P}_2$, written $\mathcal{P}_1 \sqsubseteq_{PA} \mathcal{P}_2$ as follows:*

$$\mathcal{P}_1 \sqsubseteq_{PA} \mathcal{P}_2 \overset{df}{=} \mathcal{P}_1 \|_\Sigma \mathcal{P}_2 =_{PA} \mathcal{P}_1.$$

The strictness relation can be shown to obey certain properties.

Lemma 1. *The relation $\sqsubseteq_{PA}$ is transitive, antisymmetric and reflexive.*

Example 4. Consider the policy automaton in Example 1 ($\mathcal{P}_1$) and the synchronous composition of the two automata in Example 3 ($\mathcal{P}_{12}$).

As we remarked in Example 3, the two policy automata are clearly not equivalent. However, we would expect $\mathcal{P}_{12}$ to be a stricter version of $\mathcal{P}_1$. To show this, we note that the synchronous composition of $\mathcal{P}_1$ and $\mathcal{P}_{12}$, $\mathcal{P}_1 \|_\Sigma \mathcal{P}_{12}$ (where Σ is the whole alphabet, including $\{leave(home), leave(work), enter(home), enter(work)\}$), and $\mathcal{P}_{12}$ result in identical policies after following any trace. Formally, for all traces $es \in \Sigma^* \cdot policy_{\mathcal{P}_{12}\|\mathcal{P}_1}(es) =_{SPL} policy_{\mathcal{P}_{12}}(es)$, and thus we can conclude that $\mathcal{P}_{12}$ is stricter than $\mathcal{P}_1$: $\mathcal{P}_{12} \sqsubseteq_{PA} \mathcal{P}_1$.

2.3   Conflicting Policy Automata

In a similar manner as policy equivalence can be lifted from the static policy language to evolving policies, we can extend the notion of conflicting policies. Two static policies conflict when both cannot be satisfied or enforced at the same time. For example, imagine that Alice sets the policy *"Everyone can see the posts on my timeline"* and Bob activates a policy saying *"Only my friends can see my posts"*. If Bob posts in Alice's timeline which policy would apply? If the audience of the post is only Bob's friends Alice's policy would be violated. Similarly, if the audience of the posts is everyone, Bob's policy would not be satisfied. In order to define conflicting policy automata, we require the static policy language to include the notion of conflict between policies.

Assumption 3. *The static policy language SPL must be equipped with the notion of conflicting polices* $\maltese_{SPL}$, *which is assumed to be (i) symmetric; and (ii) closed under conjunction: if* $p_1 \maltese_{SPL} p_2$ *then for any* p_1', *it also holds that* $(p_1 \,\&\, p_1') \maltese_{SPL} p_2$.

We can lift the static policy conflict relation to one on evolving policies:

Definition 7. *Given any static policy language SPL and policy automata* $\mathcal{P}_1$ *and* $\mathcal{P}_2$ *with alphabet* Σ:

$$\mathcal{P}_1 \,\maltese_{PA}\, \mathcal{P}_2 \overset{df}{=} \exists es \in \Sigma^* \cdot policy_{\mathcal{P}_1}(es) \,\maltese_{SPL}\, policy_{\mathcal{P}_2}(es).$$

The intuition behind the previous definition is simple. Any two automata are in conflict if after the execution of a sequence of events, they end up in a state where their policies conflict (at the static policy level).

Example 5. Imagine that Alice and Bob want to leverage the advantages of evolving policies, and they rewrite the previous static policies in a more precise way, *"Everyone can see the posts on my timeline during my birthday"* and *"Only my friends can see my posts when I am at home"*. Combining the policy automata representing these two policies, we can identify a conflict in a state reachable after a trace in which, Alice's birthday begins and afterwards (before the day ends) Bob goes home. Note that it is not required that Bob posts in Alice's timeline for the conflicting policies to be reached, since it is known beforehand that both policies cannot be satisfied at the same time.

Based on this definition and the assumptions we made about conflicts over static policies, we can prove that evolving policies are closed under increasing strictness.

Theorem 1. *Given the policy automata* $\mathcal{P}_1$ *and* $\mathcal{P}_2$ *the following holds*

$$\mathcal{P}_1 \,\maltese_{PA}\, \mathcal{P}_2 \;\wedge\; \mathcal{P}_1' \sqsubseteq_{PA} \mathcal{P}_1 \implies \mathcal{P}_1' \,\maltese_{PA}\, \mathcal{P}_2.$$

3   Translation of Policy Automata to DATEs

Dynamic Automata with Timers and Events (DATEs) [4] are symbolic automata aimed at representing monitors, with a corresponding compilation tool LARVA. In this section, we introduce the basic definitions (leaving out advanced element which are not necessary for this paper) enabling us to provide the translation from policy automata, effectively providing an implementation to the latter through LARVA. As a monitoring formalism, DATE transitions are *event, condition, action* triples: if a matching event occurs and the condition — based on event parameters and the automaton symbolic state — holds, then the action is carried out. The action can be used to either modify the automaton state, interact with the event-generating system, or generate an alert as appropriate.

Definition 8. *A symbolic automaton (SA) running over a system with state of type Θ, is a quintuple $\langle Q,\ q_0,\ a_0,\ \rightarrow,\ B \rangle$ with set of states Q, initial state $q_0 \in Q$, initial action to be executed $a_0 \in \Theta \rightarrow \Theta$, transition relation $\rightarrow \subseteq Q \times \text{event} \times (\Theta \rightarrow \mathbb{B}) \times (\Theta \rightarrow \Theta) \times Q$, and bad states $B \subseteq Q$. Note that the transitions between automaton states are labelled with: (i) an event expression which triggers the transition; (ii) an enabling condition on the system state — encoded as a function from the system state to a boolean value; and (iii) an action (code) which may change the state of the underlying system — encoded as a function, which given a system state returns an updated system state.*

A total ordering $<$, giving a priority to transitions, is assumed to be given so as to ensure determinism.

The behaviour of an SA M, upon receiving a set of events, consists of: (i) choosing the enabled transition with the highest priority; (ii) performing the transition (possibly triggering a new set of events); and (iii) repeating until no further events are generated, upon which the automaton waits for a system event.

3.1   Translation

Intuitively, the translation keeps the same states of the policy automaton, but introduces transitions and states for each static policy. We note that the translation below only handles the high-level enabling and disabling of policies, leaving the low-level checking and enforcement up to a static policy checker. We note that the translation below only handles conjunction of policies.

Given a policy automaton $\langle \Sigma, Q, q_0, \rightarrow, \pi \rangle$, for a given transition $(q, e, q') \in \rightarrow$, we generate an action which disables policies in the outgoing state, and enabling those in the ingoing state, as follows: $\text{action}(q, e, q') = stopEnforcing(\pi(q))$; $startEnforcing(\pi(q'))$, where $startEnforcing(p)$ and $stopEnforcing(p)$ switches on and off the enforcement of static policy p. Using this construction, we generate transitions of the SA labelled as follows: $\rightarrow_{\text{SA}} = \{(q, e, \text{true}, \text{action}(q, e, q'), q') \mid (q, e, q') \in \rightarrow\}$. The resulting DATE would be: $\langle Q, q_0, \text{start}, \rightarrow_{\text{SA}}, \emptyset \rangle$ where start is an action representing the activation of the automaton.

Example 6. Consider the policy automata presented in Example 1, which models the policy *'Co-workers cannot see my posts while I am not at work, and only family can see my location while I am at home'*. Assuming that the events *leave(work)*, *leave(home)*, *enter(work)* and *enter(home)* exist, the automaton can be directly converted to a DATE as follows:

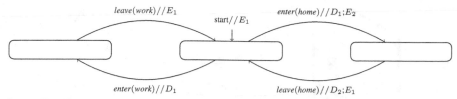

where E_1, D_1, E_2 and D_2 are defined as follows:

$$E_1 = startEnforcing(\mathcal{F}_{co\text{-}workers}(read\text{-}post))$$
$$D_1 = stopEnforcing(\mathcal{F}_{co\text{-}workers}(read\text{-}post))$$
$$E_2 = startEnforcing(\mathcal{F}_{co\text{-}workers}(read\text{-}post) \ \& \ \mathcal{F}_{\overline{family}}(see\text{-}location))$$
$$D_2 = stopEnforcing(\mathcal{F}_{co\text{-}workers}(read\text{-}post) \ \& \ \mathcal{F}_{\overline{family}}(see\text{-}location))$$

4   Implementation in Diaspora* Using LARVA

One of our objectives is to have an effective enforcement mechanism for evolving privacy policies based on policy automata in a real OSN. In this section, we describe the details of the implementation of policy automata using LARVA in the OSN Diaspora*.

We chose Diaspora* since it is open source, which allows us to implement the interaction between the OSN and LARVA. Diaspora* has a built-in mechanism for enforcing static privacy policies. Pardo and Schneider have recently extended Diaspora* with a prototype implementation of some privacy policies defined in the $\mathcal{PPF}$ framework [17,18]. $\mathcal{PPF}$ is a formal (generic) privacy policy framework for OSNs, which needs to be instantiated for each OSN in order to take into account the specificities of the OSN. $\mathcal{PPF}$ was shown not only to be able to capture all privacy policies of Twitter and Facebook, but also more complex ones involving implicit disclosure of information. $\mathcal{PPF}$ comes with a privacy policy language, $\mathcal{PPL_{SN}}$, which satisfies all the assumptions placed for the static privacy language in policy automata (cf. Sect. 2).

Using policy automata to model the evolution of the privacy policies makes it possible to define a modular enforcement of evolving policies. As we mentioned, policy automata are independent of the static policy language of the OSN (except for the assumptions on $=_{SPL}$ and $\&$), and consequently, they are also independent of the underlying enforcement of each particular static policy. Policy automata can be translated to DATEs (cf. Sect. 3). In order to implement policy automata we use the tool LARVA [5], which automatically generates a monitor from properties expressed in DATEs.

In order for the runtime enforcement to work we use a communication protocol between Diaspora* and LARVA. Every time a relevant event occurs in Diaspora* (i.e., an event that can update the state of the automata), it is reported to LARVA. Then LARVA updates the state of the privacy policies (if applicable), and whenever a privacy policy is updated LARVA reports this change to Diaspora*, which would update the corresponding (static) privacy policy (see Fig. 1).

Given that Diaspora* is implemented in Ruby and the monitors that LARVA generates are Java programs, we implement the communication protocol

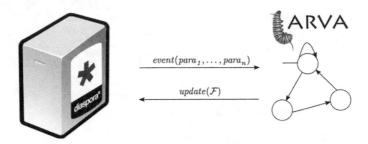

Fig. 1. High-level representation of the Diaspora*-LARVA communication

using sockets. One socket is used by Diaspora* to send a message to LARVA containing the event that has occurred, plus additional information such as the user who triggered the event; if it is a post the audience of the post, whether the post contains a location, etc. LARVA monitors detect (among other things) Java method calls corresponding to events on DATE transitions. Therefore, we have implemented a Java program, which listens to the communication socket and depending on the message sent by Diaspora* it calls a concrete method causing the LARVA automaton to update its state. When an automaton updates its state, the privacy policies to be enforced might change. There is another socket that the LARVA monitor uses to send the privacy policies that Diaspora* should enforce. The message sent by the monitor includes the policies that must be activated (policies of the incoming state) and/or deactivated (policies of the outgoing state). This part of the communication will also be handled by the Java program, which contains an auxiliary method for sending messages to Diaspora*.

5   Case Studies

As a proof-of-concept we have implemented two policy automata in the Disapora*-LARVA system presented in the previous section. Here we describe the concrete details of this prototype. The code of these case studies can be found in [8].

5.1   Case 1: Protecting Pictures During the Weekend

In this case study we describe the implementation of the following evolving privacy policy, *"My supervisor cannot see my pictures during the weekend"*. This is a simple policy that only depends on the time of the week. Let $\mathcal{F}_{supervisor}(\text{see-pictures})$ represent that my supervisor cannot see my pictures, the following DATE models the policy

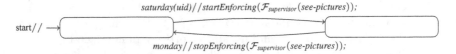

As we mentioned, Diaspora*'s privacy protection mechanism is based on an instantiation of $\mathcal{PPF}$. In this instantiation, we consider that a user appears in a picture if the user is mentioned in the post containing the picture[5]. For this policy automaton Diaspora* is required to report the events *saturday* and *monday*. Each of them represents the beginning of the day after which they are named. Every Saturday at 00:00 Diaspora* sends the message `uid;saturday` to LARVA where `uid` is a user id. This message is sent once for each user with her corresponding `uid`. At this point the automaton of each user is updated. The automaton moves to the only possible state where it replies with the message `uid;exclude-supervisor;picture`. When this message is received by Diaspora*, it activates the static privacy policy that forbids posting a picture of a user if her supervisor is part of the audience. More precisely, Diaspora*'s built-in enforcement mechanism will block any post that contains a picture and mention of a user whose supervisor is included in the audience of the post. Similarly, on Monday at 00:00, Diaspora* informs the automata with the message `monday`. All active automata update their state, therefore no `uid` parameter is needed for this event. This choice also reduces the amount of messages sent between Diaspora* and LARVA. Finally, these automata reply to Diaspora* with the message `uid;include-supervisor;picture`, which allows again the user's supervisor to be part of the audience of her pictures.

5.2   Case 2: Disclosing Location at Most 3 Times per Day

Here we describe the implementation of the policy automaton of Example 2, which we translate to a DATE (as described in Sect. 3) as follows

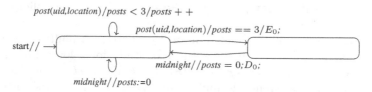

In the previous automaton $E_0 = startEnforcing(\mathcal{F}_{all}(post(uid, location)))$ and $D_0 = stopEnforcing(\mathcal{F}_{all}(post(uid, location)))$. Note that we use the variable *posts* to symbolically encode the explicit states of the real policy automata (cf. Sect. 2). There are two events present in the transitions of the automaton, which therefore need to be reported from Diaspora* to the LARVA monitors when they occur, $post(uid, location)$ and *midnight*.

In our Diaspora* $\mathcal{PPF}$ instantiation, mentioning users in a post that includes a location constitutes a disclosure of their location. Every time a user is mentioned in a post (i.e., $post(uid, location)$), a message including the message `uid;post;location` is sent to LARVA, specifying the user id and that a location of this user has been disclosed. The message is sent for each user mentioned in the post. As described before, there is one LARVA monitor per user, which

---

[5] Diaspora* does not support tagging users in pictures.

controls the policy automaton of each individual. When the message is received the automaton of the user specified by `uid` will be updated. This update will increase the value of the automaton variable *posts*, whose initial value is 0. After sending the message, Diaspora* waits for the answer of the automaton, in case an update of the privacy policies of the user is required. In case *posts* is less than 3, there is no need to update the privacy policies, therefore the message `do-nothing` is sent back. On the other hand, if *posts* is greater than 3, the automaton will move to the state where the policy forbidding the disclosure of locations must be activated, thus it will send the message `disable-posting` to Diaspora*. Note that it is not required to specify the user id in the reply since Diaspora* initiated the communication.

As for the event *midnight*, Diaspora* sends the message `midnight` to the monitors of all users every day at 23:59. If the monitors are in the state where the disclosure of location is forbidden, they take the transition to the initial state. This transition involves, firstly, resetting the variable *posts* to 0, and secondly, sending the message `uid;enable-posting;location` back to Diaspora*, which removes the privacy policy preventing the location of the user `uid` to be disclosed. If the automaton is already in the initial state, it simply resets *posts* to 0.

6   Related Work

The lack of a temporal dimension in privacy policies was already pointed out by Riesner *et al.* [19]. In their survey, they show that there is no OSN that supports policies that automatically change over time. The authors mention that Facebook allows users to apply a default audience to all their own old posts, but there is a big gap between that privacy policy and the family of evolving policies that we introduce in this paper.

Specifying and reasoning about temporal properties in multi-agent systems using epistemic logic have been the subject of study for a long time. It began with the so called *interpreted systems* (IS). In [7] Fagin *et al.* introduce IS as a model to interpret epistemic formulae with temporal operators such as box and diamond. IS have been used for security analyses of multi-agent systems. Though we do consider a temporal aspect, the focus and objectives of our work are different from the work done in interpreted systems, at least in what concerns the domain of application and the scope of the approach. In our case, the policies themselves are the ones evolving based on events, rather than the information on what is known to different agents at a given time.

Recent research has been carried out in extending IS to be able to reason about past or future knowledge. In [2] Ben-Zvi and Moses extend K_i with a timestamp $K_{i,t}$, making it possible to express properties such as "Alice knows at time 5 that Bob knew p at time 3", i.e., $K_{Alice,5}K_{Bob,3}\ p$. With the same essence but including real time, Woźna and Lomuscio present TCTLKD [22], a combination of epistemic logic, CTL, a deontic modality and real time. In these, and other related work, the intention is to be able to model the time differences in the knowledge acquired by different agents due to delay in communication channels. Although both our motivation as well as the application domain differ from those of the aforementioned logics, it is worth mentioning that they could be indeed useful to express certain real-time policies not currently supported in our formalism.

Despite the richness of both timed epistemic logics, TCTLKD [22] and the epistemic logic with timestamps [2], they would not be able to express recurrent policies as we do. We are of course adding a separate layer beyond the power of the logical formalism by using automata to precisely express when to switch from one policy to another. It remains an interesting question what would be the expressivity of policy automata if we consider an enhancement of $\mathcal{PPF}$ with timed extensions as done in some of the above works in order to express richer (static) policies.

We have not defined here a theory of privacy policies (we have not given a formal definition in terms of traces or predicates), nor have we developed a formal theory of enforcement of privacy policies. To the best of our knowledge such a characterisation does not exist for privacy policies. There is, however, work done in the context of security policies, for instance the work by Le Guernic *et al.* on using automata to monitor and enforce non-interference [9,11] or by Schneider on security automata [20]. It could be instructive to further develop the theoretical foundations of policy automata and relate it to security automata and their successors (e.g., edit automata [13]).

7   Conclusions

We have presented a novel technique to define and implement evolving privacy policies (i.e., recurrent policies that are (de)activated depending on events) for OSNs. We have defined policy automata as a formalism to express about such policies. Moreover, we have introduced the notion of parallel composition, subsumption and conflict between policy automata and we have proved some of their properties. We have defined a translation from policy automata to DATEs which enables their implementation by means of the tool LARVA. Furthermore, we have describe how to connect LARVA monitors to the OSN Diaspora* so that policy automata can effectively be implemented. In fact, the presented approach would allow to plug in policy automata to any OSN with a built-in enforcement of static privacy policies. Finally, as a proof-of-concept, we have implemented a prototype of two evolving privacy policies.

The policy automata approach has some limitations. For instance, consider that Alice enables the following policy *"Only my friends can see my pictures during the weekend"*. Imagine that Alice and Bob are not friends. If Alice shares a picture on Saturday, Bob will not have access to it. However, on Monday this policy would be deactivated. What would be the effect of turning off this policy? It might be possible that Bob gains access to all the pictures that Alice posted during the weekend, since no restrictions are specified outside the scope of the weekend. In order to address this problem we might need a policy language able to express *real-time* aspects, with an element of access memory integrated within policy automata.

We are currently also extending policy automata with timing events such as timeouts. This extension will be almost immediately implementable using LARVA since DATEs already support timeouts in their transitions. Another line of work is to extend policy automata with location events. Users normally access OSNs through mobile devices. These devices could directly report the location of users to their policy automata, which avoids having to constantly report users' location to the OSN.

Acknowledgements. This research has been supported by: the Swedish funding agency SSF under the grant *Data Driven Secure Business Intelligence*, the Swedish Research Council (*Vetenskapsrådet*) under grant Nr. 2015-04154 (*PolUser: Rich User-Controlled Privacy Policies*), the European ICT COST Action IC1402 (*Runtime Verification beyond Monitoring (ARVI)*), and the University of Malta Research Fund CPSRP07-16.

References

1. Alexa-ranking. http://www.alexa.com/topsites. Accessed 11 May 2016
2. Ben-Zvi, I., Moses, Y.: Agent-time epistemics and coordination. In: Lodaya, K. (ed.) Logic and Its Applications. LNCS, vol. 7750, pp. 97–108. Springer, Heidelberg (2013)
3. Harvard student loses Facebook internship after pointing out privacy flaws. http://www.boston.com/news/nation/2015/08/12/harvard-student-loses-facebook-internship-after-pointing-out-privacy-flaws/. Accessed 11 May 2016
4. Colombo, C., Pace, G.J., Schneider, G.: Dynamic event-based runtime monitoring of real-time and contextual properties. In: Cofer, D., Fantechi, A. (eds.) FMICS 2008. LNCS, vol. 5596, pp. 135–149. Springer, Heidelberg (2009)
5. Colombo, C., Pace, G.J., Schneider, G.: LARVA -a tool for runtime monitoring of Java programs. In: 7th IEEE International Conference on Software Engineering and Formal Methods (SEFM 2009), pp. 33–37. IEEE Computer Society (2009)
6. Diaspora*. https://diasporafoundation.org/. Accessed 11 May 2016
7. Fagin, R., Halpern, J.Y., Moses, Y., Vardi, M.Y.: Reasoning about Knowledge, vol. 4. MIT Press, Cambridge (2003)
8. Diaspora*. Test pod: https://ppf-diaspora.raulpardo.org, Code: https://github.com/raulpardo/ppf-diaspora (2016)
9. Guernic, G.L.: Automaton-based confidentiality monitoring of concurrent programs. In: 20th IEEE Computer Security Foundations Symposium (CSF 2007), pp. 218–232 (2007)
10. Johnson, M., Egelman, S., Bellovin, S.M.: Facebook and privacy: it's complicated. In: Proceedings of the Eighth Symposium on Usable Privacy and Security, SOUPS 2012, pp. 9:1–9:15. ACM, New York (2012)
11. Guernic, G., Banerjee, A., Jensen, T., Schmidt, D.A.: Automata-based confidentiality monitoring. In: Okada, M., Satoh, I. (eds.) ASIAN 2006. LNCS, vol. 4435, pp. 75–89. Springer, Heidelberg (2007). doi:10.1007/978-3-540-77505-8_7
12. Lenhart, A., Purcell, K., Smith, A., Zickuhr, K.: Social media & mobile internet use among teens and young adults. Pew Internet & American Life Project (2010)
13. Ligatti, J., Bauer, L., Walker, D.: Edit automata: enforcement mechanisms for run-time security policies. Int. J. Inf. Secur. **4**, 2–16 (2005)

14. Liu, Y., Gummadi, K.P., Krishnamurthy, B., Mislove, A.: Analyzing Facebook privacy settings: user expectations vs. reality. In: Proceedings of the 2011 ACM SIGCOMM Conference on Internet Measurement Conference, IMC 2011, pp. 61–70. ACM (2011)
15. Madejski, M., Johnson, M., Bellovin, S.: A study of privacy settings errors in an online social network. In: IEEE International Conference on Pervasive Computing and Communication Workshops (PERCOM Workshops 2012), pp. 340–345 (2012)
16. Madejski, M., Johnson, M.L., Bellovin, S.M.: The failure of online social network privacy settings. Columbia University Computer Science Technical Reports (2011)
17. Pardo, R.: Formalising privacy policies for social networks. Licentiate thesis, Department of Computer Science and Engineering, Chalmers University of Technology, p. 102 (2015)
18. Pardo, R., Schneider, G.: A formal privacy policy framework for social networks. In: Giannakopoulou, D., Salaün, G. (eds.) SEFM 2014. LNCS, vol. 8702, pp. 378–392. Springer, Heidelberg (2014)
19. Riesner, M., Netter, M., Pernul, G.: An analysis of implemented and desirable settings for identity management on social networking sites. In: 2012 Seventh International Conference on Availability, Reliability and Security (ARES), pp. 103–112, August 2012
20. Schneider, F.B.: Enforceable security policies. ACM Trans. Inf. Syst. Secur. 3(1), 30–50 (2000)
21. Weitzner, D.J., Abelson, H., Berners-Lee, T., Feigenbaum, J., Hendler, J.A., Sussman, G.J.: Information accountability. Commun. ACM 51(6), 82–87 (2008)
22. Woźna, B., Lomuscio, A.: A logic for knowledge, correctness, and real time. In: Leite, J., Torroni, P. (eds.) CLIMA 2004. LNCS (LNAI), vol. 3487, pp. 1–15. Springer, Heidelberg (2005). doi:10.1007/11533092_1

TrackOS: A Security-Aware Real-Time Operating System

Lee Pike[1]([✉]), Pat Hickey[2], Trevor Elliott[1], Eric Mertens[1], and Aaron Tomb[1]

[1] Galois, Inc., Portland, USA
{leepike,trevor,emertens,atomb}@galois.com
[2] Helium, Portland, USA
pat@helium.com

Abstract. We describe an approach to control-flow integrity protection for real-time systems. We present *TrackOS*, a security-aware real-time operating system. *TrackOS* checks a task's control stack against a statically-generated call graph, generated by an abstract interpretation-based tool that requires no source code. The monitoring is done from a dedicated task, the schedule of which is controlled by the real-time operating system scheduler. Finally, we implement a version of software-based attestation (SWATT) to ensure program-data integrity to strengthen our control-flow integrity checks. We demonstrate the feasibility of our approach by monitoring an open source autopilot in flight.

1 Introduction

Cyber-physical systems are becoming more pervasive and autonomous without an associated increase in security. For example, recent work demonstrates how easy it is to gain access to and subvert the software of a modern automobile [4]. In this paper, we focus on software integrity attacks aimed at modifying a program's control flow. Traditional methods for launching software integrity attacks include code injection and return-to-libc attacks.

Control-flow attacks are well known, and protections like canaries [5,10] and address-space layout randomization [21] have been developed to thwart them. However, for each of these protections, researchers have shown ways to circumvent them, using techniques such as return-oriented programming [4].

More recently, *control-flow integrity* (CFI), originally developed by Abadi *et al.* [1], is more difficult to exploit. CFI implements run-time checks to ensure that a program respects its statically-built control-flow graph. If the control stack is invalid, then some other program is being executed; modulo false positives, it is a program resulting from a malicious attack.

Consequently, the CFI approach to security has been favored recently as the way forward in protecting program integrity. For example, Checkoway *et al.* demonstrate how to execute return-to-libc attacks without modifying return addresses [4]. In reference to traditional kinds of defenses, the authors write:

> What we show in this paper is that these defenses would not be worthwhile even if implemented in hardware. Resources would instead be better spent deploying a comprehensive solution, such as CFI.

© Springer International Publishing AG 2016
Y. Falcone and C. Sanchez (Eds.): RV 2016, LNCS 10012, pp. 302–317, 2016.
DOI: 10.1007/978-3-319-46982-9_19

Fig. 1. *TrackOS* RTOS integration

The traditional technique for implementing CFI requires program instrumentation (the instrumentation can be done at various levels of abstraction, from the source to the binary). Instrumentation is not suitable for critical hard real-time systems code for at least two reasons. First, instrumentation fundamentally changes the timing characteristics of the program. Not only can instrumentation introduce delay, but it can introduce jitter: CFI checks are control-flow dependent. Second, safety-critical or security critical systems are often certified, and instrumenting application code with CFI checks may require recertification. Our approach allows real-time CFI without instrumenting application code.

The question we answer in this paper is how to provide CFI protections for critical embedded software. Our answer is a CFI-aware real-time operating system (RTOS) called *TrackOS*.

TrackOS has built in support for performing CFI checks over its *tasks*, as processes on an RTOS are generally known. *TrackOS* tasks do not require any special instrumentation or runtime modifications to be checked. *TrackOS* overcomes the delay and jitter issues associated with CFI program instrumentation: rather than instrumenting a program, CFI checks are performed by a separate *monitor task* as shown in Fig. 1. This task is responsible for performing CFI checks on other untrusted tasks. The monitor task is scheduled by the RTOS, just like any other task. However, the task is privileged by the RTOS and is allowed access to other tasks' memory (this is why we show the task overlapped with the RTOS in Fig. 1).

An insight of *TrackOS* is that RTOS design already addresses the problem of real-time scheduling, and CFI monitoring in a real-time setting is just an instance of the task scheduling problem. Furthermore, as an instance of the real-time task scheduling problem, the user has the freedom to decide how to temporally integrate CFI into the overall system design, given the timing constraints. For example, a developer could decide to make CFI monitoring a high-priority task if there is sufficient slack in the schedule or instead monitor intermittently as the schedule allows.

Summary of Contributions

1. *Static analysis*: Before execution, we analyze a task's executable to generate a call graph that is stored in non-volatile memory (program memory). We implement a lightweight static analysis that is able to analyze a 200 KB machine image (compiled from an approx. 10kloc autopilot) and generate a call graph in just over 10 s on a modern laptop.

2. *Control-flow integrity*: At runtime, a monitor task traverses the observed task's control stack from the top of the stack, containing the most recent return addresses, to the bottom of the stack. The control stack is compared against the static call graph stored in memory. In our approach, we do not assume frame pointers, so the analysis must parse the stack. We make optimizations to ensure checks have very low-overhead. Most importantly, the overhead is completely controllable by the user using the RTOS's scheduler, just like any other task.

   This approach implements callstack monitoring rather than just checking well-formedness of function pointers, like many rootkit dectection mechanisms [11,14,15]. The approach supports concurrency (i.e., multiple tasks can be monitored simultaneously).

3. *Program-data integrity*: Our CFI approach is only valid as long as it is executing. An attacker that can reflash a microcontroller can simply overwrite *TrackOS* and any of its tasks. Consequently, we need a check that the program memory has not been modified. We implement a *software-based* attestation framework to provide evidence to this effect. The framework is not novel to us; we borrow the *SoftWare-based ATTestation* (SWATT) approach tailored to attestation in embedded systems [19]. Our full implementation therefore answers a challenge by the authors of SWATT, in which they note that "software-based attestation was primarily designed to achieve code integrity, but not control-flow integrity" [13]. As far as we know, this is the first integration of software-based program-data integrity attestation with control-flow integrity; de Clercq *et al.* previously combine CFI and data integrity relying on hardware support [6].

Assumptions and Constraints. Regarding system assumptions, while not fundamental to our approach, we assume execution on a Harvard or modified Harvard architecture in which the program and data are stored in separate memories (e.g., Flash and SRAM, respectively). Return-oriented programming is still feasible on a Harvard architecture [8]. We do not assume the hardware supports virtual memory or provides read-write memory protections. We do not assume that programs have debugging symbols. We also do not assume the existence of frame pointers.

We assume the attacker does not have physical access to the hardware. However, she may have perfect knowledge of the software including exploitable vulnerabilities in the software, including the bootloader. She may have unlimited network access to the controller. We assume that the microcontroller's fuses allow all memory, including program memory, to be written to. Furthermore, *any* control-flow transfer technique is in-scope by the attacker.

2   Static Analysis

TrackOS compares the control stack against a statically-generated call graph of each monitored task. The call graphs are generated via binary static analysis tool called *StackApprox*; no sources or debugging symbols are required. *StackApprox* currently targets AVR binaries.

StackApprox is similar in spirit to a tool developed by Regehr *et al.* [16], although the use cases are different. In Regehr's case, the focus is on statically determining control-stack bounds, whereas our primary use case is to generate representations of call graphs as C code, although *StackApprox* approximates stack sizes, too. *StackApprox* uses standard abstraction interpretation techniques to efficiently generate a call graph; for the sake of space, we elide details about the tool's design and implementation.

Like in Regehr *et al.* [16], *StackApprox* analyzes direct jumps automatically but requires the user to explicitly itemize indirect jumps. Doing so ensures that all indirect jumps are specified and not the result of unintended or undefined (with respect to C source semantics) behavior. Moreover, large number of indirect jumps are not common in hard real-time systems (we itemized 30 targets for a 10K LOC autopilot, including interrupts).

For the purposes of CFI checking, we generate four tables or maps from the generated call graph. Only values for functions reachable from the start address are generated. Typically, the start address is the entry point for an RTOS task.

– *Loop map*: A mapping from return addresses to callers' return addresses associated with their call-sites.
– *Top map*: A mapping from call-targets (usually the start of a function definition) to the set of return addresses associated with the functions' call-sites.
– *Local stack usage map*: A mapping from call-targets to the maximum number of data bytes pushed on the stack, not including callees' stack usage.
– *Contiguous region map*: Pairs representing the start and stop address that define a contiguous region.

Our build system calls *StackApprox*, which generates C sources containing the four maps, and then integrates the generated C files into the build automatically. The basis of *TrackOS*, FreeRTOS (see Sect. 3), like many embedded RTOSes, statically links the operating system and its tasks. Consequently, there is a circular-dependency problem: because the call-graph data is statically linked into the program, it is needed to build the program, but the program binary must be available to generate the call-graph data. Our solution is to split compilation into two rounds. First, we generate dummy call-graph data that contains empty structures but provide the necessary definitions for building an ELF file. This ELF is then analyzed to extract the actual call-graph data, which is linked with the target program to produce the final ELF file.

Note that this approach requires that the call-graph data be located after the program it is linked with (i.e., the `.text` segment) to ensure the addresses are not modified by populating the call-graph data.

3   TrackOS Architecture

Before describing the CFI monitoring algorithm in the following section, we highlight here the aspects of integrating the CFI checker with the RTOS, including the definition of task control blocks, context switching, and finally, a scheduler

context

target_stack   stack end

Fig. 2. Stack layout for a swapped out task. The saved context is on the top, target_stack points to the beginning of the saved control stack, and a fixed address, 0x456, marks the bottom.

addition we call *restartable tasks*. Our prototype of *TrackOS* is a derivative of FreeRTOS, an open source commercially-available RTOS written in C and available for major embedded architectures.[1]

TrackOS *Task Control Blocks TrackOS* extends FreeRTOS's task control blocks with the following additional state:

1. *Stack location*: a pointer to the portion of a stack that comes after its saved context is added to the TCB. When a task has been swapped out by the scheduler, its control stack will first contain its saved context (i.e., its saved registers and a pointer to its task control block). The saved context is a fixed size. On the top of the stack is the task's saved context; on the bottom of the stack is a return address to the task's initialization function. A hypothetical task control stack is shown in Fig. 2.
2. *Timing*: timing variables are used to track the timing behavior of the observed task to provide *TrackOS* with the duration the task has executed in its most recent time slice. This can be used, for example, to control when stack checking is run (e.g., it might be delayed until after initialization) or even to have time-dependent stack-checking properties (e.g., "after 500 ms of execution, function f() should not appear on the stack").
3. *Restarting*: "restarting" variables allow the CFI task to be restarted as necessary; we explain the concept in Sect. 4.2. To do this, we save a code pointer to the CFI intialization code and its initial parameters as well as a pointer to a shared "restart mutex" with the observed task.

Context Switching. In Fig. 3(top right), we show FreeRTOS's context switching routine (ported to the AVR architecture), together with the extensions necessary for *TrackOS*. This routine is used to swap the context of all tasks (including the monitoring task), whether they are checked or not by the monitor task, and it may be called from the timer interrupt during preemption or explicitly by a task during a cooperative yield (interrupts are disabled when vPortYield() is called). After saving a task's context, *TrackOS* updates its pointer to the top of the stack, after the saved context. Additionally, it saves the execution time of the saved task. After scheduling a new task in (Line 10), all that has to be done is record the execution start time for the newly-scheduled task.

---

[1] http://www.freertos.org/.

```
0  void check_stack(stack_t *target_stack) {          0  void vPortYield( void ) {
      current = target_stack;                                portSAVE_CONTEXT();

      // Preemptive yield                                 #ifdef TRACKOS
      if(preemptive_yield_ret(current)) {                   pxCurrentTCB->pxStoredStack =
5       current = preemptive_stack(current);        5        pxCurrentTCB->pxTopOfStack
        stack_loop(current);                                   + portSP_TO_RET_ADDR;
      }                                                     saveTime();
      // Cooperative yield                               #endif
      else if(coop_yield_ret(current)) {
10      stack_loop(current);                          10      vTaskSwitchContext();
      }
      // Cooperative yield from an ISR                   #ifdef TRACKOS
      else if( search_ret_isrs (current) {                newStartTime();
14      current++;                                      #endif
15      current = preemptive_stack(current);        15
        stack_loop(current);                              portRESTORE_CONTEXT();
      }                                                     asm volatile ( " ret'' );
      else { error (); }                              }
    }
20
    // Check a preemptive function
    void preemptive_stack(stack_t *current) {
      current++;                                       0  void stack_loop(stack_t *current) {
      func = find_current_func(current);                  while(!(inside_main(current)) {
25    if(interrupt_in_main(func, current))                   stack_t * valid_rets =
        done(SUCCESS);                                           lookup_valid_rets (current);
      else                                                   if(NULL == valid_rets) { error(); }
        return find_caller_ret (func, current);     5        else {
    }                                                          current =
                                                                 loop_find_next(current, valid_rets );
                                                               if(NULL == current) { error(); }
                                                             }
                                                    10     }
                                                           if(at_stack_end(current)) {
                                                             done(SUCCESS);
                                                           }
                                                           else error ();
                                                    15  }
```

Fig. 3. Left: CFI procedure to discover the task's yield location. Top right: Context switch in *TrackOS*. Bottom right: *TrackOS* CFI procedure to walk the stack.

4   Control-Flow Integrity

In this section, we overview the control-flow integrity algorithm implemented in *TrackOS*, which is the heart of the approach. We begin by describing the basic algorithm in Sect. 4.1, then we describe two extensions to basic real-time stack checking in Sect. 4.2.

4.1   Basic Algorithm

The CFI algorithm described below is the heart of *TrackOS*. There are two main procedures: first, we find the top return address in the stack, resulting from an interrupt or an explicit yield by the task. Second, once a valid return address is found, it serves as an "entry point" to the rest of the control stack. The second procedure walks the control stack, moving from stack frame to stack frame.

We describe each procedure in turn. Pseudo-code representations of the two procedures are in Fig. 3. For readability, we elide details from the implementation, including hooks for performing restartable checks (see Sect. 4.2), helper functions (e.g., binary search), memory manipulations, type conversions, error codes, special-cases to deal with hardware idiosyncrasies, and other integrated stack checks for aberrant conditions. In addition, for the sake of readability, utility functions in pseudo-code listings that are underlined are described in the text without being defined.

In the following, we assume the maps generated by the *StackApprox* static analysis tool are available to the CFI checker. We do not assume that frame pointers are present, so the stack must be parsed by the CFI algorithm to distinguish data bytes from return addresses.

Yield Address Algorithm. While a task is in the task queue waiting to be executed, its context is saved on its control stack. The CFI checker's entry point is just after the saved context, pointed to by the `target_stack` variable. (The `stack_t` type is the size of stack elements, which are one byte in our implementation.)

The entry point to the stack checker algorithm is `check_stack()`, shown in Fig. 3, left. The invariant that holds after calling `check_stack()` is that either the check has been aborted due to an error, or the function returns a stack pointer to the first proper stack frame on the stack (pointing to the frame's return address). `check_stack()` is executed within a critical section, ensuring that the CFI checker, whenever it executes, always checks that the current location of the observed task's execution is valid.

There are three cases to consider at the entry point of the stack: a preemptive yield, a cooperative yield, and a cooperative yield from an interrupt service routine. These cases correspond to the three cases in the body of `check_stack()` in Fig. 3, left.

Preemptive Yield. In this case, the RTOS scheduler preempts the task via a timer interrupt. Inside the interrupt service routine (ISR), there is a call to a function that performs a preemptive context switch; if this is a preemptive yield, the top of the stack should contain the return address inside the ISR from that function. (The return address is found by *StackApprox* at compile time.) The function `preemptive_yield_ret()` performs this check.

In the case of a preemptive yield, we call `preemptive_stack()` (Line 22 in Fig. 3, left). In that function, we first increment the stack pointer: the next value on the stack following the return address inside the timer ISR is the interrupt address for the task. The function `find_current_func()` takes an arbitrary address and searches through a map containing the address ranges of reachable functions generated by *StackApprox*. If a function that contains the interrupt address cannot be found, the procedure returns an error. Assuming a reachable function is found, `interrupt_in_main()` checks that the function is not the initialization function for the task. If it is the initialization function, then there are no further stack frames to check, since no function calls have occurred. (Additionally, the function checks that the distance to the bottom of the stack is less than the maximum number of data bytes the task's initialization function pushes onto the stack.) The CFI checker completes successfully (done(SUCCESS).

If there are additional stack frames to check, from the interrupted function, the algorithm searches for the first return address on the stack. find_caller_ret() finds on the stack a return address for some caller of func. Using *StackApprox*'s *top map* (see Sect. 2), find_caller_ret() finds the set of return addresses associated with the call-sites for func; we determine the maximum stack usage for func that is also generated by *StackApprox*; call this value *max*. Then, find_caller_ret() searches for a return address appearing in the *top map* that is no more than *max* bytes from the current location in the stack, which are assumed to be data bytes. If a match is found, it is returned. At this point, we have found a return address on the stack belonging to the monitored task, and we are ready to enter the stack_loop() function in Fig. 3, bottom right.

find_caller_ret() is a heuristic for finding a valid return address. It is possible for a data byte to have the same value as a valid return address. If by malicious behavior, then the attacker may be able to cause the CFI algorithm to trace data bytes as return addresses, but these data bytes would still have to conform to *StackApprox*'s static call-graph.

Cooperative Yield. In a cooperative yield, the target task has yielded to the RTOS scheduler by directly making a yield() system call, which the function coop_yield_ret() expects to find on the top of the stack. We increment the stack pointer and call stack_loop().

Cooperative Yield From an ISR. This is a case in which the target task is preempted by an ISR, and then that ISR directly yields to the scheduler. We assume ISRs mask interrupts, so while an ISR should not be preempted, it can yield directly. Also, we assume an ISR only calls yield() just before returning, after all its local data has been popped from the stack. For each ISR that can preempt the target task, *StackApprox* generates a lookup table mapping ISRs to the return addresses for their calls to yield(). The function search_ret_isrs() searches for a match between the top of the stack and a return address from the ISR tables.

If a match is found, then after incrementing the stack pointer (Line 14), we can treat the stack the same as in the preemptive case in which we handle an interrupt to a task.

The Stack Loop Algorithm. At the entry to stack_loop() in Fig. 3, bottom right, current points to a known return address on the stack. stack_loop() "walks down" the stack in its main loop (Lines 1–10), from stack frame to stack frame.

The motivation for checking the stack in the reverse order of calls is to determine if the current location of the program is in an unexpected program location.

Unexpected return addresses further down the stack represent latent vulnerabilities in which the program may return to an unallowed program location as it pops return addresses off of its stack.

The algorithm breaks out of the loop when it reaches a return address for the entry point to the task, relying on the convention that the task entry has exactly one caller, checked by `inside_main()`. Once outside the main loop, there is a final check by `at_stack_end()` that return address of the task's `main()` function is indeed the last return address on the stack and that there are exactly the number of data bytes between the bottom of the stack and the first call by `main()`.

Inside the loop, for each return address `ret` pointed to by `current`, the function `lookup_valid_rets()` looks up the set of return addresses of calls to the function `func` containing `ret` based on the *loop map* generated by *StackApprox*. If there are known callers of `func` found, then `loop_find_next()` searches the stack for another valid return address for a call to `func`. For each return address `ret'`, `loop_find_next()` depends on knowing the number of data bytes to be expected on the stack between `ret'` and `ret`, which is provided by *StackApprox*.

4.2   Extensions

Below we describe three extensions to the basic algorithm described above.

Restartable Monitoring. The monitor task as it has been described is not reentrant. If it is swapped out by the RTOS scheduler while checking task A's stack, and task A then executes, its stack changes. When the monitor is swapped back in, the control stack it was previously checking is stale. Thus, we have designed the monitor task so that it is *restarted* when it is swapped in by the scheduler, meaning that its state is automatically reinitialized to its initial state when it is scheduled; in particular, the monitor restarts checking an observed task from the top of the stack.

The portion of the algorithm to determine a task's yield location and discover the first return address (Fig. 3, left) on the stack is executed inside of a critical section in which interrupts are disabled. Thus, each time the CFI task is enabled by the RTOS, it is guaranteed to at least perform the initial checks on the stack. This initial check is small and the execution time is fairly constant, requiring just a few thousand clock cycles in our experiments. The motivation is to ensure that if the CFI monitor is scheduled, it is not prevented from checking that the current control location is valid. While the algorithm could allow this portion to also be interruptable, it provides the attacker with the opportunity to starve the monitor.

Blacklisting. Sometimes, a code block might be reachable in a statically-generated call graph, but under nominal conditions, it should not appear on a tasks's control stack. For example, after startup, initialization code should not be executed. Similarly, error-handling code should not be executed under normal conditions. While this code cannot be eliminated from the program, it represents a security risk similar to *libc* insofar as it contains additional instructions for use in return-oriented attacks [17].

Consequently, we extend the CFI algorithm with a *blacklisting* capability. The user specifies at compile time a list of code blocks that can be called (usually these are function entry addresses), and *StackApprox* generates an array of all return addresses for callers of those blocks. The array is stored in non-volatile memory as well. Then during the execution of the CFI algorithm, for each return address found on the control stack, the algorithm makes an additional check to see whether the return address appears in the blacklist array. If it is found, then a blacklisting error is returned.

Timing Analysis. Finally, a task's control block contains hooks to keep track of a task's total execution time. This allows the programmer greater flexibility to determine when checks should occur with respect to a task's total execution time or to state control-flow properties in terms of timing behavior.

4.3   Implementation

The implementation of the CFI algorithm requires around 150 lines of code (LOC) of extensions to the RTOS, together with the implementation of a CFI monitoring task. The CFI monitor task is a privileged task, with access to the state of other tasks (and in particular, their control stack memory). Its implementation is approximately 500LOC. The monitoring task can be assigned any schedule priority level; of course, this will affect the frequency of the CFI checks.

Compiled, our implementation of the CFI task requires approximately 2000 bytes of program memory. The call-graph is stored in a special section after the `.text` segment so that instruction addresses do not change when by linking call-graph data (i.e., by "pushing" program instruction addresses down), thereby rendering the analysis on the original program useless. The size of the call graph and TCB pointers are hard-coded into the task. CFI tasks are cheap; in our implementation, adding an additional CFI task adds only 28 additional bytes to the text segment of the resulting ELF file and requires only 200–250 bytes of stack space, as noted above.

Most importantly, this approach does not require any modifications to the CFI monitoring algorithm and we can simply use the RTOS scheduler to schedule the individual CFI monitors.

5   Program-Data Integrity

As TrackOS currently targets the Harvard architecture AVR processor, it gains some measure of program protection through the separation of program and data memory spaces; typically, the program memory is flashed once at programming time, and used as read-only memory during its execution. However, assuming a bootloader is installed, the bootloader can write to program memory during execution. Francillon *et al.* demonstrate how to install malware on a Harvard architecture by exploiting the bootloader to write malicious code into program memory during execution [8]. This sort of attack can be used to simply overwrite the CFI monitor or even the entire RTOS! Even more problematic is that for embedded RTOSes on small microcontrollers, there is no memory isolation between the tasks and the RTOS itself. So a malicious task can potentially modify OS code. Consequently, for increased security, control-flow checking should be augmented by a data attestation approach.

The problem of remote attestation of low-cost embedded devices is addressed in both *Secure Code Update By Attestation* (SCUBA) [18], and *SoftWare-based ATTestation* (SWATT) SWATT [19]. SCUBA strives to provide a safe execution environment for a firmware update, while SWATT attempts to establish the state of a remote system. For our implementation of the remote-verification checksum function, we have drawn from both SWATT and SCUBA. From SWATT, we have taken the idea of verifying the entire program, and from SCUBA we have taken the implementation of a high-performance checksum function.

The checksum function itself is implemented as a simpler version of the ICE primitive from SCUBA [18] that omits the program counter and status register from the hash to simplify the implementation.

The advantage of software-based attestation (SBA) is that it requires no new hardware, which is particularly important in embedded systems with size, weight, and power constraints. SBA was thought to be impractical until the publications of SWATT and its successors, such as SCUBA. While there are shortcomings, e.g., [3], it is a comprehensive approach to ensuring data-integrity without requiring additional or modified hardware.

6   Experimental Results

In our work, the runtime overhead that is typically introduced by CFI is collected into a single RTOS task that can be scheduled at a user-defined priority, and system scheduability analysis is no different than if a new user task were introduced into the system. Because the system is general and highly-dependent on user configuration, general benchmarking is not particularly informative.

Still, to show the feasibility of our approach, we describe a case-study in which we use *TrackOS* to detect instrumented latent software vulnerabilities in ArduPilot, a popular open source autopilot [2]. ArduPilot is a full-featured autopilot that executes (at the time of the experiments) on an 8-bit ATMega2560 AVR microcontroller running at 16 MHz with 256 KB of flash, and 8 KB of SRAM. A custom board has been designed for the autopilot that contains sensors including GPS, an accelerometer, gyroscope, and a barometer and sonar to determine altitude. The ArduPilot can be used with fixed-wing and multi-rotor aircraft. It provides stabilization, GPS-guided waypoint navigation, autoland, position loitering, and communication with a ground station over a Zigbee protocol-enabled radio transmitter.

Architecture. The ArduPilot code base is just under 10K LOC of C/C++, not including standard libraries. The ArduPilot runs "bare" on the AVR hardware.

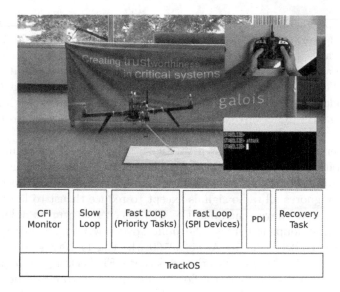

Fig. 4. Top: Attack launch configuration. Bottom: Ported ArduPilot architecture on *TrackOS*

Consequently, we ported it to run as a set of tasks on *TrackOS*. Its architecture is shown in Fig. 4. The infrastructure is decomposed into the following tasks:

- The CFI checker, integrated with *TrackOS*.
- A "slow loop" that reads GPS data, updates navigation information, updates altitude and throttle data.
- A "fast loop" that reads the pilot's radio controller, updates attitude, and writes to the servos.
- Another "fast loop" reading SPI-bus devices, the gyroscope and barometer.
- A program-data integrity task that responds SWATT challenges sent to it over a SPI bus interface.
- Finally, a recovery task. The recovery task only implements throttle control from the radio controller and is enabled if *TrackOS* detects malicious behavior. This task is not enabled until an attack is detected, at which point the slow loop task is disabled (the micro-controller does not have enough memory to support both tasks simultaneously). Thus, the recovery task is shown in the figure as a dashed component.

The CFI checker runs at priority 2, the slow loop runs at priority 1, the fast loops and recovery tasks run at priority 3, the highest priority, and the program-data integrity task runs at priority 1.

The SWATT server is implemented on an ARM Cortex M3, clocked at 60 MHz. The server has 4 MB of external flash memory, with a 50 MB/s interface to the memory over a SPI bus.

We manually annotate just under 30 indirect jumps, including the interrupt vector table.

In our experiments, we implemented two kinds of attacks. First, we implement a buffer overflow vulnerability in which an array is allocated on the stack allowing an attacker to overwrite bytes out-of-bounds. Overwriting a return address, the attack jumps to a function that is unreachable without modifying the control flow. Second, we implement a blacklist attack in which we instrument the code with a function that is supposed to be unreachable during stack checking (e.g., the function could be part of a start-up or an error-handling routine).

The experiment setup is shown in Fig. 4. The attacks are launched from a ground station (i.e., a laptop) communicating with the autopilot over the MAVLink protocol[2]. When an attack is detected on board, the recovery task begins, which ignores all radio signals except to reduce thrust to land the craft.

Even though we have scheduled the CFI checker to run at a *lower* priority than the fast loop, it detects the buffer overflow and blacklisting attacks we instrument. (Indeed, on the Atmega2560, the fast loop must be the highest priority to be schedulable.) Our work shows that CFI checking can happen intermittently and still discover control flow vulnerabilities. To evade detection, an attacker must either (1) exploit a vulnerability, perform an attack, and cleanup before the scheduler swaps the task out; or (2) starve the CFI monitor task indefinitely.

7   Related Work

Research in run-time control-flow protections for embedded software is nascent. In particular, there are few approaches that take into consideration the real-time and memory constraints present in embedded control systems. In the following, we focus specifically on the dynamic monitoring approaches. We omit related research in static analysis and software-based attestation; while *TrackOS* depends on them, we did not make novel research contributions there.

As noted in the introduction, work by Abadi *et al.* [1] addresses many of the shortcomings with earlier protection approaches. An approach that is similar in spirit to our is work by Petroni and Hicks for monitoring control-flow attacks to detect Linux kernel rootkits [14]. Their work is inspired by CFI checks as describe by Abadi *et al.* but addresses environments in which some of the assumptions made by Abadi *et al.* do not hold. Petroni and Hicks also periodically monitor the OS to reduce the timing overhead; in their case monitoring is done from a separate virtual machine hosted by a hypervisor. They focus specifically on rootkit attacks; empirically, many Linux rootkits work by modifying function pointers found in the heap. Therefore, they do not check stack-based software attacks like we do. Furthermore, their work is not focused on real-time systems. Hofmann *et al.* take a similar approach to Petroni and Hicks, also looking to detect kernel rootkits [11] in Linux. Hofmann *et al.* do consider stack-based attacks by checking return addresses on the stack for property violations (i.e., that they point to valid kernel code regions). Their approach is not suitable for

---

[2] http://qgroundcontrol.org/mavlink/start.

checking general return-to-libc attacks, like ours is. Note though that generating a call graph for something as complex as the Linux kernel is much more difficult than traditional embedded code given the prevalent use of heap-based function pointers, dynamic linking, and sheer complexity.

Two works combine CFI and data integrity checks, like ours. These include de Clercq et al. [6] and Zeng et al. [22], using hardware support and sandboxing, respectively.

With respect to CFI in embedded systems, Francillon et al. propose hardware extensions that support a distinguished control stack and data stack [9], and corresponding instruction-based memory access control. They implement a prototype hardware simulator. While hardware support like they envision simplifies the control-flow security problem, our approach works with conventional, unmodified hardware. Reeves et al. present Autoscopy, an in-kernel tool for detecting CFI violations targeted at SCADA systems [15]. Autoscopy has a five percent overhead. Their approach differs from ours insofar as we do not assume reliance on an advanced operating system mechanism, which is not available in small embedded RTOSes. Furthermore, Autoscopy learns a call graph by executing the system during a learning phase, an approach that can lead to false positives if any control paths are missed. Like the rootkit-specific approaches already described, Autoscopy focuses specifically on function-pointer hijacking rather than arbitrary CFI violations.

8 Conclusions and Future Work

We have described *TrackOS*, a unique implementation of CFI monitoring targeted at real-time embedded systems. Our research demonstrates the feasibility of CFI monitoring for low-level systems, relying on the operating system to handle scheduling, making the approach suitable even in hard real-time systems. Many research opportunities remain in the area of CFI checking for embedded systems; below, we describe research questions specifically left open in our work.

We have not addressed the resteering problem. One framework for resteering is the *Simplex architecture*, originally designed to increase the reliability of complex control systems by providing a safe and simple fallback controller [20]. Mohan et al. show how to adapt the Simplex architecture for control-flow attacks. The idea is to monitor with high fidelity the execution time of a control system, with the idea that deviations from the expected execution time are the result of malicious behavior [12]. The approach relies on having accurate timing bounds on normal execution. Our approach does not require timing analysis of the monitored task.

Our use of data attestation is partly because we there is no memory isolation between the RTOS and the tasks executing on it. On a microcontroller and kernel supporing virtual memory, this is less problematic. With a control-flow graph and timing information available to a dynamic monitor, high-level properties can be checked at run-time. For example, temporal logic analyses might be written about control flow, which can be useful for both testing as well as run-time protections of the system. For example, we might query that an authentication routine always follows updated waypoints being read from a ground station over the radio. One of the authors discusses other potential temporal logic properties in related work [7].

Acknowledgments. This work is supported in part by Air Force contract FA8650-11-C-1003. All findings herein are the authors' alone. Pat Hickey performed the work while at Galois, Inc.

References

1. Abadi, M., Budiu, M., Erlingsson, Ú., Ligatti, J.: Control-flow integrity principles, implementations, and applications. ACM Trans. Inf. Syst. Secur. **13**(1), 1–40 (2009)
2. Source code, December 2012. http://code.google.com/p/ardupilot-mega/
3. Castelluccia, C., Francillon, A., Perito, D., Soriente, C.: On the difficulty of software-based attestation of embedded devices. In: Computer and Communications Security (CCS), pp. 400–409. ACM (2009)
4. Checkoway, S., McCoy, D., Kantor, B., Anderson, D., Shacham, H., Savage, S., Koscher, K., Czeskis, A., Roesner, F., Kohno, T.: Comprehensive experimental analyses of automotive attack surfaces. In: USENIX Security (2011)
5. Cowan, C., Calton, P., Maier, D., Hintony, H., Walpole, J., Bakke, P., Beattie, S., Grier, A., Wagle, P., Zhang, Q.: Stackguard: automatic adaptive detection and prevention of buffer-overflow attacks. In: SSYM 1998: Proceedings of the 7th Conference on USENIX Security Symposium. USENIX Association (1998)
6. de Clercq, R., De Keulenaer, R., Coppens, B., Yang, B., Maene, P., de Bosschere, K., Preneel, B., de Sutter, B., Verbauwhede, S.I.: Software and control flow integrity architecture. In: Proceedings of the 2016 Conference on Design, Automation & Test in Europe (2016)
7. Diatchki, I., Pike, L., Erkök, L.: Practical considerations in control-flow integrity monitoring. In: Proceedings of the The Second International Workshop on Security Testing (SECTEST 2011). IEEE, March 2011
8. Francillon, A., Castelluccia, C.: Code injection attacks on harvard-architecture devices. In: Computer and Communications Security (CCS), pp. 15–26. ACM (2008)
9. Francillon, A., Perito, D., Castelluccia, C.: Defending embedded systems against control flow attacks. In: Proceedings of the First ACM Workshop on Secure execution of Untrusted Code, SecuCode 2009, pp. 19–26. ACM (2009)
10. Frantzen, M., Shuey, M., Stackghost: hardware facilitated stack protection. In: SSYM 2001, Proceedings of the 10th Conference on USENIX Security Symposium (2001)
11. Hofmann, O., Dunn, A.M., Kim, S., Roy, I., Witchel, E.: Ensuring operating system kernel integrity with OSck. In: Architectural Support for Programming Languages and Operating Systems (ASPLOS). ACM (2011)
12. Mohan, S., Bak, S., Betti, E., Yun, H., Sha, L., Caccamo, M., S3A: secure system simplex architecture for enhanced security of cyber-physical systems. CoRR (2012)
13. Perrig, A., van Doorn, L.: Refutation of "on the difficulty of software-based attestation of embedded devices" (2010) (Unpublished). https://sparrow.ece.cmu.edu/group/publications.html

14. Petroni, Jr., N.L., Hicks, M.: Automated detection of persistent kernel control-flow attacks. In: CCS 2007: Proceedings of the 14th ACM Conference on Computer and Communications Security, pp. 103–115. ACM (2007)
15. Reeves, J., Ramaswamy, A., Locasto, M., Bratus, S., Smith, S.: Lightweight intrusion detection for resource-constrained embedded control systems. In: Butts, J., Shenoi, S. (eds.) ICCIP 2011. IAICT, vol. 367, pp. 31–46. Springer, Heidelberg (2011). doi:10.1007/978-3-642-24864-1_3
16. Regehr, J., Reid, A., Webb, K.: Eliminating stack overflow by abstract interpretation. ACM Trans. Embed. Comput. Syst. 4(4), 751–778 (2005)
17. Roemer, R., Buchanan, E., Shacham, H., Savage, S.: Return-oriented programming: systems, languages, and applications. ACM Trans. Inf. Syst. Secur. 15(1), 1–34 (2012)
18. Seshadri, A., Luk, M., Perrig, A., van Doorn, L., Khosla, S.P.: Secure code update by attestation in sensor networks. In: ACM Workshop on Wireless Security (WiSe 2006), September 2006
19. Seshadri, A., Perrig, A., van Doorn, L., Pradeep Khosla, S.: Software-based attestation for embedded devices. In: Proceedings of the IEEE Symposium on Security and Privacy, May 2004
20. Sha, L.: Using simplicity to control complexity. IEEE Softw. 18(4), 20–28 (2001)
21. Shacham, H., Page, M., Pfaff, B., Goh, E.-J., Modadugu, N., Boneh, D.: On the effectiveness of address-space randomization. In: Proceedings of the 11th ACM Conference on Computer and Communications Security, CCS 2004, pp. 298–307. ACM (2004)
22. Zeng, B., Tan, G., Morrisett, G.: Combining control-flow integrity and static analysis for efficient and validated data sandboxing. In: Proceedings of the 18th ACM Conference on Computer and Communications Security. ACM (2011)

Leveraging DTrace for Runtime Verification

Carl Martin Rosenberg[1], Martin Steffen[1], and Volker Stolz[1,2(✉)]

[1] Inst. for Informatikk, Universitetet i Oslo, Oslo, Norway
volker.stolz@hib.no
[2] Inst. for Data- og Realfag, Høgskolen i Bergen, Bergen, Norway

Abstract. DTrace, short for "dynamic tracing", is a powerful diagnostic tool and tracing framework. It is invaluable for performance monitoring, tuning, and for getting insights into almost any aspect of a running system. In this paper we investigate how we can leverage the DTrace operating system-level instrumentation framework [9] to conduct runtime verification. To this end, we develop graphviz2dtrace, a tool for producing monitor scripts in DTrace's domain-specific scripting language D for specification formulas written in LTL_3, a three-valued variety of the well-known Linear Temporal Logic. We evaluate the tool by analyzing a small stack-implementation and a multi-process system.

1 Introduction

Runtime verification is an emergent field of research in which formal properties of concrete program or system runs are checked in an automatic manner. In order to conduct runtime verification, one must extract relevant information from the running system without harming or degrading the system in the process. We investigate using the DTrace [9] framework for this purpose.

Originally developed for Sun Microsystems, DTrace combines both static and dynamic instrumentation techniques in a unified framework spanning all aspects of a software system, from specific events in userland processes to function calls within the operating system kernel. DTrace exposes instrumentation points representing events of interest, and lets users associate actions that the computer should take when the selected events occur via a domain-specific, AWK-like, programming language, D. We investigate the suitability of DTrace for runtime verification by making the following contributions:

1. We design and implement graphviz2dtrace, a tool for generating DTrace-based monitors for properties specified in LTL_3: a three-valued variety of the well-known specification logic Linear Temporal Logic (LTL) [5]. In conjunction with the LamaConv automata library [22], graphviz2dtrace provides a complete runtime verification platform.

This article is based upon work from COST Action ARVI IC1402, supported by COST (European Cooperation in Science and Technology).

Y. Falcone and C. Sanchez (Eds.): RV 2016, LNCS 10012, pp. 318–332, 2016.
DOI: 10.1007/978-3-319-46982-9_20

2. We use `graphviz2dtrace`-based monitors to verify two software systems: A simple stack implementation written in C, and a web application consisting of a Node.js [17] web server communicating with a PostgreSQL [19] database. We demonstrate how `graphviz2dtrace`-based monitors can be used to detect property violations and analyze the performance penalty we induce by monitoring the running system.
3. Drawing on the two case studies, we discuss the possibilities and inherent limitations of `graphviz2dtrace`-based monitoring, and suggest directions for future work using DTrace for runtime verification.

The paper is organized as follows. In Sect. 2, we describe the main components of DTrace: probes, providers, and the D scripting language. We also discuss how dynamic instrumentation is possible with the `pid` and `fbt` providers. Then, we describe how to create a bridge between logical and practical concepts by associating atomic LTL propositions with DTrace *probe specifications*, and how this idea is implemented in `graphviz2dtrace`. Since `graphviz2dtrace` produces standalone scripts in the D programming language, we discuss how `graphviz2dtrace` is constrained by the inherent limitations of D, especially with respect to *concurrency*.

We describe the process of finding and specifying observable events, associating the events to atomic propositions in LTL specification formulas, and using the generated monitors to detect property violations.

We evaluate the tool in two case studies: First, we investigate a faulty stack implementation written in C, demonstrating how we can instrument a program without leaving static artifacts in the source code. Then, we investigate a system composed of a web server written in Node.js and a PostgreSQL database. We specify a safety property concerning the interaction between the web server and the database and demonstrate how to detect a violation by hooking a monitor onto the running processes. We also analyze the performance degradation we induce through monitoring, before evaluating our findings and drawing our conclusions.

Section 5 concludes with related and future work. An extended version and technical annexes can be found in the recently published Master thesis [21] and the accompanying web-page.[1]

2   DTrace

DTrace, short for "dynamic tracing", is a powerful operating system level diagnostic tool and tracing framework. It can be seen as a major step forward from older tools such as `ptrace` or `strace` in terms of versatility, sophistication, and efficiency. It offers a flexible tool set for performance monitoring, tuning and collecting comprehensive information on the behavior of a running system, from the behavior of a single process to the internals of the operating system kernel.

---

[1] http://www.mn.uio.no/ifi/english/research/groups/pma/completedmasters/2016/rosenberg/.

In its most basic form, it gives users a way of specifying events of interest and associate actions that the computer should take when those events occur. With DTrace, a user can make requests like

- *whenever a process opens this file, increment this counter and notify me when the counter exceeds a hundred*, or even something as complex as
- *whenever the Apache web server processes an HTTP request, store the response code in a data structure, and when I say so, show me a statistical distribution of the response codes.*

Requests like these are programmed in a domain-specific scripting language, D, which is heavily inspired by AWK and C. Originally written for the Sun Solaris 10 operating system, DTrace is now available for Mac OS X, FreeBSD, and other systems [13]. With DTrace installed, an administrative user can log into the system, write a DTrace script and get insights about the system without having to reboot, stop or alter the system in any way.

DTrace has two main concerns: Firstly, to give users a way of specifying the information they want, and secondly, to acquire the requested information in a safe and efficient manner. While both concerns ultimately must be met, they are treated separately within DTrace: *Producers* are DTrace components that acquire the requested data. Other components post-process the acquired data, presenting it to the user in the manner the user requested: These components are called *consumers*. One purpose of this separation is to ensure safety: producers should only be concerned with acquiring data in a safe and unintrusive way, not with how the acquired data is to be presented or used [8, p. 30-32].

At the kernel level, there are a series of producer components called *providers* that gather data about some aspect of the running system. For example, the `syscall` provider gives data about system calls that are issued to the operating system. The most important consumer is the `dtrace` program, the command-line utility that provides the most common way of interacting with the DTrace framework. This component compiles and executes D-scripts, and calls upon the underlying producers to acquire the requested data.

Specifying Events of Interest: Probes. First of all, users need a way to specify events of interest. To this end, DTrace provides the user with an enormous list of possible instrumentation points representing events of interest. These instrumentation points are called *probes*. The available probes reflect aspects of the system that can be monitored at the current point in time.

Probes are identified by a four-tuple <`provider:module:function:name`>. Users use these tuples to select the probes they are interested in, and specify actions to be taken once the associated events occur. In DTrace parlance, when the event a probe represents occurs, one says that the probe "fires".

It is also possible for application developers to employ so called User Statically Defined Tracing (USDT) to their own programs, by inserting static probes in the application source code. In this way, the application developers can create custom providers for their applications. Many notable software projects have USDT probes, including the PostgreSQL database management software, that we will visit in our case study later, as well as many programming language runtimes.

Doing Things When Events Occur: Actions. Once users have specified which probes they are interested in, they can associate actions blocks that should be executed when the selected probes fire. Users can store data in variables, collect statistics, spawn other processes, inspect system structure and analyze function parameters, to name just a few of the possibilities. Even though action statements are specified in blocks tying them to specific probes, it is possible to share variables and data structures between action blocks, making it possible to monitor complex interactions between events [13, p. 37-42]. The available action statements will vary between DTrace implementations on different platforms.

Filtering Out the Noise: Predicates. When a probe fires, an optional predicate determines if the corresponding action block should execute or not. Predicates are written as boolean expressions that can use any D operator and any D data object. A missing predicate is equivalent to the predicate /`true`/, meaning that no filter is present and the action block will be executed unconditionally when the probe fires.

Dynamic Tracing. A foundational concept in DTrace is *dynamic tracing*. Dynamic tracing permits users to instrument programs on the fly, without requiring static artifacts to be present in the software that is being instrumented [8, p. 30]. This makes it possible to analyze systems that provide limited logging capabilities, systems that are distributed in binary form only, and systems that are opaque in other ways.

In DTrace, dynamic tracing is made possible by the `fbt` and `pid` providers [12]. The previously mentioned `fbt` provider makes it possible to instrument all function return values and arguments in the operating system kernel [13, p. 163]. For userland processes, the `pid` provider gives probes that fire when a function is entered or returned from, and can also be used to create probe firings for specific instructions in the function [13, p. 788-791]. In Sect. 4.1, we use the `pid` provider to dynamically instrument a stack program in C.

The listing in Fig. 1 shows a simple D-script which matches on `read`-syscalls into the kernel. It prints the name of the process issuing the call, except of any running instance of the `dtrace`-process itself.

```
syscall::read:entry              /* probe */
/execname != "dtrace"/           /* predicate */
{ printf("%s \n ", execname); }  /* action block */
```

Fig. 1. A simple D-script

3   Design of graphviz2dtrace

The fundamental idea behind graphviz2dtrace is to let users associate the atomic propositions in LTL formulas with DTrace-observable events represented by DTrace probes (with optional predicates). Suppose, for example, that we want to ensure that a program deallocates all memory before exiting, and have expressed this property as ¬exit W dealloc using the precedence pattern identified by Dwyer et al. in [1]. Suppose that we also have produced a corresponding LTL$_3$ automaton with LamaConv. With graphviz2dtrace, we can create a concrete monitor program for this property in the following manner: First, we can map *exit* to the DTrace probe pid$target::main:return, which fires whenever the main function returns. Similarly, we can map *dealloc* to pid$::dealloc:entry, which fires whenever the dealloc function is entered. Every time DTrace registers one of the specified events, the state of the automaton is updated according to the automaton transition function (encoded in a two-dimensional array). The monitor reports a verdict the moment it detects that the property is either satisfied or violated and terminates itself.

Originally, the idea (and hence the name) of graphviz2dtrace was to provide a unified way of producing DTrace monitors from any monitor automaton encoded in Graphviz [11] dot notation[2]. However, we chose to restrict ourselves to monitor automata for LTL$_3$ since it is well suited for reasoning about *finite* traces.

LTL$_3$ differs from traditional LTL in its semantics, which is defined for *finite prefixes* of infinite traces. The semantics of LTL$_3$ is based on the notion of *good and bad prefixes* originally developed in [15]: A good prefix for a formula ϕ is a prefix such that all possible continuations of the prefix make ϕ true. Conversely, a bad prefix for ϕ is a prefix such that all possible continuations of the prefix make ϕ false. Consequently, an LTL$_3$ monitor is an automaton that *accepts* a trace if it detects a good prefix, *rejects* a trace if it detects a bad prefix or outputs *inconclusive* if the provided trace is neither a good nor a bad prefix [6].

In LTL$_3$ monitor automata produced by LamaConv, all states will be labeled either green, red or yellow. Whenever the automaton enters a red state, the automaton has detected a *bad prefix*. If the automaton enters a green state, a *good prefix* has been found. If the trace (i.e. the input to the automaton) is terminated while the automaton is in a yellow state, the verdict is inconclusive. In graphviz2dtrace-produced scripts, this is reflected in three types of probe clauses: As soon as the automaton detects that it is *about* to enter an accepting or rejecting state, the script outputs the corresponding verdict and stops itself. If the script is terminated while in a yellow state, the script outputs INCONCLUSIVE.

Concurrency-Related Limitations. The most important *limitation* with DTrace is that *there is no way to have a globally accessible yet synchronized state variable in D*: This introduces the possibility of race conditions if two or more probe

---

[2] The graphviz dot notation was chosen because LamaConv can produce it, for its ubiquity, and for the ease with which automata can be visualized.

clauses attempt to update the state variable of the automaton at the same time. A possible mitigation would be to use a thread-local rather than a global state variable, but that would make it impossible to reason about probes that are not associated with the same thread. We elected to make `graphviz2dtrace` agnostic about the provided probes: Users are responsible for preventing race conditions. While this severely restricts the properties that one can safely monitor with `graphviz2dtrace`-based scripts, we show an example that works around this limitation in Sect. 4.

4   Case Studies

In this section we use `graphviz2dtrace` to analyze simple properties in two different setups: in the first case study, we observe function calls in a simple C program that implements a stack-API. In the second, we show how our DTrace-based approach can be used to cover properties that span different operating-system level processes. Lastly, we discuss the performance penalties incurred through DTrace.

4.1   Verifying a Single Process Program

To demonstrate `graphviz2dtrace` in practice, we start by investigating a naïve implementation of the classic stack data structure, supporting the operations *push*, *pop* and *empty*. The *push* function adds an element to the top of the stack, *pop* removes the topmost element on the stack and returns the element to the user, and *empty* says whether the stack is empty or not. We will consider the following property:

$$\Box((\text{push} \land \Diamond\text{empty}) \rightarrow (\neg\text{empty } U \text{ pop}))$$

This property is chosen among the properties which Bauer et al. determined to be LTL$_3$-monitorable [6] and can be understood as saying that *for any stack that has been pushed to and is eventually found empty, a pop event must have occurred before the empty event.*

Obtaining the Automaton. First, we must obtain an automaton by using `LamaConv`. We use the following invocation to generate an automaton encoded in the Graphviz dot language:

```
rltlconv ''LTL=[]((push && <>empty) -> (!empty U pop)),
   ALPHABET=[push,pop,empty]" --formula --moore --min --dot
```

The resulting automaton and corresponding dot code are shown in Fig. 2. We observe that the resulting automaton has two yellow states and one red state. If the input to the automaton ends while the automaton is in any of the yellow states, the verdict is *inconclusive*. If the automaton is in the red state, it means that it has detected a violation of the property.

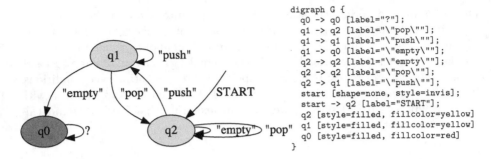

```
digraph G {
  q0 -> q0 [label="?"];
  q1 -> q2 [label="\"pop\""];
  q1 -> q1 [label="\"push\""];
  q1 -> q0 [label="\"empty\""];
  q2 -> q2 [label="\"empty\""];
  q2 -> q2 [label="\"pop\""];
  q2 -> q1 [label="\"push\""];
  start [shape=none, style=invis];
  start -> q2 [label="START"];
  q2 [style=filled, fillcolor=yellow]
  q1 [style=filled, fillcolor=yellow]
  q0 [style=filled, fillcolor=red]
}
```

Fig. 2. Automaton (left) and dot script (right) for the formula $\Box((push \wedge \Diamond empty) \rightarrow (\neg empty \; U \; pop))$ (Color figure online)

Mapping Atomic Propositions to DTrace Probe and Predicate Expressions. With the automaton in hand, we map the atomic propositions in the LTL formula (*push, pop* and *empty*) to DTrace probe and predicate expressions. We use the `pid` provider to detect function calls within the program, which lets us detect when a function is being called and when a function is returned from. In this way, we can inspect both function arguments and return values. We create the following mapping in JSON as `mapping.json`:

$$push \rightarrow \texttt{pid\$target::push:entry}$$
$$pop \rightarrow \texttt{pid\$target::pop:return}$$
$$empty \rightarrow \texttt{pid\$target::empty:return/arg1 == 1/}$$

Anytime the stack program enters the `push` function, our monitor script registers this as a *push* event and updates the internal automaton state accordingly. Similarly, whenever the stack program returns from the `pop` function, the monitor registers this as a *pop* event.

The `empty` function reports whether the stack is empty or not. It returns either 1 or 0, meaning *true* or *false*. Since we are interested in the event "the stack is empty" rather than "the `empty` function is being called", we must check the return value of `empty`. We use a predicate expression for this. The predicate checks that the return value of the function, which the `pid` provider binds to `arg1`, is 1.

We now have all the necessary ingredients. To obtain our monitor, we use the following `graphviz2dtrace` invocation:

```
$ ./graphviz2dtrace.py --mapping mapping.json automaton.dot
```

The listing in Fig. 3 shows the salient parts of the generated script, eliding generated comments, and parts of the transition table.

Detecting a Violation. To experiment with the monitor, we introduce a fault into the stack implementation. The `push` function does not increment the buffer

```
int HAS_VERDICT;
int state;
int tf[3][3];

dtrace:::BEGIN
{
        tf[0][0] = 0;
        /* ... */
        tf[2][2] = 0;
        HAS_VERDICT = 0;
        state = ($1 ? $1: 0);
}

pid$target::empty:return
/ (arg1 == 1) && (state == 2)/
{
        trace("REJECTED");
        HAS_VERDICT = 1;
        exit(0);
}
```

```
pid$target::push:entry
/state == 2 || state == 0/
{
        state = tf[state][1];
}

pid$target::empty:return
/ (arg1 == 1) && (state == 0)/
{
        state = tf[state][0];
}

pid$target::pop:return
/state == 2 || state == 0/
{
        state = tf[state][2];
}

dtrace:::END / !HAS_VERDICT /
{ trace("INCONCLUSIVE"); }
```

Fig. 3. Generated script

index after pushing a new element onto the stack, ie. the `empty` operation will yield 1 (ie. true) even though elements have been pushed onto the stack:

```
void push(int number, int* i) { buffer[*i] = number; }
```

We demonstrate this by feeding the program a test case via the standard input. Notice that the monitor is called with the `-c` parameter, which tells the monitoring script that it should start the provided program and trace until the target program finishes running. We run the program with `sudo`, as DTrace requires special privileges to run, regardless of the privilege level of the programs being monitored.

```
$ sudo ./monitor.d -c ./stack < incite_error.in
PUSHED 3
PUSHED 4
PUSHED 5
YES
REJECTED
```

Indeed, we see that the last line is REJECTED. To ensure against a false positive, we fix the stack implementation to increment on `push`, which should make the monitor output INCONCLUSIVE, we recompile the program and run the test case again:

```
$ sudo ./monitor.d -c ./stack-wpushfix < incite_error.in
PUSHED 3
PUSHED 4
PUSHED 5
NO
INCONCLUSIVE
```

As expected, the verdict is INCONCLUSIVE, since we have reached the end of the trace and stopped in neither an accepting, nor rejecting, state.

4.2 Verifying Interactions Between Programs

The previous case study concerned a single-process program. What if the system we want to analyze is realized by more than one process? To illustrate how `graphviz2dtrace` can create monitors suitable for these occasions, we will now analyze a simple system consisting of a web server written in Node.js [17] talking to a PostgreSQL [19] database. The point of this case study is not to illuminate some complex system—in fact, the system is made deliberately simplistic to emphasize how the system is instrumented—but rather to discuss what it is like to use `graphviz2dtrace` in practice on a deployed system.

The web server listens to incoming HTTP requests and stores the user-agent strings of the incoming requests in a PostgreSQL database. When the server starts up, it reports its process ID and the process ID of the attached PostgreSQL client to the terminal. Suppose we wanted to ensure that whenever the web server receiving a request, the database completes the corresponding insertion query successfully before the web server sends a response to the client. How could we do that?

In the following, we go through the process of selecting relevant probes corresponding to the events we want to study, specifying the property in LTL, creating the corresponding monitor, attaching it to the running system and detecting violations.

Both Node.js and PostgreSQL have tailor-made static probes that we can make use of. For PostgreSQL, we consulted the listing of available static probes in [20] and used DTrace to find a single probe to associate with the event that a specific PostgreSQL client is done executing a query:

```
postgresql$$1:postgres:PortalRun:query-execute-done.
```

The `$$1` lets us target a specific PostgreSQL client instance by providing the corresponding PID to the monitoring script via the command line. Furthermore, Node.js has static probes for incoming HTTP requests and responses, which can be tied to a specific Node.js instance as in these probe specifications:

```
node$target:node::http-server-request and
node$target:node::http-server-response.
```

Here, we use the `$target` macro variable to specify the PID of the relevant Node.js instance via the command line.

By not supporting parameterized properties, `graphviz2dtrace` makes it hard to reason about *distinct* events of the same type. However, the predicate mechanism in DTrace is quite expressive. Let us see if we can use the DTrace predicate mechanism to express the property as something that either *should* happen or *should never* happen, and see if we can get closer to our intended meaning.

We wanted to ensure that the server never sends a response to the client before the database management system has completed the corresponding query. Let us rephrase this property in terms of what should never happen:

1. The server should never send a response before the corresponding database query is complete.
2. There should never be an HTTP request for which the corresponding database query and HTTP response never happen.

Suppose we kept three running counters: One for registered requests, another for completed queries, and a third for completed responses. We can achieve this in a D script by adding one probe clause for each event that increments the corresponding counter:

```
int  nrequests ,  nresponses ,  nqueries ;

node$target : node :: http−server−request
    { nrequests++; }

node$target : node :: http−server−response
    { nresponses++; }

postgresql$$1 : postgres : PortalRun : query−execute−done
    { nqueries++; }
```

If we want to add this to a **graphviz2dtrace**-generated script, we must place these probe clauses *before* the clauses related to the automaton logic to get the intended result, since probe clauses associated with the same probe are processed in order. If we place them below the automaton-related clauses, the counters would be incremented *after* we check if the property is violated. Note also that global variables are initialized to 0 by default in D script.

With the counters in place, we can then express the first property as

$$\Box \neg (nresponses > nqueries)$$

What about the response property? We suggest the following: Define a tolerance level for how big the difference can be between registered requests on the one hand and registered responses and queries on the other. As a starting point, let us arbitrarily specify the tolerance level by saying that this difference should never exceed 100:

$$\Box \neg (((nrequests - nresponses) > 100) \wedge ((nrequests - nqueries) > 100))$$

Having decided on these properties, we need to find a way of associating the atomic propositions of these properties with probe firings so we can detect violations. We can associate the atomic proposition in the precedence property with the **http-server-response** probe:

```
node$target:node::http-server-response/nresponses > nqueries/
```

The response property is not as obvious, but we we can use the special **tick** provider to inspect the state of the monitoring script at a given interval. The **tick** provider fires at a fixed interval on one CPU [18, p. 177]. By associating a suitable predicate with a `tick` event, we can check if the difference between registered requests and registered queries and responses is too large. If we check the property 10 times a second, the probe and predicate specification becomes:

```
tick-10hz/((req - res) > 100) || ((req - queries) > 100)/
```

We then go on to constructing an appropriate automaton. First, we create some aliases. We call the event related to the precedence property *mismatch* and the event associated with the response property *unresponsive*. We then define our specification formula as the following conjunction:

$$(\Box\neg mismatch) \wedge (\Box\neg unresponsive)$$

We then use `LamaConv` to create the automaton, and `graphviz2dtrace` to create the corresponding script. We also add the counter logic mentioned above to get the counters to work. Finally, to make the verdicts more informative, we also add print statements helping us distinguish between when the property is violated due to the *mismatch* event and when the violation is caused by the *unresponsive* event.

Detecting a Violation. With the monitoring script in hand, let us proceed to verifying the system under scrutiny. Again, we have introduced an artificial problem in our code to give our monitor something interesting to observe. We use the following fragment in the web server source code to handle a request:

```
client.query('INSERT INTO entries(entry) VALUES($1)',
        [req.headers['user-agent']],
        function (error, result){
            if(error){
                res.end('Query failed\n');
            }
        });
res.end('Accepted entry\n');
```

Once the database finishes, the runtime executes the code in the anonymous callback function. In the meantime, the webserver can go on processing other events. However, the statement `res.end('Accepted entry\n');` which closes the HTTP response, is *outside* of the callback which fires when the database is done. Therefore it is possible that the statement above is executed *before* the database is done completing the query.

On startup, the Node.js server prints all the information that we need to subsequently attach DTrace:

```
$ node server.js
Server running at 127.0.0.1, port 1337
Node.js PID is 11509
PostgreSQL client PID is 11510
$ sudo ./monitor.d -p 11509 11510
```

The p flag binds 11509 to the $target macro variable. Similarly, 11510 will be bound to $1. With the monitor attached, we use the Apache Benchmark [2] tool ab to send the server a series of requests, and quickly trigger the monitor:

```
$ ab -n 10000 http://127.0.0.1:1337/
...
REJECTED DUE TO MISMATCH
```

We can detect a violation of the response property, too. Running a new benchmark on the server after fixing the callback error above, this time with a high number of concurrent connections via the command line option -c 200, we get immediately: REJECTED DUE TO UNRESPONSIVENESS.

The tolerance gap of 100 requests in the property was chosen arbitrarily, so this does not have to mean that there is any grave error with the software system as such. Nevertheless, we have seen that the monitor detects a violation.

On Concurrency. Since the Node.js web server and the PostgreSQL database run as separate processes on a multi-core machine it is both possible and desirable that they do tasks in parallel: Generally, this can also mean that we get two simultaneous probe firings that create a race condition on the monitor's state variable. In this specific case, we are in the clear: The clauses in the generated monitor never update the state variable, since as soon as either the *mismatch* or the *irresponsive* event is detected a bad prefix has been found and monitoring is terminated.

4.3   Performance

Finally, we would like to observe and discuss the performance of DTrace-based runtime verification. Gregg [12] analyzes the overhead of the pid provider and states the following principle about the performance overhead induced by DTrace:

> "The running overhead is proportional to the rate of probes - the more they fire per second, the higher the overhead."

He then formulates the following rules of thumb:

– "Don't worry too much about pid provider probe cost at < 1 000 events/s."
– "At > 10 000 events/s, pid provider probe cost will be noticeable."
– "At > 100 000 events/s, pid provider probe cost may be painful."

Paraphrasing our performance evaluation detailed in [21], we see that in the case of the web-server, in our benchmark the system processes roughly 2 000 requests per second, and with three probe firings associated with each request (one for the request, one for the query and one for the response), this only adds up to 6 000 probe firings per second, which is well below this threshold.

In the case of the stack example, we also compared with printf-based events (essentially how logging would be implemented). We observe that although this method of event-generation has only half the runtime overhead of using DTrace probes from the `pid` provider, it is a static instrumentation which gives less flexibility, especially in the case where the application does not need to be monitored. In that case, DTrace would have virtually no overhead, whereas the program with the `printf`-statements would have to be recompiled without them.

This shows that we can instrument a running system with DTrace without adversary performance effects, so long as we limit the number of possible probe firings per second to a reasonable level.

5   Conclusion and Future Work

DTrace offers a unique insight into running programs with little overhead. Its main design goal is unobtrusiveness, i.e., apart from a usually minor performance impact, DTrace cannot affect the program execution in any way. Here, we have used DTrace scripts to monitor events provided by the operating system runtime (function calls via C-style libraries or syscalls into the kernel), and through User Statically Defined Tracing, where developers deliberately expose relevant probes to DTrace.

As the scripts run inline with the actual program, we have chosen to encode the transition function of three-valued Linear Time Logic LTL_3 directly through a two-dimensional array in DTrace. The three-valued logic gives us the possibility to yield a verdict on an accepting/rejecting a run as soon as possible.

A major advantage of this approach is that we can associate events from different (operating system-level) processes, possibly even implemented in different languages. We have illustrated the usefulness in two small cases studies, and reflected on performance impacts.

Related Work. The main challenge in applied runtime verification is how to observe a program. Approaches can be divided into those that require access to the source code, and those that do not.

The former rely on recompilation (or byte-code transformation in case of interpreted languages) to be able to intercept relevant events at runtime. Programs are either recompiled with manual annotations or instrumentations, or through a more declarative approach like aspect-oriented programming [16]. The notions of capturing function entries and exits with the possibility to bind values in AspectJ have already been used previously together with temporal logics [24] and trace-based interface specifications [7].

In the second category of tools that can work with a binary representation only of the software, we have log-based tools [14], or those that work on a lower level, e.g. by using advanced emulation or virtualization techniques like Intel's SAE technology [10]. The latter works on the instruction-level and requires reconstruction of higher-level actions of the program from sequences of assembly instructions.

Another dimension of classification is online versus offline monitoring. In online monitoring, properties are checked in lock-step with the program execution. This also allows the monitor to interrupt, or otherwise interact with the program as soon as a violation is detected. The ability of a system to reason and reflect about its own operating modes and overall system state at runtime has also been termed *runtime reflection* in [4]. In offline monitoring, runtime verification techniques are only used to record a trace, which is then processed later, e.g. for post-mortem analyses. Our DTrace approach realises online monitoring, as scripts are executed inline, yet we have not made use of a feedback mechanism to realise reflection. However, a feedback mechanism could be achieved by connecting the output of the DTrace script to the input of the program, or making use of DTrace's so-called *destructive actions* [18, p. 114], which, among other things, offer direct manipulation of memory contents. This requires active cooperation from the program, in the sense that a developer has to program the application to respond to monitor verdicts.

In future work, we plan to extend the framework with parametrized propositions [23], or quantified event automata [3]. This will allows us to instantiate properties with events that carry values, e.g. to match corresponding identifiers in requests and responses. As we have seen in the web-server example, this is a limiting factor which can only be partially remediated through counters.

It is not clear how concurrent programs can effectively be monitored without race conditions in the action blocks. An obvious, though less elegant, solution would be to use DTrace to only *collect* the trace data, and produce a single stream of interleaved events that is *processed outside* of DTrace.

All source code to the example programs, monitors, and detailed instructions are available in [21] and the accompanying web-page http://www.mn.uio.no/ifi/english/research/groups/pma/completedmasters/2016/rosenberg/.

References

1. Aalav, H., Avrunin, G., Corbett, J., Dillon, L., Dwyer, M., Pasareanu, C.: Specification patterns. http://patterns.projects.cis.ksu.edu/. Accessed 13 Aug 2015
2. Apache Software Foundation: ab - Apache HTTP server benchmarking tool. https://httpd.apache.org/docs/2.4/programs/ab.html
3. Barringer, H., Falcone, Y., Havelund, K., Reger, G., Rydeheard, D.: Quantified event automata: towards expressive and efficient runtime monitors. In: Giannakopoulou, D., Méry, D. (eds.) FM 2012. LNCS, vol. 7436, pp. 68–84. Springer, Heidelberg (2012)
4. Bauer, A., Leucker, M., Schallhart, C.: Model-based runtime analysis of distributed reactive systems. In: 17th Australian Software Engineering Conference (ASWEC 2006). IEEE Computer Society (2006)
5. Bauer, A., Leucker, M., Schallhart, C.: Monitoring of real-time properties. In: Arun-Kumar, S., Garg, N. (eds.) FSTTCS 2006. LNCS, vol. 4337, pp. 260–272. Springer, Heidelberg (2006)
6. Bauer, A., Leucker, M., Schallhart, C.: Runtime verification for LTL and TLTL. ACM Trans. Softw. Eng. Methodol. **20**(4), 1–64 (2011)
7. Bodden, E., Stolz, V.: Tracechecks: defining semantic interfaces with temporal logic. In: Löwe, W., Südholt, M. (eds.) SC 2006. LNCS, vol. 4089, pp. 147–162. Springer, Heidelberg (2006)

8. Cantrill, B.: Hidden in plain sight. ACM Queue **4**(1), 26–36 (2006)
9. Cantrill, B., Shapiro, M.W., Leventhal, A.H.: Dynamic instrumentation of production systems. In: ATEC 2004 Proceedings of the Annual Conference on USENIX Annual Technical Conference. USENIX (2004)
10. Chachmon, N., Richins, D., Christensson, M., Cohn, R., Cui, W., Reddi, V.J.: Simulation and analysis engine for scale-out workloads. In: Proceedings of the 30th ACM on International Conference on Supercomputing. ACM (2016)
11. Ellson, J., Gansner, E.R., Koutsofios, L., North, S.C., Woodhull, G.: Graphviz - open source graph drawing tools. In: Mutzel, P., Jünger, M., Leipert, S. (eds.) GD 2001. LNCS, vol. 2265, p. 483. Springer, Heidelberg (2002)
12. Gregg, B.: DTrace pid Provider Overhead (2011). http://dtrace.org/blogs/brendan/2011/02/18/dtrace-pid-provider-overhead/
13. Gregg, B., Mauro, J.: DTrace: Dynamic Tracing in Oracle Solaris, Mac OS X, and FreeBSD. Prentice Hall Professional, Upper Saddle River (2011)
14. Havelund, K., Joshi, R.: Experience with rule-based analysis of spacecraft logs. In: Artho, C., Ölveczky, P.C. (eds.) FTSCS 2014. CCIS, vol. 476, pp. 1–16. Springer, Heidelberg (2015)
15. Kupferman, O., Vardi, M.Y.: Model checking of safety properties. Formal Meth. Syst. Des. **19**(3), 291–314 (2001)
16. Laddad, R.: AspectJ in Action, 2nd edn. Manning Publications, Cherry Hill (2009)
17. Node.js Foundation. Node.js. https://nodejs.org/en/
18. Oracle Corporation: DTrace Guide for Oracle Solaris 11. Oracle Corporation, Redwood City (2012)
19. PostgreSQL Global Development Group: PostgreSQL. http://www.postgresql.org/
20. PostgreSQL Global Development Group: PostgreSQL Documentation: Dynamic Tracing. http://www.postgresql.org/docs/current/static/dynamic-trace.html
21. Rosenberg, C.M.: Leveraging DTrace for runtime verification. Master thesis, Department of Informatics, Faculty of Mathematics and Natural Sciences, University of Oslo, May 2016
22. Scheffel, T., Schmitz, M., et al.: LamaConv-logics and automata converter library. http://www.isp.uni-luebeck.de/lamaconv
23. Stolz, V.: Temporal assertions with parametrized propositions. J. Log. Comput. **20**(3), 743–757 (2010)
24. Stolz, V., Bodden, E.: Temporal assertions using AspectJ. Electron. Notes Theoret. Comput. Sci. **144**(4), 109–124 (2006)

Finite-Trace Linear Temporal Logic: Coinductive Completeness

Grigore Roşu[⊠]

University of Illinois, Champaign, USA
grosu@illinois.edu

Abstract. Linear temporal logic (LTL) is suitable not only for infinite-trace systems, but also for finite-trace systems. Indeed, LTL is frequently used as a trace specification formalism in runtime verification. The completeness of LTL with only infinite or with both infinite and finite traces has been extensively studied, but similar direct results for LTL with only finite traces are missing. This paper proposes a sound and complete proof system for finite-trace LTL. The axioms and proof rules are natural and expected, except for one rule of coinductive nature, reminiscent of the Gödel-Löb axiom. A direct decision procedure for finite-trace LTL satisfiability, a PSPACE-complete problem, is also obtained as a corollary.

1 Introduction

Finite execution traces play an important role in several computing fields. For example, Hoare logic [12], which is at the heart of deductive program verification, defines (partial) correctness in terms of finite traces: $\{pre\}P\{post\}$ holds iff any *finite* execution trace of P starting in a state satisfying *pre* ends in a state satisfying *post*. Also, in runtime verification, formal specifications are often used to characterize the bad behaviors of a system. Then the system is monitored against monitors generated from specifications. While infinite-trace specification formalisms have occasionally been used to specify systems' bad behaviors, in the end such bad behaviors occur after a finite number of observed events, so the generated monitors need only be faithful to the finite-trace safety fragment of the property. Consequently, many temporal specification formalisms used in runtime verification (and not only) have finite-trace semantics [5,8,11,13,15,20,23].

Linear temporal logic (LTL) [18] has established itself as one of the major trace specification formalism. With few exceptions (some mentioned above, others shortly below), the semantics of LTL is typically given in terms of infinite traces or of both infinite and finite traces (see, e.g., [17]), and some of the major theoretical results of LTL have only been studied in this context. This is unfortunate, because LTL is just as suitable a specification formalism for properties over only finite traces. For example, we can specify any finite-state machine *FSM* as a finite-trace LTL formula φ_{FSM} (Example 2), so that a word is in the language of *FSM* iff (a variant of) it satisfies φ_{FSM}. Moreover, consider again a Hoare triple $\{pre\}P\{post\}$ and suppose that *FSM*, φ_{pre}, and φ_{post}, respectively, abstract the state-space of the program P (with accepting states precisely where

© Springer International Publishing AG 2016
Y. Falcone and C. Sanchez (Eds.): RV 2016, LNCS 10012, pp. 333–350, 2016.
DOI: 10.1007/978-3-319-46982-9_21

P is terminated), and *pre* and *post*. Then the formula $\varphi_{FSM} \wedge \varphi_{pre} \rightarrow \Diamond \varphi_{post}$ captures the abstract meaning of the Hoare triple quite elegantly.

When giving LTL a finite-trace semantics, one has to decide upon the semantics of the "next" operator on one-state traces, that is, when there is no next state. In a two-valued[1] setting, there are three admittedly meaningful semantics for "next φ" on one-state traces: (1) it always holds; (2) it never holds; (3) it holds iff φ holds itself on the one-state trace. The semantics (3) has the technical advantage that it reduces finite-trace to infinite-trace semantics by repeating the last state of the finite trace indefinitely, so the usual LTL reasoning remains sound. For that reason, for example, it has been used in the context of run-time verification [20], where a finite-trace semantics with sound deduction was needed. However, (3) has a major drawback: the LTL formulae cannot distinguish between terminated traces and traces which (accidentally) repeat their last state. Hence, in our view, (3) does not capture the nature of finite-trace LTL properly, so we here stick to (1) and (2). In fact, (1) and (2) are equivalent and can co-exist: if $\circ$ is the *weak* next of (1) and $\bullet$ is the *strong* next of (2), then it is easy to see that $\circ\varphi \equiv \neg\bullet\neg\varphi$ and $\bullet\varphi \equiv \neg\circ\neg\varphi$.

While first-order logic expressiveness results for LTL variants with finite-trace semantics have been studied [6,24], at our knowledge no other major theoretical aspects of finite-trace LTL have been investigated. In particular, *direct* decidability and complete deduction results are missing. By "direct" we mean ones that work directly with finite-trace LTL formulae, as opposed to ones based on translations to other logics. As an analogy, an *indirect* complete proof system for infinite-trace LTL, or for equational logic, etc., can be easily obtained by translations of these logics into first-order logic (FOL) and then using the complete proof system for FOL. Practically, such indirect results have at least two drawbacks: first, the size of the translated formulae may be larger than the original formula, thus incurring increased algorithmic complexity to solve the translated problem; second, the meaning and intuitions of the original logic and its formulae may be lost in translation, making assisted proofs more challenging and inconvenient for humans. Theoretically, direct decidable procedures and complete proof systems specialized for the logics of interest are desirable, because they help us better understand the nature of those logics and their specific challenges.

One may think that complete proof systems for finite-trace LTL should easily follow from the infinite-trace variants, because finite traces are particular infinite traces which stutter in the final state after a finite number of states. However, a careful examination reveals that the infinite-trace LTL results heavily rely on the axiom/property $\neg\circ\varphi \leftrightarrow \circ\neg\varphi$, which does *not* hold for finite-trace LTL. Only one implication holds, namely $\neg\circ\varphi \rightarrow \circ\neg\varphi$ (or its equivalent $\bullet\neg\varphi \rightarrow \neg\bullet\varphi$). Therefore, axioms need to be dropped from the infinite-trace LTL proof system. Furthermore, one may think that it suffices to just drop the implication $\circ\neg\varphi \rightarrow \neg\circ\varphi$ from the axioms of infinite-trace LTL (or replace it with a weaker one), like for the LTL variant in [17] with both infinite and finite traces, because all the other axioms and proof rules, including the powerful Induction rule

---

[1] See [2] for multi-valued variants of LTL.

$$Ind \qquad \frac{\varphi \to \circ\varphi}{\varphi \to \Box\varphi}$$

are sound for finite traces as well, and finite-trace LTL "ought to" be simpler than LTL with both finite and infinite-traces. However, it turns out that new rules are needed in order to achieve completeness, because finite-trace LTL admits new tautologies which do not hold for infinite-traces, such as $\Diamond\circ\bot$ (every trace eventually terminates).

Conceptually, the main contribution of this paper is the following Coinduction proof rule, which appears to play a central role in finite-trace temporal reasoning:

$$coInd \qquad \frac{\circ\varphi \to \varphi}{\varphi}$$

In words, it states that if we can always prove that a property holds now assuming it holds next, then the property always holds. For example, if φ is "I am happy" and $\circ$ is "tomorrow", then coinduction allows us to infer "I am happy" provided that we are able to prove "if tomorrow I am happy then today I am happy". This may seem counter-intuitive at first, but it makes full sense in the context of finite traces with the weak interpretation of $\circ$. Indeed, suppose that $\circ\varphi \to \varphi$ holds for all finite traces. Since $\circ\varphi$ always holds on one-element traces, $\circ\varphi \to \varphi$ implies that all one-element traces satisfy φ. That implies that $\circ\varphi$ always holds on two-element traces, so $\circ\varphi \to \varphi$ implies that all two-element traces satisfy φ. We can thus inductively show that traces of any length satisfy φ.

As another example of coinduction, consider program verification of partial correctness using operational semantics, as advocated in [4,19,21]. There, program partial correctness is framed as (symbolic) reachability: the desired reachability property holds iff it holds on all finite paths starting with the current (symbolic) program configuration. Consider that our property φ in the *coInd* rule above is such a reachability property, and suppose that it refers to a loop. Then $\circ\varphi$ corresponds to the same reachability property holding in the next state, which in this approach is obtained by applying an operational semantics step, which in our case means unrolling the loop once. Proving $\circ\varphi \to \varphi$ corresponds to proving the original loop program assuming the desired loop property to hold after we unroll the loop once. In other words, checking symbolically the loop invariant property. If that holds, then we can safely assume that our original reachability property φ holds, in the partial correctness sense. Indeed, if the loop does not terminate, then any reachability property can be proved for it using *coInd* (similar to Hoare logic).

Our *coInd* rule is reminiscent of the Gödel-Löb theorem/axiom, which is at the heart of provability logic [1], where the modality means "provable". We are not aware of other uses of a coinductive, Gödel-Löb-style proof rule in the context of program verification.

We show that *coInd* is strictly more powerful than *Ind*, by showing that it is equivalent to *Ind* *plus* $\Diamond\circ\bot$ (Proposition 4), and that dropping implication $\circ\neg\varphi \to \neg\circ\varphi$ from the proof system of infinite-trace LTL and replacing *Ind* with **coInd** yields a complete proof system for finite-trace LTL. Technically, the contribution is an almost complete reworking of the infinite-trace LTL decidability and completeness results, to adapt them to finite-trace LTL. The general organization and structure of our proofs follow [16].

Section 2 recalls basic facts about propositional, modal, and linear temporal logics. The syntax and semantics of finite-trace LTL are defined in Sect. 3. Section 5 defines a variant of formula closure and shows the decidability of the satisfiability problem. In fact, the decidability result is an immediate corollary of a major result of the paper, Theorem 1, which characterizes the satisfiable formulae as those admitting *complete* atom traces; this result is crucial not only for decidability, but also for completeness. Section 6 introduces our seven-rule sound proof system and proves several properties of it. Finally, Sect. 7 proves the completeness of our proof system. Section 8 concludes.

2   Preliminaries

In this section we remind some basic notions and notations about propositional and modal logic, as well as a sound and complete proof system for infinite-trace LTL.

Propositional Logic. Propositions are built with propositional variables from a countable set $PVar$, a constant symbol $\perp$ (false), and a binary operation $\rightarrow$ (implication). Other derived operations include: $\neg$ (negation), $\wedge$ (and), $\vee$ (or), $\leftrightarrow$ (equivalence). The proof system in Fig. 1 (with axiom and proof rule *schemata*) is sound and complete for propositional logic (**MP** stands for *modus ponens*). To distinguish it from other deducibility relations, we let $\vdash_{MP}$ denote the deducibility relation associated to the

A_1	$\varphi_1 \rightarrow (\varphi_2 \rightarrow \varphi_1)$
A_2	$(\varphi_1 \rightarrow (\varphi_2 \rightarrow \varphi_3))$ $\rightarrow ((\varphi_1 \rightarrow \varphi_2) \rightarrow (\varphi_1 \rightarrow \varphi_3))$
A_3	$(\neg\varphi_1 \rightarrow \neg\varphi_2) \rightarrow (\varphi_2 \rightarrow \varphi_1)$
MP	$\dfrac{\varphi_1 \quad \varphi_1 \rightarrow \varphi_2}{\varphi_2}$

Fig. 1. Propositional logic proof system

proof system above. The Deduction Theorem of propositional logic states that $\Gamma \vdash_{MP} \varphi_1 \rightarrow \varphi_2$ iff $\Gamma \cup \{\varphi_1\} \vdash_{MP} \varphi_2$. There are many equivalent proof systems for propositional logic, and all can be used in this paper in a similar way. We let **Prop** denote the set of all *theorems* of propositional logic, i.e., $\mathbf{Prop} = \{\varphi \mid \vdash_{MP} \varphi\}$.

Modal Logic. In this paper we build upon the modal logic $\mathcal{K}$ (see [10] for a thorough presentation and history of modal logics, using a modern notation), whose syntax is:

$$\varphi ::= \text{propositional logic variables } (PVar) \text{ and constructs}$$
$$\mid \Box\varphi \quad (\Diamond\varphi \text{ commonly used as syntactic sugar for } \neg\Box\neg\varphi)$$

The $\mathcal{K}$ modal logic is governed by the axiom and proof rule in Fig. 2, which together with the propositional logic proof system in Fig. 1, yield a sound and complete proof system for frame models (not discussed here; see, for example, [10]). $\mathcal{K}$ is typically enriched with additional axioms and/or proof rules. A notable axiom is $\Box\varphi \to \Box\Box\varphi$, which turns $\mathcal{K}$ into the logic known as S_4.

K	$\Box(\varphi \to \varphi') \to (\Box\varphi \to \Box\varphi')$
N	$\dfrac{\varphi}{\Box\varphi}$

Fig. 2. Modal logic proof system

An interesting modal logic extension, which is at the core of *provability logic* [1] where $\Box\varphi$ means "φ provable", is with the Gödel-Löb axiom $\Box(\Box\varphi \to \varphi) \to \varphi$, abbreviated $\boldsymbol{GL}$. It can be easily shown that $\boldsymbol{GL}$ makes the proof rule

$$\frac{\Box\varphi \to \varphi}{\varphi}$$

sound, but the converse is not true: one cannot prove $\boldsymbol{GL}$ from $\mathcal{K}$ plus the rule above.

A Proof System for Infinite-Trace LTL. Several different proof systems for infinite-trace LTL can be found in the published literature and in class lecture notes at various institutions, with no well-established winner. Our proof system is inspired from the infinite-trace LTL proof system in Fig. 3.

This proof system appears in unpublished lecture notes by Dam and Guelev, reachable from http://www.csc.kth.se/~mfd. They credit it to [16] (personal communication), although in our opinion there are several important differences between the two. The proof system in Fig. 3 is in fact quite close to the one in [9], the only difference being that the latter includes a fixed point axiom for $\Box$, in the style of $\boldsymbol{U}_2$ in Fig. 3, which, as shown by Dam and Guelev in their

proof system of propositional calculus, extended with the following:

$\boldsymbol{K_\circ}$	$\circ(\varphi \to \varphi') \to (\circ\varphi \to \circ\varphi')$
$\boldsymbol{N_\circ}$	$\dfrac{\varphi}{\circ\varphi}$
$\boldsymbol{K_\Box}$	$\Box(\varphi \to \varphi') \to (\Box\varphi \to \Box\varphi')$
$\boldsymbol{N_\Box}$	$\dfrac{\varphi}{\Box\varphi}$
$\boldsymbol{Fun}$	$\neg\circ\varphi \leftrightarrow \circ\neg\varphi$
$\boldsymbol{U_1}$	$\varphi_1\mathcal{U}_s\varphi_2 \to \Diamond\varphi_2$
$\boldsymbol{U_2}$	$\varphi_1\mathcal{U}_s\varphi_2 \leftrightarrow \varphi_2 \vee \varphi_1 \wedge \circ(\varphi_1\mathcal{U}_s\varphi_2)$
$\boldsymbol{Ind}$	$\Box(\varphi \to \circ\varphi) \to (\varphi \to \Box\varphi)$

Fig. 3. Infinite-trace LTL proof system

lecture notes, can in fact be derived. Note that $\boldsymbol{Ind}$ is given as an axiom rather than as a proof rule, but one can show them equivalent. We used the subscript s to the until operator to make it clear that *strict* until is meant. In our proof system for finite-trace LTL we prefer to work with weak until, which allows us to eliminate $\boldsymbol{U}_1$.

3   Finite-Trace LTL: Syntax and Semantics

Here we introduce the basic elements of finite-trace LTL. For notational simplicity, from here on we refer to finite-trace LTL as $\mathcal{L}$. Its core syntax is the same as that of infinite-trace LTL, that is, it consists of a unary "next" operator and of a binary "until":

$$\varphi ::= \text{usual propositional constructs}$$
$$| \quad \circ\varphi \qquad \text{(next)}$$
$$| \quad \varphi\mathcal{U}\varphi \quad \text{(until)}$$

However, the semantics is given in terms of finite-traces, where for technical simplicity both operators are interpreted *weakly*. That is, $\circ\varphi$ means: *if* there is a next state *then* φ holds in that state; and $\varphi_1\mathcal{U}\varphi_2$ means: either φ_1 holds in all future states or there is some future state in which φ_2 holds and φ_1 holds in each state until then. Formally,

Definition 1. *A **finite trace** is an element of $\mathcal{P}(PVar)^+$, that is, a non-empty finite sequence of sets of propositional variables (each such set can be thought of as a "state"). We inductively define the **satisfaction relation** between finite-traces and formulae:*

$s_1 \ldots s_n \models p$ *iff* $p \in s_1$;
$s_1 \ldots s_n \not\models \bot$;
$s_1 \ldots s_n \models \varphi_1 \to \varphi_2$ *iff* $s_1 \ldots s_n \models \varphi_1$ *implies* $s_1 \ldots s_n \models \varphi_2$;
$s_1 \ldots s_n \models \circ\varphi$ *iff* $n = 1$ *or* $s_2 \ldots s_n \models \varphi$;
$s_1 \ldots s_n \models \varphi_1\mathcal{U}\varphi_2$ *iff either* $s_i \ldots s_n \models \varphi_1$ *for all* $1 \le i \le n$ *or there is some* $1 \le i \le n$
$\qquad\qquad$ *such that* $s_i \ldots s_n \models \varphi_2$ *and* $s_j \ldots s_n \models \varphi_1$ *for all* $1 \le j < i$.

*Formula φ is **satisfiable** iff there exists some finite trace $s_1 \ldots s_n$ such that $s_1 \ldots s_n \models \varphi$, and is **valid**, or a **tautology**, written $\models \varphi$, iff $s_1 \ldots s_n \models \varphi$ for all finite traces $s_1 \ldots s_n$.*

We can now extend the syntax with several derived operators:

$$\varphi ::= \bullet\varphi \qquad \text{(strong next)} \qquad\qquad \bullet\varphi \equiv \neg\circ\neg\varphi$$
$$| \quad \Box\varphi \qquad \text{(always)} \qquad\qquad\quad \Box\varphi \equiv \varphi\mathcal{U}\bot$$
$$| \quad \Diamond\varphi \qquad \text{(eventually)} \qquad\qquad \Diamond\varphi \equiv \neg\Box\neg\varphi$$
$$| \quad \varphi\mathcal{U}_s\varphi \quad \text{(strong until)} \qquad \varphi_1\mathcal{U}_s\varphi_2 \equiv \Diamond\varphi_2 \wedge \varphi_1\mathcal{U}\varphi_2$$

It can be easily shown that these operators have the expected semantics:

$s_1 s_2 \ldots s_n \models \bullet\varphi$ iff $n > 1$ and $s_2 \ldots s_n \models \varphi$;
$s_1 \ldots s_n \models \Box\varphi$ iff $s_i \ldots s_n \models \varphi$ for all $1 \le i \le n$;
$s_1 \ldots s_n \models \Diamond\varphi$ iff $s_i \ldots s_n \models \varphi$ for some $1 \le i \le n$;
$s_1 \ldots s_n \models \varphi_1\mathcal{U}_s\varphi_2$ iff there is some $1 \le i \le n$ such that $s_i \ldots s_n \models \varphi_2$
$\qquad\qquad$ and $s_j \ldots s_n \models \varphi_1$ for all $1 \le j < i$.

It can also be easily shown that $\models \circ\varphi \leftrightarrow \neg\bullet\neg\varphi$, that is, $\circ$ and $\bullet$ are completely dual to each other. In the rest of the paper some results are easier to formulate and/or prove using the weak version of next, $\circ$, while others using the strong version, $\bullet$. Since we can easily and linearly convert a formula to use either one or the other, we will simply state which one we assume as basic construct at the beginning of each relevant section.

Another relevant and easy to prove tautology is $\models \psi_1\mathcal{U}\psi_2 \leftrightarrow \psi_2 \vee \psi_1 \wedge \circ(\psi_1\mathcal{U}\psi_2)$.

Example 1. Consider a system which performs one or more actions a followed by an action b. We want to show that whenever the system terminates, b is eventually reached. We can specify both the system and the property as the following formula:

$$\Box(a \rightarrow \bullet(a \vee b)) \rightarrow (a \rightarrow \Diamond b)$$

In words, the system is described as the formula stating that once an action a takes place then a next step *must* exist, and in that step a or b takes place. If we additionally want to state that the trace must terminate as soon as b takes place, then we write:

$$\Box((a \rightarrow \bullet(a \vee b)) \wedge (b \rightarrow \circ\bot)) \rightarrow (a \rightarrow \Diamond b)$$

For now, we can show that the above formulae are valid using Definition 1 directly. Section 6 gives a proof system which will allow us to formally derive any tautologies. Note that none of these holds under infinite-trace LTL, since a^ω does not satisfy them.

Example 2. We can, in fact, associate a formula $\varphi_{\mathcal{A}}$ over propositional variables $Q \cup A$ to any finite-state machine $FSM = (Q, A, q_0 \in Q, \delta : Q \times A \rightarrow 2^Q, F \subseteq Q)$ as follows:

$$\Box\left(\left(\bigvee_{q \in Q} q\right) \wedge \bigwedge_{q \in Q}\left(\left(q \rightarrow ((q \in F \wedge \circ\bot) \vee \bigvee_{\substack{a \in A \\ \delta(q,a) \neq \emptyset}} a)\right) \wedge \left(\bigwedge_{\substack{a \in A \\ \delta(q,a) \neq \emptyset}} q \wedge a \rightarrow \bullet \bigvee_{q' \in \delta(q,a)} q'\right)\right)\right)$$

In words, it is always the case that: (1) a state in Q is active; (2) for each final state, allow the trace to terminate there ($\circ\bot$ holds iff there is no next step); (3) for each state q which is active, its outgoing edges are also active; and (4) if a state q and an action a of that state are both active, then a step must take place to a state allowed by FSM.

It can be shown that a word $a_1 \ldots a_n$ is in the language of FSM iff there are states $q_1, \ldots, q_n \in Q$ such that $q_n \in F$ and $\{q_0, a_1\}\{q_1, a_2\} \ldots \{q_{n-1}, a_n\}\{q_n\} \models \varphi_{FSM}$. This allows us to prove properties about FSM (either directly using Definition 1 or using the subsequent proof system), such as: $\models \varphi_{\mathcal{A}} \rightarrow \Box(q_0 \rightarrow \Diamond a)$ (that is, a will be reached on any terminating path starting from q_0), or $\models \varphi_{\mathcal{A}} \rightarrow \Box(a \rightarrow \Diamond b)$ (that is, b will be reached on any terminating path starting with a from any state), etc.

4 Relationship to Infinite-Trace LTL

Before we proceed to present our novel results starting with Sect. 5, it is worth discussing alternative, indirect approaches to reason about finite-trace LTL properties. We do it in this section, at the same time also arguing for a direct approach.

There is a relatively simple way to transform any LTL formula into another LTL formula so that the former is satisfiable under the finite-trace semantics iff the latter is satisfiable under infinite-trace semantics. The idea is to conceptually complete finite traces with infinite suffixes $\$^\omega$, where $\$$ is a new propositional variable thought of as "nothing". Formally, given φ, let $\overline{\varphi}$ be the formula defined as follows:

$$
\begin{aligned}
\overline{\bot} &= \bot \\
\overline{p} &= p \wedge \neg\$ \qquad \text{where } p \text{ is a propositional variable} \\
\overline{\varphi_1 \to \varphi_2} &= \overline{\varphi_1} \to \overline{\varphi_2} \\
\overline{\circ\varphi} &= \circ(\overline{\varphi} \vee \$) \\
\overline{\varphi_1 \mathcal{U} \varphi_2} &= \overline{\varphi_1}\mathcal{U}(\overline{\varphi_2} \vee \$)
\end{aligned}
$$

Then φ is satisfiable in finite-trace LTL iff $(\neg\$)\mathcal{U}_s\$ \wedge \overline{\varphi}$ is satisfiable in infinite-trace LTL. For example, the formula (recall that $\Box\varphi$ is syntactic sugar for $\varphi\mathcal{U}\bot$, and $\Diamond\varphi$ for $\neg\Box\neg\varphi$)

$$\Box(a \to \bullet(a \vee b)) \to (a \to \Diamond b)$$

in Example 1 is satisfiable in finite-trace LTL iff

$$(\neg\$)\mathcal{U}_s\$ \;\wedge\; ((a \wedge \neg\$ \to \circ((a \vee b) \wedge \neg\$))\mathcal{U}\$ \;\to\; (a \wedge \neg\$ \to \neg((\neg(b \wedge \neg\$))\mathcal{U}\$)))$$

is satisfiable in infinite-trace LTL. Therefore, finite-trace LTL is PSPACE-decidable, like infinite-trace LTL [22], and a decidable procedure can be obtained by translation to infinite-trace LTL as above.

Following such a translation approach has, however, an important practical drawback: the size of the formula doubles, and a more complex than needed procedure is applied on the larger formula. Indeed, as seen in Sect. 5, our specialized decision procedure for finite-trace LTL reduces to checking simple reachability in a graph exponential in the size of φ, as opposed to checking for algorithmically more complex, ultimately periodic sequences in a graph exponential in twice the size of φ, as the translation to infinite-trace LTL approach would require.

Also, it can be shown that φ is valid in finite-trace LTL iff $(\neg\$)\mathcal{U}_s\$ \to \overline{\varphi}$ is valid in infinite-trace LTL. Therefore, one can indirectly obtain a complete proof system for finite-trace LTL by translation to infinite-trace LTL and then using off-the-shelf proof systems for the latter, for example [16,17] (see also Sect. 2). Besides having to prove a twice-larger formula, this translation-to-infinite-trace-LTL approach has the additional drawback that we now have to explicitly reason about $\$$ and termination of traces, departing ourselves from the basic intuitions of finite-trace LTL. For example, it seems hard to find a proof of the infinite-trace LTL formula corresponding to the finite-trace formula in Example 1, while as shown in Example 3 there is simple, direct and intuitive proof of the original formula using our new proof system.

Arguments like the above, in favor of direct procedures and reasoning systems for specific logics instead of translations to other logics, abound in the literature. Consider, for example, conventional infinite-trace LTL and its well-known translation to (a monadic fragment of) first-order logic (FOL), suggested for the first time by Kamp in his seminal 1968 thesis [14]. Specifically, each LTL formula φ can be inductively translated to an equivalent (in appropriate models) FOL formula $\varphi(x)$ over free variable x; for example,

$(\varphi \, \mathcal{U}_s \, \psi)(x)$ is the FOL formula $\exists z \, . \, x < z \land \psi(z) \land \forall y \, . \, x < y < z \to \varphi(y)$

Then we can use existing or develop new procedures for that fragment of FOL to decide satisfiability of LTL formulae, and we can use the FOL sound and complete proof system to derive any tautology of LTL. Despite the above, significant research and development effort has been spent since 1968 by the formal verification and analysis community to develop specialized, direct decision procedures and proof systems for LTL. Similarly and perhaps even more interestingly, equational logic is a well-established fragment of FOL, yet almost no equational provers are based on FOL reasoning, but on procedures and sound and complete proof systems specifically crafted for equational logic.

To push the argument to extreme, consider the seminal result by Bergstra and Tucker [3]: any computable domain, of any complexity class, is isomorphic to the initial model of a finite set of equations. Therefore, inductive equational proofs are sufficient to reason within any domain, regardless of its complexity. Such results, in spite of their beauty and insights, tend to have little practical relevance and have certainly not stopped, nor even slowed down the research and development of particular decision procedures and proof systems for particular logics. The fact that finite-trace LTL can be translated to infinite-trace LTL falls into the same category and it is, in our view, no more than an interesting observation. While one can attempt to use decision procedures and proof systems for infinite-trace LTL via the translation to infinite-trace LTL discussed above, we believe that finite trace LTL is a pivotal logic for runtime verification and thus deserves our full attention. Decision procedures and specialized sound and complete proof systems for it will provide the runtime verification researchers with understanding and insights that should carry over to other finite-trace specification formalisms, too.

5   Complete Atom Traces

In this section we show our first important result for finite-trace LTL ($\mathcal{L}$): a formula φ is satisfiable iff there is a complete (i.e., finite and terminated) trace in the tableaux of φ, where the tableaux is constructed in a way specific to the finite-trace semantics. This also gives a direct decision procedure for finite-trace LTL satisfiability, but the result is particularly important for completeness. Here we prefer to work with $\bullet$ and $\mathcal{U}$ as core formula constructs, so we assume that

$\mathcal{L}$ formulae are built with: propositional variables in $PVar$, $\bot$, $\to$, $\bullet$ and $\mathcal{U}$. As notational convenience, we use $\neg\varphi$ as a shortcut for $\varphi \to \bot$.

Definition 2. *Let $\neg'\varphi$ be either φ' when φ is $\neg\varphi'$, or $\neg\varphi$ otherwise. A set of formulae C is $\{\neg\}$-**closed** when $\varphi \in C$ implies $\neg'\varphi \in C$, is $\{\bullet\}$-**closed** when $\bullet\varphi \in C$ implies $\varphi \in C$, and is **closed** when: (1) is $\{\neg, \bullet\}$-closed; (2) $\varphi_1\to\varphi_2 \in C$ implies $\varphi_1, \varphi_2 \in C$; (3) $\bullet\varphi \in C$ implies $\bullet\neg'\varphi \in C$; and (4) $\varphi_1\mathcal{U}\varphi_2 \in C$ implies $\varphi_1, \varphi_2, \bullet(\varphi_1\mathcal{U}\varphi_2) \in C$. If φ is a formula then $Closure(\varphi)$ is the smallest closed set that includes φ.*

Note that our notion of closure is slightly stronger than the classic Fischer-Ladner closure [7], in that Fischer-Ladner does *not* require condition (3), namely that $\bullet\neg'\varphi$ is included in the closure together with $\bullet\varphi$. Thus, our closures of formulae will be slightly larger than Fischer-Ladner's, but nevertheless still linear in the formula. For example, if $\varphi_1\mathcal{U}\varphi_2 \in C$ then also $\bullet\neg(\varphi_1\mathcal{U}\varphi_2) \in C$, which is critical for the proof of Theorem 1.

Definition 3. *Let C be a $\{\bullet\}$-closed set of formulae. The $\{\bullet\}$-**generated transition relation** of C, written $R_C \subseteq \mathcal{P}(C) \times \mathcal{P}(C)$, is defined as follows: for any $A, B \subseteq C$, $(A, B) \in R_C$ iff $\bullet^{-1}A \neq \emptyset$ and $\bullet^{-1}A \subseteq B$, where $\bullet^{-1}A = \{\psi \mid \bullet\psi \in A\}$. A **complete C-trace** is a sequence $A_1 \ldots A_n$ of subsets of C with $(A_i, A_{i+1}) \in R_\varphi$ for all $1 \le i < n$ and $\bullet^{-1}A_n = \emptyset$.*

The reason C was required to be $\{\bullet\}$-closed in Definition 3, is because we want $\bullet^{-1}A \neq \emptyset$ to imply that there is some $B \subseteq C$ such that $(A, B) \in R_C$. In other words, we want the emptyness of $\bullet^{-1}A$ alone to determine whether A is terminal for R_C or not.

Definition 4. *Let C be a closed set of formulae. A **C-atom** is a set $A \subseteq C$ such that:*

1. *$\bot \notin A$;*
2. *For each $\psi \in C$, either $\psi \in A$ or $\neg'\psi \in A$;*
3. *If $\bullet^{-1}A \neq \emptyset$ then for each $\bullet\psi \in C$, either $\bullet\psi \in A$ or $\bullet\neg'\psi \in A$;*
4. *For each $\psi_1\to\psi_2 \in C$, $\psi_1\to\psi_2 \in A$ iff ($\psi_1 \in A$ implies $\psi_2 \in A$);*
5. *For each $\psi_1\mathcal{U}\psi_2 \in C$, $\psi_1\mathcal{U}\psi_2 \in A$ iff $\psi_2 \in A$ or $\psi_1 \in A$ and $\bullet\neg(\psi_1\mathcal{U}\psi_2) \notin A$.*

*Let $Atom_C$ be the set of C-atoms. If $C = Closure(\varphi)$ for some formula φ, then we write $Atom_\varphi$ instead of $Atom_{Closure(\varphi)}$ and R_φ instead of $R_{Closure(\varphi)}$. Also, a **complete atom trace of** φ is a complete $Closure(\varphi)$-trace $A_1 \ldots A_n$ such that $A_1, \ldots, A_n \in Atom_\varphi$ and $\varphi \in A_1$.*

The next theorem is a crucial result of finite-trace semantics, which is used to show both the decidability (Corollary 1) and the completeness (Theorem 4) of $\mathcal{L}$.

Theorem 1. *A formula is satisfiable iff it admits a complete atom trace.*

Theorem 1 gives us a straightforward algorithm to test the satisfiability of a formula φ: show that there is at least one node $A \in Atom_\varphi$ in the (finite) graph $(Atom_\varphi, R_\varphi)$ with $\varphi \in A$, such that there is some path from A to a node without any outgoing edges. In other words, the satisfiability problem of φ reduces to the reachability problem in graph $(Atom_\varphi, R_\varphi)$, which is decidable. Thus, like infinite-trace LTL [22], finite-trace LTL is also decidable. Although checking reachability is algorithmically simpler than checking for ultimately periodic sequences as needed for infinite-trace LTL [22], deciding finite-trace LTL satisfiability is still a PSPACE-complete problem:

Corollary 1. *The satisfiability problem for $\mathcal{L}$ is PSPACE-complete.*

6 Proof System

Figure 4 depicts our proof system for finite trace LTL. In this section we prefer to work with $\circ$ instead of $\bullet$ as core construct (so $\bullet\varphi$ desugars to $\neg\circ\neg\varphi$). We start by inheriting propositional logic and the modal logic rules corresponding to the modalities $\circ$ and $\square$. Unlike in infinite-trace LTL, $\neg\circ\varphi \leftrightarrow \circ\neg\varphi$ does not hold anymore, as both $\circ\varphi$ and $\circ\neg\varphi$ hold in one-state traces; only the implication $\neg\circ\varphi \rightarrow \circ\neg\varphi$ holds. In interesting multi-modal logics, the various modal operators tend to be connected somehow. In our case, we axiomatize the expected fact that $\varphi_1 \mathcal{U} \varphi_2$ is the fixed-point of the formula $X \leftrightarrow \varphi_2 \vee \varphi_1 \wedge \circ X$. The only unexpected rule is the Coinduction rule for $\circ$. As usual, the axioms and

proof system of propositional calculus, extended with the following:

$K_\circ$ $\qquad \circ(\varphi \rightarrow \varphi') \rightarrow (\circ\varphi \rightarrow \circ\varphi')$

$N_\circ$ $\qquad \dfrac{\varphi}{\circ\varphi}$

$K_\square$ $\qquad \square(\varphi \rightarrow \varphi') \rightarrow (\square\varphi \rightarrow \square\varphi')$

$N_\square$ $\qquad \dfrac{\varphi}{\square\varphi}$

$\neg\circ$ $\qquad \neg\circ\varphi \rightarrow \circ\neg\varphi$

Fix $\qquad \varphi_1\mathcal{U}\varphi_2 \leftrightarrow \varphi_2 \vee \varphi_1 \wedge \circ(\varphi_1\mathcal{U}\varphi_2)$

$coInd$ $\qquad \dfrac{\circ\varphi \rightarrow \varphi}{\varphi}$

Fig. 4. Finite-trace LTL proof system

rules are schemata. The fixed-point equivalence of $\square$, $\square\varphi \leftrightarrow \varphi \wedge \circ\square\varphi$, is an instance of Fix with $\varphi_1 \mapsto \varphi$ and $\varphi_2 \mapsto \bot$. To avoid inventing rule names, from now on we take the liberty to let Fix also refer to the latter equivalence. In fact, if one prefers a fragment of LTL with only $\circ$ and $\square$, then one can replace Fix with the fixed-point equivalence of $\square$ and the results in this paper still hold.

Comparing our proof system above with the one for infinite-trace LTL in Sect. 2, we note that the main difference is that the Induction rule has been replaced with the Coinduction rule. Also, the axiom $\circ\neg\varphi \rightarrow \neg\circ\varphi$ has been removed, and since we chose to work with weak instead of strong until we were able to also remove rule U_1. We argue, without proof, that our proof system above is minimal. Indeed, the rules $K_\circ$, $N_\circ$, $K_\square$, and $N_\square$ say that the $\circ$ and

$\square$ modalities form $\mathcal{K}$ logics, and $\mathcal{K}$ is the poorest modal logic. The axiom $\neg\circ$ captures the specific one-step granularity of $\circ$, which distinguishes it from $\square$ for example, so it is unlikely to eliminate it. ***Fix*** captures the recursive nature of the until operator, and it is the only axiom which does it, so again it is unlikely to be removed. Finally, note that none of the rules discussed so far is specific to finite traces, because they are in fact consequences of the infinite-trace LTL proof system, so at least one more rule is needed to allow proving finite-trace-specific properties like $\Diamond\circ\bot$. The ***coInd*** rule not only allows proving $\Diamond\circ\bot$, but as shown in Proposition 4 it also allows proving the Induction proof rule of infinite-trace LTL (which therefore also holds for finite-traces), a rule which is considered crucial for LTL and, indeed, no proof system for LTL omits it.

Let $\vdash_\mathcal{L}$ denote the induced deducibility relation. Specifically, if Γ is a set of formulae and φ a formula, then $\Gamma \vdash_\mathcal{L} \varphi$ denotes that φ is deducible from Γ using the proof system above; $\vdash_\mathcal{L} \varphi$ is a shortcut for $\emptyset \vdash_\mathcal{L} \varphi$. Let $Th_\mathcal{L} = \{\varphi \mid \vdash_\mathcal{L} \varphi\}$ be the set of all *theorems* of $\mathcal{L}$. For notational simplicity, we let ***Prop*** also denote the set of all formulae (not only propositions) deducible with the propositional logic proof subsystem; e.g., $\square\varphi \rightarrow (\circ\varphi \rightarrow \square\varphi) \in$ ***Prop*** (instance of $\boldsymbol{A_1}$ with formulae in $\mathcal{L}$). Note that ***Prop*** $= \{\varphi \mid \vdash_{MP} \varphi\} \subset Th_\mathcal{L}$.

Theorem 2. (Soundness) *For any formula φ, $\vdash_\mathcal{L} \varphi$ implies $\models \varphi$. In particular, $\bot \notin Th_\mathcal{L}$.*

Figure 5 shows a few basic properties of the next operators, which can be shown using only the $\{\boldsymbol{K_\circ}, \boldsymbol{N_\circ}, \neg\circ\}$ fragment of the proof system.

Proposition 1. *The formulae in Fig. 5 are all derivable, i.e., belong to $Th_\mathcal{L}$.*

The following says that the $\square$ modality is S_4:

Proposition 2. $\vdash_\mathcal{L} \square\varphi \rightarrow \square\square\varphi$ *for any formula φ.*

The deduction theorem of propositional logic, stating that $\Gamma \vdash_{MP} \varphi \rightarrow \psi$ iff $\Gamma, \varphi \vdash_{MP} \psi$, is technically unnecessary but quite useful in practice, because it allows us to prove impli-

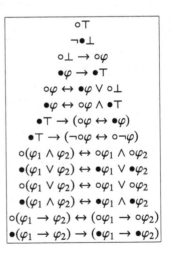

$$\circ\top$$
$$\neg\bullet\bot$$
$$\circ\bot \rightarrow \circ\varphi$$
$$\bullet\varphi \rightarrow \bullet\top$$
$$\circ\varphi \leftrightarrow \bullet\varphi \vee \circ\bot$$
$$\bullet\varphi \leftrightarrow \circ\varphi \wedge \bullet\top$$
$$\bullet\top \rightarrow (\circ\varphi \leftrightarrow \bullet\varphi)$$
$$\bullet\top \rightarrow (\neg\circ\varphi \leftrightarrow \circ\neg\varphi)$$
$$\circ(\varphi_1 \wedge \varphi_2) \leftrightarrow \circ\varphi_1 \wedge \circ\varphi_2$$
$$\bullet(\varphi_1 \vee \varphi_2) \leftrightarrow \bullet\varphi_1 \vee \bullet\varphi_2$$
$$\circ(\varphi_1 \vee \varphi_2) \leftrightarrow \circ\varphi_1 \vee \circ\varphi_2$$
$$\bullet(\varphi_1 \wedge \varphi_2) \leftrightarrow \bullet\varphi_1 \wedge \bullet\varphi_2$$
$$\circ(\varphi_1 \rightarrow \varphi_2) \leftrightarrow (\circ\varphi_1 \rightarrow \circ\varphi_2)$$
$$\bullet(\varphi_1 \rightarrow \varphi_2) \rightarrow (\bullet\varphi_1 \rightarrow \bullet\varphi_2)$$

Fig. 5. Properties of $\circ$ and $\bullet$

cations by "assuming" their hypothesis and then deriving their conclusion. We would like to also have it in our setting here. However, it is well-known that the deduction theorem does not hold by default in other logics. For example, in first-order logic, it only holds when φ is a closed formula (i.e., it has no free variables). Here we can prove the following variant of the deduction theorem:

Theorem 3. (Deduction theorem) $\Gamma \vdash_\mathcal{L} \square\varphi \rightarrow \psi$ *iff* $\Gamma, \varphi \vdash_\mathcal{L} \psi$.

When doing proofs by induction, it is often convenient to assume the property holds in *all* past moments, and not only in the *previous* one, and then prove it holds now. Dually, when doing proofs by coinduction, it is often convenient to assume the property holds in *all* future moments, and not only in the *next* one, and then prove it holds now.

The following proposition establishes that this apparently stronger variant of coinduction is in fact equivalent to the one we have now. It also gives equivalent axiomatic variants of both coinductive proof rules.

Proposition 3. *Keeping all the other axioms and rules unchanged, the rule coInd is equivalent to any of the alternative rules or axioms in Fig. 6.*

***coInd*$_\square$**	$\dfrac{\circ\square\varphi \rightarrow \varphi}{\varphi}$
***GL*$_\circ$**	$\square(\circ\varphi \rightarrow \varphi) \rightarrow \varphi$
***GL*$_\square$**	$\square(\circ\square\varphi \rightarrow \varphi) \rightarrow \varphi$

Fig. 6. Other coinductive rules

A natural question is what is the relationship between induction and coinduction. Induction is valid for infinite-traces, too, which means that it is not powerful enough to prove $\Diamond\circ\bot$ (each trace terminates); indeed, $\Diamond\circ\bot$ is equivalent to l in infinite-trace LTL. On the other hand, coinduction, as formulated here, is only valid for finite traces. We next show that coinduction is actually equivalent to *both* induction and the finite trace axiom $\Diamond\circ\bot$ *together*.

Ind	$\dfrac{\varphi \rightarrow \circ\varphi}{\varphi \rightarrow \square\varphi}$
Fin	$\Diamond\circ\bot$

Fig. 7. Induction rule and finite-trace axiom

Proposition 4. *Let **Ind** be the induction rule and **Fin** be the finite-trace axiom in Fig. 7. Keeping all the other rules unchanged, **coInd** is equivalent to **Ind** and **Fin** together.*

The properties in Fig. 8 are quite useful in practice.

Proposition 5. *The formulae in Fig. 8 are all derivable, i.e., belong to $Th_{\mathcal{L}}$.*

Example 3. Let us prove the property in Example 1, $\square(a \rightarrow \bullet(a \vee b)) \rightarrow (a \rightarrow \Diamond b)$. By the Deduction Theorem 3, it suffices to show $a \rightarrow \bullet(a \vee b) \vdash_{\mathcal{L}} a \rightarrow \Diamond b$. This follows by the **coInd** proof rule, if we can show

$\square\varphi \leftrightarrow \square\square\varphi$
$\Diamond\varphi \leftrightarrow \Diamond\Diamond\varphi$
$\square\varphi \rightarrow \varphi \wedge \circ\varphi$
$\varphi \vee \bullet\varphi \rightarrow \Diamond\varphi$
$\square(\varphi \rightarrow \bullet\varphi) \rightarrow \neg\varphi$
$\square(\varphi_1 \wedge \varphi_2) \leftrightarrow \square\varphi_1 \wedge \square\varphi_2$
$\square(\varphi_1 \rightarrow \varphi_2) \rightarrow (\Diamond\varphi_1 \rightarrow \Diamond\varphi_2)$

Fig. 8. Properties of $\square$ and $\Diamond$

$a \rightarrow \bullet(a \vee b) \vdash_{\mathcal{L}} \circ(a \rightarrow \Diamond b) \rightarrow (a \rightarrow \Diamond b)$. By propositional reasoning, it suffices to show $\vdash_{\mathcal{L}} \bullet(a \vee b) \wedge \circ(a \rightarrow \Diamond b) \rightarrow \Diamond b$, which follows by $\boldsymbol{K}_\circ$, propositional reasoning, and some theorems in Propositions 1 and 5.

7   Completeness

In this section we show that the proof system discussed in Sect. 6 is complete for finite-trace LTL ($\mathcal{L}$). The general proof scheme adopted in this section is standard: assume that φ is valid but not derivable, which implies that $\neg\varphi$ is consistent, and then use the proof system to construct a model of $\neg\varphi$ within the atom universe of the tableaux, thus contradicting the validity of φ. Like in Sect. 5, we here also prefer to work with $\bullet$ as a basic "next" construct instead of $\circ$. Recall that $\vdash_{MP}$ is the deducibility relation using only the proof subsystem of propositional logic.

Consistency, maximal consistency and related results are given below, following a pattern common to many logics (propositional logic, FOL, infinite-trace LTL, etc.).

Definition 5. Γ is **inconsistent** iff $Th_{\mathcal{L}} \cup \Gamma \vdash_{MP} \bot$, and it is **consistent** otherwise. A formula φ is **consistent** (resp. **inconsistent**) iff $\{\varphi\}$ is consistent (resp. inconsistent). Γ is **maximally consistent** iff Γ is consistent and if Γ' consistent with $\Gamma \subseteq \Gamma'$ then $\Gamma = \Gamma'$.

Therefore, Γ is inconsistent iff we can derive $\bot$ using only propositional reasoning, but all the theorems of finite-trace LTL. Once we can derive $\bot$, we can derive anything:

Proposition 6. Γ is inconsistent iff $Th_{\mathcal{L}} \cup \Gamma \vdash_{MP} \varphi$ for any formula φ.

We can always add more formulae to a consistent set of formulae which is not maximal. Once maximal, we cannot add new formulae without breaking consistency:

Proposition 7. Suppose that Γ is consistent and φ is any formula. Then:

1. $\Gamma \cup \{\varphi\}$ is consistent, or $\Gamma \cup \{\neg\varphi\}$ is consistent, or both;
2. If Γ is maximally consistent, then either $\varphi \in \Gamma$ or $\neg\varphi \in \Gamma$. In particular, $Th_{\mathcal{L}} \subseteq \Gamma$.

In particular, no new formulae can be derived from a maximally consistent set:

Corollary 2. If Γ is maximally consistent and φ is any formula, then $\Gamma \vdash_{MP} \varphi$ iff $\varphi \in \Gamma$.

Proposition 8. Suppose that Γ is maximally consistent. Then $\varphi_1 \to \varphi_2 \in \Gamma$ iff $\varphi_1 \in \Gamma$ implies $\varphi_2 \in \Gamma$, $\varphi_1 \wedge \varphi_2 \in \Gamma$ iff $\varphi_1 \in \Gamma$ and $\varphi_2 \in \Gamma$, $\varphi_1 \vee \varphi_2 \in \Gamma$ iff $\varphi_1 \in \Gamma$ or $\varphi_2 \in \Gamma$, and $\varphi_1 \mathcal{U} \varphi_2 \in \Gamma$ iff $\varphi_2 \in \Gamma$ or $\varphi_1 \in \Gamma$ and $\bullet\neg(\varphi_1 \mathcal{U} \varphi_2) \notin \Gamma$.

Any consistent set of formulae can be extended into a maximally consistent one; folklore goes that a result of this kind was first shown for predicate logic by Lindenbaum in late 1920's (according to Taski):

Proposition 9. Γ *consistent implies there is a* Γ' *maximally consistent with* $\Gamma \subseteq \Gamma'$.

The results above in this section followed a standard pattern to prove completeness in several logics. The remaining results, however, are specific to finite-trace LTL ($\mathcal{L}$).

Recall from Definition 3 that $\bullet^{-1}\Gamma = \{\psi \mid \bullet\psi \in \Gamma\}$. The next proposition tells that $\bullet^{-1}$ preserves consistency. This, with the help of Proposition 9, allows us to start with a special consistent set of formulae and iteratively "derive" it with $\bullet^{-1}$; the difficult part is to show that, for finite-trace LTL, this derivation process *can be* finite. A result similar to Proposition 10 also exists for infinite-trace LTL (see, e.g., [16]), but our proof is more involved, because of the existence of two distinct next operators. In fact, a similar result for the weak next $\circ$ operator is not possible: for example, $\circ\bot$ is consistent but $\bot$ is not.

Proposition 10. *If* Γ *is consistent then* $\bullet^{-1}\Gamma$ *is also consistent.*

To prove the completeness, we will show that any consistent formula admits a complete atom trace (see Definition 4), so we can use Theorem 1 to conclude the formula is satisfiable. Like for infinite-trace LTL [16], it is convenient to consider a subset of the atoms of the formula, namely those obtained by intersecting its closure with maximally consistent sets of formulae. Let us define the worlds of a $\{\bullet\}$-closed set:

Definition 6. *Let* C *be a* $\{\bullet\}$-*closed set of formulae and let* $W_C \subseteq \mathcal{P}(C)$ *be the set* $\{\ \Gamma \cap C \mid \Gamma$ *maximally consistent* $\}$, *whose elements are called the **worlds** of* C. *Also, let* $R_C^W \subseteq W_C \times W_C$ *be the restriction of* $R_C \subseteq \mathcal{P}(C) \times \mathcal{P}(C)$ *to* W_C.

Proposition 10 and the $\{\bullet\}$-closedness of C guarantee that for any $w \in W_C$, $\bullet^{-1}w \neq \emptyset$ iff there is some $w' \in W_C$ such that $(w, w') \in R_C^W$. Now let us show that if C is closed then its worlds are indeed particular atoms. In particular, if C is a formula closure then its worlds are among the atoms that appear in the tableaux of the formula (see Sect. 5).

Proposition 11. *If* C *is closed then* $W_C \subseteq Atom_C$.

The next result tells that we can formally derive that a world can evolve to its successors, if any. A similar result also exists for infinite-trace LTL (see, e.g., [16]), but like before our proof is more involved due to the two distinct next operators available.

Proposition 12. *Let* C *be a finite and* $\{\neg, \bullet\}$-*closed set of formulae, and let* $w \in W_C$ *such that* $\bullet^{-1}w \neq \emptyset$. *Then* $\vdash_{\mathcal{L}} \widehat{w} \rightarrow \bullet \bigvee_{(w,w') \in R_C^W} \widehat{w'}$, *where* $\widehat{A} = \bigwedge\{\psi \mid \psi \in A\}$ *for any* $A \subseteq C$.

Unlike for infinite-trace LTL, where the objective is to show the existence of a ultimately periodic infinite atom trace that satisfies the formula, for finite-trace LTL the challenge is to show the existence of *any* finite trace that satisfies the formula. This is where our proof differs completely from that for infinite-trace LTL: we show that for any world $w \in W_C$, it is impossible to have only infinite R_C^W-sequences starting with w:

Proposition 13. *If C is finite and $\{\neg, \bullet\}$-closed, then for any $w \in W_C$ there exists some complete C-trace (see Definition 3) starting with w whose elements are all in W_C.*

We can now show that formula consistency and satisfiability coincide:

Proposition 14. *A formula is consistent iff it is satisfiable.*

The completeness theorem is now a simple corollary of the above:

Theorem 4. *(Completeness) For any formula φ, $\models \varphi$ implies $\vdash_{\mathcal{L}} \varphi$.*

8   Conclusion

This paper gave direct decidability and completeness results for finite-trace LTL. Neither the PSPACE-completeness of satisfiability nor the existence of a sound and complete proof system for finite-trace LTL are surprising results in themselves, because similar results exist for other variants of temporal logics. Moreover, the presented proof architecture follows the usual pattern encountered in infinite-trace variants of temporal logic, which itself follows a pattern well-established in first-order and predicate logics (for almost 100 years now). Looked at from that angle, this paper made two contributions, one conceptual and one technical. The conceptual contribution is the Coinduction proof rule, stating that if $\circ \varphi \rightarrow \varphi$ is provable then φ is also provable. It surprised the author that it captures so well the essence of finite-trace reasoning and yields its completeness. Its simplicity and elegance suggest that Coinduction may play a central role in finite-trace temporal reasoning. The technical contribution is Proposition 13, together with Proposition 12 on which it relies, saying that a consistent formula cannot admit only infinite-trace models; it must admit some finite-trace models, too, so the formula is finite-trace satisfiable. It may look "obvious" to the hasty reader now, after the fact, but the difficulty of proving these results made the author initially believe that finite-trace LTL may in fact not allow any complete proof system within itself, that is, without translation to other (richer) logics. This would have not been unheard of: equational logic restricted to *uncondi-tional* equalities over regular expressions does *not* admit a finite axiomatization within itself, but it does admit one if we allow *conditional* equations. It could have just as well been the case that finite-trace LTL admitted no finite proof system within itself, in spite of its infinite-trace variants admitting finite proof systems.

References

1. Artemov, S.N., Beklemishev, L.D.: Provability logic. In: Gabbay, D.M., Guenthner, F. (eds.) Handbook of Philosophical Logic, vol. XIII, 2nd edn, pp. 181–360. Springer, Berlin (2005)
2. Bauer, A., Leucker, M., Schallhart, C.: Comparing ltl semantics for runtime verification. J. Log. Comput. **20**(3), 651–674 (2010)
3. Bergstra, J.A., Tucker, J.V.: Initial and final algebra semantics for data type specifications: two characterization theorems. SIAM J. Comput. **12**(2), 366–387 (1983)
4. Ştefănescu, A., Ciobâcă, C., Mereuţă, R., Moore, B.M., Şerbănută, T.F., Roşu, G.: All-path reachability logic. In: Dowek, G. (ed.) RTA-TLCA 2014. LNCS, vol. 8560, pp. 425–440. Springer, Heidelberg (2014)
5. D'Amorim, M., Roşu, G.: Efficient monitoring of omega-languages. In: Etessami, K., Rajamani, S.K. (eds.) CAV 2005. LNCS, vol. 3576, pp. 364–378. Springer, Heidelberg (2005)
6. Diekert, V., Gastin, P.: Ltl is expressively complete for mazurkiewicz traces. J. Comput. Syst. Sci. **64**(2), 396–418 (2002)
7. Fischer, M.J., Ladner, R.E.: Propositional dynamic logic of regular programs. J. Comput. Syst. Sci. **18**(2), 194–211 (1979)
8. Giannakopoulou, D., Havelund, K.: Automata-based verification of temporal properties on running programs. In: ASE, pp. 412–416. IEEE Computer Society (2001)
9. Goldblatt, R.: Logics of Time and Computation. CSLI Lecture Notes, vol. 7, 2nd edn. Center for the Study of Language and Information, Stanford (1992)
10. Goldblatt, R.: Mathematical modal logic: a view of its evolution. J. Appl. Log. **1**(5–6), 309–392 (2003)
11. Havelund, K., Rosu, G.: Efficient monitoring of safety properties. Int. J. Softw. Tools Technol. Transf. (STTT) **6**, 158–173 (2004)
12. Hoare, C.A.R.: An axiomatic basis for computer programming. CACM **12**(10), 576–580 (1969)
13. Jard, C., Jeron, T.: On-line model-checking for finite linear temporal logic specifications. In: Sifakis, J. (ed.) CAV 1989. LNCS, vol. 407, pp. 189–196. Springer, Heidelberg (1990). doi:10.1007/3-540-52148-8_16
14. Kamp, H.W.: Tense logic and the theory of linear order. Ph.D. thesis, University of California, Los Angeles (1968)
15. Lee, I., Kannan, S., Kim, M., Sokolsky, O., Viswanathan, M.: Runtime assurance based on formal specifications. In: Arabnia, H.R. (ed.) PDPTA, pp. 279–287. CSREA Press, Las Vegas (1999)
16. Lichtenstein, O., Pnueli, A.: Propositional temporal logics: decidability and completeness. Log. J. IGPL **8**(1), 55–85 (2000)
17. Lichtenstein, O., Pnueli, A., Zuck, L.: The glory of the past. In: Parikh, R. (ed.) Log. Progr. LNCS, vol. 193, pp. 196–218. Springer, Berlin, Heidelberg (1985)
18. Pnueli, A.: The temporal logic of programs. In: FOCS, pp. 46–57. IEEE (1977)
19. Roşu, G., Ştefănescu, A., Ciobâcă, C., Moore, B.M.: One-path reachability logic. In: Proceedings of the 28th Symposium on Logic in Computer Science (LICS 2013), pp. 358–367. IEEE, June 2013
20. Rosu, G., Havelund, K.: Rewriting-based techniques for runtime verification. Autom. Softw. Eng. **12**, 151–197 (2005). doi:10.1007/s10515-005-6205-y
21. Rosu, G., Stefanescu, A.: Checking reachability using matching logic. In: Proceedings of the 27th Conference on Object-Oriented Programming, Systems, Languages, and Applications (OOPSLA 2012), pp. 555–574. ACM (2012)

22. Sistla, A.P., Clarke, E.M.: The complexity of propositional linear temporal logics. J. ACM **32**(3), 733–749 (1985)
23. Sulzmann, M., Zechner, A.: Constructive finite trace analysis with linear temporal logic. In: Brucker, A.D., Julliand, J. (eds.) TAP 2012. LNCS, vol. 7305, pp. 132–148. Springer, Heidelberg (2012)
24. Thiagarajan, P., Walukiewicz, I.: An expressively complete linear time temporal logic for mazurkiewicz traces. Inf. Comput. **179**(2), 230–249 (2002)

Wireless Protocol Validation Under Uncertainty

Jinghao Shi[1][(✉)], Shuvendu K. Lahiri[2], Ranveer Chandra[2],
and Geoffrey Challen[1]

[1] University at Buffalo, Buffalo, NY 14120, USA
{jinghaos,challen}@buffalo.edu
[2] Microsoft Research, Redmond, WA 98052, USA
{shuvendu,ranveer}@microsoft.com

Abstract. Runtime validation of wireless protocol implementations
cannot always employ direct instrumentation of the device under test
(DUT). The DUT may not implement the required instrumentation, or
the instrumentation may alter the DUT's behavior when enabled. Wireless sniffers can monitor the DUT's behavior without instrumentation,
but they introduce new validation challenges. Losses caused by wireless propagation prevent sniffers from perfectly reconstructing the actual
DUT packet trace. As a result, accurate validation requires distinguishing between specification deviations that represent implementation errors
and those caused by sniffer uncertainty.

We present a new approach enabling sniffer-based validation of wireless protocol implementations. Beginning with the original protocol
monitor state machine, we automatically and completely encode sniffer uncertainty by selectively adding non-deterministic transitions. We
characterize the NP-completeness of the resulting decision problem and
provide an exhaustive algorithm for searching over all mutated traces.
We also present practical protocol-oblivious heuristics for searching over
the most likely mutated traces. We have implemented our framework and
show that it can accurately identify implementation errors in the face of
uncertainty.

1 Introduction

Custom wireless protocols are often designed and deployed to meet the specific performance and power needs of special-purpose wireless devices. Examples
include Google Iris contact lenses [14], Xbox One wireless controllers [26], and
Google Chromecast [25]. Validating that device implementations work correctly
is critical to achieve the design goals of the wireless protocol and also prevent
bugs in shipped products [7,9,12].

Runtime validation of the protocol implementations on such devices is challenging because collecting traces from the device under test (DUT) is often
infeasible. The resource limitations of embedded or battery-powered devices may
cause them to not provide trace collecting capabilities. DUT may contain propri-
etary hardware or firmware that hides the implementation details and prevents
testers from collecting traces through source code instrumentation. Even when

© Springer International Publishing AG 2016
Y. Falcone and C. Sanchez (Eds.): RV 2016, LNCS 10012, pp. 351–367, 2016.
DOI: 10.1007/978-3-319-46982-9_22

collecting trace directly from the DUT is possible, the overhead it causes may alter the behavior of the DUT due to the observer effect [21], threatening the validation results.

An attractive alternative is to use wireless sniffers to record traffic generated by the DUT during testing. Sniffers do not require direct access to the DUT or the need to alter its behavior. However, due to the fundamentally unpredictable nature of wireless communications, the packets captured by the sniffer will not exactly match those received by the DUT. The sniffer may miss packets that the DUT received, or receive packets that the DUT missed. This is true even when using multiple sniffers [3,6,19], a sniffer with multiple antennas [23], or in isolated wireless environments.

Since the sniffer trace may not perfectly match the actual trace, uncertainty arises during protocol implementation validation. For example, if the DUT fails to respond correctly to a packet in the sniffer trace, it may either because the DUT's implementation is incorrect, or the DUT did not actually receive the packet, or the DUT's response was missed by the sniffer. Whenever the DUT's behavior does not match the specification, there are now two potential explanations: either the DUT's implementation is wrong, or the sniffer trace is inaccurate. Accurate validation requires distinguishing between these two causes.

We present a new technique than enables validation of protocol implementations using wireless sniffers. Given a monitor state machine representing the protocol being validated, we describe a systematic transformation that adds non-deterministic transitions to incorporate uncertainty introduced by the sniffer. This augmented validation state machine implicitly defines a set of mutated traces, each satisfying the original state machine with a specific likelihood. If the set is empty, the implementation definitely violates the protocol. Searching over all the mutated traces is NP-complete, but the approach can be made practical by applying protocol-oblivious heuristics that limit the search to likely mutated traces.

Our paper makes the following contributions:

1. To the best of our knowledge, we are the first to identify the uncertainty problem caused by sniffers in validating wireless protocol implementations.
2. We formalize the problem using a nondeterministic state machine that systematically and completely encodes the uncertainty of the sniffer trace.
3. We characterize the NP-completeness of the validation problem, and present two protocol-oblivious heuristics to prune the search space and make validation possible in practice.
4. We implement the validation framework and evaluate it using the NS-3 network simulator [22]. Our framework accurately identifies both synthetic and previously unknown violations in NS-3's implementations of the 802.11 and ARF protocols.

Due to space limitations, we omit the proof of lemmas and theorems in this paper. They can be found in the technical report [17].

2 Background and Motivating Example

We encountered the uncertainty problem while testing the protocol implementation of a popular wireless game controller. A custom wireless communication protocol was designed to meet the low latency and low power consumption goals. As is common industry practice, the protocol specification was then handed over to wireless chipset vendors for implementation. However, neither implementation details nor trace collection capabilities are provided in the shipped firmware due to intellectual property constraints and device resource limitation. Hence using sniffers to validate the protocol implementation is the only option.

We initially developed a tool to validate certain protocol properties over the sniffer trace, yet often found unacceptable amount of false alarms due to the incompleteness of the sniffer traces, making the tool virtually useless. It was clear that we needed to account for sniffer uncertainty.

To better understand the incompleteness of sniffer trace, consider the IEEE 802.11 (also known as Wi-Fi) transmitter (DUT) state machine shown in Fig. 1. After the DUT sends $DATA_i$—a data packet with sequence number i ($s_0 \rightarrow s_1$), it starts a timer and waits for the acknowledgment packet—Ack. The DUT either receives Ack within time T_o ($s_1 \rightarrow s_0$), or it sends $DATA'_i$—retransmission of $DATA_i$ ($s_1 \rightarrow s_2$). Similarly, the DUT either receives the Ack within T_o ($s_2 \rightarrow s_0$) or aborts transmission and moves on to next packet[1] ($s_2 \rightarrow s_1$).

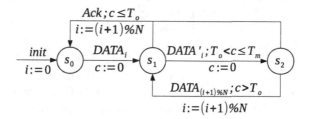

Fig. 1. Monitor state machine for 802.11 transmitter.

Given a complete log of DUT's packet transmission and reception events, it is trivial to feed such a log into the state machine in Fig. 1 and validate the correctness of DUT's protocol implementation. However, due to DUT limitations we have described earlier, this complete log is not available. As a result, we seek to validate the DUT implementation using sniffers.

There are two fundamental properties in wireless communication that bring uncertainty to sniffer's observation: packet loss and physical diversity. The sniffer could either miss packets sent from or to the DUT due to packet loss, or overhear packets that are sent to but missed by the DUT due to physical diversity.

---

[1] To represent the state machine succinctly, our example assumes that the DUT retries at most once.

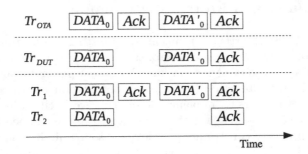

Fig. 2. Uncertainty of Sniffer Observations. Tr_{OTA} is the chronological sequence of packets sent by the DUT and the receiver. Tr_{DUT} is DUT's internal events. Tr_1 and Tr_2 are two examples of many possible sniffer traces.

Consider a correct packet exchange sequence shown in Fig. 2. The DUT first sends $DATA_0$. Suppose the receiver receives $DATA_0$ and sends the Ack which the DUT does not receive. Eventually the DUT's timer fires and it sends $DATA'_0$. This time the $DATA'_0$ reaches receiver and the DUT also receives the Ack.

Now consider two possible traces that could have been overheard by a sniffer shown in Fig. 2. In first sniffer trace Tr_1 where the sniffer *overhears* the first Ack packet, a validation *uncertainty* arises when the sniffer sees the $DATA'_0$: was the previous Ack missed by the DUT or is there a bug in DUT which causes it to retransmit even after receiving the Ack?

Similarly, consider the second possible sniffer trace Tr_2 where both the $DATA'_0$ and Ack packets were missed by the sniffer. During this period of time, it appears the DUT neither receives Ack for $DATA_0$ nor sends $DATA'_0$. Again, without any additional information it is impossible to disambiguate between the sniffer missing certain packets and a bug in DUT's retransmission logic.

Informally, the question we set out to answer in this paper is: given the protocol monitor state machine and the sniffer's observation with inherent uncertainty, how to accurately validate that the DUT behaves as specified?

3   Prerequisites and Problem Statement

3.1   Packet, Trace and Monitor State Machine

The alphabet of the monitor state machine is the finite set of all valid packets defined by the protocol, denoted as $\mathbb{P}$. A packet is a binary string of a finite number of bits, encoding interesting protocol attributes such as `src`, `dest`, `type`, `flags`, and physical layer information, such as `channel`, `modulation`, etc. The input of the state machine then corresponds to a time-ordered sequence of packets.

Definition 1. *A packet trace is a finite sequence of (timestamp, packet) tuple:* $[(t_1, p_1), (t_2, p_2), \ldots, (t_n, p_n)]$ *where* $t_i \in \mathbb{Z}^+$ *is the discrete timestamp and* p_i *is the packet observed at time* t_i. *The timestamps are strictly monotonically increasing:* $t_i < t_{i+1}$ *for* $1 \leq i < n$.

In addition to timestamp monotonicity, we also require that adjacent packets do not overlap in time, $t_{i+1} - t_i > \texttt{airtime}(p_i)$ for $1 \leq i < n$, where $\texttt{airtime}()$ calculates the time taken to transmit a packet. The timestamp represents the observer's local clock ticks, and need not to be synchronized among devices.

We use *timed automata* [1] to model the expected behaviors of the DUT. A timed automata is a finite state machine with timing constraints on the transitions: each transition can optionally start one or more timers, which can later be used to assert certain events should be seen before or after the time out event. We refer the readers to [1] for more details about timed automata.

Definition 2. *A protocol monitor state machine S is a 7-tuple* $\{\Sigma, \mathbb{S}, \mathbb{X},$ $s_0, C, E, G\}$*, where:*

- $\Sigma = \mathbb{P}$ *is the finite input alphabet.*
- $\mathbb{S}$ *is a non-empty, finite set of states.* $s_0 \in \mathbb{S}$ *is the initial state.*
- $\mathbb{X}$ *is the set of boolean variables. We use* $v = \{x \leftarrow true/false \mid x \in \mathbb{X}\}$ *to denote an assignment of the variables. Let* $\mathbb{V}$ *be the set of such values* v*.*
- C *is the set of clock variables. A clock variable can be reset along any state transitions. At any instant, reading a clock variable returns the time elapsed since last time it was reset.*
- G *is the set of guard conditions defined inductively by*

$$g := true \mid c \leq T \mid c \geq T \mid x \mid \neg g \mid g_1 \wedge g_2$$

where $c \in C$ *is a clock variable,* T *is a constant, and* x *is a variable in* $\mathbb{X}$*. A transition can choose not to use guard conditions by setting* g *to be true.*
- $E \subseteq \mathbb{S} \times \mathbb{V} \times \mathbb{S} \times \mathbb{V} \times \Sigma \times G \times \mathscr{P}(C)$ *gives the set of transitions.* $\langle s_i, v_i, s_j, v_j, p, g, C' \rangle \in E$ *represents that if the monitor is in state* s_i *with variable assignments* v_i*, given the input tuple* (t, p) *such that the guard* g *is satisfied, the monitor can transition to a state* s_j *with variable assignments* v_j*, and reset the clocks in* C' *to 0.*

A tuple (t_i, p_i) in the packet trace means the packet p_i is presented to the state machine at time t_i. The monitor *rejects a trace* Tr if there exists a prefix of Tr such that all states reachable after consuming the prefix have no valid transitions for the next (t, p) input.

As an example, the monitor state machine illustrated in Fig. 1 can be formally defined as follows:

- $\Sigma = \{DATA_i, DATA'_i, Ack \mid 0 \leq i < N\}$.
- Clock variables $C = \{c\}$. The only clock variable c is used for acknowledgment time out.
- $\mathbb{X} = \{i\}$, as a variable with $log(N) + 1$ bits to count from 0 to N.
- Guard constraints $G = \{c \leq T_o, c > T_o, T_o < c \leq T_m\}$. T_o is the acknowledgment time out value, and $T_m > T_o$ is the maximum delay allowed before the retransmission packet gets sent. T_o can be arbitrary large but not infinity in order to check the liveness of the DUT.

The monitor state machine defines a *timed language* L which consists of all valid packet traces that can be observed by the DUT. We now give the definition of protocol *compliance* and *violation*.

Definition 3. *Suppose* $\mathbb{T}$ *is the set of all possible packet traces collected from DUT, and S is the state machine specified by the protocol. The DUT violates the protocol specification if there exists an packet trace $Tr \in \mathbb{T}$ such that S rejects Tr. Otherwise, the DUT is compliant with the specification.*

The focus of this paper is to determine whether a *given* Tr is evidence of a violation.

3.2   Mutation Trace

As shown in the motivation example in Fig. 2, a sniffer trace may either miss packets that are present in DUT trace, or contain extra packets that are missing in DUT trace. Note that in the latter case, those extra packets must be all sent *to* the DUT. This is because it is impossible for the sniffer to overhear packets sent from the DUT that were not actually sent by the DUT.

We formally capture this relationship with the definition of mutation trace.

Definition 4. *A packet trace Tr' is a mutation of sniffer trace Tr w.r.t. a DUT if for all $(t, p) \in Tr \backslash Tr'$, $p.dest = DUT$, where $p.dest$ is the destination of packet p.*

By definition, either $Tr' \supseteq Tr$ (hence $Tr \backslash Tr' = \emptyset$), or those extra packets in Tr but not in Tr' are all sent to the DUT. Note that Tr' may contain extra packets that are either sent to or received by the DUT.

A mutation trace Tr' represents a *guess* of the corresponding DUT packet trace given sniffer trace Tr. In fact, the DUT packet trace must be one of the mutation traces of the sniffer trace Tr.

Lemma 1. *Let Tr_{DUT} and Tr be the DUT and sniffer packet trace captured during the same protocol operation session, and $\mathcal{M}(Tr)$ be the set of mutation traces of Tr with respect to DUT, then $Tr_{DUT} \in \mathcal{M}(Tr)$.*

3.3   Problem Statement

Lemma 1 shows that $\mathcal{M}(Tr)$ is a *complete* set of guesses of the DUT packet trace. Therefore, the problem of validating DUT implementation given a sniffer trace can be formally defined as follows:

Problem 1. VALIDATION
instance A protocol monitor state machine S and a sniffer trace Tr.
question Does there exist a mutation trace Tr' of Tr that satisfies S?

If the answer is no, a definite violation of the DUT implementation can be claimed. Nevertheless, if the answer is yes, S may still reject Tr_{DUT}. In other words, the conclusion of the validation can either be *definitely wrong* or *probably correct*, but not *definitely correct*. This is the fundamental limitation caused by the uncertainty of sniffer traces.

4   Validation Framework

4.1   Augmented State Machine

To deal with the inherent uncertainty of sniffer traces, we propose to systematically augment the original monitor state machine with non-deterministic transitions to account for the difference between the sniffer and DUT traces.

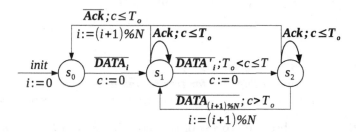

Fig. 3. Augmented Monitor State Machine. Augmented transitions are highlighted in bold face. $\overline{Pkt}$ means either ϵ or Pkt.

Before formally defining the augmented state machine, we first use an example to illustrate the basic idea. Figure 3 shows the augmented state machine for 802.11 transmitter state machine shown in Fig. 1. For each existing transition (e.g., $s_0 \rightarrow s_1$), we add an *empty transition* with same clock guards and resetting clocks. This accounts for the possibility when such packet was observed by the DUT but missed by the sniffer. Additionally, for each transition triggered by a *receiving* packet (i.e., $p.dest = DUT$), such as $s_1 \rightarrow s_0$ and $s_2 \rightarrow s_0$, we add a *self transition* with the same trigger packet and clock guards, but an empty set of resetting clocks and no assignments to variables. This allows the state machine to make progress when the sniffer missed such packets.

There are two things to note. First, self transitions are added only for packets sent *to* the DUT, since the sniffer will not overhear packets *from* the DUT if they were not sent by the DUT. Second, no augmented transitions are added for the packets that are sent to DUT yet are missed by both the DUT and the sniffer, since such packets do not cause difference between the DUT and sniffer traces.

The augmented state machine in Fig. 3 will accept the sniffer packet traces Tr_1 and Tr_2 shown in Fig. 2. For instance, one accepting transition sequence on sniffer trace Tr_1 is $s_0 \rightarrow s_1 \rightarrow_s s_1 \rightarrow s_2 \rightarrow s_0$, and the sequence for Tr_2 is $s_0 \rightarrow s_1 \rightarrow_e s_2 \rightarrow s_0$, where $\rightarrow$ is the transition from the original state machine, $\rightarrow_e$ and $\rightarrow_s$ are the augmented empty and self transitions respectively.

We now formally define the augmented state machine.

Definition 5. *An augmented state machine S^+ for a monitor state machine S is a 7-tuple $\{\Sigma^+, \mathbb{S}, \mathbb{X}, s_0, C, E^+, G\}$, where $\mathbb{S}, \mathbb{X}, s_0, C, G$ are the same as S. $\Sigma^+ = \{\epsilon\} \cup \Sigma$ is the augmented input alphabet with the empty symbol, and $E^+ \supset E$ is the set of transitions, which includes:*

Algorithm 1. Obtain Augmented Transitions E^+ from E

1: **function** AUGMENT(E)
2:    $E^+ := \emptyset$
3:    **for all** $\langle s_i, v_i, s_j, v_j, p, g, C' \rangle \in E$ **do**
4:        $E^+ := E^+ \cup \{\langle s_i, v_i, s_j, v_j, p, g, C' \rangle\}$ ▷ Type-0
5:        $E^+ := E^+ \cup \{\langle s_i, v_i, s_j, v_j, \epsilon, g, C' \rangle\}$ ▷ Type-1
6:        **if** $p.dest = DUT$ **then**
7:            $E^+ := E^+ \cup \{\langle s_i, v_i, \boldsymbol{s_i}, \boldsymbol{v_i}, p, g, \emptyset \rangle\}$ ▷ Type-2
8:    **return** E^+

- E: existing transitions (**Type-0**) in S.
- E_1^+: empty transitions (**Type-1**) for transitions in E.
- E_2^+: self transitions (**Type-2**) for transitions triggered by receiving packets.

Algorithm 1 describes the process of transforming E into E^+. In particular, Line 4 adds existing transitions in E to E^+, while line 5 and 7 add Type-1 and Type-2 transitions to E^+ respectively. We have highlighted the elements of the tuple that differ from the underlying Type-0 transition. Note that in Type-2 transitions, both the state and the variables stay the same after the transition.

With augmented state machine S^+, we can use Type-1 transitions to non-deterministically infer packets missed by the sniffer, and use Type-2 transitions to consume extra packets captured by the sniffer but missed by the DUT.

A accepting run of S^+ on sniffer trace Tr yields a mutation trace Tr' which represents one possibility of the DUT trace. Specifically, Tr' can be obtained by adding missing packets indicated by Type-1 transitions to Tr, and removing extra packets indicated by Type-2 transitions from Tr.

We show that the VALIDATION problem is equivalent to the satisfiability problem of Tr on S^+.

Theorem 1. *There exists a mutation trace $Tr' \in \mathcal{M}(Tr)$ that satisfies S if and only if Tr satisfies S^+.*

By Theorem 1, the inherent uncertainty of the sniffer traces is explicitly represented by the augmented transitions, and can be systematically explored using the well established theory of state machine.

4.2   Problem Hardness

In this section, we show that the VALIDATION problem is NP-complete. In fact, the problem is still NP-complete even with only one type of augmented transitions.

Recall that Type-1 transitions are added because the sniffer may miss packets. Suppose an imaginary sniffer that is able to capture *every* packet ever transmitted, then only Type-2 transitions are needed since the sniffer may still overhear packets sent to the DUT. Similarly, suppose another special sniffer that would not overhear any packets sent to the DUT, then only Type-1 transitions are needed to infer missing packets.

We refer the augmented state machine that only has Type-0 and Type-1 transitions as S_1^+, and the augmented state machine that only has Type-0 and Type-2 transitions as S_2^+. And we show that each subproblem of determining trace satisfiability is NP-complete.

Problem 2. VALIDATION-1
Given that $Tr\backslash Tr_{DUT} = \emptyset$ (sniffer does not overhear packets).
instance Checker state machine S and sniffer trace Tr.
question Does S_1^+ accept Tr?

Problem 3. VALIDATION-2
Given that $Tr_{DUT} \subseteq Tr$ (sniffer does not missing packets).
instance Checker state machine S and sniffer trace Tr.
question Does S_2^+ accept Tr?

Lemma 2. *Both VALIDATION-1 and VALIDATION-2 are NP-complete.*

The hardness statement of the general VALIDATION problem naturally follows Lemma 2.

Theorem 2. *VALIDATION is NP-complete.*

4.3   Searching Strategies

In this section, we present an *exhaustive* search algorithm of the accepting transition sequence of S^+ on sniffer trace Tr. It is guaranteed to yield an accepting sequence if there exists one, thus is exhaustive. In the next sections, we present heuristics to limit the search to accepting sequences of S^+ that require relatively fewer transitions from $E_1^+ \cup E_2^+$. Due to the NP-completeness of the problem, this also makes the algorithm meaningful in practice.

The main routines of the algorithm are shown in Algorithm 2. In the top level SEARCH routine, we first obtain the augmented state machine S^+, and then call the recursive EXTEND function with an empty prefix, the sniffer trace, and the S^+'s initial state. In the EXTEND function, we try to consume the first packet in the remaining trace using either Type-0, Type-1 or Type-2 transition. Note that we always try to use Type-0 transitions before other two augmented transitions (line 6). This ensures the first found mutation trace will have the most number of Type-0 transitions among all possible mutation traces. Intuitively, this means the search algorithm tries to utilize the sniffer's observation as much as possible before being forced to make assumptions.

Each of the extend functions either returns the mutation trace Tr', or *nil* if the search fails. In both EXTEND-0 and EXTEND-2 function, if there is a valid transition, we try to consume the next packet either by appending it to the prefix (line 13) or dropping it (line 26). While in EXTEND-1, we guess a missing packet without consuming the next real packet (line 20). Note that since only Type-0 and Type-2 consume packets, the recursion terminates if there is a valid Type-0 or Type-2 transition for the last packet (line 12 and line 25).

Algorithm 2. Exhaustive search algorithm of S^+ on Tr.

```
 1: function SEARCH(S, Tr)
 2:     S⁺ := AUGMENT(S)
 3:     return EXTEND([], Tr, S⁺.s₀)
 4: function EXTEND(prefix, p::suffix, s)
 5:     if not LIKELY(prefix) then return nilᵃ
 6:     for i ∈ [0, 1, 2] do
 7:         mutation := EXTEND-i(prefix, p::suffix, s)
 8:         if mutation ≠ nil then return mutation
 9:     return nil
10: function EXTEND-0(prefix, p::suffix, s)
11:     for ⟨s, s′, p⟩ᵇ∈ E do
12:         if suffix = nil then return prefix@p
13:         mutation := EXTEND(prefix@p, suffix, s′)
14:         if mutation ≠ nil then return mutation
15:     return nil
16: function EXTEND-1(prefix, p::suffix, s)
17:     for all ⟨s, s′, q⟩ ∈ E₁⁺ do
18:         if q.time > p.time then
19:             continue
20:         mutation := EXTEND(prefix@q, p::suffix, s′)
21:         if mutation ≠ nil then return mutation
22:     return nil
23: function EXTEND-2(prefix, p::suffix, s)
24:     for all ⟨s, s, p⟩ ∈ E₂⁺ do
25:         if suffix = nil then return prefix
26:         mutation := EXTEND(prefix, suffix, s)
27:         if mutation ≠ nil then return mutation
28:     return nil
```

ᵃThis check should be ignored in the exhaustive algorithm.
ᵇ$\langle s, s′, p \rangle$ is short for $\langle s, *, s′, *, p, *, * \rangle$.

It is not hard to see that Algorithm 2 terminates on any sniffer traces. Each node in the transition tree only has finite number of possible next steps, and the depth of Type-1 transitions is limited by the time available before the next packet (line 18).

4.4 Pruning Heuristics

In the face of uncertainty between a possible protocol violation and sniffer imperfection, augmented transitions provide the ability to blame the latter. The exhaustive nature of Algorithm 2 means that it always tries to blame sniffer imperfection whenever possible, making it reluctant to report true violations.

Inspired by the *directed model checking* [10] technique which is to mitigate the state explosion problem, we propose to enforce extra constraints on the mutation trace to restrict the search to only mutation traces with high likelihood.

The modified EXTEND function checks certain likelihood constraints on the prefix of the mutation trace before continuing (line 5), and stops the current search branch immediately if the prefix seems *unlikely*. Because of the recursive nature of the algorithm, other branches which may have a higher likelihood can then be explored.

The strictness of the likelihood constraint represents a trade-off between precision and recall of validation. The more strict the constraints are, the more false positive violations will potentially be reported, hence the lower the precision yet higher recall. On the contrary, the more tractable the constraints are, the more tolerant the search is to sniffer imperfection, hence the more likely that it will report true violations, thus higher precision but lower recall.

The exact forms of the constraints may depend on many factors, such as the nature of the protocol, properties of the sniffer, or domain knowledge. Next, we propose two *protocol oblivious* heuristics based on the sniffer loss probabilities and general protocol operations. Both heuristic contains parameters that can be fine tuned in practice.

NumMissing(d, l, k). This heuristic states that the number of missing packets from device d in any sub mutation traces of length l shall not exceed k ($k \leq l$). The sliding window of size l serves two purposes. First, l should be large enough for the calculated packet loss ratio to be statistically meaningful. Second, it ensures that the packet losses are evenly distributed among the entire packet trace.

The intuition behind this heuristic is that the sniffer's empirical packet loss probability can usually be measured before validation. Therefore, the likelihood that the sniffer misses more packets than prior measured loss ratio is quite low. The value of l and k can then be configured such that k/l is marginally larger than the measured ratio.

GoBack(k). This heuristic states that the search should only backtrack at most k steps when the search gets stuck using only E. The motivation is that many protocols operate as a sequence of independent transactions, and the uncertainty of previous transactions often do not affect the next transaction. For instance, in 802.11 packet transmission protocol, each packet exchange, include the original, retransmission and acknowledgment packets, constitute a transaction. And the retransmission status of previous packets has no effect on the packets with subsequent sequence numbers, hence need not be explored when resolving the uncertainty of the packets with new sequence numbers. Note that we do not require the protocol to specify an exact transaction boundary, but only need k to be sufficiently large to cover a transaction.

5   Case Studies

We present case studies on applying our validation framework on two protocols implemented in the NS-3 network simulator: 802.11 data transmission and ARF rate control algorithm. The goal is to demonstrate how our framework can avoid false alarms and report true violations on incomplete sniffer traces and report true violations.

5.1   802.11 Data Transmission

In this section, we first show that our framework can improve validation precision by inferring the missing or extra packets using the augmented transition framework. We then demonstrate the ability of our framework to detect true violations by manually introducing bugs in the NS-3 implementation and show the precision and recall of validation results.

Experimental Setup. We set up two Wi-Fi devices acting as the transmitter (DUT) and receiver respectively. Another Wi-Fi device is configured in monitor mode and acts as the sniffer. During the experiments, we collect both the DUT packet trace (the ground truth) and the sniffer trace.

Verifying Unmodified Implementation. In the original monitor state machine shown in Fig. 1, we set acknowledgment timeout $T_o = 334\,\mu s$, maximum retransmission delay $T_m = 15\,ms$ according to the protocol. We also adapt the state machine to include multiple retransmissions[2] instead of one.

Let Pr_{ds}, Pr_{es} and Pr_{ed} be the packet loss probability between the DUT and sniffer, endpoint and sniffer, endpoint and DUT respectively. Pr_{ed} represents the characteristics of the system being tested, while Pr_{ds} and Pr_{es} represent the sniffer's quality in capturing packets.

We vary each of the three probabilities, Pr_{ds}, Pr_{es} and Pr_{ed}, from 0 to 0.5 (both inclusive) with 0.05 step. For each loss ratio combination, we ran the experiment 5 times, and each run lasted 30 seconds. In total, 6655 ($11^3 \times 5$) pairs of DUT and sniffer packet traces were collected.

To establish the ground truth of violations, we first verify the DUT packet traces using the *original* state machine S. This can be achieved by disabling augmented transitions in our framework. As expected, no violation is detected in any DUT packet traces.

We then verify the sniffer traces using the augmented state machine S^+. For the $GoBack(k)$ heuristic, we set $k = 7$, which is the maximum number of transmissions of a single packet. For the $NumMissing(d, l, k)$ heuristic, we set the sliding window size $l = 100$, and $k = 80$ such that no violation is reported. The relationship of k and validation precision is studied in next section.

Next, we present detailed analysis of the augmented transitions on the sniffer traces. The goal is to study for a given system packet loss probability Pr_{ed}, how the sniffer packet loss properties (Pr_{ds} and Pr_{es}) affect the difference between

---

[2] The exact number of retransmissions is not part of the protocol, and NS-3 implementation set this to be 7.

the DUT trace and the mutation trace, which represents a guess of the DUT trace by the augmented state machine based on the sniffer trace.

For all following analysis, we divide the traces into three groups according to Pr_{ed}: low $(0 \leq Pr_{ed} \leq 0.15)$, medium $(0.20 \leq Pr_{ed} \leq 0.35)$ and high $(0.40 \leq Pr_{ed} \leq 0.50)$.

The different between two packet traces can be quantified by the Jaccard distance metric.

$$Jaccard(Tr_1, Tr_2) = \frac{|Tr_1 \ominus Tr_2|}{|Tr_1 \cup Tr_2|} \tag{1}$$

where $\ominus$ is the symmetric difference operator. The distance is 0 if the two traces are identical, and is 1 when the two traces are completely different. The smaller the distance is, the more similar the two traces are.

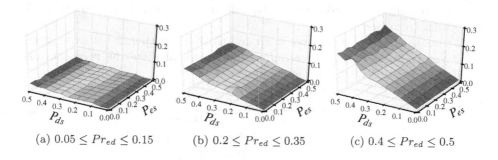

(a) $0.05 \leq Pr_{ed} \leq 0.15$ (b) $0.2 \leq Pr_{ed} \leq 0.35$ (c) $0.4 \leq Pr_{ed} \leq 0.5$

Fig. 4. Jaccard Distance Between Mutation and DUT Traces. For each data point, the mean of the 5 runs is used.

Figure 4 shows the Jaccard Distance between mutation and its corresponding DUT trace. We make the following observations. First, for a given system loss probability Pr_{ed} (each sub-figure), the lower the sniffer packet loss probability $(Pr_{ds}$ and $Pr_{es})$, the smaller Jaccard distance between the DUT and mutation trace. Intuitively, this means a sniffer that misses less packets can enable our framework to better reconstruct the DUT trace.

Second, we observe a *protocol-specific* trend that Pr_{ds} is more dominant than Pr_{es}. This is because retransmission packets of the same sequence number are identical, hence when the sniffer misses multiple retransmission packets, our framework only needs to infer one retransmission packet to continue state machine execution.

Finally, as the system loss probability Pr_{ed} increases, the Jaccard distance increases more rapidly as Pr_{ds} increases. This is because the ratio of retransmission packet increases along with Pr_{ed}.

Introducing Bugs. We have demonstrated that our framework can tolerate sniffer imperfections and avoid raising false alarms. The next question is, can it detect true violations? To answer this question, we manually introduce several bugs in NS-3 implementation that concerns various aspects of 802.11 data transmission protocol. More specifically, the bugs are:

- **Sequence Number:** the DUT does not assign sequence number correctly. For example, it may increase sequence by 2 instead of 1, or it does not increase sequence number after certain packet, etc. We choose one type of such bugs in each run.
- **Semantic:** the DUT may retransmit even after receiving *Ack*, or does not retransmit when not receiving *Ack*.

We instrument the NS-3 implementation to embed instances of bugs in each category. At each experiment run, we randomly decide whether and which bug to introduce for each category. We fix $Pr_{ds} = Pr_{es} = 0.1$ and vary Pr_{ed} from 0.0 to 0.5 with 0.01 step. For each Pr_{ed} value, we ran the experiment 100 times, of which roughly 75 experiments contained bugs. In total, 5100 pairs of DUT and sniffer traces were collected.

We use the DUT packet traces as ground truth of whether or not each experiment run contains bugs. For each Pr_{ed} value, we calculate the precision and recall of violation detection using the sniffer traces.

$$\text{Precision} = \frac{|\{\text{Reported Bugs}\} \cap \{\text{True Bugs}\}|}{|\{\text{Reported Bugs}\}|} \tag{2}$$

$$\text{Recall} = \frac{|\{\text{Reported Bugs}\} \cap \{\text{True Bugs}\}|}{|\{\text{True Bugs}\}|} \tag{3}$$

The precision metric quantifies how *useful* the validation results are, while the recall metric measures how *complete* the validation results are.

Figure 5 shows the CDF of precision and recall of the 51 experiments for various k values. For precision, as expected, the more tolerant the search to sniffer losses (larger k), the more tolerant the framework is to sniffer losses, and the more precise the violation detection. In particular, when $k = 30$, the

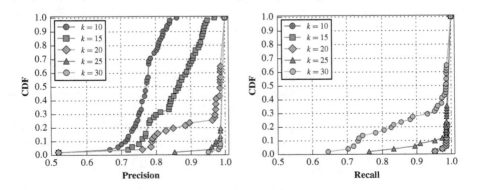

Fig. 5. Precision and recall of validation results.

precisions are 100 % for all Pr_{ed} values. Second, the recall is less sensitive to the choice of k. Except for the extreme case when $k = 30$, all other thresholds can report almost all the violations.

5.2   ARF Rate Control Algorithm

We report a bug found in NS-3 ARF [16] implementation which causes the sender to get stuck at a lower rate even after enough number of consecutive successes. The bug was detected using sniffer traces and confirmed by both the DUT trace and source code inspection.

6   Related Work

Hidden Markov Model (HMM) Approach. When considering the whole system under test (both DUT and endpoint), the sniffer only captures a subset of the all the packets (events). This is similar to the event sampling problem in runtime verification [2, 4, 5, 11, 15]. Stoller *et al.* [24] used HMM-based state estimation techniques to calculate the confidence that the temporal property is satisfied in the presence of gaps in observation.

While it seems possible to adapt the method in [24] to our problem, we note several advantages of our approach. First, the automatically augmented state machine precisely encodes the protocol specification and the uncertainty. This is intuitive to design and natural for reporting the evidence for a trace being successful. We do not require a user to specify the number of states of the underlying HMM, or accurately provide underlying probabilities. Second, we use timed automata to monitor the timing constraints which are common in wireless protocols. It may be non-trivial to encode such timing information in HMM. Finally, we can exploit domain knowledge to devise effective pruning heuristics to rule out unlikely sequences during the exhaustive search.

Network Protocol Validation. Lee *et al.* [18] studied the problem of passive network testing of network management. The system input/output behavior is only partially observable. However, the uncertainty only lies in missing events in the observation, while in the context of wireless protocol verification, the uncertainty could also be caused by extra events not observed by the tested system. Additionally, they do not provide any formal guarantees even for cases when we report a definite bug. Software model checking techniques [13, 20] have also been used to verify network protocols. Our problem is unique because of the observation uncertainty caused by sniffers. Our framework shares similarity with *angelic verification* [8] where the program verifier reports a warning only when no acceptable specification exists on unknowns.

7   Conclusions

We formally define the uncertainty problem in validating wireless protocol implementations using sniffers. We describe a systematic augmentation of the protocol state machine to explicitly encode the uncertainty of sniffer traces. We characterize the NP-completeness of the problem and propose both an exhaustive search algorithm and heuristics to restrict the search to more likely traces. We present two case studies using NS-3 network simulator to demonstrate how our framework can improve validation precision and detect real bugs.

References

1. Alur, R., Dill, D.L.: A theory of timed automata. Theor. Comput. Sci. **126**(2), 183–235 (1994)
2. Arnold, M., Vechev, M., Yahav, E.: QVM: an efficient runtime for detecting defects in deployed systems. In: ACM Sigplan Notices, vol. 43, pp. 143–162. ACM (2008)
3. Bahl, P., Chandra, R., Padhye, J., Ravindranath, L., Singh, M., Wolman, A., Zill, B.: Enhancing the security of corporate Wi-Fi networks using DAIR. In: Proceedings of the 4th International Conference on Mobile Systems, Applications and Services, pp. 1–14. ACM (2006)
4. Basin, D., Klaedtke, F., Marinovic, S., Zălinescu, E.: Monitoring compliance policies over incomplete and disagreeing logs. In: Qadeer, S., Tasiran, S. (eds.) RV 2012. LNCS, vol. 7687, pp. 151–167. Springer, Heidelberg (2013). doi:10.1007/978-3-642-35632-2_17
5. Bonakdarpour, B., Navabpour, S., Fischmeister, S.: Sampling-based runtime verification. In: Butler, M., Schulte, W. (eds.) FM 2011. LNCS, vol. 6664, pp. 88–102. Springer, Heidelberg (2011). doi:10.1007/978-3-642-21437-0_9
6. Cheng, Y.-C., Bellardo, J., Benkö, P., Snoeren, A.C., Voelker, G.M., Savage, S.: Jigsaw: solving the puzzle of enterprise 802.11 analysis, vol. 36. ACM (2006)
7. Ciabarra, M.: WiFried: iOS 8 WiFi Issue. https://goo.gl/KtRDqk
8. Das, A., Lahiri, S.K., Lal, A., Li, Y.: Angelic verification: precise verification modulo unknowns. In: Kroening, D., Păsăreanu, C.S. (eds.) CAV 2015. LNCS, vol. 9206, pp. 324–342. Springer, Heidelberg (2015). doi:10.1007/978-3-319-21690-4_19
9. digitalmediaphile. Windows 10 wifi issues with surface pro 3 and surface 3. http://goo.gl/vBqiEo
10. Edelkamp, S., Schuppan, V., Bošnački, D., Wijs, A., Fehnker, A., Aljazzar, H.: Survey on directed model checking. In: Peled, D.A., Wooldridge, M.J. (eds.) MoChArt 2008. LNCS (LNAI), vol. 5348, pp. 65–89. Springer, Heidelberg (2009). doi:10.1007/978-3-642-00431-5_5
11. Fei, L., Midkiff, S.P.: Artemis: practical runtime monitoring of applications for execution anomalies. In: ACM SIGPLAN Notices, vol. 41, pp. 84–95. ACM (2006)
12. Gizmodo. The worst bugs in android 5.0 lollipop and how to fix them. http://goo.gl/akDcvA
13. Godefroid, P.: Model checking for programming languages using verisoft. In: Proceedings of the 24th ACM SIGPLAN-SIGACT Symposium on Principles of Programming Languages, pp. 174–186. ACM (1997)
14. Google. Google contact lens. https://en.wikipedia.org/wiki/GoogleContactLens
15. Hauswirth, M., Chilimbi, T.M.: Low-overhead memory leak detection using adaptive statistical profiling. In: ACM SIGPLAN Notices, vol. 39, pp. 156–164. ACM (2004)
16. Kamerman, A., Monteban, L.: Wavelan-II: a high-performance wireless lan for the unlicensed band. Bell Labs Tech. J. **2**(3), 118–133 (1997)

17. Lahiri, S., Chandra, R., Shi, J., Challen, G.: Wireless protocol validation under uncertainty. Technical report, July 2016. https://www.microsoft.com/en-us/research/publication/wireless-protocol-validation-under-uncertainty/
18. Lee, D., Netravali, A.N., Sabnani, K.K., Sugla, B., John, A.: Passive testing and applications to network management. In: Proceedings of 1997 International Conference on Network Protocols, pp. 113–122. IEEE (1997)
19. Mahajan, R., Rodrig, M., Wetherall, D., Zahorjan, J.: Analyzing the MAC-level behavior of wireless networks in the wild. In: ACM SIGCOMM Computer Communication Review, vol. 36, pp. 75–86. ACM (2006)
20. Musuvathi, M., Park, D.Y., Chou, A., Engler, D.R., Dill, D.L.: CMC: a pragmatic approach to model checking real code. ACM SIGOPS Oper. Syst. Rev. **36**(SI), 75–88 (2002)
21. Mytkowicz, T., Sweeney, P.F., Hauswirth, M., Diwan, A.: Observer effect and measurement bias in performance analysis (2008)
22. Riley, G.F., Henderson, T.R.: The NS-3 network simulator. In: Wehrle, K., Güneş, M., Gross, J. (eds.) Modeling and Tools for Network Simulation, pp. 15–34. Springer, Heidelberg (2010). doi:10.1007/978-3-642-12331-3_2
23. Savvius Inc., Savvius Wi-Fi adapters. https://goo.gl/l3VXSx
24. Stoller, S.D., Bartocci, E., Seyster, J., Grosu, R., Havelund, K., Smolka, S.A., Zadok, E.: Runtime verification with state estimation. In: Khurshid, S., Sen, K. (eds.) RV 2011. LNCS, vol. 7186, pp. 193–207. Springer, Heidelberg (2012). doi:10.1007/978-3-642-29860-8_15
25. Wikipedia. Chromecast. https://en.wikipedia.org/wiki/Chromecast
26. Wikipedia. Xbox One controller. https://en.wikipedia.org/wiki/XboxOne Controller

Dynamic Determinacy Race Detection
for Task Parallelism with Futures

Rishi Surendran$^{(\boxtimes)}$ and Vivek Sarkar

Rice University, Houston, TX, USA
{rishi,vsarkar}@rice.edu

Abstract. Existing dynamic determinacy race detectors for task-parallel programs are limited to programs with strict computation graphs, where a task can only wait for its descendant tasks to complete. In this paper, we present the first known determinacy race detector for non-strict computation graphs, constructed using futures. The space and time complexity of our algorithm are similar to those of the classical SP-bags algorithm, when using only structured parallel constructs such as spawn-sync and async-finish. In the presence of point-to-point synchronization using futures, the complexity of the algorithm increases by a factor determined by the number of future task creation and get operations as well as the number of non-tree edges in the computation graph. The experimental results show that the slowdown factor observed for our algorithm relative to the sequential version is in the range of $1.00\times -9.92\times$, which is in line with slowdowns experienced for strict computation graphs in past work.

1 Introduction

Current dynamic determinacy race detection algorithms for task parallelism are limited to parallel constructs in which a task may wait for a child task [4,16], a descendant task [26,27] or the immediate left sibling [14]. However, current parallel programming models include parallel constructs that support more general synchronization patterns. For example, the OpenMP depends clause allows tasks to wait on previously spawned sibling tasks and the future construct in C#, C++11, Habanero Java (HJ), X10, and other languages, enables a task to wait on any previously created task to which the waiter task has a reference. Both approaches can lead to non-strict computation graphs, in general. Race detection algorithms based on vector clocks [3,17] are impractical for these constructs because either the vector clocks have to be allocated with a size proportional to the maximum number of simultaneously live tasks (which can be unboundedly large) or precision has to be sacrificed by assigning one clock per processor or worker thread, thereby missing potential data races when two tasks execute on the same worker.

The approaches in [4,16,26,27] focus on an imperative structured task-parallel model, in which tasks communicate through side effects on shared variables. In contrast, our paper focuses on enabling the use of futures for

© Springer International Publishing AG 2016
Y. Falcone and C. Sanchez (Eds.): RV 2016, LNCS 10012, pp. 368–385, 2016.
DOI: 10.1007/978-3-319-46982-9_23

functional-style parallelism, while also allowing futures to co-exist with imperative async-finish parallelism [10]. The addition of point-to-point synchronization
with futures makes the race detection more challenging than for async-finish task
parallelism since the computation graphs that can be generated using futures are
more general than those that can be generated by fork-join parallel constructs
such as async-finish constructs in X10 [10] and Habanero-Java [8], spawn-sync
constructs in Cilk [5], and task-taskwait constructs in OpenMP [24].

Existing algorithms for detecting determinacy races for dynamic task parallelism, do not support race detection for futures. For instance, data race detectors
for Cilk [4,16] handle only spawn-sync constructs where the computation graph
is a Series-Parallel (SP) dag. Although the computation graphs for async-finish
parallelism [26,27] are more general than SP dags, whether two instructions may
logically execute in parallel can still be determined efficiently by a lookup of the
lowest common ancestor of the instructions in the dynamic program structure
tree [26,27]. The computation graphs in the presence of futures may not have
any of the structures discussed above, and therefore, the past approaches are
not directly applicable to parallel programs with futures. However, parallel programs written with futures enjoy the property that data race freedom implies
determinacy, i.e., if a parallel program is written using only async, finish, and
future constructs, and is known to not exhibit a data race, then it must be determinate [12,19]. Thus, a data race detector for programs with async, finish, and
future constructs, can be used as a determinacy checker for these programs.

The main contributions of this paper[1] are as follows:

1. The first known sound and precise on-the-fly algorithm for detecting races
   in programs containing async, finish, and future parallel constructs. Instead
   of using brute force approaches such as building the transitive closure of
   the happens-before relation, our algorithm relies on a novel data structure
   called the *dynamic task reachability graph* to efficiently detect races in the
   input program. We show that the algorithm can detect determinacy races
   by effectively analyzing all possible executions for a given input. Relative to
   the SP-bags and related algorithms, the complexity of our algorithm only
   increases by a factor determined by the number of future task creation and
   get operations as well as the number of non-tree edges in the computation
   graph.
2. An implementation and evaluation of the algorithm on programs with
   structured async-finish parallelism and point-to-point synchronization using
   futures. We implemented the algorithm in the Habanero Java compiler and
   runtime system, and evaluated it on a suite of benchmarks containing async,
   finish and future constructs. The experiments show that the algorithm performs similarly to SP-bags in the presence of structured synchronization and
   degrades gracefully in the presence of point-to-point synchronization.

The remainder of the paper is organized as follows. Section 2 discusses our
programming model, and Sect. 3 defines determinacy races for our programming

---

[1] A summary abstract of this approach was presented as a brief announcement at
SPAA 2016 [28].

model. Section 4 presents the algorithm for determinacy race detection for parallel programs with futures, and Sect. 5 discusses the implementation and experimental results for our race detection algorithm. Section 6 discusses related work, and Sect. 7 contains our conclusions.

2   Programming Model

Our work addresses parallel programming models that can support combinations of functional-style futures and imperative-style tasks; examples include the X10 [10], Habanero-Java [8], Chapel [9], and C++11 languages. We will use X10 and Habanero Java's finish and async notation for task parallelism in this paper, though our algorithms are applicable to other task-parallel constructs as well. In this notation, the statement "async {S}" causes the parent task to create a new child task to execute S asynchronously (i.e., before, after, or in parallel) with the remainder of the parent task. The statement "finish {S}" causes the parent task to execute S and then wait for the completion of all asynchronous tasks created within S. Each dynamic instance T_A of an async task has a unique *Immediately Enclosing Finish (IEF)* instance F of a finish statement during program execution, where F is the innermost dynamic finish containing T_A. There is an implicit finish scope surrounding the body of main() so program execution will end only after all async tasks have completed.

A future [18] (or promise [21]) refers to an object that acts as a proxy for a result that may initially be unknown, because the computation of its value may still be in progress as a parallel task. In the notation used in this paper, the statement, "future < T > f = async < T > Expr;" creates a new child task to evaluate Expr asynchronously, where T is the type of the expression Expr. In this case, f contains a handle to the return value (future object) for the newly created task and the operation f.get() can be performed to obtain the result of the future task. If the future task has not completed as yet, the task performing the f.get() operation blocks until the result of Expr becomes available. Futures are traditionally used for enabling functional-style parallelism and are guaranteed not to exhibit data races on their return values. However, imperative programming languages allow future tasks to also contain side effects in the task bodies. These side effects on shared memory locations may cause determinacy races if the program has insufficient synchronization.

Comparison with spawn-sync and async-finish. In both spawn-sync and async-finish programming models, a join operation can be performed only once on a task (by the parent task in spawn-sync and by the ancestor task containing the immediately enclosing finish in async-finish). The class of computations generated by spawn-sync constructs is said to be *fully strict* [6], and the class of computations generated by async-finish constructs is called *terminally strict* [1].

The introduction of future as a parallel construct increases the possible synchronization patterns. Task T_2 can wait for a previously created task T_1 if T_2 has a reference to T_1 by performing the get() operation. Moreover, this join operation on task T_1 can be performed by multiple tasks. As an example, consider

```
 1 // Main task
 2 Stmt1;
 3 future<T> A = async<T> { ... }; // Task  T_A
 4 Stmt2;
 5 future<T> B = async<T>{ Stmt3;A.get();Stmt4;}; // Task T_B
 6 Stmt5;
 7 future<T> C = async<T>{ Stmt6 ; A.get(); Stmt7; B.get();}; // Task T_C
 8 Stmt8;
 9 A.get();
10 Stmt9;
11 C.get();
12 Stmt10;
```

Fig. 1. Example Program with HJ Futures. A, B and C hold references to future tasks created by the main program

the program in Fig. 1, where the main program creates three future tasks T_A, T_B, and T_C. There are three join operations on task T_A performed by sibling tasks T_B, T_C, and the parent task. Here Stmt3, Stmt6, and Stmt8 may execute in parallel with task T_A, while Stmt4, Stmt7, and Stmt9 can execute only after the completion of task T_A. Synchronization using get() can lead to transitive dependences among tasks. For example, although the main task in Fig. 1 did not perform an explicit join on task T_B, there is a transitive join dependence from T_B to the main task, because task T_C performed a get operation on task T_B due to which Stmt10 can execute only after tasks T_A, T_B, and T_C complete their execution. This example has a non-strict computation graph, because of the get operations performed by T_B and T_C on their siblings.

3   Data Races and Determinacy

In this section, we formalize the definition of data races in programs containing async, finish, and future constructs as a preamble to defining determinacy races. Our definition extends the notion of a *computation graph* [6] for a dynamic execution of a parallel program, in which each node corresponds to a *step* which is defined as follows:

Definition 1. A step is a sequence of instruction instances contained in a task such that no instance in the sequence includes the start or end of an async, finish or a get operation.

The edges in a computation graph represent different forms of happens-before relationships. For the constructs covered in this paper (async, finish, future), there are three different types of edges:

1. **Continue Edges** capture the sequencing of steps within a task. All steps in a task are connected by continue edges.
2. **Spawn Edges** represent the parent-child relationship among tasks. When task A creates task B, a spawn edge is inserted from the step that ends with the async in task A to the step that starts task B.

```
S1 ;
future<T> A = async<T> {
    S2;
    future<T> B = async<T> { S3; };
    S4;  B.get();   S5; };
S6 ;
future<T> C = async<T>{ S7;
      A.get(); S8;}
S9 ;
future<T> D = async<T>{ S10;
      C.get(); S11;}
D.get();
S12 ;
```

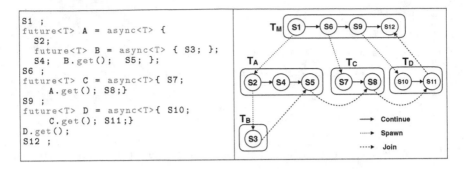

Fig. 2. Example program with futures and its computation graph. $S1$–$S12$ are steps in the program. The circles represent the steps in the program. The rectangles represents tasks. T_M is the main task and T_A, T_B, T_C and T_D are future tasks created during the execution of the program.

3. **Join Edges** represent synchronization among tasks. When task A performs a get on future B, a join edge (also referred to as a "future join edge") is inserted from the last step of B to the step in task A that immediately follows the get() operation. In addition, "finish join edges" are also inserted from the last step of every task to the step in the ancestor task immediately following the Immediately Enclosing Finish (IEF). A join edge from task B to task A is referred to as *tree join* if A is an ancestor of B; otherwise, it is referred to as a *non-tree join*. Note that all finish join edges must be tree joins, and some future join edges may be tree edges and some may be non tree edges.

All three kinds of edges have been studied in past work on computation graphs for the Cilk [5] and Habanero-Java [26] languages, except for non-tree join edges.

Definition 2. A step u is said to precede step v, denoted as $u \prec v$, if there exists a path from u to v in the computation graph.

This precedence relation is a partial order, and is also referred to as the "happens-before" relation in past work [20]. We use the notation $Task(u) = T$ to indicate that step node u belongs to task T, and $u \nprec v$ to denote the fact that there is no path from step u to step v in the computation graph. Two distinct steps, u and v may execute in parallel, denoted $u \parallel v$, iff $u \nprec v$ and $v \nprec u$.

Definition 3. A data race may occur between steps u and v, iff $u \parallel v$ and both u and v include accesses to a common memory location, at least one of which is a write.

As an example, consider the program in Fig. 2 which creates four future tasks: T_A, T_B, T_C, and T_D. $S1$–$S12$ represent the steps in the program. Here $S2 \parallel S10$ because there is no directed path from $S2$ to $S10$, or from $S10$ to $S2$, in the computation graph, and $S2 \prec S12$ since there is a directed path from

$S2$ to $S12$. The join edge from $S3$ to $S5$ is a tree join since T_A is an ancestor of T_B. The edge from $S5$ to $S8$ is a non-tree join since T_C is not an ancestor T_A.

We say that a parallel program is *functionally deterministic* if it always computes the same answer when given the same inputs. Further, we refer to a program as *structurally deterministic* if it always computes the same computation graph, when given the same inputs. Finally, following past work [12, 19], we say that a program is *determinate* if it is both functionally and structurally deterministic. If a parallel program is written using only async, finish, and future constructs, *and is guaranteed to never exhibit a data race*, then it must be determinate, i.e., both functionally and structurally deterministic. Note that all data-race-free programs written using async, finish and future constructs are guaranteed to be determinate, but it does not imply that all racy programs are non-determinate. For instance, a program with parallel writes of the same value to a common memory location is racy, yet determinate.

4 Determinacy Race Detection Algorithm

In this section, we present our algorithm for detecting determinacy races in programs with async, finish and future as parallel constructs. A dynamic determinacy race detector needs to provide mechanisms that answers two questions: for any pair of memory accesses, at least one of which is a write, (1) can the two accesses logically execute in parallel?, and (2) do they access the same memory location? To answer the first question, we introduce a program representation referred to as *dynamic task reachability graph* which is presented in Sect. 4.1. Similar to most race detectors, we use a shadow memory mechanism (presented in Sect. 4.2) to answer the second question. Section 4.3 presents our overall determinacy race detection algorithm.

4.1 Dynamic Task Reachability Graph

Since storing the entire computation graph of the program execution is usually intractable due to memory limitations (akin to storing a complete dynamic trace of a program), we introduce a more compact representation that still retains sufficient information to precisely answer all reachability queries during race detection. Our program representation, referred to as a *dynamic task reachability graph*, represents reachability information at the task-level instead of the step-level. The representation assumes that the input program is executed serially in depth-first order, and leverages the following three ideas for encoding reachability information between steps in the computation graph of the input program:

Disjoint set representation of tree joins. The reachability information between tasks which are connected by tree join edges is represented using a disjoint set data structure. Two tasks A and B are in the same set if and only if B is a descendant of A and there is a path in the computation graph from B to A which includes only tree-join edges and continue edges. Similar to the SP-bags algorithm, our algorithm uses the fast disjoint-set data structure

[11, Chap. 22], which maintains a dynamic collection of disjoint sets Σ and provides three operations:

1. MAKESET(x) which creates a new set that contains x and adds it to Σ
2. UNION(X, Y) which performs a set union of X and Y, adds the resulting set to Σ and destroys set X and Y
3. FINDSET(x) which returns the set $X \in \Sigma$ such that $x \in X$.

Any m of these three operations on n sets takes a total of $O(m\alpha(m, n))$ time [30]. Here α is functional inverse of Ackermann's function which, for all practical purposes is bounded above by 4.

Interval encoding of spawn tree. In order to efficiently store and answer reachability information from a task to its descendants, we use a labeling scheme [13], in which each task is assigned a label according to preorder and postorder numbering schemes. The values are assigned according to the order in which the tasks are visited during a depth-first-traversal of the *spawn tree*, where the nodes in the spawn tree correspond to tasks and edges represent the parent-child spawn relationship. Using this scheme, the ancestor-descendant relationship queries between task pairs can be answered by checking if the interval of one task subsumes the interval of the other task. For example, if $[x.pre, x.post]$ is the interval associated with task x and $[y.pre, y.post]$ is the interval associated with task y, then x is an ancestor of y if and only if $x.pre \leq y.pre$ and $y.post \leq x.post$. When task A performs a join operation on a descendant task B, the disjoint sets of A and B are merged together and the new set will have the label originally associated with A. Although, a label is assigned to every task when it is spawned, the labels are associated with each disjoint set in general. Compared to past work [13] which used labeling schemes on static trees, the tree is dynamic in our approach since race detection is performed on-the-fly. This requires a more general labeling scheme, where a temporary label is assigned when a task is spawned and the label is updated when the task returns to its parent.

Immediate predecessors + significant ancestor representation of non-tree joins. The non-tree joins in the computation graph are represented in the dynamic task reachability graph as follows:

- *immediate predecessors:* For each non-tree join from task A to task B, B stores A in its set of predecessors.
- *lowest significant ancestor:* We define the *significant ancestors* of task A as the set of ancestors of A in the spawn tree that have performed at least one non-tree join operation. For each task, we store only the lowest significant ancestor.

Definition 4. A *dynamic task reachability graph* of a computation graph G is a 5-tuple $R = (N, D, L, P, A)$, where

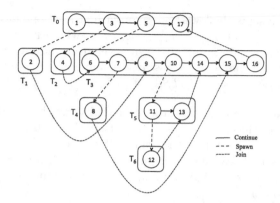

Fig. 3. A computation graph with non-tree joins. The join edges (2,9) and (4,6) are non-tree joins because T_1 and T_2 are not descendants of T_3

- N is the set of vertices, where each vertex represents a dynamic task instance.
- $D = \{D_i\}_{i=1}^n$ is a partitioning of the vertices in N into disjoint sets. $\bigcup_{i=1}^n D_i = N$. Each partition consists of tasks which are connected by tree-join edges.
- $L : N \rightarrow \mathbb{Z}_{\geq 0} \times \mathbb{Z}_{\geq 0}$ is a map from vertices to their labels, where each label consists of the preorder and postorder value of the vertex in the spawn tree. A label is also associated with each disjoint set $D_i \in D$, where the label for D_i is same as the label of u, where $u \in D_i$ and u is the node in D_i that is closest to the root of the spawn tree.
- $P : N \rightarrow 2^N$ represents the set of non-tree edges $P(u) = \{v_1, .., v_k\}$ if and only if there are non-tree join edges from tasks $v_1..v_k$ to u.

Table 1. (a) is the dynamic task reachability graph for the computation graph in Fig. 3 after execution of step 11. Task T_3 performed join operations on T_2 and T_1. Therefore $P(T_3) = \{T_1, T_2\}$. The least significant ancestor of T_4, T_5 and T_6 is T_3 because T_3 is their lowest ancestor which performed a non-tree join. (b) is the dynamic task reachability graph for the computation graph in Fig. 3 after execution of step 17. T_0, T_3, T_4, T_5 and T_6 are all in the same disjoint set because they are connected by tree join edges

Disjoint Set	Task	L (Label)	P (NT)	A (LSA)		Disjoint Set	Task	L (Label)	P (NT)	A (LSA)
0	T_0	[0, MAXINT]	()	-			T_0	[0, 13]		
1	T_1	[1, 2]	()	-			T_3	[5, 12]		
2	T_2	[3, 4]	()	-		0	T_4	[6, 7]	$\{T_1, T_2\}$	-
3	T_3	[5, MAXINT-1]	$\{T_1, T_2\}$	-			T_5	[8, 11]		
4	T_4	[6, 7]	()	T_3			T_6	[9, 10]		
5	T_5	[8, MAXINT-2]	()	T_3		1	T_1	[1, 2]	()	-
6	T_6	[9, MAXINT-3]	()	T_3		2	T_2	[3, 4]	()	-

(a)   (b)

- $A : N \to N$ represents the lowest ancestor with at least one incoming non-tree edge. $A(u) = v$, if and only if $w_1, w_2..w_k..w_m$ (where $r = w_1$, $v = w_k$ and $u = w_m$) is the path consisting of spawn edges from the root r of G to u, and $P(w_j) = \emptyset, \forall j$ such that $k + 1 \le j \le m - 1$ and $P(v) \ne \emptyset$. v is referred to as the *lowest significant ancestor (LSA)* of u.

Table 1(a) shows the dynamic task reachability graph for the computation graph in Fig. 3 after the execution of step 11. Here the postorder values assigned to T_0, T_3, T_5 and T_6 are temporary values (See Sect. 4.3). All tasks are in a separate disjoint sets, because no tree joins have been performed yet. Table 1(b) shows the dynamic task reachability graph for the computation graph in Fig. 3 after the execution of step 17.

4.2 Shadow Memory

As in past work [26, 27], our algorithm maintains a shadow memory M_s for every shared memory location M. M_s contains the following fields

- w, a reference to a task that wrote to M. $M_s.w$ is initialized to *null* and is updated at every write to M. It refers to the task that last wrote to M.
- r, a set of references to tasks that read M. $M_s.r$ is initialized to $\emptyset$ and is updated at reads of M. It contains references to all future tasks that read M in parallel, since the last write to M. It also contains a reference to one non-future (async) task which read M since the last write to M.

4.3 Algorithm

The overall determinacy race detection algorithm is given in Algorithms 1–10. As the input program executes in serial, depth-first order the race detection algorithm performs additional operations whenever one of the following actions occurs: task creation, task return, begin-finish, end-finish, get() operation, shared memory read and shared memory write. The race detector stores the following information associated with every disjoint set of tasks.

- *pre* and *post* together form the interval label assigned to the disjoint set.
- *nt* is the set of incoming non-tree edges.
- *parent* refers to the parent task.
- *lsa* represents the least significant ancestor.

Next, we describe the actions performed by our race detector:

Initialization: Algorithm 1 shows the initialization performed by our race detector when the main task M is created. The set S_M is initialized to contain task M. It assigns $[0, MAXINT]$ as the interval label for the main task. Since the postorder value of a node is known only after the full tree has unfolded, we assign a temporary postorder value $MAXINT$ (the largest integer value). The *parent* and *lsa* fields are initialized to *null*.

```
Input: Main task M
 1: dfid ← 0
 2: tmpid ← MAXINT
 3: S_M ← MAKE-SET(M)
 4: S_M.pre ← dfid
 5: dfid ← dfid + 1
 6: S_M.post ← tmpid
 7: tmpid ← tmpid − 1
 8: S_M.parent ← null
 9: S_M.lsa ← null
```

Algorithm 1. Initialization

```
Input: Parent task P, Child task C
 1: S_C ← MAKE-SET(C)
 2: S_C.pre ← dfid; dfid ← dfid + 1
 3: S_C.post ← tmpid; tmpid ← tmpid − 1
 4: S_C.parent ← S_P
 5: if S_P.nt = {} then
 6:    S_C.lsa ← S_P.lsa
 7: else
 8:    S_C.lsa ← S_P
 9: end if
```

Algorithm 2. Task creation

Task Creation: Algorithm 2 shows the actions performed by our race detector during task creation. Whenever a task P spawns a new task C, C is assigned the preorder value and a temporary postorder value. Our algorithm assigns temporary postorder values starting at the largest integer value ($MAXINT$) in decreasing order. This assignment scheme maintains the interval label property, where the label of an ancestor subsumes the labels of descendants. The set S_C is initialized to contain task C. The least significant ancestor for task C is initialized at task creation time based on whether task P has performed any non-tree joins.

Task Termination: When task C terminates, the postorder value of C is updated with the final value. This is shown in Algorithm 3.

Get Operation: Algorithm 4 shows the actions performed by the race detector at a `get()` operation. When task A performs a `get()` operation on task B, there are two possible cases: (1) A is an ancestor of B and there are join edges from all tasks which are descendants of A and ancestors of B to A. In this case, the algorithm performs a union of the disjoint sets S_A and S_B by invoking the MERGE function given in Algorithm 7, and (2) there is a non-tree join edge from B to A. In this case, B is added to the sequence of non-tree predecessors of A.

Finish: Algorithms 5 and 6 shows the actions performed by the race detector at the start and end of a finish. At the end of a finish F, the disjoint sets of all tasks with F as the immediately enclosing finish is merged with the disjoint set of the ancestor task executing the finish.

Shared Memory Access: Determinacy races are detected when a read or write to a shared memory location occurs. When a write to a memory location M is performed by step u, the algorithm checks if the previous *writer* or the previous *readers* in the shadow memory space may execute in parallel with the currently executing step and reports a race. It updates the *writer* shadow space of M with the current task and removes any reader r if $r \prec u$. This is shown in Algorithm 8. When a read to a memory location M is performed by step u, the algorithm checks if the previous *writer* in the shadow memory space may execute in parallel with the currently executing step and reports a race. It adds the current task to the set of readers of M and removes any task r

Input: Terminating task C
1: $S_C.post \leftarrow dfid$; $dfid \leftarrow dfid + 1$
2: $tmpid \leftarrow tmpid + 1$

Algorithm 3. Task termination

Input: Tasks A, B such that A performs $B.\text{get}()$
1: **if** FIND-SET$(A) =$
2:    FIND-SET$(B.parent)$ **then**
3:       MERGE(S_A, S_B)
4: **else**
5:    $S_A.nt \leftarrow S_A.nt \cup \{B\}$
6: **end if**

Algorithm 4. Get operation

Input: Start of finish F in task A
1: $F.parent \leftarrow A$

Algorithm 5. Start finish

Input: Finish F
1: $A \leftarrow F.parent$
2: **for** $B \in F.joins$ **do**
3:    MERGE(S_A, S_B)
4: **end for**

Algorithm 6. End finish

Input: Disjoint sets S_A, S_B
1: **procedure** MERGE(S_A, S_B)
2:    $nt \leftarrow S_A.nt \cup S_B.nt$
3:    $lsa \leftarrow S_A.lsa$
4:    $S_A \leftarrow S_B \leftarrow$ UNION(S_A, S_B)
5:    $S_A.nt \leftarrow nt$
6:    $S_A.lsa \leftarrow lsa$
7: **end procedure**

Algorithm 7. Merge tasks

if $r \prec u$. Our algorithm differentiates between future tasks and async tasks: async tasks can be waited upon by only ancestor tasks using the finish construct and future tasks can be waited upon using the get() operation. Given a task A as argument, IsFUTURE returns true, if A is a future task. The readers shadow memory contains a maximum of one async task, but may contain multiple future tasks. During the read of a shared memory location by step s of an async task A, the algorithm replaces the previous async reader X by A, if X precedes s. This is shown in Algorithm 9.

Given tasks A and B, PRECEDE routine shown in Algorithm 10 checks if task A must precede B by invoking routine VISIT which is also given in Algorithm 10. Lines 6–11 of VISIT routine returns true if the interval corresponding to the disjoint set of B is contained in the interval corresponding to the disjoint set of A. Lines 12–14 returns false, if the preorder value of A is greater than the preorder value of B, since the source of a non-tree join edge must have a lower preorder value than the sink of the non-tree edge. Lines 15–20 checks if B is reachable from A along the immediate non-tree predecessors of B. Lines 21–29 traverses paths which include the non-tree predecessors of the significant ancestors of B starting with the least significant ancestor of B. The routine returns true when a path from A to B is found or returns false when all the non-tree edges whose source has a preorder value greater than the preorder value of A are visited.

The following two theorems discuss the complexity and correctness of our race detection algorithm. The proofs for these theorems are given in [29].

Input: Memory location M, Task A that writes to M
1: **for** $X \in M_s.r$ **do**
2:     **if not** PRECEDE(X, A) **then**
3:         *a determinacy race exists*
4:     **else**
5:         $M_s.r \leftarrow M_s.r - \{X\}$
6:     **end if**
7: **end for**
8: **if not** PRECEDE$(M_s.w, A)$ **then**
9:     *a determinacy race exists*
10: **end if**
11: $M_s.w \leftarrow A$

Algorithm 8. Write check

Input: Memory location M, Task A that reads M
1: *update* = **false**
2: **for** $X \in M_s.r$ **do**
3:     **if** PRECEDE(X, A) **then**
4:         $M_s.r \leftarrow M_s.r - \{X\}$
5:         *update* $\leftarrow$ **true**
6:     **else if** ISFUTURE(X) **or**
7:             ISFUTURE(A) **then**
8:         *update* $\leftarrow$ **true**
9:     **end if**
10: **end for**
11: **if not** PRECEDE$(M_s.w, A)$ **then**
12:     *a determinacy race exists*
13: **end if**
14: **if** *update* **then**
15:     $M_s.r \leftarrow M_s.r \cup \{A\}$
16: **end if**

Algorithm 9. Read check

Input: Tasks A, B
1: **procedure** PRECEDE(A, B)
2:     **return** VISIT$(A, B, \{\})$
3: **end procedure**

1: **procedure** VISIT$(A, B, Visited)$
2:     **if** $B \in Visited$ **then**
3:         **return** false
4:     **end if**
5:     $Visited \leftarrow Visited \cup \{B\}$
6:     $S_A \leftarrow$ FIND-SET(A)
7:     $S_B \leftarrow$ FIND-SET(B)
8:     **if** $S_A.pre \leq S_B.pre$ **and**
9:         $S_A.post \geq S_B.post$ **then**
10:         **return** true
11:     **end if**
12:     **if** $S_A.pre > S_B.pre$ **then**
13:         **return** false
14:     **end if**
15:     **for all** x in $S_B.nt$ **do**
16:         **if** VISIT$(A, x, Visited)$
17:         **then**
18:             **return** true
19:         **end if**
20:     **end for**
21:     $sa \leftarrow B.lsa$
22:     **while** $sa \neq null$ **do**
23:         **for all** x in $sa.nt$ **do**
24:             **if** VISIT$(A, x,$
                    $Visited)$ **then**
25:                 **return** true
26:             **end if**
27:         **end for**
28:         $sa \leftarrow sa.lsa$
29:     **end while**
30:     **return** false
31: **end procedure**

Algorithm 10: Reachability check

Theorem 1. *Consider a program with async, finish and future constructs that executes in time T on one processor, creates a async tasks, f future tasks, performs n non-tree join edges and references v shared memory locations. Algorithms 1–10 can be implemented to check this program for determinacy races in $O(T(f + 1)(n + 1)\alpha(T, a + f))$ time using $O(a + f + n + v * (f + 1))$ space.*

Here α is functional inverse of Ackermann's function which, for all practical purposes is bounded above by 4. It is interesting to note that our algorithm degenerates to past complexity results for async-finish programs [26] in the case when the program creates no futures ($f = n = 0$).

Theorem 2. *Algorithms 1–10 detect a determinacy race for a given parallel program and data input if and only if a determinacy race exists.*

5   Experimental Results

In this section, we present experimental results for our determinacy race detection algorithm. The race detector was implemented as a new Java library for detecting determinacy races in HJ programs containing async, finish and future constructs. The benchmarks written in HJ were instrumented for race detection during a bytecode-level transformation pass implemented on HJ's Parallel Intermediate Representation (PIR) [23]. The PIR extends Soot's Jimple IR [31] with parallel constructs such as async, finish, and future. The instrumentation pass adds the necessary calls to our race detection library at async, finish and future boundaries, future get operations, and also on reads and writes to shared memory locations.

Our experiments were conducted on a 16-core Intel Ivybridge 2.6 GHz system with 48 GB memory, running Red Hat Enterprise Linux Server release 7.1, and Sun Hotspot JDK 1.7. To reduce the impact of JIT compilation, garbage collection and other JVM services, we report the mean execution time of 10 runs repeated in the same JVM instance for each data point. We evaluated the algorithm on the following benchmarks:

Table 2. Runtime overhead for determinacy race detection

Benchmark	#Tasks	#NTJoins	#SharedMem	#AvgReaders	Seq (millisecs)	Racedet (millisecs)	Slowdown (Racedet/Seq)
Series-af	999,999	0	4,000,059	0.75	483,224	484,746	1.00
Series-future	999,999	0	6,000,059	0.66	487,134	487,985	1.00
Crypt-af	12,500,000	0	1,150,000,682	0.74	15,375	119,504	7.77
Crypt-future	12,500,000	0	1,175,000,682	1.23	15,517	128,234	8.26
Jacobi	8,192	34,944	641,499,805	1.70	3,402	27,388	8.05
Strassen	30,811	33,612	1,610,522,196	0.94	6,281	33,618	5.35
Smith-Waterman	1,608	4,641	1,652,175,806	1.56	3,488	34,558	9.92

- **Series-af:** Fourier coefficient analysis from JGF [7] benchmark suite (Size C), parallelized using async and finish.
- **Series-future:** Fourier coefficient analysis from JGF benchmark suite (Size C), parallelized using futures.
- **Crypt-af:** IDEA encryption algorithm from JGF benchmark suite (Size C), parallelized using async and finish.
- **Crypt-future:** IDEA encryption algorithm from JGF benchmark suite (Size C), parallelized using futures.
- **Jacobi:** 2 dimensional 5-point stencil computation on a 2048×2048 matrix, where each tasks computes a 64×64 submatrix.
- **Strassen:** Multiplication of 1024×1024 matrices using Strassen's algorithm. The implementation uses a recursive cutoff of 32×32.
- **Smith-Waterman:** Sequence alignment of two sequences of size 10000. The alignment matrix computation is done by 40×40 future tasks.

The first four benchmarks were derived from the original versions in the JGF suite. The next two, Jacobi and Strassen were translated by the authors from OpenMP versions of those programs in the Kastors [32] benchmark suite. The original versions of these benchmarks used the OpenMP 4.0 *depends* clause, in which tasks specify data dependence using **in**, **out** and **inout** clauses. The translated versions of these benchmarks used future as the main parallel construct, with get() operations used to synchronize with previously data dependent tasks. In general, this kind of task dependences cannot be represented using only async-finish constructs without loss of parallelism. The Smith-Waterman benchmarks uses futures and is based on a programming project in COMP322, an undergraduate course on parallel computing at Rice University.

The results of our evaluation is given in Table 2. The first column lists the benchmark name, and the second column shows the dynamic number of tasks (#Tasks) created for the inputs specified above. The third column shows the number of non-tree joins (#NTJoins) performed by each of the applications (the subset of future get() operations that are non-tree-joins). The fourth column shows the total number of shared memory accesses (#SharedMem) performed by the applications (all accesses to instance/static fields and array elements). The fifth column (#AvgReaders) shows the average number of past parallel readers per location stored in the shadow memory when a read/write access is performed on that location. (The average is computed across all accesses and all locations.) For a given access, the number of such stored readers will be either zero or one for programs containing only async and finish constructs, thereby ensuring that the average must be in the $0 \dots 1$ range for async-finish programs. For programs with futures, the number of stored readers can be greater than one, if the location being accessed is in the read-shared state and is read by multiple tasks that can potentially execute in parallel each other. Thus, #AvgReaders can be any value that is ≥ 0, for programs with futures.

The next column (Seq) reports the average execution time of the sequential (serial elision) version of the benchmark, and the following column (Racedet) reports the average execution time of a 1-processor execution of the parallel benchmark using the determinacy race detection algorithm introduced in this paper. Finally, the Slowdown column reports the ratio of the Racedet and Seq values.

We can make a number of observations from the data in Table 2. First, if we compute the Seq/#Tasks ratio for all the benchmarks, we can see that the Crypt-af and Crypt-future benchmarks perform $\approx$100$\times$ less work per task on average, relative to all the other benchmarks. This is the primary reason why the Crypt-af and Crypt-future benchmarks exhibit slowdowns of 7.77$\times$ and 8.26$\times$. With less work per task, the overhead per task during race detection becomes more significant than in other benchmarks; further, creating data structures for large numbers of tasks puts an extra burden on garbage collection and memory management. However, it is important to note that the slowdowns for Series-af and Crypt-af are comparable to the slowdowns reported for the ESP-Bags algorithm [25] that only supported async and finish, thereby showing that our determinacy race detector does not incur additional overhead for async/finish constructs relative to state-of-the-art implementations.

Next, we see that the number of non-tree joins performed by Series-af and Crypt-af is zero, since they are async-finish programs for which all join (finish) operations appear as tree-join edges in the computation graph (Sect. 3). Since their corresponding future versions, Series-future and Crypt-future, used futures to implement async-finish synchronization, their future get() operations also appear as tree-join edges in the computation graph, thereby resulting in zero non-tree joins as well. However, the future versions of these two benchmarks have higher number of shared memory accesses than the async-finish versions, due to the additional writes and reads of future references which happened to be stored in shared (heap) locations for both benchmarks. In particular, we know that the reference to each future task must be subjected to at least one write access (when the future task is created) and one read access (when a get() operation is performed on the future), though more accesses are possible. Since Series-future creates 999,999 future tasks, we see that the difference in the #Shared-Mem values for Series-future and Series-af is 2,000,000 which is very close to the lower bound of $2 \times 999,999$. Likewise, for Crypt-future and Crypt-sf, the number of tasks created is 12,500,000 and the difference in the #SharedMem values is 25,000,000 which exactly matches the lower bound of $2 \times 12,500,000$. The slowdown for Crypt-future is higher than that of Crypt-af due to two reasons: (1) the additional number of memory accesses due to the future references and (2) the average number of readers stored in the shadow memory is higher, because of the presence of future tasks.

The slowdowns for Jacobi, Smith-Waterman and Strassen (8.05$\times$, 9.92$\times$, and 5.35$\times$) are positively correlated by the values of #SharedMem, #AvgReaders, and 1/Seq, and these correlations can help explain the relative slowdowns for the three benchmarks. A larger value of #SharedMem leads to a larger slowdown due to the overhead of processing additional shared memory accesses. A larger value of #AvgReaders leads to a larger slowdown because the number of reachability queries required per shared memory access is equal to the number of readers present in the shadow memory for that location. A larger value of 1/Seq indirectly leads to a larger slowdown due to the smaller available time to amortize the overheads of race detection.

Finally, we observe that the slowdowns are not significantly impacted by the number of non-tree edges. This is because the producer and consumer tasks of a future object happen to be closely located to each other in the computation graph (for these benchmarks), usually only requiring 1–2 hops involving non-tree edges in the graph traversal.

6   Related Work

Dynamic data race detection techniques target either structured parallelism or unstructured parallelism. Race detection for unstructured parallelism typically uses vector clock algorithms, e.g., [3,17]. Atzeni et al. [2] presented a low over-head, high accuracy vector clock race detector for OpenMP programs via a combination of static and dynamic analysis. These algorithms are impractical for task parallelism because either the vector clocks have to be allocated with a size proportional to the maximum number of simultaneously live tasks (which can be unboundedly large) or precision has to be sacrificed by assigning one clock per processor or worker thread, thereby missing potential data races when two tasks execute on the same worker.

Mellor-Crummey [22] presented the Offset-Span labeling algorithm for nested fork-join constructs, which is an extension of English-Hebrew labeling scheme [15]. The idea behind their techniques is to attach a label to every thread in the program and use these labels to check if two threads can execute concurrently. The length of the labels associated with each thread is bounded by the maximum dynamic fork-join nesting depth in the program. Our approach uses a constant size labeling scheme to store reachability information for ancestor-descendant tasks. While the Offset-Span labeling algorithm supports only nested fork-join constructs, our algorithm supports a more general set of computation graphs.

Feng and Leiserson [16] introduced the SP-bags algorithm for Cilk's fully-strict parallelism, which uses only a constant factor more memory than does the program itself. Bender et al. [4] presented the parallel SP-hybrid algorithm which uses English-Hebrew labels and SP-bags to detect races in Cilk programs. Despite its good theoretical bounds, the paper did not include an implementation of the algorithm. Raman et al. [26] extended the SP-bags algorithm to support async-finish parallelism. They subsequently proposed the parallel SPD3 algorithm [27] also for async-finish constructs. In contrast to these approaches, our data race detection algorithm handles async, finish and futures, which can create more general computation graphs than those that can be generated by async-finish parallelism.

7   Conclusions

In this paper, we presented the first known determinacy race detector for dynamic task parallelism with futures. As with past determinacy race detectors, our algorithm guarantees that all potential determinacy races will be checked so that if a race is reported for a given input in one run of our algorithm, it will always be reported in all runs. Likewise, if no race is reported for a given input, then all parallel executions with that input are guaranteed to be race-free and deterministic. Our approach builds on a novel data structure called the *dynamic task reachability graph* which models task reachability information for non-strict computation graphs in an efficient manner. We presented a complexity analysis of our algorithm, discussed its correctness, and evaluated an implementation of the algorithm on a range of benchmarks that generate both strict and non-strict computation graphs. The results indicate that the performance of our approach is similar to other efficient algorithms for spawn-sync and async-finish programs and degrades gracefully in the presence of futures. Specifically, the experimental results show that the slowdown factor observed for our algorithm relative to the sequential version is in the range of $1.00\times$–$9.92\times$, which is very much in line with slowdowns experienced for fully strict computation graphs.

References

1. Agarwal, S., Barik, R., Bonachea, D., Sarkar, V., Shyamasundar, R.K., Yelick, K.: Deadlock-free scheduling of X10 computations with bounded resources. In: SPAA 2007, pp. 229–240. ACM, New York (2007)
2. Atzeni, S., Gopalakrishnan, G., Rakamaric, Z., Ahn, D.H., Lee, G.L., Laguna, I., Schulz, M., Protze, J., Mueller, M.: ARCHER: effectively spotting data races in large OpenMP applications. In: IPDPS 2016, pp. 53–62, May 2016
3. Banerjee, U., Bliss, B., Ma, Z., Petersen, P.: A theory of data race detection. In: PADTAD 2006, pp. 69–78. ACM, New York (2006)
4. Bender, M.A., Fineman, J.T., Gilbert, S., Leiserson, C.E.: On-the-fly maintenance of series-parallel relationships in fork-join multithreaded programs. In: SPAA 2004, pp. 133–144. ACM, New York (2004)
5. Blumofe, R.D., Joerg, C.F., Kuszmaul, B.C., Leiserson, C.E., Randall, K.H., Zhou, Y.: Cilk: an efficient multithreaded runtime system. In: PPopp. 1995, pp. 207–216. ACM, New York (1995)
6. Blumofe, R.D., Leiserson, C.E.: Scheduling multithreaded computations by work stealing. J. ACM **46**(5), 720–748 (1999)
7. Bull, J.M., Smith, L.A., Westhead, M.D., Henty, D.S., Davey, R.A.: A benchmark suite for high performance Java. Concurr. Pract. Exp. **12**(6), 375–388 (2000)
8. Cavé, V., Zhao, J., Shirako, J., Sarkar, V.: Habanero-Java: the new adventures of old x10. In: PPPJ 2011, pp. 51–61. ACM, New York (2011)
9. Chamberlain, B.L., Callahan, D., Zima, H.P.: Parallel programmability and the Chapel language. Int. J. High Perform. Comput. Appl. **21**(3), 291–312 (2007)
10. Charles, P., Grothoff, C., Saraswat, V., Donawa, C., Kielstra, A., Ebcioglu, K., von Praun, C., Sarkar, V.: X10: an object-oriented approach to non-uniform cluster computing. In: OOPSLA 2005, pp. 519–538. ACM, New York (2005)
11. Cormen, T.H., Stein, C., Rivest, R.L., Leiserson, C.E.: Introduction to Algorithms, 2nd edn. McGraw-Hill Higher Education, New York (2001)

12. Dennis, J.B., Gao, G.R., Sarkar, V.: Determinacy and repeatability of parallel program schemata. In: DFM 2012, pp. 1–9. Computer Society IEEE, Washington, DC (2012)
13. Dietz, P., Sleator, D.: Two algorithms for maintaining order in a list. In: STOC 1987, pp. 365–372. ACM, New York (1987)
14. Dimitrov, D., Vechev, M., Sarkar, V.: Race detection in two dimensions. In: SPAA 2015, pp. 101–110. ACM, New York (2015)
15. Dinning, A., Schonberg, E.: An empirical comparison of monitoring algorithms for access anomaly detection. In: PPOpp 1990, pp. 1–10. ACM, New York (1990)
16. Feng, M., Leiserson, C.E.: Efficient detection of determinacy races in Cilk programs. In: SPAA 1997, pp. 1–11. ACM, New York (1997)
17. Flanagan, C., Freund, S.N.: FastTrack: efficient and precise dynamic race detection. In: PLDI 2009, pp. 121–133. ACM, New York (2009)
18. Halstead Jr., R.H.: Multilisp: a language for concurrent symbolic computation. ACM Trans. Program. Lang. Syst. **7**(4), 501–538 (1985)
19. Karp, R.M., Miller, R.E.: Parallel program schemata. J. Comput. Syst. Sci. **3**(2), 147–195 (1969)
20. Lamport, L.: Time, clocks, and the ordering of events in a distributed system. Commun. ACM **21**(7), 558–565 (1978)
21. Liskov, B., Shrira, L.: Promises: linguistic support for efficient asynchronous procedure calls in distributed systems. In: PLDI 1988, pp. 260–267. ACM, New York (1988)
22. Mellor-Crummey, J.: On-the-fly detection of data races for programs with nested fork-join parallelism. In: Supercomputing 1991, pp. 24–33. ACM, New York (1991)
23. Nandivada, V. Krishna Shirako, J., Zhao, J., Sarkar, V.: A transformation framework for optimizing task-parallel programs. ACM Trans. Program. Lang. Syst. **35**(1) (2013)
24. OpenMP specifications. http://www.openmp.org/specs
25. Raman, R., Zhao, J., Sarkar, V., Vechev, M., Yahav, E.: Efficient data race detection for async-finish parallelism. In: Barringer, H., et al. (eds.) RV 2010. LNCS, vol. 6418, pp. 368–383. Springer, Heidelberg (2010). doi:10.1007/978-3-642-16612-9_28
26. Raman, R., Zhao, J., Sarkar, V., Vechev, M., Yahav, E.: Efficient data race detection for async-finish parallelism. Form. Methods Syst. Des. **41**(3), 321–347 (2012)
27. Raman, R., Zhao, J., Sarkar, V., Vechev, M., Yahav, E.: Scalable and precise dynamic datarace detection for structured parallelism. In: PLDI 2012, pp. 531–542. ACM, New York (2012)
28. Surendran, R., Sarkar, V.: Brief announcement: dynamic determinacy race detection for task parallelism with futures. In: SPAA 2016, Pacific Grove, July 2016
29. Surendran, R., Sarkar, V.: Dynamic determinacy race detection for task parallelism with futures. Technical report TR16-01, Department of Computer Science, Rice University, Houston (2016)
30. Tarjan, R.E.: Efficiency of a good but not linear set union algorithm. J. ACM **22**(2), 215–225 (1975)
31. Vallée-Rai, R., Co, P., Gagnon, E., Hendren, L., Lam, P., Sundaresan, V.: Soot - a Java bytecode optimization framework. In: CASCON 1999. IBM Press (1999)
32. Virouleau, P., Brunet, P., Broquedis, F., Furmento, N., Thibault, S., Aumage, O., Gautier, T.: Evaluation of OpenMP dependent tasks with the KASTORS benchmark suite. In: DeRose, L., de Supinski, B.R., Olivier, S.L., Chapman, B.M., Müller, M.S. (eds.) IWOMP 2014. LNCS, vol. 8766, pp. 16–29. Springer, Heidelberg (2014)

Runtime Monitoring for Concurrent Systems

Yoriyuki Yamagata[1]([⊠]), Cyrille Artho[1,2], Masami Hagiya[3], Jun Inoue[1],
Lei Ma[4], Yoshinori Tanabe[5], and Mitsuharu Yamamoto[4]

[1] National Institute of Advanced Industrial Science and Technology (AIST),
1-8-31 Midorigaoka, Ikeda, Osaka 563-8577, Japan
{yoriyuki.yamagata,c.artho,jun.inoue}@aist.go.jp
[2] KTH Royal Institute of Technology, 100 44 Stockholm, Sweden
artho@kth.se
[3] The University of Tokyo, 7-3-1 Hongo Bunkyo-ku, Tokyo 113-8656, Japan
hagiya@is.s.u-tokyo.ac.jp
[4] Chiba University, 1-33 Yayoicho, Inage-ku, Chiba-shi, Chiba 263-8522, Japan
malei@chiba-u.jp, mituharu@math.s.chiba-u.ac.jp
[5] Tsurumi University, 2-1-3 Tsurumi, Tsurumi,
Yokohama, Kanagawa 230-0063, Japan
tanabe-y@tsurumi-u.ac.jp

Abstract. Most existing specification languages for runtime verification describe the properties of the entire system in a top-down manner, and lack constructs to describe concurrency in the specification directly. CSP_E is a runtime-monitoring framework based on Hoare's Communicating Sequential Processes (CSP) that captures concurrency in the specification directly. In this paper, we define the syntax of CSP_E and its formal semantics. In comparison to quantified event automata (QEA), as an example, CSP_E describes a specification for a concurrent system in a bottom-up manner, whereas QEA lends itself to a top-down manner. We also present an implementation of CSP_E, which supports full CSP_E without optimization. When comparing its performance to that of QEA, our implementation of CSP_E requires slightly more than twice the time required by QEA; we consider this overhead to be acceptable. Finally, we introduce a tool named stracematch, which is developed using CSP_E. It monitors system calls in (Mac) OS X and verifies the usage of file descriptors by a monitored process.

Keywords: Runtime monitoring · Parametric monitoring · CSP · Process algebra

1 Introduction

Runtime monitoring is a technique for monitoring program execution. In a subfield of run-time monitoring called specification-based monitoring [34], program execution is monitored against a given specification. The specification is given by a formal language, such as temporal logic, automata, grammar, or rule-based systems. Thus, specification-based monitoring lies somewhere between tests—which usually test only input/output contracts or assertions—and traditional

© Springer International Publishing AG 2016
Y. Falcone and C. Sanchez (Eds.): RV 2016, LNCS 10012, pp. 386–403, 2016.
DOI: 10.1007/978-3-319-46982-9_24

formal methods such as model checking or theorem proving, which try to prove the correctness of a program along all possible execution paths.

This work focuses on *parametric monitoring*. In parametric monitoring, program execution consists of a sequence of events, and each event is associated with one or more parameters, such as a file name or an IP address.

Many frameworks for parametric monitoring have been proposed. One group of frameworks is based on automata. Another is based on formal languages such as regular expressions or context-free grammars, and still others are based on temporal logic or rule-based systems. However, most of these frameworks do not allow for a direct description of the concurrency of a monitored program. Because a bug related to concurrency often surfaces only at runtime, runtime monitoring of a concurrent system is important. In this paper, we investigate the following research questions.

1. Can we design a monitoring language that specifies a concurrent system in a bottom-up fashion—in a way that first describes the specifications of components and then combines them?
2. Can process calculi, which are studied extensively to specify concurrent systems, be used for this particular purpose?

The first question is important because a concurrent system is often specified by the specifications of its components and how they interact. On the other hand, the traditional monitoring languages listed above concentrate on specifying the global properties of systems, regardless of the specifications of their components. This is useful, for instance, when we want to specify a safety property for the whole system, regardless of its components. However, it would be difficult to describe the correct interaction of the components in the system using such methods, because they lack constructs to compose the specifications of systems based on the specifications of their components.

The second question addresses using process calculi in a new context. Process calculi were developed to reason about concurrent systems. In process calculi, programs are processes, which are composed of simpler processes using sequential or concurrent composition. Processes which compose a program can communicate with each other using communication primitives such as events or channels. In particular, we focus on Hoare's Communicating Sequential Processes (CSP) [35,45]. CSP is a process calculus that uses events as communication primitives. Thus, CSP is effective for describing event sequences generated by a concurrent system.

In this paper, we introduce CSP_E, a runtime-monitoring framework based on CSP. Because it is based on CSP, CSP_E has constructs that allow for the direct description of concurrency in the specification. In this paper, we define the language of CSP_E and its formal semantics. However, our goal is not to introduce a completely new language. Rather, our goal is to show that, with a slight modification, CSP is amenable to monitoring. In fact, to obtain CSP_E from CSP, we merely add a `Failure` constant to express already-failed processes. We show that CSP_E can neatly describe a system of Unix-like processes and file descriptors.

We also implement a domain-specific language (DSL) based on CSP_E and compare its performance with quantified event automata (QEA) [5,34,43,44] implemented in [13], using a simulated event log of the Unix-like processes and file descriptors. QEA is an automata-based monitoring framework, which, according to [36], is one of the most expressive of this kind. Further, it is easiest to understand by engineers [36]. Finally, MarQ, an implementation of QEA, came top in the offline and Java track in first international competition on Runtime Verification (2014) [20]. We use an implementation [13] that is a successor of MarQ. In this comparison, our CSP_E implementation requires slightly more than twice the time that QEA takes; we consider this overhead to be acceptable.

Our DSL is shallowly embedded in the Scala programming language [41]; this language is also named CSP_E. An event monitor can be defined by using the CSP_E language. A monitor that is defined by CSP_E sequentially consumes the events from an event stream. If at some point the monitor fails to proceed, this indicates that something unexpected has occurred.

The language of CSP_E was discussed in part in [3]. In this paper, we fully explain the syntax, semantics, and implementation of CSP_E. In [3], the process construct is used for a recursive definition. In this paper, we use the built-in def construct in Scala for a recursive definition. If a process construct is needed, it can be derived from the def construct.

We develop denotational semantics for CSP_E, based on the trace semantics of CSP. Our technical contribution to formal semantics is a proof that the semantic space of CSP_E can still be defined as a complete partial order (CPO) — a mathematical structure which allows a recursive definition.

This paper is organized as follows. In Sect. 2, we discuss related work. In Sect. 3, we discuss the syntax of CSP_E using a motivating example. In Sect. 4, we discuss the formal semantics of CSP_E and prove that it forms a complete partial order. This makes it possible to define monitors recursively. In Sect. 5, we discuss our implementation of CSP_E. In Sect. 6, we show a benchmark for our CSP_E implementation and a QEA implementation [13] using the motivating example. In Sect. 7, we introduce a tool named stracematch. This tool analyzes a log of system calls and verifies the correct usage of file descriptors in a real program. Finally, Sect. 8 concludes the paper.

2   Related Work

Many specification-based runtime-monitoring frameworks have been proposed, including four approaches to parametric monitoring: an automaton-based approach [5,7,14,15,17,19,26,32,39]; a regular expression- and grammar-based approach [1,17,22]; an approach based on temporal logic [6,8,9,17–19,22,30,31,37, 39,46–48]; and a rule-based approach [4,6,33].

Qadeer and Tasiran [42] surveyed monitoring methods for multi-threaded programs. They identified several important classes of correctness criteria, such as race freedom, atomicity, serializability, linearizability and refinement. Their notion of refinement is different from the CSP context. In the CSP context, it is a relation between specification, while a refinement relation in Qadeer and Tasiran mean a relation between traces. Qadeer and Tasiran's paper [42] deals with specific properties and construction of specialized monitors, not general-purpose specification languages like ours.

Among work on monitoring distributed systems, [10,21] concentrate global properties which can be described by temporal logic. polyLarva [16] is an extension of LARVA [14,15] designed for distributed systems, by which a user can control the location of verifiers in the distributed system explicitly. LARVA specifies the properties of monitored systems by sets of automata which can communicate each other through channels. In this respect, it has a similar spirit to CSP_E, because both aim to synthesize a specification of a whole system from a specification of each component. However, LARVA is based on automata and does not support launching new automata dynamically.

Compared to these other frameworks, our approach creates a new avenue for specification languages. We employ a process calculus—namely, CSP—to describe a specification of a monitored program. The advantage of using process calculi is primarily that they are designed to describe a concurrent system, thereby providing a way to describe concurrency in a monitored system easily and directly. Another benefit is that process calculi, and in particular CSP, allow for automatic model checking [50,51]. Model checkers can check the *refinement* relation between CSP specifications. A CSP specification is a refinement of another CSP specification when the former is a more detailed specification of the latter. Thus, by checking the refinement relation, we can guarantee that the monitor will check for desirable properties that otherwise might not be able to be monitored directly, especially when they are too general.

Theoretically, any model checker based on process calculi, such as CADP [23] can be used to offline runtime monitoring. In particular, CADP has a tool called SEQ.OPEN [22], which can convert traces to Labeled Transition System (LTS). A trace can be converted to an LTS and then synchronously composed to a specification. If the system in such a way exhibits a deadlock, this indicates that the trace violates the specification. The difference of our approach is that, CSP_E does not need a full model checker, and thus is much more lightweight. Also CSP_E is a DSL which is embedded in a general-purpose programming language, thus it is easy to extend. Finally, CSP_E can be used for online monitoring. To use model-checking approach above for online monitoring, a significant development effort seems necessary. "exhibitor" and "evaluator" of CADP can check whether traces confirm given specifications, if they are used together with SEQ.OPEN, but they use regular expressions or alternation-free μ-calculus for specification languages.

Implementation-wise, CSP_E is a shallow-embedded DSL in Scala [3]. In this respect, it closely resembles TRACECONTRACT [7]. However, the application program interface (API) of CSP_E is considerably different from that of TRACE-CONTRACT.

3 Introduction to CSP_E

In this section, we introduce CSP_E using a motivating example, and we compare it to QEA [5, 34, 43, 44]. We argue that CSP_E excels at describing properties that are composed of local properties (i.e., to a process) yet interact globally.

3.1 Motivating Example

Our motivating example is a system of Unix-like processes and file descriptors. Each process and file descriptor have unique IDs. We assume that only Process 0 is running initially, and that Process 0 never exits. Each process can spawn child processes. Any process other than Process 0 can exit anytime, without waiting for its child processes to exit. Each process can open any file descriptor. If a process opens a file descriptor, it must close it before exiting. Opening the same file descriptor twice without closing it, or closing the same file descriptor twice without opening it again, is not allowed. If a file descriptor is opened by a process, the process can access it. Child processes can also access file descriptors that were opened by their parent before they were spawned. Such file descriptors must be closed by a child process before a child process exits.

3.2 CSP_E Syntax

CSP_E provides a DSL that is shallowly embedded in Scala. This DSL is also called CSP_E. Figure 1 shown the above specification in CSP_E.

The notable classes that appear in the example are **Event** and **Process**.

Event. The monitored system creates a stream of *events*. CSP_E models events using the **Event** case class, which is a subclass of **AbsEvent**. Every event takes a symbol called an *alphabet* as its first argument, and it can have any number of trailing arguments of **Any** type.

Process. A **process** class and its subclasses in CSP_E are specifications of systems that are being monitored. They describe how a system produces sequences of events. A process is often termed a *monitor*, because a process that is constructed by the CSP_E accepts an event stream and judges whether it follows the specification that the process describes. A process is constructed using methods that are defined by the CSP_E library. In Fig. 1, **system** is the description of the entire system, while **sysproc** represents a process (and its subprocesses). **uniqSysproc** guarantees that process IDs are all unique for all process. **P1 ||** **Set('Spawn, 'Exit) || P2** means that P1 and P2 run concurrently and share events which have alphabets 'Spawn and 'Exit. **?? {case ... => ...}** is a pattern match on incoming events, **P1 ||| P2** is the interleaving of P1 and P2, and **SKIP** is a process that does nothing and terminates normally. A process can be defined by recursion, using the standard Scala **def** syntax. For the full syntax, see Fig. 2 in BNF form.

```
def sysproc(pid: Int, openFiles: Set[Int]): Process = ?? {
  case Event('Spawn, 'pid', child_pid: Int) =>
    sysproc(pid, openFiles) ||| sysproc(child_pid, openFiles)
  case Event('Open, 'pid', fd: Int) if !openFiles(fd) =>
    sysproc(pid, openFiles + fd)
  case Event('Access, 'pid', fd: Int) if openFiles(fd) =>
    sysproc(pid, openFiles)
  case Event('Close, 'pid', fd: Int) if openFiles(fd) =>
    sysproc(pid, openFiles - fd)
  case Event('Exit, 'pid') if pid != 0 && openFiles.isEmpty => SKIP
}
def uniqSysproc(pidSet : Set[Int]) : Process = ?? {
  case Event('Spawn, _, child_pid : Int) if ! pidSet(child_pid) =>
    uniqSysproc(pidSet + child_pid)
  case Event('Exit, pid : Int) if pidSet(pid) =>
    uniqSysproc(pidSet - pid)
}
def system = sysproc(0, Set.empty) || Set('Spawn, 'Exit) ||
            uniqSysproc(Set(0))
var monitors = new ProcessSet(List(system))
```

Fig. 1. Motivating example in CSP_E

Intuitively, each construct has the following meaning:

- SKIP : A process that does nothing and terminates normally. For example, e
  ->: SKIP represents a process that accepts event e and terminates.
- STOP : A process that does nothing and never terminates. For example, e ->:
  STOP accepts event e but gets stuck.
- Failure : A process that has already failed. For example, e ->: Failure
  accepts event e and then fails immediately. Using a process P which does not
  consume e, the difference between STOP and Failure can be seen in the exam-
  ples e ->: STOP ||| P and e ->: Failure ||| P. Both processes accept
  event e, but subsequently, the former runs provided that P accepts events,

$$P ::= \text{SKIP} \mid \text{STOP} \mid \text{Failure} \mid$$
$$e \text{ ->: } P \mid$$
$$?? f \mid ??? f \mid$$
$$P \text{ <+> } P \mid$$
$$P \mid\mid a \mid\mid P \mid$$
$$P \mid\mid\mid P \mid$$
$$P \$ P$$

Fig. 2. Full syntax for CSP_E : Here, SKIP, STOP, Failure are constants, e is an event,
f is a partial function which maps a event to a process, and a is a set of alphabets.

whereas the latter fails immediately after event e. Using `Failure` explicitly marks that a branch leads to an impossible state.

- `e ->: P` : A process that accepts event e and behaves like P. For example, `e1 ->: e2 ->: SKIP` accepts events e1 and e2 and then terminates.
- `?? (f : Event -> Process)` : A process that accepts event e and then behaves like `f(e)`. The function f typically uses pattern matching in order to select the behavior that matches that of e. If e does not match any pattern, `?? f` behaves like `Failure`.
- `??? (f : Event -> Process)` : Similar to `??`, but unlike `??`, if the incoming event e does not match any pattern, `??? f` waits for another event.
- `P1 <+> P2` : A process that behaves like either P1 or P2, depending on which of them can accept the event that is input to `P1 <+> P2`. If both P1 and P2 can accept the event, both possibilities remain. For example, `e ->: e1 ->: SKIP <+> e ->: e2 ->: Failure` first accepts e. Then, if it accepts e1, it terminates normally; if it accepts e2, however, it fails immediately. If both processes cannot accept the event, it behaves like Failure.
- `P1 || a || P2` : Concurrent composition of P1 and P2, using events whose alphabets are elements of a as synchronization events. For example, if a contains the alphabet of e0 but a does not contain alphabets of e1 and e2, then `e0 ->: e1 ->: SKIP || a || e0 ->: e2 ->: SKIP` accepts the sequences e0, e1, e2 and e0, e2, e1 but does not accept e0, e0, e1, e2.
- `P1 ||| P2` : Interleaving of P1 and P2. `e1 ->: SKIP ||| e2 ->: SKIP` accepts the sequences e1, e2 and e2, e1.
- `P1 $ P2` : A process that first behaves as P1 and then behaves as P2. If P1 fails, then P1 $ P2 fails. For example, `e1 ->: SKIP $ e2 ->: SKIP` accepts e1 and e2 and then terminates normally.

Then, we generate a set of monitors with `new ProcessSet(...)` constructs. Because CSP_E can track multiple possible states in the monitored system, we use the set of monitors to monitor the system. Our system is similar to the one presented in [35], but with unique differences, such as the inclusion of `Failure`. Another difference is that our system has no internal choice, no τ, and no hiding. Theoretically, we can implement such constructs, but they easily lead to the state explosion of the monitors in which they are used. We designed the syntax of CSP_E in such a way that it closely resembles the original CSP syntax. However, there are syntactical limitations, owing to the fact that CSP_E is embedded [3] in Scala. In Scala, the associativity and precedence of operators are both determined by the established syntax of operators, and thus cannot be changed. For example, to make the operator $\rightarrow$ right-associative, we need to add : to `->`. Moreover, some symbols in Scala, such as `[]`, are reserved for certain kinds of operations. Thus, we use `<+>` rather than `[]` to indicate the choice operator. In the traditional CSP, the human-readable representation differs from the machine-readable representation. For CSP_E, we selected the machine-readable code as a common representation for both types for simplicity. Because the human-readable representation of CSP_E and its embedding to Scala are the same, both are termed CSP_E.

3.3   Comparison with QEA

Because our specification contains a specification on file descriptors and a specification on processes, we split these specifications into two QEA automata: fdMonitor and processMonitor. Using the textual representation used in [34], each can be defined as shown in Fig. 3.

```
qea {
  Forall(fd)
  accept skip(init) {
    spawn(parent, child) if [ parent in PS ]
      do [ PS.add(child) ] -> init
    open(pid, fd) if [ pid in PS ] -> failure
    open(pid, fd) if [ not pid in PS ]
      do [ PS.add(pid) ]-> init
    access(pid, fd) if [ not pid in PS ] -> failure
    close(pid, fd) if [ pid in PS ]
      do [ PS.remove(pid) ] -> init
    close(pid, fd) if [not pid in PS ] -> failure
    exit(pid) if [ pid in PS ] -> failure
  }
}

qea {
  accept next(init) {
    spawn(parent, child)
      if [ (parent in PS || parent = 0) && not child in PS && child = 0]
      do [ PS.add(child) ] -> init
    exit(pid) if [ pid in PS ]
      do [ PS.remove(pid) ] -> init
    open(pid, fd) -> init
    access(pid, fd) -> init
    close(pid, fd) -> init
    }
}
```

Fig. 3. QEA monitor for file descriptors and processes, respectively

Theoretically, CSP_E, and QEA can represent any Turing computable property, because we allow CSP_E and QEA to have rich data-structures such as Set; thus, we can encode a universal Turing machine using these data structures as tapes. However, such theoretical representation is of no practical interest, because such a monitor does not have much difference to a hand-coded monitor.

A major characteristic of CSP_E is that it can represent the specification in a bottom-up manner. The entire monitor is built from sysproc(pid, openFiles) monitors, which run in an interleaving fashion, and uniqProcess, which guarantees that each process has a unique ID. Moreover, sysproc(pid, openFiles) can be further decomposed into concurrent monitors. Thus, it can describe the specification in the term near its implementation yet abstracted from unnecessary details. A major characteristic of QEA is that, insofar as it is based on state machines, it requires specifying the states and transitions of the whole system in order to describe the specification.

4   Formal Semantics

In this section, we define the formal semantics of CSP_E. Because it is outside the scope of this paper to define a language that contains all of the Scala constructs, we consider a language that consists of all the constructs explicitly described in Sect. 3.2, along with purely functional Scala expressions.

In the context of a runtime-monitoring framework, the term *formal semantics* refers to the formal definition of actions of a monitor when it is given a finite sequence of events (trace). For each trace, there are three possibilities:

1. The trace is accepted as a successful and complete execution of the monitored program.
2. The trace is successful thus far, but not yet complete.
3. The trace is rejected as a failure.

Every possible trace falls into one of these three categories. To distinguish these three cases, it is enough to give a set of traces which satisfy either cases 1 or 2. We call such a set a *trace semantics* of a monitor. In the given trace semantics T, we interpret each trace as follows:

1. A trace $t \in T$ that ends with $\checkmark$ is interpreted as a successful and complete execution.
2. A trace that is contained in T and does not end with $\checkmark$ is interpreted as an incomplete trace.
3. A trace that is not contained in T is interpreted as a failure.

The semantic space $\mathcal{T}$ of all possible trace semantics consists of the set of traces T that satisfies the following:

1. If $t \in T$ and t' is a prefix of t, then $t' \in T$, and
2. for all $t \in T$, the $\checkmark$ appears only at the end of t.

This definition allows for the $\emptyset$ to be included as a member of $\mathcal{T}$, unlike the usual definition of CSP trace semantics [35, 45]. Let T^c denote all completed traces in T, T^i denote all incomplete traces in T, and T^f denote all traces that are not contained in T. We allow for the possibility that a trace $t \in T$ is interpreted as successful thus far, despite the failure of all of its successors—for example, when $\langle \rangle \in$ STOP. From here, we abuse notations and use STOP, SKIP and Failure to denote their semantics. The STOP specification is required to be used for concurrent composition. If STOP is coupled with other processes concurrently, STOP will get stuck, whereas other processes will continue to run. If Failure is coupled with other processes concurrently, on the other hand, `Failure` causes an immediate failure in the entire system.

Because we allow for a recursive definition of monitors, fixed points of reasonable sets of operators are needed in the semantic space $\mathcal{T}$. We follow the usual approach by introducing a structure known as a complete partial order (CPO) into the semantic space $\mathcal{T}$. We define the order relation $T_1 \sqsubseteq T_2$ to hold for elements T_1, T_2 in $\mathcal{T}$, if $T_1 \subseteq T_2$. CPO is a partial order of which directed subsets have supremums. A directed subset is a subset of a partial order such that it is non-empty and every pair in it has an upper bound in it. A complete lattice is a partially ordered set of which all subsets have supremums and infimums. If all subsets have supremums, they also have infimums [45].

Theorem 1. $\mathcal{T}$ *is a complete lattice.*

Proof. For a set $(T_i)_{i \in X}$ of elements in $\mathcal{T}$, its least upper bound $T = \bigsqcup_{i \in X} T_i$ is defined as $T = \bigcup_{i \in X} T_i$ (i.e., the union of $(T_i)_{i \in X}$ as sets). It is routine to check whether $T \in \mathcal{T}$.   □

It is well known that all complete lattices are CPO. We define $T_1 \sqcup T_2$ as $\bigsqcup_{i=1,2} T_i$. Here, $\mathcal{T}$ has the minimal element `Failure`, and `Failure` does not contain any trace. Moreover, `STOP` consists solely of $\langle \rangle$. In the usual trace semantics, `STOP` is the smallest element of the semantic space, but it is clear that `Failure` $\sqsubseteq$ `STOP`. We also define `SKIP` as `SKIP` $= \{\langle \rangle, \langle \checkmark \rangle\}$. Next, we define the operators $\rightarrow, \frown$ on $\mathcal{T}$ in order to define the semantic interpretations of `->:` and `$`. We use the operation $e^\wedge s$ and $s \frown t$ on an event e and traces s, t in order to define $\rightarrow$ and $\frown$. Here, $e^\wedge s$ of the concatenation of the event e to s, and $s \frown t$ is the concatenation of s and t, but if s ends with a $\checkmark$, then this $\checkmark$ is removed. Let e denote an event other than $\checkmark$, and let $T, T_1, T_2 \in \mathcal{T}$.

$$e \rightarrow T = \{\langle \rangle\} \cup \{e^\wedge t \mid t \in T\}$$
$$T_1 \frown T_2 = T_1^i \cup \{s \frown t \mid s \in T_1^c, t \in T_2\}$$

Theorem 2. *If e is an event and $T, T_1, T_2 \in \mathcal{T}$, then $e \rightarrow T, T_1 \frown T_2 \in \mathcal{T}$.*

Next, we define the concurrent composition $T_1 \|_A T_2$ ($\checkmark \notin A$) by co-induction on T_1 and T_2. $T \in \mathcal{T}$ is either empty ($T = $ `Failure`) or it can be decomposed as follows:

$$C \sqcup \bigsqcup_{e \in \mathrm{hd}(T)} e \rightarrow T^e \tag{1}$$

where C is `SKIP` if T can successfully terminate immediately or `STOP` otherwise. Here, $\mathrm{hd}(T)$ is defined as $\{e \mid \exists t, e^\wedge t \in T\}$. Intuitively, $T_1 \|_A T_2$ is defined as follows: first, we assume that T_1 and T_2 allow only one event, e_1 for T_1 and e_2 for T_2 at the first step, and after these events their behaviors are described by $T_1^{e_1}$ and $T_2^{e_2}$ respectively. If both events are not in A, we assume that $T_1 \|_A T_2$ behaves in an interleaved way, that is, $T_1 \|_A T_2 = e_1 \rightarrow (T_1^{e_1} \|_A T_2) \sqcup e_2 \rightarrow (T_1 \|_A T_2^{e_2})$. If one of them, say, e_2 fall into A but not e_1, then first e_1 occurs and the occurrence of e_2 is delayed $e_1 \to (T_1^{e_1}||_A e_2 \to T_2^{e_2})$. If both fall into A, then they must be equal otherwise $T_1||_A T_2 = \texttt{STOP}$. If $e = e_1 = e_2$, $T_1||_A T_2 = e \to (T_1^e||_A T_2^e)$. If there are multiple possibilities for events which can occur at the first step, we can write $T_1 = \bigsqcup_{e \in \mathrm{hd}(T_1)} e \to T_1^e$. We define $T_1||T_2$ by distributivity: $T_1||_A T_2 = \bigsqcup_{e \in \mathrm{hd}(T_1)} e \to T_1^e||_A T_2$. Considering the possibility of immediate termination, we reach the following conditions. Let $a, a' \in A$ and $b, b' \notin A \cup \{\checkmark\}$.

1. $\texttt{Failure}||_A T = \texttt{Failure}$
2. $\texttt{SKIP}||_A T = T$
3. $\texttt{STOP}||_A T = T \backslash T^c$
4. $a \to T_1^a||_A a \to T_2^a = a \to (T_1^a||_A T_2^a)$
5. $a \to T_1^a||_A a' \to T_2^a = \texttt{STOP}$ if $a \neq a'$
6. $b \to T_1^b||_A a \to T_2^a = b \to (T_1^b||_A a \to T_2^a)$
7. $b \to T_1^b||_A b' \to T_2^{b'} = b \to (T_1^b||_A b' \to T_2^{b'}) \sqcup b' \to (b \to T_1^b||_A T_2^{b'})$
8. $(C \sqcup \bigsqcup_{e \in \mathrm{hd}(T_1)} e \to T_e)||_A T_2 = (C||_A T_2) \sqcup \bigsqcup_{e \in \mathrm{hd}(T_1)} (e \to T_e||_A T_2)$
9. All symmetric cases of above rules.

Theorem 3. *If $T_1, T_2 \in \mathcal{T}$, $T_1||_A T_2$ exists and is an element of $\mathcal{T}$.*

Theorem 4. *The operators $\sqcup, \bigsqcup, \to, ||_A$, and $\frown$ are all monotonic.*

Thus, Tarski's fixed-point theorem can be applied, and the use of recursion is justified [45].

We interpret $\texttt{Failure}$, $\texttt{STOP}$, and $\texttt{SKIP}$ in the CSP_E notation as $\texttt{Failure}$, $\texttt{STOP}$, and $\texttt{SKIP}$ in $\mathcal{T}$, respectively, and $\texttt{->:}$, $\texttt{<+>}$, $\texttt{?? f}$, $\texttt{|| a ||}$, and $\texttt{\$}$ as $\to$, $\sqcup$, $\bigsqcup_{e:\texttt{Event}} e \to \texttt{f}(e)$, $||_{A(a)}$, and $\frown$, respectively. Here, $A(a)$ is the set of events that have elements of $\texttt{a}$ as alphabets. Moreover, $\texttt{???}$ and $\texttt{|||}$ can be defined by using the operators above and a recursive definition.

5　Implementation

In this section, we discuss an implementation of CSP_E, which is available at [52]. CSP_E was implemented as an internal shallow-embedded DSL in the Scala programming language. Artho et al. discussed in depth the use of a DSL in the context of verification [3]. The proposed CSP_E is a combinator library that can be used to define an object of the $\texttt{Process}$ class, which represents a monitor. An object of the $\texttt{Process}$ class includes a method called $\texttt{accept}$, which accepts an event object and returns new monitors. To monitor an event sequence, $\texttt{ProcessSet}$ is first instantiated by a list of monitors that are defined by CSP_E. $\texttt{ProcessSet}$ also includes a method named $\texttt{accept}$, which accepts an event and returns a new $\texttt{ProcessSet}$. $\texttt{ProcessSet}$ represents multiple possible system states that are being monitored. Each monitor contained in $\texttt{ProcessSet}$ represents one possible system state. $\texttt{ProcessSet}$ includes a method named $\texttt{isFailure}$, which returns a Boolean value. If it returns true, there is no possible state that can be interpreted as a correct system state, thus signifying the occurrence of an error. `ProcessSet` includes a method named `canTerminate`, which also returns a Boolean value. If it returns true, the system can exit at that point. If it returns false and the system exits, the exit is an error.

As stated above, the `Process` object returns new `Process` objects when it accepts a new event, rather than changing its internal state. This design simplifies the implementation of non-determinism and concurrency. However, it also requires immutable data structures for the internal state of a `Process` object. A data structure for holding sets of processes is crucial in terms of performance, especially when there are many processes running concurrently. The current implementation uses the standard Scala List, which allows for duplicate entries. A set in the standard library and multisets [49] have more efficient representations, but we found that using them degrades the performance. Removing duplicate entries appears to be unnecessary, because the current implementation generates many closures. Closures in Scala are compared by their physical equality, thus all closures which are generated at different times are distinct. Thus, the considerable amount of time needed to compute hashes and compare objects is superfluous. Furthermore, we attempted to enhance the performance and reduce memory usage by caching the results of `accept`. Alas, this slowed the library, contrary to our expectations. In that experiment, we used ScalaCache [11] together with Google Guava [25].

6   Benchmark

We compared the performance of our implementation of CSP_E with an implementation of QEA [13], using a randomly generated event sequence that correctly simulates our motivating example. The benchmark generated an event sequence and fed this into the CSP_E and QEA monitors inside the same program, without using an external log file. The program generated a sequence of `Event` objects using a `Stream` and put its first 300,000 elements into a `List` to avoid recording the time required to generate the sequence in the benchmark. Then, the benchmark program first fed these elements into the CSP_E monitor, recording the real time from the first event to each 1,000 events. The benchmark program also did the same to the QEA monitor, and finally formatted the result into the CSV format. The time required for the JVM startup and the initialization of the monitors is not included. The benchmark program is included in the `test` directory of the CSP_E distribution [52].

The benchmark uses Java `1.8.0_77-b03` and Scala 2.11.8 on Mac OS X El Capitan, which we executed on a Mac Pro (late 2013 model), with a 3.7 GHz Quad-Core Intel Xeon E5 and 64 GB of 1866 MHz DDR3 ECC.

Figure 4 shows the results of this experiment. The time required to process n events is roughly quadratic to n, because the number of processes in the monitored system increases linearly to n and for each event, checking that every process follows the specification requires time linearly to n. We can observe that QEA is slightly more than twice as fast as CSP_E. Nevertheless, because the current implementation of CSP_E has not yet been optimized, this shows that CSP_E is a feasible approach to monitoring concurrent systems.

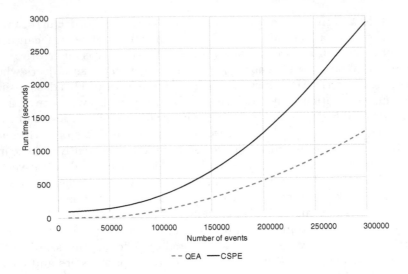

Fig. 4. Benchmark with the motivating example

7   Application: Stracematch

stracematch is contained in the example directory of the CSP_E distribution [52]. CSP_E is used to implement a complete model of open and close system calls for file descriptors, the fork system call, and the execve system call. It accepts the dtruss -f output on OS X from the standard input, and then verifies that the program correctly handles file descriptors. dtruss is based on DTrace [12]. DTrace can instrument kernel events using D-script (not related to the D programming language), and do an arbitrary complex task at each kernel event.

dtruss is a wrapper of DTrace and traces system calls and produces a log, similar to strace in Linux. However, there are limitations: (1) dtruss cannot obtain file descriptors which are created by socketpair and pipe, (2) dtruss cannot catch the invocation of execve system call, which causes errors, (3) dtruss outputs the trace to stderr, while it also outputs error messages to stderr, therefore, if an error happens, the error message has to be removed from the log manually. In the future work, we may consider using directly DTrace to circumvent these limitations.

Owing to these limitations of dtruss, stracematch verifies that (a) a process does not close the same file descriptor twice, and (b) if stracematch detects the opening of a file descriptor, it is closed in the same thread. We applied stracematch to several programs, as indicated in Table 1, where the "log size" represents the number of lines in the log, and "time" denotes the amount of time in seconds that stracematch required to analyze the log, which includes the time to start the JVM.

Table 1. Benchmark of stracematch

Program	Log size	Result	Time [s]
ls	156	Passed	0.370
wget (short)	267	Fd not closed	0.377
wget (long)	28,901	Fd not closed	1.145
Emacs	2,678	Fd not closed	0.750
Chrome	166,090	Stopped at 2,935	0.810
Ruby ehttpd	11,034	Closed fd twice at 1,168	0.648
Sinatra	3,191	Closed fd twice at 1,170	0.673
bash	1,218	Closed fd twice at 946	0.575

ls [2] is a Unix command which lists the contents of a directory. "ls" shows the result on a trace which was obtained by invoking ls -l in a directory. wget [29] is a command line tool to download the contents of a Web page or a Web site. "wget (short)" shows the result on a trace which was obtained by downloading a single web page. "wget (long)" shows the result on a trace which is obtained by downloading an entire web site recursively. Emacs [28] is a popular text editor. "Emacs" shows the result on a trace which was obtained by invoking and terminating Emacs on the terminal. Chrome [24] is a popular Web browser. "Chrome" shows the result on a trace which was obtained by starting and exiting Chrome. Ruby ehttpd is a web server which is included in the standard Ruby [38] programming language distribution. Sinatra [40] is a simple web framework. "Ruby ehttpd" and "Sinatra" shows the results on traces which were obtained by running these web servers on a simple static web site and downloading the entire web site by wget. bash is a popular Unix command shell. "bash" [27] shows the result on a trace which was obtained by running an artificial shell script which was extracted from sbt, a build system which is used mainly for Scala programming language. The shell script which was used, is available upon request.

Our tool can process any logs within less than 1.2 s. With the exception of the case of "ls", stracematch ended with errors. When stracematch encounters an error, it stops and prints the line number and the contents of the line. In Table 1, the location of each termination is indicated by the line number at which stracematch stopped. One group of errors involved some file descriptors that were still open at the end of the execution. This may be an indication of a leak of that file descriptor. Another group of errors involved closing the same file descriptor twice without re-opening it in between. This can cause a rare bug in which another thread or a signal handler opens a file descriptor after that file descriptor is closed for the first time and then the same file descriptor is closed again; thus, that other thread or that signal handler cannot use this file descriptor after that point. In the "Chrome" case, stracematch stopped because invocations of fork appeared in the log, but only for child processes; and there were no record of the invocation of fork for the parent processes. In such a case, stracematch will become confused and stop working.

We contacted the developers of wget and bash, but the bash developer answered that the error is harmless. The wget developers did not respond.

8   Conclusion

In this paper, we presented CSP_E, an event-monitoring framework for concurrent systems inspired by Hoare's CSP. Monitoring concurrent systems is important, because concurrent systems are now ubiquitous, and unit tests are incapable of detecting concurrency bugs. Unlike most of other monitoring frameworks, CSP_E can describe a concurrent system in a bottom-up fashion, by composing specifications of system components. This is often a natural way of specifying concurrent systems.

CSP_E is implemented as an internal DSL in Scala. Consequently, it can be easily adapted to the needs of specific applications. Although the current implementation has not yet been optimized, it incurs acceptable overhead, as we demonstrated by comparing it to a QEA implementation to monitor a simulated event sequence of a highly concurrent system. We presented the formal semantics for CSP_E in Sect. 4. Thus, CSP_E is amenable to theoretical analysis. The semantics are closely similar to the standard trace semantics of CSP. To interpret the Failure construct, however, we allow the $\emptyset$ as a valid element in the semantic space. We showed that even in such a setting, the semantic space forms a CPO, thus allowing for fixed-point construction.

There are several directions for future research. Currently, a CSP_E monitor can only determine whether a given event trace is correct, outputting a Boolean value. This makes it difficult to find the cause of an error. In addition, there is no mechanism for error recovery. Rather, a monitor simply terminates when it first encounters an error. We plan to add functionality that records the event sequence to the error, providing error recovery based on diagnostics. CSP_E does not currently offer an easy way to share states among monitors running concurrently. Global variables in Scala cannot be used for this purpose, because they are also shared between monitors that represent the different states of the system. We shall consider a mechanism and a language feature that can record the global states among monitors.

Acknowledgments. We are grateful to Giles Reger for helping to develop the QEA models, and to Eijiro Sumii for helping us to develop the proof of Theorem 3. Yoshinao Isobe influenced the early design of the language. This work was supported by JSPS KAKENHI Grant Number JP26280019. We would like to thank Editage (www.editage.jp) for English-language editing.

References

1. Allan, C., Avgustinov, P., Christensen, A.S., Hendren, L., Kuzins, S., Lhoták, O.V.R., De Moor, O., Sereni, D., Sittampalam, G., Tibble, J.: Adding trace matching with free variables to AspectJ. In: Johnson, R., Baniassad, E., Gabriel, R.P., Noble, J., Marick, B. (eds.) OOPSLA 2005, pp. 345–364. ACM, New York (2005)
2. Apple: ls, version 7.2.0.0.1.1447826929
3. Artho, C., Havelund, K., Kumar, R., Yamagata, Y.: Domain-specific languages with Scala. In: Butler, M., et al. (eds.) ICFEM 2015. LNCS, vol. 9407, pp. 1–16. Springer, Heidelberg (2015). doi:10.1007/978-3-319-25423-4_1
4. Barringer, H., Rydeheard, D., Havelund, K.: Rule systems for run-time monitoring: from EAGLE to RULER. J. Log. Comput. **20**(3), 675–706 (2010). Oxford University Press
5. Barringer, H., Falcone, Y., Havelund, K., Reger, G., Rydeheard, D.: Quantified event automata: towards expressive and efficient runtime monitors. In: Giannakopoulou, D., Méry, D. (eds.) FM 2012. LNCS, vol. 7436, pp. 68–84. Springer, Heidelberg (2012)
6. Barringer, H., Goldberg, A., Havelund, K., Sen, K.: Rule-based runtime verification. In: Steffen, B., Levi, G. (eds.) VMCAI 2004. LNCS, vol. 2937, pp. 44–57. Springer, Heidelberg (2004)
7. Barringer, H., Havelund, K.: TraceContract: a Scala DSL for trace analysis. In: Butler, M., Schulte, W. (eds.) FM 2011. LNCS, vol. 6664, pp. 57–72. Springer, Heidelberg (2011). doi:10.1007/978-3-642-21437-0_7
8. Basin, D., Klaedtke, F., Müller, S.: Policy monitoring in first-order temporal logic. In: Touili, T., Cook, B., Jackson, P. (eds.) CAV 2010. LNCS, vol. 6174, pp. 1–18. Springer, Heidelberg (2010)
9. Bauer, A., Küster, J.-C., Vegliach, G.: From propositional to first-order monitoring. In: Legay, A., Bensalem, S. (eds.) RV 2013. LNCS, vol. 8174, pp. 59–75. Springer, Heidelberg (2013)
10. Bauer, A., Falcone, Y.: Decentralised LTL monitoring. In: Giannakopoulou, D., Méry, D. (eds.) FM 2012. LNCS, vol. 7436, pp. 85–100. Springer, Heidelberg (2012). doi:10.1007/978-3-642-32759-9_10
11. Birchall, C.: ScalaCache. https://github.com/cb372/scalacache
12. Cantrill, B., Shapiro, M., Leventhal, A.: Dynamic instrumentation of production systems. In: USENIX 2004, pp. 15–22. USENIX (2004)
13. Cuenca, H.: QEA. https://github.com/selig/qea
14. Colombo, C., Pace, G.J., Schneider, G.: Dynamic event-based runtime monitoring of real-time and contextual properties. In: Cofer, D., Fantechi, A. (eds.) FMICS 2008. LNCS, vol. 5596, pp. 135–149. Springer, Heidelberg (2009)
15. Colombo, C., Pace, G.J., Schneider, G.: LARVA - safer monitoring of real-time Java programs (tool paper). In: Hung, D.V., Krishnan, P. (eds.) SEFM 2009. IEEE Computer Society (2009)
16. Colombo, C., Francalanza, A., Mizzi, R., Pace, G.J.: polyLARVA: runtime verification with configurable resource-aware monitoring boundaries. In: Eleftherakis, G., Hinchey, M., Holcombe, M. (eds.) SEFM 2012. LNCS, vol. 7504, pp. 218–232. Springer, Heidelberg (2012)
17. D'Amorim, M., Havelund, K.: Event-based runtime verification of Java programs. ACM SIGSOFT Softw. Eng. Notes **30**(4), 1–7 (2005)
18. Decker, N., Leucker, M., Thoma, D.: Monitoring modulo theories. In: Ábrahám, E., Havelund, K. (eds.) TACAS 2014 (ETAPS). LNCS, vol. 8413, pp. 341–356. Springer, Heidelberg (2014)

19. Drusinsky, D.: Modeling and verification using UML statecharts: a working guide to reactive system design, runtime monitoring and execution-based model checking. Newnes (2011)
20. Runtime Verification 2014: First international competition on runtime verification. http://rv2014.imag.fr/monitoring-competition/results.html
21. Francalanza, A., Seychell, A.: Synthesising correct concurrent runtime monitors. Formal Meth. Syst. Des. **46**(3), 226–261 (2014). Springer, US
22. Garavel, H., Mateescu, R.: SEQ.OPEN: a tool for efficient trace-based verification. In: Graf, S., Mounier, L. (eds.) SPIN 2004. LNCS, vol. 2989, pp. 151–157. Springer, Heidelberg (2004)
23. Garavel, H., Lang, F., Mateescu, R., Serwe, W.: CADP 2011: a toolbox for the construction and analysis of distributed processes. Int. J. Softw. Tools Technol. Transf. **15**(2), 89–107 (2013). Springer
24. Google Inc.: Chrome, version 47.0.2526.111 (64-bit)
25. Google Inc.: Guava. https://github.com/google/guava
26. Goubault-Larrecq, J., Olivain, J.: A smell of ORCHIDS. In: Leucker, M. (ed.) RV 2008. LNCS, vol. 5289, pp. 1–20. Springer, Heidelberg (2008)
27. GNU project: bash, version 4.3.42(1)-release (x86_64-apple-darwin14.5.0). https://www.gnu.org/software/bash/
28. GNU project: Emacs, version 24.5.1. https://www.gnu.org/software/emacs/
29. GNU project: wget, version 1.17.21-df7cb-dirty built on darwin14.5.0. https://www.gnu.org/software/wget/
30. Hallé, S., Villemaire, R.: Runtime enforcement of web service message contracts with data. IEEE Trans. Serv. Comput. **5**(2), 192–206 (2012). IEEE
31. Havelund, K., Roşu, G.: Monitoring programs using rewriting. In: Feather, M., Goedicke, M. (eds.) ASE 2001, pp. 135–143. IEEE CS Press, November 2001
32. Havelund, K.: Runtime verification of C programs. In: Suzuki, K., Higashino, T., Ulrich, A., Hasegawa, T. (eds.) TestCom/FATES 2008. LNCS, vol. 5047, pp. 7–22. Springer, Heidelberg (2008)
33. Havelund, K.: Rule-based runtime verification revisited. Int. J. Softw. Tools Technol. Transf. **17**(2), 143–170 (2014). Springer
34. Havelund, K., Reger, G.: Specification of parametric monitors: quantified event automata versus rule system. In: Formal Modeling and Verification of Cyber-Physical Systems, pp. 151–189. Springer Fachmedien Wiesbaden (2015)
35. Hoare, C.A.R.: Communicating Sequential Processes. Prentice-Hall International, London (1985)
36. Kassem, A., Falcone, Y., Lafourcade, P.: Monitoring electronic exams. In: Bartocci, E., et al. (eds.) RV 2015. LNCS, vol. 9333, pp. 118–135. Springer, Heidelberg (2015). doi:10.1007/978-3-319-23820-3_8
37. Lee, I., Kannan, S., Kim, M., Sokolsky, O., Viswanathan, M.: Runtime assurance based on formal specifications. In: Arabnia, H.R. (ed.) PDPTA 1999, pp. 279–287. CSREA Press (1999)
38. Matsumoto, Y.: Ruby, version 2.2.2p95 (2015-04-13 revision 50295) [x86_64-darwin14]
39. Meredith, P.O., Jin, D., Griffith, D., Chen, F., Roşu, G.: An overview of the MOP runtime verification framework. Int. J. Softw. Tools Technol. Transf. **14**(3), 249–289 (2012). Springer
40. Mizerany, B.: Sinatra, version 1.4.7. http://www.sinatrarb.com/
41. Odersky, M., Spoon, L., Venners, B.: Programming in Scala. Artima, Suffolk (2016)
42. Qadeer, S., Tasiran, S.: Runtime verification of concurrency-specific correctness criteria. Int. J. Softw. Tools Technol. Transf. **14**(3), 291–305 (2012). Springer

43. Reger, G.: Automata based monitoring and mining of execution traces. Ph.D. thesis, University of Manchester (2014)
44. Reger, G., Cruz, H.C., Rydeheard, D.: MarQ: monitoring at runtime with QEA. In: Baier, C., Tinelli, C. (eds.) TACAS 2015. LNCS, vol. 9035, pp. 596–610. Springer, Heidelberg (2015)
45. Roscoe, A.W., Hoare, C.A.R., Bird, R.: The Theory and Practice of Concurrency. Prentice Hall PTR, Upper Saddle River (1997)
46. Stolz, V.: Temporal assertions with parametrized propositions. J. Log. Comput. **20**(3), 743–757 (2008). Oxford University Press
47. Stolz, V., Bodden, E.: Temporal assertions using AspectJ. Electron. Notes Theoret. Comput. Sci. **144**, 109–124 (2006). Elsevier
48. Stolz, V., Huch, F.: Runtime verification of concurrent Haskell programs. Electron. Notes Theoret. Comput. Sci. **113**, 201–216 (2005). Elsevier
49. Stucki, N.: multisets. https://github.com/nicolasstucki/multisets
50. Sun, J., Liu, Y., Dong, J.S., Pang, J.: PAT: towards flexible verification under fairness. In: Bouajjani, A., Maler, O. (eds.) CAV 2009. LNCS, vol. 5643, pp. 709–714. Springer, Heidelberg (2009)
51. University of Oxford: FDR3, https://www.cs.ox.ac.uk/projects/fdr/
52. Yamagata, Y.: CSP_E: log analyzing tool for concurrent systems. https://github.com/yoriyuki/cspe

Decision-Theoretic Monitoring
of Cyber-Physical Systems

Andrey Yavolovsky, Miloš Žefran$^{(\boxtimes)}$, and A. Prasad Sistla

University of Illinois at Chicago, Chicago, USA
{ayavol2,mzefran,sistla}@uic.edu

Abstract. Runtime monitoring has been proposed as an alternative to formal verification for safety critical systems. This paper introduces a decision-theoretic view of runtime monitoring. We formulate the monitoring problem as a Partially Observable Markov Decision Process (POMDP). Furthermore, we adopt a Partially Observable Monte-Carlo Planning (POMCP) to compute an approximate optimal policy of the monitoring POMDP. We show how to construct the POMCP for the monitoring problem and demonstrate experimentally that it can be effectively applied even when some of the state-space variables are continuous, the case where many other POMDP solvers fail. Experimental results on a mobile robot system show the effectiveness of the proposed POMDP-monitor.

1 Introduction

Modern cyber-physical systems (CPS) are becoming increasingly complex and thus call for novel approaches to guarantee their correct functioning. An important class of CPS are autonomous systems, where an embedded control system relies on the perception of the environment through various sensors to autonomously operate the system. Correct functioning of autonomous systems is especially important for medical and transportation systems, where a failure can have catastrophic consequences.

Many cyber-physical systems are stochastic and have states that are only partially observable. Runtime monitoring is an appealing alternative to the formal verification of such systems. A monitor processes the sequence of outputs generated by the system and raises an alarm when it determines that those outputs are likely generated by a system run that violates a given property. Monitors are especially useful when fail-safe shutdown procedures can be implemented, and may serve as an attractive alternative to other traditional approaches that guarantee correctness.

In this paper, we study runtime monitoring from the decision-theoretic perspective. A monitor can be seen as a sequential decision process whose inputs

This research was supported in part by NSF grants CNS-0910988, CNS-1035914, CCF-1319754 and CNS-1314485.

Y. Falcone and C. Sanchez (Eds.): RV 2016, LNCS 10012, pp. 404–419, 2016.
DOI: 10.1007/978-3-319-46982-9_25

are the observations of the system (system outputs), and whose output is a decision whether to raise an alarm or continue with the system execution. Partially Observable Markov Decision Processes (POMDPs) are a well-known formalism for describing sequential decision processes for partially observable stochastic systems. In this paper, we formally define a POMDP that describes the monitoring process. An important departure from the traditional POMDP literature is that in monitoring, an alarm represents a terminal action.

Once the monitoring problem is formulated as a POMDP, the monitor corresponds to the optimal policy for the POMDP, a map that takes the current belief state and generates an action. Solving a POMDP, i.e., finding the optimal policy, is known to be a hard problem [14]. We adapt a Partially Observable Monte-Carlo Planning (POMCP) [19] to compute an approximate solution for the optimal POMDP policy. In particular, we outline how the POMCP approach needs to be adapted for monitoring. The POMCP has been successfully applied to the large and complex POMDPs. But what makes it particularly attractive for monitoring is that it does not need analytical models of the system and the property, a black-box (numerical) model is all that is needed. This makes the approach particularly useful for industrial applications where in many cases all that is available are Simulink or Stateflow models [9].

We use a mobile robot with a software implementation of a transmission system to demonstrate our approach. Our experiments demonstrate that POMCP is computationally efficient and sufficiently fast for monitoring in real time. We evaluate the performance of POMDP-monitors for different choices of rewards, and compare them with the threshold monitors described in [20,21]. The comparison shows that POMDP-monitors provide greater flexibility than threshold monitors.

The main contributions of the paper are as follows: (1) the monitoring problem is formulated as a sequential decision process and formally described using the POMDP formalism; (2) it is shown how POMCP framework can be adapted to compute the approximate optimal policy for the monitoring POMDP in real time; (3) experimental results illustrating the performance of the proposed POMDP-monitors are provided and a comparison with the previously proposed threshold monitors is presented.

1.1 Related Work

Safety and liveness verification for hybrid systems has been extensively studied [6,15]. It was shown that this verification problem is in general undecidable [6]. Another problem that has been extensively studied is fault detection and diagnosis of hybrid automata [4,7,10,12,24], where the aim is to detect when the automaton enters a fail state; none of these works address the problem of monitoring a system against properties specified in an expressive formalism such as Linear Temporal Logic (LTL) [5]. Control synthesis for stochastic discrete-event systems has been studied in [11,13] but only finite-state systems with directly observable state have been considered. Similarly, the literature on diagnosability of partially-observable discrete-event systems (e.g. [25]) only considers deterministic finite-state systems. Runtime monitoring for software programs modeled as (finite-state) HMMs has been studied in [23].

Issues of safety have been studied using the POMDP formalism [1,8,18]. However, in all of these works safety was considered to be a part of the system internally, i.e., actions need to be chosen to avoid or reduce the risk of failures. In our work, we are not focused on controlling the system in a safe way, but on detecting the failures accurately and in a timely fashion. Further, we consider systems with continuous state spaces.

2   Background

2.1   Definitions and Notation

System Model. In this paper, we consider stochastic dynamical systems over discrete time with both discrete and continuous state variables, and discrete outputs. We will model such a system using Extended Hidden Markov Models (EHMMs) introduced in [20].

Consider a vector $\sigma = (\sigma_0, \ldots, \sigma_{n-1})$, such that every $\sigma_i \in \{0, 1\}$. We define a hybrid domain $S_\sigma = T_0 \times \cdots \times T_{n-1}$, where $T_i = \mathbb{N}$ or $T_i = \mathbb{R}$ depending on whether $\sigma_i = 0$ or $\sigma_i = 1$ respectively. Let $n_1, n_2, m_1 \geq 0$ be integers and σ_1, σ_2 be the vectors $0^{n_1}1^{n_2}$ and 0^{m_1}, respectively. Intuitively, n_1, n_2 give the number of discrete and continuous state variables, while m_1 gives the number of discrete outputs of the system being described. An Extended Hidden Markov Model (EHMM) $\mathcal{H}$ of dimensions $(n_1, n_2, m_1, 0)$, is a triple (f, g, μ) defined as follows. The function $f : (S_{\sigma_1} \times S_{\sigma_1}) \to [0, \infty)$ is a *next state function*. For any fixed value $x \in S_{\sigma_1}$, function $f(x, y)$ represents a *probability function* (see [20] for details) on S_{σ_1} in y. A function $g : (S_{\sigma_1} \times S_{\sigma_2})$ is an *output function*. For any appropriate fixed value $x \in S_{\sigma_1}$, function $g(x, z)$ represents a probability function[1] on S_{σ_2} in z. To simplify the notation, we will denote S_{σ_1} with S, and S_{σ_2} with Σ. Finally, μ describes the probability of the initial state, i.e., it is a probability function on S_{σ_1}. EHMM is a generalization of the traditional HMM to state spaces that have both discrete and continuous components, with f, g and μ simply generalizing the analogous quantities for HMMs.

Safety Specification. In this work, we are interested in monitoring whether the run of the system is consistent with a certain safety property. Intuitively, a safety property is defined by the set of all sequences that are acceptable. We have the option whether we specify the acceptable output sequences (external monitoring), or the acceptable state sequences (internal monitoring). It turns out that the internal monitoring is a much harder problem [21] and it is the focus of the present paper.

---

[1] Since we are only considering discrete outputs, the probability function becomes a probability distribution in z.

Let S^ω be the set of all infinite sequences on S. A *run* of the EHMM $\mathcal{H}$ is any infinite sequence $\sigma \in S^\omega$ that can be generated by $\mathcal{H}$. A *property* is simply a subset $C \subseteq S^\omega$; elements of C are called *good* runs, and those not in C are *bad* sequences. Property $C \subseteq S^\omega$ is a *safety property* if every bad sequence has a prefix that can not be extended to a good sequence. A safety property can be specified using a (deterministic) *safety automaton* $\mathcal{P}$ that accepts precisely those infinite runs that are good.

Probabilistic Hybrid Systems. A hybrid system is a dynamic system whose evolution is characterized by both symbolic (discrete) and continuous variables. We are interested in a particular subclass of hybrid systems, *probabilistic hybrid systems (PHS)* [7,20]. Formally, a probabilistic hybrid system $\mathcal{A}$ is a tuple $(Q, V, \Delta t, \mathcal{E}, \mathcal{T}, c_0)$ where Q is a countable set of *discrete* states (modes); V is a disjoint union of three sets V_1, V_2 and V_3 called the continuous state variables, output variables and noise processes, respectively; Δt is the sampling time; $\mathcal{E}$ is a function that with each $q \in Q$ associates a set $\mathcal{E}(q)$ of discrete-time state equations describing the evolution of the continuous state (value of the variables in V_1) and the output (value of the variables in V_2) at time $t + \Delta t$ as functions of the state at t and the noise variables; $\mathcal{T}$ is a function that assigns to each $q \in Q$ a set of *transitions* (ϕ, p), where the *guard* ϕ is a measurable predicate over the set of continuous (and possibly discrete) state variables and p is a probability distribution over Q; and c_0 is a pair giving the initial discrete state and an initial continuous probability distribution on the variables in V_1. We require that for each $q \in Q$, the state equations in $\mathcal{E}(q)$ have noise variables on the right-hand side and that the set of guards on the transitions in $\mathcal{T}(q)$ be mutually exclusive and exhaustive.

For the theoretical development in this paper, it is important to note that we can associate an EHMM to every PHS; details are omitted in the interest of space. The semantics of the PHS is thus given by the associated EHMM.

Monitors. Let Σ be a set of output symbols generated by the monitored system modeled as an EHMM $\mathcal{H}$. Formally [21], a monitor $M : \Sigma^* \to \{0, 1\}$ is a function such that for any $\alpha \in \Sigma^*$, if $M(\alpha) = 0$ then $M(\alpha\beta) = 0$ for every $\beta \in \Sigma^*$. For an $\alpha \in \Sigma^*$, we say that M rejects α (raises an alarm), if $M(\alpha) = 0$, otherwise we say M accepts α. Thus if M rejects α then it rejects all its extensions. For an infinite sequence $\sigma \in \Sigma^\omega$, we say that M rejects σ iff there exists a prefix α of σ that is rejected by M; we say M accepts σ if it does not reject it. Let $L(M)$ denote the set of infinite sequences accepted by M.

Accuracy Measures. Let $\mathcal{P}$ be a safety automaton on states of $\mathcal{H}$. The *acceptance accuracy* [21] of M for $\mathcal{P}$ with respect to the EHMM $\mathcal{H}$, denoted by $AA(M, \mathcal{H}, \mathcal{P})$, is the conditional probability that a sequence generated by the system is accepted by M, given that it is in $L(\mathcal{P})$. The *rejection accuracy* of M for $\mathcal{P}$ with respect to $\mathcal{H}$, denoted by $RA(M, \mathcal{H}, \mathcal{P})$ represents the probability that a sequence generated by the system is rejected by M, given that it is not in $L(\mathcal{P})$. Intuitively, the *acceptance accuracy* represents the probability that good runs generated by $\mathcal{H}$ are accepted by the monitor M, while the *rejection accuracy* is the probability that bad runs are rejected.

Monitoring Time. In addition to accurately detecting a failure, the time that takes the monitor to raise an alarm plays an important role. Monitoring time has been formally defined and studied in [22]. Intuitively, it is the expected time span from the moment of system failure to the moment when the monitor raises an alarm.

Monitoring Safety Properties. Let $\mathcal{A}$ be a PHS (with the associated EHMM $\mathcal{H}_\mathcal{A}$) and assume that the property that has to be monitored is defined by the (deterministic) safety automaton $\mathcal{P}$. Let $\mathcal{B}$ be the product, $\mathcal{B} = \mathcal{A} \times \mathcal{P}$ (see [20] for details). Intuitively, the execution of $\mathcal{B}$ corresponds to the run of $\mathcal{A}$ and with $\mathcal{P}$ being simultaneously driven with the sequence of states of $\mathcal{A}$. Finally, let $\mathcal{H}_\mathcal{B}$ be the EHMM associated with $\mathcal{B}$. Threshold monitors for safety properties as defined in [20] compute the probability that a sequence of observed outputs is generated by the execution that is rejected by the property $\mathcal{P}$; this probability is approximated by the probability (belief) that the current state of $\mathcal{B}$ is bad (the second component of the combined state of $\mathcal{B}$ is a bad state of $\mathcal{P}$). If this probability is greater than the given threshold, the monitor raises an alarm.

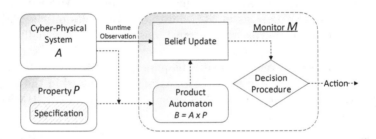

Fig. 1. Monitoring algorithm.

In this paper, we generalize the algorithm and extend it by substituting the threshold-based approach with a generic decision procedure. Figure 1 demonstrates the basic flow and building blocks of the monitoring process. Run-time observations that are generated by the system $\mathcal{A}$ are used to maintain the belief state of the product automaton $\mathcal{B}$. This belief state is used by the decision procedure to select an action.

3   Decision Theoretic Monitoring

We view the monitor as a sequential decision process [17], that makes decisions according to the principle of *maximum expected utility* (MEU) in order to achieve the best possible outcome. According to the MEU, the desirability of each action is quantified numerically, and the decision is made to pick the action that maximizes the expected utility.

A monitor has 2 possible actions to choose from. It can either *Continue* the execution of the monitored system or it may raise an *Alarm* to indicate the violation of the monitored property. The set of monitor action is thus $A = \{Alarm, Continue\}$. It is important to note that *Alarm* is a *terminal* action; that is, the execution of the system terminates once *Alarm* is chosen.

Rationality of the decision is driven by the costs assigned to each of the possible actions. We define a *reward function* for all $s \in S$ and $a \in A$ as follows. Assume that we can represent the set of states S (of $\mathcal{H}_B$) as a union $S_{good} \cup S_{bad}$, where S_{bad} is a set of states that represent a failure, and S_{good} is a complement of S_{bad}. The reward function is

$$R(s, a) = \begin{cases} R_g^c \in \mathbb{R}_{\geq 0} & s \in S_{good}, a = Continue \\ R_g^a \in \mathbb{R}_{\leq 0} & s \in S_{good}, a = Alarm \\ R_b^c \in \mathbb{R}_{\leq 0} & s \in S_{bad}, a = Continue \\ R_b^a \in \mathbb{R}_{\geq 0} & s \in S_{bad}, a = Alarm \end{cases} \tag{1}$$

where $R_g^c \geq 0 \geq R_b^c$, $R_b^a \geq 0 \geq R_g^a$. The values of rewards $(R_g^c, R_b^c, R_g^a, R_b^a)$ define the monitor and will affect its performance in terms of acceptance and rejection accuracies, and monitoring time. Given a state s, the optimal action is to *Continue* if the state is *good*, and *Alarm* if the state is *bad*. However, when system states are not fully observable, choosing any action entails certain risks. Those risks are quantified by the values of rewards so that choosing a wrong action will gain a smaller reward. To emphasize undesirability of wrong actions we assign a negative value to R_b^c and R_g^a. Note that every time when a failure has not been detected a penalty in the form of R_b^c will be accumulated. Note also that a penalty for the false alarm will only be assigned once since the action *Alarm* is terminal.

The simplest monitor makes a decision only based on the expected outcome of the immediate actions. Given a sequence of observations $\sigma[0, \ldots, n-1]$ at time n, we can compute the probability p that a system state at time n is bad (represents a failure). According to the MEU an action *Alarm* will be chosen if $pR_b^a + (1-p)R_g^a \geq pR_b^c + (1-p)R_g^c$. This directly implies the decision procedure as a function of the failure probability: $p \geq \dfrac{1}{1 + \frac{R_b^a - R_b^c}{R_g^c - R_g^a}} = rth$, where rth is a rejection threshold. This decision procedure is equivalent to the implementation of the threshold-based monitoring technique studied in [21].

A more sophisticated decision procedures might include consideration of the expected future evolution of the system by employing a system model. Evaluation of the expected rewards over the finite or infinite horizon depth is a key part of the POMDP. We represent the monitoring agent as a POMDP, and present the solution of the monitoring POMDP using adapted Partially Observable Monte-Carlo Planning (POMCP). The policy of the monitoring POMDP is the decision procedure of the monitoring agent.

4   POMDP-Monitor Design

A POMDP is a common approach in AI to describe a sequential decision process in partially observable environments. Formally, a POMDP [17] is a tuple $(S, A, T, R, O, Z, \gamma)$, where S, A and O are correspondingly a set of states, actions and observations, T and R represent transition and reward functions, Z is the observation function, and γ is a discount factor that specifies how much immediate rewards are preferred over future rewards.

We define the POMDP-monitor on the top of the EHMM associated with the product automaton $\mathcal{B} = \mathcal{A} \times \mathcal{P}$, where $\mathcal{A}$ is a system modeled as PHS and $\mathcal{P}$ is a monitored safety property automaton. For the automaton B we construct the corresponding EHMM $\mathcal{H}_\mathcal{B}$, such that $S_{\mathcal{H}_\mathcal{B}}$ is the set of states of $\mathcal{H}_\mathcal{B}$, Σ is the set of outputs, $f(x, y)$ and $g(x, z)$ represent the *next state function* and *output function* respectively. Let $S_{bad} \subset S_{\mathcal{H}_\mathcal{B}}$ represent a set of states of the product automaton such that the component representing the property $\mathcal{P}$ characterizes a failure. Sets S_{bad} and $S_{good} = S_\mathcal{B} \backslash S_{bad}$ represent the sets of the good and the bad states of the EHMM $\mathcal{H}_\mathcal{B}$ with respect to the property.

We define the set of actions of the POMDP-Monitor as $A = \{Alarm, Continue\}$. The set of states S of the POMDP-Monitor is a union $S_{\mathcal{H}_\mathcal{B}} \cup \{s_{terminal}\}$. A special state $s_{terminal}$ represents a condition after the terminal action *Alarm* is executed.

When the action *Continue* is executed, the transition function T is completely defined by the *next state function* f of the EHMM $\mathcal{H}_\mathcal{B}$.

$$T(s, s', Continue) = \begin{cases} f(s, s') & s, s' \in S \backslash \{s_{terminal}\} \\ 0 & s \neq s' \text{ and } s' = s_{terminal} \\ 1 & s = s' = s_{terminal} \end{cases}$$

Transition probabilities under the effect of action *Alarm* are defined for $\forall s \in S$ as follows:

$$T(s, s', Alarm) = \begin{cases} 0 & s' \in S \backslash \{s_{terminal}\} \\ 1 & s' = s_{terminal} \end{cases}$$

The reward function R of the POMDP is based on the rewards tuple $(R_g^c, R_g^a, R_b^c, R_b^a)$, with additional consideration of the terminal state:

$$R(s, a) = \begin{cases} R_g^c \in \mathbb{R}_{\geq 0} & s \in S_{good}, a = Continue \\ R_g^a \in \mathbb{R}_{\leq 0} & s \in S_{good}, a = Alarm \\ R_b^c \in \mathbb{R}_{\leq 0} & s \in S_{bad}, a = Continue \\ R_b^a \in \mathbb{R}_{\geq 0} & s \in S_{bad}, a = Alarm \\ 0 & s = s_{terminal}, \forall a \in A \end{cases}$$

The POMDP-monitor inherits the observation function in the form of the *output function* from the underlying EHMM and, consequently, from the monitored PHS, and extends it to consider the case of the state $s_{terminal}$. To make the

POMDP model consistent we may define a new observation $o_{terminal}$, which is deterministically observed while in the state $s_{terminal}$.

Every history, i.e., a sequence of actions and observations, may be compactly represented in the form of the belief state b - a conditional probability function of the current state given past history that can be computed recursively using Bayes belief propagation [17]. The policy of the POMDP-monitor defines an action that has to be taken for every belief state b. The optimal policy corresponds to an action that maximizes the expected utility gained by the immediate execution and by following the optimal strategy over a future time horizon: $\pi^*(b) = \arg\max_{a \in A} Q(b, a)$, where according to the Bellman equation [17]

$$Q(b, Alarm) = pR_b^a + (1 - p)R_g^a$$

$$Q(b, Continue) = pR_b^c + (1 - p)R_g^c + \gamma \sum_{o \in O} Pr(o|Continue, b)V^*(b_o^{Continue})$$

$$V^*(b) = \max_{a \in A} Q(b, a)$$

In the equations above, p represents the probability that the current state is bad (represents a failure), i.e., $p = \int_{S_{bad}} b(s)\mathrm{d}s$ (the integral needs to be understood abstractly in the sense of probability functions, see [20] for details), $Pr(o|a, b)$ is the probability that given the current belief state b and action a, the next observation equals o (it can be computed by "integrating" over the current belief state and appropriately using the transition and observation functions), and b_o^a is the belief state in the next time step given we have taken action a and that the next observed symbol is o (it can be computed using Bayes belief propagation). Note that according to the definition of the action *Alarm*, a value of the expected future reward is equal to 0 so $Q(b, Alarm)$ misses a term compared to $Q(b, Continue)$. Therefore, for the given belief state b, the optimal policy π^* will return the action *Alarm* iff the following condition holds:

$$pR_b^a + (1 - p)R_g^a > pR_b^c + (1 - p)R_g^c + \gamma \sum_{o \in O} Pr(o|Continue, b)V^*(b_o^{Continue})$$

The value of the discount factor γ has to be selected to obtain the desired property of the policy. Infinite horizon solutions require a value of $\gamma < 1$ to guarantee the convergence of the infinite sum. However, if the value function is calculated for the finite horizon it is common to assume that $\gamma = 1$.

4.1 POMDP-Monitor Rewards

The rewards that appear in the definition of the rewards function of the monitoring POMDP represent a six tuple $(R_g^c, R_g^a, R_b^c, R_b^a, R_t^c, R_t^a)$, where R_t^c and R_t^a both equal to 0 and represent reward that is assigned to an agent in the terminal state.

It can be shown that the decision rule of any POMDP is invariant with respect to rewards multiplied by some positive constant value. We omit the proof due to the space limitations, but this property of rewards may be derived by rewriting the decision rule with modified rewards and observing that the new rewards system the same decision rule.

We can always select one non-negative reward, and divide the rewards vector by its value. In this way we may assume that the absolute value of one of $R_g^c, R_g^a, R_b^c, R_b^a$ is equal to 1. Therefore, in any monitoring POMDP the decision depends on 3 free parameters.

The analysis of the effect of the values assigned to the rewards in the monitoring POMDP is not trivial. The primary complexity arises due to the non-linear operator max in the value function of the action $Continue$. To start off, we analyzed some of the rewards structures that lead the monitoring POMDP to produce a trivial policy. We assume POMDP policies for a finite horizon with discount factor $\gamma = 1$.

By studying simple reward systems that have some rewards equal to 0 we obtained a list of trivial cases. Reward tuples $(R_g^c \neq 0, R_g^a = 0, R_b^c = 0, R_b^a = 0)$, $(R_g^c = 0, R_g^a \neq 0, R_b^c = 0, R_b^a = 0)$ and $(R_g^c \neq 0, R_g^a \neq 0, R_b^c = 0, R_b^a = 0)$ represent a case when $Alarm$ is never raised. While the reward tuple $(R_g^c = 0, R_g^a = 0, R_b^c \neq 0, R_b^a = 0)$ forces $Alarm$ for every belief state. This can be easily obtained by plugging the values of zero rewards into the decision rule defined in Sect. 4.

The other assignments of rewards represent non-trivial monitors that in turn depend on the depth of the POMDP horizon and characteristics of the monitored system, such as transition and observation models.

4.2   POMDP-Monitor Policy

While many POMDP solvers assume that POMDP models are fully defined, i.e., the transition and observation functions are given, it is not obvious how to define them for systems modeled as PHS. Instead, defining a black-box simulator is straightforward. For a PHS it can be constructed by implementing the difference equations for each mode and transitions for the hybrid mode switching. Such black-box simulator is able to produce a sample of the next state and the observation, given a current state.

POMDPs with continuous state space are even more complex. In order to handle continuous spaces some algorithms have been developed that employ Monte-Carlo simulations [3,19]. Considering the lack of completely defined POMDP model but the existence of the black-box simulator, we focused on Partially Observable Monte-Carlo Planning (POMCP) to implement the POMDP-monitor. The traditional POMCP is defined for discrete state spaces, however the algorithm can be easily extended and applied to the continuous case, although the observation space has to be kept discrete. Here we define a Monitoring-POMCP, which is an adaptation of the POMCP for the POMDP-monitors.

Similarly to the traditional POMCP [19], the Monitoring-POMCP is an online POMDP planner. Rather than requiring analytically defined probability distributions it is designed to work with the black-box instantiation of the

model. The generative model that is hidden within the black-box is able to produce a sample of the future state s_{t+1}, observation o_{t+1} and reward r_{t+1}, given
the pair (s_t, a_t) of the current state and an action.

POMCP may be described similarly to any POMDP planner and consists of
the following basic steps: (1) update the belief state b_t to obtain b_{t+1} considering
the new observation o_{t+1} and the most recent action a_t, (2) for the new belief
state b_{t+1} find an action $a_{t+1} \in A$ that should be executed. In POMCP both
steps share the same Monte-Carlo simulation to propagate the belief state from
b_t to b_{t+1}. This belief propagation step may be performed efficiently by a particle
filter and Monte-Carlo simulations even for continuous state space. Provided that
there are sufficiently many particles, the approximation of the belief state will
be close to the true distribution.

The decision step of the POMCP is based on the *Monte-Carlo Tree Search*
adapted for the belief state search space [19]. The root tree node corresponds
to the current belief state of the POMDP, and every other node represents a
history h of actions and observations. Each tree node has an associated pair
$(N(h), V(h))$, where $N(h)$ is the number of times the node has been visited
during the search, and $V(h)$ is the mean return of all simulations started from
the node.

In order to limit the size of the tree and compute a good approximation
of the optimal policy, it is necessary to require a finite number of actions and
observations. The POMDP-monitor only has two actions, and we have assumed
that the continuous observation space is quantized and represented with a finite
set. Note that in practice sensors typically use an analog-to-digital converter to
produce the output, which means that the observation measurements are in fact
already quantized.

The search tree of the Monitoring-POMCP is constructed sequentially with a
number of Monte Carlo simulations starting from a state sampled from the belief
state in the root node. Every simulation represents a sequence of actions and
observations. While the observations are produced by a black-box simulation,
the action at each simulation step is selected either by a *tree policy* or by a
rollout policy (see Fig. 2).

For a history node that already has at
least one action leaf node the *tree policy* is
used. For the Monitoring-POMCP, we use
the UCB1 (Upper Confidence Bounds) [2]
algorithm. UC1 selects an action that maximizes the value of the node augmented by
the exploration bonus: $V^{\oplus}(ha) = V(ha) +$
$c\sqrt{\frac{\log N(h)}{N(ha)}}$. The scalar value c determines
the relative ratio between the exploration
and exploitation. The value of unexplored
actions is always set to ∞ so that each
action is selected for exploration at least
once. The Monitoring-POMCP uses the

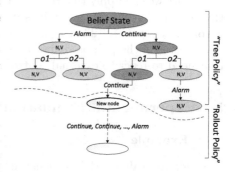

Fig. 2. POMCP search tree

exploration constant $c = R_{hi} - R_{lo}$ [19], where R_{hi} is the largest value achieved during sample runs of the POMDP with the constant $c = 0$, and R_{lo} is the smallest value returned during sample rollouts. In the context of the Monitoring-POMDP, $R_{hi} = \max(R_g^c, R_b^a)$, and $R_{lo} = \min(R_g^a, R_b^c)$.

For the case of the history node that has no action leaf nodes yet the *rollout policy* is used. In rollout, the execution proceeds up to the end of the fixed horizon. The simplest form of the *rollout policy* is a uniform random policy. However, it is not suitable for the POMDP-monitor. To see that, consider the following scenario. Assume that at some point during the construction of the search tree, the simulation is at a node with the history h that does not have any leaf nodes so that the *rollout policy* is used. Let's also assume that when this node was reached during the simulation, the system state corresponded to a failure. The random *rollout policy* will generate a finite randomly sampled sequence of actions. The sequence will be stopped either when the maximum horizon depth is reached, or a terminal action is executed. Let's assume that in the generated sequence of actions the first action is *Continue*, followed again by some number of *Continue* actions and eventually executing an *Alarm*. Such an action sequence would accumulate a significant penalty for a missed alarm, and this penalty would be associated with the new leaf node added to the tree. Now, let's assume that when this search tree node is encountered again in the search, the system state is good, i.e. there is no failure. According to the *tree policy*, at first the *Alarm* branch will be explored, but at further times it will be unlikely that *Continue* branch will be explored again. This might have a significant effect on the value of the expected reward for the action *Continue* at the root node of the tree.

Instead of selecting the action randomly during the *rollout policy* we propose to select the action to maximize the reward at every step. This can be achieved by raising the alarm only at the failure state, and continuing the execution if the system state is good. In this way it is guaranteed that the value assigned to the newly added will promote further exploration when the *tree policy* is used.

The outcome of the search is an action that produces the largest augmented reward from the root node after the predefined number of simulations have been performed.

Before we can apply the POMCP for any real-life problem we should consider that just as for any POMDP, it is designed to describe decisions of completely autonomous systems. That is, no external control input is present. While this is a limitation of the proposed approach, the extension of the procedure to systems that need to react to external control inputs is beyond the scope of this paper.

5   Experimental Evaluation

5.1   Example

In order to evaluate the efficiency of the decision-theoretic monitor, we use a mobile robot with a software implementation of a 2-gear transmission system.

By switching gears, the engine revolutions per minute (RPM) are maintained in a safe range. However, due to failures, RPM might increase and stay beyond the limit over a period of time. This may lead to the engine damage and should be promptly detected. We emphasize that while this system is rather simple, it demonstrates that decision-theoretic monitoring techniques can be used in real time and that the POMDP-monitor works well in practice.

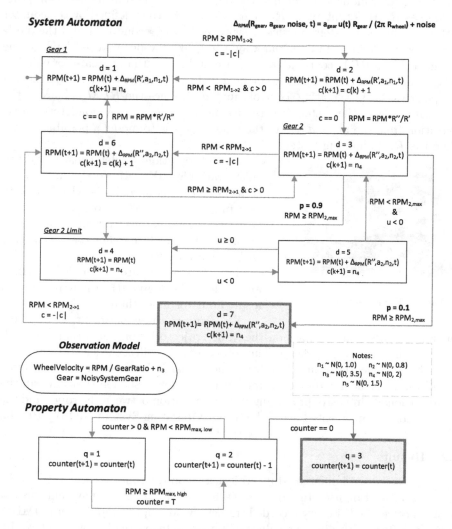

Fig. 3. Experimental model

The automatons for the system and monitored property are shown in the Fig. 3. The discrete modes of the hybrid system are described by the variable d, c is a timer, a_1 and a_2 correspond to the linear acceleration of the vehicle when in the corresponding gear, and $n_1, \ldots, n_4$ are disturbances. The function

$u(t) \in [-1, 1]$ represents the control input from the combined accelerator/brake pedal. The positive values of $u(t)$ correspond to acceleration, while the negative values correspond to braking.

The system starts from the mode $d = 1$ with acceleration dynamics of the first gear. Once the RPM is above the predefined constant $R_{1 \rightarrow 2}$ a transition to the intermediate mode $d = 2$ occurs and the timer c is set by the random variable n_4. The mode $d = 2$ models the delay due to the shifting between gears. As long as RPM is kept above $R_{1 \rightarrow 2}$ at least for the time defined by the counter c, the transmission system physically switches to the second gear and the mode $d = 3$ becomes active. In a similar way, the gear may be switched back to the first gear. If the RPM continues to increase and is eventually greater or equal to $R_{2,max}$ the system transitions into mode $d = 4$ that limits the RPM by ignoring any positive, i.e. accelerating, control input $u(t)$. Once the RPM is back to the acceptable range, the system returns to the mode $d = 3$. A nondeterministic transition from the mode $d = 3$ to the mode $d = 7$ is to model a possible failure when the RPM limiting system fails to engage.

Fig. 4. Experimental robot.

The observation model consists of two noisy variables $WheelVelocity$ and $Gear$. $WheelVelocity$ is a vehicle's wheel velocity as a function of RPM distorted by a noise. $Gear$ is a distorted observation of the transmission gear, which matches the actual gear with probability 0.9.

The property automaton is a safety automaton: the engine RPM may not exceed a safe limit for more than time T.

We conduct the experiment by applying different monitors many times on the same trajectories of states that were collected from the physical system. The robot (Fig. 4) collects wheel velocity data from the incremental rotary encoders. The transmission system was simulated in software. The acquired data is transmitted to a workstation that does all the computationally intensive processing. Communication between the robot and the workstation is implemented using the Robot Operating System (ROS) API [16].

5.2   Results

We have recorded 14 different state trajectories on the robot for the fixed predefined input function $u(t)$. In 7 of these cases, the RPM limiting system was not engaged correctly. For every recorded trajectory, we apply a number of POMDP-based monitors with different values of rewards. In particular, we explore different ratios of rewards to penalties for the selected action. In addition to the POMDP-based monitors, we also tested the threshold-based monitor described in Sect. 3. We ran each monitor 100 times for the same state trajectory so that we can assess its average performance.

Every POMCP-based monitor was configured to use the discount factor $\gamma = 1$, with a maximum depth of the search tree (search horizon) equal to 20. The total number of simulations executed to construct the search tree and determine the optimal action was 1000. We have used 1000 particles to sample the belief state both in the threshold-based and POMDP-based monitors.

For every monitor run and every system trajectory, we count how many times the alarm was raised or missed. Then, the acceptance and rejection accuracies, and monitoring time, denoted by AA, RA, and $MTIME$ respectively, were computed according to:

$$AA = \frac{g_a}{g_a + g_r} \quad RA = \frac{b_r}{b_a + b_r} \quad MTIME = \frac{\sum_{i=1}^{b_r} T_{b_r}^i}{b_r},$$

where g_a (resp., g_r) is the number of good runs that were accepted (resp., rejected), b_r (resp., b_a) is the number of bad runs that were rejected (resp., accepted), and $T_{b_r}^i$ is the from when the failure occurs to when the monitor raises an alarm. Note that g_r corresponds to the number of false alarms, and b_a to the number of missed alarms; the accuracies approach 1 as these numbers approach 0. An execution was considered good if the state of the property automaton at the end of the run was not representing a failure, and bad otherwise.

The number of raised false alarms as well as the convergence time depend on the monitor configuration. For the case of the threshold-based monitor, it depends on the value of the threshold. The lower the threshold, the larger will be the number of false alarms and the smaller will be the monitoring time. Threshold monitors do not allow these two quantities to be independently adjusted.

On the other hand, POMDP-monitors are configured by the assignment of reward values. This paper does not focus on how to obtain a monitor configuration that would result in smallest $MTIME$ for the same AA. However, our

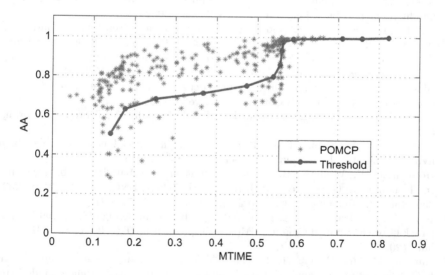

Fig. 5. Acceptance accuracy vs. monitoring time (larger AA for smaller $MTIME$ is better).

experiments confirm that POMDP-based approach is a promising direction in designing efficient monitoring algorithms. Figure 5 shows that many of configurations that have been chosen for the experiments, indeed, result in a better accuracy for the same monitoring time.

6 Conclusions

In this paper we formulate run-time monitors as sequential decision processes. We present a formal definition of the sequential decision monitoring process in the form of Monitoring-POMDP. For this POMDP model we adapt the POMCP algorithm to compute the approximate optimal policy. The POMCP algorithm can be applied to complex models, does not require an analytical model of the system, and only requires the observation space to be quantized, not the state space. Our experiments with the POMCP implementation of the POMDP-monitor show that it is computationally efficient and suitable for real-time monitoring. We have also demonstrated that POMDP based approach provides a broader spectrum of performance outcomes and can in turn be used to achieve better monitoring efficiency. Further work will focus on the theoretical analysis of POMDP-monitors and their performance, especially as compared to threshold monitors.

References

1. Agate, R., Seward, D.: Autonomous safety decision-making in intelligent robotic systems in the uncertain environments. In: Annual Meeting of the North American Fuzzy Information Processing Society, NAFIPS 2008, pp. 1–6. IEEE (2008)
2. Auer, P., Cesa-Bianchi, N., Fischer, P.: Finite-time analysis of the multiarmed bandit problem. Mach. Learn. **47**(2–3), 235–256 (2002)
3. Bai, H., Hsu, D., Lee, W.S., Ngo, V.A.: Monte Carlo value iteration for continuous-state POMDPs. In: Hsu, D., Isler, V., Latombe, J.-C., Lin, M.C. (eds.) Algorithmic Foundations of Robotics IX. Springer Tracts in Advanced Robotics, vol. 68, pp. 175–191. Springer, Heidelberg (2011). doi:10.1007/978-3-642-17452-0_11
4. Blom, H., Bloem, E.: Particle filtering for stochastic hybrid systems. In: 43rd IEEE Conference on Decision and Control, CDC, vol. 3 (2004)
5. Clarke, E.M., Grumberg, O., Peled, D.: Model Checking. MIT press, Cambridge (1999)
6. Henzinger, T.A., Kopke, P.W., Puri, A., Varaiya, P.: What's decidable about hybrid automata? J. Comput. Syst. Sci. **57**(1), 94–124 (1998)
7. Hofbaur, M.W., Williams, B.C.: Mode estimation of probabilistic hybrid systems. In: Tomlin, C.J., Greenstreet, M.R. (eds.) HSCC 2002. LNCS, vol. 2289, pp. 253–266. Springer, Heidelberg (2002). doi:10.1007/3-540-45873-5_21
8. Radu, V.: Application. In: Radu, V. (ed.) Stochastic Modeling of Thermal Fatigue Crack Growth. Applied Condition Monitoring, vol. 1, pp. 63–70. Springer, Switzerland (2015)
9. Kanade, A., Alur, R., Ivančić, F., Ramesh, S., Sankaranarayanan, S., Shashidhar, K.C.: Generating and analyzing symbolic traces of simulink/stateflow models. In: Bouajjani, A., Maler, O. (eds.) CAV 2009. LNCS, vol. 5643, pp. 430–445. Springer, Heidelberg (2009). doi:10.1007/978-3-642-02658-4_33

10. Koutsoukos, X., Kurien, J., Zhao, F.: Estimation of distributed hybrid systems using particle filtering methods. In: Maler, O., Pnueli, A. (eds.) HSCC 2003. LNCS, vol. 2623, pp. 298–313. Springer, Heidelberg (2003). doi:10.1007/3-540-36580-X_23

11. Kumar, R., Garg, V.: Control of stochastic discrete event systems modeled by probabilistic languages. IEEE Trans. Autom. Control 46(4), 593–606 (2001)

12. Lerner, U., Moses, B., Scott, M., McIlraith, S., Koller, D.: Monitoring a complex physical system using a hybrid dynamic bayes net. In: Proceedings of the 18th Annual Conference on Uncertainty in AI (UAI), pp. 301–310 (2002)

13. Pantelic, V., Postma, S., Lawford, M.: Probabilistic supervisory control of probabilistic discrete event systems. IEEE Trans. Autom. Control 54(8), 2013–2018 (2009)

14. Papadimitriou, C.H., Tsitsiklis, J.N.: The complexity of Markov decision processes. Math. Oper. Res. 12(3), 441–450 (1987)

15. Tabuada, P.: Verification and Control of Hybrid Systems: A Symbolic Approach. Springer Science & Business Media, New York (2009)

16. Quigley, M., Conley, K., Gerkey, B., Faust, J., Foote, T., Leibs, J., Wheeler, R., Ng, A.Y.: ROS: an open-source Robot Operating System. In: ICRA Workshop on Open Source Software 3 (2009)

17. Russell, S., Norvig, P., Intelligence, A.: A Modern Approach. Prentice Hall, Englewood (2009)

18. Seward, D., Pace, C., Agate, R.: Safe and effective navigation of autonomous robots in hazardous environments. Auton. Robot. 22(3), 223–242 (2007)

19. Silver, D., Veness, J.: Monte-Carlo planning in large POMDPs. In: Advances in Neural Information Processing Systems, pp. 2164–2172 (2010)

20. Sistla, A.P., Žefran, M., Feng, Y.: Runtime monitoring of stochastic cyber-physical systems with hybrid state. In: Khurshid, S., Sen, K. (eds.) RV 2011. LNCS, vol. 7186, pp. 276–293. Springer, Heidelberg (2012). doi:10.1007/978-3-642-29860-8_21

21. Sistla, A.P., Žefran, M., Feng, Y.: Monitorability of stochastic dynamical systems. In: Gopalakrishnan, G., Qadeer, S. (eds.) CAV 2011. LNCS, vol. 6806, pp. 720–736. Springer, Heidelberg (2011). doi:10.1007/978-3-642-22110-1_58

22. Sistla, A.P., Žefran, M., Feng, Y., Ben, Y.: Timely monitoring of partially observable stochastic systems. In: Proceedings of the 17th International Conference on Hybrid Systems: Computation and Control, pp. 61–70. ACM (2014)

23. Stoller, S.D., Bartocci, E., Seyster, J., Grosu, R., Havelund, K., Smolka, S.A., Zadok, E.: Runtime verification with state estimation. In: Khurshid, S., Sen, K. (eds.) RV 2011. LNCS, vol. 7186, pp. 193–207. Springer, Heidelberg (2012). doi:10.1007/978-3-642-29860-8_15

24. Verma, V., Gordon, G., Simmons, R., Thrun, S.: Real-time fault diagnosis. IEEE Robot. Autom. Mag. 11(2), 56–66 (2004)

25. Yoo, T., Lafortune, S.: Polynomial-time verification of diagnosability of partially observed discrete-event systems. IEEE Trans. Autom. Control 47(9), 1491–1495 (2002)

Precision, Recall, and Sensitivity of Monitoring Partially Synchronous Distributed Systems

Sorrachai Yingchareonthawornchai[1]([✉]), Duong N. Nguyen[1],
Vidhya Tekken Valapil[1], Sandeep S. Kulkarni[1], and Murat Demirbas[2]

[1] Department of Computer Science and Engineering, Michigan State University,
East Lansing, MI 48824, USA
{yingchar,nguye476,tekkenva,sandeep}@cse.msu.edu
[2] Department of Computer Science and Engineering, University at Buffalo,
The State University of New York, Buffalo, NY 14260-2500, USA
demirbas@cse.buffalo.edu

Abstract. Runtime verification focuses on analyzing the execution of a given program by a monitor to determine if it is likely to violate its specifications. There is often an impedance mismatch between the assumptions/model of the monitor and that of the underlying program. This constitutes problems especially for distributed systems, where the concept of current time and state are inherently uncertain. A monitor designed with asynchronous system model assumptions may cause false-positives for a program executing in a partially synchronous system: the monitor may flag a global predicate that does not actually occur in the underlying system. A monitor designed with a partially synchronous system model assumption may cause false negatives as well as false positives for a program executing in an environment where the bounds on partial synchrony differ (albeit temporarily) from the monitor model assumptions.

In this paper we analyze the effects of the impedance mismatch between the monitor and the underlying program for the detection of conjunctive predicates. We find that there is a small interval where the monitor assumptions are hypersensitive to the underlying program environment. We provide analytical derivations for this interval, and also provide simulation support for exploring the sensitivity of predicate detection to the impedance mismatch between the monitor and the program under a partially synchronous system.

1 Introduction

Runtime verification focuses on analyzing the execution of a given program by a monitor to determine if it violates its specifications. In analyzing a distributed program, the monitor needs to take into account multiple processes simultaneously to determine the possibility of violation of the specification. Unfortunately, perfect clock synchronization is unattainable for distributed systems [1,2], and distributed systems have an inherent uncertainty associated with the concept of current time and state [3]. As a result, there is often an impedance mismatch between the assumptions/model of the monitor and that

© Springer International Publishing AG 2016
Y. Falcone and C. Sanchez (Eds.): RV 2016, LNCS 10012, pp. 420–435, 2016.
DOI: 10.1007/978-3-319-46982-9_26

of the underlying program. Even after a careful analysis of the underlying distributed system/program, the model assumptions that the monitor infers for the system/program will have errors due to uncertain communication latencies (especially over multihops over the Internet), temporal perturbations of clock synchronization (especially when different multihop clock references [4] are used), and faults.

In the absence of precise knowledge about events there is a potential that the debugging/monitoring system (which we call as the monitor) would either (1) find non-existent bugs or/and (2) miss existing bugs. While some errors are unavoidable, if we cannot characterize monitor and the underlying program/system behavior precisely, there is no analysis to answer the effect of system uncertainty on predicate detection/runtime verification. Our goal in this paper is to analyze the errors caused by uncertainty of the underlying distributed system and the impedance mismatch between the monitor and the underlying distributed system.

To illustrate the role of the uncertainty and the impedance mismatch, consider the example in Fig. 1. In this computation, we want to verify that the system never reaches a state where the predicate $x > 0 \land y > 0$ is true. In Fig. 1(a), it is clear that the predicate is not true since there is a message after $x > 0$ has become false and before $y > 0$ becomes true. In Fig. 1(b), if the processes' clocks were perfectly synchronized the predicate is always false. However, if it is assumed that the processes are asynchronous or can have large clock drifts then in Fig. 1(b), the predicate is true. In other words, if the algorithm for runtime monitoring assumes that the system clock is perfectly synchronized but in reality it is not then in Fig. 1(b), the result of the monitoring algorithm will be false negative, i.e., the monitor will fail to detect that the system (possibly) reached a state where $x > 0 \land y > 0$ was true. On the other hand, if the monitoring algorithm assumes an asynchronous system but in reality, it is synchronous (and the system may be using timeouts as implicit communication) then in Fig. 1(b), the result of the monitoring algorithm is false positive, i.e., the monitor incorrectly finds that the system (possibly) reached a state where $x > 0 \land y > 0$ was true. Our goal in this work is to characterize the false positives/negatives in run-time monitoring of a distributed system due to the uncertainty and impedance mismatch. We focus on conjunctive predicates, i.e., predicates that are conjunctions of local predicates of individual processes. The disjunction of such conjunctive predicates can express any predicate in the system. Our analysis focuses on comparing the application ground truth (whether the predicate was true under the assumptions made by the application) with the monitor ground truth (whether the predicate is true under the assumptions made by the monitor). In other words, it identifies the effect of uncertainty in the *problem* of monitoring distributed programs rather the uncertainty associated with a given algorithm.

Specifically, we consider the following problems in the context of detecting weak conjunctive predicates. (1) Suppose we utilize a monitoring algorithm designed for asynchronous systems; then what is the likelihood of the result being a false positive/negative when used with an application that relies on

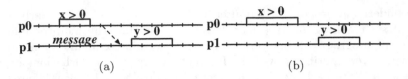

Fig. 1. Uncertainty and impedance mismatch in distributed systems.

partial clock synchronization. (2) Suppose we utilize an algorithm designed for partially synchronous systems where it is assumed that clocks of two processes are synchronized up to ϵ_{mon}, but in reality, the bound used by the application is ϵ_{app}. In this context, what is the likelihood of receiving false positive/negative detection? Moreover, if ϵ_{app} cannot be precisely identified (may have temporal perturbations), how *sensitive* is the debugging algorithm to variations in clock drift/uncertainty?

Precision, recall, and sensitivity of asynchronous monitors. We present an analytical model that characterizes the false positive rate for monitors that assume that the system is fully asynchronous (i.e., $\epsilon_{mon} = \infty$) and clock drift can be arbitrary (ϵ_{app} is finite). Under these assumptions, monitor can only suffer from false positives: The monitor will have perfect recall (i.e., there will be no false negatives) but may suffer from a lack of precision. Our analytical results show that we can classify the clock synchronization requirement in the partial synchrony model into 3 categories with respect to two parameters ϵ_{p_1} and ϵ_{p_2}. We find that if the clock drift is between $[0..\epsilon_{p_1}]$ then the precision of monitoring is very low (i.e., the rate of false positives is high). If the drift is in the range $[\epsilon_{p_2}..\infty]$ then the precision of monitoring is reasonably high. Moreover, in both of those cases, the precision is not very sensitive, i.e., changes in the clock drift of the application does not affect the rate of false positives. However, in the range $[\epsilon_{p_1}..\epsilon_{p_2}]$, the monitoring is hypersensitive and small differences between the clock drift assumed by the monitor and the underlying application can have a substantial impact on the rate of false positives. A noteworthy result in this context is that the hypersensitivity range $\frac{\epsilon_{p_2} - \epsilon_{p_1}}{\epsilon_{p_2}}$ approaches to 0 whenever number of processes $n \to \infty$.

Precision, recall, and sensitivity of partially synchronous monitors. We consider an extension of asynchronous monitors to the general case where the monitor relies on the fact that the underlying clocks are synchronized to be within ϵ_{mon}, which may be different than the timing properties ϵ_{app} of the application. We find that for small ϵ_{app} there is a tradeoff among precision, recall, and sensitivity. If the monitor tries to achieve very high recall and precision (say at 95 %) at the same time, it becomes hypersensitive with respective to both precision and recall (small mismatch between the synchrony assumptions of the monitor and the underlying program can have a substantial impact on the rate of both false positives and false negatives). In this case, the monitor would need to sacrifice from the quality of either precision and recall to avoid being hypersensitive.

We also find that for large ϵ_{app}, the tradeoff dilutes. The monitor can achieve very high recall and precision while remaining less susceptible to sensitivity for large ϵ_{app}.

Implications of our findings for monitor design/tuning. Our findings inform the monitor designer to manage the tradeoffs among precision, recall, and sensitivity according to the predicate detection task at hand. Our analytical model can inform based on ϵ_{app} and local predicate occurrence probability, whether hypersensitivity is avoidable or not. If hypersensitivity is avoidable, ϵ_{mon} can be chosen from the suitable interval to achieve both high precision and high recall. However, if it becomes necessary to make a tradeoff between precision and recall to avoid hypersensitivity, the monitor would need to decide which one is more important, and which one it can sacrifice.

The monitor may decide to prioritize recall in lieu of reduced precision. In other words, the monitor can attain better coverage of notifications of predicate detection to the expense of increased false positive notifications. This is useful for investigating predicates that occur rarely, where one cannot afford to miss occurrences of the predicate but can afford to investigate/debug some false-positive detections. This is also useful for monitoring safety predicates, which is relatively easier to debug.

The monitor may decide to prioritize precision in lieu of reduced recall. In other words, the monitor can reduce the false positive notifications of predicate detection to the expense of allowing some missed notifications of predicate detection. This is useful for predicates that occur frequently: the monitor has enough opportunities to sample and can afford to miss some occurrences of the predicate. This is also useful for monitoring liveness/progress predicates, which is harder to debug and false-positives cause wasting time with debugging.

Organization of the Paper. In Sect. 2, we present our computational model. In Sect. 3, we investigate precision and sensitivity of asynchronous monitors in partially synchronous systems. In Sect. 4, we analyze the precision, recall, and sensitivity of partially synchronous monitoring of partially synchronous systems. We discuss related work in Sect. 5 and conclude in Sect. 6.

2   System Model

We consider a system that consists of a set of n processes that communicate via messages. Each process has a local clock that is synchronized to be within ϵ of absolute time, using a protocol such as NTP [4]. Any message sent in the system is received no earlier than δ_{min} time and no later than δ_{max} time. We denote such a system as $\langle \epsilon, \delta_{min}, \delta_{max} \rangle$-system. We also use the abbreviated notion of $\langle \epsilon, \delta \rangle$-system, where δ denotes the **minimum** message delay and the maximum message delay is ∞. Observe that this modeling is generic enough to model asynchronous systems ($\epsilon = \infty, \delta_{min} = 0, \delta_{max} = \infty$) and purely synchronous systems ($\epsilon = 0, \delta_{min} = 0, \delta_{max} = 0$), as well as partially synchronous systems.

We define $hb-consistent$ to capture the requirement that two events e and f "could have" happened at the same time. Specifically, e and f are hb-consistent (also called concurrent) provided both *ehb f* and *fhb e* are false.[1] If both *ehb f* and *fhb e* are false then *e* and *f* could have happened at the same time in an asynchronous system where clock drift could be arbitrary. A global snapshot consisting of local snapshot of each process is *hb*-consistent if and only if all local snapshots are mutually *hb*-consistent.

For partially synchronous systems, we define the notion of ϵ-consistent. Two events *e* and *f* are ϵ-consistent provided they are *hb*-consistent and the difference between the physical time of *e* and *f* is no more than ϵ. A global snapshot consisting of local snapshot of each process is ϵ-consistent if and only if all local snapshots are mutually ϵ-consistent.

A conjunctive predicate $\mathcal{P}$ is defined of the form $\mathcal{P}_1 \wedge \mathcal{P}_2 \wedge \cdots \wedge \mathcal{P}_n$, where $\mathcal{P}_i$ is a local predicate at process *i*. At each process, the local predicate $\mathcal{P}_i$ can become randomly and independently true at the chosen time unit granularity (say millisecond granularity) with probability β. For instance, if $\beta = 0.1$ and time unit is selected as millisecond, then the local predicate becomes true roughly every 10 ms. We use ℓ to denote the length of an interval for which the local predicate remains true at a process once it becomes true.

3   Precision and Sensitivity of Asynchronous Monitors

In this section, we evaluate the precision and sensitivity of an asynchronous monitor in partially synchronous systems. In particular, we focus on $\langle \epsilon, \delta \rangle$ systems.

3.1   Analytical Model

Using a monitor designed for asynchronous systems in partially synchronous systems can result in a false positive. Hence, in this section, we develop an analytical model to address the following question:

> If we use a monitor for predicate detection that is designed for an asynchronous system and apply it in a partially synchronous system, what is the likelihood that it would result in a false positive?

The false positive rate is defined as the probability of a snapshot discovered by the asynchronous monitor is a false positive in $\langle \epsilon, \delta \rangle$-system. To compute this ratio for interval-based local predicates, we first define the following. Two intervals $[a_1, b_1]$ and $[a_2, b_2]$ differ by $\max(\max(a_1, a_2) - \min(b_1, b_2), 0)$. Let *c* be a snapshot consisting of a collection of intervals $[a_i, b_i]$ for each process $i = 0$ to $n - 1$. We denote $L(c)$ as the length of the snapshot *c* defined by the least value of *x* such that *c* is *x*-consistent snapshot.

An asynchronous monitor has perfect recall because every ϵ-snapshot is *hb*-snapshot as shown in Proposition 1.

---

[1] Following Lamport's definition of causality [5], for any two events *e* and *f*, we say that *ehb f* (*e* happened before *f*) if and only if (1) *e* and *f* are events in the same process and *e* occurred before *f*, (2) *e* is a send event and *f* is the corresponding receive event, or (3) there exists an event *g* such that *ehb g* and *ghb f*.

Proposition 1. *Let $\mathcal{H}$ be a set of hb-snapshots detected by an asynchronous monitor, and $\mathcal{P}$ be a set of ϵ-snapshots detected by a partially synchronous monitor. Then, $\mathcal{P} \subseteq \mathcal{H}$.*

If an hb-consistent snapshot is also ϵ-consistent, this is a true positive, which means the asynchronous monitor is precise in this case. Our first result is Precision (true positive rate) of hb-consistent snapshots in $\langle \epsilon, \delta \rangle$-systems.

Theorem 1. *For interval-based predicate, given c is an hb-consistent snapshot, the probability of c being also ϵ-consistent is $\phi(\epsilon, n, \beta, \ell) = (1 - (1 - \beta)^{\epsilon + \ell - 1})^{n-1}$.*

To prove Theorem 1, we first show, $\phi(\epsilon, n, \beta, 1)$, probability of hb-consistent snapshot being ϵ-snapshot for point-based predicate. This is equivalent to computing distribution of $L(c)$ where each interval has length 1. For point-based predicate, the result is as follows and its derivation is provided as a proof.

Lemma 1. *For point-based predicate, the probability of a hb-consistent snapshot being ϵ-consistent (true positive rate) is $\phi(\epsilon, n, \beta) = (1 - (1 - \beta)^{\epsilon})^{n-1}$.*

Proof. Given the system model, for a long execution trace of a distributed program, it follows that true positive rate will eventually converge to some value by law of large number in probability theory. The trick is we first fix process 0 to have true predicate at time 0. We define random variable x_i as the first time after time 0 that the predicate is true at process i, $1 \leq i \leq n-1$. By system model, x_i's local predicate has independent probability to be true at each time unit. Hence, x_i has geometric distribution with parameter β, i.e., $P(x_i \leq \epsilon) = 1 - (1 - \beta)^{\epsilon}$. The cut is ϵ-consistent if all points are not beyond ϵ. That is,

$$P(\max_{1 \leq i \leq n-1} x_i \leq \epsilon) = \prod_{i=1}^{n-1} P(x_i \leq \epsilon)$$
$$= (1 - (1 - \beta)^{\epsilon})^{n-1}$$

We now proceed with the proof of Theorem 1.

Proof. We calculate probability of hb-consistent snapshot being ϵ-snapshot for interval-based predicate of length ℓ. Using Lemma 1, we can obtain the following result. For convenience, we denote $\phi(x, n, \beta, \ell)$ as $f(x)$ representing the length of an interval-based predicate snapshot.

We directly compute $P(L(c) \leq \epsilon)$. In this case, $L(c) = \max(\max_i(\{a_i\}) - \min_i(\{b_i\})), 0)$ by definition of a length of the snapshot c, $L(c)$. Let c' be a snapshot of point-based predicate. Hence,

$$P(L(c) \leq \epsilon) = P(\max(\max_i(\{a_i\}) - \min_i(\{b_i\}), 0) \leq \epsilon)$$
$$= P(L(c') \leq \epsilon + \ell - 1)$$
$$= (1 - (1 - \beta)^{\epsilon + \ell - 1})^{n-1}$$

The last equation follows from Lemma 1. This completes the proof.

The formula above suggests that when n increases, snapshots that are *hb*-consistent will become less physically consistent. This is expected since the more number of processes, the harder to find *hb*-consistent snapshots as well as physically close *hb*-consistent snapshots. On the contrary, if we increase β, predicates will be more frequent and there are more physically close *hb*-consistent snapshots.

We use the characteristics of this function to compute the sensitivity of asynchronous monitors. We focus on ϵ since it is likely to vary over time. We consider the special case where predicates are point-based denoted as $\phi(x, n, \beta) = \phi(x, n, \beta, 1)$.

We identify two inflection points of $\frac{\partial \phi(\epsilon, n, \beta)}{\partial \epsilon}$, denoted as ϵ_{p_1} and ϵ_{p_2} where ϕ changes rapidly for $\epsilon \in [\epsilon_{p_1}, \epsilon_{p_2}]$. On the other hand, we observe that if $\epsilon \leq \epsilon_{p_1}$ or $\epsilon \geq \epsilon_{p_2}$, the change in ϕ is very small. That is, in the range, $[0..\epsilon_{p_1}]$, the monitor has lots of false-positives and is not very sensitive to changes in the value of ϵ. Moreover, in range $[\epsilon_{p_2}, \infty]$, the monitor has few false positives and again not sensitive to changes in the value of ϵ. However, in the range $[\epsilon_{p_1}..\epsilon_{p_2}]$, the monitor is very sensitive to changes in ϵ. In other words, except in the range $[\epsilon_{p_1}..\epsilon_{p_2}]$, we can compute the precision of the asynchronous monitor with only approximate knowledge of ϵ used in the partially synchronous model.

Our next result shows that the gap between two inflection points of $\frac{\partial \phi(\epsilon, n, \beta)}{\partial \epsilon}$ approaches zero for large n.

Theorem 2. *For $n > 1$, two inflection points of $\frac{\partial \phi(\epsilon, n, \beta)}{\partial \epsilon}$ are at*

$$\{\epsilon_{p_1}, \epsilon_{p_2}\} = \log_{(1-\beta)}(\frac{3n - 4 \pm \sqrt{5n^2 - 16n + 12}}{2(n-1)^2})$$

where $\epsilon_{p_1} < \epsilon_{p_2}$. Furthermore, the relative uncertain range approaches 0 as n increases. In other words, the relative difference of phase transition ϵ_{p_1} and post-phase transition ϵ_{p_2} converges to 0, which is independent of β. That is,

$$\lim_{n \to \infty} \frac{\epsilon_{p_2} - \epsilon_{p_1}}{\epsilon_{p_1}} = 0$$

Proof. Solve a system of equations of the third order derivative of $\phi(\epsilon, n, \beta)$ with respect to ϵ by definition of inflection points of slopes. To complete the proof, we take ratio from ϵ_{p_1} and ϵ_{p_2}. Then, we compute the limit as $n \to \infty$.

To understand the main idea of the result, we can instantiate some concrete values. For example, taking the unit of time granularity as millisecond, with $n = 50$ and $\beta = 0.001$ (i.e., the local predicate is true every second on average), the two points of inflection of slope are at 3635.41 and 5550.24 ms respectively. This means if the system has ϵ less than 3 s, then with high probability the *hb*-consistent global conjunctive predicate is not ϵ-consistent. If the system has ϵ more than 6 s, then with high probability the *hb*-consistent detection is also ϵ-consistent. As another example, with $n = 50$ and $\beta = 0.5$, the two points of inflection of slope are at 5.24 and 8.01 ms, respectively. This means with high probability *hb*-consistent predication is ϵ-consistent if the system has ϵ greater than 8 ms.

3.2   Simulation Setup

To validate the analytical model, we set up a simulation environment. The simulation code is available at https://sourceforge.net/projects/wcp-rv2016/. In our simulation, at any given instance, with a certain probability a process chooses to advance its clock as long as the synchrony requirement is not violated. When a process increments its clock, it can decide if the local predicate is true with probability β. Depending upon point-based detection and/or interval-based detection, the local predicate will remain true for just one instant or for a duration whose length is chosen by an exponential distribution. Furthermore, when a process advances its clock, it can choose to send a message to a randomly selected process with probability α. The delay of this message will be δ, the minimum message delay. Note that the analytical model predicts that the possibility that a given cut is a false positive is independent of α and δ. We find that this prediction is also valid with simulations. Hence, delivering the message as soon as it is allowed does not change the false positive rate. The values of α and δ only affect the number of snapshots identified.

For the simulation length, we run until each process advances its clock to 100,000 as we have observed that false positive rates stabilize quickly. Due to space restriction, the results of stabilization of false positive rate are not included but can be found in [6]. During a simulation run, we identify Y, the number of snapshots identified by the asynchronous monitor algorithm in [7], and Y_F, the number of snapshots that are also ϵ-consistent. Thus, the false positive rate FPR is calculated as $1 - \frac{Y_F}{Y}$.

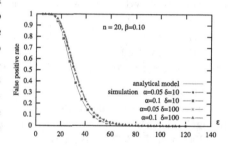

Fig. 2. The independence of false positive rates from α and δ, shown by analytical model and simulations

3.3   Sensitivity for Point-Based Predicates

Independence of False Positive Rate with Respect to α and δ. Since the analytical model predicts that the false positive rate is independent of α and δ, we validate this result with our simulation. Specifically, Fig. 2 considers the false positive rates for $n = 20, \beta = 0.10$. We consider different values of $\alpha = 0.05, 0.1$ and $\delta = 10, 100$ and compare the simulation results with the analytical model. The simulation results validate the analytically computed false positive rate as well as the fact that it is independent of α and δ.

Effect of ϵ. Figure 3(a)-(b) illustrate the effect of false positive rate for different values of ϵ. Figure 3(a), (b) consider the cases with $n = 5$, and 20 processes, respectively. In each figure, we vary β from 1% to 8%. The results validate the analytical model's prediction that values of ϵ can be divided into 3 ranges: a brief range of high false positives to the left when ϵ is small, a range of low false

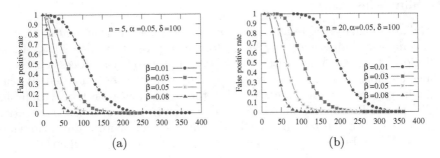

Fig. 3. Impact of β and n on false positive rates in simulations

positives to the right when ϵ is large, and a short uncertainty range in the middle where a small drift in ϵ significantly changes the false positive rates.

Effect of β. As expected from the analytical model, when the value of β is close to 0, the predicted false positive rate is 1. And, as β approaches 1, false positive rate approaches 0. We validate this result with Fig. 3(b). When considering a network of 20 processes, and β is small, say 1 %, the false positive rate at $\epsilon = 200$ is 93.51 %. By contrast if β is increased to 3 % and 5 % then the false positive rate decreases to 4.68 % and 0.08 % respectively.

Effect of n. The analytical model predicts that when n increases, the false positive rate increases. The speed of change depends on β. This result is confirmed in Fig. 3(a), (b). Let $\beta = 0.01$, when n is small, say 5, the false positive rate at $\epsilon = 200$ is 43.71 %. If n is increased to 20 then the false positive rate increases to 93.51 %.

Due to reasons of space, we only focus on scenarios where the local predicates are true for just an instant and those at different processes are independent. In an extended version of the paper [6], we consider the cases where local predicates are true for some duration of time and those associated with different processes are correlated. We note that the results for these cases are also similar to the basic case.

4   Precision, Recall, and Sensitivity of Partially Synchronous Monitors

In this section, we focus on the following problem:

Suppose we designed a monitor (predicate detection algorithm) for a $\langle \epsilon_{mon}, \delta_1 \rangle$-system and applied it in a system that turns out to be a $\langle \epsilon_{app}, \delta_2 \rangle$-system, then what are possible false positives/negatives that may occur? [2]

---

[2] As validated in Sect. 3, the value of δ is not important. Hence, we only focus on the relation between ϵ_{mon} and ϵ_{app}.

4.1   Analytical Model and Its Validation with Simulation Results

We consider the case where the monitoring algorithm assumes partially synchronous model where clocks do not differ by more than ϵ_{mon}. This algorithm is then used for monitoring an application that implicitly relies on the assumption that clocks are synchronized to be within ϵ_{app}, that is difficult to compute and is unavailable to the monitoring algorithm. Such an application may use ϵ_{app} with the use of timeouts, or even more implicitly may rely on database update and cache invalidation schemes to ensure that no two events that are more than ϵ_{app} can be part of the same global state as observed by the clients [8].

If $\epsilon_{app} < \epsilon_{mon}$, then the situation is similar to that of the asynchronous monitors, where $\epsilon_{mon} = \infty$. However, if ϵ_{mon} is finite then it will reduce the false positives as this monitor will avoid detecting some instances where the time difference between the local predicates being true is too large. Thus, a monitor that assumes that clocks are synchronized to be within ϵ_{mon}, will detect snapshots that are ϵ_{mon}-consistent. However, it is expected to identify ϵ_{app}-consistent snapshots. Hence, the precision of the algorithm, i.e., the ratio of the number of snapshots correctly detected and number of snapshots detected, can be determined by calculating the probability that an ϵ_{mon}-consistent snapshot is also an ϵ_{app}-snapshot. Also, in this case since every ϵ_{app}-consistent snapshot is also an ϵ_{mon}-consistent snapshot, the monitor will recall all correct snapshots.

If $\epsilon_{app} > \epsilon_{mon}$, the situation would be reversed, i.e., precision will always be 1. But recall would be less than 1, as the monitor may fail to find some snapshots that are ϵ_{app} consistent but not ϵ_{mon}-consistent. Thus, we have

Theorem 3. *When a monitor designed for $\langle \epsilon_{mon}, \delta \rangle$-system is used in an application that assumes that the system is $\langle \epsilon_{app}, \delta \rangle$-system, the Precision and Recall are as follows:*

$$Precision = \frac{f(\min(\epsilon_{app}, \epsilon_{mon}))}{f(\epsilon_{mon})}, False\ positive\ rate = 1 - Precision$$

$$Recall = \frac{f(\min(\epsilon_{app}, \epsilon_{mon}))}{f(\epsilon_{app})}\ False\ negative\ rate = 1 - Recall$$

$$Where\ f(x) = (1 - (1 - \beta)^{x + \ell - 1})^{n-1}$$

Proof. Precision can be calculated as follows. If $\epsilon_{mon} < \epsilon_{app}$, then Precision is 1 since all ϵ_{mon}-snapshots are ϵ_{app}-snapshots, but not vice versa. If $\epsilon_{mon} > \epsilon_{app}$, then Precision can be calculated as probability of ϵ_{mon}-snapshot being ϵ_{app}-snapshot. In other words, Precision is probability of a snapshot has length of ϵ_{app} given that the snapshot is of length ϵ_{mon}. Therefore, let $L(c)$ be length of snapshot c; Precision is given by

$$Precision = P(L(c) \leq \epsilon_{app} | L(c) \leq \epsilon_{mon})$$
$$= \frac{P(L(c) \leq \epsilon_{app} \text{ and } L(c) \leq \epsilon_{mon})}{P(L(c) \leq \epsilon_{mon})}$$
$$= \frac{P(L(c) \leq \min(\epsilon_{app}, \epsilon_{mon}))}{P(L(c) \leq \epsilon_{mon})}$$
$$= \frac{f(\min(\epsilon_{app}, \epsilon_{mon}))}{f(\epsilon_{mon})}$$

Similarly, Recall is probability of a snapshot being of length ϵ_{mon} given that the snapshot is of length ϵ_{app}. The derivation is essentially the same.

Next, we study the *sensitivity* –changes in the value of Precision and Recall based on changes in $|\epsilon_{app} - \epsilon_{mon}|$– of partially synchronous monitor. We visualize this by a diagram called PR-sensitivity Diagram using Precision and Recall. PR-sensitivity Diagram is basically a contour map of Precision and Recall given two variables $(\epsilon_{mon}, \epsilon_{app})$. If $\epsilon_{app} > \epsilon_{mon}$, the diagram shows only Recall since Precision in this area is always one. Similarly, if $\epsilon_{app} < \epsilon_{mon}$, the diagram shows only Precision. Let η be an accuracy bound, meaning that Precision and Recall are bounded by η, PR-sensitivity Diagram shows contour whose value is η.

Figure 4(a) and (b) show examples of PR-sensitivity Diagram. This diagram shows that the contour lines of Precision/Recall move closer as ϵ_{app} gets smaller. In other words, *the value of Precision and Recall is sensitive when ϵ_{app} is small.* If $\epsilon_{mon} > \epsilon_{app}$ (respectively, $\epsilon_{mon} < \epsilon_{app}$), then even minute change in ϵ_{app} can result in large change in Precision (respectively, Recall). In this case, we need to be careful when monitoring in such tight synchronization.

For scenarios where we consider intervals where local predicates are true, we obtain similar simulation results. Furthermore, we observe that the longer the intervals, the better precision and recall. The simulation results for interval scenarios are not presented here but can be found in [6].

We describe analytical result. If we want both Precision and Recall to be greater than η, the relation between ϵ_{mon} and ϵ_{app} needs to satisfy the condition in the next theorem. Observe that this theorem identifies useful range –where both precision and recall are greater than η– of a monitor.

Theorem 4. *For $\langle \epsilon_{app}, \delta \rangle$-system with n processes where each process has probability β, the monitor designed for $\langle \epsilon_{app}, \delta \rangle$ system has Precision and Recall no less than η if the following condition holds:*

$$\log_{1-\beta}(1 - \eta^{\frac{1}{n-1}} g(\beta, \epsilon_{app}, \ell)) \leq \epsilon_{mon} + \ell - 1 \leq \log_{1-\beta}(1 - \eta^{\frac{-1}{n-1}} g(\beta, \epsilon_{app}, \ell))$$

where

$$g(\beta, \epsilon_{app}, \ell) = 1 - (1 - \beta)^{\epsilon_{app} + \ell - 1}$$

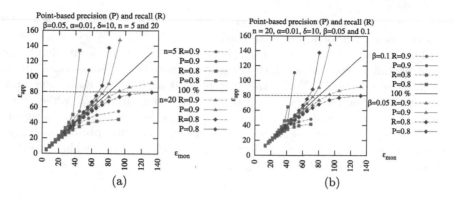

Fig. 4. Precision and Recall diagram in point-based predicate detection

Proof. We fix ϵ_{app} and then we bound the target ϵ_{mon}. If $\epsilon_{app} < \epsilon_{mon}$, then by Theorem 3 Precision is

$$\left(\frac{1 - (1 - \beta)^{\epsilon_{app}+\ell-1}}{1 - (1 - \beta)^{\epsilon_{mon}+\ell-1}}\right)^{n-1}$$

We want precision to be at least η where $0 \leq \eta \leq 1$. We establish an inequality:

$$\left(\frac{1 - (1 - \beta)^{\epsilon_{app}+\ell-1}}{1 - (1 - \beta)^{\epsilon_{mon}+\ell-1}}\right)^{n-1} \geq \eta$$

The results follow from solving the inequality for both Precision and Recall cases.

Finally, there is a phase transition such that if ϵ_{app} is too small then the precision and recall are hypersensitive, meaning that a minute change can result in drastically different accuracy. If ϵ_{app} is beyond phase transition, then the precision and recall are almost non-sensitive as the bound in Theorem 4 grows rapidly.

Theorem 5. *The Precision and Recall due to difference in ϵ_{app} and ϵ_{mon} is hypersensitive if*

$$\epsilon_{app} \leq \log_{1-\beta}(\eta^{\frac{-1}{n-1}} - 1) - \ell + 1$$

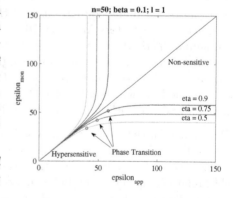

Fig. 5. PR diagram given by analytical model

Proof. We use the same technique as point of inflections of slopes to obtain the phase transition. The phase transition is defined as the point that maximizes concavity or convexity. This can be done by solving an equation given by third order derivative of the bound in Theorem 4 setting to zero. We used Computer Algebra, WolframAlpha, to derive the final expression.

Illustration of Theorems 4 and 5 is shown in Fig. 5. Suppose there are 50 processes where each local predicate truthification rate is at every 10 ms (thus, $\beta = 0.1$). The bounds are obtained by Theorem 4. Each red circle highlights the point of maximum concavity, which is the starting point of phase-transition as highlighted in Theorem 5. Notice the after phase transition for each value of η, there is virtually no sensitivity at all as we can deviate from ϵ_{app} while maintaining high precision and recall. However, if ϵ_{mon} is less than phase transition, the regions below are hypersensitive. In this case, we cannot obtain both high precision and recall simultaneously. Instead, we can choose to have high precision while sacrificing recall and vice versa.

5   Related Work

Inherent to the model of shared nothing distributed systems is that the nodes execute with limited information about other nodes. This further implies that the system developers/operators also have limited visibility and information about the system. Monitoring/tracing and predicate detection tools are an important component of large-scale distributed systems as they provide valuable information to the developers/operators about their system under deployment.

Monitoring Large-Scale Web-Services and Cloud Computing Systems.
Dapper [9] is Google's production distributed systems tracing infrastructure. The primary application for Dapper is performance monitoring to identify the sources of latency tails at scale. Making the system scalable and reducing performance overhead was facilitated by the use of adaptive sampling. The Dapper team found that a sample of just one out of thousands of requests provides sufficient information for many common uses of the tracing data.

Facebook's Mystery Machine [10] has goals similar to Google's Dapper. Both use similar methods, however mystery machine tries to accomplish the task relying on less instrumentation than Google Dapper. The novelty of the mystery machine work is that it tries to infer the component call graph implicitly via mining the logs, where as Google Dapper instrumented each call in a meticulous manner and explicitly obtained the entire call graph.

Predicate Detection with Vector Clocks. Lot of previous work has been done on predicate detection (e.g., Marzullo & Neiger [11] WDAG 1991, Verissimo [12] 1993), using vector clock (VC) timestamped events sorted via happened-before (hb) relationship. The work in [11] not only defined Definitely and Possibly detection modalities, but also provided algorithms for predicate detection using VC for these modalities. This work also showed that information about clock synchronization (i.e., ϵ) can be translated into additional happened-before constraints and fed in to the predicate detection algorithm to take into account system synchronization behavior and avoiding false positives in only VC-based predicate detection. However, that work did not investigate the rates of false-positives with respect to clock synchronization quality and event occurrence rates.

Predicate detection with physical clocks and NTP synchronization. In partially synchronized systems, Stoller [13] investigated global predicate detection using NTP clocks, showing that using NTP synchronized physical clocks provide some benefits over using VC in terms of complexity of predicate detection. The worst case complexity for predicate detection using hb captured by VC is $\Omega(E^N)$, where E is the maximum number of events executed by each process, and N is the number of processes. With some assumptions on the inter-event spacing being larger than time synchronization uncertainty, it is possible to have worst-case time complexity for physical clock based predicate detection to be $O(3^N E N^2)$ — linear in E.

Predicate Detection under Partially Synchronous System. The duality of the literature on monitoring predicates forces one to make a binary choice before hand: To go with either VC- or physical clock-based timestamping and detection [14,15]. Hybrid Vector Clocks (HVC) obviate this duality and offer the lowest cost detection of VC and physical clock-based detection at any point. Moreover while VC is of $\Theta(N)$ [16], thanks to loosely-synchronized clock assumption, it is possible with HVC to keep the sizes of HVC to be a couple entries at each process [17]. HVC captures the communications in the timestamps and provides the best of VC and physical clock worlds.

Runtime Monitoring with Imprecise Timestamp. Prior runtime-verification approaches assume timestamp to be precise. However, results from such protocol may not be correct due to uncertainty in underlying system. Recent works account for clocks' imprecision under a variety of settings. Zhang et al. [18] propose a probabilistic approach to deal with imprecise timestamp in data-stream processing. Wang et al. [19] consider imprecise trace in runtime verification due to unknown event ordering. In [20], Mostafa and Bonakdarpour have focused on the issue of verifying LTL properties in asynchronous systems. As part of this monitoring, they need to evaluate whether the current state satisfies a given global predicate. To achieve this, they utilize the structure of the given predicate to build distributed monitors. Basin et al. [21] focus on the real-time temporal logic MTL over a continuous time domain that accounts for imprecise timestamp. Implicitly, those assumptions can be too strong as well. Our result sheds light on the sensitivity of overall error rate to the errors in assumptions made about the underlying system.

6   Conclusion

We presented analytical and simulation models to capture the effect of the gap between assumptions made by the application and by the monitor. First, we investigated the effect of using a monitor designed for asynchronous systems in partially synchronous systems. We find that regarding ϵ, we can partition the system in three regions: high false positives, uncertain range, low false positives. We find that the uncertain range is hypersensitive, i.e., small changes in ϵ change the false positive rate substantially. We also showed how these ranges can be computed analytically. In particular, we show how one can compute ϵ_{p_1} and ϵ_{p_2} such that the high false positive range is $[0..\epsilon_{p_1}]$, uncertain range is $[\epsilon_{p_1}..\epsilon_{p_2}]$ and low false positive range is $[\epsilon_{p_2}..\infty]$. An interesting observation in this context was that the uncertainty range, $\frac{\epsilon_{p_2}-\epsilon_{p_1}}{\epsilon_{p_2}}$, approaches 0 as the number of processes increase or as ϵ_{app} grows. Although the analytical results focused on situations where the probability of the local predicate being true is independent, it can also be used in cases where local predicate being true is correlated.

We also considered the case where monitoring algorithm assumes that the clocks are synchronized to be within ϵ_{mon}, but the actual clock synchronization of the system/program is ϵ_{app}. One reason this may happen is that application uses clock estimation approaches to identify dynamic value of ϵ_{app} but this value is not visible to the monitor and, hence, it uses an estimated value. We identified possible ranges where the error rate caused by differences in these values is within acceptable limits. Here, we find that for specific ranges of ϵ_{mon}, the algorithm is highly sensitive. We observed tradeoffs among precision, recall, and sensitivity when ϵ_{app} is small, and found that the tradeoff dilutes as ϵ_{app} gets larger.

There are several future extensions of these results. One extension is to evaluate error probability for more complex predicates in terms of conjunctive predicate detection. Here, if the predicate was $\phi_1 \vee \phi_2$ there is a possibility that even if ϕ_1 is detected incorrectly, ϕ_2 may still be true causing detection of $\phi_1 \vee \phi_2$. Apart from conjuctive predicates, it is an open question if similar error probabilities hold for distributed runtime verification for linear temporal logic (LTL) such as in [20]. Another future extension is to consider the case for specific instances of monitors which have potential in-built errors introduced for sake of efficiency during monitoring.

Acknowledgments. This work is supported in part by NSF CNS-1329807, NSF CNS-1318678, NSF XPS-1533870, and NSF XPS-1533802.

References

1. Fan, R., Lynch, N.: Gradient clock synchronization. In: PODC, pp. 320–327 (2004)
2. Patt-Shamir, B., Rajsbaum, S.: A theory of clock synchronization (extended abstract). In: ACM Symposium on Theory of Computing (STOC), pp. 810–819 (1994)
3. Sheehy, J.: There is no now. Commun. ACM **58**(5), 36–41 (2015)
4. Mills, D.: A brief history of NTP time: memoirs of an internet timekeeper. ACM SIGCOMM Comput. Commun. Rev. **33**(2), 9–21 (2003)
5. Lamport, L.: Time, clocks, and the ordering of events in a distributed system. Commun. ACM **21**(7), 558–565 (1978)
6. Yingchareonthawornchai, S., Nguyen, D., Valapil, V.T., Kulkarni, S.S., Demirbas, M.: Precision, recall, sensitivity of monitoring partially synchronous distributed systems. CoRR, abs/1607.03369 (2016). http://arxiv.org/abs/1607.03369
7. Garg, V.K., Chase, C.: Distributed algorithms for detecting conjunctive predicates. In: International Conference on Distributed Computing Systems, pp. 423–430, June 1995

8. Lu, H., Veeraraghavan, K., Ajoux, P., Hunt, J., Song, Y.-J., Tobagus, W., Kumar, S., Lloyd, W.: Existential consistency: measuring and understanding consistency at Facebook. In: Proceedings of the 25th Symposium on Operating Systems Principles, pp. 295–310. ACM (2015)

9. Sigelman, B., Barroso, L., Burrows, M., Stephenson, P., Plakal, M., Beaver, D., Jaspan, S., Shanbhag, C.: Dapper, a large-scale distributed systems tracing infrastructure. Google Inc., Technical report (2010). http://research.google.com/archive/papers/dapper-2010-1.pdf

10. Chow, M., Meisner, D., Flinn, J., Peek, D., Wenisch, T.: The mystery machine: end-to-end performance analysis of large-scale internet services. In: 11th USENIX Symposium on Operating Systems Design and Implementation (OSDI 2014), pp. 217–231 (2014)

11. Cooper, R., Marzullo, K.: Consistent detection of global predicates. ACM SIGPLAN Not. **26**(12), 167–174 (1991)

12. Verissimo, P.: Real-time communication. In: Distributed Systems, vol. 2 (1993)

13. Stoller, S.: Detecting global predicates in distributed systems with clocks. Distrib. Comput. **13**(2), 85–98 (2000)

14. Kulkarni, S.S., Demirbas, M., Madappa, D., Avva, B., Leone, M.: Logical physical clocks. In: Aguilera, M.K., Querzoni, L., Shapiro, M. (eds.) OPODIS 2014. LNCS, vol. 8878, pp. 17–32. Springer, Heidelberg (2014). doi:10.1007/978-3-319-14472-6_2

15. Demirbas, M., Kulkarni, S.: Beyond truetime: using augmentedtime for improving google spanner. In: 7th Workshop on Large-Scale Distributed Systems and Middleware, LADIS (2013)

16. Charron-Bost, B.: Concerning the size of logical clocks in distributed systems. Inf. Process. Lett. **39**(1), 11–16 (1991)

17. Yingchareonthawornchai, S., Kulkarni, S., Demirbas, M.: Analysis of bounds on hybrid vector clocks. In: 19th International Conference on Principles of Distributed Systems, OPODIS (2015)

18. Zhang, H., Diao, Y., Immerman, N.: Recognizing patterns in streams with imprecise timestamps. Proc. VLDB Endow. **3**(1–2), 244–255 (2010). http://dx.doi.org/10.14778/1920841.1920875

19. Wang, S., Ayoub, A., Sokolsky, O., Lee, I.: Runtime verification of traces under recording uncertainty. In: Khurshid, S., Sen, K. (eds.) RV 2011. LNCS, vol. 7186, pp. 442–456. Springer, Heidelberg (2012). doi:10.1007/978-3-642-29860-8_35

20. Mostafa, M., Bonakdarpour, B.: Decentralized runtime verification of LTL specifications in distributed systems. In: 2015 IEEE International Parallel, Distributed Processing Symposium, IPDPS 2015, 25–29 May 2015 Hyderabad, India, pp. 494–503 (2015). http://dx.doi.org/10.1109/IPDPS.2015.95

21. Basin, D., Klaedtke, F., Marinovic, S., Zălinescu, E.: On real-time monitoring with imprecise timestamps. In: Bonakdarpour, B., Smolka, S.A. (eds.) RV 2014. LNCS, vol. 8734, pp. 193–198. Springer, Heidelberg (2014). doi:10.1007/978-3-319-11164-3_16

Short Papers

Falsification of Conditional Safety Properties for Cyber-Physical Systems with Gaussian Process Regression

Takumi Akazaki[✉]

The University of Tokyo, Tokyo, Japan
`ultraredrays@is.s.u-tokyo.ac.jp`

Abstract. We propose a framework to solve falsification problems of *conditional safety properties*—specifications such that "a safety property φ_{safe} holds whenever an antecedent condition φ_{cond} holds." In the outline, our framework follows the existing one based on *robust semantics* and numerical optimization. That is, we search for a counterexample input by iterating the following procedure: (1) pick up an input; (2) test how robustly the specification is satisfied under the current input; and (3) pick up a new input again hopefully with a smaller robustness. In falsification of conditional safety properties, one of the problems of the existing algorithm is the following: we sometimes iteratively pick up inputs that do not satisfy the antecedent condition φ_{cond}, and the corresponding tests become less informative. To overcome this problem, we employ *Gaussian process regression*—one of the model estimation techniques—and estimate the region of the input search space in which the antecedent condition φ_{cond} holds with high probability.

1 Introduction

1.1 Falsification

In design of Cyber-Physical Systems (CPSs), the importance of quality assurance of these systems is ever-rising, thus employing *model-based development (MBD)*—making virtual models (e.g. Simulink/Stateflow blocks) of products, and on these models, verifying properties by mathematical methodologies—has become standard. However, currently at least, the complexity of these virtual models in industry are overwhelm the scalability of the state-of-art formal verification methodologies.

Under such current situation, *falsification* is gathering attention as a viable approach to quality assurance [2,6,9,11]. The falsification problem is formulated as follows.

- **Given:** a system *model* $\mathcal{M}$ with its input domain D, and a *specification* φ
- **Return:** a counterexample input $x \in D$ such that its corresponding output $\mathcal{M}(x)$ violates the specification φ (if such an input exists).

© Springer International Publishing AG 2016
Y. Falcone and C. Sanchez (Eds.): RV 2016, LNCS 10012, pp. 439–446, 2016.
DOI: 10.1007/978-3-319-46982-9_27

Through solving the above falsification problem, we expect to obtain the following insights: (1): we detect errors in which the system violates the specification φ; and (2): in case that such an error could not be found, we would say "the violation of the specification φ unlikely happens."

1.2   Robustness Guided Falsification

As a formal expression of real-time specification on CPSs, *metric interval temporal logic (MITL)* [1], and its adaptation *signal temporal logic (STL)* [12] are actively studied. For these specifications, one common class of algorithms to solve falsification is *robustness guided falsification* [2,6]. Here, one technical core of these algorithms is employing *robust semantics* [7,8] on these logics. In robust semantics, in contrast to conventional Boolean semantics, a truth value takes a quantitative one $[\![\mathcal{M}(x), \varphi]\!] \in \mathbb{R}$ such that it is greater than 0 if the formula φ is satisfied, and its magnitude denotes "how robustly the current output $\mathcal{M}(x)$ satisfies φ." With this robust semantics, we could attribute falsification problems to numerical optimization problems, that is, we search for a counterexample input $x \in D$ by iterating the following steps (for $t = 1 \ldots N$).

1. Pick an input $x_t \in D$ (in stochastic manner.)
2. Compute the output $\mathcal{M}(x_t)$ by numerical simulation (e.g. sim function on Simulink)
3. Check the robustness $[\![\mathcal{M}(x_t), \varphi]\!]$
4. If the robustness is less equal than 0, then return x_t. Otherwise pick a new input x_{t+1} hopefully with which the robustness becomes smaller.

In industrial practice, a system model $\mathcal{M}$ is often huge and complex, hence among the above four steps, the second one, numerical simulation step tends to be the most costly in time—it sometimes takes several tens of seconds for each simulation. Therefore, reducing the number of iterations in minimization of the robustness $[\![\mathcal{M}(x_t), \varphi]\!]$ is essential. To this end, application of various numerical optimization algorithms (e.g. Simulated Annealing [2], Cross-entropy method [14], and so on) is actively studied.

In this paper, as one of the powerful numerical optimization algorithms, we mainly employ *Gaussian process upper confidence bound (GPU-CB)* [15, 16]. Actually, applying **GP-UCB** and other Gaussian process regression based optimization techniques for falsification of temporal logic properties is actively studied. [3–5] We give further illustration of **GP-UCB** in Sect. 3.

1.3   Our Motivation: Falsification of Conditional Safety Property

In this paper, as a class of specifications to be falsified, we have an eye on *conditional safety properties*—common class of specifications in development of CPSs.

Whenever a model satisfies an antecedent condition φ_{cond}, then at that time, the model also satisfies a safety property φ_{safe}.

With this class of formulas, we could express various requirements of behavior of the system under various specific conditions. Hence, for a given system, verifying conditional safety property is as important as for safety property.

On **STL**, we usually encode such a condition into a **STL** formula in the form of $\Box_I(\neg\varphi_{\text{cond}} \vee \varphi_{\text{safe}})$. Note that, in conventional Boolean semantics, the formula is equivalent to $\Box_I(\varphi_{\text{cond}} \to \varphi_{\text{safe}})$. In robustness guided falsification, we search for a counterexample by minimizing the robustness of the formula $\neg\varphi_{\text{cond}}$ and φ_{safe} simultaneously.

However there exists the following gap between this straightforward attribution to the numerical optimization and what we expect to obtain through the falsification: if we write down a conditional safety property, we would like to say something meaningful about dynamics of the model when the antecedent condition φ_{cond} holds; but in the iteration of simulation, *we could not guarantee that enough number of behavior are observed in which the system satisfies the antecedent condition* φ_{cond}. From this point of view, we would expect an optimization algorithm that solves conditional safety property

– with as small as number of iteration to find a counterexample $x \in D$; and
– with picking up enough number of inputs $x_{j_1} \ldots x_{j_n}$ that steers the whole model to satisfy the antecedent condition φ_{cond}.

To this end, we propose a novel algorithm to pick up a suitable input in each step of the iteration with satisfying the above twofold requirements. A technical highlight is that, with Gaussian process regression, we estimate the function $F^* : x \mapsto [\![\mathcal{M}(x), \Box_I\neg\varphi_{\text{cond}}]\!]$, and obtaining the input subspace $D' \subset D$ such that, for any input $x \in D'$, the output $\mathcal{M}(x)$ satisfies the antecedent condition φ_{cond} with high probability.

Related Work. The difficulty of the falsification is to observe the rare event (here, conditional safety property is false). Our technique is based on the following idea: we consider a superset-event that happens much likely than the original one (φ_{cond} holds), and from the input space, we "prune" the region in which the superset-event does not happen. This idea is common with importance sampling. Actually, our Proposition 2.4 is an instance of decomposition in Sect. 4.1 in [10].

While importance sampling explores the input by stochastic sampling, **GP-UCB** deterministically chooses the next input, hence combining these two optimization algorithms are not straightforward. One of our contributions is that we realize the above "pruning" in GP-UCB style optimization by employing regression.

2   Signal Temporal Logic (STL)

Definition 2.1 (syntax). Let **Var** be a set of variables. The set of **STL** *formulas* are inductively defined as follows.

$$\varphi ::= f(v_1, \ldots, v_n) > 0 \mid \bot \mid \top \mid \neg\varphi \mid \varphi \vee \varphi \mid \varphi\,\mathcal{U}_I\,\varphi$$

where f is an n-ary function $f : \mathbb{R}^n \to \mathbb{R} \cup \{-\infty, \infty\}$, $v_1, \ldots, v_x \in \mathbf{Var}$, and I is a closed non-singular interval in $\mathbb{R}_{\geq 0}$, i.e. $I = [a, b]$ or $[a, \infty)$ where $a < b$ and $a \in \mathbb{R}$. We also define the following derived operators, as usual: $\varphi_1 \wedge \varphi_2 \equiv \neg(\neg \varphi_1 \vee \neg \varphi_2)$, $\varphi_1 \, \mathcal{R}_I \, \varphi_2 \equiv \neg(\neg \varphi_1 \, \mathcal{U}_I \, \neg \varphi_2)$, $\Diamond_I \varphi \equiv \top \, \mathcal{U}_I \, \varphi$, and $\Box_I \varphi \equiv \bot \, \mathcal{R}_I \, \varphi$.

Definition 2.2 (robust semantics of STL). Let $\sigma \colon \mathbb{R}_{\geq 0} \to \mathbb{R}^{\mathbf{Var}}$ be a signal and φ be an **STL** formula. We define the *robustness* $[\![\sigma, \varphi]\!] \in \mathbb{R}_{\geq 0} \cup \{-\infty, \infty\}$ inductively as follows. Here $\sqcap$ and $\sqcup$ denote infimums and supremums of real numbers, respectively.

$$[\![\sigma, f(v_1, \cdots, v_n) > 0]\!] \triangleq f\big(\sigma(0)(v_1), \cdots, \sigma(0)(v_n)\big)$$
$$[\![\sigma, \bot]\!] \triangleq -\infty \qquad\qquad [\![\sigma, \top]\!] \triangleq \infty$$
$$[\![\sigma, \neg\varphi]\!] \triangleq -[\![\sigma, \varphi]\!] \qquad\qquad [\![\sigma, \varphi_1 \vee \varphi_2]\!] \triangleq [\![\sigma, \varphi_1]\!] \sqcup [\![\sigma, \varphi_2]\!]$$
$$[\![\sigma, \varphi_1 \, \mathcal{U}_I \, \varphi_2]\!] \triangleq \bigsqcup_{t \in I}\big([\![\sigma^t, \varphi_2]\!] \sqcap \bigsqcap_{t' \in [0, t)} [\![\sigma^{t'}, \varphi_1]\!]\big)$$

Notation 2.3. Let $f : \mathbb{R}^n \to \mathbb{R} \cup \{-\infty, \infty\}$. We define *the Boolean abstraction of* f as the function $\overline{f} : \mathbb{R}^n \to \mathbb{B}]$ such that as $\overline{f}(v) = \top$ if $f(v) > 0$, otherwise $\overline{f}(v) = \bot$. Similarly, for an **STL** formula φ, we denote by $\overline{\varphi}$ the formula which is obtained by replacing all atomic functions f occurs in φ with the Boolean abstraction $\overline{f}$. We see that $[\![\sigma, \varphi]\!] > 0$ implies $[\![\sigma, \overline{\varphi}]\!] > 0$.

As we see in Sect. 1.3, conditional safety properties are written as **STL** formulas in the form of $[\![\sigma, \Box_I(\neg\varphi_{\mathsf{cond}} \vee \varphi_{\mathsf{safe}})]\!]$, and its intuitive meaning is "φ_{safe} holds whenever φ_{cond} is satisfied." To enforce our algorithm in Sect. 4 to pick inputs satisfying the antecedent conditions φ_{cond}, we convert the formula to the logically equivalent one. The converted formula consists of mainly into the two parts such that one of them stands for "the antecedent condition φ_{cond} is satisfied or not."

Proposition 2.4. *For any signal σ and **STL** formulas φ_1, φ_2, the following holds.*

$$[\![\sigma, \Box_I(\neg\varphi_1 \vee \varphi_2)]\!] > 0 \iff [\![\sigma, \Box_I \neg\varphi_1]\!] \sqcup [\![\sigma, \Box_I(\neg\overline{\varphi_1} \vee \varphi_2)]\!] > 0$$

3   Gaussian Process Upper Confidence Bound (GP-UCB)

As we mentioned in Sect. 1.3, in robustness guided falsification to minimize F^* : $x \mapsto [\![\mathcal{M}, \varphi]\!]$, we pick inputs iteratively hopefully with smaller robustness value. For this purpose, *Gaussian process upper confidence bound (**GP-UCB**)* [15,16] is one of the powerful algorithm as we see in [3–5].

The key idea in the algorithm is that, in each iteration round $t = 1, \ldots, N$, we estimate the *Gaussian process* [13] $\mathrm{GP}(\mu, k)$ that most likely to generate the points observed until round t. Here, we call two parameters $\mu : D \to \mathbb{R}$ and $k : D^2 \to \mathbb{R}$ as the *mean function* and the *covariance function* respectively.

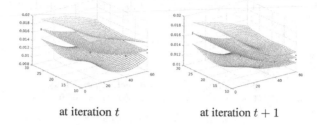

at iteration t at iteration $t+1$

Fig. 1. An intuitive illustration of **GP-UCB** algorithm. Each figure shows the estimated Gaussian process $\mathrm{GP}(\mu, k)$ at iteration round t and $t+1$: the middle curve is a plot of the mean function μ, and the upper and lower curve are a plot of $\mu + \beta^{1/2}k$, $\mu - \beta^{1/2}k$. In each iteration round t, we pick the point $x[t]$ (red point in the left figure) that minimizes the lower curve. Once we observe the value $F^*(x[t])$, the uncertainty at $x[t]$ becomes smaller in the next round $t+1$. In general, as a confidence parameter β we choose an increasing function to guarantee the algorithm not to get stuck in local optima (e.g. $\beta(t) = 2\log(ct^2)$ for some constant c). See [15,16]) (Color figure online)

Very roughly speaking, for each $x \in D$, the value $\mu(x)$ of mean function stands for the expected value of $F^*(x)$, and the value $k(x, x)$ of co variance function at each diagonal point does for the magnitude of uncertainty of $F^*(x)$.

Pseudocode for the **GP-UCB** algorithm is found in Algorithm 1. As we see in the code, we pick $x[t] = \mathsf{argmin}_{x \in D} \mu(x) - \beta^{1/2}(t)k(x, x)$ as the next input. Here, the first term try to minimize the expected value $F^*(x[t])$, and the second term try to decrease uncertainty globally. In Fig. 1, we see an illustration of how the estimated Gaussian process is updated in each iteration round of optimization. Thus, the strategy balancing exploration and exploitation helps us to find a minimal input with as small as number of iteration.

Algorithm 1. The GP-UCB algorithm for falsification

Hyper parameters: A confidence parameter $\beta : \mathbb{N} \to \mathbb{R}$; Maximal number of iteration N;
Input: Input space D; An uncertain function $F : D \to \mathbb{R}$ to be minimized;
Output: An input $x \in D$ such that $F(x) \leq 0$
    for $t = 1 \ldots N$ **do**
        $x[t] = \mathsf{argmin}_{x \in D} \mu(x) - \beta^{1/2}(t)k(x, x)$;   ▷ Choose a new sample input
        $y[t] = F(x[t])$;   ▷ Observe the corresponding output
        if $y[t] \leq 0$ **then**
            return $x[t]$;
        end if
        $(\mu, k) = \mathsf{regression}\big((x[1], y[1]), \ldots (x[t], y[t])\big)$;
                 ▷ Perform Bayesian update to obtain new mean and covariance function
    end for

---

4 Our Algorithm: GP-UCB with Domain Estimation

Now we give our algorithm for falsification of conditional safety properties with enough number of testing in which the model satisfies the antecedent condition.

Algorithm 2. The GP-UCB algorithm for falsification with domain estimation

---

Hyper parameters: A confidence parameter $\beta : \mathbb{N} \to \mathbb{R}$ and its bound $\beta_{min}, \beta_{max} \in \mathbb{R}$; Maximal
number of iteration N; Target hit rate $R \in (0, 1)$
Input: Input space D; Uncertain functions $F, G : D \to \mathbb{R}$;
Output: An input $x \in D$ such that $\max(F(x), G(x)) \leq 0$
    for $t = 1 \dots N$ **do**
        $r = (R \times N - n_{hit})/(N - t)$
                ▷ Calculate the current objective probability r of satisfying $F(x) \leq 0$
        $\beta_F = \min(\max(\sqrt{2}\mathrm{erf}^{-1}(1 - 2r), \beta_{min}), \beta_{max})$ where erf is the error function
        $D' = \{x \in D \mid \mu_F(x) - \beta_F k_F(x, x) \leq 0\}$
                ▷ Estimate a region in which $F(x) \leq 0$ holds with probability r
        if $D' == \emptyset$ **then**
            $x_F[t] = \mathrm{argmin}_{x \in D}\, \mu_F(x) - \beta_F k_F(x, x);$
        else
            $x_G[t] = \mathrm{argmin}_{x \in D'}\, \mu_G(x) - \beta^{1/2}(t) k_G(x, x);$
        end if   ▷ Choose a new sample input
        $y_F[t] = F(x_t);$
        if $y_F[t] \leq 0$ **then**
            $n = n + 1; x_G[n] = x_F[t]; y_G(x_G[n]);$
            if $y_G[n] \leq 0$ **then**
                return $x_G[n];$
            end if
        end if   ▷ Observe the corresponding output
        $(\mu_F, k_F) = \mathrm{regression}((x_F[1], y_F[1]), \dots (x_F[t], y_F[t]));$
        $(\mu_G, k_G) = \mathrm{regression}((x_G[1], y_G[1]), \dots (x_G[n], y_G[n]));$
            ▷ Perform Bayesian update to obtain new mean and covariance function
    end for

As we show in Proposition 2.4, falsification of the specification $\Box_I(\neg\varphi_{\mathsf{cond}} \vee \varphi_{\mathsf{safe}})$ could be reduced to the following problem.

Find x such that $[\![\mathcal{M}(x), \Box_I \neg\varphi_{\mathsf{cond}}]\!] \sqcup [\![\mathcal{M}(x), \Box_I(\neg\overline{\varphi_{\mathsf{cond}}} \vee \varphi_{\mathsf{safe}})]\!] \leq 0.$

A key observation here is that, when the first part of the robustness $[\![\mathcal{M}(x), \Box_I \neg\varphi_{\mathsf{cond}}]\!]$ becomes less than zero, then with this input x, the corresponding behavior of the system $\mathcal{M}(x)$ satisfies the antecedent condition φ_{cond}.

Based on this observation, we propose the **GP-UCB** with domain estimation algorithm. Pseudocode of the algorithm is available in Algorithm 4. This algorithm takes a hyper parameter R which stands for a target hit rate, that is, how large ratio of the input $x[1], \dots, x[N]$ steer the model to satisfy the antecedent condition. In each iteration round of the falsification, to guarantee both fast minimization and enough testing on which φ_{cond} holds, we pick the next input by the following strategy: (1) calculate how many ratio r of the input should make φ_{cond} true through the remaining iteration; (2) estimate the input subdomain $D' \subset D$ in which the antecedent condition φ_{cond} holds with probability r; (3) from the restricted domain $x \in D'$, pick a new input x to falsify the whole specification in the **GP-UCB** manner.

5 Experiments

To examine that our **GP-UCB** with domain estimation algorithm achieves both fast minimization and enough testing with the antecedent condition φ_{cond}.

As a model of the CPSs, we choose the powertrain control verification benchmark [11]. This is an engine model with a controller which try to keep the air/fuel ratio in the exhaust gas. This model has 3-dimensional input parameters, and the controller have mainly two modes—feedback mode and feed-forward mode. As conditional safety specifications to falsify, we experiment with the following **STL** formula φ. In this formula, the antecedent condition is mode = feedforward, that is, we would like to observe behavior of the system in the feed-forward mode.

$$\Box_{[\tau,\infty)}\left(\neg(\text{mode} = \text{feedforward}) \vee |\text{ratio}_{A/F}| < 0.2\right) \tag{1}$$

In fact of the model, the formula (1) does not have any counterexample input, and with the original **GP-UCB** algorithm, about 58 % of the input leads the whole systems to feed-forward mode. Then, we run our **GP-UCB** with domain estimation algorithm with setting the target hit rate as $R = 0.8$, and observe that about 79 % of the inputs satisfy the antecedent condition.

6 Conclusion

To solve falsification of conditional safety properties with enforcing the generated inputs to satisfy the antecedent condition, we provide an optimization algorithm based on Gaussian process regression techniques.

References

1. Alur, R., Feder, T., Henzinger, T.A.: The benefits of relaxing punctuality. J. ACM **43**(1), 116–146 (1996)
2. Annpureddy, Y., Liu, C., Fainekos, G., Sankaranarayanan, S.: S-TaLiRo: a tool for temporal logic falsification for hybrid systems. In: Abdulla, P.A., Leino, K.R.M. (eds.) TACAS 2011. LNCS, vol. 6605, pp. 254–257. Springer, Heidelberg (2011)
3. Bartocci, E., Bortolussi, L., Nenzi, L., Sanguinetti, G.: On the robustness of temporal properties for stochastic models. In: Dang, T., Piazza, C. (eds.) Proceedings Second International Workshop on Hybrid Systems and Biology, HSB 2013, Taormina, Italy, 2nd September 2013, vol. 125 of EPTCS, pp. 3–19 (2013)
4. Bartocci, E., Bortolussi, L., Nenzi, L., Sanguinetti, G.: System design of stochastic models using robustness of temporal properties. Theor. Comput. Sci. **587**, 3–25 (2015)
5. Chen, G., Sabato, Z., Kong, Z.: Active requirement mining of bounded-time temporal properties of cyber-physical systems. CoRR abs/1603.00814 (2016)
6. Donzé, A.: Breach, a toolbox for verification and parameter synthesis of hybrid systems. In: Touili, T., Cook, B., Jackson, P. (eds.) CAV 2010. LNCS, vol. 6174, pp. 167–170. Springer, Heidelberg (2010)
7. Donzé, A., Maler, O.: Robust satisfaction of temporal logic over real-valued signals. In: Chatterjee, K., Henzinger, T.A. (eds.) FORMATS 2010. LNCS, vol. 6246, pp. 92–106. Springer, Heidelberg (2010)
8. Fainekos, G.E., Pappas, G.J.: Robustness of temporal logic specifications for continuous-time signals. Theor. Comput. Sci. **410**(42), 4262–4291 (2009)
9. Hoxha, B., Abbas, H., Fainekos, G.: Benchmarks for temporal logic requirements for automotive systems. In: Proceedings of Applied Verification for Continuous and Hybrid Systems (2014)

10. Jegourel, C., Legay, A., Sedwards, S.: Importance splitting for statistical model checking rare properties. In: Sharygina, N., Veith, H. (eds.) CAV 2013. LNCS, vol. 8044, pp. 576–591. Springer, Heidelberg (2013)

11. Jin, X., Deshmukh, J.V., Kapinski, J., Ueda, K., Butts, K.: Powertrain control verification benchmark. In: Fränzle, M., Lygeros, J. (eds.) 17th International Conference on Hybrid Systems: Computation and Control (part of CPS Week), HSCC 2014, Berlin, Germany, 15–17 April 2014, pp. 253–262. ACM (2011)

12. Maler, O., Nickovic, D.: Monitoring temporal properties of continuous signals. In: Lakhnech, Y., Yovine, S. (eds.) FORMATS 2004 and FTRTFT 2004. LNCS, vol. 3253, pp. 152–166. Springer, Heidelberg (2004)

13. Rasmussen, C.E., Williams, C.K.I.: Gaussian Processes for Machine Learning (Adaptive Computation and Machine Learning). The MIT Press, Massachusetts (2005)

14. Sankaranarayanan, S., Fainekos, G.: Falsification of temporal properties of hybrid systems using the cross-entropy method. In: Proceedings of the 15th ACM International Conference on Hybrid Systems: Computation and Control, HSCC 2012, pp. 125–134. ACM, New York (2012)

15. Srinivas, N., Krause, A., Kakade, S., Seeger, M.W.: Gaussian process optimization in the bandit setting: no regret and experimental design. In: Fürnkranz, J., Joachims, T. (eds.) Proceedings of the 27th International Conference on Machine Learning (ICML 2010), 21–24 June 2010, Haifa, Israel, pp. 1015–1022. Omnipress (2010)

16. Srinivas, N., Krause, A., Kakade, S.M., Seeger, M.W.: Information-theoretic regret bounds for Gaussian process optimization in the bandit setting. IEEE Trans. Inf. Theor. **58**(5), 3250–3265 (2012)

Reactive Property Monitoring of Hybrid Systems with Aggregation

Nicolas Rapin[⊠]

CEA LIST, Boîte Courrier 174, 91191 Gif sur Yvette, France
nicolas.rapin@cea.fr

Abstract. This work is related to our monitoring tool called ARTi-Mon for the property monitoring of hybrid systems. We explain how the aggregation operator of its language derives naturally from a generalization of the eventually operator as introduced by Maler and Nickovik for $MITL_{[a,b]}$. We present its syntax and its semantics using an interval-based representation of piecewise-constant functions. We define an on-line algorithm for its semantics calculus coupled with an elimination of irrelevant intervals in order to keep the memory resource bounded.

1 Introduction

Property monitoring is a unified solution in order to detect failures at many stages of systems life-cycle. Supervision, applied during exploitation phase, requires *reactive* monitoring: monitors have to run on-line, in real time and indefinitely. The motivation of our work is to define an expressive specification language suitable for systems evolving in dense time, like continuous and hybrid systems, coupled to an effective monitoring approach suitable for supervision purpose. In this short paper we restrict the presentation of this approach to one single operator, called the aggregation operator, which makes more expressive real time temporal logics restricted to the boolean type or to a booleanization [5] of non-boolean types. Our presentation is strongly based on a work due to Maler and Nickovic [4]. *Signals* and the *eventually* operator are recalled and discussed in Sect. 2. Section 3 is dedicated to the *aggregation* operator and gives some examples of properties. Section 4 describes an algorithm for reactive monitoring of aggregation properties.

2 Signals

In [4] Maler and Nickovik study $MITL_{[a,b]}$ a bounded version of $MITL$ and its interpretation over behaviors of continuous and hybrid systems modelled by *signals* defined as partial piecewise-constant boolean time functions satisfying the *finite variability* property. Formally, a signal s is a function ranging in $\mathbb{B} = \{\bot, \top\}$ and whose time definition domain is a bounded interval of $\mathbb{R}$, noted $|s|$. This domain is bounded because, in the context of monitoring a running system always delivers a partial trace. But as time elapses the monitoring process extends the domain

Y. Falcone and C. Sanchez (Eds.): RV 2016, LNCS 10012, pp. 447–453, 2016.
DOI: 10.1007/978-3-319-46982-9_28

of signals i.e. $|s|$ is successively of the forms $\emptyset$, δ_1, $\delta_1 \cup \delta_2$, ... where δ_i, δ_{i+1} are adjacent intervals ($\delta_i \cup \delta_{i+1}$ is an interval and $\delta_i \cap \delta_{i+1} = \emptyset$) satisfying $\delta_i \prec \delta_{i+1}$ (which holds if $t < t'$ holds for any $t \in \delta_i$, $t' \in \delta_{i+1}$). Of course monitoring produces only *conservative* extensions: noting s_n the signal s at the nth extension, for any $n > 1$, the restriction of s_{n+1} to $|s_n|$ is s_n. The *finite variability* property ensures that any signal can be represented by a finite and minimal set of intervals carrying the value $\top$ (called *positive* intervals). Notice that finite variability does not imply the *bounded variability* property which is satisfied when the function changes with a bounded rate $\chi \in \mathbb{N}$ (i.e. at most χ variations over any interval of length 1). A signal changing n times on $[n, n+1[$ satisfies finite variability but not bounded variability. The *eventually* operator is derived from the *until* operator primary in $MITL_{[a,b]}$. Its syntax is $\Diamond_i \phi$ where ϕ is a boolean sub-term and i a bounded interval of $\mathbb{R}^+$. Its semantics is defined with $\models$ called the *satisfaction relation*: $(s,t) \models \Diamond_i \phi$ iff $\exists t' \in t \oplus i.(s,t') \models \phi$ where $t \oplus i$ denotes the interval i shifted of t (for example $t \oplus [a,b[$ is $[t+a, t+b[$). Notice that notation $(s,t') \models \phi$ is equivalent to $s(t') = \top$ when s is a time function. As far as we know the relation $\models$ comes from model theory. Using it subsumes that signals are considered as models and that all terms of the logic should be interpreted with respect to those models. Our approach, which constitutes one of our contribution, is different. We do not really interpret terms over models as usual. Instead we consider there exists a set of *ground signals* and that operators of a logic proceed as constructors for building new time functions or, as it will be proven, new signals. According to this point of view the term $\Diamond_i \phi$ builds a time function noted $(\Diamond_i \phi)$ (we add parenthesis to the term to denote the function it builds) which derives inductively from (ϕ). Let us begin by the definition of $(\Diamond_i \phi)(t)$ and secondly we will focus on its definition domain. Derived from the above definition based on $\models$ relation, a first definition is: $(\Diamond_i \phi)(t) = \top$ iff $\exists t' \in (t \oplus i).(\phi)(t') = \top$. Another equivalent definition can be given by introducing the set of values taken by a time function over a restriction of its domain. Let g be a signal and r satisfying $r \subseteq |g|$ then $g(r)$ denotes the set $\{g(t)/t \in r\}$. The semantics definition of an eventually terms at a time instant becomes:

Definition 1 (Eventually as Aggregation). $(\Diamond_i \phi)(t) = \bigvee_{b \in (\phi)(t \oplus i)} b$

Since (ϕ) is a boolean function we have $(\phi)(t \oplus i) \subseteq \{\bot, \top\}$. It suffices that $\top \in (\phi)(t \oplus i)$ for $(\Diamond_i \phi)$ being true at t. This definition emphasis the fact that the eventually modality is the result of the aggregation of a set of values using *disjunction*. Extending this aggregation notion, which is the main idea of this work, will be studied below. For now let us define $|(\Diamond_i \phi)|$. We consider that $(\Diamond_i \phi)$ is *reliable* at time instant t if $(t \oplus i) \subseteq |(\phi)|$. We define $|(\Diamond_i \phi)|$ as the set of all reliable time instants, so $|(\Diamond_i \phi)| = \{t/t \oplus i \subseteq |(\phi)|\}$. We will note this latter set $i \leftrightsquigarrow |(\phi)|$ in the sequel. As $|(\phi)|$ is a bounded interval it is also a bounded interval.

Definition 2 (Eventually Semantics). Let ϕ be a boolean signal.
$$|(\Diamond_i \phi)| = i \leftrightsquigarrow |(\phi)| \qquad (\Diamond_i \phi)(t) = \bigvee_{b \in (\phi)(t \oplus i)} b$$

Remark. A important point to notice here, which constitutes one of our contribution, is that the completeness and reliability of the domain enables an incremental and inductive computation of signals. *Basic Case*: as mentioned in Sect. 2 the extension of a ground signal is conservative. *Induction Step*: consider the conservative extension of (ϕ) from domain D to $D \cup \lambda$. According to Definition 2 the domain $|(\Diamond_i \phi)|$ is extended from $i \rightsquigarrow D$ to $i \rightsquigarrow (D \cup \lambda)$. By induction hypothesis (ϕ) remains the same on D. It follows that $(\Diamond_i \phi)$ remains the same on $i \rightsquigarrow D$. Hence the extension of $(\Diamond_i \phi)$ is also conservative. Thus one has to compute $(\Diamond_i \phi)$ only on $\Delta = (i \rightsquigarrow (D \cup \lambda)) \setminus (i \rightsquigarrow D)$ in order to know the function $(\Diamond_i \phi)$ on $i \rightsquigarrow (D \cup \lambda)$. One can already feel the benefit of such a restriction for the on-line calculus. It will be detailed below in Sect. 4.

Lemma 1 (Signal Property Conservation). *If (ϕ) is a signal then the time function $(\Diamond_i \phi)$, as defined in Definition 2, is also a signal.*

We have already mentioned that $|(\Diamond_i \phi)|$ defined as $i \rightsquigarrow |(\phi)|$ is bounded (in the algorithm below we give an operational calculus for $i \rightsquigarrow |(\phi)|$). What remains to be proved is that $(\Diamond_i \phi)$ satisfies the finite variability property. To establish this we need to describe the operational semantics calculus of $(\Diamond_i \phi)$. The so-called *backward propagation* proposed in [4] plays an important role in this calculus. For the ease of the presentation, in an algorithmic context, any signal is assimilated to its interval based representation being a chronologically ordered list of positive intervals (i.e. ordered by $\prec$). It is also useful to formalize intervals and their associated operations before introducing backward propagation. Formally an interval is a 4-tuple (l, lb, ub, u) of $\mathbb{B} \times \mathbb{R} \times \mathbb{R} \times \mathbb{B}$ (for example $(\top, a, b, \bot)$ stands for $[a, b[$. We use pointed notation to denote interval attributes: $(l, a, b, u).ub$ denotes b. The opposite of i, noted $-i$ is $(i.u, -i.ub, -i.lb, i.l)$; notation $t \oplus i$ stands for $(i.l, t + i.lb, t + i.ub, i.u)$ and $t \ominus i$ for $t \oplus -i$. The $\oplus$ operation can be extended to an interval: given k, i two intervals, $k \oplus i$ denotes $\bigcup_{t \in k} t \oplus i$ which is $(k.l \wedge i.l, k.lb + i.lb, k.ub + i.ub, k.u \wedge i.u)$. A valued interval is an interval carrying a value. $val(i)$ denotes the value carried by i. For example a boolean positive interval is an interval carrying the value $\top$.

Backward Propagation. Let us suppose that for $t' \in |(\phi)|$ we have $\phi(t') = \top$ then also $(\Diamond_i \phi)(t) = \top$ provided t satisfies $t' \in t \oplus i$ i.e. $t \in t' \oplus -i$. The interval $t' \oplus -i$, also noted $t' \ominus i$, is the *backward propagation* of the true value of ϕ at t'. This can be extended to an interval: if ϕ is valid over k then also $(\Diamond_i \phi)$ over $k \ominus i$. Given that signals representations are based on positive intervals, an algorithm for computing $(\Diamond_i \phi)$ could be the following. *Init* : $(\Diamond_i \phi) = \emptyset$. *Iteration* : for all interval k of (ϕ) aggregate $j = k \ominus i$ to $(\Diamond_i \phi)$. *Post$-$Treatment* : merge adjacent intervals of $(\Diamond_i \phi)$ (until no more adjacent can be found). We will refer to this algorithm as the *off-line* algorithm as (ϕ) is assumed to exist as an input. In the Iteration step *aggregate* has different meanings depending on how j covers the existing positive intervals of $(\Diamond_i \phi)$: if covers none it is purely added to $(\Diamond_i \phi)$; if covers some empty spaces, each empty space covered by j is converted into a positive interval added to $(\Diamond_i \phi)$. The merging step is achieved in order to obtain minimality of the representation. It follows that the backward propagation of one interval of ϕ produces three kind of modifications of $(\Diamond_i\phi)$: (1) it adds one interval (2) it extends one interval (3) it reduces the number of intervals (when j fills the gap between intervals which are merged). By induction hypothesis (ϕ) is a signal; it satisfies the finite variability property and hence its interval representation is composed of a finite number of positive intervals. So according to modifications $(1),(2),(3)$ it is also the case for $(\Diamond_i\phi)$ which satisfies the finite variability assumption; hence it is a signal. With the same argumentation we can prove that bounded variability is preserved.

3   Aggregation Operator

Our idea, firstly appearing in [6], of the aggregation operator stems from the algorithm described in the previous Section. Let us interpret propagation as an aggregation process. Distinguishing $(\Diamond_i\phi)$ before (with superscript bf) the propagation of k and after (with superscript af) we have $\forall t \in k \ominus i.(\Diamond_i\phi)^{af}(t) = \top \vee (\Diamond_i\phi)^{bf}(t)$. This equality shows that $\top$ is aggregated by disjunction to the value of $(\Diamond_i\phi)^{bf}$ for every t of $k \ominus i$. This is coherent with Definition 2 relating eventually modality with disjunction. Now ϕ could have another type than boolean type and the aggregation could be based on other functions than disjunction. This is what we investigate in the remainder. A non-boolean signal differs from a boolean one by its range which is of the form $E = E' \times \{\emptyset\}$ where E' gives the type of the signals. Notice that a non-boolean signal may takes the value $\emptyset$ which stands for the *undefined* value. Interval based representations of non-boolean signals is also based on positive intervals whose definition is extended to intervals not carrying the special value $\emptyset$. The syntax for an aggregation term is $\mathcal{A}\{f\}_i\phi$ where f is an aggregation function, i is an interval of $\mathbb{R}$ with finite bounds and ϕ is a term. An aggregation function is any binary function $f(e,a)$ which aggregates an element e to an aggregate a (where a can be the special value $\emptyset$). Formally it is a function of $E \times A \to A$ where E and A are sets, both containing the special value noted $\emptyset$, and satisfying $f(\emptyset,a) = a$. A term $\mathcal{A}\{f\}_i\phi$ is well formed if ϕ and f are compatible regarding their types: if range of ϕ is E then f must be of the form $E \times A \to A$. Then $\mathcal{A}\{f\}_i\phi$ type is $A \setminus \{\emptyset\}$. **Examples of aggregation functions**. Let $max\_min : \mathbb{R} \times ((\mathbb{R} \times \mathbb{R}) \cup \{\emptyset\}) \to ((\mathbb{R} \times \mathbb{R}) \cup \{\emptyset\})$ be the aggregation function satisfying: $max\_min(x,(M,m)) = (max(x,M),min(x,m))$, $max\_min(x,\emptyset) = (x,x)$. Let $sum(e,a) : \mathbb{R} \times (\mathbb{R} \cup \{\emptyset\}) \to (\mathbb{R} \cup \{\emptyset\})$ satisfying $sum(e,a) = e+a$, $sum(e,\emptyset) = e$; $disj$ satisfying $disj(e,a) = e \vee a$, $disj(e,\emptyset) = e$. For aggregation the backward propagation satisfies: $\forall t \in k \ominus i.(\mathcal{A}\{f\}_i\phi)^{af}(t) = f(val(k),(\mathcal{A}\{f\}_i\phi)^{bf}(t))$. If f is an aggregation function we note $\overline{f}$ its extension to finite sequences. For $e_1, \ldots, e_n$ being elements of E it satisfies: $\overline{f}(()) = \emptyset$ and $\overline{f}((e_1,\ldots,e_n)) = f(e_n,\overline{f}((e_1, \ldots, e_{n-1})))$. For Definition 1 we introduced $g(r)$ denoting a set of values, for general aggregation we need to denote a sequence. Let g be a signal and $r \subset |g|$ be an interval, it follows that the restriction of g to r is the concatenation of a finite number of constant functions $g_1 \to c_1, \ldots, g_n \to c_n$ satisfying $|g_w| \prec |g_{w+1}|$ for $w \in [1, n-1]$. We note $g_{seq}(r)$ the sequence $(c_1, \ldots, c_n)$.

Definition 3 (Aggregation). Let ϕ be a signal of range E, i a bounded interval of $\mathbb{R}$, and f an aggregation function of $E \times A \to A$ then: $|(\mathcal{A}\{f\}_i\phi)| = i \looparrowright |(\phi)|$, $(\mathcal{A}\{f\}_i\phi)(t) = \overline{f}((\phi)_{seq}(t \oplus i))$

Though Maler and Nickovic introduce also in [4] non-boolean signals in their logic, those are always composed with non-temporal predicative functions reducing the composition to the boolean framework. We claim that with the aggregation the logic is more expressive as one can form terms with a spread temporal dependency (not reduced to current time). The off-line semantics calculus for $(\mathcal{A}\{f\}_i\phi)$ can be obtained by achieving a slight modification of the backward propagation in the algorithm described for the eventually modality. Iteration over intervals of (ϕ) is achieved in the chronological order. At each step of the iteration, it aggregates $j = k \ominus i$ with value $val(k)$ to $(\mathcal{A}\{f\}_i\phi)$. Due to the chronological iteration, there is only three cases: (1) j covers an empty space beyond (w.r.t $\prec$), if any, all positive intervals of $(\mathcal{A}\{disj\}_i\phi)$; this space is converted into an interval with value $f(val(k), \emptyset)$ and added (2) the value of any interval $m \subseteq j$ is changed to $f(val(k), val(m))$ (3) it may exists one interval m partially covered by j, it is split in two, the uncovered part value is set to $val(m)$ and the covered to $f(val(k), val(m))$. It follows that one propagation adds at most two intervals into $(\mathcal{A}\{disj\}_i\phi)$. The number of intervals of $(\mathcal{A}\{disj\}_i\phi)$ is then at most the double of (ϕ).

Examples. Notice that $\Diamond_i\phi$ and $\mathcal{A}\{disj\}_i\phi$ are equivalent. Invariant $a \Rightarrow \mathcal{A}\{disj\}_{[-1,1]}\ b$ specifies that b should be always present around a in a the time window $[-1, 1]$. Notice that our logic supports pairing of signals and the application of functions and predicates like STL [5]. For example if (s, s') is a pair of signals and g a binary function or predicate $g(s, s')(t) = g(s(t), s'(t))$. For readability we may note $s\ g\ s'$ instead of $g(s, s')$ (typically $s < s'$ for $< (s, s')$). Example 2. *The variation of the flow over* 60 s *should be under* 10 *percent*. Let us consider this term $\div(\mathcal{A}\{max\_min\}_{[-60,0]}\ flow)$. At t its value is $\div(M, m) = M \div m$ where M and m are respectively the max and the min values of $flow$ over $t \oplus [-60, 0]$. The invariant is then formalized by: $\div(\mathcal{A}\{max\_min\}_{[-60,0]}\ flow) < 1.1$. Example 3. *When the temperature is under* 10 *degrees the motor should not be started more than* 3 *times during the next hour*. Here we consider that *motor_starts* function has the form of a Dirac function (its value is 0 except at some time instants where its value is 1). The invariant is formalized by: $(temp < 10) \Rightarrow (\mathcal{A}\{sum\}_{[0,3600]}\ motor\_starts \leq 3)$. Example 4. With $inc(e, a)$ satisfying $inc(e, \emptyset) = (\top, e)$, $inc(e, (b, a)) = ((e > a) \wedge b, e)$ the invariant $motor\_starts \Rightarrow (\mathcal{A}\{inc\}_{[0,150]}temp)[0]$ formalizes *temperature should not decrease for* 150 s *after the motor starts*. Example 5. $\mathcal{A}\{owr\}_{[c,c]}\phi$ where owr (for *overwrite*) satisfies: $owr(x, \emptyset) = x$, $owr(x, y) = x$ shifts (ϕ) of c in time.

4 On-Line Monitoring

For us supervision consists in checking that some invariants remain true. To achieve this we exploit the remark made in Sect. 2 about an incremental semantics calculus completed it with a garbage collection mechanism which, assuming ground signals satisfy also the bounded variability property (see Sect. 2), keeps the memory bounded. Our on-line algorithm for $(\mathcal{A}\{f\}_i\phi)$ is called after (ϕ) has been extended. *start* denotes an interval of ϕ or *nil* and $nxt(i)$ denotes, if exists, the next interval in the list containing i else *nil*. *Dom* is an interval initially being $\emptyset$. Basically the algorithm restricts the off-line calculus to the domain extension and remembers, thanks to *start*, where to restart the iteration. $(\phi).last$ denotes the last interval of the interval representation of (ϕ).

Step 0. If $Dom \neq \emptyset$ goto Step 2.

Step 1. If $Dom = i \looparrowright |(\phi)|$ is equal to $\emptyset$ then RETURN else perform off-line calculus on Dom; make *start* refers to $(\phi).last$; RETURN.

Step 2. $\Delta = (i \looparrowright |(\phi)|) \setminus Dom$. While $((start \ominus i) \prec \Delta$ and $nxt(start) \neq nil)$ do $start = nxt(start)$.

Step 3. Perform the off-line algorithm on domain Δ by iterating on (ϕ) from *start*. Concatenate result over Δ to Dom. $Dom = (i \looparrowright |(\phi)|)$. RETURN.

Now let us examine which part of (ϕ) is irrelevant regarding the computation of any extension of $(\mathcal{A}\{f\}_i\phi)$ i.e. regarding the next call. It is clear that t' is *irrelevant* if its propagation $t' \ominus i$ does not exceed Dom i.e. if $t' \ominus i$ is included in $Dom^{-\infty} = (\bot, -\infty, (i \looparrowright |(\phi)|).ub, (i \looparrowright |(\phi)|).u)$ being the left-unbounded version of Dom. This is equivalent to have $t' \in (-i \looparrowright Dom^{-\infty})$ or $t' \in (i.u \Rightarrow \bot, -\infty + i.ub, |(\phi)|.ub - i.ub + i.lb, i.l \Rightarrow (i.u \Rightarrow |(\phi)|).u))$. The main interesting data is the upper bound $|(\phi)|.ub - i.ub + i.lb = |(\phi)|.ub - (i.ub - i.lb)$ revealing the constant value $(i.ub - i.lb)$. Finally for computing further extension of $(\mathcal{A}\{f\}_i\phi)$ only the definition of (ϕ) over is useful $Dom \setminus (-i \looparrowright Dom^{-\infty})$ proved to have always the constant length $(i.ub - i.lb)$. If ϕ is sub-term of several terms each determining a relevant interval we choose the larger one. Suppose now that ground signals satisfy bounded variability and that their extension are always bounded (in length or in number of new intervals). With our definition of time domains and the argumentation used for Lemma 1 one can show it is preserved for complex terms. Then firstly the number of intervals over the relevant interval is bounded, say by K_ϕ. And secondly an extension of ϕ is bounded in number of new intervals, let us say by $N_\phi \in \mathbb{N}$. So, when the extension of (ϕ) is computed the monitor must preserve K_ϕ intervals for upper terms and create at most N_ϕ new intervals, for a total cost of $K_\phi + N_\phi$ intervals. This principle, extended to all operators of our logic and applied to all sub-terms of invariants ensures that the memory resource remains bounded.

Related Works. We firstly introduced aggregation in [6]. It has been studied by Basin et al. in [1,2] for discrete sequences of data. In this work aggregation calculus is based on sliding windows bringing potentially some complexity reduction for associative functions. Earlier Finkbeiner et al. [3] studied an extension of LTL with aggregation in order to collect statistics over runtime executions.

5   Conclusion and Future Works

Starting from the eventually operator of $MITL_{[a,b]}$, we defined an aggregation operator suitable for specifying complex invariants about hybrid systems. Main principles of our reactive monitoring approach have been presented, though only focused on the bounded aggregation of our logic. In future works we plan to expose how the same principles extend to conventional modalities like *since, until*, or to less conventional like the unbounded aggregation operator and to operators strongly inspired by the interval based operational calculus, like for example the *incremental length* operator which, combined with aggregation, can express properties involving integrals.

References

1. Basin, D., Klaedtke, F., Marinovic, S., Zălinescu, E.: Monitoring of temporal first-order properties with aggregations. Form. Meth. Syst. Des. **46**(3), 262–285 (2015)
2. Basin, D., Klaedtke, F., Zălinescu, E.: Greedily computing associative aggregations on sliding windows. Inf. Process. Lett. **115**(2), 186–192 (2015)
3. Finkbeiner, B., Sankaranarayanan, S., Sipma, H.B.: Collecting statistics over runtime executions. Form. Meth. Syst. Des. **27**(3), 253–274 (2005)
4. Maler, O., Nickovic, D.: Monitoring temporal properties of continuous signals. In: Lakhnech, Y., Yovine, S. (eds.) FORMATS 2004 and FTRTFT 2004. LNCS, vol. 3253, pp. 152–166. Springer, Heidelberg (2004)
5. Nickovic, D., Maler, O.: AMT: a property-based monitoring tool for analog systems. In: Raskin, J.-F., Thiagarajan, P.S. (eds.) FORMATS 2007. LNCS, vol. 4763, pp. 304–319. Springer, Heidelberg (2007). doi:10.1007/978-3-540-75454-1_22
6. Rapin, N.: Procede et dispositif permettant de generer un systeme de controle a partir de comportements redoutes specifies. PCT/Ep. 2011/072221, December 2011

Integration of Runtime Verification into Metamodeling for Simulation and Code Generation (Position Paper)

Fernando Macias[1](✉), Torben Scheffel[2](✉), Malte Schmitz[2](✉), and Rui Wang[1](✉)

[1] Bergen University College, Bergen, Norway
{fernando.macias,rui.wang}hib.no
[2] Institute for Software Engineering and Programming Languages,
University of Lübeck, Lübeck, Germany
{scheffel,schmitz}@isp.uni-luebeck.de

Abstract. Runtime verification is an approach growing in popularity to verify the correctness of complex and distributed systems by monitoring their executions. Domain Specific Modeling Languages are a technique used for specifying such systems in an abstract way, but still close to the solution domain. This paper aims at integrating runtime verification and domain specific modeling into the development process of complex systems. Such integration is achieved by linking the elements of the system model with the atomic propositions of the temporal correctness properties used to specify monitors. We provide a unified approach used for both the code generation and the simulation of the system through instance model transformations. This unification allows to check correctness properties on different abstraction levels of the modeled system.

1 Introduction

Modeling is a well-established practice in the development of big and complex software systems. Some of the more widespread approaches (e.g. Unified Modeling Language, UML) comprise the use of several general-purpose modeling languages. The models created with each of these modeling languages are then interconnected or related to one another. In recent years, general-purpose modeling languages are being replaced by Domain Specific Modeling Languages in many cases [6]. These languages define the structure, semantics and constraints for models related to the same application domain [12]. Among the reasons for the adoption of DSMLs one can mention their understandability by domain experts, capacity for high-level abstraction, user friendliness and tailoring to the problem space [6]. Besides, DSMLs inherit some of the advantages of general-purpose modeling, such as an improvement of efficiency for development and simulation.

This work is supported in part by the European Cooperation in Science and Technology (COST Action ARVI) and the BMBF project CONIRAS under number 01IS13029.

Y. Falcone and C. Sanchez (Eds.): RV 2016, LNCS 10012, pp. 454–461, 2016.
DOI: 10.1007/978-3-319-46982-9_29

However, the use of DSMLs does not completely shield the produced software from bugs or man-made mistakes. Software failures may still occur on complex systems due to a variety of reasons such as design errors, hardware breakdown or network problems. These failures require that verification methods are integrated into the development process. The use of such methods during the specification of a system can greatly improve their reliability. Unfortunately, testing is seldom exhaustive and cannot always guarantee correctness. An exhaustive option to check every execution path is model checking. But this alternative may suffer the state space explosion problem [10], especially relevant in distributed systems due to their inherent non-determinism. Yet another possibility in the system verification domain is to use runtime verification (RV). RV can cope with the inadequacies of testing by reacting to systems' failures as soon as they occur [9]. Also, it is a much more lightweight technique when compared to model checking, since only one execution path is checked. RV can be used to check whether an execution of a system violates a given correctness property. Such checking can be typically performed by using a monitor [10]. In its simplest form, a monitor decides whether the execution of a system satisfies a given correctness property by outputting either true or false. With runtime verification, the actual execution of the complex system may then be easily checked to ensure that the program does not violate given correctness properties.

This paper aims to effectively integrate runtime verification and domain specific modeling into the development of complex systems. This integration is achieved by linking the elements of domain specific models with the temporal correctness properties.

Related Work. Using models and runtime verification during the development of complex systems is not new. For example, in [8], common concepts of runtime models and the provision of a basis for the metamodeling are described, and a metamodeling process for runtime models is presented, which guides the creation of metamodels combining design time and runtime concepts. In [3], a system modeling approach is developed to allow design-time system models to be reused by an autonomous system, and a runtime verification framework is also proposed. A combination of runtime verification and a specific DSML has been used in [5]. The authors used their own modeling framework for component-based systems and extended it by an RV framework. Their approach has a similar direction, but our approach aims at modeling more abstractly while keeping the possibility of verifying low-level properties, with any DSML.

The rest of this paper is organized as follows: Sect. 2 recaps some basic notion of RV and DSMLs which are used throughout the paper. Section 3 presents the main contribution of this paper: the integration of runtime verification and DSMLs. Finally, a conclusion and an outlook are given in the last section.

2   Background

We view a system as having a state consisting of a set of atomic propositions. Thereby each atomic proposition can either be true or false, and the state of the

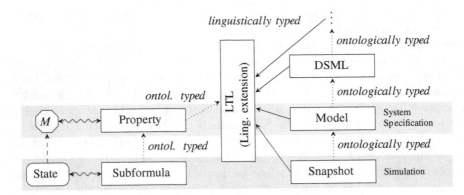

Fig. 1. Underlying multilevel model hierarchy with linguistic extension. Correctness properties of the system can be formulated in LTL, which is connected with the model as a linguistic extension. The property can be translated into a monitor, which accepts prefixes of the words in the language of the property. The System Specification is the abstraction layer of the most specific models which is used for the code generation. A Snapshot of the Model together with the not yet fulfilled Subformula or a State of the Monitor forms one state of the Simulation.

system at a certain point in time is given by the current value of each atomic proposition. Thus, a run of the system can be seen as an infinite sequence of those states and an execution is a finite prefix of such a run. In RV, we specify correctness properties based on the atomic propositions and generate monitors from them. With this, monitor statements about the correctness of the current execution of the system can then be made.

To be compatible with this view of a system, we define a multilevel modeling hierarchy [1] where the DSML and the actual model of the system are included. Moreover, the hierarchy includes instances of the system model that represent the particular state of the system at a given point in time (see Fig. 1). As presented in [11], this hierarchy borrows the concepts of multilevel modelling (with *ontological* typing relations), deep metamodelling [1] and linguistic extension [15] (hence the *linguistic* typing relations). To avoid ambiguities, we call the instances of the system model *snapshots*. A snapshot is also a model, and contains the set of active elements of the system. The way in which the system evolves during the simulation is described using model transformations (MT) that generate a new snapshot from the previous one. See [7,20] for similar approaches. In a simplistic way, this MTs remove elements which are not active anymore and create new active ones (see Fig. 2). To link both RV and DSMLs, we associate the atomic propositions, used in RV, with the current state of the system, represented as a snapshot of a domain specific model.

This is done by *matching*: this concept is defined as finding a particular set of elements in the current snapshot (match) or not (no match) in [11].

Snapshot *n*   Snapshot *n* + 1

Fig. 2. Sketch of the model transformation for transition triggering. A transition is triggered (its instance appears in a new snapshot) if it is connected to a task and an input in the model, which have active instances in the current snapshot.

3   Combining RV and DSMLs

DSMLs used for behavior generally have concepts along the lines of actions being executed and connections among them that define the flow sequence in which the actions are executed. In this section, we introduce our approach using an example DSML which is a simple realization of both kinds of concepts. Together with this DSML, we define the integration of its behavioral semantics with the evaluation of temporal properties. We achieve such integration by linking the elements of the DSML with the atomic propositions used in Linear Temporal Logic (LTL) formulas. All these parts are included in the modeling hierarchy depicted in Fig. 1.

3.1   Example of Behavioural DSML

The DSML used in the example defines three types of elements:

Input. Used to incorporate information from the environment into the model. Inputs allow the system to react to external stimuli, such as sensor information in a robot. Hence, inputs appear in a snapshot when any of the aforementioned happens, and disappear afterwards. Their appearance cause generally a change of state in the system (new snapshots).

Task. A specific action or set of actions executed by the system. A task is running if an instance of it appears in the current snapshot. Multiple tasks can run at the same time.

Transition. Represents the order in which tasks are executed. Every transition is connected to a source and a target task, and associated to one input. When the source task is running (i.e. appears in the current snapshot) and the associated input appears, the transition is triggered. After a transition is triggered, a new snapshot is generated in which the transition and the target task start running. Notice that a task may have more than one incoming transition, as well as multiple outgoing transitions. In the first case, as soon as any of the incoming transitions is fired, the target of that transition is activated. In the second case, all of the transitions with the same input are fired at the same time. That is, the target tasks of all fired transitions start running in parallel.

When the system is simulated, new snapshots are generated using model transformations. These transformations are not explained in detail here due to space limitations. A richer example similar to ours can be found in Table III of [16]. We adapted the syntax that the authors use in our example. Generally speaking, these model transformations are responsible for the simulation of inputs appearing, transitions being fired and tasks finishing (disappearing). Figure 2 shows an illustrative example of the MT for the triggering of a transition.

Inputs are used in our DSML to model all the possible happenings that may cause a change of state. The monitors used to evaluate temporal properties require that a snapshot is generated only when there is a change of state of the system, i.e. no two consecutive snapshots are the same. Besides, the monitors need to be aware of any registered input, even if it does not trigger any transition. Hence, inputs are modeled as triggers for transitions, but the appearance of an input in a snapshot is independent from the transitions that it may trigger.

Note that the execution of our system does not include any notion of time. In some cases it is nevertheless useful to model the expiration of a certain amount of time. We do this by introducing timers which raise a timeout after a specified time. A timer may be started on activating a task. In the model we abstract away from the time passing by and represent timeouts as regular inputs. The timeout inputs can be used like any other input in order to trigger a transition. In a nutshell, this allows us to handle time while keeping the discrete LTL semantics defined on a sequence of states.

3.2 Linking a DSML with Temporal Properties

As presented in [11], we implement the syntax of a temporal logic as a linguistic extension. This extension is orthogonal to the model hierarchy composed by the DSML, the particular system model, and the current snapshot (see Fig. 1).

The key concept of a linguistic extension for our work is the possibility to connect *any* type of element or set of elements in the modeling hierarchy to the model representing a temporal property. In this work, we will connect single elements in the snapshots to the temporal properties. As a consequence of this way of modeling LTL properties, an atomic proposition is a fragment of a model instance that may appear in a snapshot. The atomic propositions are evaluated as follows: If at least one match of the fragment appears in the current snapshot of the system, the atomic proposition is evaluated to true otherwise to false.

This connection of elements and atomic propositions allows us to look at the sequence of snapshots of a system as the execution of that system, from both RV and modelling points of view. So we can do runtime verification with temporal logics in a natural way based on those snapshots because they represent the states of the system during the execution. An example for this can be seen in Fig. 3. In this example we modeled a robot driving around. The figure shows how inputs are part of the model of the system, and at the same time are linked to the atomic propositions of the LTL formula. The correctness property given in Fig. 3 states that obstacles found in front of the robot disappear if the robot moves backwards. Otherwise the robot has found a moving obstacle coming after

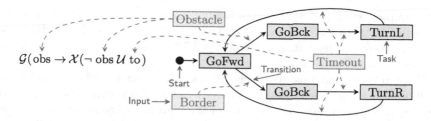

Fig. 3. Modeling of the behavior of a robot with an attached correctness property detecting moving obstacles. The robot can move forwards (GoFwd), move backwards (GoBck) and turn left or right (TurnL, TurnR). The transitions are activated by the inputs and activate the subsequent task. Obstacle and Input represent sensor inputs and Timeout represents the expiration of a timer started by GoBck, TurnL and TurnR. That is, Timeout is used to represent the amount of time that a Task takes to finish.

it. This property describes the environment of the robot and hence is specified using atomic propositions linked to inputs. Atomic propositions can be linked to tasks in the same way if the property expresses the behavior of the robot in a more direct way.

The connection of the atomic propositions to the elements enables us to expand our approach to different LTL semantics like LTL₃ [2] in order to report final fulfillment or violation of the correctness properties as soon as possible when monitoring. Also, we can expand to LTL extensions like timed LTL [14] that allows us to express real-time properties or add other theories for using variables instead of only boolean propositions [4], and quantified propositions [19].

Notice that the possibility of connecting any element (or set of them) to atomic propositions greatly enriches LTL via its atomic propositions.

4   Conclusion and Outlook

Our approach integrates behavioral models of DSMLs and correctness properties for RV through the whole software engineering process of design, simulation and code generation. For design, we provide a framework which allows to specify correctness properties as a linguistic extension of the DSML modeling hierarchy. In the simulation, a monitor and a model can be executed at once by synchronizing the model simulation and the monitor execution. Thereby the simulation is defined as a sequence of snapshots which are enriched with atomic propositions based on the match of certain elements in the snapshots. Finally, this synchronization between correctness properties and model execution is reused in order to execute the monitors and the designed system in the generated code for the target platform. The connection between the correctness property and the modeled behavior of the system is kept consistent throughout the whole software engineering process.

We implemented this approach in Eclipse EMF[1] and generated Python code for the ev3dev platform[2] in order to control Lego EV3 robots. The Python code for the monitors is generated by using the LTL_3 semantics with the logic and automata library LamaConv[3].

We plan to extend this approach for designing and verifying asynchronous distributed systems. Such systems generally have a huge state space generated by the environmental influence because of the high asynchronous fashion. Hence static verification approaches become difficult to use. With metamodeling, such systems can be designed in a more abstract way and monitors can be connected on multiple abstraction layers to the agents they should observe. To achieve such extension, we need to be able to model single agents of the distributed system and connect their actions with each other such that we can model their communication. Our goal is to increase the applicability of existing approaches of RV for asynchronous distributed systems like the ones in [13,17,18] by combining them with DSMLs as presented in this paper.

References

1. Atkinson, C., Kühne, T.: Reducing accidental complexity in domain models. Softw. Syst. Model. **7**(3), 345–359 (2008)
2. Bauer, A., Leucker, M., Schallhart, C.: Runtime verification for LTL and TLTL. ACM Trans. Softw. Eng. Methodol. **20**(4), 14:1–14:64 (2011)
3. Callow, G., Watson, G., Kalawsky, R.: System modelling for run-time verification and validation of autonomous systems. In: Proceedings of System of Systems Engineering (SoSE), pp. 1–7. IEEE (2010)
4. Decker, N., Leucker, M., Thoma, D.: Monitoring modulo theories. Softw. Tools Technol. Transf. (STTT) **18**(2), 205–225 (2016)
5. Falcone, Y., Jaber, M., Nguyen, T.H., Bozga, M., Bensalem, S.: Runtime verification of component-based systems in the BIP framework with formally-proved sound and complete instrumentation. Softw. Syst. Model. **14**(1), 173–199 (2015)
6. Fowler, M.: Domain-Specific Languages. Pearson Education, Essex (2010)
7. Ghamarian, A.H., de Mol, M., Rensink, A., Zambon, E., Zimakova, M.: Modelling and analysis using GROOVE. Softw. Tools Technol. Transf. (STTT) **14**(1), 15–40 (2012)
8. Lehmann, G., Blumendorf, M., Trollmann, F., Albayrak, S.: Meta-modeling runtime models. In: Dingel, J., Solberg, A. (eds.) MODELS 2010. LNCS, vol. 6627, pp. 209–223. Springer, Heidelberg (2011)
9. Leucker, M.: Teaching runtime verification. In: Khurshid, S., Sen, K. (eds.) RV 2011. LNCS, vol. 7186, pp. 34–48. Springer, Heidelberg (2012)
10. Leucker, M., Schallhart, C.: A brief account of runtime verification. J. Logic Algebraic Program. **78**(5), 293–303 (2009)
11. Macias, F., Rutle, A., Stolz, V.: A property specification language for runtime verification of executable models. In: Nordic Workshop on Programming Theory (NWPT). pp. 97–99, Technical report. RUTR-SCS16001, School of Computer Science, Reykjavik University (2015)

---

[1] www.eclipse.org/modeling/emf.
[2] www.ev3dev.org.
[3] www.isp.uni-luebeck.de/lamaconv.

12. Mellor, S.J.: MDA Distilled: Principles of Model-driven Architecture. Addison-Wesley Professional, Boston (2004)
13. Mostafa, M., Bonakdarpour, B.: Decentralized runtime verification of LTL specifications in distributed systems. In: Proceedings of Parallel and Distributed Processing Symposium (IPDPS), pp. 494–503. IEEE (2015)
14. Raskin, J., Schobbens, P.: The logic of event clocks - decidability, complexity and expressiveness. J. Autom. Lang. Comb. 4(3), 247–286 (1999)
15. Rossini, A., de Lara, J., Guerra, E., Rutle, A., Wolter, U.: A formalisation of deep metamodelling. Formal Aspects Comput. 26(6), 1115–1152 (2014)
16. Rutle, A., MacCaull, W., Wang, H., Lamo, Y.: A metamodelling approach to behavioural modelling. In: Proceedings of Behaviour Modelling-Foundations and Applications, pp. 5:1–5:10. ACM (2012)
17. Scheffel, T., Schmitz, M.: Three-valued asynchronous distributed runtime verification. In: Proceedings of Formal Methods and Models for Codesign, MEMOCODE, pp. 52–61. IEEE (2014)
18. Sen, K., Vardhan, A., Agha, G., Rosu, G.: Efficient decentralized monitoring of safety in distributed systems. In: Proceedings of Software Engineering (ICSE), pp. 418–427. IEEE (2004)
19. Stolz, V.: Temporal assertions with parametrized propositions. J. Log. Comput. 20(3), 743–757 (2010)
20. Wang, H., Rutle, A., MacCaull, W.: A formal diagrammatic approach to timed workflow modelling. In: Proceedings of Theoretical Aspects of Software Engineering (TASE), pp. 167–174. IEEE (2012)

Applying Runtime Monitoring for Automotive Electronic Development

Konstantin Selyunin[1(✉)], Thang Nguyen[2], Ezio Bartocci[1], and Radu Grosu[1]

[1] Vienna University of Technology, Treitlstr.3, Vienna, Austria
{konstantin.selyunin,ezio.bartocci,radu.grosu}@tuwien.ac.at
[2] Infineon Technologies Austria AG, Siemenstrasse 2, Villach, Austria
thang.nguyen@infineon.com

Abstract. This paper shows how runtime monitoring can be applied at different phases of electronic-product development in automotive industry. Starting with concept development, runtime monitors are generated from the product requirements and then embedded in a chip simulation to track the specification compliance at an early stage. In the later phase when a prototype or a product is available, the runtime monitors from the concept development are reused for synthesis into FPGA for monitoring the implementation correctness of the product/system during runtime tests at real-time speeds. This is advantageous for long-term test scenarios where simulation becomes impractical or where evaluation of large amounts of data is required. For example, about 480 K frames/min are exchanged between a sensor and an ECU. This is beyond the capability of an engineer to check the specification conformance of every frame even for one minute of the system run. We embed monitors in a real-world industrial case study, where we runtime-check the requirements of an automotive sensor interface both in simulation and for the test chip.

1 Introduction

Electronic components and software systems in the automotive industry are increasingly prominent: They already encompass up to 35 % of the costs of a car and they will continue to expand [1]. The compliance with the stricter safety standards (e.g. ISO 26262 [2]), the increase in the number of functions that the electronic systems of a vehicle must fulfill (ADAS [3], X-by-wire [4]), the tight time-to-market schedule, and the enlarged system complexity challenge the automotive electronic industry as never before. To overcome these challenges, chip manufacturers strive for solutions that help capture errors at all stages of the development cycle.

Sensors build up the front-end between the analog world and the digital electronic systems. They provide the required level of safety and comfort while driving: E.g., they detect the rotation angle of a steering wheel, the position of pedals, the pressure for launching airbags [5], the distance to surrounding objects (high-speed radar sensor), air pressure in tires (tire pressure monitor sensor, TPMS), etc. In this paper we show how runtime verification [6], a light-weight

Y. Falcone and C. Sanchez (Eds.): RV 2016, LNCS 10012, pp. 462–469, 2016.
DOI: 10.1007/978-3-319-46982-9_30

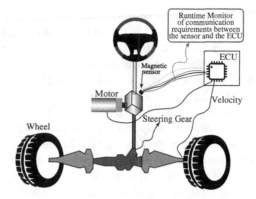

Fig. 1. Electronic power steering: two magnetic sensors measure the rotation angle of the steering wheel. The rotation angle is then sent to the electronic control unit (ECU). Based on the speed and the sensor data, the ECU activates the motor. The lower the speed, the more the motor is activated. This affects the ease of rotating the steering wheel.

state-of-the-art technique for checking compliance between a specification and a system at runtime, can be applied during sensor chip development. We consider a sensor that measures a magnetic field, from which the angle of the steering wheel can be calculated in an electronic power-steering application (Fig. 1).

The contributions of this paper can be summarized as follows:

1. To the best of our knowledge, we are the first to showcase runtime verification techniques in automotive sensor chip design and provide two use cases: Simulation and lab measurement.
2. In the first use case, the runtime monitors which are formalized and generated from product requirements are embedded in the test bench of a chip concept simulation. The implementation's correctness with respect to the requirements is then possible to monitor during simulation runtime.
3. In the second use case, the runtime monitors are reused and synthesized into an FPGA hardware for monitoring implementation correctness in the lab.
4. We demonstrate our approach on a real-world industrial case study, checking the communication protocol between a magnetic sensor and an ECU.

The rest of the paper is organized as follows: Sect. 2 discusses the related work. Section 3 elaborates on the use cases of runtime verification during chip design. Section 4 presents the case study and the experimental results. Section 5 offers our concluding remarks.

2   Related Work

Evaluating a temporal-logic specification φ over a trace or a signal is usually associated with either an automaton construction [7,8] or with the concept of a temporal tester [9]. In [7] the authors present a technique to build a deterministic timed automaton that accepts traces that satisfy an MTL formula φ. In [9] the authors proposed a compositional, transducer-like way of evaluating temporal logic formulas, threafter applied in hardware runtime monitoring [10].

Hardware runtime monitors for temporal logic properties [10–12] are usually generated directly in HDL languages (VHDL or Verilog). In this paper we apply High-Level Synthesis for RTL generation from the C/C++ code. Moreover, the application domains of hardware temporal logic monitoring in [11,12] are quite different from the chip design for the automotive industry.

FPGA-based development and emulation [13–15] are increasingly used in safety critical automotive electronic system development, as accelerated hardware models support real-time testing of both hardware and software at an early stage of the development and help overcome simulation bottlenecks.

3   Industrial Use Case

In this section we ellaborate on how runtime monitoring of signal-temporal-logic (STL) [16] requirements can be applied for both checking the conformance of a chip model and for testing the chip later on against the formalized requirements.

Figure 2 shows the flow of the runtime-monitors generation for the two use cases at Infineon Technologies Austria AG. In a first step, we formalize time-invariant product requirements, and obtain a set of temporal logic formulas. We use bounded-time STL as a specification language, due to its ability to handle analog-mixed-signal properties. In a next step we produce an equisatisfiable past STL formula [17], which will be used as formal specification for the use cases.

3.1   Use Case 1: Runtime Monitors in Simulation

The first use case, *Runtime Monitors in Simulation*, checks the implementation correctness of the developing electronic product. The use case draws inspiration from the offline monitoring framework [13]. However, simulation traces are simultaneously generated and checked against the product's requirements during the simulation runtime. Monitors are embedded in the toplevel test bench and are being simulated together with the Design-Under-Test. This allows one to run the chip model and the monitors at once and observe whether the chip model satisfies its formalized specification for different test cases (that correspond to various environmental conditions, power supply quality or fault injections).

We use the SystemC implementation of the STL temporal-operators ("behavior" Fig. 2). This allows us to speed up the implementation and to use the facilities of the SystemC and C++ libraries.

3.2   Use Case 2: Runtime Monitors for Lab Evaluation

At a later phase of the development, the chip is taped-out in the so-called engineering samples. These samples still need to be verified in the lab environment.

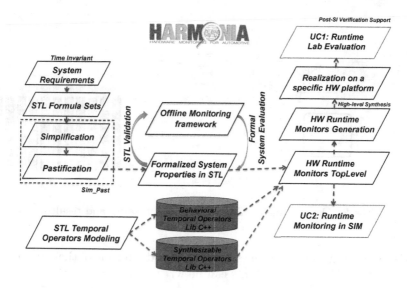

Fig. 2. Runtime monitoring generation flow

The key concept of use case 2 is to synthesize the monitors from use case 1 into FPGAs, to be used as an extended lab-equipment support for lab evaluation activities. This is especially true for the scenarios in which errors can be seen only after a certain test time. For example, hardware runtime errors, or scenarios including large amounts of data exchange between sensor and ECU. The aim is to guarantee that the implementation satisfies the requirements, under its operational condition, and sometimes under a stress condition.

In this use case runtime monitors are synthesized in an FPGA and run in parallel with the test hardware to keep up with the real-time sensor-ECU data exchange requirements. The C++ code ("synthesizable" in Fig. 2) is supplied to High-Level Synthesis [18] to generate RTL that can be put in FPGA. To be able to obtain efficient hardware implementation the code must use hardware precise data types and must not dynamically allocate memory.

4   Case Study: Automotive Sensor Interface

This section describes the runtime monitoring, both in simulation and in hardware, of the magnetic sensor used in electronic power steering (Fig. 1).

We monitor the temporal requirements of the communication protocol (PSI5) between the sensor and the ECU. To demonstrate our approach we build STL monitors for checking the shape of the data and synchronization pulses. The ECU sends synchronization pulse to the sensor via the voltage line. The sensor produces the reply by modulating the current. We monitor both, the voltage from

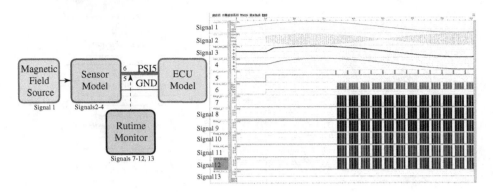

Fig. 3. The runtime monitor in simulation: setup and results

the ECU and the current from the sensor: raise and fall time of these pulses must not exceed t_{rise}. These requirements can be written in the past-STL:

rise_req: $\text{enter}(\text{high}) \rightarrow \text{trans} \, \mathcal{S}_{[0,t_{\text{rise}}]} \text{exit}(\text{low})$

fall_req: $\text{enter}(\text{low}) \rightarrow \text{trans} \, \mathcal{S}_{[0,t_{\text{rise}}]} \text{exit}(\text{high}),$

where $\text{enter}\varphi$ and $\text{exit}\varphi$ are syntactic sugar for $\ominus \neg \varphi \wedge \varphi$ and $\ominus \varphi \wedge \neg \varphi$.

Figure 3 shows the simulation setup and the result of a run of the chip model. A magnetic field - Signal 1 in Fig. 3 - is supplied to the sensor. Then the field values are sampled by an ADC and passed through a filter for internal processing in a sensor, Signals 2–4. After powering the chip and a passed stabilization time, the ECU sends synchronization pulses to the sensor (Signal 5, Fig. 3). In synchronization mode, each synchronization pulse sent by the ECU is responded by modulated sensor frames: Signal 6. Signals 7–12 in Fig. 3 are intermediate outputs of the sub-formula of the specification "rise_req" ("fall_req" is omitted from the picture for conciseness). Signal 13 is the output of the monitor, which, in this case, indicates that the requirement has been met.

To demonstrate the second use case, we generate the runtime monitors in FPGA and check the test chip. Figure 4 illustrates the lab setup: To emulate the ECU we use a signal generator that sends synchronization pulses to the test chip. The sensor replies with data packets, which are handled by an Analog Front-End (AFE). In the FPGA the transmission line between the sensor and the ECU is modeled (Fig. 1) to facilitate an evaluation of various system integration scenarios. We generate hardware monitors using Vivado HLS and integrate them to the output of the transmission line, where we check the same requirements as in the chip simulation (i.e. "req_rise"). We use the Xilinx debug core to observe the communication between the sensor and the ECU and the outputs of our monitors on the ChipScope (Fig. 5).

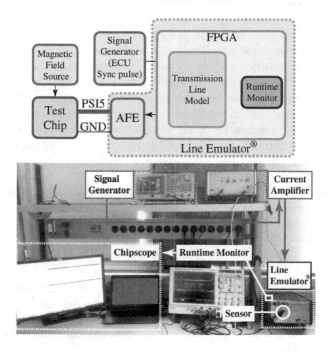

Fig. 4. Runtime monitor in hardware: lab setup

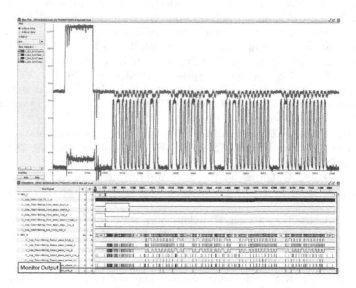

Fig. 5. Runtime monitor in hardware: chip scope results

5 Conclusion

In this paper we proposed and illustrated *the two use cases of runtime monitoring in the automotive electronic development*, and demonstrated their usefulness by checking the communication interface requirements of a steering-wheel magnetic sensor. We showed that runtime monitors can be included in a chip-concept simulation and that they can be later reused for requirements-monitoring in-the-lab after applying High Level Synthesis. Runtime monitoring in automotive electronic industry promises to speed up the verification process and can be considered as an additional tool to capture runtime bugs which could be very challenging to catch by classical in-the-lab approaches.

Acknowledgment. This research is supported by the project HARMONIA (845631), funded by a national Austrian grant from FFG (Österreichische Forschungsförder ungsgesellschaft) under the program IKT der Zukunft and the EU ICT COST Action IC1402 on Runtime Verification beyond Monitoring (ARVI).

References

1. Kolbe, M., Schoo, J.: Industry overview the automotive electronics industry in Germany. Germany Trade and Invest (2014)
2. ISO 26262: road vehicles Functional safety. International Organization for Standardization (ISO) (2011)
3. Okuda, R., Kajiwara, Y., Terashima, K.: A survey of technical trend of adas and autonomous driving. In: Proceedings of International Symposium on VLSI Design, Automation and Test (VLSI-DAT) 2014, pp. 1–4, April 2014
4. Sans, M.: X-by-wire park assistance for electric city cars. In: Proceedings of World Electric Vehicle Symposium and Exhibition (EVS27) 2013, pp. 1–9, November 2013
5. Infineon Technologies AG: Sensing the world: sensor solutions for automotive, industrial and consumer applications. Infineon Technologies AG (2016)
6. Leucker, M.: Teaching runtime verification. In: Khurshid, S., Sen, K. (eds.) RV 2011. LNCS, vol. 7186, pp. 34–48. Springer, Heidelberg (2012)
7. Ničković, D., Piterman, N.: From MTL to deterministic timed automata. In: Chatterjee, K., Henzinger, T.A. (eds.) FORMATS 2010. LNCS, vol. 6246, pp. 152–167. Springer, Heidelberg (2010)
8. Maler, O., Nickovic, D., Pnueli, A.: From MITL to timed automata. In: Asarin, E., Bouyer, P. (eds.) FORMATS 2006. LNCS, vol. 4202, pp. 274–289. Springer, Heidelberg (2006)
9. Pnueli, A., Zaks, A.: On the merits of temporal testers. In: Grumberg, O., Veith, H. (eds.) 25 Years of Model Checking. LNCS, vol. 5000, pp. 172–195. Springer, Heidelberg (2008)
10. Jaksic, S., Bartocci, E., Grosu, R., Kloibhofer, R., Nguyen, T., Nickovic, D.: From signal temporal logic to FPGA monitors. In: Proceedings of 13 ACM/IEEE International Conference on Formal Methods and Models for Codesign, pp. 218–227 (2015)
11. Geist, J., Rozier, K.Y., Schumann, J.: Runtime observer pairs and Bayesian network reasoners on-board FPGAs: flight-certifiable system health management for embedded systems. In: Bonakdarpour, B., Smolka, S.A. (eds.) RV 2014. LNCS, vol. 8734, pp. 215–230. Springer, Heidelberg (2014). doi:10.1007/978-3-319-11164-3_18

12. Reinbacher, T., Függer, M., Brauer, J.: Runtime verification of embedded real-time systems. Formal Meth. Syst. Des. **44**(3), 203–239 (2014)
13. Nguyen, T., Ničković, D.: Assertion-based monitoring in practice–checking correctness of an automotive sensor interface. In: Lang, F., Flammini, F. (eds.) FMICS 2014. LNCS, vol. 8718, pp. 16–32. Springer, Heidelberg (2014)
14. Nguyen, T., Wooters, S.N.: FPGA-based development for sophisticated automotive embedded safety critical system. SAE Int. J. Passeng. Cars Electron. Electr. Syst. **7**, pp. 125–132 (2014)
15. Nguyen, T., Basa, A., Hammerschmidt, D., Dittfeld, T.: Advanced mixed-signal emulation for complex automotive ICs. In: AIRBAG Conference, pp. 1–8 (2014)
16. Donzé, A., Maler, O., Bartocci, E., Nickovic, D., Grosu, R., Smolka, S.: On temporal logic and signal processing. In: Chakraborty, S., Mukund, M. (eds.) ATVA 2012. LNCS, vol. 7561, pp. 92–106. Springer, Heidelberg (2012)
17. Maler, O., Nickovic, D., Pnueli, A.: On synthesizing controllers from bounded-response properties. In: Damm, W., Hermanns, H. (eds.) CAV 2007. LNCS, vol. 4590, pp. 95–107. Springer, Heidelberg (2007)
18. Vivado High-Level Synthesis. http://www.xilinx.com/products/design-tools/vivado/integration/esl-design.html. Accessed 25 May 2016

Regular Tool Papers

A Monitoring Tool for a Branching-Time Logic

Duncan Paul Attard[(✉)] and Adrian Francalanza

CS, ICT, University of Malta, Msida, Malta
{duncan.attard.01,adrian.francalanza}@um.edu.mt

Abstract. We present the implementation of an experimental tool that automatically synthesises monitors from specifications written in MHML, a monitorable subset of the branching-time logic μHML. The synthesis algorithm is compositional *wrt* the structure of the formula and follows closely a synthesis procedure that has been shown to be correct. We discuss how this compositionality facilitates a translation into concurrent Erlang monitors, where each individual (sub)monitor is an actor that autonomously analyses individual parts of the source specification formula while still guaranteeing the correctness of the overall monitoring process.

1 Introduction

Runtime Verification (RV) is a lightweight verification technique that compares the execution of a system against correctness specifications. Despite its advantages, this technique has limited expressivity and cannot be used to verify arbitrary specifications such as (general) liveness properties [6]. These limits are further explored in [3] *wrt.* the branching-time domain for a logic called μHML, describing properties about the *computational graph* of programs. The work identifies a syntactic logical subset called MHML, and shows it to be monitorable and maximally-expressive *wrt.* the constraints of runtime monitoring.

This paper discusses the implementation of a prototype tool that builds on the results of [3]. A pleasant by-product of these results is the specification of a synthesis procedure that generates *correct* monitor descriptions from formulas written in MHML. Our tool investigates the implementability of this synthesis procedure, instantiating it to generate executable monitors for a specific general-purpose programming language. This instantiation follows closely the procedure described in [3], thereby giving us higher assurances that the generated executable monitors are indeed correct. Furthermore, we exploit the compositional structure of the procedure in [3] and refine the synthesis so as to enable it to produce *concurrent* monitors wherein (sub)monitors autonomously analyse individual parts of the global specification formula while still guaranteeing the correctness of the overall monitoring process. Through our tool, we show how these concurrent components can be naturally mapped to Erlang [2] actors that monitor a running system with minimal instrumentation efforts.

This work was partly supported by the project "TheoFoMon: Theoretical Foundations for Monitorability" (nr.163406-051) of the Icelandic Research Fund.

Y. Falcone and C. Sanchez (Eds.): RV 2016, LNCS 10012, pp. 473–481, 2016.
DOI: 10.1007/978-3-319-46982-9_31

This paper is structured as follows. Section 2 reviews the logic and synthesis procedure from [3]. Subsequently, Sect. 3 presents changes by which this synthesis procedure can achieve higher detection coverage. The challenges encountered while implementing a synthesis procedure that follows closely the formal description developed in Sect. 3, are discussed in Sect. 4. Finally, Sect. 5 concludes and briefly reviews related work.

2   Preliminaries

The syntax of $\psi \in$ MHML, a monitorable subset of μHML, is given in Fig. 1. It consists of two syntactic classes, sHML, describing *invariant* properties, and cHML, describing properties that hold *eventually* after a *finite* number of events. The logical formula $[\alpha]\theta$ states that *for all* system executions producing event α (possibly none), the subsequent system state must then satisfy θ, whereas the formula $\langle\alpha\rangle\pi$ states that there *exists* a system execution with event α whereby the subsequent state then satisfies π. E.g., $[\alpha]\mathbf{ff}$ describes systems that *cannot* produce event α, whereas $\langle\alpha\rangle\mathbf{tt}$ describes systems that *can* produce event α. $\mathbf{max}\, X.\theta$ and $\mathbf{min}\, X.\pi$ resp. denote maximal and minimal fixpoints for recursive

Monitorable Logic Syntax

$$\theta, \vartheta \in \text{sHML} ::= \mathbf{tt} \quad | \; \mathbf{ff} \quad | \; [\alpha]\theta \quad | \; \theta \wedge \vartheta \quad | \; \mathbf{max}\, X.\theta \quad | \; X$$

$$\pi, \varpi \in \text{cHML} ::= \mathbf{tt} \quad | \; \mathbf{ff} \quad | \; \langle\alpha\rangle\pi \quad | \; \pi \vee \varpi \quad | \; \mathbf{min}\, X.\pi \quad | \; X$$

Monitor Syntax and Semantics

$$m \in \text{Mon} ::= v \; | \; \alpha.m \; | \; m_1 + m_2 \; | \; \mathbf{rec}\, x.m \; | \; x \qquad v \in \text{Verd} ::= \mathbf{end} \; | \; \mathbf{no} \; | \; \mathbf{yes}$$

$$\frac{}{v \xrightarrow{\alpha} v} \qquad \frac{}{\alpha.m \xrightarrow{\alpha} m} \qquad \frac{}{\mathbf{rec}\, x.m \xrightarrow{\tau} m[\mathbf{rec}\, x.m/x]} \qquad \frac{m_1 \xrightarrow{\mu} m_1'}{m_1 + m_2 \xrightarrow{\mu} m_1'}$$

Monitor synthesis

$$(\!|\mathbf{ff}|\!) \stackrel{\text{def}}{=} \mathbf{no} \qquad\qquad (\!|\mathbf{tt}|\!) \stackrel{\text{def}}{=} \mathbf{yes} \qquad\qquad (\!|X|\!) \stackrel{\text{def}}{=} x$$

$$(\!|[\alpha]\psi|\!) \stackrel{\text{def}}{=} \begin{cases} \alpha.(\!|\psi|\!) & \text{if } (\!|\psi|\!) \neq \mathbf{yes} \\ \mathbf{yes} & \text{otherwise} \end{cases} \qquad (\!|\langle\alpha\rangle\psi|\!) \stackrel{\text{def}}{=} \begin{cases} \alpha.(\!|\psi|\!) & \text{if } (\!|\psi|\!) \neq \mathbf{no} \\ \mathbf{no} & \text{otherwise} \end{cases}$$

$$(\!|\psi_1 \wedge \psi_2|\!) \stackrel{\text{def}}{=} \begin{cases} (\!|\psi_1|\!) & \text{if } (\!|\psi_2|\!) = \mathbf{yes} \\ (\!|\psi_2|\!) & \text{if } (\!|\psi_1|\!) = \mathbf{yes} \\ (\!|\psi_1|\!) + (\!|\psi_2|\!) & \text{otherwise} \end{cases} \quad (\!|\psi_1 \vee \psi_2|\!) \stackrel{\text{def}}{=} \begin{cases} (\!|\psi_1|\!) & \text{if } (\!|\psi_2|\!) = \mathbf{no} \\ (\!|\psi_2|\!) & \text{if } (\!|\psi_1|\!) = \mathbf{no} \\ (\!|\psi_1|\!) + (\!|\psi_2|\!) & \text{otherwise} \end{cases}$$

$$(\!|\mathbf{max}X.\psi|\!) \stackrel{\text{def}}{=} \begin{cases} \mathbf{rec}\, x.(\!|\psi|\!) & \text{if } (\!|\psi|\!) \neq \mathbf{yes} \\ \mathbf{yes} & \text{otherwise} \end{cases} \quad (\!|\mathbf{min}X.\psi|\!) \stackrel{\text{def}}{=} \begin{cases} \mathbf{rec}\, x.(\!|\psi|\!) & \text{if } (\!|\psi|\!) \neq \mathbf{no} \\ \mathbf{no} & \text{otherwise} \end{cases}$$

Fig. 1. The logic MHML, the monitor syntax, and compositional synthesis function

formulas; these act as binders for X in θ (*resp.* π), where we work up to α-conversion of bound variables while assuming recursive formulas to be guarded.

Monitors are expressed as a standard process calculus where $m \xrightarrow{\alpha} m'$ denotes a monitor in state m observing event α and transitioning to state m'. The action τ denotes internal transitions while μ ranges over α and τ. For instance, $m_1 + m_2$ denotes an external choice where $m_1 + m_2 \xrightarrow{\mu} m'$ if either $m_1 \xrightarrow{\mu} m'$ or $m_2 \xrightarrow{\mu} m'$ (Fig. 1 omits the symmetric rule). The only novelty is the use of verdicts v: persistent states that do not change when events are analysed, modelling the *irrevocability* of a verdict v (see [3] for details).

The synthesis function $(\!|-|\!)$ from MHML formulas to monitors is also given in Fig. 1. Although the function covers both sHML and cHML, the syntactic constraints of MHML mean that synthesis for a formula ψ uses at most the first row (*i.e.*, the logical constructs common to sHML and cHML) and then either the first column (in the case of sHML) or the second column (in case of cHML). It is worth noting that the monitor synthesis function is compositional wrt. the structure of the formula, *e.g.*, the monitor for $\psi_1 \wedge \psi_2$ is defined in terms of the submonitors for the subformulas ψ_1 and ψ_2. Finally, we highlight the fact that conditional cases used in the synthesis of conjunctions, disjunctions, necessity and possibility formulas, and maximal and minimal fixpoints are necessary to handle logically equivalent formulas and generate correct monitors.

Example 1. The sHML formula φ_1 describes the property stating that "*after any sequence of service requests* (req) *and responses* (ans)*, a request is never followed by two consecutive responses*", i.e., subformula [ans][ans]ff. The synthesis function in Fig. 1 translates φ_1 into the monitor process m_1.

$$\varphi_1 = \mathbf{max}\, X.\big([\mathsf{req}]([\mathsf{ans}]X \wedge [\mathsf{ans}][\mathsf{ans}]\mathbf{ff})\big) \quad m_1 = \mathbf{rec}\, x.\big(\mathsf{req}.(\mathsf{ans}.x + \mathsf{ans}.\mathsf{ans}.\mathbf{no})\big)$$

$$\varphi_2 = \mathbf{min}\, X.\big(\langle\mathsf{ping}\rangle X \vee \langle\mathsf{cls}\rangle\mathbf{tt} \vee (\mathbf{min}\, Y.\mathbf{ff} \vee \langle\mathsf{cls}\rangle\mathbf{ff})\big) \quad m_2 = \mathbf{rec}\, x.\big(\mathsf{ping}.x + \mathsf{cls}.\mathbf{yes}\big)$$

The cHML formula φ_2 describes a property where after a (finite) sequence of ping events, the system closes a channel connection cls. The subformula $\mathbf{min}\, Y.\mathbf{ff} \vee \langle\mathsf{cls}\rangle\mathbf{ff}$ is semantically equivalent to $\mathbf{ff}$; accordingly the side conditions in Fig. 1 take this into consideration when synthesising monitor m_2. ∎

Note that although the synthesis employs both acceptance and rejection verdicts, it only generates *uni-verdict* monitors that only produce acceptances or rejections, *never both*; [3] shows that this is essential for monitor correctness.

3   Refining the Monitor Synthesis

The first step towards implementing our tool involved refining the existing synthesis function to improve monitor detections. Specifically, there are cases where the synthesis function in Fig. 1 produces monitors with non-deterministic behaviour. For instance, monitor m_1 of Example 1 may exhibit the following behaviour:

$$\mathbf{rec}\, x.\mathsf{req}.(\mathsf{ans}.x + \mathsf{ans}.\mathsf{ans}.\mathbf{no}) \xrightarrow{\tau} \cdot \xrightarrow{\mathsf{req}} \mathsf{ans}.m_1 + \mathsf{ans}.\mathsf{ans}.\mathbf{no}$$

at which point, upon analysing action ans, it may non-deterministically transition to either m_1 or ans.**no**. The latter case can raise a rejection if it receives another ans event but the former case, *i.e.*, m_1, does *not* — this results in a missed detection. Although this behaviour suffices for the theoretical results required in [3], it is not ideal from a practical standpoint. The problem stems from a limitation in the choice construct semantics, $m_1 + m_2$, which forces a selection between submonitor m_1 or m_2 upon the receipt of an event.

We solve this problem by replacing external choice constructs with a parallel monitor composition construct, $m_1 \times m_2$ that allows *both* submonitors to process the event without excluding one another. The semantics of the new combinator is defined by the following rules (again we omit symmetric cases):

$$\frac{m_1 \xrightarrow{\alpha} m_1' \quad m_2 \xrightarrow{\alpha} m_2'}{m_1 \times m_2 \xrightarrow{\alpha} m_1' \times m_2'} \qquad \frac{m_1 \xrightarrow{\alpha} m_1' \quad m_2 \xrightarrow{\alpha} \quad m_2 \xrightarrow{\tau}}{m_1 \times m_2 \xrightarrow{\alpha} m_1'}$$

$$\frac{m_2 \xrightarrow{\tau} m_2'}{m_1 \times m_2 \xrightarrow{\tau} m_1 \times m_2'} \qquad \frac{}{v \times m \xrightarrow{\tau} v}$$

The first rule states that both monitors proceed in lockstep if they can process the *same* action. The second rule states that if only one monitor can process the action and the other is stuck (*i.e.*, it can neither analyse action α, nor transition internally using τ), then the able monitor transitions while terminating the stuck monitor. Otherwise, the monitor is allowed to transition silently by the third rule. The last rule terminates parallel monitors once a verdict is reached.

We define a second synthesis function $[\![-]\!]$ by structural induction on the formula. Most cases are identical to those of $(\!|-|\!)$ in Fig. 1 with the exception of the two cases below, substituting the choice construct for the parallel construct:

$$[\![\psi_1 \wedge \psi_2]\!] \stackrel{\text{def}}{=} \begin{cases} [\![\psi_1]\!] & \text{if } [\![\psi_2]\!] = \textbf{yes} \\ [\![\psi_2]\!] & \text{if } [\![\psi_1]\!] = \textbf{yes} \\ [\![\psi_1]\!] \times [\![\psi_2]\!] & \text{otherwise} \end{cases} \quad [\![\psi_1 \vee \psi_2]\!] \stackrel{\text{def}}{=} \begin{cases} [\![\psi_1]\!] & \text{if } [\![\psi_2]\!] = \textbf{no} \\ [\![\psi_2]\!] & \text{if } [\![\psi_1]\!] = \textbf{no} \\ [\![\psi_1]\!] \times [\![\psi_2]\!] & \text{otherwise} \end{cases}$$

The two monitor synthesis functions correspond in the sense of Theorem 1. In [3], verdicts are associated with logic satisfactions and violations, and thus Theorem 1 suffices to show that the new synthesis is still correct.

Theorem 1. *For all* $\psi \in \text{MHML}$, $(\!|m|\!) \xrightarrow{\alpha_1} \ldots \xrightarrow{\alpha_n} v$ *iff* $[\![m]\!] \xrightarrow{\alpha_1} \ldots \xrightarrow{\alpha_n} v$.

Proof. By induction on the strucure of ψ. Most cases are immediate because the *resp.* translations correspond. In the case of $\psi_1 \wedge \psi_2$ where the synthesis yields $(\!|\psi_1|\!) + (\!|\psi_2|\!)$, a verdict is reached only if $(\!|\psi_1|\!) \xrightarrow{\alpha_1} \ldots \xrightarrow{\alpha_n} v$ or $(\!|\psi_2|\!) \xrightarrow{\alpha_1} \ldots \xrightarrow{\alpha_n} v$. By I.H. we obtain $[\![\psi_1]\!] \xrightarrow{\alpha_1} \ldots \xrightarrow{\alpha_n} v$ (or $[\![\psi_2]\!] \xrightarrow{\alpha_1} \ldots \xrightarrow{\alpha_n} v$) which suffices to show that $[\![\psi_1]\!] \times [\![\psi_2]\!] \xrightarrow{\alpha_1} \ldots \xrightarrow{\alpha_n} v$. A dual argument can be constructed for the implication in the opposite direction. $\square$

Example 2. For ψ_1 in Example 1, we now only have the following monitor behaviour:

$$\textbf{rec } x.\text{req}.\big(\text{ans}.x \times \text{ans}.\text{ans}.\textbf{no}\big) \xrightarrow{\tau} \cdot \xrightarrow{\text{req}} \text{ans}.m_1 \times \text{ans}.\text{ans}.\textbf{no} \xrightarrow{\text{ans}} m_1 \times \text{ans}.\textbf{no} \xrightarrow{\text{ans}} \textbf{no}$$

■

4   Implementation

We implement a RV tool which analyses the correctness of concurrent programs developed in Erlang. Actions, in the form of Erlang trace events, consist of two types: outputs $i \, ! \, d$ and inputs $i \, ? \, d$, where i corresponds to process (*i.e.*, actor) identifiers (PID), and d denotes the data payload associated with the action in the form of Erlang data values (*e.g.*, PID, lists, tuples, atoms, *etc.*). Specifications, defined as instantiations of MHML terms, make use of *action patterns* which possess the same structure as that of the aforementioned actions, but may also employ variables (alphanumeric identifiers starting with an uppercase letter) in place of values; these are then bound to values when pattern-matched to actions at runtime. Action patterns require us to synthesise a slightly more general form of monitors with the following behaviour: if a pattern e matches a trace event action α, thereby binding a variable list to values from α (denoted as σ), the monitor evolves to the continuation m, substituting the variables in m for the values bound by pattern e (denoted by $m\sigma$); otherwise it transitions to the terminated process **end**.

$$\frac{\mathbf{match}(e, \alpha) = \sigma}{e.m \xrightarrow{\alpha} m\sigma} \qquad \frac{\mathbf{match}(e, \alpha) = \bot}{e.m \xrightarrow{\alpha} \mathbf{end}}$$

MHML formulas are synthesised into *Erlang code*, following closely the synthesis function discussed in Sect. 3. In particular, we exploit the inherent concurrency features offered by Erlang together with the modular structure of the synthesis to translate submonitors into independent concurrent *actors* [2] that execute in *parallel*. An important deviation from the semantics of parallel composition specified in Sect. 3 is that actors execute *asynchronously* to one another. For instance, one submonitor may be analysing the second action event whereas another may forge ahead to a stage where it is analysing the fourth event. The moment a verdict is reached by any submonitor actor, all others are terminated, and said verdict is used to declare the final monitoring outcome. This alternative semantics still corresponds to the one given in Sect. 3 for three main reasons: (i) monitors are univerdict, and there is no risk that one verdict is reached before another thereby invalidating or contradicting it; (ii) processing is local to each submonitor and independent of the processing carried out by other submonitors; (iii) verdicts are irrevocable and monitors can terminate once an outcome is reached, safe in the knowledge that verdicts, once announced, cannot change.

Monitor recursion unfolding, similar to the work in [4], constitutes another minor departure from the semantics in Sect. 3, as the implementation uses a process environment that maps recursion variables to monitor terms. Erlang code for monitor **rec** $x.m$ is evaluated by running the code corresponding to the (potentially open) term m (where x is free in m) in an environment with the map $x \mapsto m$.

Figure 2 outlines the compilation steps required to transform a formula script file (`script.hml`) into a corresponding Erlang source code monitor implementation (`monitor.erl`). To be able to adhere the compositional synthesis of Sect. 3

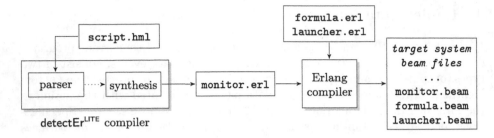

Fig. 2. The monitor synthesis process pipeline

the tool had to overcome an obstacle attributed to pattern bindings. Specifically, in formulas such as $[e]\psi$ or $\langle e \rangle \psi$, subformula ψ may contain free (value) variables bound by the pattern e. For instance, in [Srv ? {req, Clt}] [Clt ! ans]ff, the Erlang monitor code for the subformula [Clt ! ans]ff would contain the free variable Clt bound by the preceding pattern Srv ? {req, Clt}. Since Erlang does *not* support dynamic scoping [2], the synthesis cannot simply generate open functions whose free variables are then bound dynamically at the program location where the function is used. To circumvent this issue, the synthesis generates an *uninterpreted* source code string composed using the util:format() string manipulation function. Compilation is then handled normally (using the static scoping of the *completed* monitor source code) via the standard Erlang compiler.

The Monitor constructs and the corresponding Erlang code (excerpt)

The tool itself, written in Erlang, is organised into two main modules. The synthesis in Fig. 2 is carried out by the function synth in module compiler.erl. This relies on generic monitor constructs implemented as function macros inside the module formula.erl (Fig. 2). Table 1 outlines the mapping for two of these constructs. Parallel composition is encoded by spawning two parallel actors (lines 2–3) followed by forking trace events to these actors for independent processing (line 4). Action prefixing for pattern e is encoded by generating a

Table 1. The Monitor constructs and the corresponding Erlang code (excerpt).

Monitor construct	formula module code
$\llbracket \psi_1 \rrbracket \times \llbracket \psi_2 \rrbracket$	1 mon_and(Psi1, Psi2) -> 2 fun(Env) -> Pid1 = spawn_link(fun() -> Psi1(Env) end), 3 Pid2 = spawn_link(fun() -> Psi2(Env) end), 4 fork(Pid1, Pid2) 5 end.
$e.\llbracket \psi \rrbracket$	6 mon_nec(ActMatcher) -> 7 fun(Env) -> 8 receive Act -> Psi = ActMatcher(Act), 9 Psi(Env) end 10 end.

pattern-and-continuation specific function `ActMatcher` that takes a trace event `Act`, pattern-matches it with the translation of pattern e (line 8) and executes the continuation monitor returned by `ActMatcher` in case of a successful match (line 9). Note that the execution of a monitor always takes a map environment `Env` as argument.

The function `synth` in module `compiler.erl` consumes the formula parse-tree (encoded as Erlang tuples), generates the Erlang source code string of the respective monitor and writes it to `monitor.erl`. Table 2 outlines the tight correspondence between this compilation and the synthesis function of Sect. 3. To encode the branching cases of the synthesis function, the compilation returns a *tuple* where the first element is a *tag* ranging over `yes`, `no` and `any`, and the second element, the monitor source code string. The correspondence is evident for $[\![\psi_1 \wedge \psi_2]\!]$, where the code on line 7 performs the necessary string processing and calls the function `mon_and` presented in Table 1. For formula $[\![[e]\psi]\!]$, the translation inserts directly the function corresponding to `ActMatcher` (lines 13–15) alluded to in Table 1 — this is passed as an argument to `mon_nec` from `formula.erl` (line 17), thereby addressing the aforementioned limitation associated with open functions and dynamic scoping. Pattern `Pat` is extracted from the parse tree (line 9), while the continuation monitor source code string `Mon` is synthesised from the subtree of `Phi` (line 10).

The tool instruments the generated monitors to run with the system in asynchronous fashion, using the native tracing functionality provided by the Erlang Virtual Machine (EVM). Erlang directives instruct the EVM to report events of

Table 2. The monitor synthesis function cases and corresponding compiler functions.

Synthesis subcase	`compiler` module function

$[\![\psi_1 \wedge \psi_2]\!] \stackrel{\text{def}}{=}$
 	
 $\begin{cases} [\![\psi_1]\!] & \text{if } [\![\psi_2]\!] = \textbf{yes} \\ [\![\psi_2]\!] & \text{if } [\![\psi_1]\!] = \textbf{yes} \\ [\![\psi_1]\!] \times [\![\psi_2]\!] & \text{otherwise} \end{cases}$
	<pre>1 synth({and_op, Psi1, Psi2}) ->
	2 case {synth(Psi1), synth(Psi2)} of
	3 {{Tag, Mon}, {yes, _}} -> {Tag, Mon};
	4 {{yes, _}, {Tag, Mon}} -> {Tag, Mon};
	5 {{Tag1, Mon1}, {Tag2, Mon2}} ->
	6 {join_tag(Tag1, Tag2),
	7 util:format("mon_and(~s,~s)", [Mon1, Mon2])}
	8 end;</pre>

$[\![[e]\psi]\!] \stackrel{\text{def}}{=}$
 	
 $\begin{cases} e.[\![\psi]\!] & \text{if } [\![\psi]\!] \neq \textbf{yes} \\ \textbf{yes} & \text{otherwise} \end{cases}$
	<pre>9 synth({nec, Pat, Phi}) ->
	10 case synth(Phi) of
	11 {yes, _} -> {yes, "mon_tt()"};
	12 {Tag, Mon} ->
	13 Fun = util:format(
	14 "fun(Act) -> case Act of ~s -> ~s;
	15 _ -> mon_id() end end", [pat_to_str(Pat), Mon]),
	16 {join_tag(nec, Tag),
	17 util:format("mon_nec(~s)", [Fun])}
	18 end;</pre>

interest from the system execution to a *tracer* actor executing in parallel; this in turn forwards said events to the monitor (also executing in parallel). Crucially, this type of instrumentation requires *no changes to the monitor source code* (or the target system binaries) increasing confidence of its correctness. In the tool, compiled monitor files together with their dependencies (*e.g.*, `formula.erl`) are placed alongside other system binary files. Instrumentation is then handled by a third module, `launcher.erl`, tasked with the responsibility of launching the system and corresponding monitors in tandem.

The initial distribution of the tool is available from https://bitbucket.org/duncanatt/detecter-lite, and requires a working installation of Erlang.

5   Conclusion

We discuss the implementation of a tool that synthesises and instruments asynchronous monitors from specifications written in MHML, a monitorable subset of the logic μHML. The implementation follows very closely a correct monitor synthesis specification described in [3]. This tight correspondence gives us high assurances that the executable monitors generated by our tool are also correct.

Discussion and Related work: Monitors form part of the trusted computing base of a system and generally, their correctness is *sine qua non* [5]. Despite its importance, tools prioritising this aspect often prove correctness for a high level abstraction of the monitor but do not put much effort towards showing that the *resp.* monitor implementation corresponds to this abstraction. To our knowledge, the closest work that attempts to bridge this correctness gap is [4], wherein the authors formalise an operational semantics of a subset of the target language and then show monitor correctness within this formalised language subset. Their tool shares a number of common aspects with our work (*e.g.*, they also synthesise subsets of μHML, use Erlang as a target language and also asynchronous instrumentation), but differs in a few main aspects: (i) we consider a substantially larger syntactic monitorable subset of μHML (*e.g.*, we can specify *positive* properties such as "the system can perform action α"); (ii) our notion of monitor correctness is formalised in terms of a language agnostic abstraction — a process calculus; (iii) we consider action patterns, which complicate the modularity of the synthesis process. In other related work, [1] explores *synchronous* monitor instrumentations within a similar setting to ours; this requires changes to the monitor and system code, which can potentially affect correctness.

References

1. Cassar, I., Francalanza, A.: On synchronous and asynchronous monitor instrumentation for actor-based systems. In: FOCLASA, pp. 54–68 (2014)
2. Cesarini, F., Thompson, S.: Erlang Programming. O'Reilly, Sebastopol (2009)
3. Francalanza, A., Aceto, L., Ingolfsdottir, A.: On verifying Hennessy-Milner logic with recursion at runtime. In: Bartocci, E., et al. (eds.) RV 2015. LNCS, vol. 9333, pp. 71–86. Springer, Heidelberg (2015). doi:10.1007/978-3-319-23820-3_5

4. Francalanza, A., Seychell, A.: Synthesising correct concurrent runtime monitors. Formal Met. Syst. Des. **46**(3), 226–261 (2015)

5. Laurent, J., Goodloe, A., Pike, L.: Assuring the guardians. In: Bartocci, E., et al. (eds.) RV 2015. LNCS, vol. 9333, pp. 87–101. Springer, Heidelberg (2015). doi:10.1007/978-3-319-23820-3_6

6. Manna, Z., Pnueli, A.: Completing the temporal picture. Theor. Comput. Sci. **83**(1), 97–130 (1991)

SMEDL: Combining Synchronous and Asynchronous Monitoring

Teng Zhang$^{(\boxtimes)}$, Peter Gebhard, and Oleg Sokolsky

University of Pennsylvania, Philadelphia, PA 19104, USA
{tengz,pgeb,sokolsky}@cis.upenn.edu

Abstract. Two major approaches have emerged in runtime verification, based on synchronous and asynchronous monitoring. Each approach has its advantages and disadvantages and is applicable in different situations. In this paper, we explore a hybrid approach, where low-level properties are checked synchronously, while higher-level ones are checked asynchronously. We present a tool for constructing and deploying monitors based on an architecture specification. Monitor logic and patterns of communication between monitors are specified in a language SMEDL. The language and the tool are illustrated using a case study of a robotic simulator.

Keywords: Monitor generation · Synchronous monitoring · Asynchronous monitoring

1 Introduction

Runtime verification(RV) [1] has emerged as a powerful technique for correctness monitoring of critical systems. Numbers of approaches have been proposed among which *synchronous* monitoring [2] and *asynchronous* monitoring [3] are broadly used. Synchronous monitoring will block the execution of the system being monitored until validity of an observation is confirmed, ensuring that potentially hazardous behavior is not propagated to the system environment. This makes this method suitable for safety- and security-related contexts. However, synchronous monitoring incurs high execution overhead for the target system, and less critical properties may not require such strict guarantees. On the other hand, asynchronous monitoring may allow to check the properties with less overhead for the target system, but as the system continues its execution while checking is performed, it may not be suitable for some critical properties. Moreover, the error point is hard to locate: when the monitor reports the violation of the property, the target system may have already left the position causing the problem. Most RV tools target one of these two approaches. Furthermore, synchronous monitoring may not be suitable for distributed systems. In many practical cases, it is desirable to combine the two approaches to get the benefits of both and reduce effects of drawbacks.

The contribution of this paper is a tool for construction and deployment of hybrid monitoring. The tool uses the language SMEDL to specify monitoring

Y. Falcone and C. Sanchez (Eds.): RV 2016, LNCS 10012, pp. 482–490, 2016.
DOI: 10.1007/978-3-319-46982-9_32

architecture and individual monitors. Properties to be checked are represented in a state-machine style in monitors. Generated monitors can be integrated with the target system or deployed separately, according to the architecture specification. Execution within a monitor is synchronous while the communication among monitors is asynchronous. This allows us to monitor properties on multiple time scales and levels of criticality.

Related work. MaC (Monitoring and Checking) [4] is an architecture for asynchronous runtime monitoring. A distributed version of MaC, DMaC [5], is proposed mainly for monitoring the properties of network protocols. MOP (Monitoring Oriented Programming) [6] is a generic framework for properties specification and the checking of the properties at runtime. Based on the work of MOP, RV-Monitor [7] can monitor hundreds of properties of Java API specifications at the same time. Using the concepts of AOP [8] and MOP, MOVEC [9] is compiler supporting the parametric runtime verification for systems written in C. [10] proposes an architecture allowing for switching between synchronous and asynchronous monitoring but it is not clear how to use synchronous and asynchronous monitoring simultaneously. [11] proposed PT-DTL, a temporal logical to describe the temporal properties of distributed system, and a decentralized monitoring algorithm for PT-DTL. However, the proposed tool, DIANA, only supports the asynchronous monitoring for distributed program with a fixed architecture. [12] presents a method for monitoring multi-threaded component-based systems described in BIP but it is not suitable for distributed systems. [13] proposes a primitive condition rule-based system RuleR which supports the hierarchy architecture of monitors but asynchronous monitoring is not supported. Thus, despite the variety of available tools, there is presently no support for combining synchronous and asynchronous monitoring.

The paper is organized as follows. Section 2 gives an overview of SMEDL. Section 3 introduces the implementation of the SMEDL tool. Section 4 uses the case study of simple robot simulator to evaluate the performance of the tool. Section 5 concludes the paper and presents the future work.

2 Overview of SMEDL

2.1 SMEDL Concepts

A SMEDL monitoring system can be divided as four parts: target system, monitoring specification, SMEDL code generator and runtime checkers, as illustrated in Fig. 1. Target system is the system to be monitored and checked. The SMEDL specification contains a set of monitoring objects and an architecture that captures patterns of communication between them. A monitoring object can be an abstraction of a system object or an abstract entity that represents interactions between multiple system objects. Objects can include a set of parameters whose values are fixed when the object is instantiated. Internal state can be maintained in an object to reflect the history of its evolution. SMEDL events are instantaneous occurrences that ultimately originate from observations of the execution

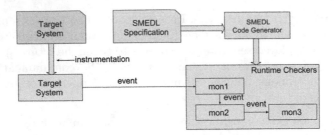

Fig. 1. SMEDL overview

of target system. Events can also be raised by monitors in response to other events. Raised events can be delivered to other monitors for checking or serve as alarms. A SMEDL specification is independent from the system implementation so that the monitoring specification does not need to be changed as long as the specification remains the same, even if the implementation has been changed. Instead, the definition of events in terms of observations on the target system is modified. Each monitoring object is converted to executable code by the SMEDL code generator and can be instantiated multiple times with different parameters, either statically during the target system startup or dynamically at run time, in response to system events such as the creation of a new thread in the target system.

2.2 Brief Description of the Language

The SMEDL specification contains two parts: a definition for each monitor object and a description of the monitor network that specifies monitor instances and connections between them.

Monitoring objects. A SMEDL monitoring object is a collection of extended finite state machines (EFSMs) sharing a set of internal state variables and events. More precisely, a monitoring object is a tuple ⟨*interface, implementation*⟩, where *interface* contains the name, unchangeable identity parameters and event declarations; *implementation* contains state variables and state machines of the monitor. In SMEDL syntax, illustrated in the case study, state machines are represented as *scenarios*. Three kinds of events, *imported*, *exported* and *internal*, can be specified in the event declaration. *Imported* events of a monitor can be received and used to trigger the execution of the monitor; *exported* events are raised in the monitor and are sent to other monitors; *internal* events are processed within the monitor instance. State machines are used to define the behavior of the monitor. Transitions of the state machines are labelled with events that trigger the transition. In addition to an event, each transition may also be labeled by a guard, which is a predicate over state variables and event attributes, and a set of actions, each action is either an assignment to a local variable, or a statement that raises an event. Semantics for single monitors determines *macro-steps*, that is, synchronous compositions of individual transitions of state machines (referred to as *micro-steps*) in response to an imported event from delivered from the environment. After finishing all enabled transitions, the monitor will output the exported events raised during the macro-step and wait for the next imported environment. Formal description of the semantics can be found in [14].

Architecture. A monitor network is a directed tree $G = \langle V, E \rangle$ where V contains the target system and a set of monitor instances which can receive or raise events; E is a set of directed edges connecting event ports from the target system to the monitors or between monitors. Monitors may receive events either from the target system or from other monitors. Monitors directly connecting with the target system will execute synchronously with the target system, while all others have their own execution threads and can be deployed locally or over a network. Events are delivered to monitor instances based on the values of instance parameters or event attributes. Thus, an architecture description language is provided for specifying event connection patterns between monitor instances. Apart from the source and target monitoring objects and events, connection patterns also specify matching rules between source and target monitor instances according to instance parameters or attributes of the event. [15] gives a detailed description of the language.

3   Tool Implementation

We have developed a toolchain for deploying monitors based on SMEDL specifications, shown in Fig. 2. The tool contains two parts: *monitor generator* and *configurator*. The monitor generator generates the code for a single monitor object, while the configurator is responsible for integrating monitor instances and target program, based on the SMEDL architecture specification.

The monitor generator produces C code for the monitor object. The monitor API consists of a set of function calls corresponding to imported events of the

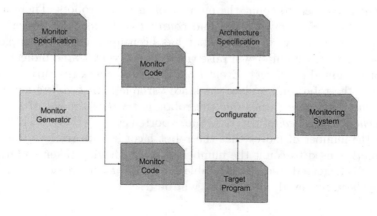

Fig. 2. SMEDL toolchain

monitor object. Calls to event functions trigger execution of the monitor state machines. To support the asynchronous communication between monitors, we use the publish-subscribe mechanism of the RabbitMQ middleware [16]. Each event in the architecture specification is represented as a topic. Events raised by a monitor are published to a topic according to the architecture specification. Topic names include information about names of parameters of raising monitors and event attributes. We rely on filtering provided in RabbitMQ subscriptions: monitor instances subscribing to an event can specify values of parameters and attributes that are relevant for them, according to the architecture specification.

We have developed a prototype of SMEDL toolchain which can generate the C code of single monitors. The toolchain and the case study used in this paper is available for downloading.[1]

4   Explorer: A Case Study

Explorer is a multi-threaded program for simulating robots locating and retrieving targets on a two-dimensional map. Each robot, running in its own thread, will start in a specified position on the map and has to retrieve a number of targets in a limited number of moves across the map. The goal of monitoring for this program is twofold. First, we want to check that each robot is following the search-and-retrieve protocol and, second, we collect statistics about the number of moves needed to retrieve the target. We thus define two monitor objects: one checks behavior of each robot thread and another is a statistic monitor that collects events from all behavior checking monitors. The behavior checking monitor is deployed synchronously with each new thread, while the statistic monitor is asynchronous.

Monitor specification. *ExplorerMon*, defined in Listing 1.1, directly connects to each robot for synchronous checking. The monitor has three *scenarios Main*, *Explore* and *Count*. *Main* is used to check whether robot has found the target in its view and begun to retrieve it. *Explore* is used to describe the behavior of robots. *Count* is used to count the number of moves of robots. There are four imported events, *view*, *drive*, *turn* and *count*. Event *view* will be sent to the monitor whenever the view of the robot has been updated. If the target is in the robot's view, the monitor will raise the internal event *found* indicating that the robot has found the target. Event *turn* is used to check the current heading direction of the robot and update the state variable *mon_heading* accordingly. Event *drive* is triggered whenever the robot is trying to move. If the helper function *check_retrieved* returns true, the exported event *retrieved* will be raised carrying the number of moves that the robot has taken to retrieve this target. Event *count* is used to count the number of robots having taken so far. Every time *count* is triggered, the state variable *move_count* is increased by 1. Once a target has been retrieved, *move_count* will be reset.

---

[1] https://gitlab.precise.seas.upenn.edu/tengz/SMEDLTool.

Listing 1.1. SMEDL specification for ExplorerMon

```
object ExplorerMon
identity
  opaque id;
state
  int mon_x, mon_y, mon_heading, move_count;
events
  imported view(pointer),drive(int,int,int),turn(int),count();
  internal found();
  exported retrieved(int);
scenarios
  Main:
    Explore -> found() -> Retrieve
    Retrieve -> retrieved(cnt) -> Explore
  Explore:
    Look->view(view_pointer) when contains_object(view_pointer) {raise found();}->Move
      else -> Move
    Move -> turn(facing) when facing != heading{mon_heading = facing;} -> Look
      else -> Move
    Move -> drive(x, y, heading, map) when check_retrieved(map,x,y)
      { raise retrieved(move_count); mon_x = x; mon_y = y; move_count = 0; } -> Look
      else {mon_x = x;mon_y = y;} -> Look
  Count:
        Start -> count(){move_count=move_count+1;}->Start
}
```

To check if all robots retrieve all targets in the map and calculate the average number of moves the robots have used, asynchronous monitor *ExplorerStat* is defined in Listing 1.2. In the system, there is only one instance of *ExplorerStat* which will receive events *retrieved* from instances of *ExplorerMon*. Whenever *retrieved* is delivered into the monitor, state variable *sum* will be increased by 1 and the number of moves will also be added to the variable *count*. If the sum is equal to the overall number of targets, the exported event *output* will be raised with the average number of moves of a robot as an attribute.

Listing 1.2. SMEDL specification for ExplorerStat

```
object ExplorerStat
state
    int sum,count,targetNum;
events
    imported retrieved(int);
    internal reachNum();
    exported output(float);
scenarios
    stat:
        Start -> retrieved(move_count){sum=sum+1;count=count+move_count
                                      ;raise reachNum();}-> Start
    check:
        CheckSum -> reachNum() when (sum < targetNum) -> CheckSum
                    else{raise output(count/sum);sum=0;count=0;}->CheckSum
```

Figure 3a, shows the corresponding runtime architecture. The two monitoring objects communicate via a single event *retrieved*. Figure 3b, shows a runtime view of the architecture, where $ex\_mon\_1, \ldots, ex\_mon\_k$ are instances of *ExplorerMon* associated with threads $robot\_1, ldots, robot\_k$ simulating k robots. The single instance of *ExplorerMon* receive events from all instances ex_mon_i. The implementation introduces an additional thread *sender* that publishes events from all instances to the broker of RabbitMQ.

Performance evaluation. The experiment is done on a single core virtual machine with CPU of speed 2.5 GHz and memory of 4 GB. The operating system is Ubuntu 14.04LTS and RabbitMQ is used as the communication middleware API. Overhead is one of the most important measurements that can show the performance of the monitoring system. There are three sources of overhead for synchronous monitoring: instantiation of monitors, checking of observations, and

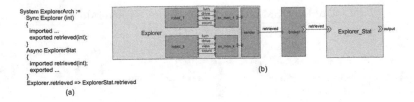

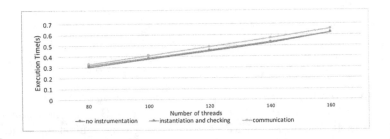

Fig. 3. Monitor network of explorer

communication. Communication overhead is incurred only when asynchronous monitors are present and events need to be sent to the asynchronous monitors via the middleware. The overhead of publishing events depends on the choice of middleware. Note that the initialization of connection in the main thread is incorporated into the communication overhead. Checking overhead increases with the number of observations produced by the target system. In our case study, the number of observations depend on two tunable factors: the number of robot threads in the system and the size of the map. We expect overhead to increase linearly with the number of threads, since the number of observations from each thread is independent of others. Increasing the size of the map tends to reduce overhead, since robots tend to move straight over longer distances on a larger map, without generating observations. This reduces the frequency of events, on average. In this experiment, the size of map is fixed to 40×80 and there are 5 targets in the map.

We describe two experiments that consider these factors separately. The first experiment varies the number of threads, with the size of map is fixed to 40×80 and 5 targets on the map. Figure 4 shows that the overhead is approximately linear with the number of threads. The overall relative overhead of monitor instantiation and synchronous checking is about 2 %, while communication overhead is approximately 3 %, respectively. In absolute terms, processing of an average event with and without communication overhead is 2.11 μs vs. 1.93 μs.

The second experiment considers the overhead as a function of the map size. Table 1 shows that overhead quickly becomes negligible with the size of map

Fig. 4. Execution time vs. number of threads

Table 1. Relation between input size and overhead

Input size #	Avg moves	Checking	Communication
30 × 60	43306	3.2 %	6 %
40 × 80	75205	1.9 %	3.3 %
50 × 100	112943	< 1 %	2 %
60 × 120	161918	< 1 %	2 %

increasing. However, communication overhead remains about twice as high as checking overhead.

We discuss results of the case study in the next section.

5 Discussion and Conclusions

We presented a tool to support generation and deployment of hybrid, i.e., synchronous and asynchronous, monitors specified in the language SMEDL. The SMEDL specification describes a network of monitors. Within the single monitor, the execution is synchronous while the communication between monitors is asynchronous. A prototype of the tool has been implemented. The paper describes evaluation of the tool using the case study of a robot simulator.

We first discuss some of our design decisions. We implement asynchronous communication using middleware, which allows us to exchange events across the network. This restricts synchronous monitoring to a single computing node. It is possible that some security-critical applications may require synchronous monitoring of multiple nodes. However, in our experience, such configurations are subject to high overhead and should be avoided when possible. In our tool, extension to synchronous monitoring over a network would be a simple extension to consider in the future. We assume that each monitor object in the architecture is deployed either synchronously or asynchronously. That is, either all imported events are supplied by the target system, or all are supplied by other monitors through the middleware. Potentially, deployments could be mixed, however implementation of the monitor becomes substantially more complicated.

From the case study, we note the choice balance between synchronous and asynchronous monitors in an architecture is not straightforward. The most surprising lesson from the case study, for us, was that the overhead of sending an event to a separate monitor can be larger than checking the event synchronously within the same monitor. Thus, intuitively, delegating checking to an asynchronous monitor makes sense only if it involves complex computation.

The presented toolset remains in active development. We are working on automatic instrumentation of C code, using an approach similar to [9]. We are also improving automatic deployment of asynchronous monitors, as well as reducing both checking and communication overheads.

References

1. Leucker, M., Schallhart, C.: A brief account of runtime verification. J. Logic Algebraic Program. **78**(5), 293–303 (2009)
2. Francalanza, A.: A theory of monitors. In: Jacobs, B., Löding, C. (eds.) FOSSACS 2016. LNCS, vol. 9634, pp. 145–161. Springer, Heidelberg (2016). doi:10.1007/978-3-662-49630-5_9
3. Francalanza, A., Gauci, A., Pace, G.J.: Distributed system contract monitoring. J. Logic Algebraic Program. **82**(5–7), 186–215 (2013)
4. Kim, M., Kannan, S., Lee, I., Sokolsky, O., Viswanathan, M.: Java-MaC: a runtime assurance approach for Java programs. Formal Methods Syst. Des. **24**(2), 129–155 (2004)
5. Zhou, W., Sokolsky, O., Loo, B.T., Lee, I.: *DMaC*: distributed monitoring and checking. In: Bensalem, S., Peled, D.A. (eds.) RV 2009. LNCS, vol. 5779, pp. 184–201. Springer, Heidelberg (2009). doi:10.1007/978-3-642-04694-0_13
6. Meredith, P.O., Jin, D., Griffith, D., Chen, F., Roşu, G.: An overview of the MOP runtime verification framework. Int. J. Softw. Tools Technol. Transfer **14**(3), 249–289 (2012)
7. Luo, Q., Zhang, Y., Lee, C., Jin, D., Meredith, P.O.N., Şerbănuţă, T.F., Roşu, G.: RV-Monitor: efficient parametric runtime verification with simultaneous properties. In: Bonakdarpour, B., Smolka, S.A. (eds.) RV 2014. LNCS, vol. 8734, pp. 285–300. Springer, Heidelberg (2014)
8. Kiczales, G., Lamping, J., Mendhekar, A., Maeda, C., Lopes, C., Loingtier, J.-M., Irwin, J.: Aspect-oriented programming. In: Akşit, M., Matsuoka, S. (eds.) ECOOP 1997. LNCS, vol. 1241, pp. 220–242. Springer, Heidelberg (1997). doi:10.1007/BFb0053381
9. Chen, Z., Wang, Z., Zhu, Y., Xi, H., Yang, Z.: Parametric runtime verification of C programs. In: Chechik, M., Raskin, J.-F. (eds.) TACAS 2016. LNCS, vol. 9636, pp. 299–315. Springer, Heidelberg (2016). doi:10.1007/978-3-662-49674-9_17
10. Colombo, C., Pace, G.J., Abela, P.: Compensation-aware runtime monitoring. In: Barringer, H., Falcone, Y., Finkbeiner, B., Havelund, K., Lee, I., Pace, G., Roşu, G., Sokolsky, O., Tillmann, N. (eds.) RV 2010. LNCS, vol. 6418, pp. 214–228. Springer, Heidelberg (2010)
11. Sen, K., Vardhan, A., Agha, G., Rosu, G.: Efficient decentralized monitoring of safety in distributed systems. In: Proceedings of the 26th International Conference on Software Engineering, pp. 418–427. IEEE Computer Society (2004)
12. Nazarpour, H., Falcone, Y., Bensalem, S., Bozga, M., Combaz, J.: Monitoring multi-threaded component-based systems. Technical report TR-2015-5, Verimag Research Report (2015)
13. Barringer, H., Rydeheard, D., Havelund, K.: Rule systems for run-time monitoring: from Eagle to RuleR. J. Logic Comput. **20**(3), 675–706 (2010)
14. Zhang, T., Gebhard, P., Sokolsky, O.: Semantics of SMEDL monitor objects. Technical report MS-CIS-16-02, University of Pennsylvania (2016)
15. Zhang, T., Gebhard, P., Sokolsky, O.: Architecture description language for SMEDL. Technical report MS-CIS-16-06, University of Pennsylvania (2016)
16. Videla, A., Williams, J.J.: RabbitMQ in Action. Manning, Shelter Island (2012)

Tool Exhibition Papers

Runtime Visualization and Verification in JIVE

Lukasz Ziarek[1]([⊠]), Bharat Jayaraman[1], Demian Lessa[1], and J. Swaminathan[2]

[1] Department of Computer Science and Engineering,
State University of New York at Buffalo, Buffalo, USA
{lziarek,bharat}@buffalo.edu, demian@lessa.org
[2] Amrita Vishwa Vidyapeetham University, Coimbatore, India
swaminathanj@am.amrita.edu

Abstract. JIVE is a runtime visualization system that provides (1) a visual representation of the execution of a Java program, including UML-style object and sequence diagrams as well as domain specific diagrams, (2) temporal query-based analysis over program schedules, executions, and traces, (3) finite-state automata based upon key object attributes of interest to the user, and (4) verification of the correctness of program execution with respect to design-time specifications. In this paper we describe the overall JIVE tool-chain and its features.

Keywords: Runtime visualization · Object · Sequence · State diagrams · Finite state model extraction · Runtime verification

1 Introduction and JIVE Overview

We present in this paper a tool called JIVE for runtime visualization and verification of Java and real-time Java programs running on the Fiji VM [9]. JIVE provides visual debugging, visual dynamic analysis through temporal queries, and visual model synthesis and validation for object oriented programs. The toolchain and associated tutorials and installation instructions are publicly available at: http://www.cse.buffalo.edu/jive/. JIVE is based upon a model-view-controller architecture; the controller component interfaces with the Java Platform Debugger Architecture (JPDA), an event-based debugging architecture, in order to receive debug event notifications such as method entry and exit, field access and modification, object creation, and instruction stepping. JIVE supports two modes of operation, an interactive mode where the user can debug while the program is executing, and an offline mode where a program execution trace (represented as a sequence of events) can be loaded and introspected. JIVE's form-based queries and its reverse step/jump feature allow past program states to be explored without restarting the program [5].

JIVE has been extend to support offline analysis of real-time Java programs. The extension is called JI.FI [2,3], and takes offline traces of events as input. Unlike the vanilla version of JIVE, JI.FI supports precise notions of time and assumes timestamps present in events are gathered from a real-time clock. The JI.FI system is agnostic to both SCJ and RTSJ, offering support for either specification's memory model [4] and linguistic constructs. Our initial work on JI.FI

© Springer International Publishing AG 2016
Y. Falcone and C. Sanchez (Eds.): RV 2016, LNCS 10012, pp. 493–497, 2016.
DOI: 10.1007/978-3-319-46982-9_33

has resulted in some preliminary specialized visual representations of real-time Java programs, specifically focusing on scoped memory, a region based memory allocation strategy that is highly error prone. The true power of JI.FI lies in its temporal query analysis engine. By leveraging precise timestamps as well as the temporal database for storing execution events, JI.FI is able to detect schedule drift of periodic tasks due to contention on shared monitors between threads of differing priority. The JI.FI system does also offer a preliminary sequence diagram that can illustrate visually contended monitors and schedule drift.

Java Path Finder (JPF) [7] is a specialized virtual machine for Java that can simulate the nondeterminism inherent in features such as thread scheduling and selection of random numbers. Although JPF is a very powerful tool and incorporates several execution efficiencies, its textual output is not always easy to follow, especially for long executions. JIVE provides a visualization mechanism for JPF's output, which we call the *scheduling tree diagram*. The scheduling tree diagram depicts the choices made (nodes) and the paths traversed by the JPF virtual machine in order to uncover a bug. The paths of this scheduling tree are traversed by the JPF virtual machine in a depth-first left-right manner, and the rightmost leaf node in the search tree corresponds to a property violation. The edges of the search tree are annotated with the JPF instructions that lead to a choice generation. The path leading to the property violation is shown by JIVE in more detail using a SD, which summarizes at a high-level the calling sequence leading to the violation. Thus, the three diagrams (scheduling tree, sequence, and object) allow the user to progressively explore different levels of detail in the execution of a concurrent Java program, and together serve as a useful tool for understanding concurrency bugs.

2   Runtime Models: Visualization and Verification

While object and sequence diagrams are useful in clarifying different aspects of run-time behavior, they each have some limitations. Sequence diagrams do not have any state information while object diagrams may be too detailed and also do not convey a sense of how the state changes over time. To remedy these shortcomings, a state diagram is proposed as a more concise way to summarize the evolution of execution than either the object or sequence diagram. A state diagram is an especially appropriate visualization for the class of programs that have a repetitive behavior, especially servers and embedded system controllers.

In order to cater to different summarizations of execution, we let the user specify at a high level which attributes of which objects/classes are of interest. These are referred to as *key attributes* and they typically are a subset of the attributes that get modified in some loop. Given a set of key attributes and an execution trace of Java program for a particular input, we systematically construct a state diagram that summarizes the program behavior for that input. Each field write event in the execution trace could potentially lead to a new state in the diagram. Since the number of field writes is bounded by the number of events n, the complexity of state diagram construction is $O(n)$.

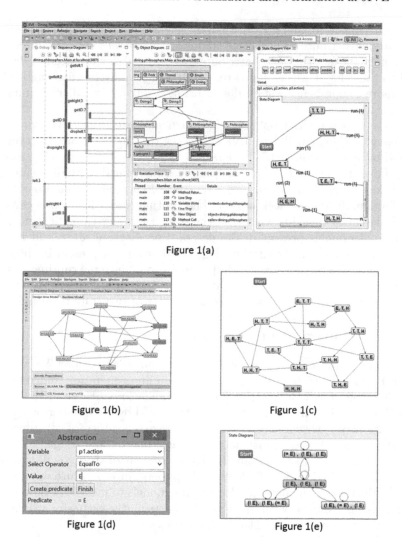

Figure 1(a)

Figure 1(b)   Figure 1(c)

Figure 1(d)   Figure 1(e)

Fig. 1. (a) JIVE user interface showing a fragment of sequence, object, and state diagrams, along with execution trace. (b) JIVE model-checking view showing the states for three dining philosophers and the result of checking EG[T1∧T2]. (c) Finite state model extraction from a Java execution of the three philosophers, with attributes of interest being the philosopher states. (d) Specifying predicate Abstraction in JIVE. (e) Reduced state machine after performing predicate abstraction WRT 'p1.action = E and p2.action = E and p3.action = E'.

We briefly mention some refinements that can help construct more concise and insightful state diagrams: (1) *Predicate Abstraction* helps reduce the state space by reducing the number of possible values for one or more key attributes. (2) *Range Reduction* is similar to Predicate Abstraction and is applicable for a totally-ordered set of values, e.g., integers. By grouping values in ranges, e.g., less than 0, equal to 0, and greater than 0, we can reduce the state space for the integer-valued attribute to just three values. (3) *Masking* some attributes allows us to capture the fact that a key attribute was changed during execution without regard to the value it was assigned to. (4) *Merging Multiple Runs* enables us to obtain more comprehensive state diagrams, as a union of smaller of finite-state machines.

In order to close the loop between design and execution, JIVE provides a consistency-checking capability. JIVE allows the design-time state diagram to be authored by an open-source UML tool, such as Papyrus UML (which is available as an Eclipse plug-in), or the state diagram may be defined textually using a simple notation, referred to as JSL, for JIVE State Language. Given a design-time state diagram, JIVE can check whether the runtime state diagram is consistent with the design by checking whether every state and every transition in the runtime state diagram is present in the design-time diagram. JIVE will highlight states and transitions in the runtime diagram that are not present in the design, thereby signaling a possible error in implementation. Since the runtime state diagram may not exercise all possible states and transitions, the consistency check is an 'inclusion' test rather than an 'equality' test of two state diagrams.

3   Conclusions and Future Work

In this paper we presented an overview of JIVE and its extensions. We described the latest additions to the JIVE toolchain, including generation and refinement of runtime models as well as verification and validation of those models against design time models. The system has been developed over a number of years and the website http://www.cse.buffalo.edu/jive is a repository of all information about the system, including instructions for installation and usage. We provide in Fig. 1 a few screen shots from the latest version of JIVE to illustrate the mechanism described in Sect. 2 of the main paper. For our future work we plan to extend the runtime models and design time models to include notions of time. This extensions, coupled with JI.FI will be particularly useful for validation of real-time system designs against execution traces.

TuningFork [1] is a visual debugger for real-time systems, and much like our JI.FI extension it provides basic visualizations over event streams. A number of tools for enhancing program comprehension of object-oriented programs have appeared over the last two decades. Jinsight [8] provides dynamic views for detecting execution bottlenecks (Histogram View), displaying execution sequences (Execution View), showing interconnections among objects based on pattern recognition algorithms (Reference Pattern View), and displaying profiling information for method calls (Call Tree View). Shimba [10] represents traces as scenario diagrams, extracts state machines from scenario diagrams, detects repeated sequences of events (i.e., behavioral patterns), and compresses contiguous (e.g., loops) and non-contiguous (e.g., subscenarios) sequences of events. Ovation [6] visualizes traces as execution pattern views, a form of interaction diagram depicting program behavior; it supports various levels of detail through filtering, collapsing/expanding, and pattern matching.

References

1. Bacon, D.F., Cheng, P., Frampton, D., Pizzonia, M., Hauswirth, M., Rajan, V.T.: Demonstration: on-line visualization and analysis of real-time systems with TuningFork. In: Mycroft, A., Zeller, A. (eds.) CC 2006. LNCS, vol. 3923, pp. 96–100. Springer, Heidelberg (2006)
2. Blanton, E., Lessa, D., Arora, P., Ziarek, L., Jayaraman, B.: JIFI: visual test and debug queries for hard real-time. Concurrency Comput. Pract. Exper. **26**(14), 2456–2487 (2014)
3. Blanton, E., Lessa, D., Ziarek, L., Bharat Jayaraman, J.: Visual test and debug queries for hard real-time. In: Proceedings of the 10th International Workshop on Java Technologies for Real-Time and Embedded Systems. ACM, New York, October 2012
4. Cavalcanti, A., Wellings, A., Woodcock, J.: The safety-critical Java memory model: a formal account. In: Butler, M., Schulte, W. (eds.) FM 2011. LNCS, vol. 6664, pp. 246–261. Springer, Heidelberg (2011). doi:10.1007/978-3-642-21437-0_20
5. Czyz, J.K., Jayaraman, B.: Declarative and visual debugging in eclipse. In: Proceedings of the 2007 OOPSLA Eclipse Technology eXchange Workshop (ETX 2007), pp. 31–35. ACM, New York (2007)
6. De Pauw, W., Lorenz, D., Vlissides, J., Wegman, M.: Execution patterns in object-oriented visualization. In: Proceedings of the 4th USENIX Conference on Object-Oriented Technologies and Systems (COOTS 1998), pp. 219–234, April 1998
7. Havelund, K.: Java PathFinder User Guide. NASA Ames Research, California (1999)
8. Zheng, C.-H., Jensen, E., Mitchell, N., Ng, T.-Y., Yang, J.: Visualizing the execution of Java programs. In: Diehl, S. (ed.) Software Visualization. LNCS, vol. 2269, pp. 151–162. Springer, Heidelberg (2002)
9. Pizlo, F., Ziarek, L., Blanton, E., Maj, P., Vitek, J.: High-level programming of embedded hard real-time devices. In: Proceedings of the 5th European conference on Computer systems, EuroSys 2010, pp. 69–82. ACM, New York (2010)
10. Systä, T., Koskimies, K., Müller, H.: Shimba–an environment for reverse engineering Java software systems. Softw. Pract. Exper. **31**, 371–394 (2001)

An Overview of MarQ

Giles Reger[⊠]

University of Manchester, Manchester, UK
giles.reger@manchester.ac.uk

Abstract. MarQ is a runtime monitoring tool for specifications written as quantified event automata, an expressive automata-based specification language based on the notion of parametric trace slicing. MarQ has performed well in the runtime verification competition and implements advanced indexing and redundancy elimination techniques. This overview describes the basic structure and functionality provided by MarQ and gives a brief description of how to use the tool.

1 Introduction

Runtime monitoring [3,7] is the process of checking whether an execution trace produced by a running system satisfies a given specification. This paper gives an overview of the MarQ tool [12] for monitoring specifications written as quantified event automata (QEA) [1,6,9]. QEA is an expressive formalism for *parametric* properties i.e. those concerned with events parameterised by data.

MarQ is available from

$$\text{https://github.com/selig/qea}$$

This includes instructions on how to perform online and offline monitoring and a collection of specifications used in the runtime verification competitions.

This overview briefly describes the QEA formalism (Sect. 2), how to write and use these to monitor log files and Java programs using MarQ (Sect. 3) and its performance (Sect. 4). It concludes with remarks about its future (Sect. 5).

2 Quantified Event Automata

Quantified event automata [1] combine a logical notion of quantification with a form of extended finite state machine. To demonstrate the expressiveness of this formalism, Fig. 1 gives three (simple) example QEA specifications for the following properties:

1. *SafeIterator.* An iterator created from a collection of size *size* should only be iterated at most *size* times.
2. *SafeMapIterator.* There should not be a map m, collection c and iterator i such that c is created from m, i is created from c, m is updated and then i is used. This demonstrates the use of multiple quantifiers.

© Springer International Publishing AG 2016
Y. Falcone and C. Sanchez (Eds.): RV 2016, LNCS 10012, pp. 498–503, 2016.
DOI: 10.1007/978-3-319-46982-9_34

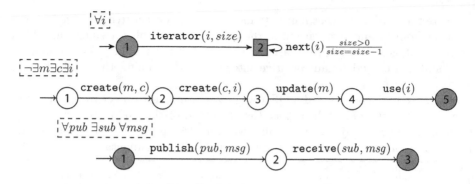

Fig. 1. Example quantified event automata.

3. *PublisherSubscriber.* For every publisher there exists a subscriber that receives all of that publisher's messages. This demonstrates how alternating quantification can be used to concisely capture a complex property about related objects.

See related publications [1,6,9] for further examples and a full description of their semantics. Note that QEA have a (may valued) finite-trace semantics so liveness properties (like *PublisherSubscriber*) are implicitly bounded by an end of trace event.

3   Using MARQ

Here we briefly describe how to use MARQ. These examples (and others) are available online. We describe how to construct QEAs and their corresponding monitor objects and then how to use these objects to monitor log files and Java programs.

3.1   Creating QEAs and Monitors

Currently MARQ provides a builder API for constructing QEA properties. Event names are specified as integers and there is a library of predefined guards and assignments that can be used in transitions. Below is an example of how the *SafeIterator* QEA can be constructed in this way. Sect. 5 discusses future plans to improve this.

```
QEABuilder q = new QEABuilder("safeiter");

int ITERATOR = 1; int NEXT = 2;
final int i = -1;
final int size = 1;
q.addQuantification(FORALL, i)

q.addTransition(1,ITERATOR, i, size, 2);
q.addTransition(2,NEXT, i, isGreaterThanConstant(size,0), decrement(size), 2);

q.addFinalStates(1, 2); q.setSkipStates(1);

QEA qea = q.make();
```

Here there are two event names (which must be consecutive positive integers) starting from 1) and two variables, the quantified variable i (which must be a negative integer) and the free variable $size$ (which must be a positive integer). Two states are used (again positive integers) with 1 being the implicit start state.

Once we have constructed a QEA we create a monitor object by a call to the MonitorFactory. This will inspect the structure of the QEA and produce an optimised monitor object. Optionally, we can also specify garbage and restart modes on monitor creation (some of these are still experimental).

```
Monitor monitor = MonitorFactory.create(qea);
Monitor monitor = MonitorFactory.create(qea,GarbageMode.LAZY,RestartMode.REMOVE);
```

The garbage mode indicates how the monitor should handle references to monitored objects e.g. should weak references be used. By default the garbage mode is off, which is optimal for offline monitoring. The restart mode tells the monitor what should be done with a binding that fails the specification. For example, the REMOVE value here allows a *signal-and-continue* approach to monitoring safety properties.

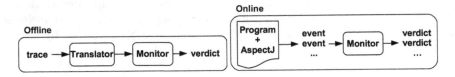

Fig. 2. Two different monitoring modes.

3.2 Monitoring a Trace Offline

To monitor a trace we construct an appropriate FileMonitor (which reads in the trace) and call monitor() to produce a verdict. As illustrated in Fig. 2, offline monitoring of traces makes use of an optional Translator object to produce events in the form expected by the monitor constructed above. This allows parameters to be parsed as integers, reordered or filtered.

MARQ accepts trace files in the formats specified by the runtime verification competition [4]. Therefore, any system that can be intrumented to produce such traces can be monitored offline. The following code can be used to construct a monitor for a CSV trace for the *SafeIterator* property. The translator object will parse the size parameter as an integer and other parameters as (interned) strings (objects with a notion of equality).

```
String trace = ''trace_dir/trace.csv'';
QEA qea = builder.make(); //see above
OfflineTranslator translator = TranslatorFactory.makeParsingTranslator(
                  event("iterator",param(0,OBJ),param(1,INT)),
                  event("next",param(0,OBJ))));
CSVFileMonitor m = new CSVFileMonitor(trace_name, qea, translator);
Verdict v = m.monitor();
```

3.3 Monitoring Online via AspectJ

For monitoring Java programs MᴀʀQ is designed to be used with AꜱᴘᴇᴄᴛJ
i.e. using a *pointcut* for each event and submitting the necessary information
directly to the monitor object as in the following extract. For other examples
of how instrumentation and monitoring using AꜱᴘᴇᴄᴛJ can be achieved see the
online examples and [12].

```
after (Collection c) returning (Iterator i) :
    call(Iterator Collection+.iterator()) && target(c) {
    synchronized(monitor){ check(monitor.step(ITERATOR,i,c.size())); }
}
before(Iterator i) : call(* Iterator.next()) && target(i) {
    synchronized(monitor){ check(monitor.step(NEXT,i)); }
}
private void check(Verdict verdict){
    if(verdict==Verdict.FAILURE){ <report error here> }
}
```

4 Performance

We briefly discuss the performance of MᴀʀQ, see [9,12] for experiments.

Implementation. MᴀʀQ has a number of features related to efficiency:

- *Structural specialisation.* MᴀʀQ analyses the QEA and constructs a monitoring algorithm suited to its structure. For example, particular indexing
  mechanisms can be employed. This is an ongoing area of research.
- *Symbol-based indexing.* Whilst other tools for parametric trace slicing use
  value-based indexing to lookup monitoring state, MᴀʀQ uses a symbol-based
  technique inspired by discrimination trees from automated reasoning.
- *Redundancy elimination.* MᴀʀQ analyses the QEA to determine which states
  are *redundant* and eagerly discards redundant information during monitoring.
- *Garbage removal.* As mentioned earlier, MᴀʀQ can be configured to weakly
  reference monitored objects and remove these from indexing structures when
  they become garbage. It is an ongoing area of research to extend these ideas
  to offline monitoring.

See [12] for further details.

Competitions. MᴀʀQ performed well in the 2014, 2015 and 2016 iterations of
the runtime verification competition. It came joint first in the Java division in
2014[1] with JᴀᴠᴀMOP [8] and in 2015[2] and 2016 [13] it came second to Mᴜꜰɪɴ
[2] (which is very efficient on certain forms of *connected* properties). In 2014 and
2016 it came first in the Offline division and in 2015 it came second to LᴏɢFɪʀᴇ
[5] (although performed better on benchmarks jointly entered).

---

[1] See http://rv2014.imag.fr/monitoring-competition/results.html.
[2] See https://www.cost-arvi.eu/?page_id=664.

5   Conclusion

MARQ is an efficient tool for parametric runtime verification of QEA. The development of MARQ is an ongoing project and the tool will continue to be updated and improved. The current planned areas for improvement are as follows:

- Improve the current method for defining QEA to remove the dependency on arbitrary details such as quantified variables being negative integers. Furthermore, providing a more general purpose method for defining guards and assignments rather than the current pre-defined library.
- Implement alternative front-end specification languages that compile into QEA. For example, a form of first-order temporal logic [14].
- Incorporate methods for explaining violations in terms of edits to the trace [10].
- Explore integration with specification mining techniques [11].

Please contact the author with comments or suggestions.

References

1. Barringer, H., Falcone, Y., Havelund, K., Reger, G., Rydeheard, D.: Quantified event automata: towards expressive and efficient runtime monitors. In: Giannakopoulou, D., Méry, D. (eds.) FM 2012. LNCS, vol. 7436, pp. 68–84. Springer, Heidelberg (2012). doi:10.1007/978-3-642-32759-9_9
2. Decker, N., Harder, J., Scheffel, T., Schmitz, M., Thoma, D.: Runtime monitoring with union-find structures. In: Chechik, M., Raskin, J.-F. (eds.) TACAS 2016. LNCS, vol. 9636, pp. 868–884. Springer, Heidelberg (2016). doi:10.1007/978-3-662-49674-9_54
3. Falcone, Y., Havelund, K., Reger, G.: A tutorial on runtime verification. In: Broy, M., Peled, D. (eds.) Summer School Marktoberdorf - Engineering Dependable Software Systems (2012). IOS Press (2013, To appear)
4. Falcone, Y., Nickovic, D., Reger, G., Thoma, D.: Second international competition on runtime verification. In: Bartocci, E., Majumdar, R. (eds.) RV 2015. LNCS, vol. 9333, pp. 405–422. Springer, Heidelberg (2015). doi:10.1007/978-3-319-23820-3_27
5. Havelund, K.: Rule-based runtime verification revisited. Int. J. Softw. Tools Technol. Transf. (STTT) 17(2), 143–170 (2014)
6. Havelund, K., Reger, G.: Formal modeling and verification of cyber-physical systems. In: Drechsler, R., Kühne, U. (eds.) Specification of parametric monitors. Springer, Wiesbaden (2015). doi:10.1007/978-3-658-09994-7_6
7. Leucker, M., Schallhart, C.: A brief account of runtime verification. J. Log. Algebraic Program. 78(5), 293–303 (2008)
8. Meredith, P., Jin, D., Griffith, D., Chen, F., Roşu, G.: An overview of the MOP runtime verification framework. J. Softw. Tools Technol. Transf. 1–41 (2011)
9. Reger, G.: Automata based monitoring and mining of execution traces. PhD thesis, University of Manchester (2014)
10. Reger, G.: Suggesting edits to explain failing traces. In: Bartocci, E., Majumdar, R. (eds.) RV 2015. LNCS, vol. 9333, pp. 287–293. Springer, Heidelberg (2015). doi:10.1007/978-3-319-23820-3_20

11. Reger, G., Barringer, H., Rydeheard, D.: A pattern-based approach to parametric specification mining. In: Proceedings of the 28th IEEE/ACM International Conference on Automated Software Engineering, November 2013
12. Reger, G., Cruz, H.C., Rydeheard, D.: MARQ: monitoring at runtime with QEA. In: Baier, C., Tinelli, C. (eds.) TACAS 2015. LNCS, vol. 9035, pp. 596–610. Springer, Heidelberg (2015). doi:10.1007/978-3-662-46681-0_55
13. Reger, G., Hallé, S., Falcone, Y.: Third international competition on runtime verification CRV. In: Falcone, Y., Sánchez, C. (eds.) Runtime Verification - 16th International Conference. RV 2016. LNCS, pp. 21–37, Springer, Switzerland (2016, to appear)
14. Reger, G., Rydeheard, D.: From first-order temporal logic to parametric trace slicing. In: Bartocci, E., Majumdar, R. (eds.) RV 2015. LNCS, vol. 9333, pp. 216–232. Springer, Heidelberg (2015). doi:10.1007/978-3-319-23820-3_14

Runtime Analysis with R2U2:
A Tool Exhibition Report

Johann Schumann[1]([⊠]), Patrick Moosbrugger[2], and Kristin Y. Rozier[3]

[1] SGT, Inc., NASA Ames, Moffett Field, Mountain View, CA, USA
Johann.M.Schumann@nasa.gov
[2] Vienna University of Technology, Vienna, Austria
moosbrugger@cps.tuwien.ac.at
[3] Iowa State University, Ames, IA, USA
kyrozier@iastate.edu

Abstract. We present R2U2 (Realizable, Responsive, Unobtrusive Unit), a hardware-supported tool and framework for the continuous monitoring of safety-critical and embedded cyber-physical systems. With the widespread advent of autonomous systems such as Unmanned Aerial Systems (UAS), satellites, rovers, and cars, real-time, on-board decision making requires unobtrusive monitoring of properties for safety, performance, security, and system health. R2U2 models combine past-time and future-time Metric Temporal Logic, "mission time" Linear Temporal Logic, probabilistic reasoning with Bayesian Networks, and model-based prognostics.

The R2U2 monitoring engine can be instantiated as a hardware solution, running on an FPGA, or as a software component. The FPGA realization enables R2U2 to monitor complex cyber-physical systems without any overhead or instrumentation of the flight software. In this tool exhibition report, we present R2U2 and demonstrate applications on system runtime monitoring, diagnostics, software health management, and security monitoring for a UAS. Our tool demonstration uses a hardware-based processor-in-the-loop "iron-bird" configuration.

1 Introduction and Tool Overview

The Realizable, Responsive, Unobtrusive Unit (R2U2) is a framework for runtime System Health Management (SHM) of cyber-physical systems. R2U2 is unique in that it combines several different runtime reasoning "building blocks" to provide a more effective runtime analysis than can be accomplished via any one of them alone; [10,11] give an overview of the building block architecture and provide ideas and examples for tool configurations. Building blocks include temporal logic runtime observers, Bayes Net (BN) decision-makers, and sensor filters; the framework is extensible in that it is easy to connect the inputs and outputs of different types of reasoning blocks. Other notable advantages of R2U2 are its zero-overhead hardware implementation, dual-encodings of temporal logic observers to include both time- and event-triggered results, implementations of

© Springer International Publishing AG 2016
Y. Falcone and C. Sanchez (Eds.): RV 2016, LNCS 10012, pp. 504–509, 2016.
DOI: 10.1007/978-3-319-46982-9_35

future-time and past-time observers, and efficient use of Bayesian reasoning over observer outputs to provide temporal diagnostics.

R2U2 reasons efficiently about temporal behaviors using temporal logic runtime observers. These observers encode Metric Temporal Logic (MTL) [5] and Mission-Time Linear Temporal Logic (LTL) [6] formulas. MTL adds discrete time bounds to the temporal operators of LTL formulas; for R2U2 we bound operators in units of ticks of the system clock, so a singular bound of [100] designates the operator holds for the next 100 clock ticks and a paired bound of [5, 20] designates that the operator holds from 5 to 20 clock ticks from now. We defined Mission-Time LTL [6] in recognition that many requirements for missions of air- and spacecraft, for example, are most naturally written in LTL but there is an (often unspecified) assumption that the eventualities guaranteed by strong operators ($\Diamond$ and $\mathcal{U}$) are fulfilled during the mission. Therefore, we consider such formulas to be in Mission-Time LTL, where we automatically fill in MTL-like time bounds on eventualities to give an appropriate finite-trace semantics that guarantees satisfaction during the current mission, or mode of flight. Uniquely, R2U2 encodes every future-time temporal logic specification twice: once as an asynchronous observer and once as a synchronous observer. Asynchronous, or event-triggered, observers return a verdict (*true* or *false*) in the first clock-tick that the formula can be evaluated. Their output is a tuple including the clock-tick(s) they have a verdict for and that verdict, where the clock-tick(s) may be in the past in the case of future-time formulas for which there was not previously sufficient information to evaluate fully. Asynchronous observers resemble traditional runtime monitors with one important difference: they always report both success *and* failure of the formula (rather than just reporting failures) as both evaluations provide valuable information to influence the probabilistic evaluations of the BNs. Synchronous, or time-triggered, observers return a three-valued verdict (*true*, *false*, or *maybe*) at every tick of the system clock. This is useful to provide intermediate information for probabilistic BN reasoning as well as a "liveness" check that the monitoring framework is responsive. We defined and proved correct FPGA-based implementations of asynchronous and synchronous runtime observers [6].

R2U2 expands upon the failure reporting of traditional runtime monitors to provide advanced diagnostics by combining the temporal logic observers with light-weight Bayesian Networks (BNs) that reason over the observer outputs and (possibly filtered) sensors signals. Our R2U2 model can have modular, usually rather small Bayesian networks for groups of highly-related faults that might occur for one hard- or software component. We designed and experimentally evaluated efficient FPGA-based encodings of our BNs in [4], demonstrating their ability to perform efficient diagnostics for safety and performance requirements. Recognizing that violations of security properties that occur through tampering with sensor inputs may also have unique temporal patterns, we expanded on this work with a series of case studies for UAS in [8]. A possibly innocuous off-nominal reading or event, followed by a specific temporally-displaced pattern of behavior is often indicative of a hard-to-diagnose security threat, such as dangerous MAV

(Micro Air Vehicle) commands, ground station denial-of-service attempts, or GPS spoofing; [8] defines and demonstrates R2U2 configurations that efficiently diagnose these during runtime.

2   Tool Architecture

In its usual configuration, R2U2 obtains data from sensors, actuators, and the flight software using a read-only (serial) interface (Fig. 1A). This enables R2U2 to continuously monitor multiple signals during runtime with minimal instrumentation of the flight software. Altering safety-critical software or hardware components can cause difficulties maintaining flight certification. R2U2 itself is implemented in VHDL that is compiled into an FPGA configuration. For our experiments, we use an Adapteva Parallella board [1] that provides a suitable FPGA and runs a Linux system for data logging and development. Software-only versions of R2U2 are available and can be executed on any Linux-based system, preferably on a separate hardware unit to avoid interaction with the flight software and hardware.

R2U2 models consist of temporal logic formulas, Bayesian networks, and specifications of signal-preprocessing and filtering. These models can be designed in a modular and hierarchical manner to enable the designer to easily express properties containing temporal, model-based, and probabilistic aspects. For graphical modeling of the Bayesian networks, we use the freely available tool SamIam [2]. With the other parts of the model in textual format, our tool-chain (Fig. 1C) compiles temporal formulas and Bayesian network reasoners into a compact and efficient binary format. The compiled model then can be directly downloaded onto the R2U2 execution engine without having regenerate code or configuration, which could take considerable time for an FPGA.

MTL and LTL formulas are compiled into code for a special purpose processor that is instantiated on the FPGA or emulated in software. Efficient and correct

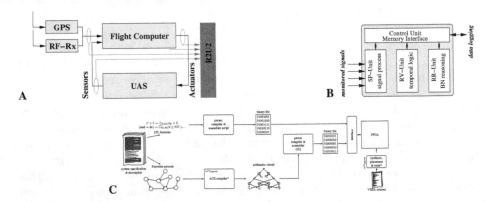

Fig. 1. A: Schematics of R2U2 for a small UAS. **B**: R2U2 architecture **C**: R2U2 tool chain

algorithms for the temporal operators [6] avoid the construction of potentially large finite state machines. The Bayesian network is compiled into an arithmetic circuit [3], which can be efficiently evaluated in bounded time using a special purpose processor on the FPGA. Filtering and thresholding of the (floating-point) input signals is done by the SP-Unit. Figure 1B shows the high-level architecture of the R2U2 engine. All algorithms of R2U2 are fully static, do not require any dynamic structures or memory allocation, and have known and bounded runtime behavior, making the tool suitable for execution on embedded architectures.

3   Examples and Applications

R2U2 has been used for UAS to continuously monitor numerous properties and perform root cause analysis [4]. These properties typically address safety ("Is the airspeed always higher than the stall-speed?"), performance ("Have we reached our desired waypoint within 10 s of ETA?"), or security ("Has our GPS system be spoofed?").

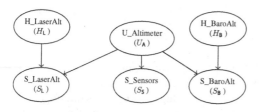

Fig. 2. Sensor failure detection BN from [6]

For example, the relationship property "A pitch-up should cause the UAS to climb within 5 s" can be expressed by the following MTL formula: $\Box(pitch^{up} \rightarrow \Diamond_{[0,5]}(\Box_{[2]}(v_z^b > 20\,\text{ft/min})))$, where v_z^b is the vertical speed measured by the baro-altimeter. Here, we have refined the requirement that within the last 5 s, we have to encounter at least a 2 s stretch of uninterrupted climbing in order to filter out short-term effects like turbulence.

Checking the consistency of several sensors can be an important help to figure out if a sensor is broken, and if so, which one. In our example (see [6]), the UAS is equipped with a barometric altimeter, a laser altimeter, and an inertial measurement unit (IMU) for navigation. Because of sensor noise, it would be hard to directly compare the values. We rather abstract the readings from each sensor into "climbing" and "descending". We feed these data to the sensor nodes of our the Bayesian network model (Fig. 2, bottom row). Given this information, R2U2 can calculate, in real-time, the posteriors of the health nodes (H_LaserAlt and H_BaroAlt) indicating their most likely health status. This Bayesian network allows us to incorporate domain knowledge (e.g., the laser altimeter is more likely to fail than the barometric altimeter) and complex interrelationships between components. For details of this example see [6,7].

The tool demonstration website [7] contains a number of relevant examples illustrating the monitoring of safety and performance properties, monitoring a UAS for possible cyber-attacks [8], and incorporating battery prognostics [9]. We will demonstrate multiple examples with R2U2 on our "iron-bird," which contains the Arduino flight hardware including sensors and servos, and the Parallella board with R2U2 running on FPGA or in software.

4 Summary

R2U2 is designed for continuous runtime analysis of safety-critical and embedded cyber-physical systems, for example, UAS. The modeling framework uses a synergistic combination of past- and future-time MTL, mission-time LTL, Bayesian Networks, and prognostics models. The R2U2 framework and tool is demonstrated on our UAS iron-bird, a processor-in-the-loop setup for a small UAS. R2U2 can be instantiated on an FPGA or as a software application and can be used for monitoring safety, security, and performance properties, as well as performing diagnostics for wide ranges of software and cyber-physical systems.

Detailed information about R2U2, documentation, examples, and demo scripts can be found at [7]; we are in the application process for a NASA Open Source License.

Acknowledgments. The development of R2U2 was in part supported by NASA ARMD grant NNX14AN61A, ARMD 2014 I3AMT Seedling Phase I NNX12AK33A, and NRA NNX08AY50A.

References

1. Adapteva: The Parallella System (2016). http://adapteva.com
2. Automated Reasoning Group, UCLA: SamIam Sensitivity Analysis, Modeling, Inference and More (SamIam) (2016). http://reasoning.cs.ucla.edu/samiam/
3. Darwiche, A.: A differential approach to inference in Bayesian networks. J. ACM **50**(3), 280–305 (2003)
4. Geist, J., Rozier, K.Y., Schumann, J.: Runtime observer pairs and Bayesian network reasoners on-board FPGAs: flight-certifiable system health management for embedded systems. In: Bonakdarpour, B., Smolka, S.A. (eds.) RV 2014. LNCS, vol. 8734, pp. 215–230. Springer, Heidelberg (2014). doi:10.1007/978-3-319-11164-3_18
5. Koymans, R.: Specifying real-time properties with metric temporal logic. Real-Time Syst. **2**(4), 255–299 (1990)
6. Reinbacher, T., Rozier, K.Y., Schumann, J.: Temporal-logic based runtime observer pairs for system health management of real-time systems. In: Ábrahám, E., Havelund, K. (eds.) TACAS 2014 (ETAPS). LNCS, vol. 8413, pp. 357–372. Springer, Heidelberg (2014). doi:10.1007/978-3-642-54862-8_24
7. Schumann, J., Moosbrugger, P., Rozier, K.Y.: Runtime Analysis with R2U2: A Tool Exhibition Report (Tool Demonstration Website) (2016). http://temporallogic.org/research/RV16/
8. Schumann, J., Moosbrugger, P., Rozier, K.Y.: R2U2: monitoring and diagnosis of security threats for unmanned aerial systems. In: Bartocci, E., Majumdar, R. (eds.) RV 2015. LNCS, vol. 9333, pp. 233–249. Springer, Heidelberg (2015). doi:10.1007/978-3-319-23820-3_15
9. Schumann, J., Roychoudhury, I., Kulkarni, C.: Diagnostic reasoning using prognostic information for unmanned aerial systems. In: Proceedings of PHM 2015 (2015)

10. Schumann, J., Rozier, K.Y., Reinbacher, T., Mengshoel, O.J., Mbaya, T., Ippolito, C.: Towards real-time, on-board, hardware-supported sensor and software health management for unmanned aerial systems. In: Proceedings of PHM 2013, pp. 381–401 (2013)
11. Schumann, J., Rozier, K.Y., Reinbacher, T., Mengshoel, O.J., Mbaya, T., Ippolito, C.: Towards real-time, on-board, hardware-supported sensor and software health management for unmanned aerial systems. Int. J. Prognostics Health Manage. (IJPHM) **6**(1), 1–27 (2015)

Author Index

Printed in the United States
By Bookmasters